Java™ Servlet Programming Bible

Java™ Servlet Programming Bible

Suresh Rajagopalan, Ramesh Rajamani,
Ramesh Krishnaswamy, and Sridhar Vijendran

Hungry Minds™

est-Selling Books • Digital Downloads • e-Books • Answer Networks • e-Newsletters • Branded Web Sites • e-Learning

New York, NY ✦ Cleveland, OH ✦ Indianapolis, IN

Java™ Servlet Programming Bible

Published by
Hungry Minds, Inc.
909 Third Avenue
New York, NY 10022
www.hungryminds.com

Library of Congress Control Number: 2001093386

ISBN: 0-7645-4839-5

Printed in the United States of America

10 9 8 7 6 5 4 3 2 1

1B/RV/QS/QS/IN

Distributed in the United States by Hungry Minds, Inc.

Distributed by CDG Books Canada Inc. for Canada; by Transworld Publishers Limited in the United Kingdom; by IDG Norge Books for Norway; by IDG Sweden Books for Sweden; by IDG Books Australia Publishing Corporation Pty. Ltd. for Australia and New Zealand; by TransQuest Publishers Pte Ltd. for Singapore, Malaysia, Thailand, Indonesia, and Hong Kong; by Gotop Information Inc. for Taiwan; by ICG Muse, Inc. for Japan; by Intersoft for South Africa; by Eyrolles for France; by International Thomson Publishing for Germany, Austria, and Switzerland; by Distribuidora Cuspide for Argentina; by LR International for Brazil; by Galileo Libros for Chile; by Ediciones ZETA S.C.R. Ltda. for Peru; by WS Computer Publishing Corporation, Inc., for the Philippines; by Contemporanea de Ediciones for Venezuela; by Express Computer Distributors for the Caribbean and West Indies; by Micronesia Media Distributor, Inc. for Micronesia; by Chips Computadoras S.A. de C.V. for Mexico; by Editorial Norma de Panama S.A. for Panama; by American Bookshops for Finland.

For general information on Hungry Minds' products and services please contact our Customer Care department within the U.S. at 800-762-2974, outside the U.S. at 317-572-3993 or fax 317-572-4002.

For sales inquiries and reseller information, including discounts, premium and bulk quantity sales, and foreign-language translations, please contact our Customer Care department at 800-434-3422, fax 317-572-4002 or write to Hungry Minds, Inc., Attn: Customer Care Department, 10475 Crosspoint Boulevard, Indianapolis, IN 46256.

For information on licensing foreign or domestic rights, please contact our Sub-Rights Customer Care department at 212-884-5000.

For information on using Hungry Minds' products and services in the classroom or for ordering examination copies, please contact our Educational Sales department at 800-434-2086 or fax 317-572-4005.

For press review copies, author interviews, or other publicity information, please contact our Public Relations department at 317-572-3168 or fax 317-572-4168.

For authorization to photocopy items for corporate, personal, or educational use, please contact Copyright Clearance Center, 222 Rosewood Drive, Danvers, MA 01923, or fax 978-750-4470.

About the Authors

Suresh Rajagopalan recently completed his B.S. in Computer Science at the University of Technology Sydney in Australia. His specialty is in eCommerce, which is also his minor. He has worked as a Web and Java developer at the eFunds Corporation in St. Paul, Minnesota. Suresh is also an active member of the Programmers Society of UTS. He wrote Chapters 1, 4, 5, and 10 and Appendixes B, C, and E. He also contributed to Chapter 2 and Appendix D.

Ramesh Rajamani is a designer and developer of software products for financial institutions. He has expertise with servlets, JSPs, and J2EE. He is also trains and mentors employees in his company to get them acquainted with the latest Java technologies. Ramesh spends his spare time studying and researching design patterns and their applicability to enterprise Java applications. He wrote Chapters 6, 13, 14, and 15. He also contributed to Chapter 2 and Appendix D.

Ramesh Krishnaswamy is a software architect who designs and develops business applications for the financial industry. His prime focus is server-side Java and Enterprise application design. Apart from development, he is involved in training people on Java, enterprise applications, object-oriented technologies, and databases. Ramesh wrote Chapters 8 and 11 and Appendix F, and he also contributed to Chapter 2.

Sridhar Vijendran is an ardent computer programmer and a keen chess fanatic. He wrote Chapters 3, 7, 9, and 12.

Credits

Acquisitions Editor
Grace Buechlein

Project Editors
Gus Miklos
Sharon Nash
Hugh Vandivier

Technical Editor
David Williams

Copy Editors
William A. Barton
C. M. Jones

Editorial Manager
Mary Beth Wakefield

Senior Vice President, Technical Publishing
Richard Swadley

Vice President and Publisher
Joseph B. Wikert

Project Coordinator
Regina Snyder

Graphics and Production Specialists
Melanie DesJardins, Joyce Haughey,
Stephanie D. Jumper, Barry Offringa,
Jill Piscitelli, Betty Schulte,
Jeremey Unger, Mary J. Virgin

Quality Control Technicians
Laura Albert, David Faust,
Andy Hollandbeck, Susan Moritz

Permissions Editor
Laura Moss

Media Development Specialist
Travis Silvers

Proofreading and Indexing
TECHBOOKS Production Services
Fran Blauw
Mary Lagu

Cover Image
Murder By Design

To my Lord, Ganesh: Thank you for all I have been given. —Suresh Rajagopalan

I would like to dedicate my writings to my family and friends. —Ramesh Rajamani

I would like to dedicate this book to my parents. —Ramesh Krishnaswamy

Dedicated to Sharayu, sweet little daughter of my beloved sister, Srividhya Ravi. —Sridhar Vijendran

Preface

Welcome to *Java Servlet Programming Bible*. Our aim in this book is to cover a broad range of topics in which servlet technology can be used to build Web-based applications or components. This book touches on the essential topics that pertain to servlet technology.

Servlets and JSP technology are currently the most popular options in developing Web-based applications. This book is designed to acquaint you with this technology so that you can develop your own servlets or convert existing applications. There are a number of choices in server-side application development, and after you delve into servlets, we believe you will find them one of the superior choices among these.

This book is aimed toward developers who want to get their hands dirty with servlets and JSP technologies, so be prepared to see a lot of code.

What You Need to Know

In writing this book, we have assumed you have the following minimum requisites:

- Knowledge of the Java programming language at a basic level
- Knowledge of HTML at a basic level
- Knowledge of database concepts

In addition, experience with any other programming language is beneficial.

In this book, we try to address readers and developers at various levels so that everyone can gain something by reading it.

How This Book Is Organized

This book is organized into three main parts and five appendixes. Each chapter in the book assumes that you are aware of concepts discussed in previous chapters.

Part I: Servlet Programming Fundamentals

This part consists of Chapters 1 through 4 and introduces the essential concepts you need to know before commencing programming with servlets.

The following essential concepts are discussed in this part of the book:

- ✦ How the Internet works using the client-server paradigm
- ✦ How to set up a development environment for developing and executing servlets
- ✦ An introduction to the servlet lifecycle and Application Programming Interface (API)
- ✦ The basics of the Hypertext Transfer Protocol (HTTP)

A beginning-level reader might find this part of the book most useful.

Part II: Working with Servlets

The more exciting part of the book begins here, where we demonstrate the use of other technologies such as Remote Method Invocation (RMI). We also show you how servlets can perform various services in conjunction with HTML and databases: for example, collecting and storing form data into a database. We explore the slightly older technology of Server-Side Includes that makes use of servlets. You learn how you can start, manage, and control a Web-application session. The final chapter of this part explores how to develop secure Web applications (with the use of HTTPS services).

Readers at an intermediate level should start at this point.

Part III: Beyond Servlets: JavaServer Pages

This part explores another technology, JavaServer Pages (JSPs), based on servlets. It shows how you can use servlets, JavaBeans, and JSPs to build Web applications. Another chapter in this part discusses important design concepts and patterns for building Web applications. More specifically, it delves into a specific architecture that is ideal for building Web applications. We conclude the book by introducing various concepts that can reduce maintenance work on your application.

Acknowledgments

Suresh Rajagopalan: I would like to thank the team at Hungry Minds who have helped make this book possible. Grace Buechlein in particular deserves special thanks for being able to coordinate all the activities needed to get this book together. The other members of this team include Sharon Nash, Gus Miklos, Hugh Vandivier, Eric Newman, C. M. Jones, and David Williams. They have all added their insight and steered the book on the right course.

Most important, I would like acknowledge the efforts and talents of the co-authors who have helped me put this book together. It has been both fun and a learning experience to work with Ramesh Rajamani, Ramesh Krishnaswamy, and Sridhar Vijendran. It has also been an interesting experience to work with a team writing from different geographical locations.

I would like to add a special mention of the D2C Team at eFunds, who have contributed their wisdom and experiences and helped me form my own as a developer.

Finally, I would like to acknowledge my parents, who have supported me throughout the writing of this book.

Ramesh Rajamani: I thank Grace Buechlein for giving us this opportunity. She and the team at Hungry Minds have been very cooperative and helpful throughout. I thank Suresh Rajagopalan, Ramesh Krishnaswamy, and Sridhar Vijendran for working together and putting it all together in completing this book. I thank all my friends who have given me support and help throughout the writing of this book. I thank my mom, dad, brother, and my sisters, who have encouraged me and supported me in taking up this opportunity. Last, but not least, I thank God, who has given me this wonderful opportunity.

Ramesh Krishnaswamy: I would like to thank Suresh Rajagopalan and Ramesh Rajamani for giving me an opportunity to get involved in the writing of this book. I would also like to thank Sridhar Vijendran, R. Rengarajan, and S. Karthigai Balan for their support. A special thanks to Grace Buechlein for her patience and encouragement when I was unable to meet deadlines for various reasons. I end by thanking my parents, sister, and friends, whose well wishes have helped me in the successful completion of the book.

Sridhar Vijendran: My sincere thanks to co-authors and to S. Karthigai Balan and Rengarajan Ramasamy for their timely technical assistance.

Contents at a Glance

Contents

Servlet Programming Fundamentals

PART

I

✦ ✦ ✦ ✦

In This Part

✦ ✦ ✦ ✦

Servlets and Web Application Development

✦ ✦ ✦ ✦

In This Chapter

How the Web works

The benefits of servlets

How servlets are used

Factors in choosing a server-side scripting language

Advantages to building Web-based applications

✦ ✦ ✦ ✦

Review of Internet Fundamentals

Essentially, the Internet (inaccurately known to many as the Web or the Net) is a *Global Area Network* (GAN). In fact, the Internet is the only GAN today. This GAN consists of many smaller networks around the world that are interconnected through regional Internet Service Providers (ISPs) that make up the Internet. The Internet operates over a number of shared Transmission Control Protocol/Internet Protocol (TCP/IP) protocols. TCP/IP is used to break data into packets (or smaller parcels of data) and to route these packets to their destination. Higher-level protocols use TCP/IP to send and route data to their destination. Table 1-1 contains examples of higher-level protocols that make use of TCP/IP.

Note

The term *protocol* refers (in this context) to the rules that govern communication between the client and server.

Packets are basically parcels of the data stream being sent or received that have been broken up before transmission.

Table 1-1
TCP/IP Protocols

Protocol	*Purpose*
http:// (HyperText Transfer Protocol)	Used for Web browsing through retrieval of hypertext documents
ftp:// (File Transfer Protocol)	Used for remote file transfers
telnet://	Used to connect and work on a remote system
News:	Used to read and post messages on newsgroups
SMTP (Simple Mail Transfer Protocol)	Use to send e-mail
https:// (Secure HTTP)	Used for secure transactions (It's an extension of the HTTP)

This book deals primarily with the HTTP protocol. Of various Internet protocols, TCP/IP are the most important because every computer connected to the Web understands and uses TCP/IP protocols to transmit and receive data from other computers on the network.

Today, the Internet is thriving and growing due to the e-commerce explosion. As the number of Internet users is growing at an exponential rate, the market potential for e-commerce is growing at extraordinary rates as well. The Internet has become a cheap medium for sending and receiving information; also, the Internet allows users to perform transactions regardless of geographical location. Having a presence on the Web has become critical to many traditional brick-and-mortar businesses.

Benefits of Java programming

The Java programming language is a popular choice in Web-application development (as well as traditional application development). Java is popular for many reasons, one being its object-oriented approach. This allows developers to develop modules of code that need only be written once and can then be used anywhere. In addition to this, the Java language provides many packages/libraries that can be used to work with other technologies more easily. Other benefits that Java offers (that make it of great interest to organizations) is that it is scalable (can be extended to meet increased loads), it is a free language to use and develop with, and it is platform independent.

The client/server paradigm

The Internet operates in a client/server paradigm. The server operates in a rather passive way. The server waits for somebody to make a request. As a request comes in, the server processes it; then the server waits for more requests or processes subsequent requests.

Server is used interchangeably to describe the program that handles request processing and the physical hardware on which the program runs.

In this context, a *user agent* is essentially the software that is used to make requests to servers.

The *client* is a type of user agent that a user runs to access the Web. A browser is also a type of user agent. There are, however, other types of user agents, such as search-engine robots or chat/messenger programs. The client makes requests to servers and renders the resulting data in a manner that varies depending on the type of user agent . For example, a browser takes the resulting HTML and renders a Web page. A typical scenario of the client/server paradigm is shown in Figure 1-1.

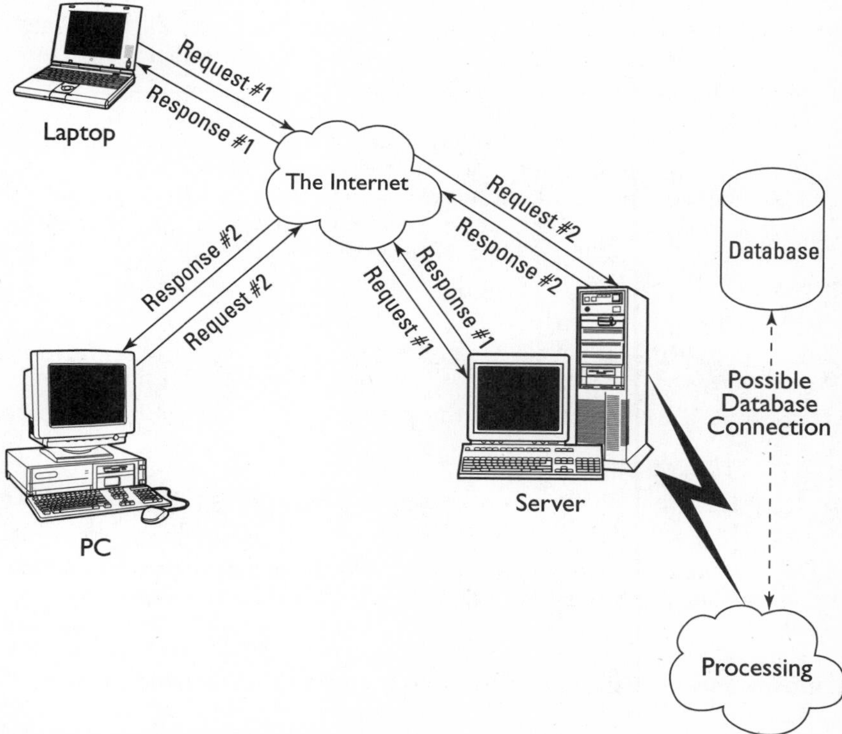

Figure 1-1: The client/server paradigm

The following steps take place when the client makes a request for a Web page:

1. A client (a PC in the preceding scenario) makes a request through the Web browser.

2. The server listens on a socket and port for incoming HTTP requests. Port 80 is the default port on the server on which HTTP requests are accepted.
3. The server processes the request in the order in which the request arrives.
4. The server transmits a response (most likely in HTML).
5. The client receives the response, and the view is rendered in the browser.

HTTP is the primary protocol for Web pages. It is a connectionless protocol, meaning no permanent connection is retained between the client and the server. Each document is handled as a separate request and in a separate session that is terminated after the request is processed. A Web page may contain several elements within it such as images, sounds and video. In the processing of this document, separate HTTP requests are made to each element (that is, the images, sounds and video contained in the document). The user (being the person entering the URL of the document) does not explicitly make requests to these document elements, however his or her user-agent (being the Web browser in this case) will automatically send requests for these elements in order to render the document view. The server then transmits each of these elements to the client.

The Internet is a common network which clients can servers can log onto in order to transmit data (consisting of requests and responses) to each other. In layman's terms, clients and servers use the Internet to communicate with each other. The client/server paradigm is important to understand because, as the developer, you will be responsible for handling client requests and sending back appropriate responses to the client.

Data transmission over the Internet

Data is transmitted and received over the Internet through the TCP/IP protocols, as shown in Figure 1-2.

By *sender* we are referring to the physical machine sending data packets. This may either be the client who is sending a request or the server sending a response.

By *receiver* we are referring to a physical machine receiving data packets. This can again be either the client receiving the response or the server receiving the request.

The following occurs as data is transmitted from sender to receiver:

1. The sender breaks data into *packets*.
2. These packets are sent through the Internet to the destination address via *routers*. Routers calculate the most efficient route for the packet (based on network congestion and traffic) and forward the packet to the next router until the packet reaches its destination.
3. The receiver then reassembles the data.

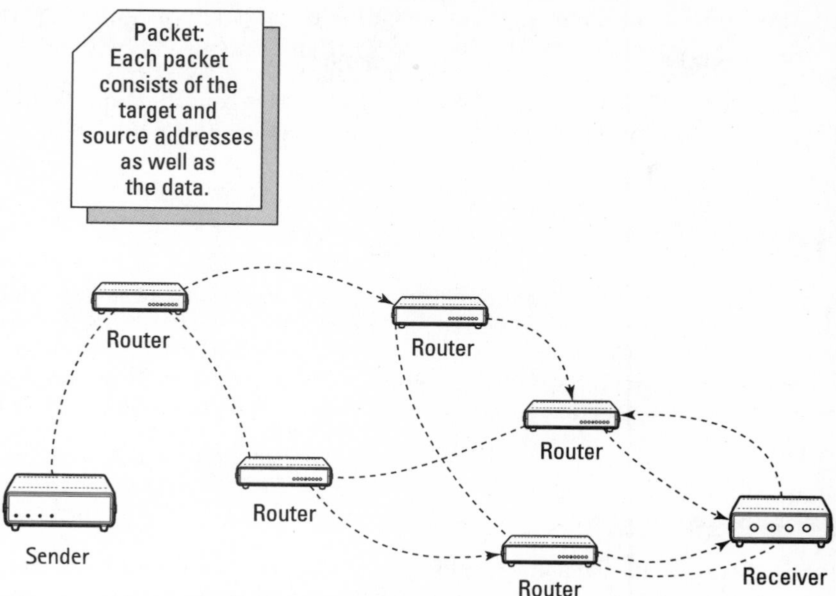

Figure 1-2: Data transmission using TCP/IP protocols

Packets may not travel the same paths to arrive at their destinations. The receiver requests that any lost packets be retransmitted. The job of the sender and receiver is to break up and reassemble packets by using the TCP. The IP is used to forward packets between networks and routers so the packets arrive at their destinations. The TCP/IP protocols are much more complicated than explanations suggest here. This is simply a summary of what happens.

The future of the Web

With the Wireless Application Protocol (WAP) in place, the Web can be accessed with wireless devices such as mobile phones and personal digital assistants (PDAs). Currently, protocols to take the Internet into space are being developed. These will allow us to receive information and images directly from space stations and telescopes via the Internet or to send e-mail to astronauts in space. New protocols are being developed to take the Internet into every corner of our lives.

Despite these advances the Web browser will still be the common and familiar interface many people will use throughout the world. It is an interface that remains the same across various platforms, whether you're a MAC, PC, or UNIX user. The browser caters well to a wide range of computer users; both computer experts and novices are familiar with using the Internet through a Web browser. For these reasons, the Internet has become the means for which most applications are developed. This book shows you how to use servlet technology (in conjunction with the Web interface) to deliver dynamic content to a user using a Web browser—whether the user is a corporate manager trying to access reports about Web-site performance or an online customer browsing the company's product catalog.

An Introduction to Servlets

The servlet Application Programming Interface (API) is one area of Java technology that provides developers with a mechanism for extending the functionality of a Web server. As a Java technology, servlets have access to the entire Java API. Java servlets and JSP are becoming an increasingly popular choice for Web-application development and an important technology for both Web and Java developers to learn.

What are servlets?

A servlet is a server-side Java application that operates within a network service, like a Web server. If you are familiar with Java applets, think of a servlet as an applet that runs on the server side (rather than the client side) and on the visual part of the servlet as a Web page.

Unlike CGI programs, Java servlets are executed inside the application or Web-server process. Servlets provide a component-based and platform-independent approach for building Web applications.

Servlets technology is not proprietary to a particular platform or server, thus providing freedom to select the best choice of platforms, servers, and so on. Also, servlets technology provides freedom to integrate servlets with existing architecture. Java servlets have a role to play in the J2EE Architecture, which is becoming a popular and effective architecture for Enterprise Web-application solutions. Servlets are part of the `javax.servlet` and `javax.servlet.http` packages in the J2EE Architecture.

Client-side scripting

Client-side scripting allows a developer to control events and responses (to a limited extent) on the client side of the Internet's client/server paradigm. The most widely supported scripting language on all browsers is JavaScript. VBScript is another popular option; however, VBScript is supported only in Microsoft's Internet Explorer. For examples in this book, JavaScript is used.

Client-side scripting takes advantage of the client's CPU resources to perform some routines the server handles otherwise. The server receives the consequential benefit, as the server now has a significantly reduced workload. For example, a validation routine that prevents users from submitting blank fields in a form reduces the workload of the server in a number of ways. The server does not have to detect blank fields, thus saving validation modules executed on the server. In addition, the server does not have to generate appropriate responses to send to the client. This time and resource saving can be better spent on serving other requests. This makes the application run more efficiently. These savings make a significant difference in cases where the server handles large volumes of traffic. Figure 1-3 shows a situation for one request where the client side is taking care of managing events, validation, and calculation. Now imagine that these were not taken care of by the client; many requests would have to be sent to the server instead. Now multiply this by the number of machines making simultaneous requests. The server would clearly be burdened with unnecessary work. This would result in the server taking a longer time to process each request, and thus you would have to wait longer for your response.

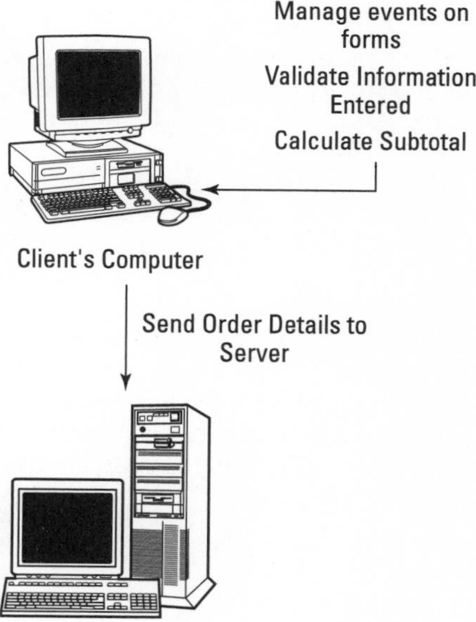

Figure 1-3: Client-side processing

Does Your Browser Run JavaScript?

Though it is rare to encounter browsers that have JavaScript disabled, a good developer should cover all scenarios.

JavaScript is embedded in an HTML document between the `<SCRIPT LANGUAGE="JAVASCRIPT">` and the ending `</SCRIPT>` tag.

Where JavaScript is disabled, content should be included within the starting `<NOSCRIPT>` and closing `</NOSCRIPT>` tags.

All JavaScript-enabled browsers recognize `<NOSCRIPT>` tags; if JavaScript is enabled on the browser, the content encapsulated between the `<NOSCRIPT>` tags is ignored. Browsers that do not recognize JavaScript ignore the `<NOSCRIPT>` tags and render the content between the `<NOSCRIPT>` tags. The following code detects whether JavaScript is enabled on the browser. If JavaScript is not enabled (or supported), this information is displayed in a message to the user.

```
<HTML>
<HEAD>
<TITLE>JavaScript Enabled or Disabled?</TITLE>
<SCRIPT LANGUAGE="JavaScript">
<!--
window.location.href = "javascript.html";
// -->
</SCRIPT>
</HEAD>
<BODY>
<NOSCRIPT>
<H2> Your browser does not support JavaScript for one of the
following reasons: </H2>
<UL>
<LI> JavaScript has been disabled on your browser.
<LI> You need a JavaScript enabled browser.
</UL>
 <BR>
 <B> To view this page a JavaScript enabled browser is required.
</NOSCRIPT>
</BODY>
</HTML>
```

When JavaScript is enabled on the browser, the preceding code forwards a client to the `javascript.html` page.

Activities such as maintaining state (limited), validation, and numeric calculations can be handled on the client side. Server resources can prove an expensive cost per request; therefore, it is wise to conserve server resources. The server should handle only activities that the client cannot perform and activities that need to run in a secure environment, such as sending e-mail and making database updates or entries. As a Web or Java developer, you should use all the tools and resources available; so we recommend that JavaScript be used to reduce the server's overall workload.

Server-side scripting

The more interesting part of Web-applications development is what happens on the server side. This is where the action is! Server-side scripting or programming can be used very effectively to provide interactivity and dynamic content for a client.

In server-side scripting, it's important to remember that the connection between the client and server exists only during a page request. As the request is fulfilled by the server, the connection is broken. All activity on the server (effected by the user) occurs at the page-request level. Often pages requested have scripts embedded within them (this code can only been seen on the server). When a request is made for such pages the code within the page is firstexecuted. This may result in subsequent processing of business logic on the server side. Upon completion, an HTML response is transmitted back to the client. Scripted pages may contain user-defined variables, subroutines, and functions. Some scripting engines allow objects to be defined and permit these objects to interact with each other.

Note By *scripting engine* we refer to the software container/component that can support and execute the scripted pages.

The ultimate purpose of server processing is to

- ✦ Update the business state of the server (that is, allow information concerning and affecting the business operations to be updated).
- ✦ Respond with an HTML-formatted page (user interface) for the requesting browser

An important and subtle part of Web-application design is understanding and accommodating this paradigm of client/server interaction. Business objects are not always accessible when handling individual user-interface requests. For example, you may have a module that performs some validation using some business logic or rules. This object may be residing on a different server and have reached its peak in servicing requests, so new requests have to wait. These waits then translate into a delay for the client who is waiting for a response. Requests should be pooled and synchronized to avoid deadlock.

The limitations of HTML

HTML is simple but inefficient for Web programmers, as it requires pages to be prepared in advance. Let's say you are building an online store and you want to display a catalog of all your products; it is extremely inefficient and expensive to update the HTML constantly to maintain a catalog with new products. Some of the benefits a server-side language offers are to allow you to connect to a database, retrieve product lists and image names, and display the products in the client's browser in HTML format. In other words, you can develop completely database-driven Web sites. Updating the Web site becomes easier because adding products requires only database updates with the new product information; recoding is unnecessary.

HTML is limited in functionality and is restricted to defining the presentation and layout of a Web page. When serving HTML pages, little or no interaction exists between the client and server (other than the request for the Web page). Server-side scripting also provides mechanisms for collecting or gathering client information. Let's say you want to gather feedback from your customers about their shopping experiences on your online shop front and to store their feedback in a database. HTML provides the mechanism to build forms or surveys but not to e-mail or deliver the information. Server-side programming fills these gaps. Depending on the choice of language, all server-side scripting languages can offer many features that prove both useful and convenient to developers.

Choosing a server-side scripting/programming language

There are numerous options in choosing a server-side programming language these days; however, all languages provide the mechanism for delivering dynamic Web content. The following factors are important in choosing a server-side language:

✦ **Cost:** This is a key issue from a management standpoint. Some costs to evaluate are the cost of setting up software and server(s) to be able to develop and deploy the application, the cost of hiring developers, and the cost of future maintenance.

✦ **Ease to Use/Easy to learn:** It is more beneficial to have a language that avoids cryptic syntax and semantics. These benefits occur in development and more so in maintenance. Less time is wasted in understanding or reviewing code and more time can be spent on design. You want to avoid situations where you forget what the code you wrote months ago does! This also makes it easier on other developers to pick up where you left off.

✦ **Documentation:** Documentation of the language should be adequate or abundant. In turn, this benefits developers. Languages that have abundant documentation often have a larger developer community, making it easier to find developers.

- **Scalability:** Often, developers don't consider scalability. How much traffic growth do you expect? How far can you extend the efficiency, performance, and workload of your Web-based application? The answers to these questions can depend on your choice of language.
- **Platform:** NT? UNIX? Some languages are platform-dependent. For example, an ASP application may not be ported directly to a UNIX OS as Java is ported. Java provides the benefit of being platform independent.
- **Industry Support:** How widely is the language you have chosen supported in the I.T. industry? Are there going to be future upgrades, enhancements, and support for the language you choose? Industry support of the language is closely tied with the companies that sponsor, create, and enhance a language. Also, this issue is tied closely with developer availability and cost to develop applications using the language.
- **Portability:** Portability is an issue related mainly to deployment across various server environments. Your code should be relatively easy to deploy.
- **Features:** This is a key issue for developers. Some languages offer more features to provide convenience. ColdFusion is a great example of this. ColdFusion has a large number of tags, and each tag provides a functionality that does not need to be coded. Customization is another factor to consider in this area. Customization provides the opportunity to extend the capability of the language by allowing the developer to create customized components that can be reused.
- **Integration:** How far and easily can you integrate code from this language with legacy, existing technologies, and future technologies?

When evaluating a server-side programming language, consider striking a balance or making tradeoffs with the preceding factors. Java provides numerous benefits that cater to all these issues.

Web Application Development

Web-based applications are becoming increasingly popular. This is partly due to the fact that there is a rapid deployment of technologies to develop Web-based applications. It is easy to be confused between a Web site and a Web application. The difference is that a Web application uses a Web site as an interface (or front end). In a typical application, user input (in this case, from a Web site) directly affects the state of the business (processing occurs at the application level). In other words, business logic is triggered through the submission of user input. Processing a request through the interface requires a business application to execute business logic. After execution is complete, a response is transmitted back to the client. The response can be the source of subsequent requests.

Forms

The most common and effective way for Web applications to accept user input is through forms and form submission. A form consists of a number of fields (of various types such as check boxes, radio buttons, and text areas). A user fills out a form and submits the information via the interface, along with a request for the subsequent page (often called an *action page*). Often, form submission occurs when a Submit button is clicked (the submission can also take place through JavaScript links). The action page's code is then executed. The action page has access to the information submitted through the form and can use and store this information. This is the primary method Web applications use to gather user input and information. Usually, the response generated is based on the information submitted through the form.

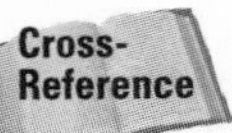

Form creation and elements are discussed in detail in Chapter 5.

Advantages of Web applications

The growing popularity of Web applications is due mainly to the advantages they offer over traditional applications. Table 1-2 summarizes the benefits of Web-based applications that are not readily available through traditional applications. The advantages and benefits of Web-based applications (shown in Table 1-2) result in overall reduced costs for development and maintenance.

Table 1-2
The Advantages of Web-based Applications

Advantages	*Description*
Information delivery	Because of its hypertext capabilities, the Web is an effective communications tool for delivering dynamic content in a variety of formats. Objects can be viewed online or downloaded and viewed at the convenience of the client. Web-site information can be database driven and current.
Distribution and distribution overheads	Updates can be made once and received everywhere at the client's request. Thus, there is little or no overhead for distribution of application updates (including content).
Remote access	The application can be accessed in any remote location that has Internet access. The application becomes independent of physical location.
Platform-independent user agent	The most common and widely-used browsers are available for a variety of platforms; the Web application becomes platform independent (in the context of running the application).

Advantages	*Description*
Reduced development efforts and costs	The development effort and cost of the application are significantly reduced. More emphasis is placed on business logic and user interface than on network programming. Users are not required to have access to costly WAN's or modem-telephone banks. With SSL, security becomes transparent to the programmer.
Centralized maintenance efforts	The centralized maintenance of Web-based applications is another key benefit. Often, the cost of coordinating the maintenance of distributed applications and distribution costs for maintenance upgrades can dwarf the initial development cost of the application.
Instant upgrades	Changes made to Web-based applications on the server take effect immediately for all users, eliminating issues of incompatibility due to version differences. Web applications that take advantage of client-side processing by using downloadable components, such as Java controls, allow the Web browser to download modified components immediately, making an instant upgrade possible when changes are made. All upgrades to software or hardware can be made without the end user knowing that the upgrade has been made.
Interface changes	The client interface can be modified without affecting the rest of the application.

Issues to consider

Although a Web-application approach provides numerous benefits, developers have challenging issues to deal with in a Web application. The main issues are: handling synchronization concurrency; maintaining state or session information; dealing with clients running old browser versions; and dealing with programming issues on various platforms.

Handling synchronization and concurrency

In the client/server paradigm, each server handles multiple and concurrent clients. In addition, each server accesses common services in the application. Such services can include files, databases, and e-mail services. It is important that clients do not tread on each other. For example, clients tread on each other when one client is reading data from a file while another client is writing to the file. Web-based applications should be developed to manage these types of situations.

Maintaining state

As the Web (in the context of the HTTP) is stateless, determining the state of the client becomes challenging. How do you know where the client is in the application and what page the client is on? Most good scripting languages define the session object in some way. There are several ways to maintain session and state information. The main methods are Cookies, Hidden form fields, and URL Rewriting.

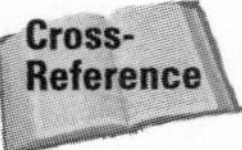

Maintaining state and session information is discussed in Chapter 11.

Multiple platforms

As the Web application can be accessed on multiple browsers and platforms, avoiding coding that may work only on one type of browser or platform is a good idea (unless it is deliberate for some reason). Such coding causes problems for clients or customers using the Web application. For example, writing JavaScript into your Web page that is specific to Internet Explorer restricts functionality (provided by the JavaScript) to users using Netscape Navigator.

Even HTML is handled slightly differently in Internet Explorer versus Netscape. Internet Explorer 5.x + is more liberal (and allows you to get away with mistakes) where Netscape Navigator does not.

Scripting Options

Essentially, server-side programming and scripting is what many Web applications are built on. As discussed previously, there are a number of options when choosing a server-side programming language for developing Web-based applications. The most common options used in industry (and discussed in this chapter) are CGI (Perl), ASP, PHP, ColdFusion, and servlets and JSP. Each of these languages is designed for a specific purpose, and any of them can get the job done. You need to evaluate these options in detail to determine which best suits the needs of the Web application and the business.

Common Gateway Interface (CGI)

CGI was the first server-side scripting language to be developed. The idea of dynamic content delivery from the server side was spawned from the advent of CGI. CGI scripts being on the server side have access to all the resources contained on the server. These resources can be used to perform tasks and help to generate responses. CGI is most commonly executed in a UNIX environment; however, with the ActivePerl product, CGI scripts can be executed in a windows environment. Being the first and oldest server-side scripting language, CGI is supported by most Web servers today.

The main advantages of CGI are:

- A CGI program can be written in a number of languages such as C, C++, UNIX shell scripts, or Perl. Perl, however, is the most popular choice.
- The fact that CGI can be written in a number of languages makes it easier for an experienced programmer to learn CGI.
- CGI interfaces work well with a many UNIX programs (such as sendmail) and legacy systems.

CGI has some drawbacks, particularly in performance.

The main disadvantages of CGI are:

- CGI has a large process overhead. For every request for a CGI page, a new process has to be started. When the CGI script concludes, the process has to be shutdown, so there is a large startup and shutdown overhead.
- Maintaining state becomes difficult in CGI, due to the fact that each CGI process is shutdown after each request.
- CGI (Perl) can be cryptic both in syntax and semantics and can be difficult to learn.
- CGI has security vulnerabilities that the developer must minimize. Because of these vulnerabilities, many ISPs restrict access to CGI scripts. If you don't have control over the server that hosts your application, CGI may not be a viable choice for you.

CGI's performance drawbacks make it a poor choice for developing any serious Web application.

These disadvantages make servlets a superior alternative to CGI.

Active Server Pages (ASP)

ASP is a scripting technology developed by Microsoft. ASP is a very popular choice among Visual Basic developers for Web-application development.

The main advantages of ASP are:

- The syntax of ASP is based on VBScript that (arguably) makes it easier to learn than Java coding, especially for existing VB programmers.
- Like Java, ASP is an inexpensive option.
- ASP constructs components quickly.
- ASP has no constraints on the client-side.
- ASP can use ODBC to connect to any data source.

- ASP offers fast execution.
- ASP offers visual-authoring tools and development tools.

The main disadvantages of ASP are:

- In choosing ASP, you are pretty much tied to the Microsoft and NT Platforms, as you need an IIS Web server (unless you are using Chillisoft's products).
- ASP is not as well suited as Java for building complex applications.
- Because ASP ties you to a Windows Platform, you cannot take advantage of other platforms such as UNIX.
- Often, logic and presentation are tied together in ASP code. ASP lacks the structure needed to form well-designed programs.

ASP is a viable and popular choice for Web-application development; however, ASP may not be as well suited as Java for building complex and scalable Web applications. Complex applications require reusable components that are more intuitively built and designed in Java.

Hypertext Preprocessor (PHP)

PHP is a server-side, cross-platform, HTML-embedded scripting language. Like the other major scripting options, PHP has a large developer base and has been around for quite a while.

PHP has these main advantages:

- PHP is open source and completely free.
- PHP is platform independent.
- PHP was designed as a rapid Web-application development tool. If it takes about two months to code a Web application in C++, you can develop the same Web application in about one to two weeks using PHP.
- PHP has excellent database connectivity to all SQL database servers, in particular to mySQL.

PHP has these main disadvantages:

- PHP is not a pure OO scripting language; therefore, maintenance becomes an issue for large applications that contain large amounts of code.
- PHP is interpreted; therefore, it cannot offer the performance other scripting languages can offer (despite the fact that you can get a performance boost with the Zend optimizer).

VB developers can pick up ASP. Java developers can pick up servlets and JSP, and C/C++ developers can get up to speed with CGI; however, development in PHP requires the developer to learn a whole new language.

ColdFusion (CFML)

ColdFusion is completely tag-based markup language. Its syntax resembles HTML and XML. Allaire's ColdFusion application server works with common Web servers to process ColdFusion (`.cfm` or `.cfml`) pages. To develop and use ColdFusion pages, the ColdFusion application server is required. This application server is available for both NT and UNIX platforms.

The advantages of ColdFusion are

- ✦ As ColdFusion is tag based, it is relatively easy to learn, especially if you know HTML. New developers might find programming complex constructs in cfml relatively easy.
- ✦ ColdFusion is ideal for a rapid Web-application development environment, as it features around 70 or more tags and 200 functions that can be used to develop applications quickly.
- ✦ ColdFusion is highly extensible through custom tags and CFX extensions. It provides the ability to integrate with COM, CORBA, and EJB. Java objects can be directly invoked.

The disadvantages of ColdFusion are

- ✦ One of the biggest disappointments with ColdFusion is cost. ColdFusion server(s) must be purchased for development and deployment. Often, the IDE, although not required, is an additional cost.
- ✦ Separating code for business logic and presentation is not intuitive in ColdFusion.
- ✦ ColdFusion ties you to a particular range of Web servers that are configurable with the ColdFusion application server.
- ✦ For every page request, the cfm page must be interpreted and executed. Optimizing the performance of a ColdFusion application is often tied to hardware optimization.

The Power of Servlets

As part of the family of Java API, servlets have the full *power* of Java and inherit the object-oriented advantages of Java technologies. Servlets were introduced as a superior replacement for CGI; however, they have become a popular alternative to Web development and Web-application development.

Java servlets are direct extensions to the Web server. They are simply Java objects that the Web server's Java Virtual Machine (JVM) loads dynamically (see Figure 1-4).

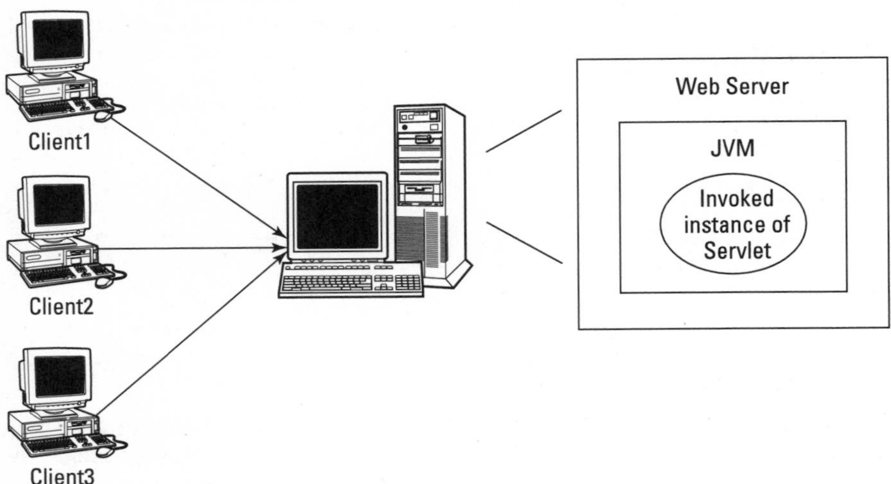

Figure 1-4: Servlet Invocation

Advantages that make servlet technology a superior choice as a server-side programming language are: platform independence; scalability; persistence; extensibility; reusability, performance; security; portability; intuitive design; industry-wide support; protocol independence; and cost efficiency. These advantages are explained and discussed in the remainder of this section.

Platform independence

Essentially, platform independence is the Java promise of *write once and run anywhere*. This means that you will be able to develop your application and deploy it on various platforms (for example, UNIX or NT), and it will run the same way in either environment. You may find that this may not always hold true (for example, if the code in the application does something operating system (OS)-specific or uses OS-specific resources. In such cases some tweaking may be required to use the program. But application modules will be able to be used (with or without tweaking) and reused without the need for a complete rewrite.

Scalability

Scalability refers to the ability to be able to handle/cater for various loads that could either be large volumes or small traffic. Servlets offer scalability because they are object oriented and can be designed and synchronized to meet the needs of a Web application. Servlets can operate within the JVM of any small Web server or even within giants such as IBM's Websphere.

Persistence

Persistence is the ability to maintain information for a duration (the duration may be specified). Servlets offer persistence because the Web server loads them only once; therefore, servlets can maintain information among multiple requests. This simplifies session tracking and maintaining services such as database connections. Servlets have the capability to share data, to persist data (by using Java Beans), to forward requests, and to generate responses of various formats (MIME types).

Extensibility

Extensibility is the ability to extend existing modules in order to create new modules. As a Java technology, servlets can extend classes as needed. This provides maintenance and cost benefits.

Reusability

As Java is an object-oriented language, its components can be designed and reused across the Web application or across multiple applications, again driving down development efforts, maintenance efforts, and cost. The reuse occurs at a programming level with one component/module using another in order to perform some task. That way code does not need to be replicated over multiple programs/applications.

Performance

One of the biggest benefits Java offers is performance. Java is truly the best performer in terms of server-side scripting options.

In a typical CGI environment, each request creates a new process that loads the Perl interpreter (typically over 500 KB in size). Subsequently, the Perl interpreter loads the Perl script, compiles it, and executes it. If the application communicates with a database, a new connection needs to be established for each Perl script (a rather expensive process for some databases). This adds tremendous overhead to the application.

When deployed, a servlet is loaded once and used many times. With each request, servlets start a new thread (rather than a new process).

A new process is an expensive system overhead. Threads are cheap in the way of system resources.

To execute a servlet, the JVM must be running on the server at all times. This allows servlets to use significantly fewer system resources. In addition, it allows better scalability and optimal performance.

Security

Servlets are in a compiled form, unlike CGI/Perl, so the source code is protected when the `.jar` or `.class` files are deployed. Servlets are more secure than CGI/Perl, as they are not prone to security vulnerabilities; also, only the Web server can invoke servlets (as they act as a direct extension to the Web server). This makes servlets a very secure choice in the server-side programming environment.

Portability

The Servlet API is standard and consistent across platforms and server implementations, thus allowing applications to be moved easily from one operating system to another. Many companies are looking for a portable solution. Perhaps they want developers to use Linux or Windows NT while their production server runs a Solaris OS. Or perhaps they want to sell their Web application to as many customers as possible, on as many platforms as possible. Java presents an unparalleled option in portability.

Intuitive design

Because Java is an OO language, its design is intuitive. Components can be designed, extended, and reused many times. The Unified Modeling Language (UML) provides a mechanism for simplifying the OO-design process. Combined with an abundance of documentation and specifications (including J2EE architecture), Java's intuitive design provides an easy way to apply the industry's best practices to your application.

Industry-wide support

Java now has industry-wide support from all the big names (Sun, IBM, and even Microsoft) and many of the small names. Finding Web servers, software, tools and other technologies to support your needs poses no problem. There is an abundance of both open source (free) and commercially supported technologies for servlets. Thorough documentation is also abundant.

Protocol independence

The servlet API assumes nothing about the protocol being used to transmit on the Internet.

The `javax.servlet.GenericServlet` is not tied to HTTP or to any protocol. Do not confuse it with `javax.servlet.HttpServlet`, which is tied to HTTP.

This protocol independence is advantageous in that responses can be generated for a variety of clients, such as Web browsers or mobile phones.

Cost efficiency

Ultimately, all of these benefits drive down the cost of a Web application powered by Java servlets versus other server-side languages. However, a major cost when using Java technology is hiring Java developers.

The role of servlets

Servlets act as a middle layer or *tier* between any type of thin client and business or enterprise services. Servlets are invoked through the HTTP services (via HTTP Requests) of a Web server and can generate HTTP Responses.

Typically, servlets are used for the following tasks:

- Reading client input and HTTP request information
- Tracking sessions (establishing the session, then tracking the session through cookies or URL rewriting)
- Connecting to back-end systems for data or business services
- Sending and receiving client information to the back end. This information may be necessary for either data storage or application logic
- Generating content (setting the appropriate response parameters, then either outputting or forwarding the appropriate page to the client)

Often, although it might be minimal, application logic is embedded in the servlet.

In enterprise-level Web-application development, servlets play a major role in providing the necessary connection between Web servers and enterprise-wide services. On their own, servlets are applicable only for small to medium scale Web-application development.

Summary

In this chapter, you have learned how the Web works and the advantages that Java/servlet technology offers to Web-application development. The key points you should take from this chapter are

- The Internet works on a client/server paradigm.
- That TCP/IP protocols are the backbone data transmission on the Internet.
- JavaScript can be used to reduce server workload.

- There are various options and considerations to be made when choosing a server-side programming language for Web-application development.
- Servlets are part of the `javax.servlet` and `javax.servlet.http` packages.
- Creating threads is more efficient than creating new processes, as processes have a larger overhead.
- Servlets play various roles in Web applications.

In the next chapter, you learn to set up a servlet development environment to begin creating your own servlets.

✦ ✦ ✦

Setting up a Servlet Development Environment

✦ ✦ ✦ ✦

In This Chapter

Learning which Web servers support servlet technology

Setting up and administering a Web server to run servlets

Creating and running your first servlet

✦ ✦ ✦ ✦

This chapter focuses on learning which Web servers support servlet technology and setting up and administering a Web server to run servlets. The chapter also discusses installing and configuring the JRun 3.02 application server to run servlets. All the examples in this book are tested with JRun 3.02. This chapter ends with a simple example of creating and running your first servlet.

Note From this point forward, we assume that you have your Java Development Kit version 1.2.2 or higher set up correctly on your machine or that you have an IDE (such as JBuilder or Visual Age for Java) that has appropriate compiler configurations.

What You Need to Run Servlets

A *servlet* is a Java program that uses the servlet packages (*javax.servlet*) in the `servlet.jar` file. Like any other Java program, you need to compile a servlet by using the Java compiler *javac*. The `servlet.jar` file does not come as a part of the Java Development Kit (JDK). The servlet.jar package is available for free download from Sun's Java servlet site: `http://java.sun.com/products/servlet/`.

You can find the `servlet.jar` file on this book's CD-ROM.

The Java compiler needs to know the location of the `servlet.jar` file, so the path where the file is physically present needs to be present in the `CLASSPATH` environment variable. Java looks for this variable to locate classes. To find whether the `CLASSPATH` environment variable exists, try issuing the following command at the prompt:

In UNIX:

`-printenv CLASSPATH (csh/tcsh shells)` or

`echo $CLASSPATH (for sh/bash shells)`

In Windows 2000/NT/98/95:

```
set CLASSPATH
```

Assuming the `CLASSPATH` variable exists, you can add the `servlet.jar` reference using the following commands:

In UNIX, for `csh/tcsh` shells:

```
setenv CLASSPATH .:$CLASSPATH:<servlet.jar directory>/servlet.jar
```

or for `bash/sh` shells:

```
CLASSPATH=$CLASSPATH:<servlet.jar directory>/servlet.jar
```

In Windows 2000/NT/ME/98/95:

```
set CLASSPATH=%CLASSPATH%;<servlet.jar directory>/servlet.jar
```

We use `%CLASSPATH%` or `$CLASSPATH` to preserve `CLASSPATH` and to avoid overwriting it. If the `CLASSPATH` variable does not exist already, we can omit the `%CLASSPATH%` or `$CLASSPATH` references.

The servlets and other necessary classes you develop might be under an alternate directory, so you might want to append the top-level directory to the `CLASSPATH` variable. This ensures that all classes necessary to implement a servlet are available to the Java compiler.

To run servlets, we require a Web server with support for servlets. A number of Web servers that support servlets are available on the market. You can view a reference to servers that support servlets at the following address: `http://java.sun.com/products/servlet/industry.html`. Some Web servers are freely downloadable.

Note

If you are developing servlets for commercial use, you need a high-quality, reliable Web server. However, if you want to learn servlets, a Web server that has basic servlet-handling functionality and can be installed on a desktop is quite sufficient.

The following are commonly used Web servers that support servlets:

- **Java Server Web Development Kit (JSWDK)**—This Web server can be used to test servlets and JSP pages. It has been implemented according to the official servlet 2.1 and JSP 1.0 specification. It is free for downloading but is a bit complex to set up. Point your browser to `http://java.sun.com/products/servlet/download.html`.
- **Java Web Server (JWS)**—This Web Server has been widely used and completely developed using Java. In addition, it has been developed in accordance with the servlet 2.1 and JSP 1.0 specifications. It comes with maximum security features. Sun's Java site provides a link to a free trial version of JWS at `http://www.sun.com/software/jwebserver/`.
- **Apache Tomcat**—Tomcat can act as a standalone server for testing servlets and can be integrated with the Apache Web Server. As of early 2001, Tomcat 3.2.1 is the latest release that supports servlet 2.2 and JSP1.1. A freely downloadable shareware, Tomcat is difficult to configure. You can download Tomcat and get more information about it at `http://jakarta.apache.org/tomcat/index.html`.
- **Allaire JRun**—A servlet and JSP engine, JRun is powerful and can be plugged into most popular servers, such as Netscape Enterprise Server, IIS, and Microsoft Personal Web Server (PWS). A fully functional evaluation and a licensed version JRun is available. JRun includes powerful visual tools called JRun Studio that can be used for developing rapid Web applications. The next section provides a detailed description of setting up JRun. You can find JRun at `http://www.allaire.com/products/jrun/`.
- **Unify eWave ServletExec**—This is a popular Web server that can be used for Solaris, Windows, Mac OS, HP-UX, and Linux. Although a free evaluation version disables administration utilities and advanced features, a fully functional ServletExec is available for purchase. It provides HTML-based remote administration for maximum browser compatibility and is easy to use. Unify eWave, in unison with its Web server, provides a free servlet debugger also. For further information, you can browse `http://www.unifyewave.com/servletexec/index.htm`.
- **Caucho Technology's Resin**—The latest version of Resin is 1.2.2, which supports servlet 1.2 and JSP 1.1. This Web server is available for a free download. Resin provides the flexibility for Web developers to choose the right language for their tasks. Resin has its built-in XSL (XML Stylesheet Language) parser that can be used to format XML (eXtensible Markup Language). More information is available at `http://www.caucho.com/`.
- **LiteWebServer**—This is a pure, Java-based Web server that provides support for servlet 2.2 and JSP 1.1 APIs. It is small and free is easy to set up and use. This server is recommended for use in servlet development, personal use, or for a small Intranet and can be found at `http://www.gefionsoftware.com`.

Of the Web servers mentioned here, JSWDK and JWS are primarily used by developers who want to learn working with Web servers. The configuration of these servers is console-based. Apache is widely used but requires expertise to configure. Resin is used mainly with XML and XSL, and parsing has to be done on the server side. JRun is both a Web server and an application server and has a good Web-based UI to configure. JRun Developer Edition is available for free and can be used by developers to test their applications. This book takes JRun as the server to deploy and test all the examples because of the ease in configuring. The next section covers in depth how to configure and manage JRun.

Appendix F presents in detail how to configure and manage Apache and Tomcat servers.

Setting up a Web Server with JRun

Allaire's JRun comes with its own Web server that is sufficient for development purposes. It also has a built-in servlet engine that is quite popular on the servlet-engine market. JRun comes in three flavors. Each varies depending upon the license you procure when purchasing JRun.

At the time of writing this book, JRun 3.0 (service pack 2) is the latest edition released by Allaire. The Developer edition is limited to three concurrent connections and is available for free download from `http://www.allaire.com/products/jrun/`. The Development edition can be used only for developing and testing Web applications. It is not licensed for deployment and hence cannot be used for production purposes.

You can find the setup file for JRun on the book's CD-ROM.

The Professional edition allows an unlimited number of concurrent connections and can be used to deploy Web applications.

The Advanced edition builds on the Professional edition and adds features such as load balancing, fail over, and clustering to satisfy the needs of an enterprise. The licenses for both Professional and Advanced editions have to be procured on a per-processor basis. For the purposes of this discussion, we will use the JRun Developer edition.

Installing the JRun Web server

In this section, we look at how to install the JRun Web server and servlet engine on a Windows 2000/NT/98/95 system.

When you download the JRun software from the Web site, it will be saved under the name `jr302.exe`. Alternatively, you can search for this file on the accompanying CD-ROM. Launch the executable setup file (`jr302.exe`) by double-clicking it. This brings up the window shown in Figure 2-1.

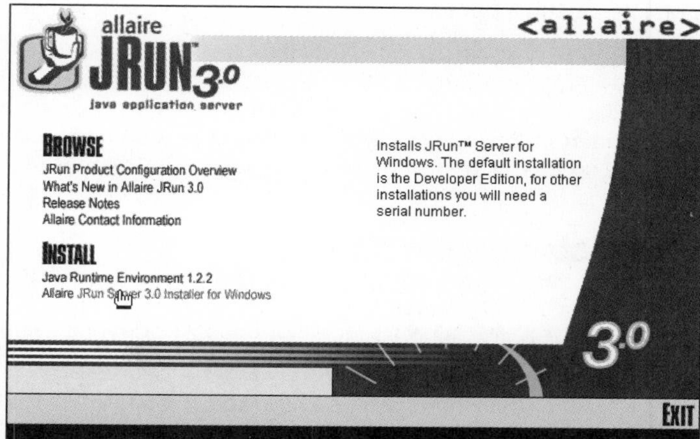

Figure 2-1: The JRun main installation window

Select Allaire JRun Server 3.0 Installer for Windows. The License Agreement dialog box is displayed in Figure 2-2. Choose Yes after reading the license agreement. The next step in the installation prompts for a license key. Since we will be using only the Developer edition of JRun, you can leave the entry blank.

Setup
JRun Product Serial Number
Please enter the JRun product serial number
allaire JRUN
Please enter the JRun product serial number. A serial number is not required to install the JRun Developer Edition.
Serial Number
InstallShield
< Back Next > Cancel

Figure 2-2: JRun license information and serial number window

Figure 2-3 shows the JRun Setup Type dialog box, which allows you to select the type of JRun installation required. There are three options:

✦ **Full Installation** — Installs all the components in JRun and is the recommended option for developers.

✦ **Typical Installation** — Installs minimal components needed for deploying a Web application.

✦ **Custom Installation** — Allows you to choose all the components yourself. This option is recommended only for advanced users who are very proficient with the JRun server. In a custom installation, you can select server components, EJB components, and so forth separately based on your requirements.

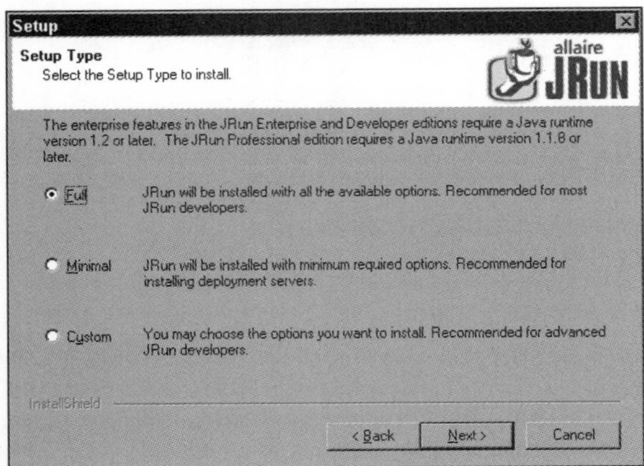

Figure 2-3: Select the type of JRun installation you require.

After specifying the installation type, setup copies all the files to the specified destination directory. Once copying is complete, setup asks if you want JRun Services installed, as shown in Figure 2-4. By selecting this option, JRun Web server runs as a Windows service and starts automatically when the system boots up. Windows 95/98/ME does not have the feature of running software components as a service. A Windows 2000/NT machine has the feature, but to install a component as a service, you must have local-administration privileges.

If JRun is not installed as a service, the Web server can be started and stopped manually by selecting a menu option from the JRun menu, which is accessed from the Start menu. For development environments that require frequent starting and stopping of the Web server, the recommended option is to start and stop the server manually, not to install it as a service. For production environments, it best to run the server as a service; in the event of a system crash or reboot, the server can automatically continue running when the system is back online.

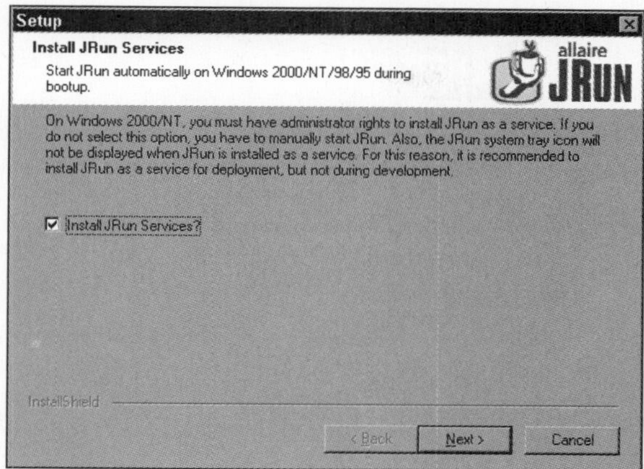

Figure 2-4: Installing the JRun services option

The next step in the installation process (see Figure 2-5) allows you to select the Java runtime environment for the JRun servlet engine to execute the server-side Java components (servlets, JSP, Enterprise JavaBeans, and so on). Installing a Java runtime of 1.2.2 or higher is a good idea so that all components of JRun work properly.

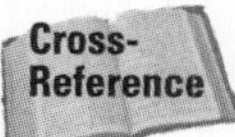

JSPs are components that are used for dynamic presentation. JSPs are covered in detail in Chapter 12.

Enterprise Java Beans are a special kind of JavaBean component and are reusable across applications. EJBs are run by special containers, which have the capability to do transaction management. Hence, they reduce the programmer's burden of managing transactions in his or her code.

The Java runtime of 1.2.2 or higher is specifically required for running EJB components deployed in JRun.

Setup prompts you for the port where the JRun administration routine listens for incoming requests to the admin server. It prompts you also for the JRun administration password.

Figure 2-6 shows the JRun Setup Complete dialog box, which gives you the option to configure external Web servers now or later. An external Web server is usually required when this Web server cannot process a request. For example, when XML/XSL parsing has to be done at the server side, external Web servers such as Apache or Resin could be configured as external Web servers to JRun. Once configured, when a request of type XML/XSL occurs, JRun automatically transfers the control to the external Web server. At present, we do not require external Web servers. Select "Start the JRun Management Console, I'll configure my Web server later" option. With this step, JRun installation is complete.

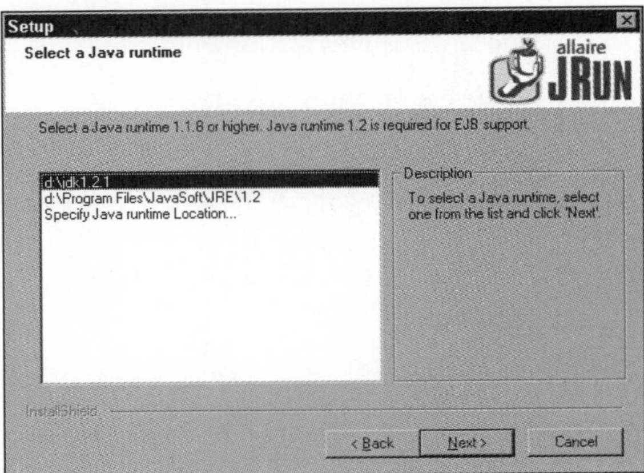

Figure 2-5: Select a Java runtime environment.

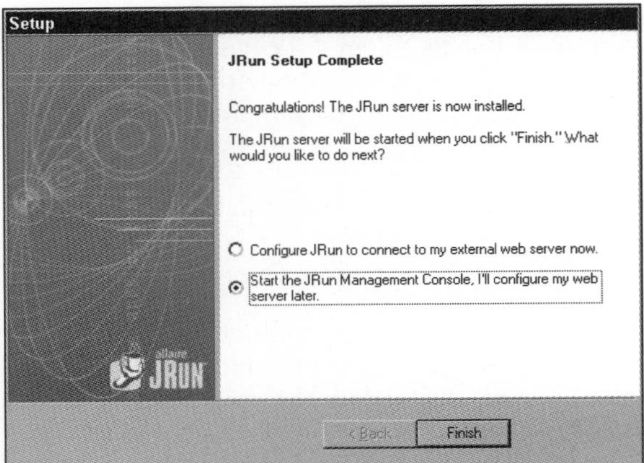

Figure 2-6: The JRun Setup Complete dialog box gives you the option of configuring external Web servers now or later.

JRun directory structure

After installation, JRun components are organized in the manner listed in Table 2-1. This table lists the directories that exist under the root directory (under which JRun has been installed) and describes the files they contain.

Table 2-1
JRun Web Server Directory Structure

Directory	*Description*
Bin	Contains all the executable files JRun needs
Connectors	Contains information on the necessary connector files required for configuring external Web servers to work with JRun
Docs	Contains documentation relevant to JRun
Lib	Contains .jar files and properties files that define default properties for all JRun applications
lib/ext	Contains .jar files, including servlet.jar and ejb.jar
Logs	Contains the JRun log files
samples	Contains the JRun sample files
servers	Contains the JRun servers and their applications
servers/admin	Defines the administration JRun server
servers/admin/deploy	Stores Enterprise JavaBeans (EJBs) to be deployed. Once deployed, EJBs are copied to the runtime directory at startup.
servers/admin/jmc-app	Contains the JRun Management Console (JMC) application
servers/admin/lib	Contains .jar and .class files accessed by all applications within the administration server
servers/admin/runtime	Runtime directory that contains classes to run EJB components.
servers/admin/tmp	Contains temporary subdirectories for each application in this JRun server. Removing these directories is *not* recommended.
servers/default	Defines the default JRun server
servers/default/default-app	Contains the default JRun application. Use this application to build and test Java servlets and JSPs.
servers/default/demo-app	Contains the JSP/servlet sample applications
servers/default/deploy	Stores deployed Enterprise JavaBeans (EJBs). Deployed EJBs are copied to the runtime directory at startup.

Continued

Table 2-1 (continued)

Directory	***Description***
`servers/default/lib`	Contains `.jar` and `.class` files accessed by all applications within the default server
`servers/default/runtime`	Deployed EJBs are copied to the runtime directory at startup.
`servers/default/runtime/classes`	Contains `.class` files for dynamically loaded EJB implementations
`servers/default/tmp`	Contains temporary subdirectories for each application in this JRun server. *Do not* remove the temporary directories.
`Servers/lib`	Contains `.jar` and `.class` files accessed by all JRun servers. This is a good location to store shared database drivers and other shared files. JRun stores the tag library in this directory.
`Servlets`	Contains `.class` files accessible to the default Web application. This directory is included for backward compatibility. The `.class` files for a new application should be arranged in a structured hierarchy as defined by the servlet 2.2 specification.
`Uninst`	Contains JRun uninstallation information

Starting the Web server

Depending on the installation, JRun can be started in different ways. If JRun Services are installed as part of the installation process, the Web server and the administration server are started automatically after the OS gets booted. Otherwise, you can use the shortcut items under the JRun menu to start the servers as follows:

1. To start the JRun Admin server, click Start ➪ Programs ➪ JRun 3.0 ➪ JRun Admin server.
2. To start the JRun Web server, click Start ➪ Programs ➪ JRun 3.0 ➪ JRun Default server.

Web server administration

The Web administrator can configure and optimize the JRun Web Server, as driven by application requirements. This can be done using the browser-based administration tool in JRun. Even though this tool ultimately writes information to properties files, it is easier for the end user to do it with the help of a user interface.

The JRun Admin server listens at port 8000 (default) to handle administration-related activities. To start the administration module, run the browser and, in the URL, specify the host name and port number in the following format:

```
http://host name:administration tool port number/
```

For example, if the host name is Bob and the port number is the default (that is, 8000), type the URL as:

```
http://BOB:8000/
```

If the host is the same client machine, the host can be referred by `localhost`. The URL would be

```
http://localhost:8000/
```

The module can also be invoked if the IP address of the host is known. In the case of `localhost`, the IP is 127.0.0.1, which represents that the host is the client:

```
http://127.0.0.1:8000/
```

This invokes the JRun Administration login dialog box, as depicted in Figure 2-7.

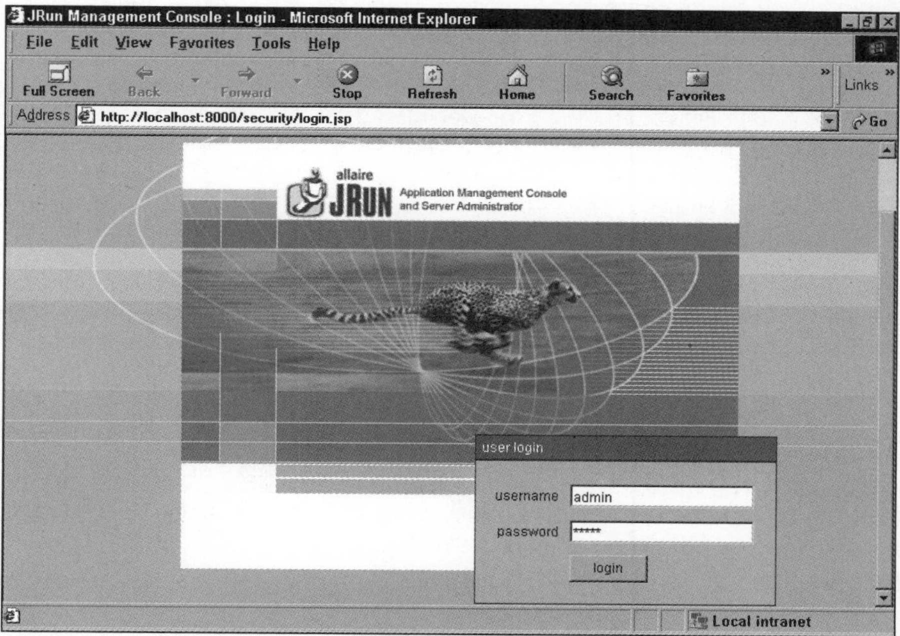

Figure 2-7: JRun Administration login

The built-in user name for the administrator is `admin`. Enter the password provided during installation time, and click the Login button. Once the authentication is successful, the JRun Application Management console and Server Administrator window are displayed, as shown in Figure 2-8.

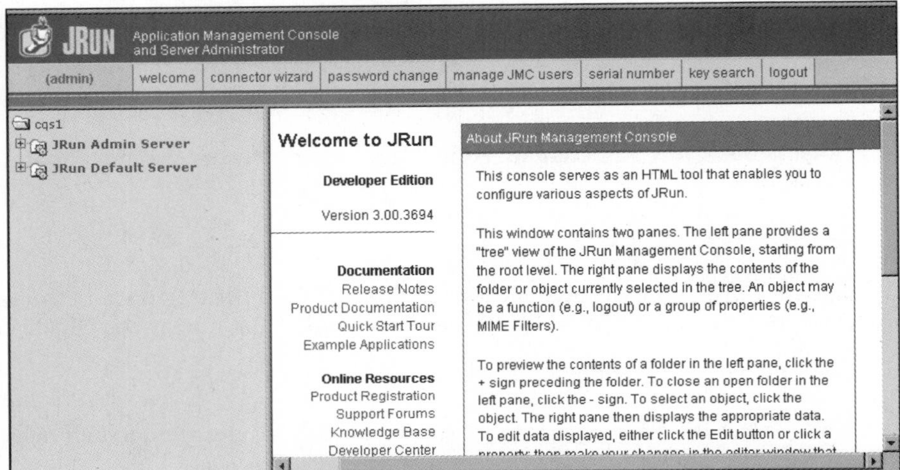

Figure 2-8: The JRun Application Management console and Server Administrator window

By default, two servers are set up automatically when JRun is installed. They are the JRun Admin Server and the JRun Default Server. A separate instance of the JRun executable (`jrun.exe` on the Windows platform) is run for each of the servers. More servers can be added to JRun as needed. Adding servers is relevant in situations in which a separate development server, testing server, and production server are required, but we have just one processor license for the JRun installation.

The JRun Admin Server hosts the JRun Management console Web administration application. Only through this application are we able to configure the parameters for JRun servers. The JRun Admin Server listens to a default port of 8000 unless specifically changed during the installation or through the administration module.

The JRun Default Server hosts all user applications. The Default server, by default, listens to port 8100. The number of Web applications that can be hosted per server is unlimited. The various parameters that can be configured are shown in Figure 2-9. Clicking on the links that are listed below the Default Server link can configure these parameters. The following sections cover these parameters in detail.

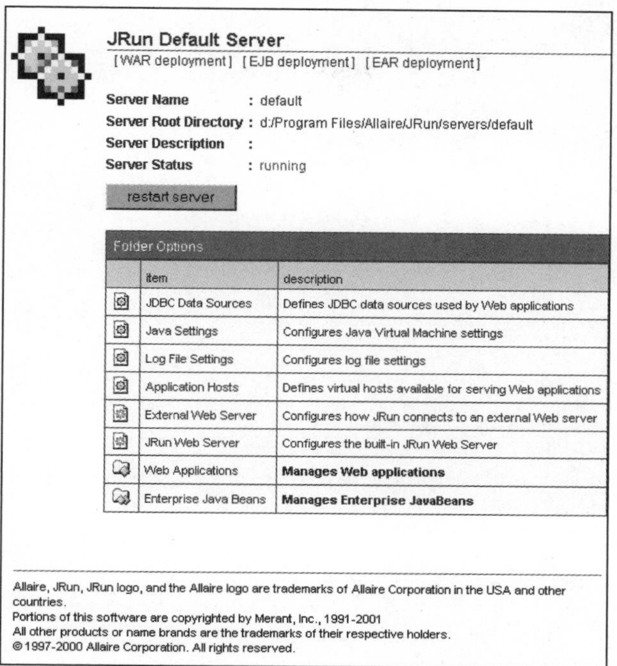

Figure 2-9: Use the JRun Default Server Application to configure Web-application parameters.

To go to the page displayed previously, you have to click the JRun Default Server link in the left pane of the JRun Application Management Console window. We will now look into each of the settings in detail.

JDBC data sources

The JDBC Data Sources page lets you define data sources that can be used in servlets and JSP programs to connect to a database. The advantage of defining data sources in such a manner is that when you change the details regarding a data source, the servlet programs using this need not be recompiled. At the same time, a servlet, which uses such data sources, does not run in a different servlet engine such as Tomcat or Resin. The JDBC Data Source screen is shown in Figure 2-10.

The JDBC Data Sources wizard guides you through creating a data source successfully. Important parameters are described in Table 2-2.

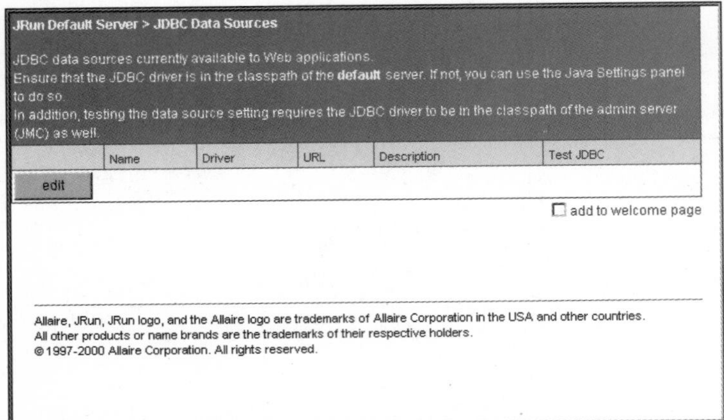

Figure 2-10: The JDBC Data Sources page allows you to define data sources to be used in servlets and JSP programs.

Table 2-2
JDBC Data Source Parameters

Parameter	*Description*
RDBMS Server Name	Select the name of the database driver this data source will use from the drop-down list provided.
Data Source Name	Enter the name for the data source you are creating. Use this name to connect to the database in a servlet program.
Description	Enter the description of the data source. This is an optional parameter and can be left blank.
Driver	Enter the name of the JDBC driver the data source will use to connect to the database (for example, `sun.jdbc.odbc.JdbcOdbcDriver`).
Username	If the database you are connecting to requires authentication, provide the username required to connect to the database.
Password	Enter a password corresponding to the username if one is provided.
Vendor Arguments	This parameter lets you specify vendor-specific arguments while connecting to the data source. Consult the database vendor documentation to find out the vendor arguments that can be provided.

The `.jar` files needed by the JDBC driver specified while creating the data source have to be added to the `CLASSPATH` of the default server and admin server, so that the data source can be used in a Web application.

Java settings

The Java Settings panel, shown in Figure 2-11, allows you to configure the Java Virtual Machine (JVM) parameters for the Web server and servlet engine.

JRun Default Server > Java Settings

Java Virtual Machine settings for this server.

Name	Value	Summary
Java Executable	d:\PROGRA~1\JavaSoft\JRE\1.2\bin\javaw.exe	Path to your JVM executable
System.out Log File	{jrun.rootdir}/logs/{jrun.server.name}-out.log	Location where System.out messages appear
System.err Log File	{jrun.rootdir}/logs/{jrun.server.name}-err.log	Location where System.err messages appear
JRun Control Port	53000	Port used by JRun to send server commands
Classpath	{jrun.rootdir}/servers/lib	Additional classpath entries
Java Arguments		Additional command-line arguments passed to the Java Executable
Library Path	{servlet.jnipath};{ejb.jnipath}	Directory of native JNI

edit

add to welcome page

Figure 2-11: Java Settings for Web server parameters

The Web server parameters are described in Table 2-3.

Table 2-3
Java Settings

Parameter	*Description*
Java Executable	Specify the name of the Java executable in this location. The JRun installer defaults this to the location of the JDK specified during installation.
`System.out` Log file	This entry reveals the location of the file that contains all the `System.out` messages printed in a servlet program.
`System.err` Log file	This entry reveals the location of the file that contains all the `System.err` messages printed in a servlet program.
JRun control port	Port used by JRun internally to communicate with the different components within itself.
`CLASSPATH`	Specify the classpath for all the packages that will be used by your applications here.
Java Arguments	Specify additional Java arguments that have to be passed to the Java executable in this location.

Log file settings

The log file settings specify the location of the JRun server log files. All JRun server messages are logged in the file specified at this location.

Application hosts

The Application Hosts section allows you to define the virtual hosts through which Web applications can be accessed. The virtual hosts can be mapped to different Web site addresses. Web administrators in a clustering environment primarily use this.

External Web server

The external Web server option allows you to plug in the JRun servlet engine to a different Web server, thereby taking advantage of the powerful features of the target Web server. This also enables the target Web server to host Web applications written using server-side Java technologies.

JRun Web server

The JRun Web server link allows you to activate the built-in Web server that is part of the JRun default server. If you use an external Web server to host your Web site and use JRun primarily as a connector to host server-side Java applications, this Web server can be turned off. By default, the Web server is turned on and listens on a particular port (8100). The port number can, however, be changed. Other parameters that can be configured are shown in Figure 2-12.

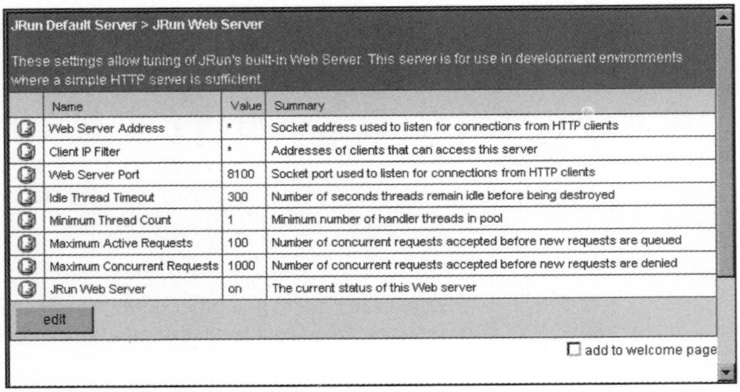

JRun Default Server > JRun Web Server

These settings allow tuning of JRun's built-in Web Server. This server is for use in development environments where a simple HTTP server is sufficient

Name	Value	Summary
Web Server Address	*	Socket address used to listen for connections from HTTP clients
Client IP Filter	*	Addresses of clients that can access this server
Web Server Port	8100	Socket port used to listen for connections from HTTP clients
Idle Thread Timeout	300	Number of seconds threads remain idle before being destroyed
Minimum Thread Count	1	Minimum number of handler threads in pool
Maximum Active Requests	100	Number of concurrent requests accepted before new requests are queued
Maximum Concurrent Requests	1000	Number of concurrent requests accepted before new requests are denied
JRun Web Server	on	The current status of this Web server

edit

add to welcome page

Figure 2-12: The JRun Web Server configuration parameters window

Web applications

The servlet 2.2 API specification defines the notion of a Web application. "*A Web application is a collection of servlets, HTML pages, classes, and other resources that can be bundled and run on multiple containers from multiple vendors.*" Because JRun 3.0 supports the servlet API 2.2, it provides support for creating and deploying Web applications. The Web application window is shown in Figure 2-13.

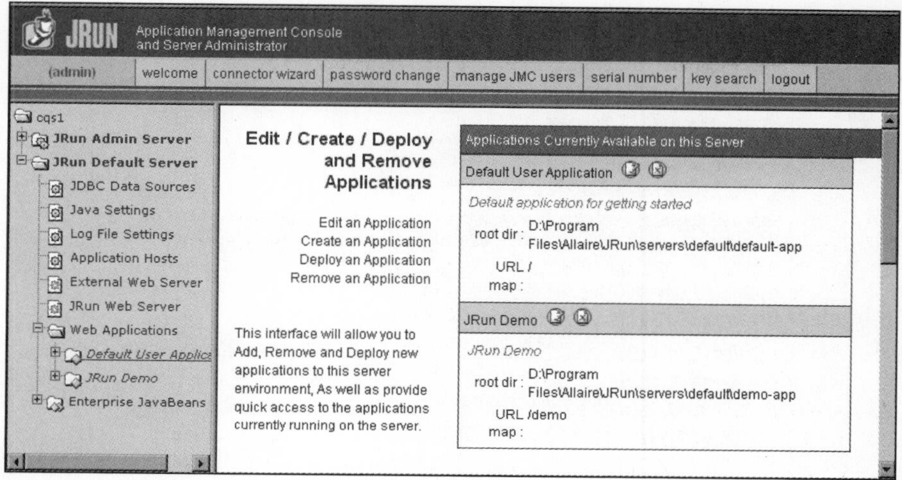

Figure 2-13: The Web application window displays all of the Web applications on the JRun servers.

The Web application window displays all the Web applications that are part of the JRun servers. You can edit any of the applications or create new ones. To create a Web application, click the "Create an application" link and provide the necessary information. The fields are self-explanatory. If you have a completed Web application to be deployed as a `.war` file, you can select "Deploy an application" to set up the Web application archive. JRun creates two Web applications at setup time in the JRun default server:

✦ **Default User Application —** If you are not creating a separate application and want to use JRun just to deploy and test your servlets and JSP, you can use the Default User Application

✦ **JRun Demo —** This is an application that hosts all the JRun samples that come with JRun. It can be accessed by using the following URL:

```
http://localhost:8100/demo/
```

Any Web application you create will have a standard set of properties. This is shown in Figure 2-14.

Application variables

You can define variables that are accessible throughout your Web application in this section. These variables can be accessed using the servlet context's `getInitParameter()` method.

File settings

As shown in Figure 2-15, the File Settings window lets you specify the directory-browsing options and default documents for this Web application.

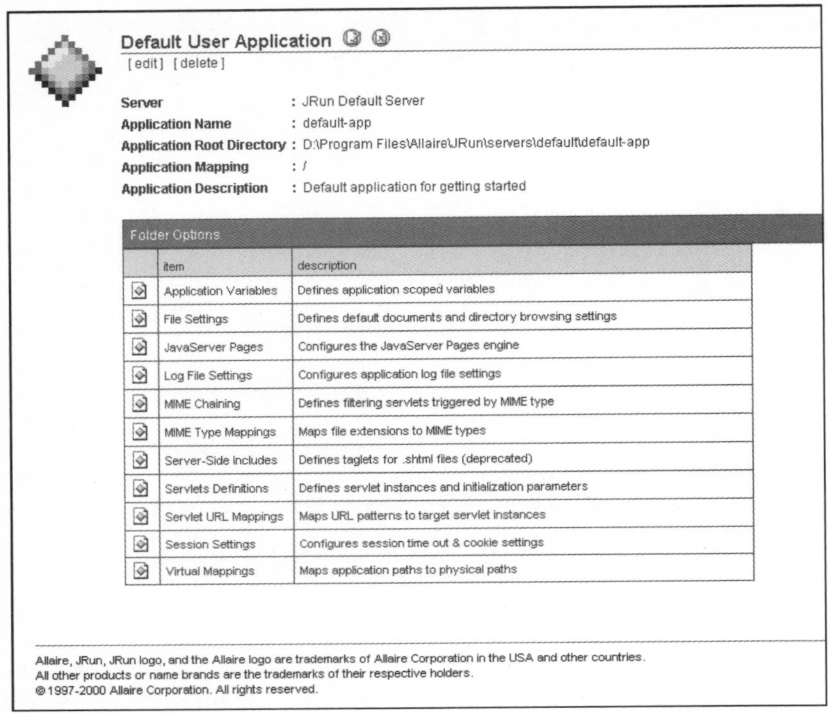

Figure 2-14: The Default User Application screen displays a standard set of properties for a Web application.

JRun Default Server > Web Applications > Default User Application > File Settings

These settings allow you to toggle the directory browsing and set default documents for the built-in JRun Web Server.

Name	Value	Summary
Directory Browsing Allowed	true	Shows directory contents upon directory access
Default Documents	index.jsp	Defines documents to serve upon directory access

edit

add to welcome page

Figure 2-15: You can specify directory-browsing options in the File Settings window.

Java server pages

The Java Server pages link allows you to instruct JRun to look for a `global.jsa` file while this Web application is loaded. The `global.jsa` file can be used to store application-level variables used by servlets and JSP. In addition, you can specify the Java compiler to be used to compile the JSP files. The Java compiler settings window and examples of specifying external Java compiler are shown in Figure 2-16.

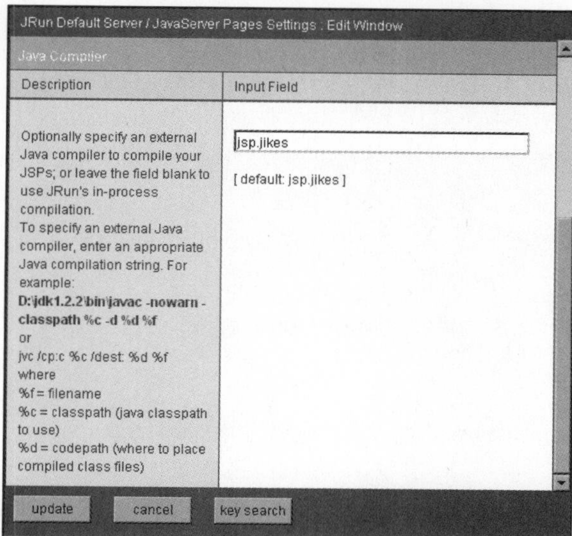

Figure 2-16: The Java Server Pages Settings window allows you to set up storage for Web application variables used by servlets and JSP.

Log file settings

The Log File Settings window shown in Figure 2-17 allows you to enable the logging of various events and errors related to your Web application. The types of messages that can be logged can be selected by choosing the Logging Level link. The Event log link allows you to specify the location of the log file. By default, the log file exists in the JRun logs directory.

JRun Default Server > Web Applications > Default User Application > Log Settings

Settings for log files used by this application.

	Name	Value	Summary
	Logging Level	info,warning,error	Types of events written to the event log
	Event Log	{jrun.rootdir}/logs/{jrun.server.name}-event.log	Location where messages from the server appear

edit

☐ add to welcome page

Figure 2-17: You can enable the logging of various Web-application events by using the Log File Settings window.

MIME type chaining

MIME Type Chaining lets you chain servlets based on the MIME type of the response generated from another servlet or JSP (see Figure 2-18).

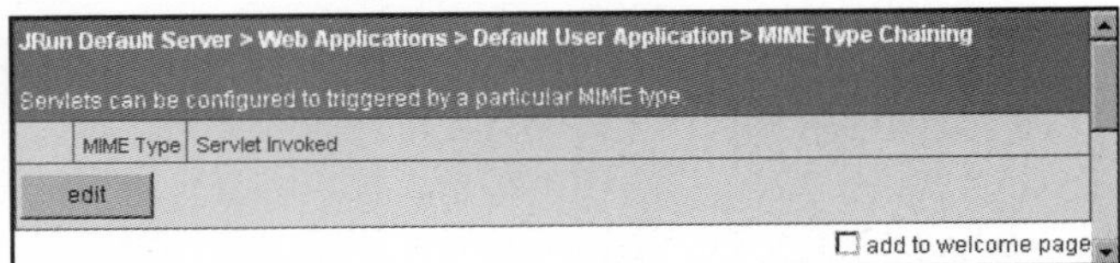

Figure 2-18: The MIME Type Chaining window allows you to chain servlets based on the given MIME type.

MIME type chaining mechanisms are discussed in detail in Chapter 9.

Multipurpose Internet Mail Extensions (MIME) type mappings

MIME type mappings allow you to associate files having a particular extension with a predefined code (see Figure 2-19). When JRun receives a request for a file with the specified extension, the MIME part of the request identifies the type of file requested.

JRun Default Server > Web Applications > Default User Application > MIME Type Mappings

Configure MIME type mappings.

MIME Type Extension	MIME Type
txt	text/plain
html	text/html

edit

add to welcome page

Figure 2-19: The MIME Type Mappings window lets you map MIME types to file types.

Server-side includes

Server-side includes are tags in an HTML file that are processed on the server side. A typical example is the `<SERVLET>` server-side tag in Java Web Server. When this tag is present, JWS automatically invokes a servlet to execute the instruction specified in the servlet tag and includes the output of the servlet. JRun lets you do the same by defining new tags (Figure 2-20).

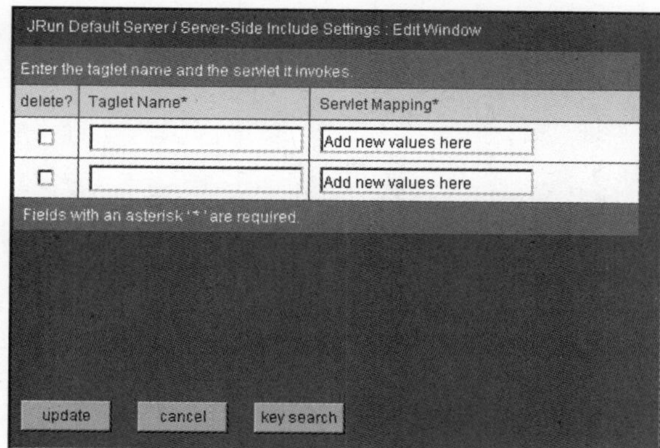

Figure 2-20: The Server-Side Includes window lets you define new tags.

Servlet definitions

The Servlet Definitions window shown in Figure 2-21 allows you to give alias names to a servlet. It also gives you an option to load a servlet automatically upon startup. Servlet initialization arguments can also be set here.

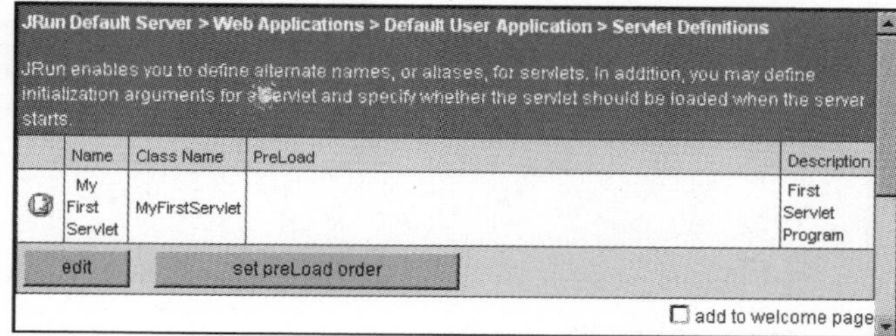

Figure 2-21: You can give servlets alias names by using the Servlet Definitions window or by specifying that you want a servlet to load on startup.

Servlet URL mappings

Servlet URL mappings allows you to map a virtual path or extension to a particular servlet. For example, if you use Cocoon to process XML files on the server side and transform those files to HTML, you can map an `.xml` extension to the `cocoon` servlet. This process is shown in Figure 2-22.

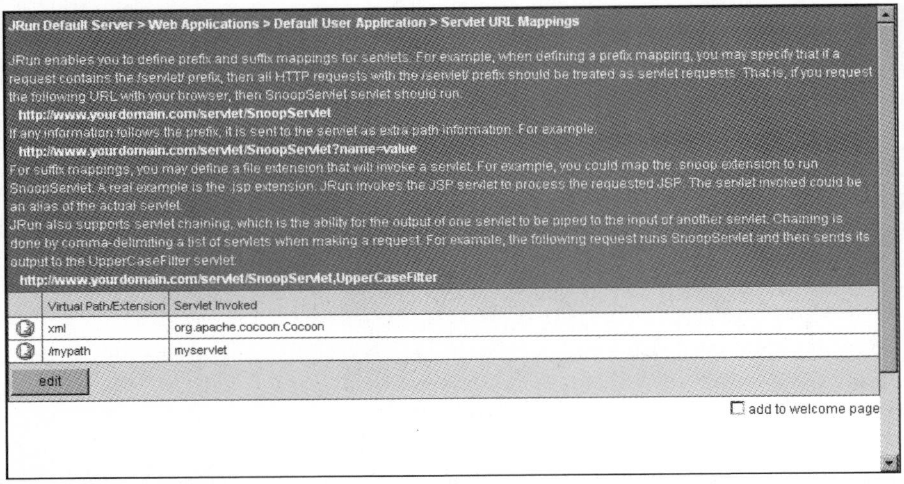

JRun Default Server > Web Applications > Default User Application > Servlet URL Mappings

JRun enables you to define prefix and suffix mappings for servlets. For example, when defining a prefix mapping, you may specify that if a request contains the /servlet/ prefix, then all HTTP requests with the /servlet/ prefix should be treated as servlet requests. That is, if you request the following URL with your browser, then SnoopServlet servlet should run:

http://www.yourdomain.com/servlet/SnoopServlet

If any information follows the prefix, it is sent to the servlet as extra path information. For example:

http://www.yourdomain.com/servlet/SnoopServlet?name=value

For suffix mappings, you may define a file extension that will invoke a servlet. For example, you could map the .snoop extension to run SnoopServlet. A real example is the .jsp extension. JRun invokes the JSP servlet to process the requested JSP. The servlet invoked could be an alias of the actual servlet.

JRun also supports servlet chaining, which is the ability for the output of one servlet to be piped to the input of another servlet. Chaining is done by comma-delimiting a list of servlets when making a request. For example, the following request runs SnoopServlet and then sends its output to the UpperCaseFilter servlet:

http://www.yourdomain.com/servlet/SnoopServlet,UpperCaseFilter

Virtual Path/Extension	Servlet Invoked
xml	org.apache.cocoon.Cocoon
/mypath	myservlet

edit

add to welcome page

Figure 2-22: The Servlet URL Mappings window maps a virtual path to a particular servlet.

Session settings

You can use the Session Settings window to configure session attributes. By default, session information is stored as a cookie in the sessions directory. The properties allow users to change the location where these cookies are stored and to change other information, such as the session time out, the time interval (when the cookie is updated), and so on. Figure 2-23 shows all the properties and their default values.

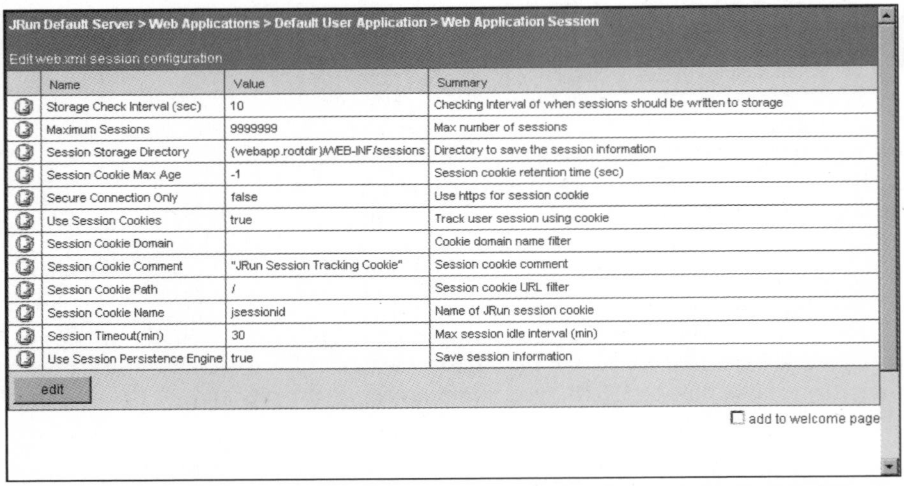

JRun Default Server > Web Applications > Default User Application > Web Application Session

Edit web.xml session configuration

Name	Value	Summary
Storage Check Interval (sec)	10	Checking Interval of when sessions should be written to storage
Maximum Sessions	9999999	Max number of sessions
Session Storage Directory	{webapp.rootdir}/WEB-INF/sessions	Directory to save the session information
Session Cookie Max Age	-1	Session cookie retention time (sec)
Secure Connection Only	false	Use https for session cookie
Use Session Cookies	true	Track user session using cookie
Session Cookie Domain		Cookie domain name filter
Session Cookie Comment	"JRun Session Tracking Cookie"	Session cookie comment
Session Cookie Path	/	Session cookie URL filter
Session Cookie Name	jsessionid	Name of JRun session cookie
Session Timeout(min)	30	Max session idle interval (min)
Use Session Persistence Engine	true	Save session information

edit

add to welcome page

Figure 2-23: Configure session attributes by using the Session Settings window.

Virtual mappings

The Virtual Mappings section shown in Figure 2-24 allows you to define mappings that convert the portion of a URL (relative URL) to a physical directory location. By doing this, you can organize your files in separate directories as required and can access them from the server by referring to the relative URL.

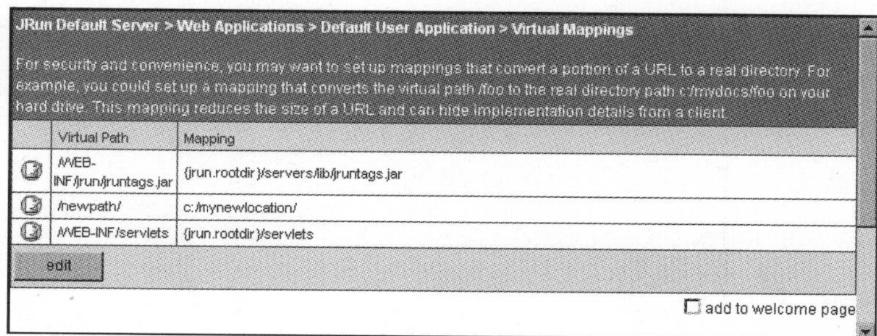

Figure 2-24: The Virtual Mappings window allows you to map a portion of a relative URL to a physical directory.

Enterprise JavaBeans

The Enterprise JavaBeans section shown in Figure 2-25 allows you to deploy EJB components in JRun.

Deploy Enterprise Java Beans
Deploy your EJBs in JRun
Please Note:
You need to restart the JRun server after deploying EJBs.
Enterprise JavaBeans Deployment Information
EJB Jar File: Browse...
JRun Server Name: JRun Default Server
Deploy Properties:
deploy
Welcome
Use this tool to deploy new Enterprise JavaBeans.

Figure 2-25: Deploy Enterprise JavaBeans components in JRun.

Essential Servlet Documentation for Developers

Developers should make thorough use of the documentation available on servlets when developing servlet modules and applications. The key documents a developer should have follow:

- ✦ The Servlet API
- ✦ The Java Servlet Specification
- ✦ Java 2 Enterprise Edition (J2EE) Documentation

The Servlet API defines the classes (and their methods) of the *java.servlet* and *javax.servlet.http* packages. It summarizes these classes and available methods of the servlet packages.

The Java Servlet Specification is aimed at developers that need to know in detail the underlying mechanisms of servlet technology.

The preceding documents can be found at `http://java.sun.com/products/servlet/download.html`.

The Servlet API is a required component of the Java 2 Enterprise Edition. J2EE documentation describes how to develop and deploy J2EE applications. A number of documents, from a FAQ to developer's guides, are available at `http://java.sun.com/j2ee/docs.html/`.

Creating Your First Servlet

All HTTP servlets require that you import the *javax.servlet*, the *javax.servlet.http*, and the *java.io* packages. This is required because all HTTP servlets extend (and make use of) the following abstract classes: *GenericServlet*, *HttpServlet*, *ServletInputStream*, and *ServletOutputStream*. The following section describes how to build a simple servlet.

Basic servlet template

A basic servlet can be constructed simply by the following steps:

1. Import the `java.io`, the `javax.servlet`, and the `javax.servlet.http` packages.
2. Extend the abstract class `HttpServlet`.
3. Override either the `doGet()` or `doPost()` method, or override both methods.

In Listing 2-1, we override both methods.

Listing 2-1

```
package servletbible.ch02.examples;

import java.io.*;
import javax.servlet.*;
import javax.servlet.http.*;

/**
 * An example of a basic Servlet
 */
public class ServletTemplate extends HttpServlet {

    /**
     * Here we override the doGet method
     *
     * @param request the client's request
     * @param response the servlet's response
     */
    public void doGet(HttpServletRequest request, HttpServletResponse
response) throws ServletException,IOException {
        PrintWriter out = response.getWriter();
    }

    /**
     * Here we override the doPost method
     *
     * @param request the client's request
     * @param response the servlet's response
     */

    public void doPost(HttpServletRequest request,
HttpServletResponse response) throws
ServletException,IOException {
        PrintWriter out = response.getWriter();
    }
} // End of ServletTemplate.java
```

Both the `doGet()` and `doPost()` methods take *HttpServletRequest* and *HttpServletResponse* as arguments. The *HttpServletRequest* argument is the HTTP request the client makes; the request contains HTTP-protocol specified header information as well as form data.

The *HttpServletResponse* allows you to manipulate HTTP-protocol specified information and return data to the client.

Both the doGet() and doPost() methods throw the ServletException and IOException.

The most important part of the servlet is the PrintWriter (obtained from the *HttpServletResponse*) to send content back to the client.

The "Hello World!" servlet

Here in Listing 2-2 you see the "Hello World!" servlet in action. The servlet prints "Hello World!" after setting the content type as text/html.

Listing 2-2

```
package servletbible.ch02.examples;
import javax.servlet.*;
import javax.servlet.http.*;
import java.io.*;

/**
* Hello World Servlet. Prints "Hello World!" to the browser.
*/

public class HelloWorldServlet extends HttpServlet
{


    public String message = "Hello World!";


     /**
     * Here we override the doGet method
     *
     * @param request the client's request
     * @param response the servlet's response
     */
    public void doGet(HttpServletRequest request, HttpServletResponse
response) throws ServletException, IOException
        {
            /**
                * Sets the content type
                */
        response.setContentType("text/html");

                PrintWriter out = response.getWriter();

                /**
                * Prints the html document and Hello World!
                */
```

```
                out.println("<html><head><title>Hello World
Servlet</title></head><body>");
                out.println("<h1>"+getMessage()+"</h1>");
                out.println("</body></html>");
            out.close();
        }

        public String getMessage()
        {
            return message;
        }
} //End of HelloWorldServlet
```

Figure 2-26 shows what you see in the browser when you access the servlet by typing the servlet's URL. Before calling this servlet in your browser, compile it in the servlet directory of your server. To do the compilation, open the DOS prompt and go to the directory where you have the servlet code saved. Give the following command:

```
javac HelloWorldServlet.java
```

After compiling the servlet successfully, copy the `HelloWorldServlet.class` file generated into the directory *<JRun rootdirectory>*`\webapp\servers\default\default-app\web-inf`.

Once you have done this, you are can call the servlet in your browser.

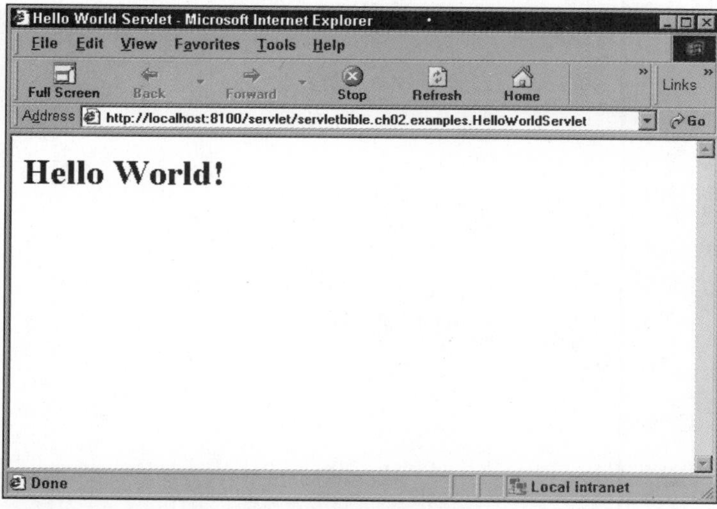

Figure 2-26: Running the "Hello World!" servlet

We are able to access this servlet by typing the URL into the browser because this is a GET request. When we override the doPost() method in place of the doGet() method in the HelloWorldServlet, we are not able to access the servlet in this manner.

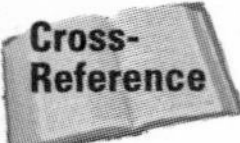

GET and POST requests are discussed in detail in Chapter 3.

Other basic servlet examples

This section contains some simple examples that demonstrate how servlets can use other parts of the Java API.

The date servlet

Listing 2-3 shows the code for a simple servlet that displays the date in a particular string format. Figure 2-27 shows the results of running this servlet in the browser.

Listing 2-3

```
package servletbible.ch02.examples;

import java.io.*;
import java.text.*;
import java.util.*;
import javax.servlet.*;
import javax.servlet.http.*;

/**
 * This is a simple servlet that displays the date in a
 * particular string format.
 */
public class DateServlet extends HttpServlet {
    String todaysDate;
    String dateFormat = "MMMMMMMMM dd yyyy"; //Holds the format the
Date will be displayed as

public void doGet(HttpServletRequest request, HttpServletResponse
response) throws ServletException,IOException {
        PrintWriter out = response.getWriter();
        response.setContentType("text/plain");
        SimpleDateFormat d2cformatter = new
SimpleDateFormat(dateFormat);
        todaysDate = d2cformatter.format(new Date());

        out.println("<html><head><title>Date
Servlet</title></head><body>");
        out.println("Todays Date is "+todaysDate);
        out.println("</body></html>");
```

```
        out.close();

    }
}
```

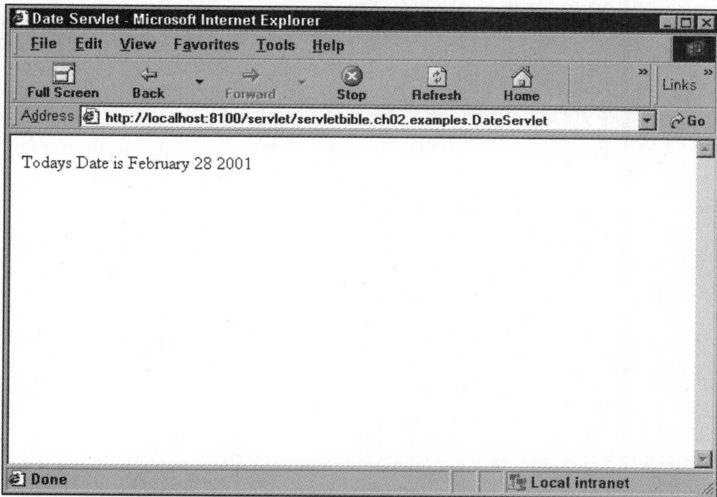

Figure 2-27: The Date servlet displays today's date in Internet Explorer.

Greetings, Suresh!

Listing 2-4 is another example of a servlet overriding both the `doPost()` and `doGet()` methods; you can, therefore, call this servlet in two ways. Figure 2-28 and 2-29 show the results of compiling and running this servlet.

Listing 2-4

```
package servletbible.ch02.examples;

import java.io.*;
import javax.servlet.*;
import javax.servlet.http.*;

public class NameServlet extends HttpServlet {

  public void doGet(HttpServletRequest req, HttpServletResponse
res)throws ServletException, IOException {
```

Continued

Listing 2-4 (continued)

```
    getName(req, res);
  }

  public void doPost(HttpServletRequest req, HttpServletResponse res)
throws ServletException, IOException {
    getName(req, res);
  }

public String getName(HttpServletRequest request, HttpServletResponse
response)
throws ServletException, IOException {


     response.setContentType("text/html");

     PrintWriter out = response.getWriter();
     String name = request.getParameter("name");
     out.println("<HTML>");
     out.println("<HEAD><TITLE>Greetings " + name +
"!</TITLE></HEAD>");
     out.println("<BODY>");
     out.println("Greetings " + name+ "!");
     out.println("</BODY></HTML>");
     return name;
  }

} // End of NameServlet
```

One way in which `NameServlet` can be called is through a form that submits a `POST` request. The following is the HTML code snippet that actually does a `POST`.

```
<form
name=callNameServlet method=POST
action="\servlet\servletbible.ch02.examples.NameServletlet">
```

When I enter my name and submit the form, the servlet greets me as shown in Figure 2-29.

Another way to call the servlet is by typing the URL along with the name parameter on the query string as shown in Figure 2-30. The query string is made up of the name-value pairs and appears after the question mark (?). Multiple parameters are separated by an ampersand (&).

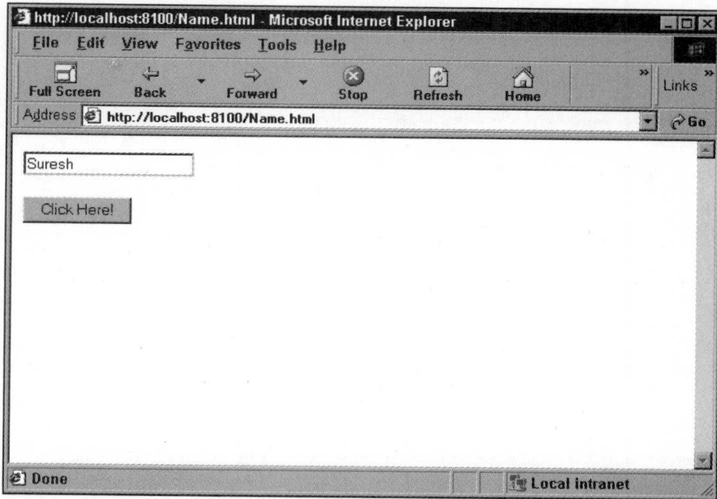

Figure 2-28: The NameServlet input form

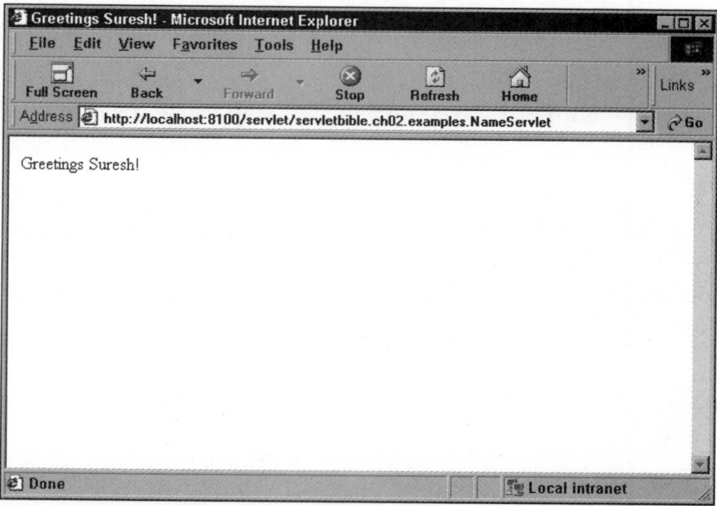

Figure 2-29: The NameServlet displays "Greetings" to the name the user enters.

Using `POST` or `GET` produces the same result, as they are just two different methods to send the data.

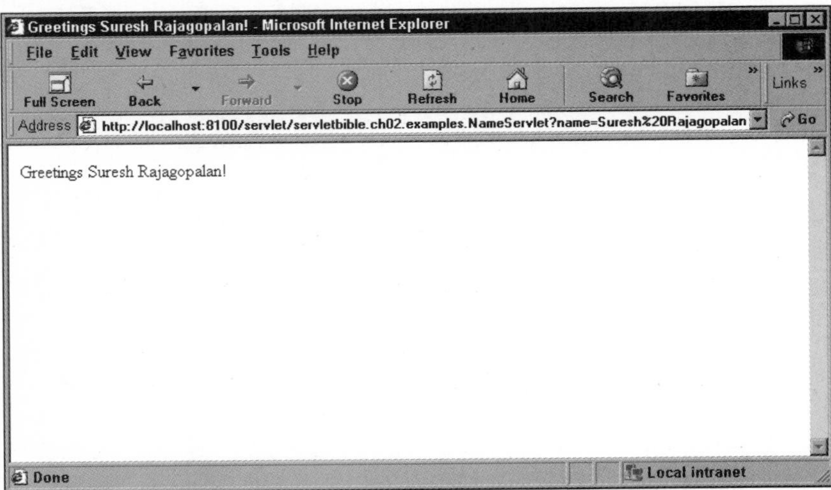

Figure 2-30: Running NameServlet by using the GET request and by entering a query string in the URL

Print a file

Another example is to print a text file on the client machine by using servlets. The text file resides on the server. The code shown in Listing 2-5 does the functionality of printing a text file taken from the server.

Listing 2-5

```
package servletbible.ch02.examples;

import java.io.*;
import javax.servlet.*;
import javax.servlet.http.*;

public class FileRead extends HttpServlet
{
    public void doGet(HttpServletRequest req,HttpServletResponse
resp) throws ServletException, IOException {
        PrintWriter out;
        File inputFile = new File("default-app/Name.html");
        FileReader fr = new FileReader(inputFile);
        resp.setContentType("text/html");
        out = resp.getWriter();
        out.println("<HTML>");
        out.println("<TITLE>");
        out.println("Read a file and display in browser");
        out.println("</TITLE>");
```

```
        out.println("<BODY>");
        out.println("<H3>");
        out.println("<I>");
        out.println("Name.html file for Name Servlet example")
        out.println("</I>");
        out.println("</H3>");
        int ch;
        boolean flag=false; // to identify when new line is
encountered
        while((ch = fr.read()) != -1) {
        //    Discard all new lines and insert a single break
            while(ch == 13 || ch == 10) {
                flag = true;
                ch = fr.read();
            }
            if(ch == -1) break;
            if(flag) {
                out.print("<BR CLEAR=None>");
                flag = false;
            }
            if((char)ch == '<')
                out.print("&lt;");
            else if((char)ch == '>')
                out.print("&gt;");
            else
                out.print((char)ch);
        }
        out.println("</body>");
        out.println("</html>");
        fr.close();
        out.close();
    }
}
```

The File object opens the Name.html file and is passed to the FileReader object. Note that when the servlet is executed, and if a file is referred without a path, the file is searched under the JRun's Default Server root directory (which is JRun\servers\default). Here, the Name.html file resides under the default-app directory; hence, the path is given as default-app/Name.html.

The while loop executes until the file ends. The statements inside the while loop discard extra newline characters (checks for ASCII 10, which is carriage return, and ASCII 13, which is line feed). The flag Boolean variable identifies whether or not newline characters have been encountered. If the flag is true, a <BR> is output to the client; otherwise the character is output.

Figure 2-31 shows the output the FileRead servlet displays.

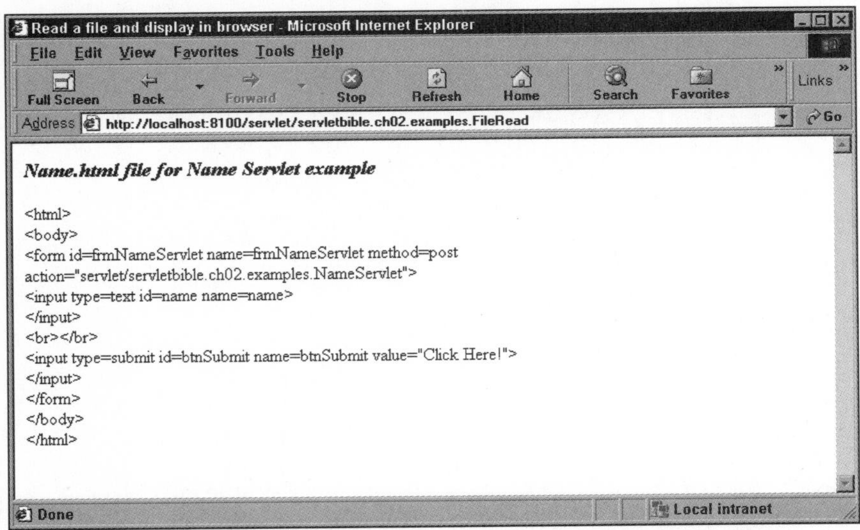

Figure 2-31: Running the FileRead servlet to read and display the Name.html file

Summary

In this chapter, you read about the requirements for executing a servlet, setting up the `CLASSPATH` environment variable for proper compilation and execution of servlets, and Web servers that support servlets. You also configured the JRun Web server to begin development of your servlets. You learned about the documentation and specifications for servlets necessary for developers and saw a few simple examples to get going on servlets.

In the next chapter, you learn about the servlet life cycle, the methods inside a servlet, the `PrintWriter` object, and how threading helps in servlet execution.

✦ ✦ ✦

The Servlet Life Cycle

In This Chapter

Basic servlet architecture

GET and POST requests in detail

Servlet life cycle

Essential classes in the servlet package

Threading

Basic Servlet Architecture

Web servers are merely capable of serving static Web pages. This means that they can present to the browser only the files available on the local system. They need an extension mechanism to generate dynamic content. Servlet technology is the Java way of abstracting this extension mechanism in a simple, platform-independent fashion. Java servlets, residing on the server side, provide an extension of Web servers to process requests and to generate a response dynamically.

Servlet containers contain, manage, and deploy servlets. They manage the servlets throughout their life cycle and should be able to act in conjunction with Web servers. The servlet container receives HTTP requests from the Web server, delegates them to the appropriate method of the servlet, and returns the response from the servlet to the Web server.

Although this native support for HTTP is obligatory for servlet containers, they can choose whether or not to support the HTTPS (HTTP Secure) protocol. Servlets can adapt to any other request/response-oriented protocol, provided that the servlet container supports the protocol. The servlet container provides the necessary plumbing to encapsulate most of the protocol-specific functionality to the servlet developer. Also, it encapsulates the developer from MIME decoding and encoding of requests and responses, respectively.

Technically, a servlet is a Java class that implements the `javax.servlet.Servlet` interface. Generally, all the servlets indirectly implement the `javax.servlet.Servlet` interface by extending from one of the classes -`javax.servlet.GenericServlet` or `javax.servlet.http.HttpServlet`. The inheritance hierarchy typically looks like this:

```
javax.servlet.Servlet➪
javax.servlet.GenericServlet➪
javax.servlet.http.HttpServlet➪YourServlet
```

GET and POST Requests in Detail

HTTP is the de facto protocol of the Web. It operates as a request/response-oriented protocol. The most common ways to request resources from a Web server are through HTTP `GET` and `POST` requests. HTTP requests and responses have message headers that describe the message.

Refer to Chapter 4 for more details about HTTP headers.

GET request

A `GET` request is used to request a resource from the server. The syntax outline of the `GET` request is `GET <URL> HTTP/<Version Number>` followed by HTTP headers.

`GET` requests do not consist of any entity body portion.

Let's see a sample `GET` request:

```
GET /index.html HTTP/1.0
Accept: text/html
Connection: Keep-Alive
Host: www.hungryminds.com
User-Agent: Mozilla/4.02 [en] (Win95; I)
```

✦ The `Accept` header specifies the MIME types the user agent supports. This is useful for a Web server/servlet engine to determine the user agent capabilities and to return responses in a format the user agent can understand.

✦ `Connection: Keep-Alive` indicates the intention of the user agent for persistent connection. If the server supports persistent connections, then the response also contains the same header name and value pair.

✦ `Host` denotes the server to which the request is made.

✦ The `User-Agent` field implies the browser or device from which the request is made. In this age of proliferation of WAP, you can know the type of client (whether it is a browser on a regular PC or is made from your WAP-enabled mobile phone) by checking the `User-Agent` field.

A `GET` request sends only the HTTP header to the Web server. Form data, if any, is encoded in the form of a query string and is appended to the URL. Let's see another sample `GET` request that illustrates this:

```
GET /index.html?authorname=Suresh&bookname=ServletBible
HTTP/1.0
Accept: text/html
```

```
Connection: Keep-Alive
Host: www.hungryminds.com
User-Agent: Mozilla/4.02 [en] (Win95; I)
```

A variant of the `GET` request is `Conditional GET`, which has an additional `If-Modified-Since` header field. The server returns a not-modified message if the content has not been modified since the time specified in the field.

POST request

A `POST` request is made to pass the user input to the server. The syntax outline of the `POST` request is `POST <URL> HTTP/<Version Number>` followed by HTTP headers and entity body. The form data constitutes the body of the request, and the `Content-Length` header field confines the boundary of the entity-body portion. Unlike a `GET` request, the size of a `POST` request is not limited. A sample `POST` request follows:

```
POST /index.html HTTP/1.0
Accept: text/html
Connection: Keep-Alive
Host: www.hungryminds.com
User-Agent: Mozilla/4.02 [en] (Win95; I)
Content-Length=30
authorname=Suresh&bookname=bible
```

When to GET and when to POST

You may be wondering by now when to use `GET` and when to use `POST` to develop form-based, interactive Web applications. Generally, you should use the `GET` method when your request does not make any marked change on the state of the server; you should use the `POST` method otherwise.

The server is said to change its state when operations such as database modification, service subscription, and so on are performed on the server.

The term *Idempotent* in the mathematical world means being a quantity that remains identical even if particular operations are applied on it. In the RPC (Remote Procedure Call) realm, it means no side effects on the server despite multiple calls.

`GET` requests should be idempotent on the server in the sense that two or more identical `GET` requests should not affect the status quo of the server state. This aspect of `GET` makes it ideal for read-only operations. For example, an address-lookup application that queries the telephone-directory database and retrieves the address given the phone number should use the `GET` method to make the request.

If the processing of an HTTP request has side effects like database modifications on the server state, you should go for the POST method. Browsers usually prompt before resubmitting a POST request, so the chances of inadvertently repeating the operation are fewer. For instance, a telephone bill payment form uses the POST method.

You should choose the method of making the request based on the nature of the operation. If you are using the GET method in the form to make the request for, say a payment instruction or purchase order, an innocuous refresh by the end user might lead to the repetition of the operation without any warning.

Consider two limitations while you choose the GET method. Because the request parameters are appended to the query string, they become visible to the end user, as it is appended with URL and displayed in the address bar of the browser. The GET method has limited request size because the query string that is passed in a GET request is stored in environment variables in the server. The operating system on which the server resides imposes limitations on the maximum number of bytes an environment variable can hold; a GET request query string is bound by that limitation.

The Servlet Life Cycle

A servlet module extends the Web server under which it runs. All the servlet containers should conform to the life-cycle contract the servlet interface imposes. The servlet is invoked and initializes calling of the `init ()` method. The servlet processes a client's request through calls to the `service()` method. The servlet is terminated by calling the `destroy()` method. After this, the servlet is garbage collected.

Let's see the methods of the servlet life cycle contract in detail.

init()

The servlet container calls the `init()` method either during load time or at the first request. It is possible that the servlet container has taken the servlet out of memory for optimal usage of memory or for some other performance considerations. In all cases, `init()` is called before the servlet takes up a service request.

service()

The servlet container calls the `service()` method to handle requests and to write the formatted response to be sent to the client. The servlet container constructs a request object out of the HTTP request either as `ServletRequest` or `HttpServletRequest`, and it constructs a response object to format the response as the `ServletResponse` or `HttpServletResponse` object. These objects are passed to the `service()` method; the `service()` method examines the request and responds accordingly.

destroy()

The `destroy()` method is the place to release acquired resources such as database connections, if any. The servlet container calls the `destroy()` method before expelling a servlet out of core. After the `destroy()` method is called, the servlet object is marked for garbage collection and, when it is taken out of memory, is left to the garbage-collector algorithm.

Although strict adherence to this life-cycle contract is mandatory for servlet containers, they have a lot of flexibility in determining how they conform to the contract. For instance, the servlet container can choose to create servlet instances at the time of the request, or it can choose to create all the defined servlets at the time of initialization of the servlet container itself.

As long as the servlet container makes sure the servlet instances are initialized before they serve a request, it is free to choose whether or not to make the life of servlet instances transient or timeless. It can opt for initializing servlet instances once to serve all the impending requests; it can take servlet instances out of memory once instances are have completed processing requests; or it can use any non-deterministic algorithm to determine the lifetime of a servlet instance. For example, the servlet container can destroy the servlet instance if the instance is idle for a particular time.

If a single instance of a servlet eternally serves client requests, the requests can be served instantaneously without the time overhead associated with object creation. As there are no multiple instances, memory can be efficiently managed. Also, the persistent nature of the servlet facilitates the initialization of certain things during the inception. For illustration, a servlet communicating with a database can open the database connection while initializing and can use the connection throughout the lifetime while handling service requests.

Figure 3-1 depicts a typical servlet life-cycle scenario. The HTTP requests coming to the server are delegated to the servlet container. The servlet container loads the servlet before invoking the `service()` method of the servlet. And the servlet container handles multiple requests by spawning multiple threads, each thread executing the `service()` method of a single instance of the servlet.

In the preceding diagram, the servlet container hosts the servlets in the same JVM in which it is running. If the Web server also happens to run in the same JVM, the entire scheme of things is more efficient because of less context-switching overhead.

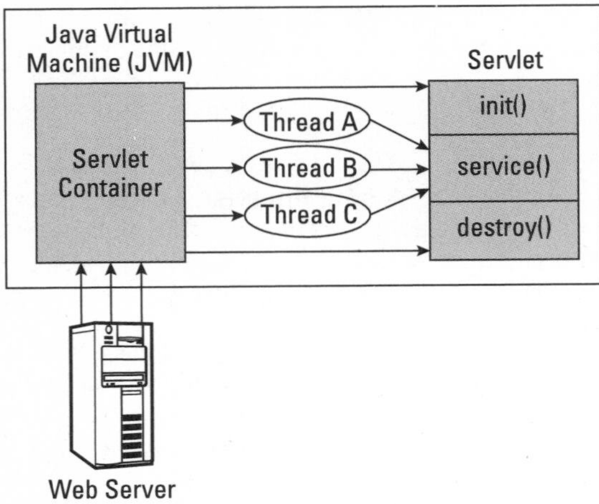

Figure 3-1: Servlet life cycle

Essential Classes in the Servlet Package

Let's examine the major classes of the servlet package and their accompanying methods.

GenericServlet

The `GenericServlet` class extends the `javax.servlet.GenericServlet` framework implementation. It implements the servlet and the `ServletConfig` interface.

The `ServletConfig` object has methods to access the initialization parameters. The initial configuration information is generally available from a configuration-properties file. The process of configuring the initialization parameters is server-dependent.

init()

As we have discussed, this method is called before processing requests. The `GenericServlet` framework implementation logs the servlet initialization apart from commonplace servlet initialization activities.

The `init()` method takes the `ServletConfig` object as an argument for anachronistic reasons. If you override this method in your servlet, you should call the `super.init()` to ensure that the ancestor's `init(ServletConfig config)` method is called.

```
public void  init ( ServletConfig  config ) throws ServletException
  {
        super.init ( config );
  }
```

Because the ServletConfig interface is implemented by the GenericServlet class and you can choose to use an overloaded init() that does not take any argument, there is no need to call super.init(...) explicitly.

service()

The service() method is called by the servlet container to handle requests and to write the formatted response to be sent back to the client. The default implementation of the service() method in the GenericServlet class does nothing, so you have to override this method if you need to handle requests in a useful way.

```
public void service(ServletRequest request , ServletResponse response)
```

destroy()

The servlet container calls this method when the servlet is taken out of memory. You can override this method and free resources if necessary. Servlet destruction is logged.

Table 3-1 outlines a few other useful methods of the GenericServlet class.

Table 3-1
A Few Other Useful Methods of the GenericServlet Class

Method	*Purpose*
GetInitParameter	Used to get the value of an initialization parameter of the servlet, given the name of the parameter
GetInitParameterNames	Used to get the names of all initialization parameters as an enumeration of string objects
GetServletConfig	Used to get servlet start-up configuration information as a ServletConfig object
GetServletContext	Used to get servlet runtime environment information as a ServletContext object
log(String message),log (String message , Throwable t)	Used to write string messages to servlet log file
GetServletName	Returns the name by which the servlet is identified

HTTPServlet

`HTTPServlet` is a class that extends the `javax.servlet.HTTPServlet` implementation. The `javax.servlet.HTTPServlet` implementation, in turn, extends from `javax.Servlet.GenericServlet`. Let's see the methods of the `HTTPServlet` class.

service()

The `service()` method of the `HTTPServlet` class overrides the `service()` method of the `GenericServlet` class. The default implementation of the `service()` method has the boilerplate code that redirects the HTTP requests such as `GET` and `POST` to methods such as `doGet()` and `doPost()`. Although you usually override the `service()` method in the case of a generic servlet, you should not do so while developing an `HTTPServlet`; doing so interferes with the delegation architecture of the framework discussed previously.

doGet()

The servlet container, upon receiving a `GET` request container, calls the `service()` method of `HTTPServlet`, which in turn, redirects the request to the `doGet()` method. In case the `doGet()` method is not overridden, an HTTP `BAD_REQUEST` error is returned to the client. To handle `GET` requests, override the `doGet()` method.

This method is used for handling conditional `GET` requests and `HEAD` requests under certain conditions. Conditional `GET` operations are `GET` requests with the `If-Modified-Since` header field in the HTTP header. The user agent receives `304 NOT MODIFIED` messages in case the content has not changed until the time specified in the `If-Modified-Since` header field. In this scenario, you receive a cached page from your browser. This method also processes the `HEAD` requests if your servlet implementation does not override the `doHead()` method.

doPost()

The servlet container redirects `POST` requests to the `doPost()` method. To handle `POST` requests, override this method. If the `doPost()` method is not overridden and a `POST` request is received, an HTTP `BAD_REQUEST` error is returned to the client.

Other methods

So far, you have had a look at commonly used methods of the servlet interface. A few other methods are used infrequently.

The HTTP `DELETE` request deletes resources on the server, and a `doDelete` method handles those requests. `PUT` is used to place resources on the server, and a `doPut` method handles these requests.

PrintWriter is a specialized class for text-output streams; it provides Unicode support, but this cannot be used for writing raw binary data in the stream. The most methods you are likely to use most frequently are print() and println(). The difference between these two methods is that println adds a line separator after outputting the String argument passed. Some systems use both carriage returns and line feeds as line separators, and some systems use just the newline character as a line separator. The println method adapts based on the platform in which it is running while writing the line separator.

HTTPServletRequest

Form data, regardless of whether they are part of the query string of a GET request or are part of the body of a POST request, are stored as a set of name/value pairs.

The following methods of the HTTPServletRequest interface can be used to retrieve this information:

```
public abstract String getParameter(String name)

public abstract Enumeration getParameterNames()

public abstract String[] getParameterValues(String name)
```

The first method, getParameter(String Name), is used to get the value of a particular parameter, the name of which is passed as an argument. The value of the parameter is returned as a String, and the method returns null if the parameter is not there.

An illustrative snippet follows with its result shown in Figure 3-2:

```
package servletbible.ch03.examples;
import java.io.*;
import javax.servlet.*;
import javax.servlet.http.*;


public class GetParameterExample extends HttpServlet
{
     public void service(HttpServletRequest httpRequest , HttpServletResponse
httpResponse) throws
          ServletException ,   IOException
     {
          // Set the content type of response
          httpResponse.setContentType("text/plain");
          // Attach the response to PrintWriter object
          PrintWriter outputStream =
               httpResponse.getWriter();
          // Get the value of the parameter named MyParameter
          String parameterValue =
               httpRequest.getParameter("MyParameter");
```

```
            if (parameterValue == null)
             {
                 outputStream.println(" The request does not contain any
parameter" ) ;
              }
            else
          {
                     outputStream.println(" The value of the parameter MyParameter
is " +  parameterValue ) ;
          }
          outputStream.close();
      }

}
```

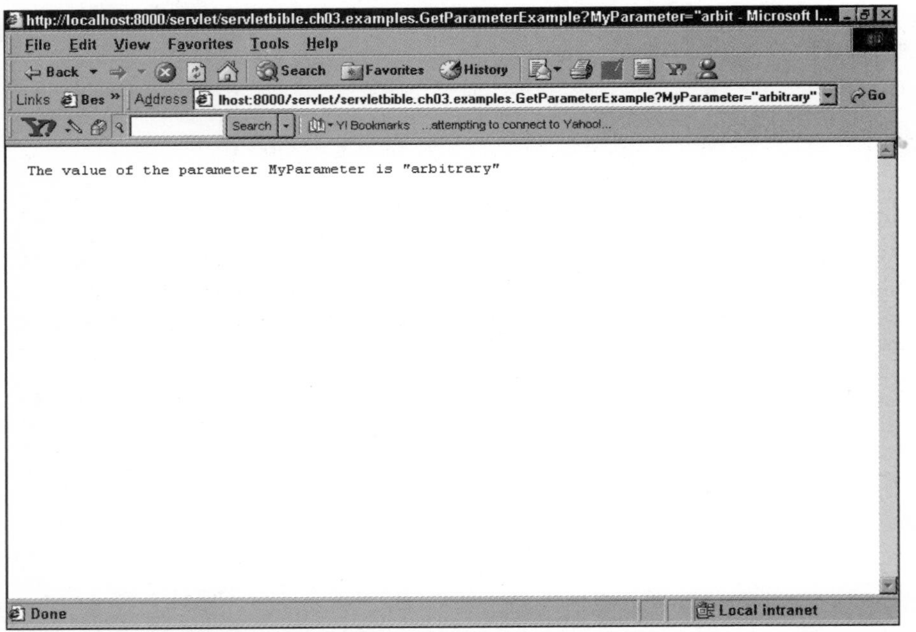

Figure 3-2: A particular GET parameter passed to the servlet

The `getParameterNames()` method returns an enumeration of all the parameter names as a `String` array. The returned `String` array does not contain an element if the request does not have a parameter.

A sample snippet follows:

```
package servletbible.ch03.examples;
import java.io.*;
import javax.servlet.*;
import javax.servlet.http.*;
import java.util.*;


public class GetParameterNamesExample extends HttpServlet
{
     public void service(HttpServletRequest httpRequest ,
HttpServletResponse httpResponse) throws
     ServletException ,   IOException
     {
          httpResponse.setContentType("text/plain");
          PrintWriter outputStream =
               httpResponse.getWriter();
          Enumeration  parameterNames  =
               httpRequest. getParameterNames();
          int paramNumber = 0 ;
          if ( parameterNames.hasMoreElements() == false )
          {
               outputStream.println(" The request does not contain any
parameter" ) ;
            }
          else
          {
               while(parameterNames.hasMoreElements() == true)
               {
                    outputStream.println(" The name of parameter number " +
++paramNumber + " is :" + parameterNames.nextElement() ) ;
               }
          }
          outputStream.close();
     }


}
```

You can see the parameters passed to the servlet enlisted in the screen shown in Figure 3-3.

The `getParameterValues()` method returns the values of the specified parameter. The values of all parameters are returned as a `String` array, and the method returns null if there are no parameters.

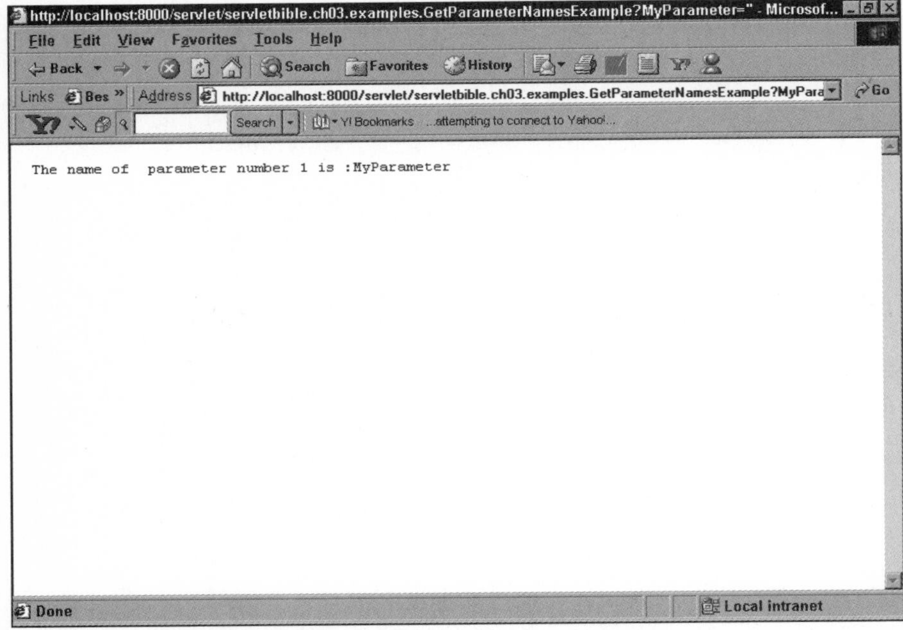

Figure 3-3: All GET parameter names passed to the servlet

The following code snippet prints all the parameter names and the corresponding values as a table. This assumes there is no duplication of parameter names.

```
package servletbible.ch03.examples;
import java.io.*;
import javax.servlet.*;
import javax.servlet.http.*;
import java.util.*;


public class GetParameterValuesExample extends HttpServlet
{
     public void service(HttpServletRequest httpRequest ,
HttpServletResponse httpResponse) throws
     ServletException ,   IOException
     {
          httpResponse.setContentType("text/html");
          PrintWriter outputStream = httpResponse.getWriter();
          Enumeration parameterNames = httpRequest.getParameterNames();
          int paramNumber = 0;
          if(parameterNames.hasMoreElements() == false)
          {
               outputStream.println(" The request does not contain any
parameter");
```

```
        }
          else
          {
                String paramName;
                outputStream.println("<HTML> <TABLE border=1>");
                while(parameterNames.hasMoreElements() == true)
                {
                      outputStream.println("<TR><TD>");
                      paramName = (String)parameterNames.nextElement();
                      outputStream.println(paramName);
                      outputStream.println("</TD><TD>" +
httpRequest.getParameterValues(paramName)[0]);
                      outputStream.println("</TD></TR>");
                      paramNumber++;
                }
                outputStream.println("</TABLE></HTML>");
          }
          outputStream.close();
     }


}
```

Find the screen snapshot of the `GET` parameters as a table of name-value pairs in Figure 3-4.

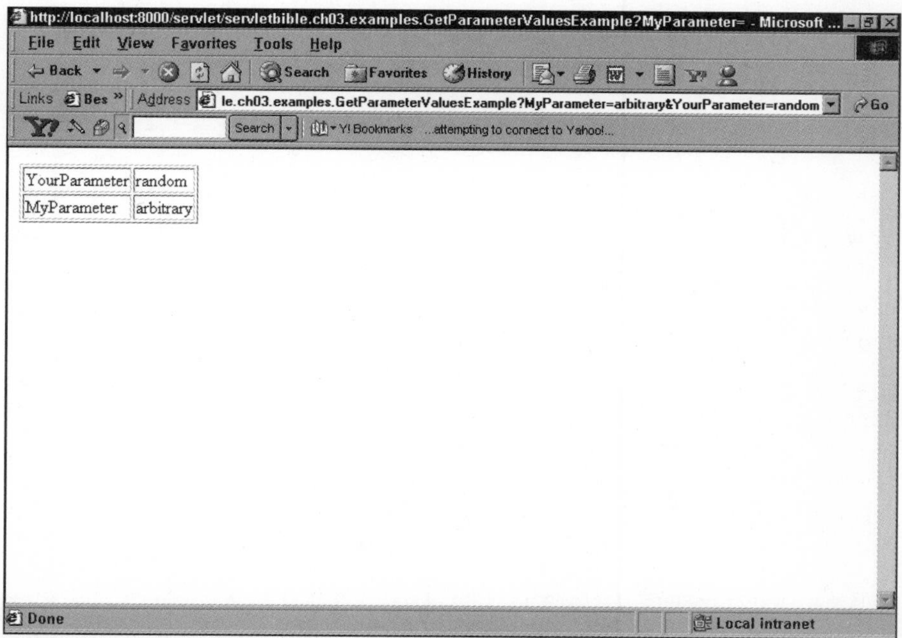

Figure 3-4: Values of GET parameters in tabular form

Also, using the `ServletRequest` object, the servlet can get information such as the scheme/protocol the client uses, requesting the host name and receiving the server name:

```
public abstract String getScheme()
```

This method returns the scheme (that is, the protocol used by the requesting user agent to make the request). Typically it is "http."

Schemes include, but are not limited to, "ftp" and "telnet."

The requesting host name can be obtained by the following method:

```
public abstract String getRemoteHost()
```

This returns a fully qualified name.

The IP address of the requesting host is returned by the following method:

```
public abstract String getRemoteAddr()
```

We can get the name of the server in which the servlet is hosted by calling the following method:

```
public abstract String getServerName()
```

The port in which the servlet is listening for the request is returned by:

```
public abstract int getServerPort()
```

Let's see an example snippet that elucidates these methods:

```
public void service(HttpServletRequest httpRequest ,
HttpServletResponse httpResponse) throws
 ServletException ,   IOException
{
       httpResponse.setContentType("text/plain");
       Printwriter outputStream =
httpResponse.getWriter();

outputStream.println("Server " +
httpRequest.getServerName() ) ;
            outputStream.println("Listening at " +
          httpRequest.getServerPort() );
      outputStream.println("Request coming from" +
          httpRequest.getRemoteHost());
             outputStream.println("Of IP address"

          + httpRequest.getRemoteAddr());
      outputStream.println("The Scheme/Protocol
 of the request is " + httpRequest.getScheme());
  }
```

Content-related methods

The following method returns the length of the request's data portion. If this is unknown, the method returns –1:

```
public abstract int getContentLength()
```

This is useful in the context of the HTTP POST and PUT requests.

The following method returns the MIME type of the request. If the request is devoid of form data, null is returned.

```
public abstract String getContentType()
```

Using the MIME media type, you can determine the request format (such as whether it is plain ASCII text, an HTML document, a JPEG image, or a GIF image).

Data stream–related methods

The data the client passes by using the POST and PUT methods are available to the servlet through the input stream ServletInputStream. The following method returns it:

```
public abstract ServletInputStream getInputStream() throws
IOException
```

This is used to read binary data from the body of the request.

On the other hand, to read text data from the body of the request, the following method of ServletRequest comes in handy:

```
public abstract BufferedReader getReader() throws IOException
```

BufferedReader provides the necessary plumbing for translating character-set encodings.

So far, we have seen the description of the ServletRequest object in general. The HTTPServletRequest that extends from the HTTPServletRequest interface has more in stock specific to HTTP:

```
public abstract String getHeader(String Name)
public abstract Enumeration getHeaders(String Name)
public abstract Enumeration getHeaderNames()
```

getHeader returns the header value upon passing the header name. If there are multiple values, only the first name is returned.

But getHeaders(...) returns an enumeration of Strings upon passing the name, when multiple header values are present.

The following code snippet prints all the header names and the corresponding values as a table, assuming there are no duplicate header names:

```
public abstract int getIntHeader(String name)
public abstract long getDateHeader(String name)
```

The `getIntHeader` method translates the header value corresponding to the name passed to an integer and returns the translation. If the `getIntHeader` method cannot translate the header value to an int, a `NumberFormatException` is thrown.

The `getDateHeader` method translates the header value corresponding to the name passed to `Date` and returns the translation as the number of milliseconds since GMT January 1, 1970. If the `getDateHeader` method cannot translate the header to a `Date` object, an `IllegalArgumentException` is thrown.

Both of these methods return –1if the header name does not exist.

For long values returned from `getDateHeader` as the number of milliseconds since GMT January 1, 1970, an overloaded constructor is available in the Java `Date` object that can convert this value to a Java `Date` object.

The following method returns the authentication scheme:

```
public abstract String getAuthType()
```

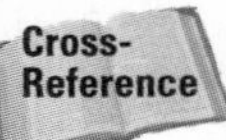

We deal with this method in detail in Chapter 14.

Also, there is a method that returns the cookies from the request:

```
public abstract Cookie[] getCookies()
```

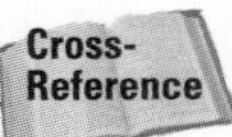

We deal with this method in detail in Chapter 11.

The following method returns the method type of the HTTP request:

```
public abstract String getMethod()
```

The boilerplate code in the service method of an HTTP servlet uses this method to find the method type of the request; the boilerplate code dispatches the request to appropriate methods, such as `doGet` or `doPost`.

Path-related methods

The request path that leads to a servlet servicing a request is composed of the following:

- **Context Path:** The path prefix associated with the `ServletContext` of which this servlet is a part
- **Servlet Path:** The path section that directly corresponds to the mapping that has activated this request
- **PathInfo:** The part of the request path that is not part of the context path or the servlet path

Their values are respectively returned from:

```
public abstract String getContextPath()
public abstract String getServletPath()
public abstract String  getPathInfo()
```

The following method returns the real path information of `Pathinfo`.

```
public abstract String getPathTranslated()
```

The ServletResponse interface

The `ServletResponse` interface has methods for replying to the client. It allows the servlet to set the content length and MIME type of the reply.

The `setContentLength()` method sets the value of the `Content-Length` in the header of the response:

```
public abstract void setContentLength(int len)
```

The `setContentType()` method is used to set the MIME type of the response in the `Content-Type` header:

```
public void service(HttpServletRequest httpRequest ,
HttpServletResponse httpResponse) throws
 ServletException ,   IOException
{
       httpResponse.setContentType("text/html");
       Printwriter outputStream =
httpResponse.getWriter();
      String response = "<HTML><HEAD><TITLE> Java Servlet
     Bible </TITLE> <BODY> Get consummate in Servlets
</BODY></HTML>" ;
       httpResponse.setContentLength(response.getLength());

       outputStream.println(response) ;
}
```

This interface provides an output stream, `ServletOutputStream`, to send binary-reply data and a `Writer` through which the servlet can send text-reply data.

The `getOutputStream()` method is used to get the `ServletOutputStream`:

```
public abstract ServletOutputStream getOutputStream() throws IOException
```

This method is particularly useful for sending images to the client. The widely used image formats of GIF and JPEG are binary.

To send text responses to the client, use the `getWriter()` method:

```
public abstract PrintWriter getWriter() throws IOException
```

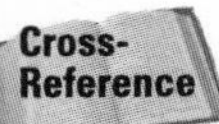

The `PrintWriter` object is discussed in detail elsewhere in this chapter.

Interfaces that extend the `ServletResponse` interface give the servlet more protocol-specific capabilities. For example, the `HttpServletResponse` interface contains methods that allow the servlet to manipulate HTTP-specific header information.

The following method can be used to set your own HTTP headers:

```
public void setHeader(String Name , String Value)
public abstract void addCookie(Cookie cookie)
```

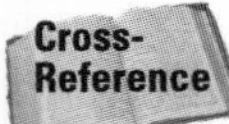

We deal with this method in detail in Chapter 11.

To check whether the response consists of a particular header, use the following method:

```
public abstract boolean containsHeader(String Name)
```

To return specific error codes to the client, use the `sendError` method of the `HttpServletResponse` interface.

Two overloaded methods exist:

```
public abstract void sendError(int sc ) throws IOException
```

and

```
public abstract void sendError(int sc , String msg) throws
IOException
```

Some of the common error-status codes returned are `SC_BAD_REQUEST`, which denotes the incorrect syntax of the client request, and `SC_FORBIDDEN`, which denotes that the server has for some reason refused the request.

A similar method, `setStatus`, is used to set the HTTP status code in the response:

```
public abstract void setStatus(int sc)
public abstract void (int sc,String sm)
```

If you are in the habit of frequent Web surfing, you probably have come across the message that the Web site has moved temporarily to some other location; your browser redirects the page to the other URL. You can achieve this behavior in servlets by using the `sendRedirect()` method:

```
Example :
httpResponse.sendRedirect("http://www.hungryminds.com");
```

The `setDateHeader()` method, while adding a new header to the response, sets the date argument passed as its value:

```
public abstract void setDateHeader(String name , long date)
```

The `setHeader()` method, while adding a new header to the response, sets the second argument passed as its `String value`:

```
public abstract void setHeader(String name , String value)
```

The `setIntHeader()` method, while adding a new header to the response, sets the second argument passed as its integer value:

```
public abstract void setIntHeader(String name , int value)
```

Threading

Recall from Chapter 1 that one of the primary advantages of the servlet approach is that it uses threads, rather than processes, to handle HTTP requests. This gives servlets a significant performance edge because threads are less resource consuming.

Usually, a single instance of a servlet handles all incoming HTTP requests simultaneously by handling each request in a separate thread. The `service()` method is called from within that thread to process the request.

The implementation of the servlet container determines whether a new thread is created and destroyed for handling each request or whether threads are taken and returned from a thread pool to handle requests. The latter approach has the advantage of lessening the burden of thread-creation overhead at the time of handling the request.

But there can be multiple instances of servlets being created in certain scenarios. If the servlet inherits `SingleThreadModel`, Java guarantees that only one thread can access the methods of the servlet at a time. In this case, more than one instance of servlets are created to handle multiple requests. Generally, servlet containers go for instance pooling in this situation to maximize performance gain.

This also means that the servlet developer has to make certain methods thread-safe. The `init()` method of the servlet is called either during the load time of the servlet or at the time of first request. Hence, there is a guarantee that it can be called by only one thread at a time, and it does not need to take care of synchronization.

The `service()` method, too, of the generic servlet needs to be thread-safe. So do the methods of the HTTP servlet to which calls are dispatched from the generic servlet when a request comes. In other words, methods such as `doGet()` and `doPost()` need to be thread-safe.

The `destroy()` method of the servlet also needs to be thread-safe, as the servlet container should not execute any service requests when the servlet container intends to expel the servlet from memory.

Making the method thread-safe does not mean that the entire method needs to be thread-safe. Instead, it is enough to synchronize the critical section of the code that accesses shared resources in a thread-unsafe manner.

Summary

In this chapter, you have seen the essential concepts you need to learn before delving deeply into servlets through your experimentation. Also you have come to grips with nuances of servlet life cycle.

In the next chapter, we go into detail about the HTTP, HTTP headers, and status codes.

✦ ✦ ✦

CHAPTER

Handling HTTP

✦ ✦ ✦ ✦

In This Chapter

HTTP transactions at work

HTTP request headers

HTTP response headers

HTTP status codes

Sending a controlled response

✦ ✦ ✦ ✦

This chapter will discuss in brief how HTTP works, and what makes up a HTTP request and HTTP response. This chapter will also outline the various HTTP status codes and what they indicate.

An Overview of HTTP and SSL

To make use of servlet technology effectively, it is key to understand how to make use of the HTTP, as servlets operate over HTTP. HTTP is the communication method clients use to communicate with the server. HTTP is one of a number of application-layer protocols that run over the TCP/IP. The default port the protocol operates on is 80.

HTTP provides the necessary means for the following to take place:

- ✦ Determining client capabilities
- ✦ Retrieving hypertext documents along with Last Modified Date/Timestamp
- ✦ Determining access rights and basic user authentication
- ✦ Negotiating content/data representation
- ✦ Returning the status of transaction success through status codes; a number of status codes are used to indicate or signal an event. For example, if the request is successful, the status code 200 is returned.
- ✦ Establishing a single transaction per connection; often, a single document may embed several elements that must be retrieved separately.

The formal set of rules of HTTP can be found at `http://www.freesoft.org/CIE/index.html`. The documents available here are known as RFCs (Request For Comments). The RFCs pertaining to HTTP are 1945, 2068, and 2616.

Secure Sockets Layer (SSL) is a variation of HTTP designed by Netscape Communications. It was designed to protect transmissions of any higher-level protocol (including HTTP) that uses sockets. SSL is used to encrypt transmissions between the client and server. SSL does well in protecting particular forms of attacks: brute force, text crypt-analysis, replay, and man in the middle. SSL provides and uses functions for mutual authentication (using digital certificates), data encryption, and data integrity. The primary benefit of SSL is its high level of transparency, which is achieved as SSL operates at the network layer of the ISO model.

HTTP transactions

HTTP transactions (requests and responses) contain HTTP headers followed by data. These headers provide a mechanism for clients/servers to indicate information about themselves or the transaction. Figure 4-1 illustrates how HTTP transactions are made between the client and server and the header information that is passed between the client and server.

Request:

GET /webappcomponents.gif

HTTP/1.0

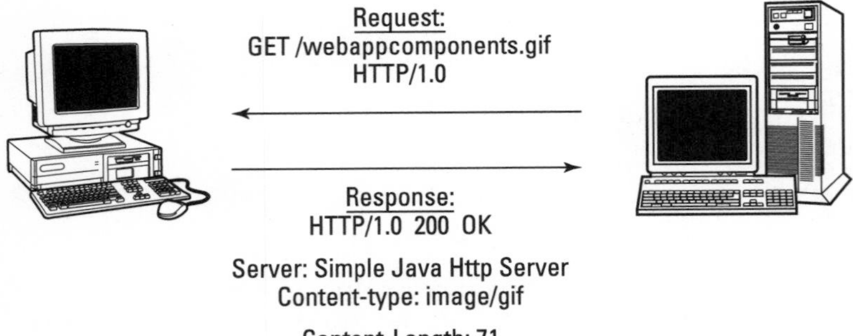

Figure 4-1: HTTP transaction flow between the client and server

Response:

HTTP/1.0 200 OK

Server: Simple Java HTTP Server

Content-type:image/gif

Content-Length: 71

The file webappcomponents would be supplied from the server here.

Simple HTTP server

Listing 4-1 demonstrates the request-response paradigm in action. When you run the simple HTTP Server, you have a Web server listening on a particular port (defaults to 1500) for incoming requests. When the browser makes a request to the server for a particular resource (which may be an HTML page, an image, or any other file), the server binds the request to a particular socket. It then fulfills the request by locating the requested file. If the file is found, it sends back to the browser a status code 200 and the file itself. If the file is not found, the server sends back to the browser a status code 404, which indicates to the browser that the file cannot be found. The browser loads the appropriate page to display a message to the client that the file cannot be found.

Listing 4-1

```
/*
* Simple Java HTTP Server, implements GET method
*
*  This example is based on the code provided by
*  Frederic Pont at http://pont.net"
*/
package servletbible.ch04.examples;

import java.net.*;
import java.io.*;
import java.util.*;
import java.lang.*;


public class httpServer
{

    public static void main(String args[]) {

     int port;
     ServerSocket server_socket;


     try {
              /**
* Here we read the port number specified by the user
* if any, otherwise default to listening on port 1500
```

Continued

Listing 4-1 (continued)

```
*/
port = Integer.parseInt(args[0]);
     }
     catch (Exception e) {
         port = 1500;
     }


     try {

         server_socket = new ServerSocket(port);
         System.out.println("httpServer running on port " +
                      server_socket.getLocalPort());

         // server infinite loop
         while(true) {
          Socket socket = server_socket.accept();
          System.out.println("New connection accepted " +
                       socket.getInetAddress() +
                       ":" + socket.getPort());

          // Construct handler to process the HTTP request
message.
          try {
              httpRequestHandler request =
               new httpRequestHandler(socket);
              // Create a new thread to process the request.
              Thread thread = new Thread(request);

              // Start the thread.
              thread.start();
          }
          catch(Exception e) {
              System.out.println(e);
          }
         }
     }

     catch (IOException e) {
         System.out.println(e);
     }
    }
}


class httpRequestHandler implements Runnable
{
```

```
    final static String CRLF = "\r\n";
    Socket socket;
    InputStream input;
    OutputStream output;
    BufferedReader br;

    // Constructor
    public httpRequestHandler(Socket socket) throws Exception
    {
     this.socket = socket;
     this.input = socket.getInputStream();
     this.output = socket.getOutputStream();
     this.br =
         new BufferedReader(new
InputStreamReader(socket.getInputStream()));
    }

    // Implement the run() method of the Runnable interface.
    public void run()
    {
     try {
         processRequest();
     }
     catch(Exception e) {
         System.out.println(e);
     }
    }

    private void processRequest() throws Exception
    {
     while(true) {

         String headerLine = br.readLine();
         System.out.println(headerLine);
         if(headerLine.equals(CRLF) || headerLine.equals(""))
break;

         StringTokenizer s = new StringTokenizer(headerLine);
         String temp = s.nextToken();

         if(temp.equals("GET")) {

          String fileName = s.nextToken();
          fileName = "." + fileName ;

          // Open the requested file.
          FileInputStream fis = null ;
          boolean fileExists = true ;
          try
              {
```

Continued

Listing 4-1 *(continued)*

```
        fis = new FileInputStream( fileName ) ;
        }
    catch ( FileNotFoundException e )
        {
        fileExists = false ;
        }

    // Construct the response message.
    String serverLine = "Server: Simple Java Http Server";
    String statusLine = null;
    String contentTypeLine = null;
    String entityBody = null;
    String contentLengthLine = "error";
    if ( fileExists )
        {
        statusLine = "HTTP/1.0 200 OK" + CRLF ;
        contentTypeLine = "Content-type: " +
            contentType( fileName ) + CRLF ;
        contentLengthLine = "Content-Length: "
            + (new Integer(fis.available())).toString()
            + CRLF;
        }
    else
        {
        statusLine = "HTTP/1.0 404 Not Found" + CRLF ;
        contentTypeLine = "text/html" ;
        entityBody = "<HTML>" +
            "<HEAD><TITLE>404 Not Found</TITLE></HEAD>" +
            "<BODY>404 Not Found"
            +"<br>usage:http://yourHostName:port/"
            +"fileName.html</BODY></HTML>" ;
        }

    // Send the status line.
    output.write(statusLine.getBytes());
          System.out.println(statusLine);

    // Send the server line.
    output.write(serverLine.getBytes());
          System.out.println(serverLine);

    // Send the content type line.
    output.write(contentTypeLine.getBytes());
          System.out.println(contentTypeLine);

    // Send the Content-Length
    output.write(contentLengthLine.getBytes());
          System.out.println(contentLengthLine);
```

```
            // Send a blank line to indicate the end of the header
lines.
            output.write(CRLF.getBytes());
                  System.out.println(CRLF);

            // Send the entity body.
            if (fileExists)
                {
                 sendBytes(fis, output) ;
                 fis.close();
                }
            else
                {
                 output.write(entityBody.getBytes());
                }

           }
       }

       try {
           output.close();
           br.close();
           socket.close();
       }
       catch(Exception e) {}
      }

      private static void sendBytes(FileInputStream fis,
OutputStream os)
       throws Exception
      {
       // Construct a 1K buffer to hold bytes on their way to the
socket.
       byte[] buffer = new byte[1024] ;
       int bytes = 0 ;

       // Copy requested file into the socket's output stream.
       while ((bytes = fis.read(buffer)) != -1 )
           {
            os.write(buffer, 0, bytes);
           }
      }

      private static String contentType(String fileName)
      {
          if (fileName.endsWith(".htm") || fileName.endsWith(".html") ||
             fileName.endsWith(".txt"))
           {
            return "text/html";
           }
```

Continued

Listing 4-1 *(continued)*

```
        else if(fileName.endsWith(".jpg") || fileName.endsWith(".jpeg")){
            return "image/jpeg";
        }

        else if(fileName.endsWith(".gif")) {
            return "image/gif";
        }

        else {
        return "application/octet-stream";
        }

    }

}
```

HTTP headers contain request/response information. You can view what HTTP request and response headers look like when you use the simple HTTP server to access the image webappcomponents.gif in Figure 4-2.

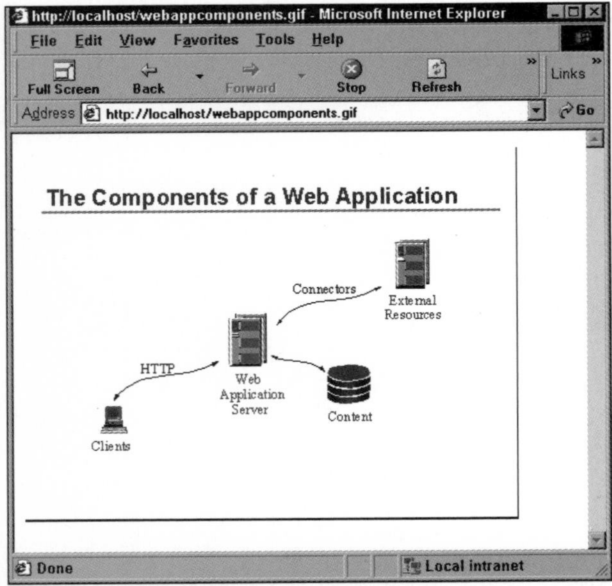

Figure 4-2: Browser accessing server requesting an image

Figure 4-3 shows the DOS Prompt containing the HTTP request and response headers when attempting to access the webappcomponents.gif image through the browser.

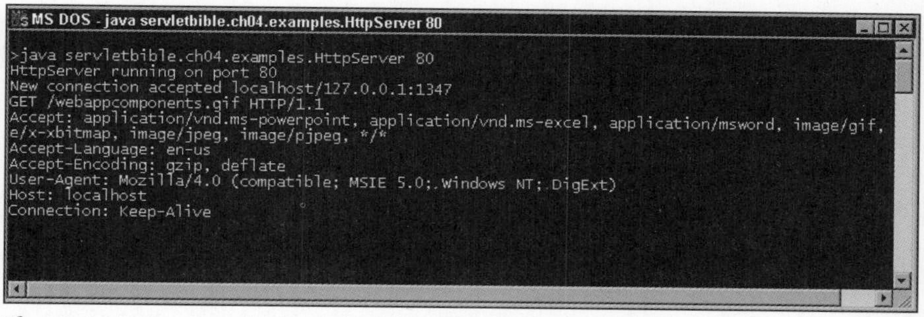

```
MS DOS - java servletbible.ch04.examples.HttpServer 80
>java servletbible.ch04.examples.HttpServer 80
HttpServer running on port 80
New connection accepted localhost/127.0.0.1:1347
GET /webappcomponents.gif HTTP/1.1
Accept: application/vnd.ms-powerpoint, application/vnd.ms-excel, application/msword, image/gif,
e/x-xbitmap, image/jpeg, image/pjpeg, */*
Accept-Language: en-us
Accept-Encoding: gzip, deflate
User-Agent: Mozilla/4.0 (compatible; MSIE 5.0; Windows NT; DigExt)
Host: localhost
Connection: Keep-Alive
```

Figure 4-3: Request-response headers for a Simple HTTP Server running in an MS-DOS window

HTTP Request Headers

The request header is very beneficial to us in that it allows us to obtain client data and information about the request and to read the HTTP header. HTTP request-header information is accessible through the `javax.servlet.http.HttpServletRequest` interface. The `HttpServletRequest` is essentially a representation of an HTTP Servlet Request (as the name implies) and the equivalent of the CGI variable `REQUEST_METHOD`.

Printing request headers

Listing 4-2 shows a servlet that prints all header information available from the client.

Listing 4-2

```
package servletbible.ch04.examples;

import javax.servlet.*;
import javax.servlet.http.*;
import java.net.*;
import java.io.*;
import java.util.Enumeration;

public class PrintHeader extends HttpServlet
{
```

Continued

Listing 4-2 (continued)

```
        /**
        * doGet implementation, calls printHeader function
        *
        * @param request
        * @param response
        * @throws IOException
        * @throws ServletException
        *
        */

        public void doGet (HttpServletRequest request, HttpServletResponse
response) throws IOException, ServletException
        {
        printHeader(request, response);
        }

        /**
        * doPost implementation, calls printHeader function
        *
        * @param request
        * @param response
        * @throws IOException
        * @throws ServletException
        *
        */


         public void doPost (HttpServletRequest request,
HttpServletResponse response) throws IOException, ServletException
         {
                printHeader(request, response);
         }

        /**
        * Prints client header information that is available
        *
        * @param request
        * @param response
        * @throws IOException
        * @throws ServletException
        *
        */

        public void printHeader(HttpServletRequest request,
HttpServletResponse response) throws IOException, ServletException {

                String headers = null;
                String htmlHeader = "<HTML><HEAD><TITLE> Request Headers
</TITLE></HEAD><BODY>";
                String htmlFooter = "</BODY></HTML>";
```

```
                response.setContentType("text/html");

                PrintWriter out = response.getWriter();
                Enumeration enum = request.getHeaderNames();

                out.println(htmlHeader);
                out.println("<TABLE ALIGN=CENTER BORDER=1>");
                out.println("<tr><th> Header </th><th> Value </th>");

                while (enum.hasMoreElements())
                {
                    headers = (String)enum.nextElement();
                    if (headers != null)
                    {
                    out.println("<tr><td align=center><b>"
+headers+"</td>");
                    out.println("<td align=center>"
+request.getHeader(headers)+"</td></tr>");
                    }
                }
                out.println("</TABLE><BR>");
                out.println(htmlFooter);

        }

} // end of PrintHeader
```

Figure 4-4 depicts in the browser the various request headers available from the client's HTTP request.

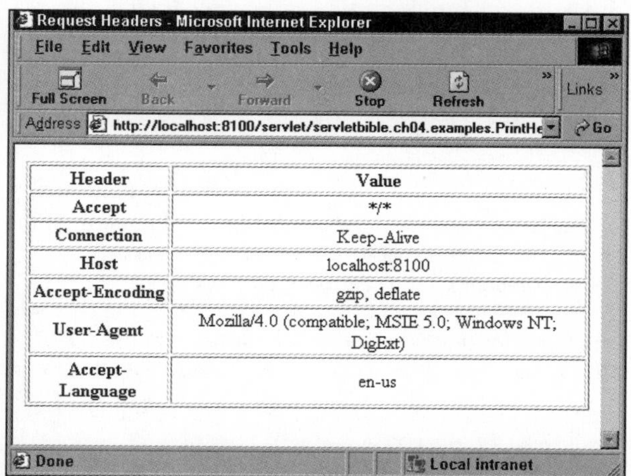

Header	Value
Accept	*/*
Connection	Keep-Alive
Host	localhost:8100
Accept-Encoding	gzip, deflate
User-Agent	Mozilla/4.0 (compatible; MSIE 5.0; Windows NT; DigExt)
Accept-Language	en-us

Figure 4-4: Client information is displayed in the browser by the PrintHeader servlet.

Table 4-1 summarizes many of the available HTTP request headers and what these headers indicate.

Table 4-1
HTTP Request Header Fields

Header Name	*Header Purpose*
`Accept`	Used to indicate the media or MIME types acceptable as a response by the client. The "*" character is used to group MIME types into ranges. A header value of */* indicates all MIME types. A *type/** indicates support for all subtypes of the *type*.
`Accept-Charset`	Used to indicate the supported character sets of the client. For example: iso-8859-5, unicode-1-1, and so on.
`Accept-Encoding`	Defines the content coding acceptable by the client.
`Accept-Language`	Defines the set of client-preferred natural languages. These are represented by codes such as en (english) and da (Danish).
`Authorization`	A client can use this field in order to authenticate itself with the server.
`Cache-Control`	Contains cache-control directives that must be followed by caching mechanisms through the request-response chain. This header field is not much use to servlets.
`Connection`	Contains the preferred options for a particular connection. The Keep-Alive option signals that a persistent connection be used. HTTP 1.1 provides for the close option that signals for the closure of the connection and indicates that a persistent connection is not required.
`Content-Length`	Indicates the size of data sent along with the request headers in bytes.
`Content-Type`	Indicates the media type of the data sent.
`Expect`	Indicates the particular behaviors the client requires. If the server determines that it cannot support a particular extension sent by the client, a status code (`SC_EXPECTATION_FAILED`) 417 is sent. In the case where the file extension is supported, a status code (`SC_CONTINUE`) 100 is sent. This field is used in the case of file attachments.
`From`	Contains the e-mail address of the person controlling the user agent making the HTTP request.
`Host`	Specifies the host and port number of the client that can be obtained from the original URI/URL or referring resource. This field must be included in all HTTP 1.1 requests.

Header Name	*Header Purpose*
`If-Match`	A client that has obtained one or more resources can verify that those entities are current by including a list of their associated entity tags in this header field. This header is useful in PUT requests.
`If-Modified-Since`	Indicates to the server that the client wants the requested resource only if it has changed after the specified date. If the resource has not been modified, a status code (`SC_NOT_MODIFIED`) 304 is returned.
`If-None-Match`	Associated with If-Match; if none of the entity tags match a status code (`SC_PRECONDITION_FAILED`), 412 should be returned.
`If-Range`	If the client has a partial/partially current copy of the requested documents, this field can be used to retrieve only the out-of-date documents.
`If-Unmodified-Since`	Similar to the If-Modified-Since field. If the requested resource/document has been modified since the specified date, the server must not perform the requested operation. A status code (`SC_PRECONDITION_FAILED`) 412 is returned. Most useful in PUT requests/operations.
`Proxy-Authorization`	Allows clients to identify themselves to proxies requiring authorization.
`Range`	An optional field that can be used by the client to obtain missing parts of the requested document.
`Referer`	A field that lets the client specify (optional) the URL from which the request URL has been obtained.
`TE`	Used to indicate the extension transfer codings (if any) that the client is willing to accept in the response.
`User-Agent`	Contains information about the user agent and the type of user agent originating the request.

For further information on request headers, refer to the HTTP 1.1 RFCs at `http://www.freesoft.org/CIE/RFC/2068/index.htm` or at `http://www.freesoft.org/CIE/RFC/Orig/rfc2616.txt`.

Printing CGI environment variables

Client-header lines are placed into CGI environment variables by the server in the format of the header name prefixed by *HTTP_*. Headers that the server has already processed may be excluded from this process.

Table 4-2 outlines the methods available to access the CGI Environment variables and the information contained in those variables.

Table 4-2
Useful Request Methods

Method	*Information Accessible*
getAuthType	Returns the authentication type used to protect the servlet (either BASIC, SSL, or null if there is no protection)
getContentType	Returns the content type
getContentTypeLength	Returns the content length
getCookies	Retrieves an array of cookie objects the client sends
getHeader, getHeaders, getHeaderNames, getIntHeader	Retrieves header names and values
getMethod	Retrieves the request method (for example, GET, POST, HEAD, and so on)
getQueryString	Retrieves the query string contained in the URL after the path
getRemoteAddr	Retrieves clients IP address
getRemoteHost	Retrieves client host name
getRemoteUser	Queries the client-user information
getRequestURI	Retrieves the request URL, excluding the query string
getServletPath	Returns the servlet path information
getServerName	Retrieves the server host name
getServerPort	Retrieves the port number the request has been made on

Listing 4-3 shows a servlet that prints some of the CGI environment variables by using the *HttpServletRequest* interface.

Listing 4-3

```
package servletbible.ch04.examples;

import javax.servlet.*;
import javax.servlet.http.*;
import java.io.*;

public class PrintCGI extends HttpServlet
```

```
{

        /**
        * doGet implementation, calls printCGIValues
        *
        * @param request
        * @param response
        * @throws IOException
        */


        public void doGet (HttpServletRequest request, HttpServletResponse
response) throws IOException
        {
         printCGIValues(request, response);
        }

        /**
        * doPost implementation, calls printCGIValues
        *
        * @param request
        * @param response
        * @throws IOException
        */


        public void doPost (HttpServletRequest request, HttpServletResponse
response) throws IOException
        {
                printCGIValues(request, response);
        }

        /**
        * Prints CGI Environment Variables in a table
        *
        * @param request
        * @param response
        * @throws IOException
        */

        public void printCGIValues (HttpServletRequest request,
HttpServletResponse response) throws IOException
        {
            String headers = null;
            String htmlHeader =
"<HTML><HEAD><TITLE> CGI Environment Variables </TITLE></HEAD><BODY>";
            String htmlFooter = "</BODY></HTML>";

            response.setContentType("text/html");

            PrintWriter out = response.getWriter();
```

Continued

Listing 4-3 (continued)

```
            out.println(htmlHeader);
            out.println("<TABLE ALIGN=CENTER BORDER=1>");
            out.println("<tr><th> CGI Variable </th><th> Value </th>");

            out.println("<tr><td align=center>Authentication Type</td>");
            out.println("<td align=center>"
+request.getAuthType()+"</td></tr>");

            out.println("<tr><td align=center>Content Type</td>");
            out.println("<td
align=center>"+request.getContentType()+"</td></tr>");

            out.println("<tr><td align=center>Content Type Length</td>");
            out.println("<td align=center>"
+request.getContentLength()+"</td></tr>");

            out.println("<tr><td align=center>Query String</td>");
            out.println("<td align=center>"
+request.getMethod()+"</td></tr>");

            out.println("<tr><td align=center>IP Address</td>");
            out.println("<td align=center>"
+request.getRemoteAddr()+"</td></tr>");

            out.println("<tr><td align=center>Host Name</td>");
            out.println("<td align=center>"
+request.getRemoteHost()+"</td></tr>");

            out.println("<tr><td align=center>Request URL</td>");
            out.println("<td align=center>"
+request.getRequestURI()+"</td></tr>");

            out.println("<tr><td align=center>Servlet Path</td>");
            out.println("<td align=center>"
+request.getServletPath()+"</td></tr>");

            out.println("<tr><td align=center>Server's Name</td>");
            out.println("<td align=center>"
+request.getServerName()+"</td></tr>");

            out.println("<tr><td align=center>Server's Port</td>");
            out.println("<td align=center>"
+request.getServerPort()+"</td></tr>");

            out.println("</TABLE><BR>");
            out.println(htmlFooter);

        }

} // end of PrintCGI
```

Figure 4-5 depicts the various CGI variables that have been requested by the servlet.

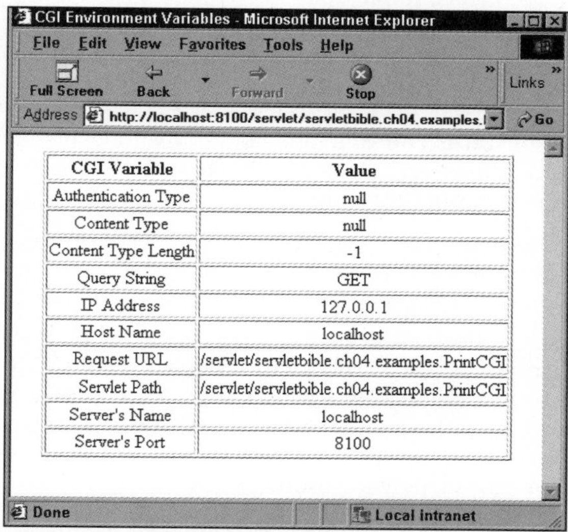

CGI Variable	Value
Authentication Type	null
Content Type	null
Content Type Length	-1
Query String	GET
IP Address	127.0.0.1
Host Name	localhost
Request URL	/servlet/servletbible.ch04.examples.PrintCGI
Servlet Path	/servlet/servletbible.ch04.examples.PrintCGI
Server's Name	localhost
Server's Port	8100

Figure 4-5: Various CGI Environment Variables available via the `HTTPServletRequest` interface

HTTP Response Headers

Common elements in a successful response consist of:

- ✦ The protocol accepted (for example, HTTP/1.1, followed by a status code, for example, 200 OK); this makes up the status line
- ✦ The server name that makes up the status line
- ✦ The content-type (for example, `text/html`)
- ✦ The content length in bytes (for example, 1234)
- ✦ Followed by a blank line (A carriage return/line feed CRLF or `\r\n`)
- ✦ The response data (that is, HTML code, requested file/resource)

The `javax.servlet.http.HttpServletResponse` interface is a representation of an HTTP servlet response. This interface can be used to modify HTTP response-header information and subsequently control the response sent to the client making the request.

Status codes

HTTP status codes are part of the response header and indicate to the client the status of the request made or the resource requested.

HTTP defines many status codes, but there are five general classes of status codes as follows:

- The 1*xx* (i.e. 100-199) range of status codes is informational and is available in HTTP 1.1 but not in HTTP 1.0. This range (available in HTTP 1.1) of status codes is used to indicate a provisional response.
- The 2*xx* range of status codes is used to indicate to the client that the request has been successfully received and accepted. A successful request is denoted by status code `200 OK`, or, in the case of a `POST` operation, a `201` is returned.
- The 3*xx* range is used in the case of redirection or cases whereby further action is needed by the client in order to process the request. Typically if the requested resource has changed in location, the server may respond with the current location of the resource in the response header. The client may make a subsequent request for the resource with the new location, or the server may simply redirect the client to the new location.
- The 4*xx* range of status codes is used by the server to indicate to the client that there is an error with the client or with the request the client has made. This status code is followed by an explanation of the error. For example, `401 Unauthorized` indicates that the client is not allowed to access the requested resource; in addition, we all know the infamous 404 status code that indicates that the page or resource cannot be found at the URL the client has entered.
- The 5*xx* range indicates an error with the server in the attempt to process the request. These codes are accompanied by a reason why the request cannot be fulfilled. For example, `500 Internal Server Error` indicates that the server has encountered an unexpected situation that prevents the processing of the request.

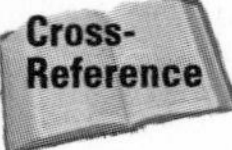

Refer to Appendix E for more detail on specific HTTP status codes.

The `HttpServletResponse` interface defines HTTP status codes as constants. The interface can be used to manipulate the status code sent to the client and thus to control the response. Table 4-3 outlines some methods of the `HttpServletResponse` interface that enable you to control aspects of the response to the client.

Table 4-3
Useful Methods of the HTTPServletResponse Interface

Method	*Purpose*
`addCookie`	Adds a cookie to the response, subsequently setting the cookie in the client
`encodeURL`	Used to encode the URL with the session ID. This method is useful in session tracking through URL rewriting.
`eetWriter`	A well-known and widely used method in servlets, used to get the `PrintWriter` object. The `PrintWriter` object is used to print character text to the client.
`setContentType`	Another widely used method by servlets to set the type of content sent to the client (for example, `text/html`)
`sendError(int sc)`, `sendError(int sc, String msg)`	Used to send an error response to the client. After you call this method, no further response should be written to the client, or an `IllegalStateException` is thrown.
`setHeader`, `setIntHeader`	Used to send response-header names and values
`sendRedirect`	Useful in sending a redirect response to the client to the specified location/URL
`setStatus(int sc)`	Used to set the status code in the response header, where `sc` is the status-code constant of the `HttpServletResponse` interface (for example, in the format `SC_OK`)

Using the HttpServletResponse interface for redirection

The examples in this section demonstrate how you can send a controlled response to the client by using the `HttpServletResponse` interface. In this case the examples are for redirection purposes. Redirection is as the name suggests re-directing or sending the user to a new location or URL programmatically. You may wish to redirect for various reasons. For example making sure that whenever users access a page that is no longer available on the server (via an old bookmark), they can be sent to the main URL of the site.

These examples require you to set various configuration parameters. These are outlined at the end of the examples in this chapter.

Listings 4-4 and 4-5 demonstrate how a page that has been requested has been moved on the server and how the servlet provides a response that provides the client with the new location of the resource.

Listing 4-4

```
package servletbible.ch04.examples;

import java.io.*;
import javax.servlet.*;
import javax.servlet.http.*;

public class RedirectWithLinkServlet extends HttpServlet
{
        public void doGet(HttpServletRequest request,
HttpServletResponse response)
        throws ServletException, IOException
        {

         /**
          * Status code (302) indicating that the resource has temporarily
          * moved to another
          * location, but that future references should still use the
          *original URI to access
          * the resource
          */

                PrintWriter out = response.getWriter();


                response.setContentType("text/html");
                out.println("<html><body>");
                out.println("<H1>The page you have requested is not found
at this location currently.</H1><BR>");
                out.println(
"<a href=\"http://localhost:8100/readme.html\">Click here</a>");
                out.println(" to go to the new location.<BR>");
                out.println("</body></html>");

                return;
        }
}
```

Figure 4-6 shows that when the readme.html file is accessed a message and link to the new location is provided on the Web page.

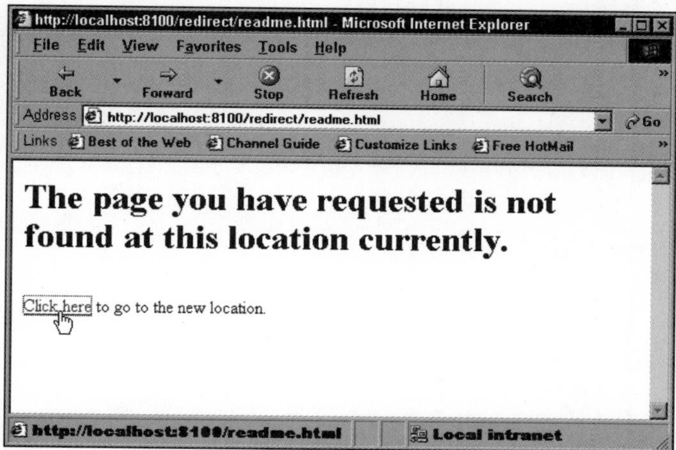

Figure 4-6: Redirecting a user by providing a link to the new location

Listing 4-5 shows how you can automatically redirect a user transparently to the new location. This method may be more useful if you are not worried about the user updating their bookmarks or references to the old location.

Listing 4-5

```
package servletbible.ch04.examples;

import java.io.*;
import javax.servlet.*;
import javax.servlet.http.*;

public class RedirectNewLocation extends HttpServlet
{
        public void doGet(HttpServletRequest request, HttpServletResponse
response) throws ServletException, IOException
        {

          /**
          * Status code (302) indicating that the resource has temporarily
          * moved to another
          * location, but that future references should still use the
          * original URI to access
          * the resource
          */
```

Continued

Listing 4-5 *(continued)*

```
                PrintWriter out = response.getWriter();

                response.setStatus(response.SC_MOVED_TEMPORARILY);
                response.setHeader("Location",
"http://localhost:8100/readme.html");

                response.setContentType("text/html");
                return;
        }
}
```

Figure 4-7 shows what the user may see prior to redirection (if there is a slow network connection or the computer system is slow) when they have entered in the URL the old location. This location is where you wish to redirect them away from.

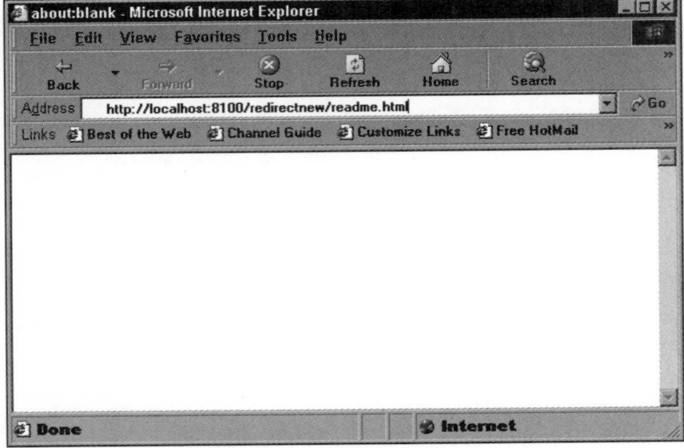

Figure 4-7: User accessing the readme.html from the old location

Figure 4-8 depicts the actual readme.html from its new location. The redirection is complete here and the user has been redirected to the new location successfully.

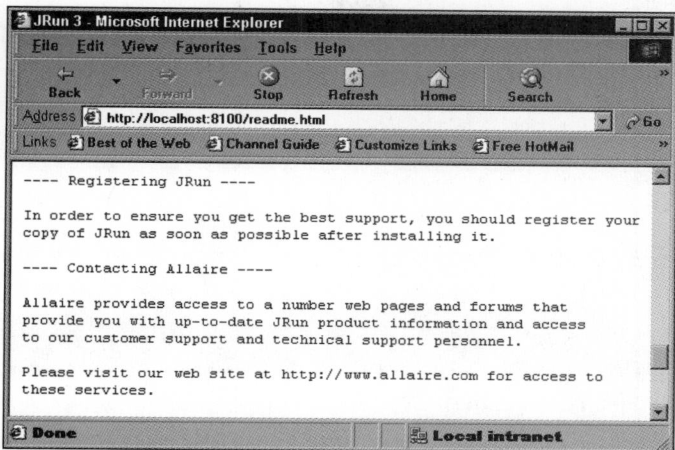

Figure 4-8: The new location of the readme.html file

Redirection servlet configuration

The following steps configure the server so that the redirection examples work:

1. Compile RedirectWithLinkServlet.java and RedirectNewLocation.java.
2. Create a directory structure as follows under JRun3.0:

   ```
   {jrun-installation-dir}\servers\default\default-app\
   WEB-INF\classes\servletbible\ch04\examples
   ```

3. Copy the .class files of RedirectWithLinkServlet.java and RedirectNewLocation.java to the directory created in the preceding step.
4. Open the JRun Management Console by typing the following URL in the browser:

   ```
   http://localhost:8000
   ```

5. Select the JRun default server ➪ Web Applications ➪ Default User Application ➪ Servlet Definitions.
6. Add the entries under this link as shown in Figure 4-9.

Note

The class name entry in Figure 4-9 should have the complete path name with package references.

For example, RedirectWithLinkServlet is present under package servletbible. ch04.examples. So the complete class name is servletbible.ch04.examples. RedirectLinkWithServlet.

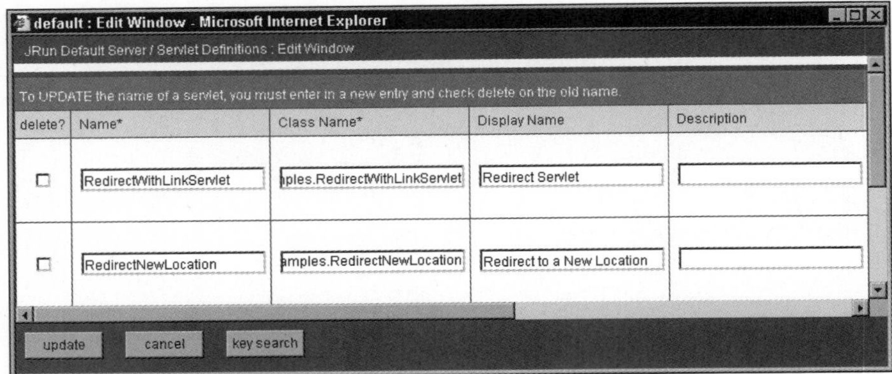

Figure 4-9: Servlet definitions entries

7. Once servlet definitions are added, add a servlet URL Mapping entry. Select JRun default server ➪ Web Applications ➪ Default User Application ➪ Servlet URL Mapping.

   Add the entries as shown in Figure 4-10.

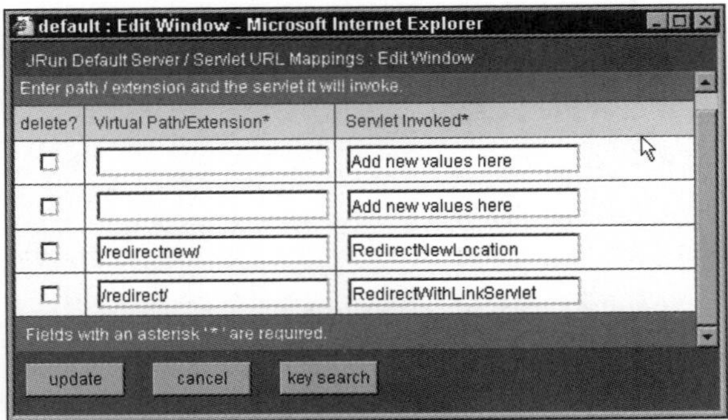

Figure 4-10: Servlet URL mappings

Once the preceding configuration steps are completed, access the two servlet programs by typing the URLs shown in Figure 4-6 and Figure 4-7.

Using the HttpServletResponse interface for restriction

Listing 4-6 shows how you can deliberately restrict a user (using the 401 status code). In this case, we are using the IP of our computer to restrict ourselves to the normal execution of the servlet. The precondition to restrict can be anything, such as a password or the client's host name. Restricting a user access to a resource can be programmatically done this way. One might want to allow access to certain resources only if they come from a specific domain or network and therefore deny everyone else access.

Listing 4-6

```
package servletbible.ch04.examples;
import java.io.*;
import javax.servlet.*;
import javax.servlet.http.*;

public class RestrictUser extends HttpServlet
{
        public void doGet(HttpServletRequest req,HttpServletResponse resp)
throws ServletException, IOException{
                PrintWriter out;
                /**
                 *Status code (401) indicating that the request requires
                 * HTTP authentication.
                 */

//                Check if the client's IP is not 172.30.81.78

                if(req.getRemoteAddr().equals("172.30.81.78")) {
                resp.sendError(HttpServletResponse.SC_UNAUTHORIZED);
                }
//                ...otherwise display the client's IP
                resp.setContentType("text/html");
                out = resp.getWriter();
                out.println("<HTML>");
                out.println("<BODY>");
                out.println("<H1>");
                out.println("Hello!");
                out.println("<BR>");
                out.println("Your IP Address: " +req.getRemoteAddr());
                out.println("</H1>");
                out.println("</body>");
                out.println("</html>");
                out.close();
        }
}
```

Figure 4-11 shows what all users not having the IP address 172.30.81.78 accessing this servlet would see. In other words they have been granted access programmatically to the servlet resource. In this case it merely greets the user and prints out their actual IP address.

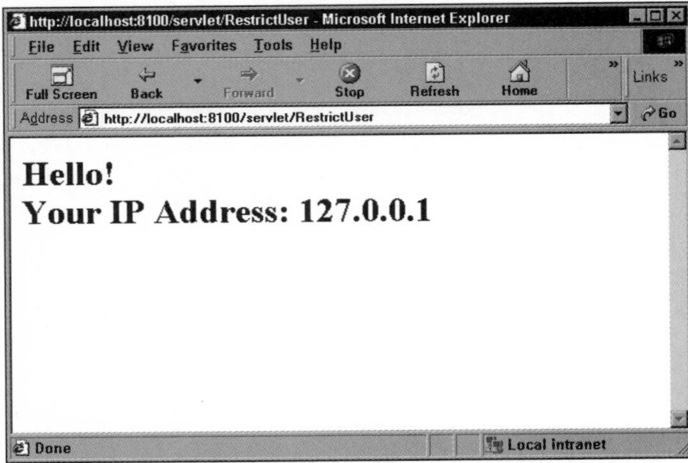

Figure 4-11: Code accessed from an alternate machine that does not have the IP 172.30.81.78

Figure 4-12 shows what a user having the IP address 172.30.81.78 would see. In this case we have in the servlet programmatically restricted the user of this IP address from having access to this resource.

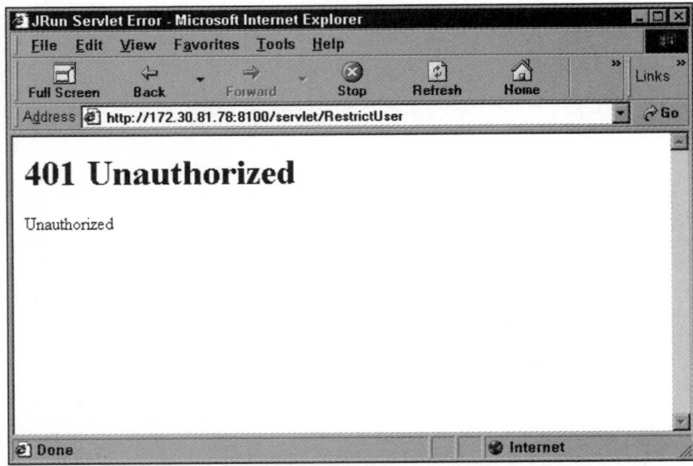

Figure 4-12: Code accessed from the same machine that has the IP 172.30.81.78

Summary

In this chapter, you have learned more about HTTP as it relates to servlet programming. You should now have a good understanding of the elements of a request and its header information and the elements of a response and its header information. You should also know how the request-response paradigm works, the information you can read from the client, and status codes and their place in HTTP. Finally, you should know how to send a controlled response by using the `HTTPServletResponse` interface.

The next chapter shows you the key elements of HTML documents and HTML forms. You also learn how HTML and servlets work together to provide an interactive Web application.

✦ ✦ ✦

P A R T

Working with Servlets

✦ ✦ ✦ ✦

In This Part

✦ ✦ ✦ ✦

Using Servlets with HTML

In This Chapter

Create and use HTML forms

Retrieve and use information entered in forms

Use servlets to generate HTML efficiently

Learn how various form elements are used

Validate forms by using JavaScript

Upload files

Use servlets with JavaMail to send e-mail

This chapter introduces the basics of HTML, more specifically how to create HTML forms. You will also learn how you can validate your form with JavaScript and how to use JavaMail to send e-mail.

HTML Forms

HTML is the language browsers use to render a view to the client. Its syntax is tag based and it is based on Standard Generalized Markup Language (SGML). HTML forms are what we use to gather input from the client. Servlets can make use of this information to execute some logic, perform some task(s), and return a view to the client's browser.

HTML is essentially the Graphical User Interface (GUI) for a servlet. Although the Java applet uses the `java.awt` package for its GUI, the servlet uses HTML pages instead.

A simple HTML document is shown in Listing 5-1.

Listing 5-1

```
<HTML>
<HEAD>
<TITLE> Simple HTML Page</TITLE>
</HEAD>
<BODY>
This is a simple HTML page.
<ul>
<li> <b>Here is some text in bold</b>
<li> <i> Here is some text in italics </i>
<li> <A href= "http://www.hungryminds.com"> This text links
to
```

Continued

Listing 5-1 (continued)

```
the Hungry Minds website </A>
</ul>

</BODY>

  </HTML>
```

All HTML documents consist of the starting <HTML> and closing </HTML> tags. HTML content is embedded between these tags. The title of the document that appears in the browser's title bar is defined by the <TITLE> tags. The main content of the HTML page appears between the starting <BODY> and </BODY> tags. Figure 5-1 depicts the HTML page from Listing 5-1 as it appears when viewed in your browser.

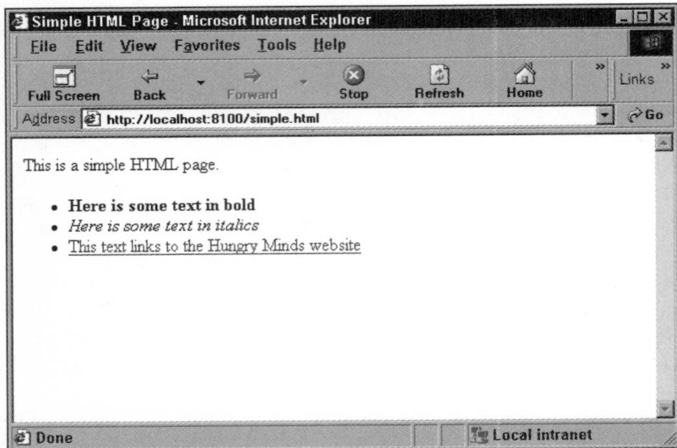

Figure 5-1: A simple HTML document viewed in a browser

For detailed or current information on HTML, visit the HTML home page at `http://www.w3.org/MarkUp/`.

Basic form elements

You may have realized by now that most HTML tags consist of starting and closing tags. Forms follow the same pattern with a starting <FORM> tag and closing </FORM> tag. Between these tags is where you place user-input elements of your choice. Elements available in HTML forms include

✦ `<input>`

✦ `<select>`, `<option>` (`<option>` is used as a property of select)

✦ `<textarea>`

These elements will be covered in more detail in the latter part of this section.

One limitation with forms is that they can't be nested; in other words, you cannot place `<FORM>` tags inside another `<FORM>` tag.

The basic form structure is as follows:

```
<FORM Name = "FormName" Action = "../servlet/PackageName.ServletName"
Method ="GET|POST" Enctype = "MIME type">
```

After the `<FORM>` tag, place the input elements:

```
<input type = "Submit" value = "Send">
<input type = "Reset" value = "Clear">
</FORM>
```

The *`Name`* attribute is optional and is used to specify the name of the form. This can be useful in a situation in which you have multiple forms on an HTML page and you need to refer to a particular form.

The *`Action`* attribute is used to define the location (absolute or relative URL) of the server-side program that processes the form's request. This attribute is required if the form request is to be processed.

The *`Method`* attribute is used to specify the way the URL specified in the action attribute is accessed. The value of this attribute can be either `GET` or `POST`. This attribute is required for form processing. If the form is submitted to a servlet, the method attribute determines whether the `doGet()` or `doPost()` methods are called.

The *`Enctype`* (Encoding Type) specifies the MIME type in which the form data is encoded. This attribute is optional and is not often explicitly specified. The default value implied, if not specified, is `application/x-www-form-urlencoded`.

Form input elements

The first category of form input elements is defined with the `<input>` tag. The `<input>` tag consists of the following attributes:

✦ `Type` — This attribute is specified as one of the following:

- `checkbox`
- `file`

- hidden
- image
- password
- radio
- reset
- submit
- text

✦ Name — This is a string/symbolic name that should be specified to refer to the field on the server side.

✦ Value — A value string/numerical can be entered here to give the field a default value.

✦ Checked — This applies to checkboxes and radio-button types, where specifying CHECKED makes the default state of the checkbox or radio button selected.

Checkboxes and radio buttons that are not selected in a form do not return a name/value pair when the form is submitted.

✦ Size — This is a numerical value that contains the size or dimension of the input field view.

✦ Maxlength — The number of characters that would be allowed to be entered in the input field would be restricted to the numerical value of this attribute. If this attribute is not defined, the number of characters that can be entered into the input field are unrestricted. This value is independent of the size attribute; the size attribute simply defines the size of the view of the field rendered in the browser.

✦ Src — This is the URL associated with the image (used where the input type is an image).

✦ Align — This attribute may be specified as one of the following:

- top
- middle
- bottom
- left
- right

There are a number of input types available. Table 5-1 outlines these types and how they are used.

Table 5-1 **Input Types**	
Input Types	***Purpose***
`checkbox`	The checkbox has two states: `ON` or `OFF`. The `ON` state occurs when the checkbox is checked. This is often placed in forms to offer a Boolean selection choice.
`file`	Supported by fourth-generation browsers, this type allows the inclusion of files along with form data. An accept attribute included with an input of this type is used to specify the file type (for example, `accept = "application/msword"`, indicating a word document).
`hidden`	This is a nonvisible element in the form the user cannot see in his or her browser. You should note that the HTML source of the hidden element can be seen if a user views the page source code through their browser. The hidden element contains a value of importance to the server-side application. Hidden elementsare mainly used to hold the client's state/session information.
`image`	This is a clickable image that can be used to submit forms. The `name` attribute is required for this input type.
`password`	This is identical to a text field; however, it masks any text entered, so the text typed in this field is not visible in the browser.
`radio`	This is useful in allowing the user to select from a small number of options. Specifying the `CHECKED` attribute makes this type selected for the initial state.
`reset`	Clicking this button resets the values of all the fields in the form (in which this type is included) to their initial states.
`submit`	When clicked, this input type sends form data according to the method specified in the `Method` attribute.
`text`	This is a single line text-entry field.

Other types of form input elements not covered by the `<input>` tag are `<select>`, `<option>` and `<textarea>`.

The `<select>` tag is used to render a drop-down selection menu, which may be used when there are numerous selectable options that may fit into the same category. The options available in the drop-down menu are defined with the `<option>` tags and are enclosed by the ending `</select>` tag.

The <textarea> type is used for multiline text entries (for example, feedback about users' Web site experiences). The WRAP attribute is used to control word-wrapping in the field. If WRAP is set to Virtual, the words wrap in the textarea; however, the field is sent as one line when the form is submitted. If WRAP is set to physical, the text wraps and is sent as typed in the textarea.

Listing 5-2 shows the HTML for a feedback form that contains some of the preceding form elements; we use this feedback form in other examples in this chapter.

Listing 5-2

```
<HTML><HEAD><TITLE> feedback Form </TITLE></HEAD>

<BODY>

<DIV ALIGN="CENTER"><H1> Feedback Form </H1></DIV>
<HR>
<BR>

<FORM NAME="ParameterPost"
ACTION="/servlet/servletbible.examples.ch05.PrintFormParams"
METHOD="POST">
<TABLE BGCOLOR="BLANCHEDALMOND" ALIGN="CENTER" BORDER="0">
    <TR>
    <TD ALIGN="CENTER"><B>Name:</B></TD>
    <TD ALIGN="CENTER"> <INPUT TYPE="TEXT" SIZE="25"
NAME="Person"></TD>
    </TR>

    <TR>
    <TD ALIGN="CENTER"><B>Email:</B></TD>
    <TD ALIGN="CENTER"> <INPUT TYPE="TEXT" SIZE="25"
MAXLENGTH="40" NAME="emailaddress"></TD>
    </TR>


    <TR>
    <TD ALIGN="CENTER"><B>How did you find this site?</B></TD>
    <TD ALIGN="CENTER">
        <SELECT NAME="from" SIZE="1">
        <OPTION VALUE = "Website" SELECTED>Another
Website</OPTION>
        <OPTION VALUE = "search engine">A search
engine</OPTION>
        <OPTION VALUE = "friend">A friend told you</OPTION>
        <OPTION VALUE = "email">From an email</OPTION>
        <OPTION VALUE = "unlisted">Another way not listed
here</OPTION>
</SELECT>
    </TD>
    </TR>
```

```
    <TR>
    <TD ALIGN="CENTER"><B>How would you rate my
website:</B></TD>
    <TD ALIGN="CENTER">
    <INPUT TYPE="radio" NAME = "rating" VALUE = "Excellent">
Excellent
    <INPUT TYPE="radio" NAME = "rating" VALUE = "Good"> Good
    <INPUT TYPE="radio" NAME = "rating" VALUE = "Average"
CHECKED> Average
    <INPUT TYPE="radio" NAME = "rating" VALUE = "Poor"> Poor
    <INPUT TYPE="radio" NAME = "rating" VALUE = "Overhaul">
Needs an Overhaul
    </TD>
    </TR>

    <TR>
    <TD ALIGN="CENTER"><B>Comments or Suggestions:</B></TD>
    <TD ALIGN="CENTER">
    <TEXTAREA ROWS="6" COLS="40" WRAP="PHYSICAL"
Name="suggestions">Enter any comments or suggestions you have
here.</TEXTAREA>
    </TD>
    </TR>

    <TR>
    <TD ALIGN="CENTER"><B>Do you think this form looks
nice?</B></TD>
    <TD ALIGN="CENTER">
    <INPUT TYPE="CHECKBOX" NAME="formrating" VALUE="yes">
    </TD>
    </TR>



    <TR>

    <TD ALIGN="CENTER">
     
    </TD>

    <TD ALIGN="LEFT">

    <INPUT TYPE="SUBMIT" VALUE="Send Comments" ALIGN="MIDDLE">
       
    <INPUT TYPE="RESET" VALUE="Clear Form" ALIGN="MIDDLE">

    </TD>
    </TR>

</FORM>
</BODY>
</HTML>
```

Figure 5-2 shows the form in Listing 5-2 when viewed in your browser.

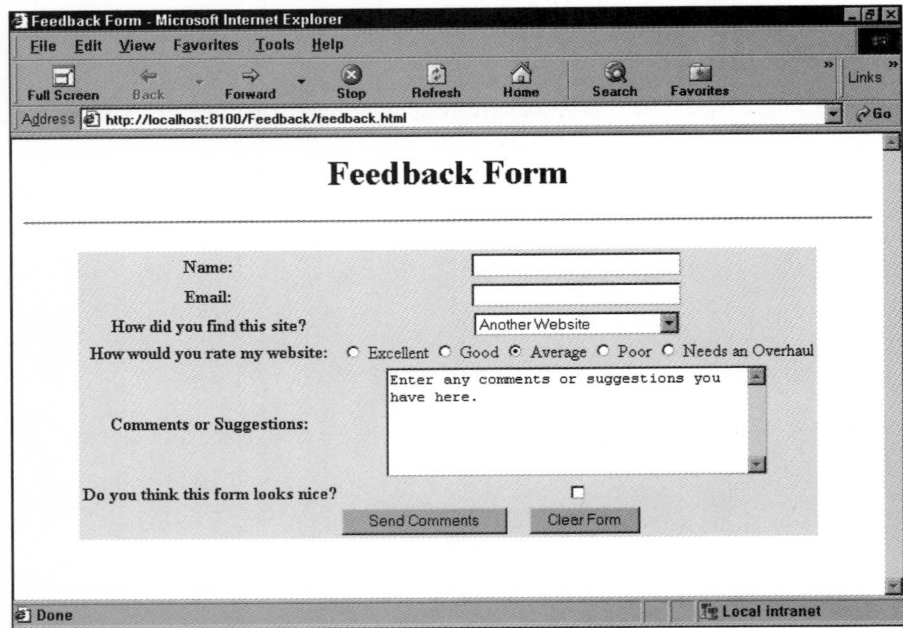

Figure 5-2: Feedback form

Now we will move on to demonstrating how you can access form data that has been sent from the user.

Processing Form Data

In this section you will be shown how you can process form data. More specifically in this case gather the form data entered by the user and record this input into a file.

Reading form input

Listing 5-3 shows you how to use a Java servlet to read and display data from the form we create in the previous section. In other words, we read and display the name/value pairs of the feedback form-input elements we create in Listing 5-2.

Listing 5-3

```
package servletbible.ch05.examples;

import java.io.*;
import javax.servlet.*;
import javax.servlet.http.*;
import java.util.Enumeration;

/**
 * Prints out the form paramters
 */

public class PrintFormParams extends HttpServlet {


    public void doGet(HttpServletRequest request, HttpServletResponse
response) throws ServletException,IOException {
        PrintParams(request, response);

    }



    public void doPost(HttpServletRequest request, HttpServletResponse
response) throws ServletException,IOException {

        PrintParams(request, response);
    }

    public void PrintParams(HttpServletRequest request, HttpServletResponse
response) throws IOException {

        response.setContentType("text/html");
        PrintWriter out = response.getWriter();

        String htmlHeader =
"<HTML><HEAD><TITLE> Printed Form Parameters </TITLE></HEAD><BODY>";
        String htmlFooter = "</BODY></HTML>";

        out.println(htmlHeader);
        out.println("<TABLE ALIGN=CENTER BORDER=1>");
        out.println("<tr><th> Input Name </th><th> Value </th>");

        Enumeration enum = request.getParameterNames();

        while (enum.hasMoreElements()) {
            String inputName = (String)enum.nextElement();
            String value = request.getParameter(inputName);

             if (value.length() != 0)
                  {
```

Continued

Listing 5-3 *(continued)*

```
                out.println("<tr><td align=center>"+inputName+"</td>");
                out.println("<td align=center>"+value+"</td></tr>");
                }
            else {
                out.println("<tr><td align=center>"+inputName+"</td>");
                out.println("<td align=center><i>Null</i></td></tr>");
            }

        }

        out.println("</TABLE><BR>");
        out.println(htmlFooter);

    } //end of PrintParams

} // End of PrintFormParams.java
```

Figure 5-3 shows the feedback form with data being entered, prior to submitting the data.

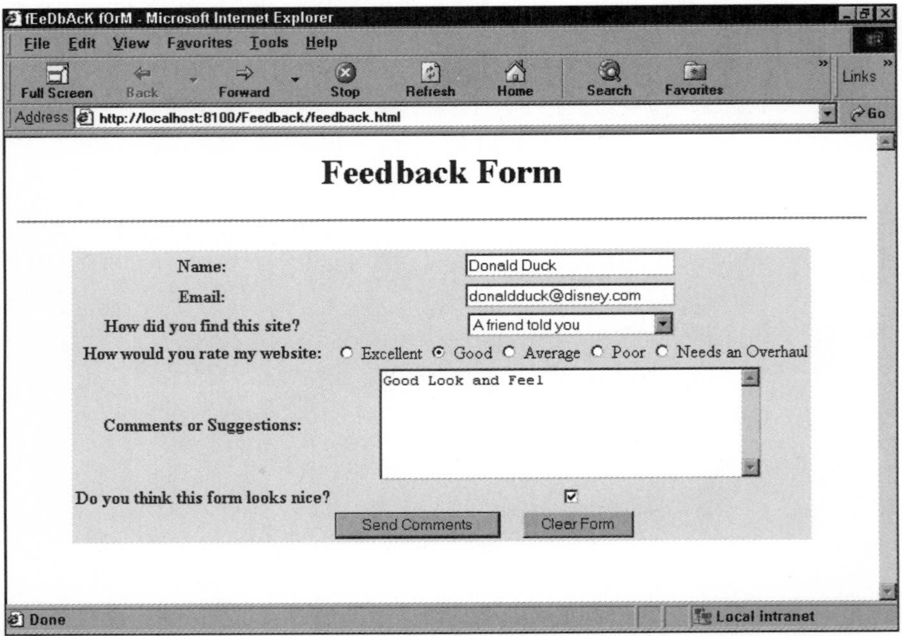

Figure 5-3: Feedback form with data entered

Figure 5-4 shows the feedback form data as name/value pairs in tabular format.

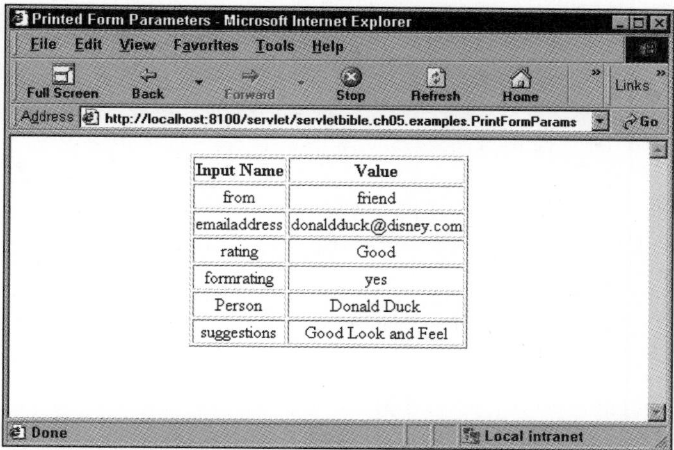

Figure 5-4: Feedback form name/value pairs displayed

Writing form input to a file

Now let's use the information gathered in this feedback form. In this section, we create a new servlet, FeedbackServlet, to write user feedback into a file. First, we must modify the feedback form from Listing 5-2 to POST the information to the new servlet as follows:

```
<FORM NAME="ParameterPost"
ACTION="/servlet/servletbible.examples.ch05.FeedbackServlet"
METHOD="POST">
```

Listing 5-4 shows the FeedbackServlet program that writes user feedback information to a file.

Listing 5-4

```
package servletbible.ch05.examples;

import java.io.*;
import javax.servlet.*;
import javax.servlet.http.*;
import java.util.*;

/**
 * The Feedback Servlet records form feedback into a file.
```

Continued

Listing 5-4 (continued)

```
 */

public class FeedbackServlet extends HttpServlet {

public static String fileName = "/home/suresh/lws/feedback_entries.txt";
public File fname  = new File(fileName);
public String fileEntry = null;


    public void doGet(HttpServletRequest request, HttpServletResponse
response) throws ServletException,IOException {

       /* Here we include a file to show the user that the form can not be
        * accessed via a GET request
        */

       getServletContext().getRequestDispatcher("/Noget.html")
.include(request, response);
    }



    public void doPost(HttpServletRequest request, HttpServletResponse
response) throws ServletException,IOException {

        response.setContentType("text/html");
        PrintWriter out = response.getWriter();

        servletbible.utils.HtmlUtils hu =
        new servletbible.utils.HtmlUtils();

        // new String Writer
        StringWriter tempEntry = new StringWriter();

        String Name = request.getParameter("Person");
        String emailAddress = request.getParameter("emailaddress");
        String Rating = request.getParameter("rating");
        String Suggestions = request.getParameter("suggestions");

        String formRating = null;
        formRating = request.getParameter("formrating");

        tempEntry.write("Name:\t"+Name+"\n");
        tempEntry.write("Email Address:\t"+emailAddress+"\n");
        tempEntry.write("Rating:\t"+Rating+"\n");
        tempEntry.write("Suggestions:\t"+Suggestions+"\n");


        if (formRating != null )
        {
        tempEntry.write("Was the form Nice?\t"+formRating+"\n");
```

```
        }

        else {
        tempEntry.write("Was the form Nice?\t No \n");
        }

        String dt = new Date().toString();

        tempEntry.write("----- Entry recorded at "+ dt +"-------");

        fileEntry = tempEntry.toString();


        if (fileExists(fname))
         {
             AppendFile(fname, fileEntry);
         }
        else {
            CreateFile(fileName, fileEntry);
        }

        tempEntry.flush();
        tempEntry.close();

        out.print(hu.createHtmlHeader("Thankyou"));
        out.print("<CENTER>");
        out.print(hu.getHead(1, "Thankyou,"));
        out.print(hu.getBR(2));
        out.print("for your comments. Your feedback has been recorded.");
        out.print("</CENTER>");
        out.print(hu.getBR(1));
        out.print(hu.getHtmlFooter());
    }


public static synchronized void CreateFile(String fname, String fileEntry)
    {

        BufferedWriter bw = null;

        try
        {
            bw = new BufferedWriter(new FileWriter(fname));
            bw.write(fileEntry);
            bw.newLine();
            bw.flush();
            bw.close();


        } catch (IOException e)
        {
            System.err.println("IOException: " + e);
        }
```

Continued

Listing 5-4 *(continued)*

```
    }

  public static synchronized void AppendFile(File fname,String fileEntry) {

        BufferedWriter bw = null;

        try
        {
            bw = new BufferedWriter(new FileWriter(fileName, true));
            bw.write(fileEntry);
            bw.newLine();
            bw.flush();
            bw.close();

        }
        catch (IOException ioe) {
        System.out.println(ioe);
        }

    }

    public static synchronized boolean fileExists(File fname) {

        FileInputStream fs = null ;

                    try
                    {
                        fs = new FileInputStream(fname) ;
                        return true;
                    }
                    catch (FileNotFoundException e)
                    {
                        return false;
                    }
    }


} // End of FeedbackServlet.java
```

Figure 5-5 depicts what you will see if you attempt to access the servlet via a GET request on the URL address bar of your browser.

Upon a successful writing of data to a file the user will get a confirmation as shown in Figure 5-6. In order to get this confirmation the data needs to have been sent via the HTTP POST method, which is the method type indicated in the form source code.

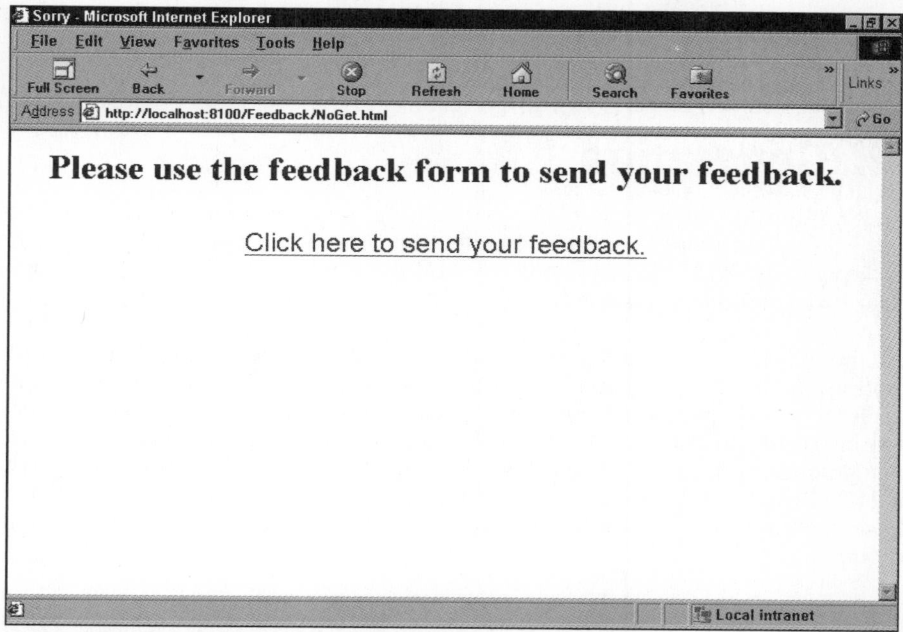

Figure 5-5: Get request to feedback servlet

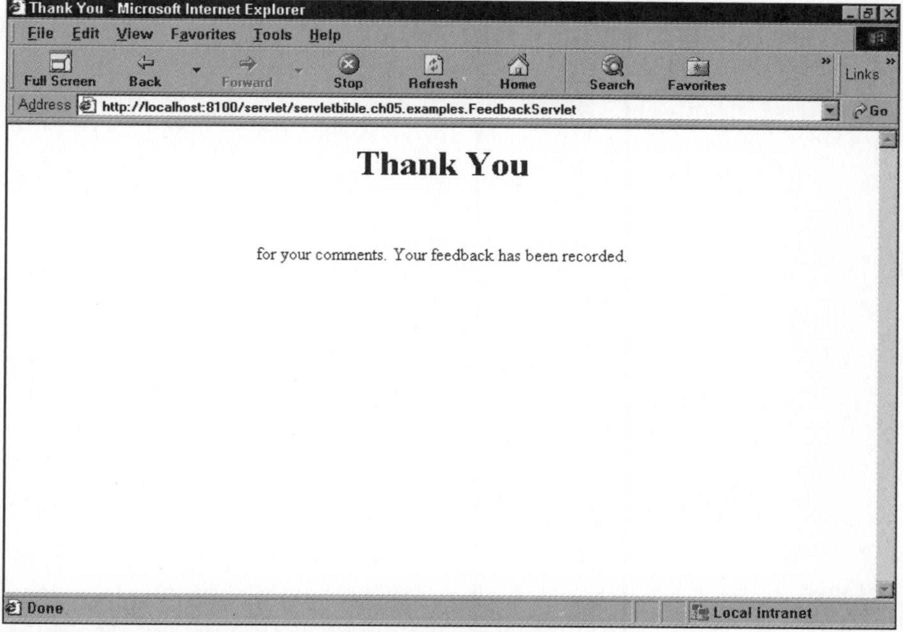

Figure 5-6: HTTP POST request to feedback servlet

Now we will move on to demonstrating how you can use servlets to generate HTML and send it to the client.

HTML Generation

Generating HTML in a servlet is a very tedious and inefficient task. We can break this process into functional components that generate the necessary code. This makes generating HTML more efficient and structured. You can add to Listing 5-5 your own methods to customize the utility.

In Listing 5-4, we use a utility class, `HtmlUtils`, to generate the required HTML. Listing 5-5 contains the code for this utility class. The HTML utility class is most useful if you are implementing an application whereby the servlet itself will be generating HTML. In Part 3 of this book you will be shown how you can render HTML dynamically, using JSP and servlets. This will prove a more efficient way of generating HTML and better also from a design standpoint. This class can be used as a basis to show you can how you can generate your own XML tags if the application requires.

Listing 5-5

```
package servletbible.utils;

import java.io.*;
import java.util.*;

/**
* This is a utility class is used to simplify the process of generating
* HTML code in Servlets.
*
*/

public class HtmlUtils {

    public String createHtmlHeader(String title) {

          String htmlHeader = null;
     htmlHeader = "<HTML><HEAD><TITLE> "+ title +" </TITLE></HEAD><BODY>";
          return htmlHeader;
    }

    public String getHtmlFooter() {

        String htmlFooter = "</BODY></HTML>";
        return htmlFooter;
    }
```

```
public String getHead(int level, String heading) {
    return "<H"+level+"> " + heading + "</H"+level+">";
}

public String getTableHead(String align, int border) {

    String tableHeader = null;
    tableHeader = "<TABLE align="+align+" border="+border+">";
    return tableHeader;

}

public String getTR(String align) {
    String TRCell = null;
    TRCell = "<TR align="+align+">";
    return TRCell;
}

public String getTR() {
    String TRCell = null;
    TRCell = "<TR>";
    return TRCell;
}

public String getTD(String align, String value) {
    String TDCell = null;
    TDCell = "<TD align="+align+"> "+value+" </TD>";
    return TDCell;
}

public String getTD() {
    String TDCell = null;
    TDCell = "<TD>";
    return TDCell;
}

public String getTD(int width) {
    String TDCell = null;
    TDCell = "<TD WIDTH="+width +">";
    return TDCell;
}

public String getTH(String align, String value) {
    String THCell = null;
    THCell = "<TH align="+align+"> "+value+" </TH>";
    return THCell;
}

/**
* This method will convert a vector into a table.
* The elementCounter is the number of data elements per row.
*/
```

Continued

Listing 5-5 *(continued)*

```
    public String getTableContents(String align, Vector values, int
elementCounter) throws IOException {

        StringWriter Cells = new StringWriter();
        String contents = new String();
        int vsize = values.size();

        Cells.write("<TR>");

        for (int i=0; i<vsize; i++)
        {
            String value = values.elementAt(i).toString();

            if (i!=0)
            {
                if(i>=elementCounter){

             if (i%elementCounter==0)
            {
                Cells.write("</TR>\n\n<TR>");
            }
                }
            }

            Cells.write("<TD align="+align+"> "+value+" </TD> \n");
        }

        Cells.write("</TR>");

        contents = Cells.toString();
        Cells.flush();
        Cells.close();

        return contents;
    }

    public String getClosedTR() {
        String TRCell = null;
        TRCell = "</TR>";
        return TRCell;
    }

    public String getClosedTD() {
        String TDCell = null;
        TDCell = "</TD>";
        return TDCell;
    }

    public String getBR(int lines) {
```

```
        StringWriter lineBR = new StringWriter();
        String lineBRs = new String();

        for (int i=0; i<=lines; i++)
        {
            lineBR.write("<BR>\n");
        }
        lineBRs = lineBR.toString();

        return lineBRs;
    }

    public String getLI(String item) {

        String li = new String("<LI>");
        li += item;
        return li;

    }

} //end of HtmlUtils.java
```

One of the most useful methods of this utility is the `getTableContents()` method. By supplying the Vector and the `elementCounter` (the number of data elements per row, that is, the number of columns in the table) this method can generate the table. For purposes of demonstration, Listing 5-6 shows an arbitrary Vector being populated manually; then the `getTableContents()` method is called to generate the table. This Vector may be populated with a database in typical applications. For example in an automated assignment marking system I recently developed the vector object was populated with a list of available markers for a particular subject in which a student was enrolled.

A Vector can be found in the java.utils package. A Vector is similar to an array but is different in that it can hold objects of different types.

Listing 5-6

```
package servletbible.ch05.examples;

import java.io.*;
import javax.servlet.*;
import javax.servlet.http.*;
import java.util.*;


public class PrintTable extends HttpServlet {
```

Continued

Listing 5-6 *(continued)*

```
    public void doGet(HttpServletRequest request, HttpServletResponse esponse)
throws ServletException,IOException {

        PrintTable(request, response);
    }



    public void doPost(HttpServletRequest request, HttpServletResponse
response) throws ServletException,IOException {

        PrintTable(request, response);

    }


    public void PrintTable(HttpServletRequest request, HttpServletResponse
response) throws IOException {

        response.setContentType("text/html");
        PrintWriter out = response.getWriter();

      servletbible.utils.HtmlUtils hu = new servletbible.utils.HtmlUtils();

        out.print(hu.createHtmlHeader("Print Table"));

        out.print(hu.getTableHead("center", 1));

        out.print(hu.getTH("center", "First Name"));
        out.print(hu.getTH("center", "Last Name"));
        out.print(hu.getTH("center", "Favorite Color"));
        out.print(hu.getTH("center", "Gender"));


        /*
        * Here will set up an arbitrary vector, containing four elements
        * Firstname, Lastname, Favorite Color, Gender.
        */

        Vector av = new Vector();

        av.addElement("John");
        av.addElement("Do");
        av.addElement("Purple");
        av.addElement("Male");

        av.addElement("Joe");
        av.addElement("Bloggs");
```

```
        av.addElement("Green");
        av.addElement("Male");

        av.addElement("Fanny");
        av.addElement("May");
        av.addElement("Blue");
        av.addElement("Female");

        av.addElement("Joeline");
        av.addElement("Bloggs");
        av.addElement("Red");
        av.addElement("Female");


       out.print(hu.getTableContents("center", av, 4));
       out.print(hu.getHtmlFooter());

    }

} // End of PrintTable.java
```

In the `PrintTable` class we set up an arbitrary Vector with arbitrary values and then pass this Vector to the `getTableContents()` of the `HtmlUtils class`. The `getTableContents()` method will return a HTML formatted table according to the values passed. This table is shown in Figure 5-7.

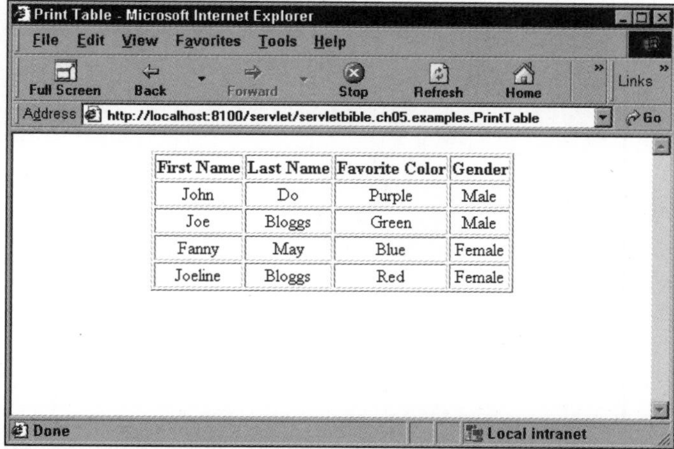

Figure 5-7: Table generated from the arbitrary Vector

Now we will move on to demonstrating how you can validate your HTML form so that unwanted data is not sent to the servlet for processing. For example we can use JavaScript to determine whether all required fields have information entered before sending this to the servlet. If we did not do this with JavaScript the servlet would have to take care of dealing with these types of conditions. This would subsequently place a greater load on the server, as explained in Chapter 1. This validation is done by embedding JavaScript code in the HTML document.

Validation with JavaScript

Despite the similarity of their names, JavaScript and Java have little to do with each other, except that JavaScript makes use of Java-reserved words. JavaScript is used to provide interactivity between the Web page and the client without any interaction with the server. The advantage of JavaScript is that it makes use of the client's system resources. JavaScript is useful to us in that it prevents unnecessary server-side validation.

We use the feedback form as our example for validation. The `FeedbackServlet` does not handle the situation where a name or e-mail address is left blank on the form. So we add the JavaScript into the HTML for the form that checks whether or not the required fields (`Name`, `Emailaddress` and `suggestions`) have been entered correctly). The new form handler with JavaScript validation is shown in Listing 5-7.

Listing 5-7

```
<HTML><HEAD>

<SCRIPT LANGUAGE="JavaScript">
<!--
function validate(){
var requiredfields = "";
if (document.ParameterPost.Person.value.length == 0) {
     /*
     * the value.length returns the length of the information
entered
     * in the Person field.
     */
    requiredfields += "\n   *  Name";
}
if ((document.ParameterPost.emailaddress.value.length == 0) ||
(document.ParameterPost.emailaddress.value.indexOf('@') == -1)
||
(document.ParameterPost.emailaddress.value.indexOf('.') == -1))
{
     /*
     * here we look to make sure the email address field
contains
```

```
     * the @ symbol and a . to determine that it is in the
correct format
     */
    requiredfields += "\n   *  Email address";
}
if(document.ParameterPost.suggestions.value == "Enter any
comments or suggestions you have here.") {
requiredfields += "\n   *  Comments or Suggestions";
}

if (requiredfields != "") {
requiredfields ="Please correctly enter the following
fields:\n" + requiredfields;
alert(requiredfields);
// the alert function will popup the alert window
return false;
}
else return true;
}
// -->
</SCRIPT>

<TITLE> Feedback Form </TITLE>
</HEAD>

<BODY>

<DIV ALIGN="CENTER"><H1> Feedback Form </H1></DIV>
<HR>
<BR>

<FORM NAME="ParameterPost"
ACTION="/servlet/servletbible.examples.ch05.FeedbackServlet"
METHOD="POST" onSubmit="return validate();">
    <TABLE BGCOLOR="BLANCHEDALMOND" ALIGN="CENTER" BORDER="0">
    <TR>
    <TD ALIGN="CENTER"><B>Name:</B></TD>
    <TD ALIGN="CENTER"> <INPUT TYPE="TEXT" SIZE="25"
NAME="Person"></TD>
    </TR>

    <TR>
    <TD ALIGN="CENTER"><B>Email:</B></TD>
    <TD ALIGN="CENTER"> <INPUT TYPE="TEXT" SIZE="25"
MAXLENGTH="40" NAME="emailaddress"></TD>
    </TR>


    <TR>
    <TD ALIGN="CENTER"><B>How did you find this site?</B></TD>
    <TD ALIGN="CENTER">
        <SELECT NAME="from" SIZE="1">
```

Continued

Listing 5-7 *(continued)*

```
        <OPTION VALUE = "Website" SELECTED>Another
Website</OPTION>
        <OPTION VALUE = "search engine">A search
engine</OPTION>
        <OPTION VALUE = "friend">A friend told you</OPTION>
        <OPTION VALUE = "email">From an email</OPTION>
        <OPTION VALUE = "unlisted">Another way not listed
here</OPTION>
        </SELECT>
    </TD>
    </TR>

    <TR>
    <TD ALIGN="CENTER"><B>How would you rate my
website:</B></TD>
    <TD ALIGN="CENTER">
    <INPUT TYPE="radio" NAME = "rating" VALUE = "Excellent">
Excellent
    <INPUT TYPE="radio" NAME = "rating" VALUE = "Good"> Good
    <INPUT TYPE="radio" NAME = "rating" VALUE = "Average"
CHECKED> Average
    <INPUT TYPE="radio" NAME = "rating" VALUE = "Poor"> Poor
    <INPUT TYPE="radio" NAME = "rating" VALUE = "Overhaul">
Needs an Overhaul
    </TD>
    </TR>

    <TR>
    <TD ALIGN="CENTER"><B>Comments or Suggestions:</B></TD>
    <TD ALIGN="CENTER">
    <TEXTAREA ROWS="6" COLS="40" WRAP="PHYSICAL"
Name="suggestions">Enter any comments or suggestions you have
here.</TEXTAREA>
    </TD>
    </TR>

    <TR>
    <TD ALIGN="CENTER"><B>Do you think this form looks
nice?</B></TD>
    <TD ALIGN="CENTER">
    <INPUT TYPE="CHECKBOX" NAME="formrating" VALUE="yes">
    </TD>
    </TR>



    <TR>

    <TD ALIGN="CENTER">
     
    </TD>
```

```
    <TD ALIGN="LEFT">

   <INPUT TYPE="SUBMIT" VALUE="Send Comments" ALIGN="MIDDLE">

   
   <INPUT TYPE="RESET" VALUE="Clear Form" ALIGN="MIDDLE">

   </TD>
   </TR>

</TABLE>
</FORM>

</BODY>

  </HTML>
```

The code in the validate() function is executed sequentially after the form is submitted. The validate() function peforms the actual validation of required fields and alerts the user appropriately. The validate() function is called using the onSubmit() event handler located inside the <FORM> tag. Figure 5-8 depicts what will occur if the form is not filled out correctly, i.e. not entering values for the required fields.

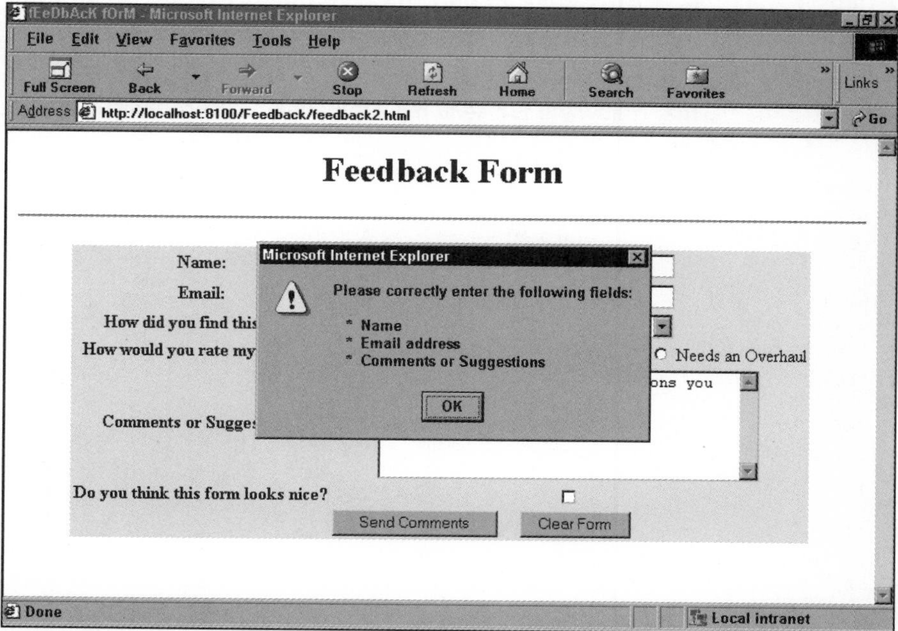

Figure 5-8: A JavaScript alert is fired when an invalid form-field entry is detected.

Moving on to a slightly different topic we will now demonstrate how you can upload a file using HTML forms and servlets.

Uploading Files

In this section we will construct a very simple file uploading mechanism using an HTML form and a servlet. You will also been shown how HTTP works in relation to sending a file as well form information to a servlet (on the server side).

Note that providing the ability to upload files is a decision that should be made carefully. Without proper precautions, both programming and otherwise, you may be providing the client with the ability to upload any type of file (for example, one that could contain a virus or large files). Providing the client with the ability to upload large files can pose various problems. For example, it can tie up network resources or pose a problem in relation to network disk space availability.

We can construct an upload module by using the HTML form element:

```
<input type = file>
```

This form input type is supported by Netscape 3.x and Internet Explorer 4.x and higher versions. Internet Explorer 3.x supports this input type with a Microsoft ActiveX control.

Listing 5-8 is a basic HTML form with only the `file` input type. We use this in our file-upload example to send a document to the server.

In Listing 5-8, the form is submitted with an encoding type of `multipart/form-data`. That is how we can send regular input types in conjunction with the `file` input type.

Listing 5-8

```
<HTML>
<HEAD>
<TITLE> Upload form </TITLE>
</HEAD>

<BODY>
<DIV ALIGN="CENTER"><H1> Upload Form </H1></DIV>
<HR>
<BR>

<form action=/servlet/com.servletbible.examples.ch05.SimpleUploadServlet
method=POST enctype=multipart/form-data>
```

```
<BR><BR>
<TABLE BGCOLOR="BLANCHEDALMOND" ALIGN="CENTER" BORDER="0">
    <TR>
    <TD ALIGN="CENTER"><B>File to Upload:</B></TD>
    <TD ALIGN="CENTER">
    <INPUT TYPE="file" SIZE="25" NAME="filename">
    </TD>
    </TR>

    <TR>

    <TD ALIGN="CENTER">
     
    </TD>

    <TD ALIGN="LEFT">

    <INPUT TYPE="SUBMIT" VALUE="Send File" ALIGN="MIDDLE">
       
    <INPUT TYPE="RESET" VALUE="Clear Form" ALIGN="MIDDLE">

    </TD>
    </TR>

</TABLE>
</FORM>
</BODY></HTML>
```

This input type is rendered with a Browse button adjacent to the text area where the path and file name are entered by the user as depicted in Figure 5-9.

It is important to understand how file data is transmitted over the Internet with HTTP. When the form is posted, HTTP headers appear in the following format:

```
header name1=value
header name2=value
header name3=value
```

Following the header name/value pairs, we have the boundary header, the content disposition, and the content type (of the file being uploaded), which might look something like this:

```
-----------------------------7d138ed49c
Content-Disposition: form-data; name="filename";
filename="C:\code\a.java"
Content-Type: application/octet-stream
then here would be a blank line
```

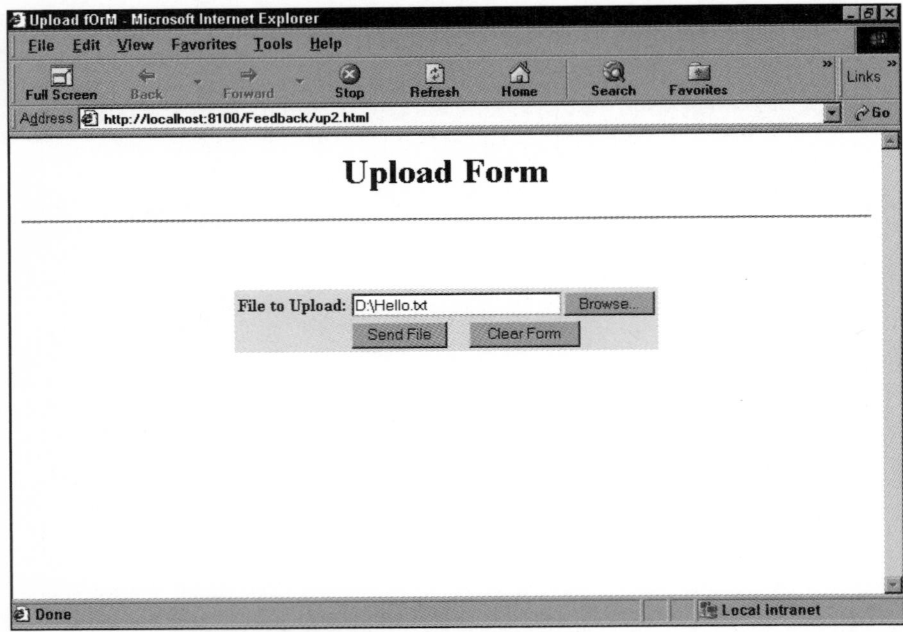

Figure 5-9: File upload form with a Browse button

Following this, we have the file data:

```
public class a {...
```

And at the end of the file data (assuming we have two text fields submitted: `Name` and file `Description`), we again have the boundary; it looks as follows:

```
-----------------------------7d138ed49c
Content-Disposition: form-data; name="Name"

Suresh Rajagopalan
-----------------------------7d138ed49c
Content-Disposition: form-data; name="Description"

A Java Program
-----------------------------7d138ed49c--
```

The terminating boundary header ends with the two dashes.

In this example the headers for the uploading of a.java was illustrated. However this HTTP process is the same for any type of file.

In developing an upload module, we need to deal with the HTTP headers and to extract only the file name and file data itself, discarding the parts we don't need, such as the boundary and blank lines. When you download a file from the Internet, the file is copied by first reading the file itself and then writing it to disk. The upload process works in the same way. You can see this in the example in Listing 5-9.

Listing 5-9

```
package servletbible.ch05.examples;

import javax.servlet.*;
import javax.servlet.http.*;
import java.io.*;
import java.util.*;

public class SimpleUploadServlet extends HttpServlet {


public void doGet(HttpServletRequest req, HttpServletResponse res)
throws ServletException,IOException {

// Here we forward to the appropriate page using the request dispatcher

getServletContext().getRequestDispatcher("/Noget.html").forward(req, resp);
}

public void doPost(HttpServletRequest req, HttpServletResponse res)

throws ServletException, IOException

{

res.setContentType("text/html");

PrintWriter out = res.getWriter();
servletbible.utils.HtmlUtils hu = new servletbible.utils.HtmlUtils();

String contentType = req.getContentType();

// the starting position of the boundary header
int ind = contentType.indexOf("boundary=");

String boundary = contentType.substring(ind+9);
int contentLength=req.getContentLength();

// a place holder of unwanted lines
String pLine = new String();
```

Continued

Listing 5-9 *(continued)*

```
String UploadLocation = new String("/home/suresh/lws/");

// a temporary holder of the file name
String pFilename = new String();


// the final holder of the file name
String fFilename = new String();


boolean uploadFlag = true;

// the maximum size of the file can only be 50K  (1024 bytes = 1K * 50)
int Max = 51200;


// the reason the file failed to upload
String reason = null;

//System.out.println("contentLength = "+ contentLength);


        /**
        * Here we compare to see that file going to be uploaded is
        * not greater than the maximum file size allowed.
        */

        if(contentLength>Max)
        {
        reason = "File too large for upload. File not uploaded.";
        uploadFlag = false;
        }

        /**
        * Here we compare verify that content type is multipart form data
        */

  if(contentType!=null && contentType.indexOf("multipart/form-data") == -1)
        {
      reason = "Encoding type not multipart/form-data. File not uploaded.";
            uploadFlag = false;
        }


    if (uploadFlag == true)
    {
     /* here we use the bufferedreader object to read in the Servlet's
      * Inputstream
      */
    BufferedReader br=new BufferedReader(
new InputStreamReader(req.getInputStream()));
```

```
    /**
    * Here we read and hold Http headers that are not used to create the
    * file itself.
    */

    pLine = br.readLine();
    pLine = br.readLine();

    /**
    * Below we extract the filename from the
    * Http headers read so far.
    */

    String filename = pLine.substring(10+pLine.lastIndexOf("filename="),
pLine.lastIndexOf("\""));
    // if the file is being uploaded from a windows OS
    if (filename.indexOf("\\") != -1)
    {
        pFilename = pLine.substring(pLine.lastIndexOf("\\"),
pLine.lastIndexOf("\""));
        fFilename = pFilename.substring(1);

    }

    else {
      fFilename = filename;
    }

    pLine = br.readLine();
    pLine = br.readLine();


        for (String line; (line=br.readLine())!=null; )
            {

                    if (line.indexOf(boundary) == -1)
                    {
                    AppendFile(UploadLocation+fFilename, line);
                    }
                    else {

                    /**
                    * If the file has been submitted in a form
                    * containing form input fields
                    * we want to strip these and not have it write to the
                    * file.
                    */
                        pLine = br.readLine();
                        pLine = br.readLine();
                        pLine = br.readLine();
```

Continued

Listing 5-9 *(continued)*

```
                    }


                } //end of for loop


    out.print(hu.createHtmlHeader("Upload Successful"));
    out.print("<CENTER>");
    out.print(hu.getHead(1, "Upload Status:"));
    out.print(hu.getBR(1));
    out.print(fFilename+" was successfully uploaded");
    out.print("</CENTER>");
    out.print(hu.getBR(1));
    out.print(hu.getHtmlFooter());


    }


    else
    {

    out.print(hu.createHtmlHeader("Upload UnSuccessful"));
    out.print("<CENTER>");
    out.print(hu.getHead(1, "Upload Status:"));
    out.print(hu.getBR(1));
    out.print(reason);
    out.print("</CENTER>");
    out.print(hu.getBR(1));
    out.print(hu.getHtmlFooter());
    }

}


/**
* The append method you may be familiar with by now,
* used to append a file and if it doesn't exist
* to create a new file.
*/

public static synchronized void AppendFile(String fname,String fileEntry) {

        BufferedWriter bw = null;

        try
        {
            bw = new BufferedWriter(new FileWriter(fname, true));
            bw.write(fileEntry);
            bw.newLine();
            bw.flush();
```

```
            bw.close();

        }
        catch (IOException ioe) {
        System.out.println(ioe);
        }

    }


} // end of SimpleUploadServlet.java
```

Tip

You may have noticed that `SimpleUploadServlet` does some condition checking. For example, it checks that the file submitted is not larger than 50KB. Any precautionary measures you wish to take can be written into the program prior to executing the upload process. You may wish to allow only certain types of files to be uploaded (such as text files). This can be done by checking the content type or checking the filename extension of the file being submitted by using `fFilename.endsWith()`.

Now when we upload a file (less than 50KB in size) to the server, the servlet uses the `BufferedWriter` object to create and write the file data. We see the status message in the browser, as shown in Figure 5-10.

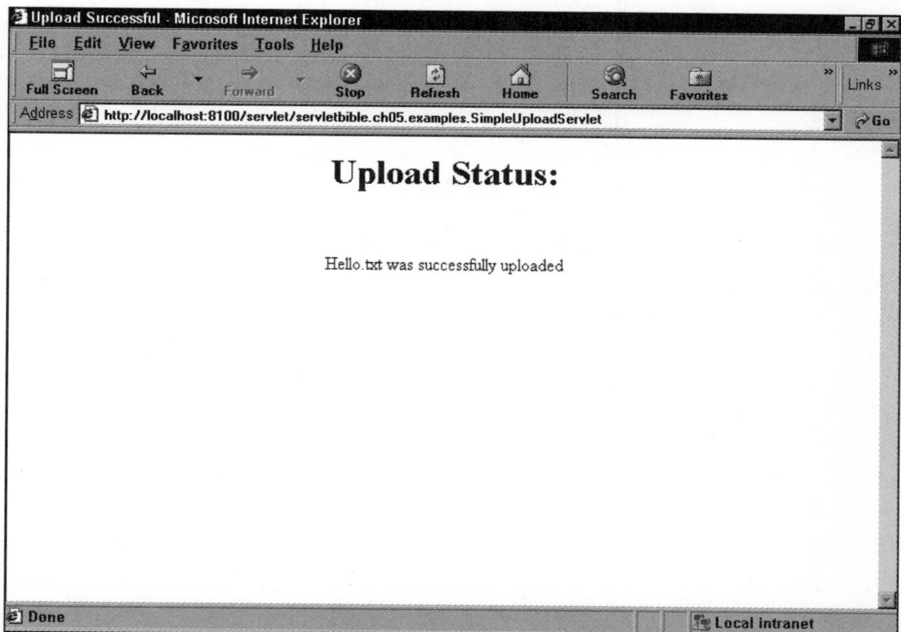

Figure 5-10: Successful file-upload status displayed in the browser

Redirections and Includes Using the Request Dispatcher

Recall from Listings 5-4 and 5-9 either of the following lines of code:

```
getServletContext().getRequestDispatcher("/Noget.html").include
(request, response);

getServletContext().getRequestDispatcher("/Noget.html").forward
(request, response);
```

These are the ways to call the request dispatcher. The request dispatcher's main function is to provide a way to send the request and response to another resource. That resource can be another servlet, an HTML page, or a JSP (which may, in turn, use/modify the request/response or again pass it on). The request and response can be passed on with the use of the `include()` method or the `forward()` method. The request dispatcher is particularly useful in a chaining process, i.e.when you are forwarding control through various servlets.

The `forward()` method should be used when you want another resource to generate or to modify the response to the client.

The `include()` method should be used when you want the other resource to form a part of the response.

A servlet calling the `forward()` method that also attempts to use the `PrintWriter` or `ServletOutputStream` objects throws an `IllegalStateException` in the calling method.

Any resource being included (by the source servlet) that attempts to modify the response object itself (for example, through the setting of response headers) may not have the modifications take effect in the response.

One way to use the request dispatcher is for domain blocking — where you want users of a particular domain to have access and others to be forwarded to a new location that fulfills their request as follows:

```
/*
*If the user is not of a particular domain we will forward
* their request
*/

if(isValidHost(request.getRemoteHost()))
{
getServletContext().getRequestDispatcher("/login.jsp").include(
request, response);
}
else
{
```

```
getServletContext().getRequestDispatcher("/public_user.jsp").fo
rward(request, response);

}
}

boolean isValidHost(String host)
{
return(host.endsWith(".edu") || host.endsWith(".gov") ||
(host.indexOf(".")==-1));
}
```

This example deals with user requests coming from public domains, in a different way than those coming from educational or government domains, by dispatching the request/response to a different JSP.

In this next section we will discuss the various important classes of the JavaMail API and demonstrate how you can send mail (via SMTP) using the JavaMail API.

Sending SMTP Mail with JavaMail

The Simple Mail Transfer Protocol (SMTP), defined by the RFC 821 at `http://www.freesoft.org/CIE/RFC/821/index.htm`, provides an efficient way to transfer e-mail reliably.

The default port SMTP operates on is 25.

A typical scenario of sending e-mail might look like this:

```
HELLO sending host smtp server

MAIL FROM: sender's e-mail address

RCPT TO: recipient e-mail address

DATA
... the e-mail message itself of any number of lines...
...
.
QUIT
```

The period at the end on a line by itself is the terminator and ends the message body of the e-mail.

The JavaMail API is Sun's answer to providing developers with a means to integrate mail and messaging capabilities into their applications in a protocol-independent manner. The beauty of the JavaMail API is that it presents a standardized, extensible interface to deal with all current and future MIME types.

Some of the classes we can use in sending e-mail include `Message`, `MimeMessage`, `Session`, `Transport`, `Multipart`, and `MimeBodyPart`.

Message

The class `Message` is abstract and models an e-mail message; therefore, it encompasses the characteristics of all messages (such as sender and receiver). It is lightweight and is filled up on demand by using the `get`*`Xxx`*`()`, `set`*`Xxx`*`()`, and `add`*`Xxx`*`()` methods. To send a message, instantiate an implementation of this class (as it is abstract) such as `MimeMessage`.

MimeMessage

`MimeMessage` is a subclass of `Message` and implements the `MimePart` interface, which provides the ability to add numerous body parts of various Mime types. This class is not abstract and can be instantiated.

Session

This class is a representation of a mail session. When you use the `getDefaultInstance()` method, a mail session can be created with the appropriate properties, such as the SMTP e-mail server.

Transport

This is an abstract class that models message-transport mechanisms such as SMTP or IMAP.

Multipart

This abstract class is a container that can hold a number of body parts. `Multipart` provides methods to retrieve and set its subparts, such as `getBodyPart()` and `addBodyPart(`*`part`*`)`.

MimeBodyPart

The `MimeBodyPart` class is a representation of a body part of an e-mail message. It has methods to get and set its content (which may include files of various types) and headers.

To use JavaMail, use the Java activation framework and the JavaMail package(s), which can be found on the CD-ROM. Extract the `jar` files (such as `activation.jar` and `mail.jar`), and add them to your `CLASSPATH`.

Now we modify the feedback form from the previous sections so that it sends feedback to an e-mail address. We modify the <FORM> tag as follows:

```
<FORM NAME="ParameterPost"

ACTION="/servlet/com.servletbible.examples.ch05.EmailServlet"

METHOD="POST">
```

As shown in Listing 5-10, we use the information entered into the form, generate the e-mail message body, and send the e-mail.

Listing 5-10

```
package servletbible.ch05.examples;

import java.io.*;
import java.util.*;

import javax.servlet.*;
import javax.servlet.http.*;

import javax.activation.*; //here we import the java activation framework
import javax.mail.*; // here we import that JavaMail packages
import javax.mail.internet.*;

public class EmailServlet extends HttpServlet {

public void doGet(HttpServletRequest request, HttpServletResponse response)
    throws ServletException,IOException {

    doPost(request, response);
}

public void doPost(HttpServletRequest req, HttpServletResponse res)
throws ServletException, IOException

{
   String to = new String("your@emailaddress.com");
   String from = new String();
   String SmtpServer = "yourSMTPserver.com";
   String subject = new String("Feedback Form Example");

   String msgBody = null;
   String FormRating = null;

   PrintWriter out = res.getWriter();
   res.setContentType("text/html");
```

Continued

Listing 5-10 *(continued)*

```
String name = req.getParameter("Person");
from = req.getParameter("emailaddress");
String arrivedFrom = req.getParameter("from");
String ratings = req.getParameter("rating");
String comments = req.getParameter("suggestions");
FormRating = req.getParameter("formrating");

// Below we assemble the Message Body of the email

msgBody = "Name: "+name+"\n"
+ "Found this site from: "+ arrivedFrom +"\n"
+ "Rates this site as: "+ ratings + "\n"
+ "Has the following comments about the site: \n" + comments +"\n";


if (FormRating != null )
{
msgBody += "Was the form Nice?\t"+FormRating+"\n";
}

else {
msgBody +="Was the form Nice?\t No \n";
}


Properties props = new Properties();
props.put("mail.smtp.host", SmtpServer);

try {

    Session session = Session.getDefaultInstance(props, null);

    // create a new message
    Message msg = new MimeMessage(session);

     // an array of addresses for the email to be sent to of size 1.
    InternetAddress ia[] = new InternetAddress[1];


    ia[0] = new InternetAddress(to, "YourName");


    msg.setFrom(new InternetAddress(from, name));

    msg.setRecipients(Message.RecipientType.TO, ia);

    /**
    * If you wish to send copies of the email to another email
    * address(es)
    * uncomment the following lines
    */
```

```
        //InternetAddress copies[] = new InternetAddress[2];

     //copies[0] = new InternetAddress("copy1@anemailaddress.com", "Name1");
     //copies[1] = new InternetAddress("copy2@anemailaddress.com", "Name2");

        //msg.addRecipients(Message.RecipientType.CC, copies);

        msg.setSubject(subject);

  //here we set the msgBody variable is set as the body of the email message
        msg.setText(msgBody);

        Transport transport = session.getTransport("smtp");
        transport.connect();
        transport.send(msg); //send the email message

       servletbible.utils.HtmlUtils hu = new servletbible.utils.HtmlUtils();

         out.print(hu.createHtmlHeader("Thankyou"));
         out.print("<CENTER>");
         out.print(hu.getHead(1, "Thankyou,"));
         out.print(hu.getBR(2));
         out.print("for your comments. Your feedback has been sent.");
         out.print("</CENTER>");
         out.print(hu.getBR(1));
         out.print(hu.getHtmlFooter());

       }

    catch (SendFailedException sfe) {
        sfe.printStackTrace();
        out.println("Mail Failed for the following reason: "+sfe);
    }

    catch (MessagingException mex) {
           mex.printStackTrace();
           Exception ex = null;
             if ((ex = mex.getNextException()) != null) {
              ex.printStackTrace();
              out.println("Mail Failed for the following reason: "+ex);
               }
    }

    catch (Exception ex) {
           ex.printStackTrace();
           out.println("Mail Failed for the following reason: "+ex);
       }

} // end of doPost

} // end of EmailServlet.java
```

You may have noticed in Listing 5-10 some of the JavaMail exceptions we can catch. The JavaMail API has a number of exceptions that allow you to deal with e-mail being sent, or the response provided to the client, in different ways. For example, you may want an application to log certain types of mail-delivery failures, or you may want to resend the e-mail after a scheduled interval. Table 5-2 lists some JavaMail exceptions and what they indicate.

Table 5-2
JavaMail Exceptions

JavaMail Exception	*Indicates*
`AddressException`	An e-mail address in the incorrect format
`AuthenticationFailedException`	If authentication is used and an incorrect username or password is supplied
`MessagingException`	The base exception thrown by all messaging classes
`NoSuchProviderException`	Thrown when an incorrect service provider is supplied when the session is being established
`ParseException`	If an error occurs in parsing MIME headers
`SendFailedException`	Message cannot be delivered, perhaps due to the fact that the recipient's address is invalid

Listing 5-11 shows an example of an `EmailServlet` sending e-mail with an attachment.

Listing 5-11

```
package servletbible.ch05.examples;

import java.io.*;
import java.util.*;

import javax.servlet.*;
import javax.servlet.http.*;

import javax.activation.*; //here we import the java activation framework
import javax.mail.*; // here we import that JavaMail packages
import javax.mail.internet.*;

public class EmailAttachmentServlet extends HttpServlet {
```

```
public void doGet(HttpServletRequest request, HttpServletResponse response)
    throws ServletException,IOException {

    doPost(request, response);
}

public void doPost(HttpServletRequest req, HttpServletResponse res)
throws ServletException, IOException

{
String to = new String("your@emailaddress.com");
   String from = new String();
   String SmtpServer = "yourSMTPserver.com";
   String subject = new String("Feedback Form Example");

   String msgBody = null;
   String FormRating = null;

   PrintWriter out = res.getWriter();
   res.setContentType("text/html");


   String name = req.getParameter("Person");
   from = req.getParameter("emailaddress");
   String arrivedFrom = req.getParameter("from");
   String ratings = req.getParameter("rating");
   String comments = req.getParameter("suggestions");
   FormRating = req.getParameter("formrating");

   // Below we assemble the Message Body of the email
   msgBody = "Name: "+name+"\n"
   + "Found this site from: "+ arrivedFrom +"\n"
   + "Rates this site as: "+ ratings + "\n"
   + "Has the following comments about the site: \n" + comments +"\n";


   if (FormRating != null )
   {
   msgBody += "Was the form Nice?\t"+FormRating+"\n";
   }

   else {
   msgBody +="Was the form Nice?\t No \n";
   }


   Properties props = new Properties();
   props.put("mail.smtp.host", SmtpServer);

   try {

       Session session = Session.getDefaultInstance(props, null);
```

Continued

Listing 5-11 *(continued)*

```
// create a new message
 Message msg = new MimeMessage(session);

 // create a new message body part
 MimeBodyPart messageBodyPart = new MimeBodyPart();

 Multipart multipart = new MimeMultipart();
 multipart.addBodyPart(messageBodyPart);


 // an array of addresses for the email to be sent to, of size 1
InternetAddress ia[] = new InternetAddress[1];


ia[0] = new InternetAddress(to, "Suresh Rajagopalan");

msg.setFrom(new InternetAddress(from, name));

msg.setRecipients(Message.RecipientType.TO, ia);



msg.setSubject(subject);

// here we set the msgBody text as the first body part of the email
messageBodyPart.setText(msgBody);

String fileAttachment = new String("file.txt");

// Here we create a new body part
 MimeBodyPart messageBodyPart2 = new MimeBodyPart();
 DataSource dsource = new FileDataSource(fileAttachment);
 messageBodyPart2.setDataHandler(new DataHandler(dsource));
 messageBodyPart2.setFileName(fileAttachment);


 // now we add the 2nd message body part which is a file attachment
 multipart.addBodyPart(messageBodyPart2);

 // Put parts into the message

 msg.setContent(multipart);


Transport transport = session.getTransport("smtp");
transport.connect();
transport.send(msg);

servletbible.utils.HtmlUtils hu = new servletbible.utils.HtmlUtils();
```

```
            out.print(hu.createHtmlHeader("Thankyou"));
            out.print("<CENTER>");
            out.print(hu.getHead(1, "Thankyou,"));
            out.print(hu.getBR(2));
            out.print("for your comments. Your feedback has been sent.");
            out.print("</CENTER>");
            out.print(hu.getBR(1));
            out.print(hu.getHtmlFooter());

        }

    catch (SendFailedException sfe) {
        sfe.printStackTrace();
        out.println("Mail Failed for the following reason: "+sfe);
    }

    catch (MessagingException mex) {
           mex.printStackTrace();
           Exception ex = null;
             if ((ex = mex.getNextException()) != null) {
              ex.printStackTrace();
              out.println("Mail Failed for the following reason: "+ex);
               }
    }

    catch (Exception ex) {
           ex.printStackTrace();
           out.println("Mail Failed for the following reason: "+ex);
        }

} // end of doPost

} // end of EmailAttachmentServlet.java
```

Summary

In this chapter, you have seen how you can use various API's with servlets. You should now understand how to create HTML forms, use HTML forms with servlets, access form data the user enters, and generate HTML more efficiently. You should also now know how to create and write to a file, use the request dispatcher, and send e-mail with servlets.

The next chapter covers some basics of JDBC, connecting to various databases, and using servlets with databases to create database-driven content.

✦ ✦ ✦

Data Access with Servlets

In This Chapter

Evolution of database systems

Understanding client/server architecture

Discussing ODBC architecture

Discussing JDBC architecture

Looking into types of JDBC drivers

JDBC-ODBC bridges

Connecting to MS-Access and Oracle

Servlets and databases

Connection pooling

Personal information maintenance servlet

This chapter introduces JDBC by discussing the JDBC architecture and the types of JDBC drivers. We then discuss how to connect to Microsoft Access and Oracle databases. We then explain the use of databases in servlets and how connection pooling is important. The chapter finally ends with a simple personal information maintenance application.

Evolution of Database Systems

There were times when programmers used flat files for storing and retrieving information for processing. This made applications slow because they needed to interact directly with the data, and the code became complicated when multiple users accessed the data at the same time. Computer applications have passed through generations, and there has been considerable change in the way information is stored, retrieved, and processed. After the flat-file generation came the 4GLs, most popularly called Database Management Systems (DBMS). The main advantage of a 4GL was that information could be accessed using simple queries. The DBMS worked on what are called *databases*. A *database* is a collection of information. The DBMS not only had queries but simple statements that could process and update information. Using simple statements, a database can be created with much ease. What's more, database operations are intelligent enough to reflect changes where information is related and interdependent.

4GL's functional areas include query and reporting tools, graphic tools, database management tools, and spreadsheets. An example of a 4GL is the popular FoxPro, through which many applications are still running. But DBMS had certain disadvantages:

- Data integrity — This ensures that the database remains in a consistent state throughout the operations performed on it. An enterprise application might have *n* number of users operating on a single piece of information. A DBMS does not have high measures in maintaining data integrity.

✦ Quality — The end user of an application plays an important role in keying the correct information. When the number of users increases, the possibility of incorrect or fraudulent data coming into the system is likely. The quality of information in the database degrades as the user tries to insert or update incorrect data. DBMS does not have suitable controls in maintaining the quality of the database.

✦ Security — A database system should be powerful enough to restrict unauthorized users from accessing or misusing key data. When a database can be accessed remotely, the system should have high security to prevent trespassers and protect information. DBMS does not have administration tools to empower security measures.

Relational Database Management Systems (RDBMS) were created as a consequence of the major disadvantages of DBMS. RDBMS is built around the Relational Model built by E. F. Codd in 1970. A database in a RDBMS is a formalized structure that can hold information. The information under this structure can be accessed and altered at any time, and in many ways, without the need to change the structure.

E. F. Codd suggested 12 rules famously called *Codd's rules*, which suggest that to be a perfect RDBMS, the system should satisfy these rules. The point is that till now not even a single RDBMS has been able to satisfy all 12 rules. Oracle leads with a score of 11.5. All the disadvantages of DBMS were overcome by an RDBMS. What's more, the system is dedicated purely for database operations. This reduces the burden on both the server and the application by splitting data, presentation, and business logic into separate components.

The advantages of an RDBMS include accessibility, flexibility, high security, data integrity, concurrency, transaction management, backup and recovery. A standard language for the RDBMS is Structured Query Language (SQL). It consists of simple statements in English that help the user communicate with the database. Even though every RDBMS extends SQL to its needs, certain statements, such as `INSERT`, `UPDATE`, `DELETE`, `CREATE`, `DROP`, and so forth, are standard and follow the same syntax the American National Standards Institute (ANSI) defines.

Client/server architecture

The client/server paradigm came to the limelight once RDBMS emerged and became widely used. The concept teaches that a client makes a request that is passed to the server. The server processes the request and satisfies the client by sending a response with the relevant information the client requires. The client/server architecture has gained momentum and has probed further. As a result, the following architectures have evolved.

✦ two-tier architecture — This is a basic architecture, as shown in Figure 6-1, in which an application is split into two parts. The presentation and the business logic are handled on one end, which is the client. The data is handled on the other end, which is the server.

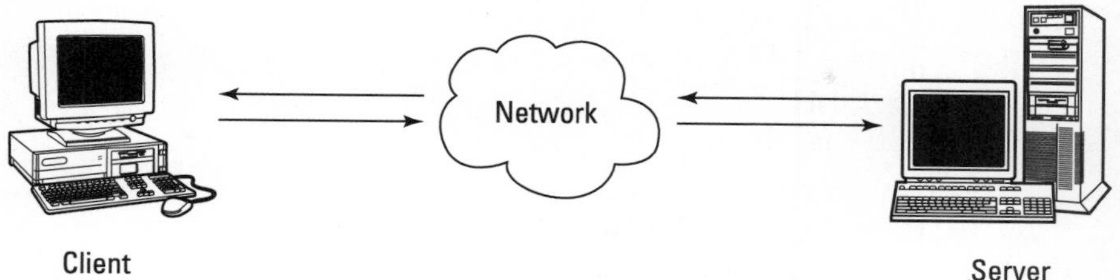

Figure 6-1: Two-tier architecture

✦ three-tier architecture — An expansion of two-tier architecture, three-tier architecture (see Figure 6-2) has a middle layer that reduces the burden of the client and the server. The middle tier initially processes the request from the client. Its responsibility is to optimize the request from the client and to process the response from the server. By this, the server receives a query that needs no or less optimization, and the client receives information in a more meaningful format that has to be presented.

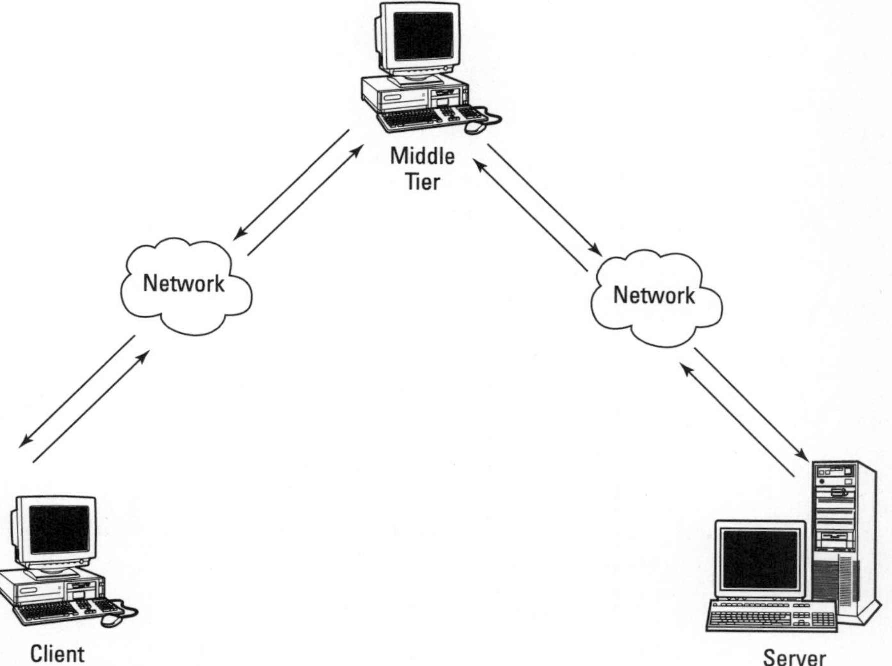

Figure 6-2: Three-tier architecture

✦ n-tier architecture — This architecture has multiple middle layers that are designated to perform a particular function, as shown in Figure 6-3. A good example is a component that receives requests for stock prices of a particular company. The requests might be from clients of various applications. The component might have caches of most popular stock quotes, or it might request from a server or another component that is more specialized in maintaining and processing stocks.

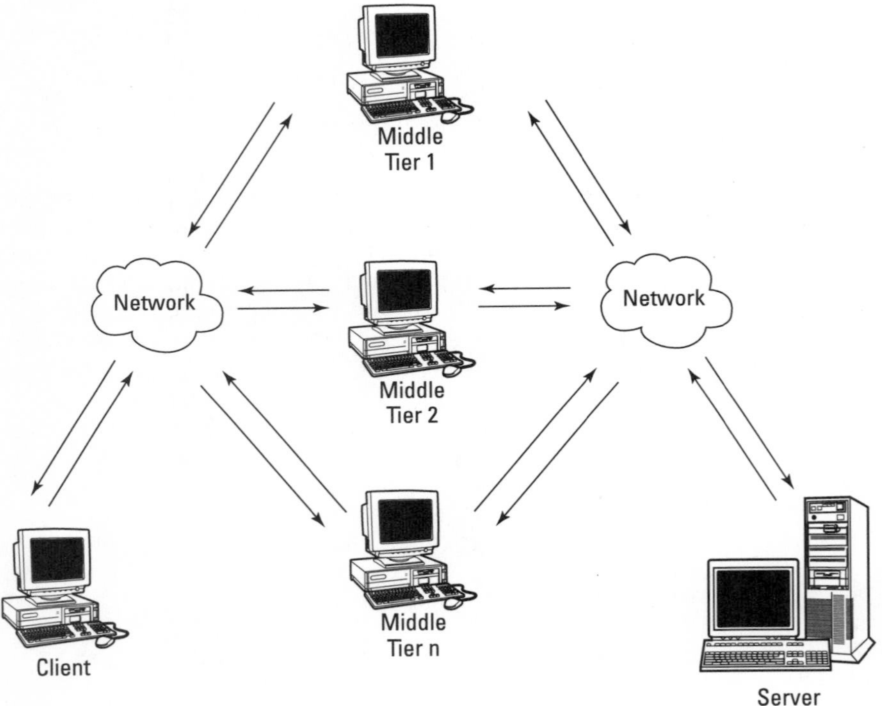

Figure 6-3: N-tier architecture

Client/server architecture became the de facto standard for developing applications, which involved voluminous data. Even though the burden on the application is considerably reduced as the database operations are carried out on the server end, the server can be remote anywhere; programmers found it difficult to connect to the database. What if tomorrow a new RDBMS more efficient than the others comes up and there is a requirement to move the database to the new system. In such a situation, programmers had to make necessary changes in their application and make it suitable to the new system.

SQL Access Group (SAG) consists of software and hardware vendors working on how to define a simple and standard method to communicate between a client and server. The result is a standard that has to be followed by bridging software that acts between a client and a server. Microsoft took the core of SAG's output and developed a set of APIs called Open Database Connectivity (ODBC).

ODBC architecture

ODBC allows users to call low-level APIs that can connect the client and server, enabling both to interact. The client and server need not know about each other and need not be the same machine or in the same location. ODBC allows a single application to interact with more than one database system simultaneously in an easier way, thus enabling maximum interoperability. Another advantage is that a programmer can create an application without specifying what database system the application is going to interact with. The end user, during the runtime, can specify the *database driver*, which establishes the connection between the application and a specific database system.

So what does the ODBC interface contain? It's a set of library functions that can connect to a database, optimize SQL statements, and pass them on to the database system or process by itself and retrieve results for the client. The method of connecting to a database is standard on any application regardless of the database system the application is going to communicate with. But each and every database system has its own way of defining data types; hence, the resulting data types of a query are dependent upon the underlying database system. This problem is overcome by ODBC by providing a standard set of data types to which results are converted, thereby reducing the burden upon the application to cast data types. The application can construct queries dynamically as well as statically. This means the application can give flexibility to the end user in choosing information. An example of this is to allow the user to select the list of fields he wants in the report. Based on the selection, the SQL is built during the runtime, and the ODBC parses it and retrieves the information from the database system. The application can send data in the format of its convenience, and the ODBC converts "it" to the format the database system it links to can understand.

The overall architecture of a client/server application using ODBC can be represented as in Figure 6-4.

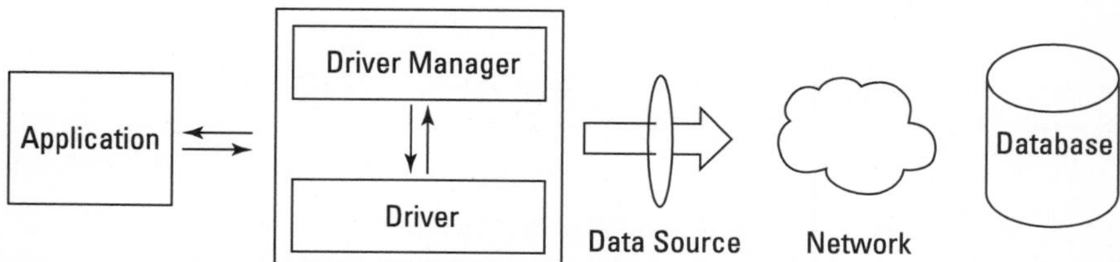

Figure 6-4: ODBC architecture

The components represented in Figure 6-4 are as follows:

✦ Application — The application can be anything such as spreadsheets, word processors, languages, and so on. The application passes the request for data to the ODBC and receives the result.

✦ Driver manager — The driver manager is responsible for loading the driver the application specifies.

✦ Drivers — The driver receives function calls from the application through the driver manager. It passes the request to the data source. Before it passes, it ensures that the request is in the form the data source understands. "It" makes any necessary changes. The driver is also responsible for query optimization. Query optimization ensures that the query is efficient and requires minimal processing time. A driver can be categorized into three.

  • Single tier — Here the driver processes the SQL and retrieves information from the database. Examples of single-tier drivers are popular DBMS such as DBASE, Paradox and FoxPro. Here the data source can be in the same machine or in the network. The client processor has the burden of processing the application as well as the driver. The components in either case are represented in Figure 6-5.

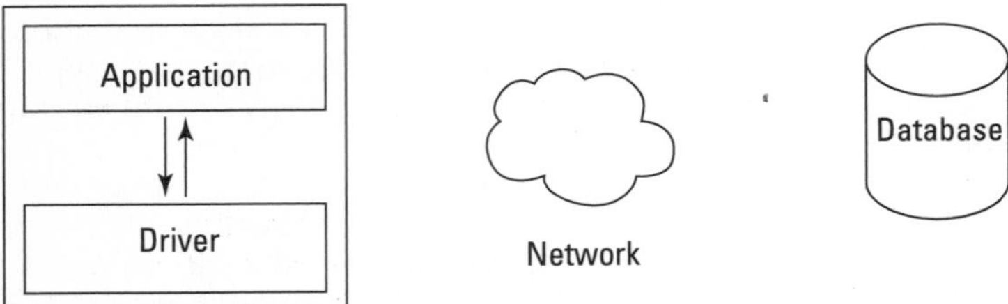

Figure 6-5: Single-tier driver

  • Multiple tier — In multiple tier, the driver passes the processing of the query to the database. The driver formats the query and optimizes it before passing it to the data source for processing.

  • Gateway — This is an expansion of the multiple tier. A gateway can either be hardware or software, which passes the query to the data source. Here the gateway takes the responsibility of optimizing the query.

✦ Data source — A data source is a representation of the DBMS, the operating system it runs on, the network address (if it runs remotely), and a unique name.

ODBC is completely written in C, so there is no object-oriented approach. It is difficult to call the right procedure or function. Moreover, the ODBC driver manager and drivers have to be installed in all the clients. For this reason, Sun introduced Java Database Connectivity (JDBC), which helps in establishing a connection between a client and a server regardless of the platforms on which they run. We take a closer look at JDBC in the next section.

JDBC Concepts

Compared to ODBC, JDBC has more flexible APIs programmers can use in their application. JDBC has all the advantages that ODBC has and caters to the needs of programmers under a variety of platforms. On the client side, nothing has to be configured. A client application or applet needs a JDBC URL or a data source registered with Java Naming and Directory Interface (JNDI). JNDI enables a simple centralized registry where applications can look up information on connection to another application or a source. As in ODBC, JDBC has an underlying driver manager that takes care of bridging the application with the DBMS. The driver manager supports multiple drivers connecting to many databases. The drivers can be written either in Java or by using native methods. A driver written purely in Java can be used in any platform by downloading or being a part of an applet. A driver written using native methods gets tied up to the underlying platform in which the application or the applet runs.

JDBC models

JDBC works under two models, two-tier model and three-tier model.

JDBC two-tier model

The client consists of the application and the JDBC driver(s). The client takes the responsibility of presentation, business logic, transaction management, and resource management. Transaction management can be either for a single statement, multiple statements, or distributed statements. The JDBC driver also resides on the client, receives the request from the application, and makes the necessary transformation (see Figure 6-6). This transformed request is passed to the DBMS. Because the application and the driver reside on the same machine, the connection between the two is direct. The application takes care of establishing a connection and specifying the details of the data source to which it is connected.

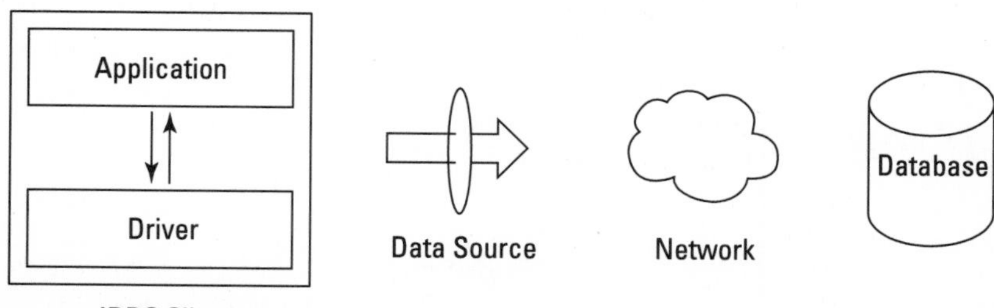

Figure 6-6: JDBC under the two-tier architecture model

The server is the DBMS, which receives the request from the client in a format it can understand. The major disadvantage of this model is that there is a heavy burden on the client, as it takes care of both the presentation as well as the business logic. In addition, the application must know the different implementations of the drivers if it needs to connect to multiple DBMS. Also, the number of concurrent connections is limited because the connections are held by the application.

JDBC three-tier model

This model consists of a client, a middle tier, and a server (see Figure 6-7). The client holds the application, which concentrates on the presentation and communicates with the middle tier requesting data. The application on the client can be a Java program, a browser, or a wireless device application.

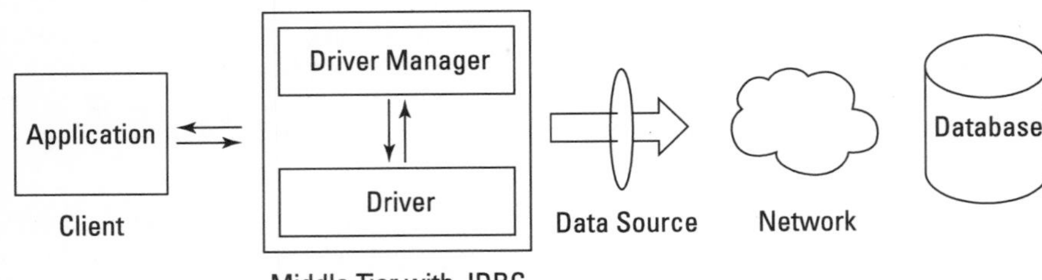

Figure 6-7: JDBC three-tier architecture model

The middle tier takes care of the business logic, communicating with the data source, handling transactions, and connection pooling. The middle tier consists of an application, an application server, and the JDBC driver. The application takes care of the business logic and provides abstract details about the data source but does not implement low-level APIs. The application server manages transactions, handling concurrent connections and identifying which driver the request has to be sent to. This helps when the application server connects to multiple DBMS. The JDBC driver provides the connectivity to the data source. It implements the JDBC API and sends the request in the form the data source can understand.

The third layer is the actual data source, which can be either a DBMS, an RDBMS, a spreadsheet, or any information system that has a necessary driver that supports JDBC.

JDBC drivers

There are four types of JDBC drivers:

✦ *Type 1 JDBC-ODBC bridge* — This provides communicating to the database through the ODBC drivers. The advantage here is that still the Java API can be used, and the conversion to the necessary driver API occurs automatically.

- *Type 2 Native API/partly Java driver*— Drivers that implement native APIs come under this category. Before the application executes, some native binary APIs have to be loaded.
- *Type 3 Net-protocol/All Java driver*— The client translates the database requests to a standard request that is independent of any DBMS requests. The receiving server parses this request back to a specific DBMS. With type 3 drivers, many clients can connect to many databases, and this type of driver is the most flexible one. Type 3 drivers are written purely in Java.
- *Type 4 Native-protocol/All Java driver*— Purely Java based, type 4 drivers or thin drivers translate the database requests into a specific DBMS-understandable format. There is a direct call on the DBMS from the client. Type 4 drivers are useful when the application falls under an Intranet setup.

As of now, JDBC supports 135 drivers mapping to different DBMS. The site `http://industry.java.sun.com/products/jdbc/drivers` gives a list of vendors who have driver APIs that support JDBC for a particular DBMS.

Standard interfaces in JDBC

The `java.sql` package consists of the necessary classes and interfaces to work with JDBC. Table 6-1 lists some of the interfaces defined in the `java.sql` package.

Table 6-1
Common Interfaces Defined in the java.sql Package

Interface	*Description*
`java.sql.CallableStatement`	A `CallableStatement` object is useful for executing stored procedures. A stored procedure is a function in the DBMS that executes a set of statements.
`java.sql.Connection`	The `Connection` object holds the session between the application and the data source. The `Connection` object holds many properties such as information about tables, stored procedures, capabilities of the connection and so on.
`java.sql.DatabaseMetaData`	This object holds information about the database. Many methods in this interface return a `ResultSet` object whose method can be used to get further information.

Continued

Table 6-1 *(continued)*

Interface	*Description*
`java.sql.Driver`	This interface is implemented by all drivers. A class implementing this interface has to register itself with the `DriverManager`.
`java.sql.PreparedStatement`	A `PreparedStatment` is similar to `Statement`, but it can be used multiple times. The SQL statement is precompiled and can be executed whenever needed. The SQL can contain a parameter that can be set during the execution of the statement by using relevant methods provided in the interface.
`java.sql.ResultSet`	A `ResultSet` object holds the result upon execution of an SQL statement. Typically, a result is a set of records with the `ResultSet` object pointing to the first row. A record contains fields, which can be retrieved using relevant methods using this interface.
`java.sql.ResultSetMetaData`	This object has methods to retrieve information about a field in the record.
`java.sql.Statement`	A `Statement` object is used to execute a static SQL statement. The execution result is returned in the form of a `ResultSet` object. At any point, only one `ResultSet` object can be open for a `Statement`.

A driver must implement all of the preceding interfaces to be a JDBC driver. The following sections explain how the interfaces in the `java.sql` package can be used to connect to a database and perform operations on it.

Connecting to a Database

This section explains step by step how a connection to the database can be established in Java. It then explains how to connect to Microsoft Access and Oracle databases.

Connecting to a database consists of the following steps:

1. Load the JDBC driver. The driver class should be in the `CLASSPATH` environment variable. A class can be loaded by using the `Class` object's `forName()` method. Typically, the code is:

```
Class.forName(<driver class>);
```

2. Connect to the database by using the `getConnection()` method of the `DriverManager` object. The parameter to this method is the database's URL, username, and password. The database's URL contains the address of the database residing in the network and any other information such as subprotocol and the port number the middle tier is listening to (in case it is a three-tier model). The following is the basic construct:

   ```
   DriverManager.getConnection(<dbURL>,username,password);
   ```

   The `getConnection()` method comes in three prototypes:

   - `getConnection(String url)`—The URL contains the protocol, the subprotocol, and any other properties such as the port number the driver is listening to. A database URL can be in the following form:

     ```
     <protocol>:<sub-protocol>:<url>:<port number>:<machine
     name>
     ```

   - `getConnection(String url, Properties info)`—The info parameter here is a pair of key-value attributes, usually the user name and the password for logging into the database system, and any other properties.

   - `getConnection(String url, String user, String password)`—Here the username and password are passed as `String` objects.

3. Perform the necessary operations, such as creating statements, executing statements, and manipulating the `ResultSet` object. All this can be done only when the connection is live. A detailed explanation of `Statements` and `ResultSets` is provided in later sections.

4. Connections are costly. When all necessary operations are complete, it is safe and advisable to close the `Statements`, `ResultSets`, and `Connections`.

Connecting to Microsoft Access

Connecting to MS Access is possible through ODBC, as the Access driver supports ODBC. As of now, no driver can be used to connect to an Access database through JDBC. Thus, the connection to an Access database through JDBC falls under the type 1 JDBC-ODBC bridge category. The next section provides information about creating an ODBC data source on Windows machines.

Creating an ODBC data source in Windows 2000/NT/98/95

To create an ODBC data source, open the control panel, and select the ODBC Data Sources item. Double click to open the ODBC Data Source Administrator window. Figure 6-8 shows this window.

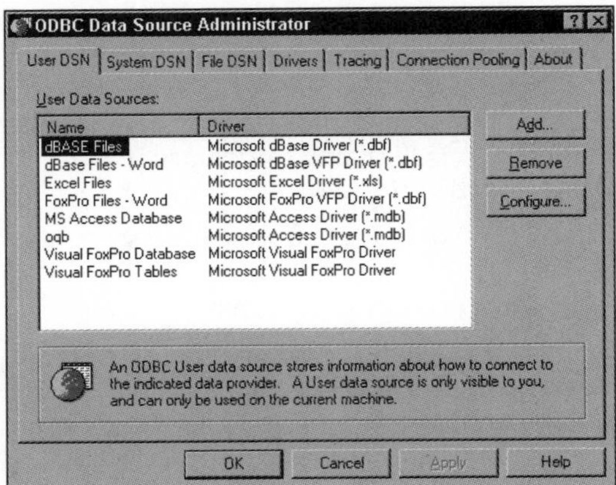

Figure 6-8: The ODBC Data Source Administrator window

A data source can be created under three categories depending upon on who is going to use it. A Data Source Name (DSN) is a lookup to the data source that is used when connecting to a database using JDBC-ODBC.

- ✦ User DSN — A user DSN can be used only by the current user on the machine on which the DSN is created.
- ✦ System DSN — All users using the machine under which the DSN is created can use a system DSN.
- ✦ File DSN — A file DSN can be shared across the network, and users having the database driver can use DSN information to connect to the database.

In the ODBC Administrator window, select one of the tabs: User, System, or File. Click the Add button to add a new data source. This brings up the window showing the list of drivers available. The list contains the driver name, the version, the company name, the driver file name, and the date of creation, as shown in Figure 6-9 (to view all of the driver information, you may have to use the horizontal scroll bar).

Select "Microsoft Access Driver (`*.mdb`)" from the list, and click the Finish button. This opens a new window, prompting for information on the data source as you can see in Figure 6-10. Type the data source name, `Inventory`, in our case, and enter a description. Click the Select button and provide the location and the file name of the database (`.mdb` file).

Click OK. The DSN name is listed under the User, System, or File DSN, whichever you chose. You can change the properties anytime by selecting the Configure button. In case of a file DSN, the user is prompted for the location where the information is stored in a `.dsn` file.

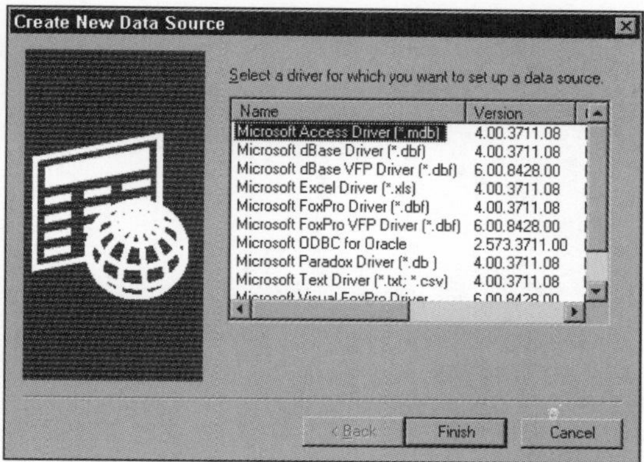

Figure 6-9: List of ODBC drivers

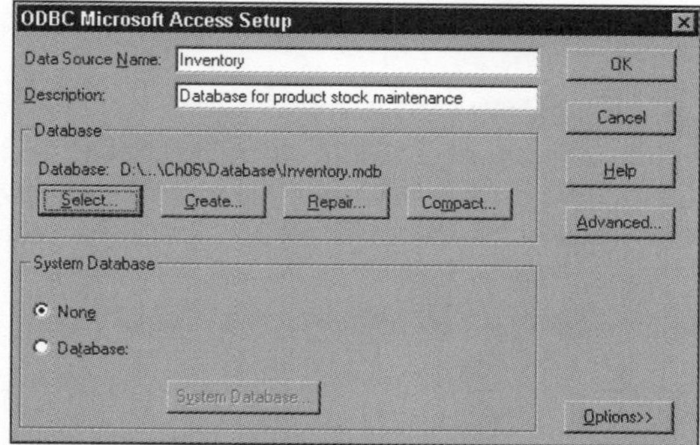

Figure 6-10: ODBC Microsoft Access Setup dialog box

Other information and attributes are present in the ODBC Data Source Administrator window:

- ✦ Drivers — The list shows the available drivers for use installed in this machine. A new driver can be installed using its setup but cannot be added from this tool.
- ✦ Tracing — This allows you to enable tracing of ODBC calls and to save them in a log file. You can enable Visual Studio tracer to start tracing ODBC calls. This is helpful in debugging with respect to connection and database problems.
- ✦ Connection pooling — This lists all the drivers and their pooling timeout in seconds, as shown in Figure 6-11. Connection pooling is explained in detail later in this chapter, but for now it is a pool of open connections that can be reused when a request for connection comes. The pool timeout marks the time until which the connection is kept alive. You can enable performance monitoring and mention the time until which the driver waits before opening a new connection.

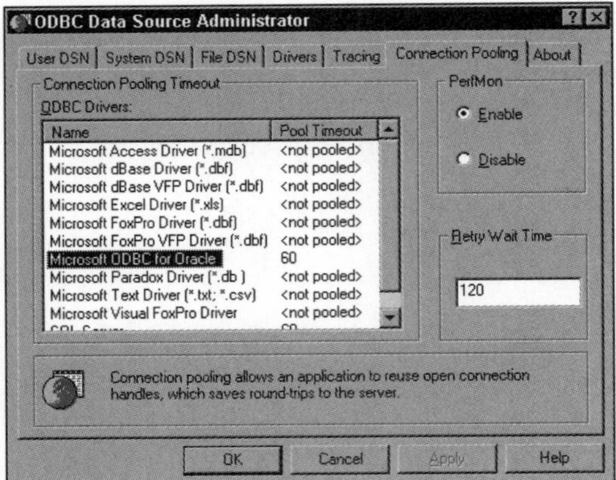

Figure 6-11: Connection pooling on ODBC Data Source Administrator

Using JDBC-ODBC Bridge to connect through DSN

Once the DSN is created, it's very simple to connect to the database using the JDBC-ODBC Bridge. JDK 1.2 comes with a built-in JDBC-ODBC driver. The following code helps in connecting to the ODBC data source we have created.

```
// Load the JDBC-ODBC driver
Class.forName("sun.jdbc.odbc.JdbcOdbcDriver");
//Use DriverManager to obtain a connection.
Connection con =
DriverManager.getConnection("jdbc:odbc:Inventory");
// Use the connection object to create statements
// and execute queries


// Close the connection object
con.close();
```

Note the database URL in the `getConnection()` method. Whatever follows the `jdbc` keyword represents the subprotocol, which is `odbc` in the case of the JDBC-ODBC Bridge. After this follows our DSN name `Inventory`.

Connecting to an SQL Server through the JDBC-ODBC Bridge is also possible. Select the SQL Server driver from the list of drivers shown on the screen. The wizard guides you through the rest of the process.

You need to create the Inventory DSN in order to run the examples that use this DSN.

Connecting to Oracle

Connecting to an Oracle database can be done by using a thin (type 4) JDBC driver. You can download the Oracle driver from the Oracle Web site. The following line of code loads the Oracle driver.

```
Class.forName(oracle.jdbc.driver.OracleDriver());
```

The database URL for getting the connection is a little different from how we connect using ODBC.

```
"jdbc:oracle:thin@(DESCRIPTION = (ADDRESS_LIST = (ADDRESS =
(PROTOCOL = <protocol>)(HOST = <Host Name/IP Address>)(PORT =
<Port number>))) (CONNECT_DATA = (SERVICE_NAME = <service
name>)))"
```

Note that we mention that we are going to use the Oracle JDBC driver and that the driver is thin. The previous description looks more clear when viewed as a tree structure that is given as follows:

```
DESCRIPTION
    ADDRESS_LIST
        ADDRESS
            PROTOCOL=protocol
            HOST=host name/IP address
            PORT=port number
    CONNECT_DATA
            SERVICE_NAME=service name
```

Take a look at the following sample code statements to connect to an Oracle database server residing at 125.39.145.56, listening for JDBC calls at port number 3489 through the TCP protocol. Oracle runs this as a service under the name `orcl`. This value is assigned to the `SERVICE_NAME` attribute.

```
Class.forName("oracle.jdbc.odbc.OracleDriver");
String connURL = (DESCRIPTION = (ADDRESS_LIST = (ADDRESS =
(PROTOCOL = TCP)(HOST = 125.39.145.56)(PORT = 3489)))
(CONNECT_DATA = (SERVICE_NAME = orcl)))
Connection con =
DriverManager.getConnection("jdbc:oracle:thin@" +
connURL,"rramesh","password");
```

Once you are connected to the database, you can perform database operations. The next section explains how to set and retrieve values to and from the database.

Retrieving Data

This section explains how data can be accessed from the database using common interfaces and classes in the `java.sql` package.

Executing SQL statements

Execution of SQL statements is done through the `Statement` interface. A `Statement` object can be created by using the `connection.createStatement()` method. The method has two variations:

- *`createStatement()`*—This method creates an empty `Statement` object.
- *`createStatement(int resultSetType,int resultSetconcurrency)`*—This method creates a `Statement` object with the mentioned type of result set and concurrency.

The `ResultSet` interface defines the following result set types:

- `TYPE_FORWARD_ONLY`—A `ResultSet` object opened with this type can move the cursor only forward.
- `TYPE_SCROLL_INSENSITIVE`—The `ResultSet` object is scrollable but is insensitive to changes made by users. This means that other users have access and can modify the tables involved in this query.
- `TYPE_SCROLL_SENSITIVE`—The `Resultset` object is scrollable but is sensitive to changes. This means that other users cannot modify or delete the tables involved in this query.

The following are the concurrency types defined:

- `CONCUR_READ_ONLY`—A `ResultSet` object opened with this mode cannot be updated.
- `CONCUR_UPDATABLE`—The `ResultSet` can be used for updating data.

As mentioned previously, the `Statement` object holds static SQL statements that can be executed using the *`execute()`* method. There are four methods to execute a query, but their purposes of execution differ.

- *`execute(String sql)`*—This method executes any kind of SQL statement and returns a Boolean value indicating whether the execution has been successful or not.
- *`executeQuery(String sql)`*—This method is used to execute queries that return results. The result is of `ResultSet` object type. Fetching and manipulating the result can be done using the `ResultSet` object.
- *`executeUpdate(String sql)`*—This method is used to execute SQL statements that make changes in the database, such as adding new information, modifying existing information, or deleting information. `Insert`, `Update` and `Delete` are the SQL statements typically used with this method. This method returns the number of rows affected if any of the preceding SQL statements have been executed; otherwise, it returns zero.

✦ *executeBatch()* — This method executes a batch of SQL statements. The method returns an array of integers identifying the number of rows affected for execution of each statement in the batch. An SQL statement is added to the current batch using the `addBatch(String sql)` method.

Prepared statements

A prepared statement consists of precompiled SQL statements, which can be effectively used whenever needed. A query passed to a prepared statement consists of parameters that need to be filled in before passed for execution. The parameters can be set using the `setXXX` methods in the `PreparedStatement` interface, where `XXX` identifies the type of the parameter, say, `integer`, `float`, `double`, and so forth. An example of using a prepared statement follows:

```
PreparedStatement ps = con.prepareStatement("select * from
Products where productId = ? and price > ?");
ps.setInt(1,20);
ps.setDouble(2,120.75);
ResultSet rs = ps.executeQuery();
```

The previous statement is equivalent to the following code:

```
Statement st = con.createStatement();
ResultSet rs = st.executeQuery("Select * from Products where
productId = 20 and price > 120.75");
```

The same `PreparedStatement` object `ps` can be used again anywhere within its scope to set another set of values and to execute the query to get a different result set. But in the case of using a statement, the object has to be instantiated again, passing in the query with new value.

If the parameter to be set does not have an equivalent type in the target database system, the `setObject()` method can be used, passing in the type of the parameter in the underlying system this value has to be converted to. A list of SQL datatype constants is defined in the Types class under the `java.sql` package. All the `setXXX()` methods throw an `SQLException` exception if a database error occurs. This might be due to an incompatibility between the value and the resulting type expected in the database system.

The `PreparedStatement` interface contains the `execute()` methods as in the `Statement` interface, but here it does not take the SQL statement as a parameter, as it is passed during the creation of the object through the `prepareStatement()` method in the Connection object.

The ResultSet interface

The outcome of executing a query statement is a ResultSet object. The ResultSet object is used to traverse the records and fetch the data on an individual record. The getXXX() methods help in retrieving individual fields from a record. *XXX* represents the data type of that field. The parameter to the getXXX() method can either be the column number, starting from 1, or the column name. Thus, there are two methods for each getXXX() method taking in a different parameter.

A ResultSet can be traversed with the help of the next() method. Initially, a ResultSet object positions itself in the beginning of record list, which is usually called Beginning of File (BOF) in file-accessing terms. It is necessary to use the next() method to position the cursor to the first record. When the next() method returns false, you have reached the end of the record list. This state is called End of File (EOF). A typical block of code for retrieving records is as follows:

```
.
.
try {
// create Statement Object
Statement st = con.createStatement();

//Pass query to Statement and get back ResultSet object
ResultSet rs = st.executeQuery("Select * from employee");

//Go through the ResultSet
while(rs.next()) {
.
// process the record using getXXX methods
.
.
}
// close the ResultSet and Statement object
rs.close();
st.close();
} catch (SQLException se) // Error during database access
    se.printStackTrace();
}
```

Note that we use next() in the while statement. If the result of executing the query is empty, rs.next() returns false, and the execution comes out of while.

Any database operation has to be caught for SQLException. An SQLException encapsulates the error message, the SQL state, the error code associated with the error message, and an option to set the next exception that occurs after this exception. The error code can be vendor specific by prefixing a specific vendor code to it. The JDBC driver documentation, if any, should help in identifying a list of vendor-specific error codes. A chain of exceptions can be set by using the setNextException() method.

Servlets and databases

All database operations that can be performed on a stand-alone application can be performed on "servlets" too. Because a "servlet" is a kind of application that gets executed on the server, it can be treated as an individual application. All database operations are performed on the server side, and only data is passed to the client. The client does not have a single hint where the information has come from. The following sections give two simple examples illustrating data from the database displayed on the client browser.

Example servlet to view records in a table

Listing 6-1 shows an example servlet that displays all records in a table. We use an Access database called `Inventory` that contains tables for `Product`, `Purchase`, and `Sales`.

You can find the `inventory.mdb` file on the book's companion CD-ROM. See Appendix A and the CD installation instructions at the back of the book for more information on how to copy these files to your system.

Listing 6-1

```
package servletbible.ch06.examples;

import javax.servlet.*;
import javax.servlet.http.*;
import java.io.*;
import java.sql.*;

/**
* Table View Servlet. Displays the records in the Product
* table from the Inventory database
*/

public class TableViewServlet extends HttpServlet
{

    //    Connection object to hold the database connection.

    Connection con;
     /**
     * Here we override the doGet method
     *
     * @param request the client's request
     * @param response the servlet's response
     */
    public void init() {
            try {
```

Continued

Listing 6-1 (continued)

```
                // Get the JDBC-ODBC connection

    Class.forName("sun.jdbc.odbc.JdbcOdbcDriver");
                // Inventory is the DSN name
                con =
DriverManager.getConnection("jdbc:odbc:Inventory");
            } catch (ClassNotFoundException cnfe) {
                System.out.println("Could not load Jdbc-Odbc
driver");
            } catch(SQLException se) {
                System.out.println("SQL Exception caught!");
            }

    }
    public void doGet(HttpServletRequest request,
HttpServletResponse response) throws ServletException,
IOException
        {
            /**
                * Sets the content type
                */
            response.setContentType("text/html");

                PrintWriter out = response.getWriter();

                /**
                * Prints the records in Product table.
                */
                out.println("<html><head><title>Table View
Servlet</title></head><body>");
                out.println("<H1>Table: Prodcut</H1>");

                /**
                * getRecords method gets the detail from the
                * table and forma a html table
                */
                out.println(getRecords());

                out.println("</body></html>");
                out.close();
    }

    private String getRecords()
    {
        String html = "";
        try {
            // Create a statement
            Statement stmt = con.createStatement();

            // Create a resultset passing the query to
executeQuery method
```

```
            ResultSet rs = stmt.executeQuery("Select * from
product");

            /**
            * ResultSetMetaData stores information about
            * the column names, their types etc.
            */
            ResultSetMetaData rsmd = rs.getMetaData();

            //get the column count
            int colCount = rsmd.getColumnCount();
            html = "<table cellspacing=0 cellpadding=0
border=1>";

            // take the field names to display them as table
header
            for(int i=1;i<=colCount;i++) {
                html += "<th>";
                html += rsmd.getColumnName(i);
                html += "</th>";
            }

            // Go through the result set to fetch records
            while(rs.next()) {
                html += "<tr>";
                /**
                * Get the data type of each column and based
on that
                * use the getXXX method in the ResultSet
object
                */
                for(int i=1;i<=colCount;i++) {
                    html += "<td>";

                    // Types object has the list of all
data types supported in standard SQL
                    // getColumnType gets a data type for
a particular column
                    switch(rsmd.getColumnType(i)) {
                        case Types.INTEGER:
                            html += rs.getInt(i);
                            break;
                        case Types.FLOAT:
                            html += rs.getFloat(i);
                            break;
                        case Types.DOUBLE:
                                html +=
rs.getDouble(i);
                            break;
                        case Types.VARCHAR:
                            html += rs.getString(i);
                            break;
```

Continued

Listing 6-1 *(continued)*

```
                    }
                    html += "</td>";
                }
                html += "</tr>";
            }
            html += "</table>";

            // Close the result set and statement
            rs.close();
            stmt.close();

            // return HTML
            return html;
        } catch(SQLException se) {
            // some error occurred during database operation
            System.out.println(se.getMessage());

            // return error message
            return se.getMessage();
        }
    }
    public void destroy() {
        try {
            // Close the connection
            con.close();
        } catch(SQLException se) {
            System.out.println("SQL Exception caught!");
        }
    }
}
//End of TableViewServlet Servlet
```

We get the connection in the init() method. This ensures that once the servlet is called for the first time, the connection object is created and is closed only when the servlet gets destroyed. In the doGet() method, we frame the HTML. The method getRecords() fetches data from the table and frames it in inside the `<TABLE>` tag, returning the HTML code, which then displays the records in the browser as shown in Figure 6-12.

This example also illustrates the use of the `ResultSetMetaData` object. Here we try to display all the records without knowing what the field name is. This is possible only when we use the `ResultSetMetaData` object. The `getMetaData()` method in the `ResultSet` interface returns an object of type `ResultSetMetaData`. This interface has methods for getting the properties and data types of the fields in a table. The `getColumnCount()`, `getColumnName()`, and `getColumnType()` methods are used in the preceding program to retrieve the number of columns in the table, each column name, and the data type of each column, respectively.

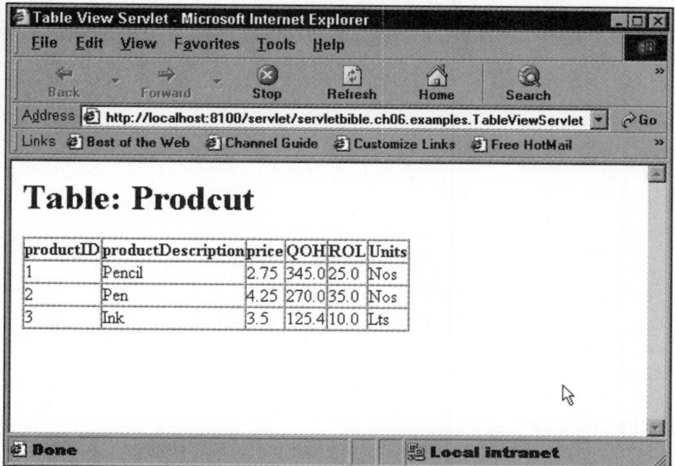

Figure 6-12: TableViewServlet displaying all the records in the Product table

The Types class in the `java.sql` package has fields identifying the standard data types used in SQL. The `getColumnType()` method returns an individual value that maps to a constant value in the `Types` class. Refer to the Java API documentation for the constants, members, and methods of all relevant classes and interfaces in the `java.sql` package.

TableViewServlet extended

Let's extend the preceding servlet to display records from any table in the database. We create one more servlet that displays all the tables in the inventory database. Clicking the table name takes us to a servlet that displays all the records from the table chosen. First, in Listing 6-2, we look at the servlet code for displaying all the tables from the database.

Listing 6-2

```
package servletbible.ch06.examples;

import javax.servlet.*;
import javax.servlet.http.*;
import java.io.*;
import java.sql.*;

/**
  * Table View Servlet. Displays all the tables
  * in the Inventory database.
  */
```

Continued

Listing 6-2 *(continued)*

```
public class AllTableViewServlet extends HttpServlet
{

    //    Connection object to hold the database connection.

    Connection con;

    public void init() {
        try {
            // Get the JDBC-ODBC connection
            Class.forName("sun.jdbc.odbc.JdbcOdbcDriver");

            // Inventory is the DSN name
            con =
                 DriverManager.getConnection("jdbc:odbc:Inventory");
        } catch (ClassNotFoundException cnfe) {
            System.out.println(
                "Could not load Jdbc-Odbcdriver");
        } catch(SQLException se) {
            System.out.println("SQL Exception caught!");
        }
    }

    /**
      * Here we override the doGet method
      *
      * @param request the client's request
      * @param response the servlet's response
      */

    public void doGet(HttpServletRequest request,
            HttpServletResponse response)
            throws ServletException,IOException
    {
        /**
          * Sets the content type
          */
        response.setContentType("text/html");

        PrintWriter out = response.getWriter();

        /**
          * Prints the records in Product table.
          */
        out.println("<html><head><title>List Tables in
                    the Database</title>");
        out.println("</head><body>");
        out.println("Database: Inventory");
        out.println("<H3>Click on any of the table
                to view the records </H3>");
```

```
        /**
          * getTables method gets all the
          * tables in the database
          */
        out.println(getTables());
        out.println("</body></html>");
        out.close();
    }

    private String getTables()
    {
        String html = "";
        final String[] tableTypes = {"TABLE","VIEW"};
        try {
            html = "<p>";

            // DatabaseMetaData holds information about database
            DatabaseMetaData dbMD = con.getMetaData();

            /**
              * getTables method returns all the Tables
              * in the database. The result is a ResultSet
              * object containing the table name and details
              * about the table.
              */

            ResultSet rs =
            dbMD.getTables(null,null,"%",tableTypes);

            // Frame the result in a Table
            html += "<table cellpadding=0 cellspacing=0 border=0>";
            html += "<th>Table Name</th>";
            String tableName="";
            while(rs.next()) {
                html += "<tr>";
                html += "<td>";

                // Get the table name
                tableName = rs.getString("TABLE_NAME");

                // Frame the link passing the table name to
                // the TableViewServlet2 Servlet
                html += "<a
href=\"/servlet/servletbible.ch06.examples.TableViewServlet2
                    ?TableName=" + tableName + "\">";
                html += tableName;
                html += "</a>";
                html += "</td>";
                html += "</tr>";
            }
            html += "</table>";
            html += "</p>";
```

Continued

Listing 6-2 *(continued)*

```
            // Close the ResultSet object
            rs.close();

            return html;
        } catch(SQLException se) {
            // Some error during database operation
            System.out.println(se.getMessage());

            // return what error it is
            return se.getMessage();
        }
    }

    public void destroy() {
        try {
                // Close the connection
                con.close();
        } catch(SQLException se) {
            System.out.println("SQL Exception caught!");
        }
    }
}
// End of AllTableViewServlet Servlet
```

Figure 6-13 shows `AllTableViewServlet`'s main page, which displays all the tables available for viewing in a database.

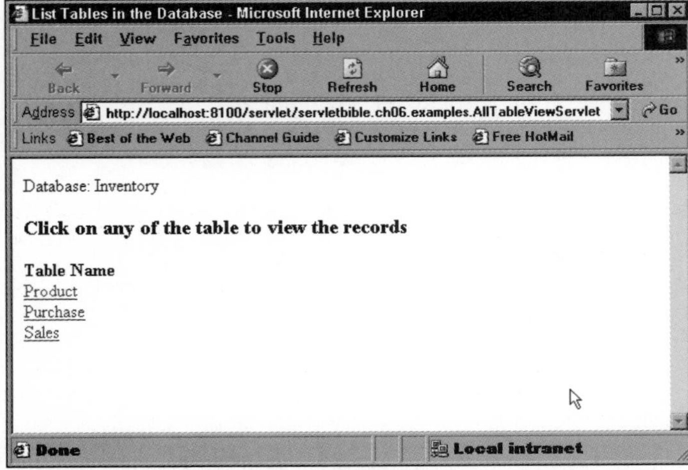

Figure 6-13: AllTableViewServlet gives the user the option to display all the tables in a database.

The getTables() method is of more interest to us in this servlet. Here we see one more interesting interface, DatabaseMetaData. This is similar to the ResultSetMetaData class except that this gives information about the database. The interface has methods for finding information about tables, indexes, procedures, database drivers, and system functions supported by the DBMS. Most of the methods in this interface return a ResultSet object. Thus, the information returned is in the form of rows and columns. In this servlet program, we are concerned with getting table information. The getTables() method comes to our aid. The method takes four parameters:

- String catalog — This refers to the catalog name where the list of tables have to be retrieved. The term *catalog* here varies depending on the DBMS. For example, to an Access DBMS, this is a database. The method getCatalogTerm() retrieves the exact term used by the underlying DBMS. If this parameter is an empty string (""), the method retrieves tables, which are not under a catalog. If the value is null, the method omits this parameter as a filter for getting the table list.
- String schemaPattern — Again, this term varies with the underlying DBMS. Usually, this represents the ownership pattern. The getSchemaTerm() method returns the term used by the DBMS. A pattern can have two special characters. A % can be replaced with zero or any number of characters, and any character can replace an underscore (_) character.
- String tableNamePattern — This is a table name pattern to filter the selection list. The % and _ characters apply here too.
- String[] types — This array identifies the types of tables to retrieve. The valid values can be one or more of "TABLE", "VIEW", "SYSTEM TABLE", "GLOBAL TEMPORARY", "LOCAL TEMPORARY", "ALIAS" and "SYNONYM".

The getTables() method returns a ResultSet object with the following columns:

- TABLE_CAT — The data type is String and has the catalog name. This column may be null.
- TABLE_SCHEM — This represents the schema name, and the data type is String. The column may contain null values.
- TABLE_NAME — This provides the table name, and the data type is String.
- TABLE_TYPE — This is a String data type representing one of the following: "TABLE", "VIEW", "SYSTEM TABLE", "GLOBAL TEMPORARY", "LOCAL TEMPORARY", "ALIAS", or "SYNONYM".
- REMARKS — This is a string value containing comments about the table.

We need the table name, so we get that column alone in our program. We frame the table name as a hyperlink and the hyperlink refers to the TableViewServlet2 servlet with the parameter TableName containing the table name.

We need to make minor changes in TableViewServlet. The changes are reflected in a new servlet TableViewServlet2.java, shown in Listing 6-3.

Listing 6-3

```
package servletbible.ch06.examples;

import javax.servlet.*;
import javax.servlet.http.*;
import java.io.*;
import java.sql.*;
import java.text.*;

/**
* Table View Servlet. Displays all the records in the
* table from the Inventory database. The table name is
* obtained from the TableName parameter
*/

public class TableViewServlet2 extends HttpServlet
{

    // Connection object to hold the database connection.

    Connection con;
    /**
      * Here we override the doGet method
      *
      * @param request the client's request
      * @param response the servlet's response
      */

    public void init()
    {
        try {
            // Get the JDBC-ODBC connection

            Class.forName("sun.jdbc.odbc.JdbcOdbcDriver");
            // Inventory is the DSN name
            con = DriverManager.getConnection("jdbc:odbc:Inventory");
        } catch (ClassNotFoundException cnfe) {
            System.out.println("Could not load Jdbc-Odbc driver");
        } catch(SQLException se) {
            System.out.println("SQL Exception caught!");
        }

    }

    public void doGet(HttpServletRequest request,
        HttpServletResponse response) throws ServletException,IOException
    {
        /**
          * Sets the content type
          */
        response.setContentType("text/html");
```

```
        PrintWriter out = response.getWriter();

        /**
          * Prints the records in Product table.
          */
        out.println("<html><head><title>Table View
                Servlet</title></head><body>");
        String tableName = request.getParameter("TableName");
        out.println("<H1>Table: " + tableName + "</H1>");
        if(tableName == null) {
            out.println("Error: Unspecified table name");
        } else {
            /**
              * getRecords method gets the detail from the
              * table and forma a html table
              */
              out.println(getRecords(tableName));
        }
        out.println("</body></html>");
        out.close();
    }

    private String getRecords(String tableName)
    {
        String html = "";
        try {
            // Create a statement
            Statement stmt = con.createStatement();

            // Create a resultset passing the query to executeQuery method
            ResultSet rs = stmt.executeQuery
                ("Select * from " + tableName);

            /**
              * ResultSetMetaData stores information about
              * the column names, their types etc.
              */
            ResultSetMetaData rsmd = rs.getMetaData();

            //get the column count
            int colCount = rsmd.getColumnCount();
            html = "<table cellspacing=0 cellpadding=0 border=1>";

            // take the field names to display them as table header
            for(int i=1;i<=colCount;i++) {
                html += "<th>";
                html += rsmd.getColumnName(i);
                html += "</th>";
            }

            // Go through the result set to fetch records
```

Continued

Listing 6-3 *(continued)*

```
        // DateFormat object can be used to format the date.
        // Here we format it in DD-MMM-YYYY format
        DateFormat df = DateFormat.getDateInstance(DateFormat.MEDIUM);
        while(rs.next()) {
            html += "<tr>";
            /**
              * Get the data type of each column and based on that
              * use the getXXX method in the ResultSet object
              */
            for(int i=1;i<=colCount;i++) {
                html += "<td>";

                // Types object has the list of all
                // data types supported in standard SQL
                // getColumnType gets a data type for
                // a particular column

                switch(rsmd.getColumnType(i)) {
                    case Types.INTEGER:
                        html += rs.getInt(i);
                        break;
                    case Types.FLOAT:
                        html += rs.getFloat(i);
                        break;
                    case Types.DOUBLE:
                        html += rs.getDouble(i);
                        break;
                    case Types.VARCHAR:
                        html += rs.getString(i);
                        break;
                    case Types.DATE:
                    case Types.TIME:
                    case Types.TIMESTAMP:
                        Date dt = rs.getDate(i);
                        html += df.format(dt);
                        break;
                }
                html += "</td>";
            }
            html += "</tr>";
        }
        html += "</table>";

        // Close the result set and statement
        rs.close();
        stmt.close();

        return html;
    } catch(SQLException se) {
        // Some error occured during database operation
        System.out.println(se.getMessage());
```

```
            // return error message
            return se.getMessage();
        }
    }

    public void doPost(HttpServletRequest request,
            HttpServletResponse response) throws ServletException,IOException
    {
        // Call doGet
        doGet(request,response);
    }

    public void destroy()
    {
        try {
            // Close the connection
            con.close();
        } catch(SQLException se) {
            System.out.println("SQL Exception caught!");
        }
    }
}
//End of TableViewServlet2 Servlet
```

Figure 6-14 shows all the records for a table being displayed in the browser.

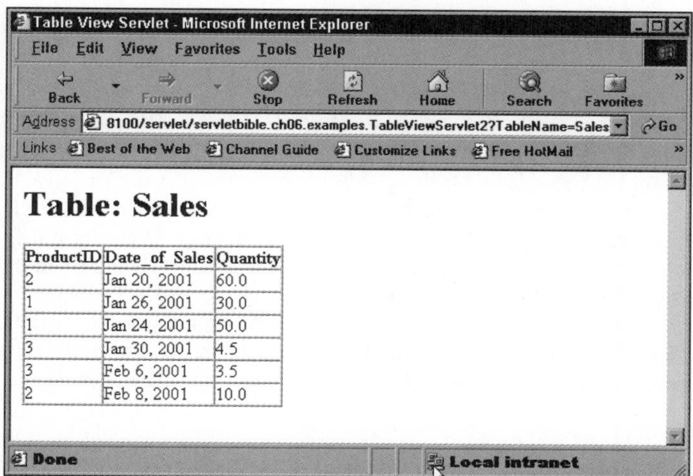

Figure 6-14: TableViewServlet2 displaying all the records for a table name passed as a parameter

We have two main changes here. One is that we use the `request.getParameter()` method to obtain the table name from the `AllTableViewServlet` servlet. The second is that we have included the `Types.DATE`, `Types.TIME`, and `Types.TIMESTAMP` in the `switch-case` block. This takes care of date and time fields. Note that we have created a `DateFormat` object before we process the `ResultSet`. The `DateFormat` object is in the `java.text` package, which is used to format the date in the required format. The `getInstance` static method returns a reference to the newly created `DateFormat` object. You can pass in one of the following styles to the `getInstance()` static method:

✦ `DateFormat.SHORT`—Displays completely in numeric form, such as `10:10 p.m.`

✦ `DateFormat.MEDIUM`—Displays in longer format, such as `Apr 04, 2001`

✦ `DateFormat.LONG`—Displays in longer format, such as `April 04, 2001`

✦ `DateFormat.FULL-`—Displays the whole date or time, such as `Wednesday, April 04, 2001 A.D.`

The format, which takes in a Date parameter, formats the date to the specified style returning a String.

We discussed the most commonly used interfaces from the `java.sql` package. Next, we look into connection pooling, an important concept in efficiently handling connections to database from applications.

Connection Pooling

An application using databases as storage for information requires a lot of communication among the database engines to retrieve the information. When multiple clients access the same Web application, the burden falls on the server to satisfy the entire client request and to dispatch the requested information. For this, the server should also be efficient enough to handle the connection between itself and the DBMS. Connections are costly and take considerable time to establish. It is important that the client be sent back the requested information as early as possible. Thus, it is wise to have a connection ready and to pass it on to the server when it requires one for processing. Creating a number of connections and storing them for future purposes is called *connection pooling*. A connection pool can also maintain information on each connection and can make sure each connection is valid until it dies.

A number of third-party connection-pooling packages are available. The known ones are pool-driver packages, available from WebLogic, and the one from Java Exchange called `DbConnectionBroker`. Connection pooling takes processing and maintenance time, but it's worth the time lost in establishing a new connection when needed.

In Listing 6-4, we implement a simple connection pool. We take in the driver, the database URL, the user name, the password, and the number of connections to create in the constructor. The connections created are stored in a hash table. Each connection forms the key in the hash table. The value for this key is a flag indicating whether this connection is currently under use or not. Initially, this is set to `false`.

Note A *hash table* is a common data structure used to store collection of data. `Hashtable` is the class in the `java.util` package that is commonly used to store collection of data.

The `getConnection()` method returns an unused connection from the hash table. Before returning the connection, the flag is set to `true` so that this connection is not returned again for use. The `takeBackConnection()` method marks the returned connection with a `false` value in the hash table so that it can be reused again.

Listing 6-4

```
package servletbible.ch06.examples;

import java.util.*;
import java.io.*;
import java.sql.*;

/**
* This class creates a connection pool.
* It takes in as parameter the
* number of connections to create
* in the constructor and creates them
* and stores them in a hashtable.
* The connection is marked by a
* boolean flag with false being unused
* and true being used
*/

public class ConnectionPool {
    private Hashtable connections = null;

    ConnectionPool(String driver,String dbURL, String dbUser,
        String dbPassword, int numberOfConnections) throws
        ClassNotFoundException,SQLException
    {
        /**
          * driver is the JDBC driver to load
          * dbURL specifies the database URL
          */
        // Instantiate Hashtable
```

Continued

Listing 6-4 *(continued)*

```
        connections = new Hashtable();

        // Load the JDBC Driver
        Class.forName(driver);

        // create numberOfConnections connections
        for(int i=0;i<numberOfConnections;i++) {
            // call different constructor if user name is empty or not
            if(!(dbUser.equals("")))
                connections.put(DriverManager.getConnection(dbURL,dbUser,
                    dbPassword),Boolean.FALSE);
            else
                connections.put(DriverManager.getConnection(dbURL),
                    Boolean.FALSE);
        }
        // Pool created
        System.out.println("Pool ready for use");
    }

    public Connection getConnection()
    {
        /**
          * Checks for availability of connection
          * and returns an unused connection.
          * Returns null if unused connection is not available
          */

        Connection connect;
        Enumeration enum = connections.keys();

        // Lock connections
        synchronized (connections)
{
            // Loop through the hashtable
            while(enum.hasMoreElements())
            {
                // Get the connection
                connect=(Connection)enum.nextElement();

                // Get status of connection
                Boolean flag=(Boolean)connections.get(connect);

                // Check if unused
                if (flag==Boolean.FALSE)
                {

                    // This connection can be used.
                    // Before returning the connection mark this
                    // connection as used
                    connections.put(connect,Boolean.TRUE);
```

```
                    //Return the connection
                    return connect;

                    // this connection is used
                }
            }
        }
        // Pool does not have unused connection
        return null;
    }

    public void takeBackConnection(Connection returnedConnection)
    {
        /**
          * Marks the connection returned to unused
          */
        Connection connect;
        Enumeration enum=connections.keys();

        //Go through the hashtable
        while (enum.hasMoreElements())
        {

            // Get next connection
            connect=(Connection)enum.nextElement();

            // Check if this connection is what returned
            if (connect==returnedConnection)
            {
                // yes this is the one returned, mark it as unused
                connections.put(connect,Boolean.FALSE);

                // come out of loop
                break;
            }
        }
    }
}
// End of ConnectionPool class
```

We will be using the connection pool class in the example in the next section.

Personal Address Book

To end this chapter, let's look at one more servlet example. This is an Address Book servlet. The database AddressBook contains a PersonalInformation table, which holds the first names, last names, nicknames, dates of birth, e-mail addresses, and hobbies of users. A PersonID uniquely identifies each person. The `AddressBook` servlet performs addition, modification, deletion, and viewing of the `PersonalInformation` table. What's eye catching here is that we are going to accomplish this in a single servlet. We show an HTML that divides the entire page in two. On the top frame, we have two links: one for showing the Add screen and the other for Modify, Delete, and View screens. Initially, the Add screen is loaded in the bottom frame.

On the CD-ROM, you'll find the `AddressBook.mdb` file and the HTML files `AddressBook.html` and `AdBookMenu.html`.

Figure 6-15 shows the Address Book main page.

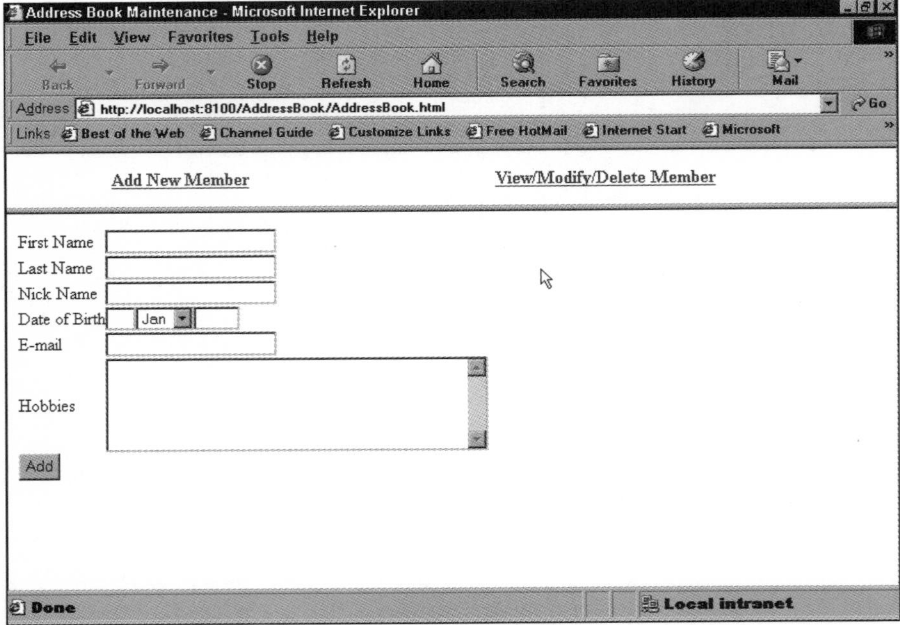

Figure 6-15: Address Book application main page

The code for client-side validations is not included in the Address Book example for this section. However, the following validations can be added as an exercise for the reader: text-field validations—to make sure the user has entered valid characters in the text fields, and first and last name validations—these fields are required.

See Chapter 5 for detailed information on client-side validation with JavaScript.

Listing 6-5 shows the `AddressBook.java` servlet code for maintaining our Address Book. The remainder of this section examines each method in detail.

Listing 6-5

```
package servletbible.ch06.examples;

import javax.servlet.*;
import javax.servlet.http.*;
import java.io.*;
import java.sql.*;
import java.util.*;

/**
  * This Servlet handles Addition, Modification, Deletion and Viewing
  * Personal information from the Address
  * NOTE: Client side validations are not written and are
  * left as exercise to the reader
  */

public class AddressBook extends HttpServlet
{
    // pool is the connection pool from where a
    //free connection can be obtained
    ConnectionPool pool;

    // Constants to identify the current module
    final int MODULE_ADD = 1;
    final int MODULE_ADDED = 2;
    final int MODULE_VIEW = 3;
    final int MODULE_VIEWED = 4;
    final int MODULE_MODIFIED = 5;
    final int MODULE_DELETED = 6;

    // Connection object to hold the database connection.
    Connection con;

    /**
      * Here we override the doGet method
      *
      * @param request the client's request
      * @param response the servlet's response
      */
    public void init()
    {
        /**
```

Continued

Listing 6-5 *(continued)*

```
        * Create the pool, passing the driver,
        * the database URL and number of connections.
        */
      try {
          pool = new ConnectionPool(
              "sun.jdbc.odbc.JdbcOdbcDriver",
              "jdbc:odbc:AddressBook","","",5);
      } catch (ClassNotFoundException cnfe) {
          System.out.println("Could not load Jdbc-Odbc driver "
              + cnfe.getMessage());
      } catch(SQLException se) {
          System.out.println("SQL Exception caught! " + se.getMessage());
      }
  }

  public void doGet(HttpServletRequest request,
          HttpServletResponse response) throws ServletException,IOException
  {
      /**
        * Sets the content type
        */
      response.setContentType("text/html");
      int module;
      PrintWriter out = response.getWriter();
      // Get the connection from the pool
      con = pool.getConnection();

      // If con is null, then the pool is exhausted.
      // Throw a message stating the request cannot be satisfied now.
      if(con == null) {
          out.println(
              "Connection to the database is not possible at this moment.
              Please try again later");
          return;
      }
      // Parameter Module identifies what Module is to be displayed now
      String strModule = request.getParameter("Module");

      // By default the screen is in the Add mode
      if(strModule == null)
          module = MODULE_ADD;
      else
          module = Integer.parseInt(strModule);

      out.println("<html>");
      out.println("<head>");

      /**
        * Write Java script method if this screen is going
```

```
     * to be for Modify or Delete, to set the hidden fields
     */
    if(module == MODULE_VIEWED) {
        out.println("<script language=javascript>");
        out.println("function model(module,personId) {");
        // Set the module number, here
        // it would be 5 (Modify) or 6 (Delete)
        // personId represents which member to modify or delete

        out.println("document.FormEntry.Module.value = module;");

        out.println("document.FormEntry.PersonId.value = personId;");

        // Submit this form
        out.println("document.FormEntry.submit()");
        out.println("}");
        out.println("</script>");
    }
    out.println("</head><body>");
    out.println("<form id=FormEntry name=FormEntry method=Get
        action=\"servletbible.ch06.examples.AddressBook\">");

    /**
     * The display as well as the processing
     * is decided based on the module. The module comes
     * in as a parameter from the previous screen.
     */
    switch(module) {
        /**
         * In case of adding new member the
         * screen remains in the addition mode
         * even after adding a record
         */
        case MODULE_ADD:
        case MODULE_ADDED:
            if(module == MODULE_ADDED) {
            /**
             * In case a record is added display a message
             * addNewRecord returns true if its successful
             */
            if(addNewRecord(request))
                out.println("<h3> New member added </h3>");
            else
                out.println(
                    "<h3> Could not complete Database operation </h3>");
    }

    // getEntryScreen displays text fields for entering information
    out.println(getEntryScreen());

    // Add button submits this form for adding new record
    out.println("<input type=Submit id=btnAdd name=btnAdd value='Add'>");
```

Continued

Listing 6-5 (continued)

```
        out.println("</input>");
        /**
          * Hidden field for holding the next module.
          * Here we directly assign value 2 because adding
          * press is going to bring up the add module again
          */
out.println("<input type=hidden id=Module name=Module value=2>");
        out.println("</input>");
        break;
        /**
          * We show the view screen (displaying all member's first name
          * last name and email address) on click of the view/modify/delete
          * link or after a member information is modified or deleted
          */
        case MODULE_VIEW:
        case MODULE_MODIFIED:
        case MODULE_DELETED:
            /**
              * updateRecord, deleteRecord does modification and deletion
              * respectively and returns true if its successful. The PersonId
              * identifies which member to modify, delete or view.
              */
            String personId = request.getParameter("PersonId");
            if(module == MODULE_MODIFIED) {
                if(updateRecord(personId,request))
                    out.println("<h3> Member Modified </h3><br>");
                else
                    out.println(
                        "<h3> Could not complete Database operation </h3>");
            }
            if(module == MODULE_DELETED) {
                if(deleteRecord(personId))
                    out.println("<h3> Member Deleted </h3><br>");
                else
                    out.println(
                        "<h3> Could not complete Database operation </h3>");
            }
            out.println(
                "<h3> Click on the First Name to
                View/Modify/Delete Personal Information </h3>");
            out.println("<p>");
            // viewRecords displays the data entry screen with
            // data filled for a PersonId
            out.println(viewRecords());
            out.println("</p>");
            break;
        case MODULE_VIEWED:
            // This module displays all the records.
            personId = request.getParameter("PersonId");
```

```
            // getEntryScreenWithData retrieves the entry screen filled up
            // for a personId
            out.println(getEntryScreenWithData(personId));

            // Modify Button. Note onclick of this button
            // we call model javascript function
            out.println("<input type=Button
                id=btnModify name=btnModify value='Modify'
                onclick=\"moddel('5','" + personId + "')\">");
            out.println("</input>");
            out.println(" ");

            // Delete button. Note onclick of
            // this button we call moddel javascript function
            out.println("<input type=Button
                id=btnDelete name=btnDelete value='Delete'
                onclick=\"moddel('6','" + personId + "')\">");
          // Hidden text field to hold the
          //next Module, would be Modify or Delete
          out.println("<input type=hidden
               id=Module name=Module>");
          out.println("</input>");
          // Hidden field to hold person id
          out.println("<input type=hidden
               id=PersonId name=PersonId>");
          out.println("</input>");
          break;
    }
    // end HTML
    out.println("</form>");
    out.println("</body></html>");
    out.close();
    // return the connection back to pool
    pool.takeBackConnection(con);
}
// End of AddressBook servlet
```

In the method, we instantiate our connection pool object. We pass an argument of *5* to tell the pool class to prepare *5* connections.

Because a single servlet handles all four modules, the servlet needs to know for which module it has been requested. We keep track of the module by passing the module number through a hidden field or by directly passing it in the query string. Each module is assigned a number and is represented through one of the following constants.

✦ `MODULE_ADD`—When the servlet receives this module number, it sends back the data entry screen for the personal information. This module is the default when the `AddressBook` servlet is called initially. This is also the module when the "Add Personal Information" link is clicked.

✦ `MODULE_ADDED`—When the servlet receives a module number of *2*, the Add button has been clicked, and the information from the previous screen has to be updated to the database. Note that we also frame the hidden field again, setting it to *2*, as from this screen you can only add again.

✦ `MODULE_VIEW`—When the servlet finds a module number of 3, it displays all the records from the table. Only the fields First Name, Last Name and E-Mail are displayed. The first name acts as a link to take you to the View/Modify/Delete page.

✦ `MODULE_VIEWED`—A screen with filled-in data appears once the user clicks on one of the links in the view page. The module number is 4 in this case. We display two buttons, one for modifying and one for deleting the record currently viewed. We also include a JavaScript function model that sets the value in the Module hidden field whether modify or delete is clicked. It also sets another hidden field, PersonId, to indicate to the servlet which person has to be deleted.

✦ `MODULE_MODIFIED`—This module is similar to `MODULE_VIEW` except that before displaying the records, it has to update a record, getting the values from the previous screen. It comes with a module value of *5*.

✦ `MODULE_DELETED`—This module is similar to `MODULE_VIEW` except that before displaying the records, it has to delete a record shown in the previous screen. It comes with a module value of *5*.

The `switch-case` block identifies which module number has come; based on that, the framing of the HTML and the database operation is performed as shown in Listing 6-6.

Listing 6-6

```
    public String getEntryScreen(){
        /**
        * This method returns html framing the data entry
        *
        */
        // Store month names in an array
        final String months[] =
{"Jan","Feb","Mar","Apr","May","Jun","Jul","Aug","Sep","Oct",
"Nov","Dec"};

        String html = "";
```

```
        // Display in a table setting the border to 0.
        // This will align the labels and text boxes.
        html += "<table cellpadding=0 cellspacing=0 border=0>";
        html += "<tr>";
        html += "<td>";
        html += "First Name";
        html += "</td>";
        html += "<td>";
        html += "<input type=text id=FirstName
name=FirstName>";
        html += "</input>";
        html += "</tr>";
        html += "<tr>";
        html += "<td>";
        html += "Last Name";
        html += "</td>";
        html += "<td>";
        html += "<input type=text id=LastName name=LastName>";
        html += "</input>";
        html += "</tr>";
        html += "<tr>";
        html += "<td>";
        html += "Nick Name";
        html += "</td>";
        html += "<td>";
        html += "<input type=text id=NickName name=NickName>";
        html += "</input>";
        html += "</tr>";
        html += "<tr>";
        html += "<td>";
        html += "Date of Birth";
        html += "</td>";
        html += "<td>";
        /**
        * Date of birth is displayed with
        *    Date as a text box
        *    Months in a combo box
        *    Year in a text box
        */

        html += "<input type=text id=Date name=Date size=2
maxvalue=2>";
        html += "</input>";
        html += "<select id=Month name=Month>";
        // Fill the months in a combo box
        for(int i=0;i<12;i++) {
            html += "<option ";
            // By default let Jan be selected
            if(i==0) html+= "selected ";
            // value is used to set the corresponding month
```

Continued

Listing 6-6 (continued)

```
number.
              // This value will be returned when a request for
this
              // field is used.
              html += "value=" + (i+1) + ">" + months[i] +
"</option>";
          }
          html += "</select>";
          html += "<input type=text id=Year name=Year size=4
maxvalue=4>";
          html += "</input>";
          html += "</tr>";
          html += "<tr>";
          html += "<td>";         html += "E-mail";
          html += "</td>";
          html += "<td>";
          html += "<input type=text id=EMail name=EMail>";
          html += "</input>";
          html += "</tr>";
          html += "<tr>";
          html += "<td>";
          html += "Hobbies";
          html += "</td>";
          html += "<td>";
          // A Text Area to hold the Hobbies
          html += "<TextArea id=Hobbies name=Hobbies rows=5
cols=40>";
          html += "</TextArea>";
          html += "</tr>";
          html += "</table>";
          // return the HTML
          return html;
     }
```

The `getEntryScreen()` method does not have database processing and returns an HTML form containing text fields for data entry, as shown in Figure 6-16. For the date, we use a text box for the day, a combo box for the month, and again a text box for the year. We set "Jan" to be the default month in the combo box. Listing 6-7 presents the code for the `addNewRecord()` method, which, as the name implies, adds a new record to the database.

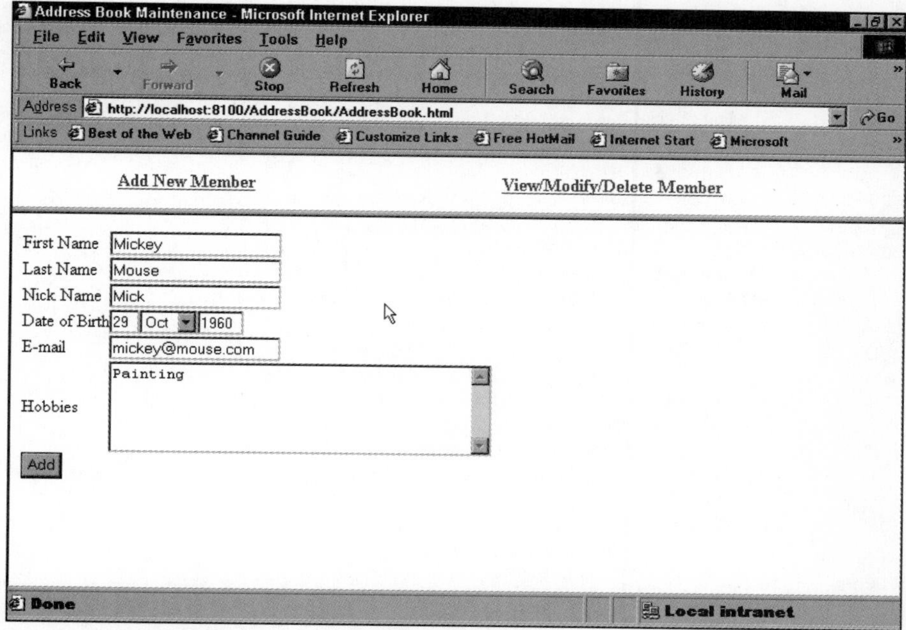

Figure 6-16: Add Entry form for Address Book application

Listing 6-7

```
    private boolean addNewRecord(HttpServletRequest request) {
        /**
        * This method adds a new record into the table.
        * The request parameter is used to get the information
        * from the previous screen.
        */
        int nextPersonID = 0;
        try {

            // getNextID returns the next member id by
            // taking the maximum member id + 1
            nextPersonID = getNextID();

            // if nextPersonID is zero then an error has
occured.
            // So send back false indicating the operation as
unsuccessful
            if(nextPersonID == 0) return false;
```

Continued

Listing 6-7 *(continued)*

```
            // Get all the values from the previous page
            String firstName =
request.getParameter("FirstName");
            String lastName =
request.getParameter("LastName");
            String nickName =
request.getParameter("NickName");
            String date = request.getParameter("Date");
            String year = request.getParameter("Year");
            String dob;

            /**
            * Date of birth is handled differently.
            * Get date, month and year individually
            * and concatenate. If any one field is missing
            * its treated as empty and not provided
            */
            if(date != null && year != null)
                dob = request.getParameter("Month") + "/" +
date + "/" + year;
            else
                dob = null;
            String eMail = request.getParameter("EMail");
            String hobbies = request.getParameter("Hobbies");

            // Frame the SQL
            String SQL = "Insert into PersonalInformation
values(";
                    SQL += nextPersonID + ",'";
                    SQL += firstName + "','";
                    SQL += lastName + "',";

                    // Check for null
                    if(nickName != null &&
(!nickName.equals("")))
                        SQL += "'" + nickName + "',";
                    else
                        SQL += "null,";

                    // Check for null
                    if(dob != null)
                        SQL += "'" + dob + "',";
                    else
                        SQL += "null,";

                    // Check for null
                    if(eMail != null &&
(!eMail.equals("")))
```

```
                        SQL += "'" + eMail + "',";
                    else
                        SQL += "null,";

                    // Check for null
                    if(hobbies != null &&
(!hobbies.equals("")))
                        SQL += "'" + hobbies + "')";
                    else
                        SQL += "null)";

            // Create Statement object
            Statement st = con.createStatement();

            // executeUpdate returns the number of rows
affected.
            int rowsAffected = st.executeUpdate(SQL);

            // Addition successful, close the Statement
object
            st.close();

            // tell the calling method, successful addition
            return true;
        } catch (SQLException se) {
            // Some problem with database operation
            se.printStackTrace();
            // tell the calling method, unsuccessful addition
            return false;
        }
    }

    private int getNextID() {
    /**
    * This method generates the next Person Id
    * by getting the maximum of PersonId
    * and incrementing by 1
    */
        int nextId;
        try {

            // Create Statement
            Statement st = con.createStatement();

            // Frame query to get maximum of PersonId
            ResultSet rs = st.executeQuery("Select
max(personID) as pID from PersonalInformation");

            /**
            * If the resultset is not empty then get the
            * person id number and increment it by 1
```

Continued

Listing 6-7 *(continued)*

```
            * else the table does not have records,
            * hence the next person Id is set to 1
            */
            if(rs.next())
                nextId = rs.getInt(1) + 1;
            else
                nextId = 1;

            // Close ResultSet and Statement
            rs.close();
            st.close();

            // return the next Person ID
            return nextId;
        } catch(SQLException se) {
            // Some problem with database operation
            se.printStackTrace();

            // return 0 to indicate that error has occurred
            return 0;
        }
    }
```

The `addNewRecord()` method adds a new record. This method is called when the module number is 2. Before we can add a new record, we must be aware that for each new person added we need a unique PersonId. Hence, we call the method `getNextId()`, which generates an Id. The `getNextId()` method posts a query requesting the maximum number in the table for the PersonId column. It increments this value by 1 and sends it back to the addNewRecord() method. If the table is empty, the method returns 1. Figure 6-17 shows the results of a successful addition of a new record to the database.

In the next step, we request information for all the fields from the previous entry screen and store it in temporary variables. Before we frame an insert query, we ensure that the fields do not contain `null` or empty values; if we get one, we make sure `null` is updated. The method returns `true` if the addition of record has been successful. If it has not been successful, a `false` value is sent back, and the calling function displays a general database error message. Listing 6-8 is the code for the method that displays all the records from the table.

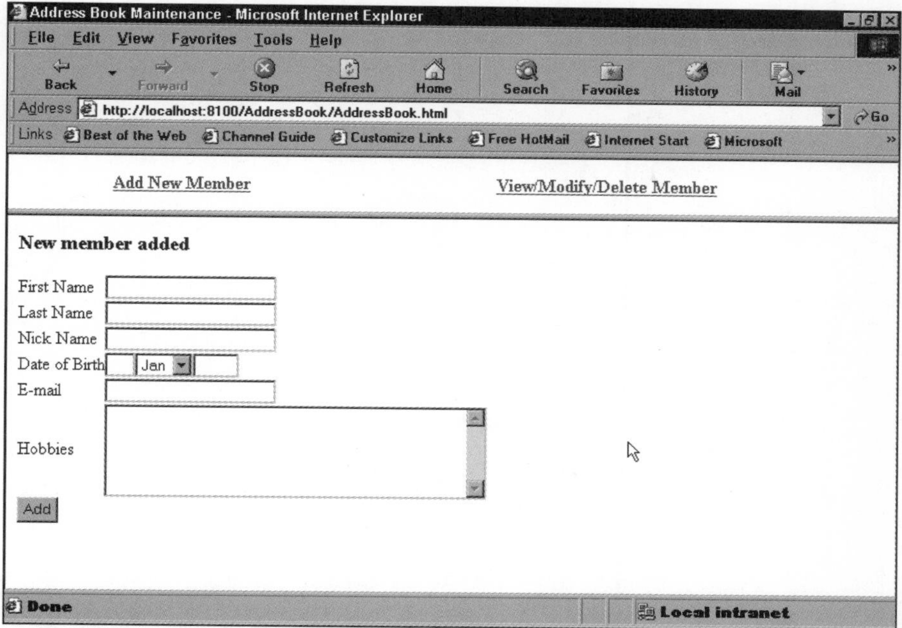

Figure 6-17: After the successful addition of a new record, the form is cleared, and the "New member added" message is displayed in the browser.

Listing 6-8

```
private String viewRecords() {
    /**
    * This method displays all the records
    * from the table. Only the First Name
    * Last Name and EMail address is displayed.
    * The First Name acts as a link. Clicking
    * on the link takes to the complete view of
    * information.
    */

    String html = "";

    // Create a table for viewing the list
    html = "<table cellpadding=0 cellspacing=0 border=1>";
    html += "<tr>";

    // Header
    html += "<th>First Name</th>";
    html += "<th>Last Name</th>";
```

Continued

Listing 6-8 *(continued)*

```
        html += "<th>E-Mail</th>";
        html += "</tr>";
        try {

            // Create the Statement object
            Statement st = con.createStatement();

            // Get PersonId, FirstName, LastName and
EMailAddress
            ResultSet rs = st.executeQuery("Select
PersonId,FirstName,LastName,EMailAddress from
PersonalInformation");

            // Go through the ResultSet
            while(rs.next()) {
                html += "<tr>";
                html += "<td>";

                    /**
                    * Frame the link for FirstName passing
the
                    * Module number and the Person Id
                    */
                    html += "<a
href='servletbible.ch06.examples.AddressBook?Module=4&PersonId=
" + rs.getInt(1) + "'>";

                    // get FirstName
                    html += rs.getString(2);
                    html += "</a>";
                html += "</td>";
                html += "<td>";

                // get LastName
                html += rs.getString(3);
                html += "</td>";
                html += "<td>";

                //get EMailAddress
                String eMail = rs.getString(4);

                // if eMail is null then display it as
unspecified instead of null
                if(eMail == null)

                    // &lt; and &gt; put the word
Unspecified between < and > symbol
                    eMail = "&lt;Unspecified&gt;";
                html += eMail;
                html += "</td>";
                html += "</tr>";
```

```
            }
            html += "</table>";

            // Close ResultSet and Statement
            rs.close();
            st.close();

            // return HTML
            return html;
        } catch(SQLException se) {
            // Some problem with database operation
            se.printStackTrace();

            // return error message
            return "Error during Database operation";
        }
    }
```

The `viewRecords()` method displays all the records in the table. We frame a hyperlink with the first name. The hyperlink reference contains this servlet name, and we append it with the query string containing the module number and the PersonId value. In case the `EMail` field is `null`, we display it in the table as "<Unspecified>" as shown in Figure 6-18.

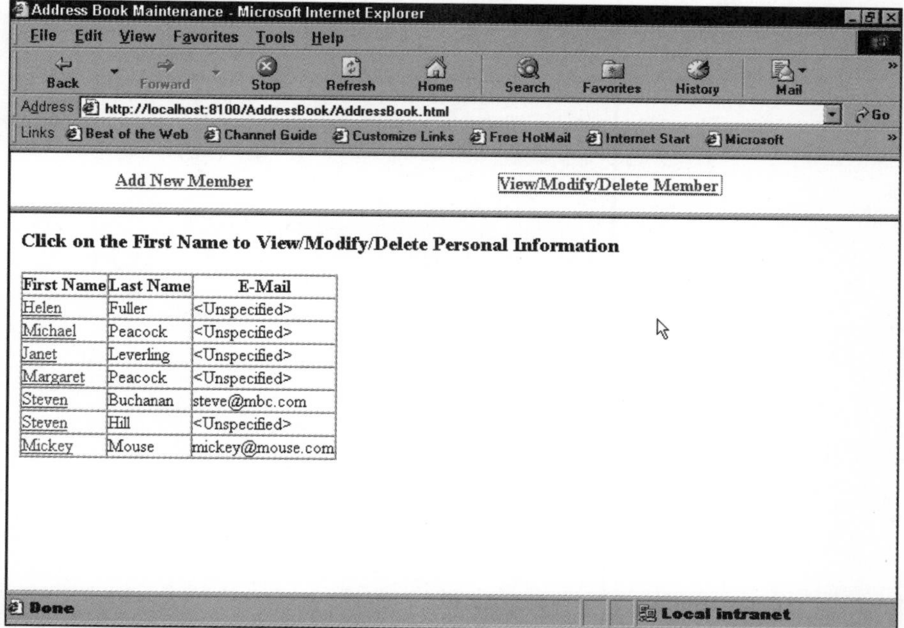

Figure 6-18: View all records from table

The next method we see is the `getEntryScreenWithData()`, which is similar to the `getEntryScreen()` method except that it fills up the data for the PersonId value passed as parameter. Listing 6-9 is the `getEntryScreenWithData()` method.

Listing 6-9

```
    private String getEntryScreenWithData(String personId){
    /**
    * This method is similar to getEntryScreen
    * method except that it fills in the data
    * for a particular person ID
    */
        String html = "";

        // Store months in an array
        final String months[] =
{"Jan","Feb","Mar","Apr","May","Jun","Jul","Aug","Sep","Oct",
"Nov","Dec"};
        try {

            // Create Statement
            Statement st = con.createStatement();

            // Frame query to get information for a person ID
            ResultSet rs = st.executeQuery("Select * from
PersonalInformation where PersonId = " + personId);

            // Go through the ResultSet
            if(rs.next()) {

                // Display in a table setting the border to
0.
                // This will align the labels and text
boxes.
                html += "<table cellpadding=0 cellspacing=0
border=0>";
                html += "<tr>";
                html += "<td>";
                html += "First Name";
                html += "</td>";
                html += "<td>";

                // Get FirstName
                html += "<input type=text id=FirstName
name=FirstName value='" + rs.getString(2) + "'>";
                html += "</input>";
                html += "</tr>";
                html += "<tr>";
```

```
                html += "<td>";
                html += "Last Name";
                html += "</td>";
                html += "<td>";

                // Get LastName
                html += "<input type=text id=LastName
name=LastName value='" + rs.getString(3) +"'>";
                html += "</input>";
                html += "</tr>";
                html += "<tr>";
                html += "<td>";
                html += "Nick Name";
                html += "</td>";
                html += "<td>";

                // Get NickName
                html += "<input type=text id=NickName
name=NickName value='";
                String nickName = rs.getString(4);
                if(nickName != null)
                    html += nickName;
                html += "'>";
                html += "</input>";
                html += "</tr>";
                html += "<tr>";
                html += "<td>";
                html += "Date of Birth";
                html += "</td>";
                html += "<td>";

                //Get Date of Birth
                java.util.Date dt = rs.getDate(5);
                String day="";
                int month=0;
                String year="";

                // Split the date into day, month and year
                if(dt != null) {
                    Calendar cal = Calendar.getInstance();
                    cal.setTime(dt);
                    // Day
                    day = "" +
cal.get(Calendar.DAY_OF_MONTH);

                    //Month
                    month = cal.get(Calendar.MONTH);
```

Continued

Listing 6-9 *(continued)*

```
                    //Year
                    year = "" + cal.get(Calendar.YEAR);
                }

                // Fill day
                html += "<input type=text id=Date name=Date
size=2 value='" + day + "'>";
                html += "</input>";

                // Fill all the months in a combo box
                html += "<select id=Month name=Month>";
                for(int i=0;i<12;i++) {
                    html += "<option ";

                    // Check if this month number is what
is in database
                    // If yes set this month as selected
                    if(month == i) html += "selected ";

                    // value is used to set the
corresponding month number.
                    // This value will be returned when a
request for this
                    // field is used.
                    html += "value=" + (i+1) + ">" +
months[i] + "</option>";
                }
                html += "</select>";

                // Fill Year
                html += "<input type=text id=Year name=Year
size=4 value='" + year + "'>";
                html += "</input>";
                html += "</tr>";
                html += "<tr>";
                html += "<td>";

                // Get EMailAddress
                html += "E-mail";
                html += "</td>";
                html += "<td>";
                String email = rs.getString(6);
                html += "<input type=text id=EMail
name=EMail value='";

                // Check for null
```

```
                if(email != null)
                    html += email;
                html += "'>";
                html += "</input>";
                html += "</tr>";
                html += "<tr>";
                html += "<td>";

                // Get Hobbies
                html += "Hobbies";
                html += "</td>";
                html += "<td>";
                String hobbies = rs.getString(7);
                html += "<TextArea id=Hobbies name=Hobbies
rows=5 cols=40>";

                // Check for null
                if(hobbies != null)
                    html += hobbies;
                html += "</TextArea>";
                html += "</tr>";
                html += "</table>";
            }

            // Close ResultSet and Statement
            rs.close();
            st.close();
            return html;
        } catch(SQLException se) {

            // Some problem with database operation
            se.printStackTrace();

            // return error message
            return "Error occured during Database operation";
        }
    }
```

The PersonId is passed as a parameter to this method. The method retrieves the information for that PersonId from the table and fills the fields as shown in Figure 6-19.

The next method is the `updateRecord()`, which updates the data entered in the screen for that PersonId. Listing 6-10 is the code for `updateRecord()` method.

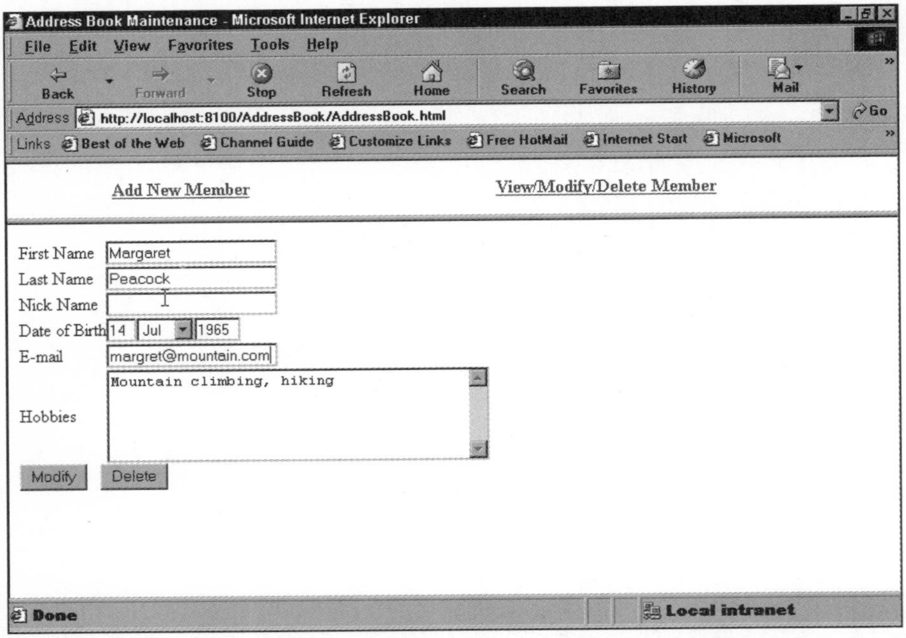

Figure 6-19: Address Book main screen with View, Modify, and Delete functions added

Listing 6-10

```
    private boolean updateRecord(String
personId,HttpServletRequest request) {
    /**
    * This method updates a record for a person id.
    * The request parameter is used to get the values
    */
        try {

            // Get all the information
            String firstName =
request.getParameter("FirstName");
            String lastName =
request.getParameter("LastName");
            String nickName =
request.getParameter("NickName");
            String date = request.getParameter("Date");
            String year = request.getParameter("Year");
            String dob;
```

```
            // Check if Date of Birth is available
            if(date != null && year != null &&
!(date.equals("") || date.equals("")))
                dob = request.getParameter("Month") + "/" +
date + "/" + year;
            else
                dob = null;
            String eMail = request.getParameter("EMail");
            String hobbies = request.getParameter("Hobbies");

            // Frame Query for Updating the information
            String SQL = "Update PersonalInformation set ";
                    SQL += "FirstName = '" + firstName +
"',";

                    SQL += "LastName = '" + lastName +
"',";

                    SQL += "NickName = ";

                    // Check for null
                    if(nickName != null
&&(!nickName.equals("")))
                        SQL += "'" + nickName + "',";
                    else
                        SQL += "null,";

                    SQL += "BirthDate = ";

                    // Check for null
                    if(dob != null)
                        SQL += "'" + dob + "',";
                    else
                        SQL += "null,";

                    SQL += "EMailAddress = ";

                    // Check for null
                    if(eMail != null &&
(!eMail.equals("")))
                        SQL += "'" + eMail + "',";
                    else
                        SQL += "null,";

                    SQL += "Hobbies = ";

                    //Check for null
                    if(hobbies != null &&
(!hobbies.equals("")))
                        SQL += "'" + hobbies + "' ";
                    else
                        SQL += "null ";
```

Continued

Listing 6-10 *(continued)*

```
                    SQL += "where PersonId = " + personId;

            // Create Statement
            Statement st = con.createStatement();

            // executeUpdate returns the number of rows
affected
            int rowsAffected = st.executeUpdate(SQL);

            // Updation successful, close the Statement
object
            st.close();

            // tell the calling method, successful addition
            return true;
        } catch (SQLException se) {

            // Some problem with database operation
            se.printStackTrace();

            // return error message
            return false;
        }
    }

    private boolean deleteRecord(String personId) {
    /**
    * This method deletes a record who has the ID of personId
    */
        try {

            // Create Statement
            Statement st = con.createStatement();

            // Frame query for deleting record with this
personId
            // executeUpdate returns the number of rows
affected
            int rowsAffected = st.executeUpdate("Delete from
PersonalInformation where PersonId = " + personId);

            // Deletion successful, close the Statement
object
            st.close();

            // tell the calling method, successful deletion
            return true;
        } catch(SQLException se) {
            // Some problem with database operation
```

```
            se.printStackTrace();

            // return error message
            return false;
        }
    }
}
// End of AddressBook Servlet
```

The updateRecord() method modifies a record. This method is called when the servlet is called with a module value of *5*. The method takes in the PersonId and the HttpServletRequest object as parameters. We frame the Update query after checking for null values and replacing appropriate values before it is executed. The method returns a Boolean value to indicate whether or not the operation has been successful.

The deleteRecord() method deletes a record. The person who has to be deleted is identified with the help of the PersonId parameter. A successful deletion returns a true value to the calling method and returns false in case of errors. Figure 6-20 shows successful deletion.

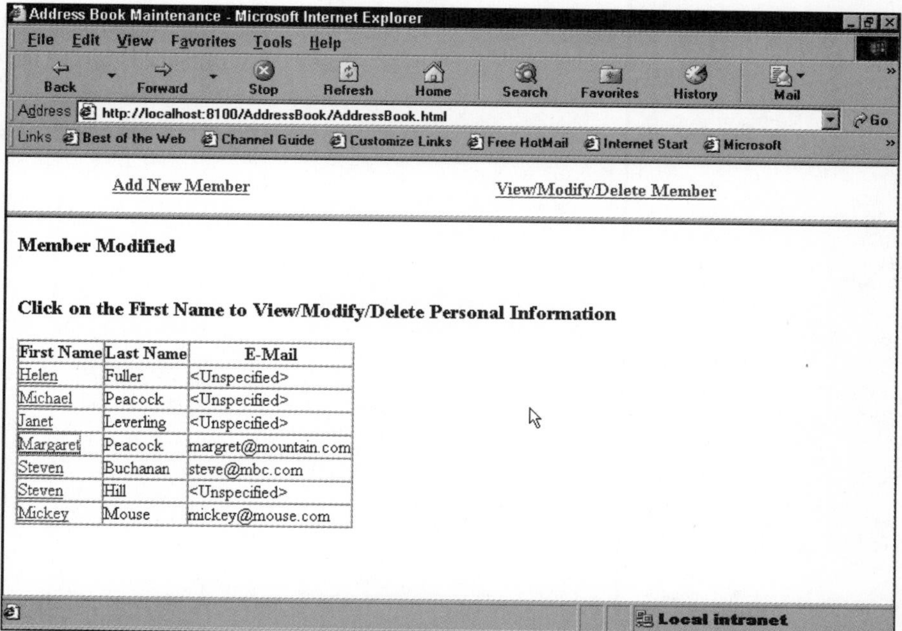

Figure 6-20: After successful modification of a record, the table is displayed in the browser along with the "Member Modified" message.

Summary

In this chapter, we learned the evolution of database systems and discussed the advantages and disadvantages of them. We discussed ODBC and its importance in applications communicating to various DBMS. We learned about JDBC, its architecture and types of drivers and their importance for Java-based applications. We learned about the JDBC-ODBC Bridge and how to set up a Data Source Name to connect to a Microsoft Access database. We covered an example of a thin (Type 4) driver using the Oracle JDBC driver. We learned the important interfaces in the `java.sql` package such as the Connection, Statement, PreparedStatement, and ResultSet interfaces. We discussed connection pooling and how important it is in effectively utilizing and maintaining connections to the database servers. We also saw a good example of database usage in "servlets" through the `AddressBook` servlet.

✦ ✦ ✦

CHAPTER 7

Exception Handling

✦ ✦ ✦ ✦

In This Chapter

Exceptions defined

Java exception handling in brief

Built-in exceptions relevant to servlets

Exception handling in servlets

Creating your own exceptions

A few general guidelines

Performance implications of exceptions

✦ ✦ ✦ ✦

Understanding Exceptions

An *exception* is an abnormal condition that occurs during runtime execution of a program. The term *exception* means exemption or omission. In software parlance it means unexpected disruption of program flow.

An exception may be thrown when the program deviates from its expected normal behavior. For instance, absence or limitation of required resources can cause an exception. Also, defects in the design or implementation of the software system can cause exceptions. Exceptions affect the normal flow of execution. Any nontrivial application should anticipate and handle the exceptions to minimize potential damages.

Servlets are written in Java and are run in a restricted environment in case access privileges are not sufficient. Hence, the chances of servlets corrupting the server are very low even if they are run in-process. Java's native-memory protection and security management guard the server process. Servlets should handle exceptions for user notification and graceful degradation of the system.

Java Exception Handling in Brief

Java's exception handling is akin to that of C++. It follows the `try`, `throw` and `catch` models. The originating method that `throws` the exception should be enclosed in the `try` block. `catch` blocks handle thrown exceptions. Java's unique concept is the `finally` block, defining the code that is always executed at end:

```
try
{
    // Code that may throw the exception
}
catch( Exception e )
```

```
{
    // Exception handling logic
}
finally
{
    // Code executed at end under all circumstances
}
```

All exceptions in Java are subclassed from the `Throwable` class.

A method that does not intend to catch an exception it throws should declare the exception in the `throws` clause as illustrated here:

```
static void SomeMethod() throws SomeException {...}
```

If a statement in the `try` block throws an exception, control goes to the `catch` block. If the block does not handle the exception, it is passed to the method's caller. In a servlet, typically this goes until it reaches a `doGet()` or `doPost()` before the execution is terminated. If the `catch` block can handle the exception, the `catch` block is executed.

Java exceptions are of two kinds: checked and unchecked. *Checked exceptions* are compiler-enforced; the exceptions must either be declared in the `throws` clause or should be caught. This way the programmer is forced to pay attention to the exceptions. *Unchecked exceptions* are runtime exceptions and their derivatives. The compiler does not mandate the handling of unchecked exceptions.

Built-in Exceptions Relevant to Servlets

Built-in exceptions are part of the Java language specification. You will frequently use certain of the following built-in exceptions for servlet exception handling.

IOException

Even though `IOException` is not specific to servlets alone, we should see a brief description of this, as it is thrown by primary servlet methods in case of network errors. When it comes to networking, socket errors can occur anytime. `IOException` is thrown by the main servlet methods to denote such communication errors. Because `IOException` is outside the domain of general servlet issues, the servlet container, rather than servlets themselves, should handle it.

ServletException

The class hierarchy of `ServletException` is

```
java.lang.Object➪java.lang.Throwable➪java.lang.Exception➪
javax.servlet.ServletException
```

The servlet throws `ServletException` to indicate a general servlet problem. If an exception is not intently thrown by the servlet, the servlet container handles it. It is good design to catch the common exceptions and to handle them gracefully.

The `ServletException` class has two constructors: one that takes a `String` parameter and another that takes none:

```
public ServletException(String msg)
public ServletException()
```

The `String` passed is a brief description of the error message.

UnavailableException

The Class hierarchy of `UnavailableException` is

```
java.lang.object➪java.lang.Throwable➪java.lang.Exception➪
javax.servlet.ServletException➪
javax.servlet.UnavailableException
```

The servlet throws `UnavailableException` to indicate its unavailability, both permanently and temporarily.

Unrecoverable errors such as configuration issues and missing required resources make the servlet permanently unavailable. One of the overloaded constructors of the `UnavailableException` class is used to indicate permanent unavailability:

```
public UnavailableException(Servlet servlet, String msg)
```

You can pass the `this` object as the first parameter.

A servlet may be temporarily unavailable due to a momentary resource crunch or network load. The following constructor should be used to indicate temporary unavailability:

```
public UnavailableException(int seconds, Servlet servlet,
String msg)
```

The extra parameter with respect to the other constructor, `int seconds`, is used to denote how long the servlet is estimated to be temporarily unavailable in seconds. Pass zero or a negative value if no estimate is available.

The servlet environment's handling of `UnavailableException` is implementation specific. Typically, the servlet container/Web server environment handles the `UnavailableException` by throwing a polite message. If you want the system to behave consistently across all implementations, you can choose to handle the `UnavailableException` on your own as described in the next section.

Exception Handling in Servlets

In this section, you will learn some of the possible servlet exception-handling strategies. Based on your specific requirements, you can choose and combine the techniques to chalk your own exception-handling strategy.

Leaving the ServletException unhandled

As a good development practice, a `ServletException` should be caught and handled by the servlet. The way servlet containers treat unhandled exceptions in tandem with the Web server depends on the implementation. Certain containers write the stack trace to the client, whereas certain containers just log the exception. Certain other containers discard and then reload the servlet. The idiosyncratic behavior of a particular servlet container might result in inconsistencies while porting to other servlet-engine implementations.

Listing 7-1 shows an example servlet that constructs and throws a `ServletException` without handling it.

Listing 7-1

```
package servletbible.ch07.examples;
import java.io.*;
import javax.servlet.*;
import javax.servlet.http.*;

public class Unhandled extends HttpServlet
{
     public void doGet(HttpServletRequest request,
HttpServletResponse response) throws ServletException, IOException
     {

     /**
```

```
        * Construct and throw a ServletExpetion object
        * that is not caught by the Servlet
        * and left to be handled by the Server
        */

          throw new ServletException("Exception not handled by
Servlet");
     }
}
```

JRun handles the exception by setting the HTTP status code to `500 - SC_INTERNAL_SERVER_ERROR`. Figure 7-1 shows Internet Explorer displaying an error page that contains the following message:

```
HTTP 500 - Internal server error
```

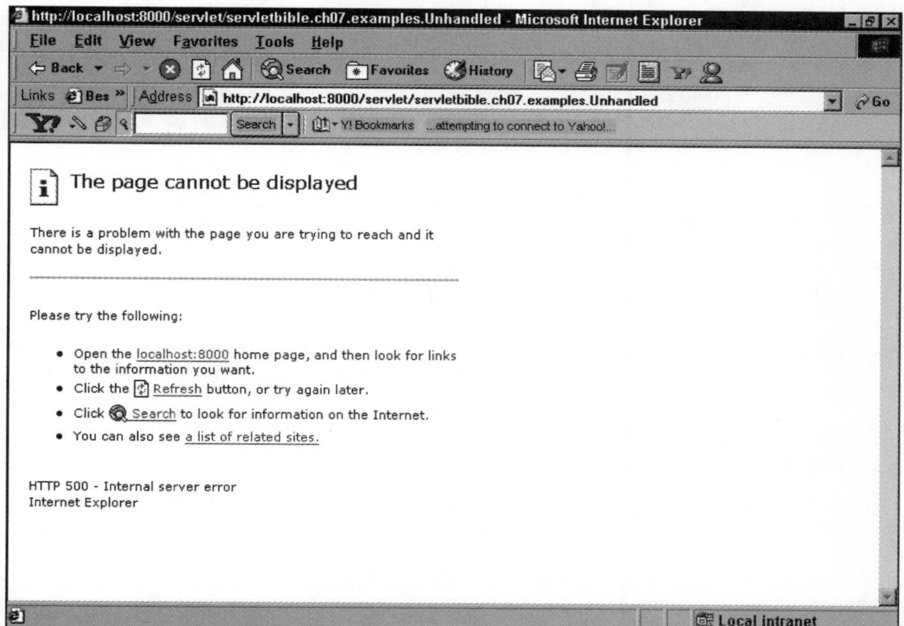

Figure 7-1: ServletException handled by Web Server

JRun logs the exception message in the error log. You can find the JRun error log file `error.log` in the directory `<JRun InstallDir>\jsm-default\services\jseweb\logs`. The stack trace is printed in the log (that is, method invocations by the thread are recorded right from the first method to the current method). Listing 7-2 shows the portion of `error.log` written when the example servlet is executed.

Listing 7-2

```
Mon Jan 24 18:17:13 GMT+05:30 2000: Running servlet
{ (Running servlet) javax.servlet.ServletException: Exception not
handled by Servlet
     at servletbible.ch07.examples.Unhandled.doGet(Unhandled.java:18)
     at javax.servlet.http.HttpServlet.service(Compiled Code)
     at javax.servlet.http.HttpServlet.service(Compiled Code)
     at com.livesoftware.jrun.JRun.runServlet(Compiled Code)
     at com.livesoftware.jrun.JRunGeneric.handleConnection(Compiled
Code)
     at
com.livesoftware.jrun.service.web.JRunWebServiceHandler.handleOutput
(Compiled Code)
     at
com.livesoftware.jrun.service.web.JRunWebServiceHandler.handleRequest
(Compiled Code)
     at
com.livesoftware.jrun.service.ThreadConfigHandler.run(Compiled Code)
    }
```

Handling the ServletException

You can handle the `ServletException` by catching the exception from within the servlet. The error can be explained to the client in the following ways:

- ✦ Return an error code using the `sendError()` method of `HttpServletResponse`.
- ✦ Set the status code `setStatus()` method of `HttpServletResponse`, and return a response explaining the error.
- ✦ Log the error to the server's log file by using the `log()` method of `ServletContext`.
- ✦ Print the stack trace in the response during development.

Previously, we saw that JRun logs the unhandled exceptions in the error log. Exceptions the servlet handles are not recorded in the error log. A caveat to consider while using the status-code approach is that nothing should be in the response object while setting the status code.

Using HttpServletResponse's sendError()

A servlet can return an HTTP status code as an error code by using the `sendError()` method of `HttpServletResponse`. Typically, Web servers generate a response body that explains the error to the client based on the error code. Listing 7-3 shows an example servlet that illustrates this idea.

Listing 7-3

```
package servletbible.ch07.examples;
import java.io.*;
import javax.servlet.*;
import javax.servlet.http.*;

public class SendError extends HttpServlet
{
     public void doGet(HttpServletRequest request,
HttpServletResponse response) throws ServletException, IOException
     {
       try
       {
       /**
       * Construct and throw a ServletException object
       */
          throw new ServletException("Exception in Servlet");
       }
       catch(ServletException exception)
       {
       /**
       * Set the response status code to 404 (File not found )
       */
            response.sendError(response.SC_NOT_FOUND);
       }

     }
}
```

`SC_NOT_FOUND` maps to the common HTTP status code 404, implying that the file has not been found. When you invoke the servlet, you find the following error message displayed in the browser (See Figure 7-2):

```
HTTP 404 - File not found.
```

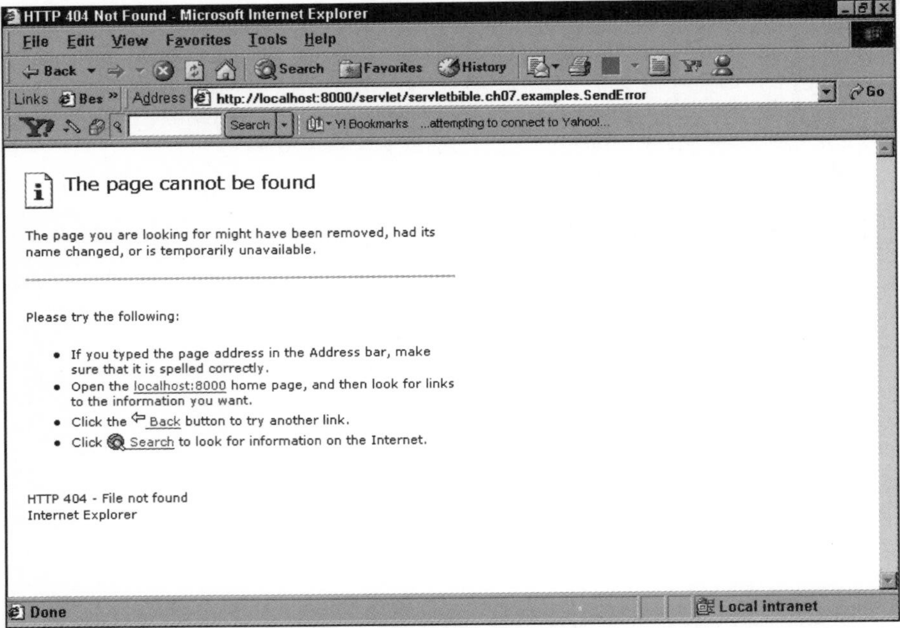

Figure 7-2: Error reported using HttpServletResponse

Setting the status and writing your own response

If the servlet intends to return a response formatted ad-hoc rather than relying on the Web server's way of formatting based on error code, the servlet can return a status code with `HttpServletResponse's setStatus()` and a response body explaining the error (shown in Listing 7-4).

Listing 7-4

```
package servletbible.ch07.examples;
import java.io.*;
import javax.servlet.*;
import javax.servlet.http.*;

public class SetStatus extends HttpServlet
{
     public void doGet(HttpServletRequest request,
HttpServletResponse response) throws ServletException, IOException
     {
       try
       {
       /**
       * Construct and throw a ServletException object
       */
```

```
            throw new ServletException("Exception in Servlet");
        }
        catch(ServletException exception)
        {
        /**
        * Set the status code and format the response
        */
            response.setStatus(response.SC_GONE);
          response.setContentType("text/plain");
          PrintWriter out = response.getWriter();
          out.println("Running out of resources");
          out.close();
        }


    }
}
```

You can see the response as formatted in your way. The client displays the following message (as seen in Figure 7-3):

```
Running out of resources.
```

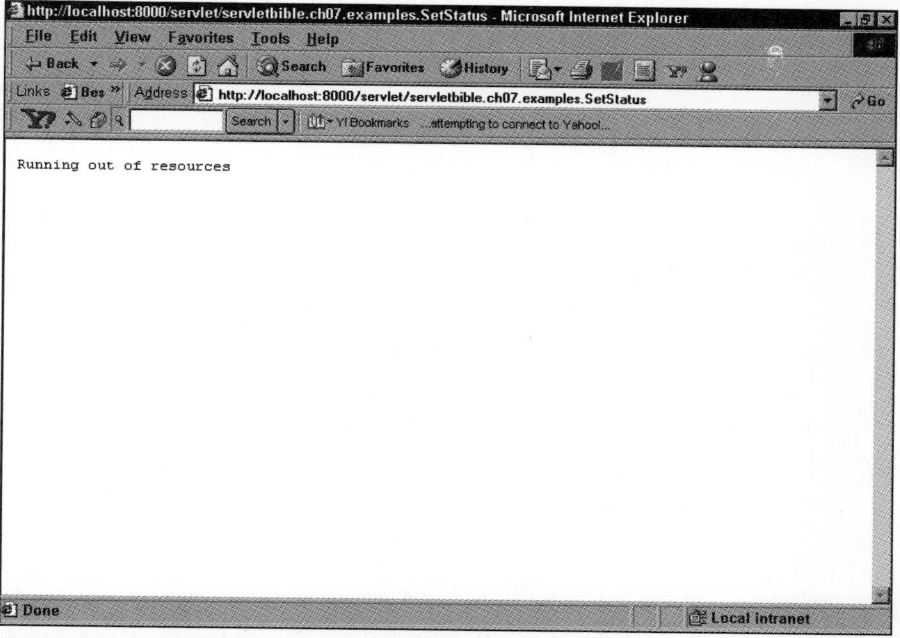

Figure 7-3: Exception reported using your own response

Logging the error

You can log the exception in the log file of a servlet container. The following overloaded methods of `ServletContext` are used for logging the exception:

```
public void log(String msg)
public void log(Exception e, String msg)
```

The first method writes an error message to the log, whereas the second messages prints the stack trace in the log apart from writing the message. The output format of the log message, the name of the log file, and the location of the log file depend on the implementation. For JRun, the location of the log file is `<JRun InstallDir>\jsm-default\services\jseweb\logs`, and the name of the log file is `event.log`. Listing 7-5 shows a servlet that illustrates the logging functionality.

Listing 7-5

```
package servletbible.ch07.examples;
import java.io.*;
import javax.servlet.*;
import javax.servlet.http.*;

public class LogError extends HttpServlet
{
     public void doGet(HttpServletRequest request,
HttpServletResponse response) throws ServletException, IOException
     {
       try
       {
       /**
       * Construct and throw a ServletExpetion object
       */
          throw new ServletException("Exception for log");
       }
       catch(ServletException exception)
       {
       /**
       * Log the thrown exception
       */
            getServletContext().log(exception,"Sent to Log");
          response.setContentType("text/plain");
          PrintWriter out = response.getWriter();
          out.println("Please see the log");
          out.close();
       }

     }
}
```

Invoke the preceding servlet, and view the event log file. You find a log message similar to Listing 7-6 as the latest entry.

Listing 7-6

```
Mon Jan 24 22:45:09 GMT+05:30 2000: Sent to Log
{ (Sent to Log) javax.servlet.ServletException: Exception for log
     at servletbible.ch07.examples.LogError.doGet(LogError.java:15)
     at javax.servlet.http.HttpServlet.service(HttpServlet.java:715)
     at javax.servlet.http.HttpServlet.service(HttpServlet.java:840)
     at com.livesoftware.jrun.JRun.runServlet(Compiled Code)
     at
com.livesoftware.jrun.JRunGeneric.handleConnection(JRunGeneric.java:
116)
     at com.livesoftware.jrun.service.web.JRunWebServiceHandler.handleOutput
(JRunWebServiceHandler.java:266)
     at com.livesoftware.jrun.service.web.JRunWebServiceHandler.handleRequest
(Compiled Code)
     at com.livesoftware.jrun.service.ThreadConfigHandler.run(Compiled Code)
 }
```

Printing the stack trace

Even though there are ways to log the exception stack trace, during development, you may find it easier to see the stack trace in the response to the client. You can't directly convert a stack trace to `String`, but you may print it directly to a `PrintWriter` object (as shown in Listing 7-7).

Listing 7-7

```
package servletbible.ch07.examples;
import java.io.*;
import javax.servlet.*;
import javax.servlet.http.*;

public class PrintTrace extends HttpServlet
{
     public void doGet(HttpServletRequest request,
HttpServletResponse response) throws ServletException, IOException
     {
       try
       {
       /**
```

Continued

Listing 7-7 (continued)

```
        * Construct and throw a ServletExpetion object
        */
           throw new ServletException("Exception for Stack Trace");
        }
        catch(ServletException exception)
        {
        /**
        * Print the Stack Trace into response
        */
              response.setContentType("text/plain");
           PrintWriter out = response.getWriter();
           exception.printStackTrace(out);
           out.close();
        }

    }
}
```

Figure 7-4 shows the stack trace printed in the response body upon invoking the servlet.

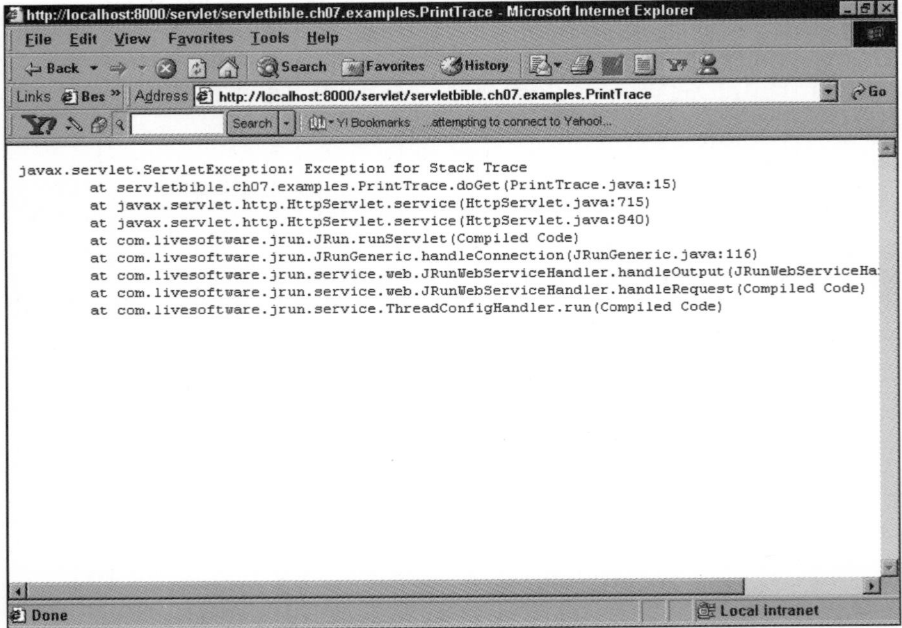

Figure 7-4: The stack trace

Creating Your Own Exceptions

Not all exceptions in the servlet are due to general servlet problems. Exceptions may occur because of XML parsing, database connectivity, incorrect parameters to a business object, and so on. Although certain abnormal conditions can be indicated by throwing standard Java exceptions provided off the shelf, certain conditions are best indicated by custom exceptions. A good design strategy is to handle all major exceptions by a common-handler method. This may necessitate a custom-exception hierarchy.

To create your own exception, subclass from `Throwable` and provide constructor(s). Then you can use the `CustomException` as you would use the built-in Java exception (as in Listing 7-8).

Listing 7-8

```
public class CustomException extends Throwable
{
     public CustomException(String str)
     {
          super(str);
     }
}



package servletbible.ch07.examples;
import java.io.*;
import javax.servlet.*;
import javax.servlet.http.*;


public class YourOwnException extends HttpServlet
{
     public void doGet(HttpServletRequest request,
HttpServletResponse response) throws ServletException, IOException
     {

     /**
       * Construct and throw a CustomException object
       */
       try
       {
          throw new CustomException("Custom Exception");
       }
       catch(CustomException exception)
       {
```

Continued

Listing 7-8 *(continued)*

```
        /**
        * Print the Stack Trace into response
        */
              response.setContentType("text/plain");
            PrintWriter out = response.getWriter();
            exception.printStackTrace(out);
            out.close();

        }


      }
}
```

The `CustomException` class is a publicly defined class visible to all Java programs, provided that the `CLASSPATH` contains the `.class` file (see Figure 7-5).

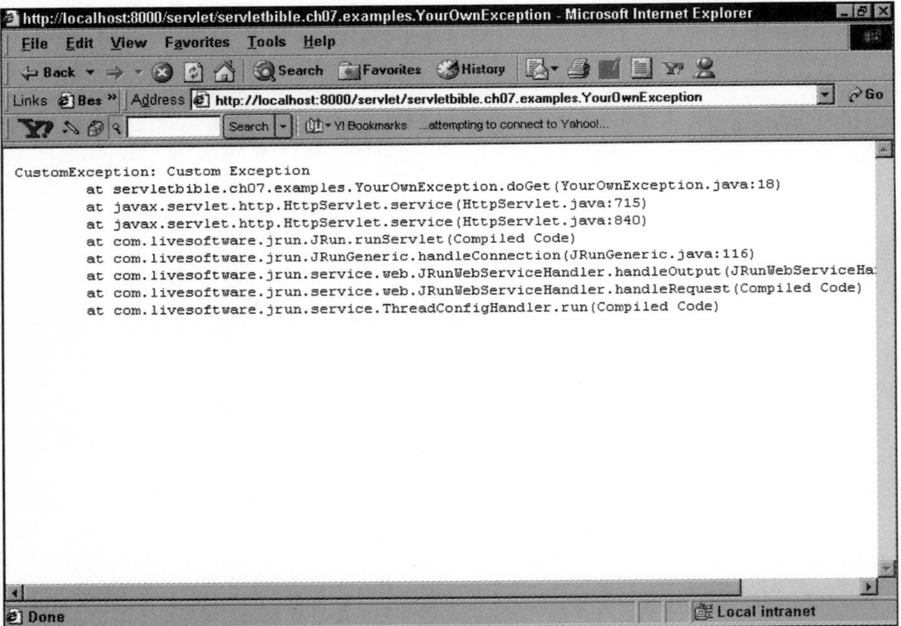

Figure 7-5: Custom Exception thrown in a Servlet

We have seen how to create a custom exception subclassed from the `Throwable` class.

A Few General Guidelines

You find a few general guidelines regarding servlet exception handling in this section. Please note that although these general guidelines work well under most circumstances, the specifics of your system may require you to depart from them.

Let the exceptions trickle to the top

Consider the following skeleton servlet snippet, which involves `doGet()` calling a number of methods – the methods handling the exceptions within themselves:

```
     public void doGet(HttpServletRequest req, HttpServletResponse
res) throws ServletException, IOException
     {
          try
          {
               method1();
               method2();
               method3();
          }
   }
method1()
{
try
{
           // Do something
}
catch( Exception exception)
{
// Handle the exception by writing the error message to // HTML
denoting 'exception' occurred in 'method1'

}
}
```

Here the exception is handled in the method in which it has occurred intending to indicate the exact context of the exception. The potential issue with this approach is that control goes to the calling method, where it may catch another exception. A better way is to let the exception trickle to the top and to handle it in the top level at one place, say, the `doGet()` method of the servlet. The stack trace indicates where the exception has occurred if need be.

Rethrow the exceptions

After a `catch` block is executed, its subsequent statement is executed. If you have a sequence of methods called from `doGet()`, `doPost`, or `service()` that handle the exceptions within themselves, control returns to the subsequent method after the exception is handled. To avoid this, rethrow the exception in the `catch` block so that execution terminates after an exception is handled:

```
     public void doGet(HttpServletRequest req, HttpServletResponse
res) throws ServletException, IOException
     {
          method1();
          method2();
          method3();
   }
method1()
{
try
{
            // Do something
}
catch( Exception exception)
{
            // Handle the exception
// RETHROW THE EXCEPTION
throw exception;
}
}
```

Handle all exceptions at one place, but one by one

Although it is better to handle all exceptions in one place, this does not mean exceptions should be handled with a single handler. This does not add value to the exception scheme, as it is not expressive. By subclassing exceptions neatly, you can handle each exception class in its own `catch` handler block. This improves code readability, and you can handle each exception differently.

Handle user interruption of servlet execution

You should add a `finally` block in the servlet that contains code to free up all the allocated resources. Using the `checkError()` method of the `PrintWriter` object, you should frequently check whether there is any error writing to the output. If so, the servlet should terminate.

Performance Implications of Exceptions

Java Virtual Machine (JVM) maintains a method-invocation stack or call stack. The call stack enlists the methods invoked by the thread en route as the exception bubbles to the top of the order. The path of the exception can be traced by using the call stack.

Java methods keep the state in stack. Each method is endowed with a stack frame used as method local storage. The stack frame is pushed onto the stack as the method is invoked and is popped from the stack as the method invocation ends.

The normal execution of a servlet does not cause any significant performance issues as stack frames are pushed and popped out of the stack. But an exception at the lower level does cause the JVM to pop methods one by one out of the stack until the right handler is found. If the exception is permitted to trickle to the top, it means more effort in terms of stack unwinding and maintaining stack trace.

Summary

This chapter covered the breadth of exceptions: Java exception handling, built-in exceptions relevant to servlets, and exception handling in servlets. You also learned how to create your own exceptions, their general guidelines, and their performance implications.

In the next chapter, we delve into sockets, procedure calls, and remote method invocation.

✦ ✦ ✦

Working with RMI

✦ ✦ ✦ ✦

In This Chapter

Sockets

Remote procedure calls

RMI

RMI architecture

Locating remote objects

Up and running with RMI (an echo server example)

RMI compiler

RMI and security

Example RMI stock quote server

Example servlet accessing the stock quote server

✦ ✦ ✦ ✦

"The Network is the computer" and "Java is the platform" read the latest slogans from Sun Microsystems. Computers have become an inevitable part of industrialized living, and it is very obvious that a standalone computer is of no use. Network programming has been an arefor whiz-kids for a long time. A person who wants to write a network application has to know a lot of things to write it successfully. In particular, he or she has to bother about the protocols that must be implemented.

A protocol is a set of rules that two applications agree upon to communicate with each other. As an example, let's look into how a telephone conversation occurs.

1. Person one who wants to talk to person two lifts the receiver.
2. Person one dials person two's number.
3. Person two's telephone rings.
4. Person two lifts the receiver.
5. Person two says, "Hello."
6. Person one acknowledges and identifies himself to person two.
7. Person two starts talking to person one and vice-versa.

Things have changed a lot since then, and network programming has become simpler. The predominant network protocol, TCP/IP, exposed a low-level set of APIs known as *socket APIs*, which can be used by application programmers to write distributed/networked applications. However, because the socket APIs were C-based libraries, most of the network applications were written using the C programming language. The Java programming language broke this constraint by providing access to the socket libraries as part of the Java language itself. Thus, the language enabled the application programmer to exploit the power of object-oriented concepts while creating distributed applications. The Java programming language has a separate package related to network programming, which is part of the JDK API specification. In this chapter, we look into the various methods available for writing networked applications. We also look in detail at the remote method invocation (RMI) in Java. Finally, we look into how RMI and servlets are used together.

Sockets

Sockets can be called the assembly language for network programming. The socket APIs provide the lowest-level interface to write network programs. The socket API helps you use the network protocol features and enables you to have fine-grained control over the programs you write.

In a socket-based application, data is transmitted over the network as a stream of bytes. The receiving end of the application interprets the byte stream and takes appropriate action. A stream is a sequence of bytes. The socket-based communication represents a full-duplex communication, which provides a means of exchanging data between two applications running in different machines located remotely.

Remote Procedure Calls

Remote procedure calls (RPCs) go a step beyond socket-based communications. Instead of sending streams of data over the network, which other applications interpret, RPC enables you to call procedures located remotely. It defines a mechanism for how methods should be called and how to pass the parameters to those methods. RPC is used primarily in C-based distributed applications. RPC is a procedure-oriented method for writing distributed applications.

Remote Method Invocation

Remote method invocation is an object-oriented, Java-based method for writing distributed applications. Using RMI, applications running in one Java virtual machine can communicate with applications running in a different Java virtual machine. The biggest advantage in this is that RMI makes life very simple, and the programmer need not be bothered about the intricacies of making the two applications communicate over a network. Using RMI, the method call on an object located in a different virtual machine appears the same as a method call for the same object running in the same virtual machine.

RMI Architecture

The primary objectives in the RMI architecture's design are to

- ✦ Keep the architecture as simple as possible
- ✦ Hide the complications of establishing a network communication and exchange of data between two applications
- ✦ Provide a seamless and natural integration of the concept with the Java language
- ✦ Make remote method calls on a remote object look the same as local method calls on a local object
- ✦ Ensure that remote method calls are secure and comply with the Java security model

RMI and interfaces

RMI architecture is based on one important concept in Java: interfaces. Interfaces define a template for the behavior an object exhibits; an interface defines names of methods and the parameters that have to be passed to methods. If an object is said to support a particular interface, it has to implement all methods defined in the interface.

Let's look at an example to understand this concept.

Consider the following interface:

```
public interface Car
{
    void drive(void);
    void turnLeft();
    void turnRight();
}

public class Ford implements Car
{
    void drive(void)
    {
          .
          .
          .
    }

    void turnLeft()
    {
          .
          .
          .
    }
```

```
        void turnRight()
        {
            .
            .
            .
        }

    }
```

The Car interface defines the features to be provided by a Car. How these features are provided depends on the Car manufacturer. A Honda City manufacturer has its own way of implementing the drive, turnLeft, and turnRight methods. A Ford manufacturer provides a different implementation for the same methods. Thus, interfaces help in providing a blueprint, which can be used to develop applications in an effective and fast manner. Interfaces help to separate the definition of the behavior of an object from its actual implementation.

By separating method definitions from the implementation, it becomes easy to handle changes to an object implementation. Client code uses interfaces to refer to the actual object rather than referring directly to the object itself. When we require changes to be made to an object, we change only the object's implementation class, not the interface. Because there is no change in the interface the client uses, the client continues work without problems.

RMI makes extensive use of this concept. In fact, RMI mandates the usage of interfaces as a paradigm for method definitions. Any remote method call the client invokes is issued on an interface. It is not possible to invoke a call on the remote object implementation directly.

In RMI, the server object exposes the methods clients can access through interfaces. Clients need not know about the implementation details of the server. Interface details are sufficient for clients to invoke methods on the server object. Figure 8-1 illustrates the relationship between a client, server, and an interface in the RMI world.

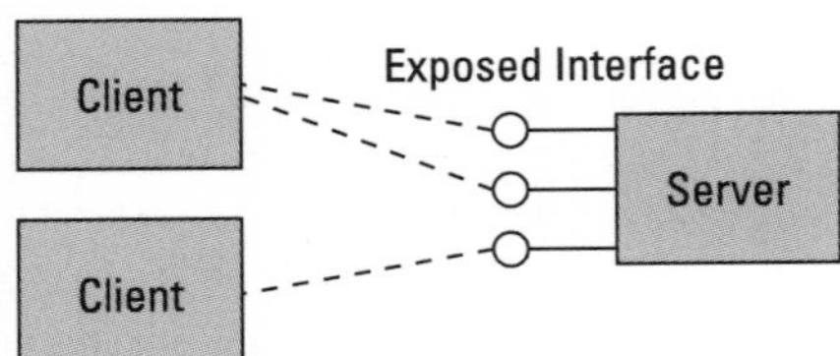

Figure 8-1: Interfaces

RMI architecture layers

The diagram in Figure 8-2 shows the various levels and components in the RMI architecture.

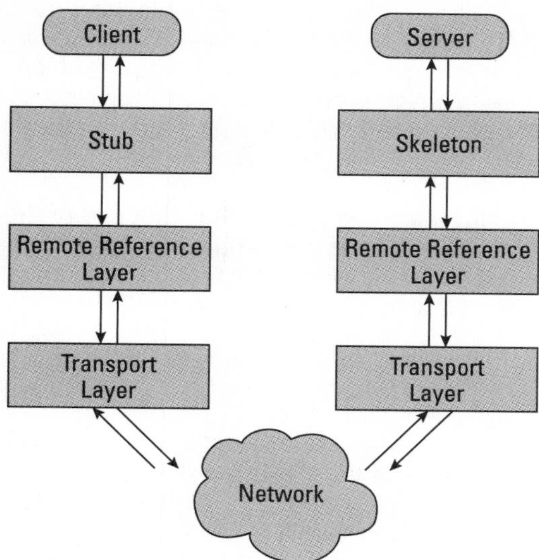

Figure 8-2: RMI architecture layers

The RMI architecture is based on a layered approach. The various layers in the RMI architecture are explained as follows:

- ✦ Layer 1 — This layer is also called the *application layer*. All applications (clients and servers) execute in this layer. Clients, which access a remote object, and server programs, which expose services and are called by clients from the network, reside at this layer.
- ✦ Layer 2 — Layer 2 is also called the *proxy layer*. This layer is very important in the RMI architecture. Client-invoked remote method calls come to this layer. The stub, which exists on the client side, is responsible for accepting the remote method call the client initiates and for sending the request to the server. It also takes care of marshaling all the parameters the client passes to the server. The skeleton exists on the server side of the architecture and is responsible for receiving all the information the stub sends. The skeleton unmarshals all the parameters it receives and calls the appropriate method on the server. Upon completion of execution of the remote method on the server, the skeleton receives the response from the server and sends it back to the client. The client receives the data the skeleton sends and passes it back to the application.

✦ Layer 3—The *remote reference layer* is responsible for handling all the semantics of remote invocations. The remote reference layer acts as the interface between the stub/skeleton layer and the transport layer and translates all the information the stub/skeleton provides to a form the transport layer can understand.

✦ Layer 4—The *transport layer* is responsible for machine-to-machine communication in the RMI architecture. The ultimate goal in a network communication is the transfer of data from one machine to another. The transport layer achieves this task by establishing a physical connection with the remote server and passes the data from the client to the transport layer in the remote server.

An important advantage we gain by using a layered approach is that any of the layers can be replaced by a different implementation without affecting the other layers. For example, the transport layer, which uses TCP/IP for transferring data to and from the remote machine, can be replaced with a combination of UDP/IP.

Stubs and skeletons

The stub/skeleton layer lies just beneath the application layer in the RMI architecture. At this point, let's recall one of the goals of designing the RMI architecture.

> Remote method calls on a remote object should look the same as local method calls on a local object.

This is popularly referred to as *location transparency*. Any data in a network can pass as a stream only (that is, as a sequence of bytes from one machine to another). RMI has to abstract this process and provide a local object for the client to invoke. This is called the stub.

The stub is the client-side representation of the remote server object. The stubclass contains all the methods the server exposes. Rather than having the exact implementation of the methods in the server, the stub provides an abstraction of the remote server methods on the client side. The stub takes the responsibility of fulfilling network-communication requirements so that the remote method call is issued on behalf of the client.

In particular, the stub is responsible for performing the following steps after a remote method call is issued from the client:

1. Receives the remote method call on behalf of the client
2. Initiates the call on the remote server through the remote reference layer
3. Marshals all the parameters relevant to the remote method call for dispatch by the remote reference layer. *Marshaling* is the process of streaming all the parameters and other information as a sequence of bytes so that it can be transported over the network. Marshaling is achieved by using serialization.

4. Signals to the remote reference layer that the call is complete so that the remote reference layer can take over.

After the remote method call is complete and returns control to the client, the stub does the following things before the control returns to the client:

1. Receives the returned response stream from the remote reference layer
2. Unmarshals all the parameters and returns values and exception information sent back
3. Determines the action to be taken based on the return stream. For example, if the remote method call has generated an exception, the same has to be passed back to the client. If the call is successful and the server has passed some return values, the same has to be constructed by the client and returned to the client.
4. Returns control to the client

There is one additional responsibility for the client stub. Because the stub acts as a proxy on behalf of the server, the stub has to compulsorily implement all the remote interfaces the remote object implements. There are tools (`rmic`) provided as part of the RMI implementation, which takes care of generating the stub/skeleton programs given a server program. Hence, the programmer need not bother about the implementation details of the stub/skeleton classes.

Listing 8-1 shows a sample code for a stub class generated by the `rmic` compiler.

Listing 8-1

```
// Stub class generated by rmic, do not edit.
// Contents subject to change without notice.

public final class RMIExampleServer_Stub
    extends java.rmi.server.RemoteStub
    implements RMIExample, java.rmi.Remote
{
    private static final java.rmi.server.Operation[] operations = {
    new java.rmi.server.Operation("java.lang.String sayHello()")
    };

    private static final long interfaceHash = 6486744599627128933L;

    private static final long serialVersionUID = 2;

    private static boolean useNewInvoke;
    private static java.lang.reflect.Method $method_sayHello_0;

    static {
```

Continued

Listing 8-1 *(continued)*

```
    try {
        java.rmi.server.RemoteRef.class.getMethod("invoke",
        new java.lang.Class[] {
            java.rmi.Remote.class,
            java.lang.reflect.Method.class,
            java.lang.Object[].class,
            long.class
        });
        useNewInvoke = true;
        $method_sayHello_0 = RMIExample.class.getMethod("sayHello",
new java.lang.Class[] {});
    } catch (java.lang.NoSuchMethodException e) {
        useNewInvoke = false;
    }
    }

    // constructors
    public RMIExampleServer_Stub() {
    super();
    }
    public RMIExampleServer_Stub(java.rmi.server.RemoteRef ref) {
    super(ref);
    }

    // methods from remote interfaces

    // implementation of sayHello()
    public java.lang.String sayHello()
    throws java.rmi.RemoteException
    {
    try {
        if (useNewInvoke) {
        Object $result = ref.invoke(this, $method_sayHello_0, null,
6043973830760146143L);
        return ((java.lang.String) $result);
        } else {
        java.rmi.server.RemoteCall call =
ref.newCall((java.rmi.server.RemoteObject) this, operations, 0,
interfaceHash);
        ref.invoke(call);
        java.lang.String $result;
        try {
            java.io.ObjectInput in = call.getInputStream();
            $result = (java.lang.String) in.readObject();
        } catch (java.io.IOException e) {
            throw new java.rmi.UnmarshalException("error
unmarshalling return", e);
        } catch (java.lang.ClassNotFoundException e) {
```

```
            throw new java.rmi.UnmarshalException("error
unmarshalling return", e);
        } finally {
            ref.done(call);
        }
        return $result;
        }
    } catch (java.lang.RuntimeException e) {
        throw e;
    } catch (java.rmi.RemoteException e) {
        throw e;
    } catch (java.lang.Exception e) {
        throw new java.rmi.UnexpectedException("undeclared checked
exception", e);
    }
    }
}
```

Now let's talk about what happens in the server after the request is received. As stated previously for the client, the server also should not be bothered about taking care of network specifics while writing a remote object. The RMI architecture introduces skeletons on the server side to take care of this.

After a remote method call is received, the skeleton performs the following tasks to fulfill the RMI request:

1. Receives the RMI request from the remote reference layer
2. Unmarshals the parameters passed to the remote method
3. Invokes the call on the remote method on behalf of the client
4. Waits until the remote method completes processing

After the remote method completes processing, the skeleton does the following things before returning the control to the client:

1. Receives the return response from the remote method
2. Marshals the return response from the server to the client
3. Signals the remote reference layer so that it picks up the marshaled stream and sends it back to the client.

Listing 8-2 shows a sample code of the corresponding skeleton class generated by the `rmic` compiler.

Listing 8-2

```
// Skeleton class generated by rmic, do not edit.
// Contents subject to change without notice.

public final class RMIExampleServer_Skel
    implements java.rmi.server.Skeleton
{
    private static final java.rmi.server.Operation[] operations = {
    new java.rmi.server.Operation("java.lang.String sayHello()")
    };

    private static final long interfaceHash = 6486744599627128933L;

    public java.rmi.server.Operation[] getOperations() {
    return (java.rmi.server.Operation[]) operations.clone();
    }

    public void dispatch(java.rmi.Remote obj,
java.rmi.server.RemoteCall call, int opnum, long hash)
    throws java.lang.Exception
    {
    if (opnum < 0) {
        if (hash == 6043973830760146143L) {
        opnum = 0;
        } else {
        throw new java.rmi.UnmarshalException("invalid method hash");
        }
    } else {
        if (hash != interfaceHash)
        throw new
java.rmi.server.SkeletonMismatchException("interface hash mismatch");
    }

    RMIExampleServer server = (RMIExampleServer) obj;
    switch (opnum) {
    case 0: // sayHello()
    {
        call.releaseInputStream();
        java.lang.String $result = server.sayHello();
        try {
        java.io.ObjectOutput out = call.getResultStream(true);
        out.writeObject($result);
        } catch (java.io.IOException e) {
        throw new java.rmi.MarshalException("error marshalling
return", e);
        }
        break;
    }

    default:
```

```
        throw new java.rmi.UnmarshalException("invalid method
number");
    }
    }
}
```

Remote reference layer

The remote reference layer takes care of the semantics of the RMI. After all the parameters are marshaled, the stub and skeleton layer passes control to the remote reference layer. The remote reference layer then determines how the request can be fulfilled. It determines whether the remote server is running or not. If the remote server is not running, the remote reference layer determines if the remote server can be instantiated. (This is achieved through the `java.rmi.activation.Activatable` interface defined in the RMI specification.) If the remote server can be instantiated, the remote reference layer sends appropriate instructions to instantiate the remote server in memory and invokes the remote method.

Transport layer

The Transport layer is responsible for establishing the actual communication between the client and server in an RMI system. The transport layer uses the TCP/IP protocol for communication. The transport layer creates a stream that can be accessed by the remote reference layer for sending and receiving data to and from the server. The transport layer sets up the connection between two machines, monitors the connection for failure, listens for incoming requests, and so on.

In addition to TCP/IP, RMI uses a proprietary protocol to represent data. This protocol is known as Java Remote Method Protocol (JRMP). JRMP is a stream-based protocol. Sun and IBM worked jointly in the next version of RMI called RMI-IIOP, which was released with Java 2 SDK version 1.3. In this version, RMI uses the Object Management Group's Internet Inter-ORB Protocol (IIOP) to represent on the wire format of the data. This enables RMI objects to interoperate with CORBA objects.

Locating Remote Objects

So far, we have looked at the basic RMI architecture and the various components involved in an RMI system. We have safely assumed that the client is able to identify where the server is running and to establish the connection with the server. One of the objectives of RMI is location transparency. We have looked at this point when we discussed the invocation semantics of the remote method from the client.

Another objective of location transparency is that the client should not be concerned about where exactly the server is running. This brings us to an important question: If the client is not aware of where the server is running, how can the client establish the connection to the server? RMI provides an answer to this question with the naming service.

The naming service runs on a well-known host machine and port number. It contains information about all the RMI servers and their locations. Clients can connect to the naming service and obtain information about the server to which they wish to connect. A wide variety of naming services, including JNDI, can be used by the RMI system. RMI also provides a built-in naming service called the RMI registry, which we can use.

RMI registry

Whenever an object needs to be remotely accessible by clients, it has to register itself with the RMI registry. This process of registering the server with the RMI registry is known as *bootstrapping*. When a server registers itself with the registry, it has to provide a unique name for itself. After the registration is successful, all requests to the registry with a particular name are redirected to the server that has been registered with this name.

RMI registry accomplishes this task by running in a well-known port and listening for incoming connections. When a client connects to the RMI registry and requests a particular name, the registry searches its list of registered names to see if the requested name can be found. If it finds the name, the registry returns the stub for the requested object to the client and continues to listen for connections from other clients. After the stub for the remote object is available to the client, the client is able to communicate with the server and invoke remote methods. Figure 8-3 shows how the client and the server use the RMI registry to enable communication between them.

We can have as many RMI registries as required in a single machine, but only one registry can run for a single JVM. The default port under which the RMI registry runs is 1099. You can start the RMI registry by using the following command from the command prompt:

```
c:\> start rmiregistry
```

As an alternative, calling the `createRegistry` method from within a Java program can start the RMI registry. This method is available in the `LocateRegistry` class, which is part of the `java.rmi.Registry` package. Listing 8-3 describes the parameters createRegistry takes and the return value.

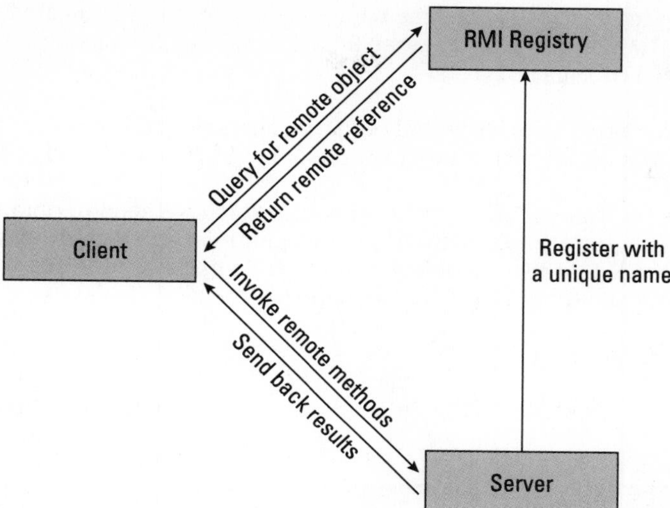

Figure 8-3: Locating remote objects using the RMI registry

Listing 8-3

```
public static Registry createRegistry(int port)
throws java.rmi.RemoteException;
```

Accessing the registry

Having discussed the registry, the next logical question that arises is: "How does one access the registry and perform the necessary operations?" RMI provides us a Uniform Resource Locator (URL) with which we can access the registry. A URL is a naming convention that defines a standard way to access a resource available on the Internet. The general form a URL takes is

```
<protocol>://<host name>:<port number>/<resource name>
```

RMI uses the `rmi` protocol to communicate between the server and the client.

The following is an example of a URL that uses the RMI protocol:

```
rmi://<hostname>:<port number>/<resource name>
```

Host name is a name identifying the machine where the RMI registry is located. It can be a name on the LAN or a DNS name or an IP address. If the host name is not specified, it is defaulted to `localhost`.

Port number is the number at which the RMI registry is listening to incoming requests from the clients. If the port number is not specified, it is defaulted to 1099.

The resource name is the name of the remote object to which we need to obtain a reference so that we can perform remote method invocations. For example, if we need to obtain a reference to a remote object bound with a name of `HelloObject` in the RMI registry, we need to refer to it as follows:

```
rmi://127.0.0.1:1099/HelloObject
```

Both clients and servers should use this syntax to refer to objects in the registry.

Binding objects to the registry

We have seen that any object that needs to be remotely accessible by the clients must register itself with the registry. In RMI terms, this is called *binding the object with the registry*. When an object needs to be bound to the registry, the following things are required:

- ✦ A reference to the instance of the object to be bound
- ✦ The location of the registry, with the port number to which the object is being bound.
- ✦ A unique name by which this object is identified in the registry

The RMI system provides a `Naming` class, which can be used to perform different operations with the RMI registry. It is available in the `java.rmi` package. One of the methods available in the `Naming` class is `bind()`, which can be used to bind an object to the registry. It takes two arguments. The first argument is a URL that refers to the name of the object in the registry. The second argument is a reference to the object to be bound.

What follows is a sample code snippet for binding an object with the registry:

```
try {
        RemoteObject myobj = new RemoteObject();
        java.rmi.Naming.bind("rmi://127.0.0.1:1099/Myobject", myobj);
}
catch(AlreadyBoundException e) {
        // Thrown if the name with which the object is bound already
exists in the registry
}
catch(MalformedURLException e) {
        // Thrown if there is a error in the URL format that was
passed.
```

```
}
catch(RemoteException e) {
        //
}
catch(Exception e) {
        // All other exceptions
}
```

In this example, `"rmi://127.0.0.1:1099/Myobject"` is the name with which the object is registered. `myobj` is the reference to the object registered.

It is not necessary that the name with which an object is registered in the registry match the class name or the instance name of the object registered. The only constraint is that an object registered with the `bind()` method call should have a unique name. If we try to register an object with a name already existing in the RMI registry, an `AlreadyBoundException` is thrown. A good practice is to use package-naming conventions while registering an object with the RMI registry so that name clashes can be avoided. The `Naming` class provides a `rebind()` method call, which is same as the `bind()` method call except that it overwrites the reference to a name if it already exists in the registry. The preceding code looks as follows with the `rebind()` method call:

```
try {
        RemoteObject myobj = new RemoteObject();
        java.rmi.Naming.rebind("rmi://127.0.0.1:1099/Myobject",
myobj);
}
catch(MalformedURLException e) {
        // Thrown if there is a error in the URL format that was
passed.
}
catch(RemoteException e) {
        //
}
catch(Exception e) {
        // All other exceptions
}
```

In this case, if the name `"rmi://127.0.0.1:1099/Myobject"` already exists, it is overwritten with the reference to `myobj`.

Looking up objects from the registry

After the object is registered with the registry, the clients can access it by querying the registry and obtaining a reference to the remote object from the registry. To do this, the client must supply the following information:

- ✦ The location of the registry that contains information about the remote object
- ✦ The name of the remote object as identified in the registry

The `java.rmi.Naming` class provides a method called `lookup()`, which clients can use to lookup and obtain references to the remote object. The `lookup()` method takes a single parameter, which is the URL reference to the remote object. The following code snippet illustrates a simple lookup being performed from the client:

```
try {
        RemoteObject robj = (RemoteObject)
java.rmi.Naming.lookup("rmi://127.0.0.1:1099/MyObject")
.
.
.
}
catch(NotBoundException e) {
       // Thrown if the registry does not contain a name that was
queried using the lookup method call
}
catch(MalFormedURLException e) {
        // Thrown if there is a error in the URL format that was
passed.
}
catch(RemoteException e) {

}
catch(Exception e) {
        // All other exceptions.
}
```

The `lookup()` method always returns an object of type `Object`. It has to be explicitly typecast to the correct type so that we can invoke methods on the object.

The diagram in Figure 8-4 gives a representation of the various steps involved in developing and using a distributed RMI application. Here are the various steps specified in the picture:

1. The remote object implementation / RMI server registers itself with the registry with a `bind()` call.
2. The client application performs a lookup for a particular remote object identified by a name.
3. The RMI registry returns the reference to the remote object.
4. When the client calls the remote method, the stub intercepts the call and receives all the arguments that need to be passed to the remote object.
5. The stub marshals the arguments and sends the data as a stream of bytes to the server.
6. The skeleton residing on the server receives the marshaled data stream, unmarshals the data, and passes the argument to the remote object implementation.

7. After the remote method execution is complete, the return values and exceptions, if any, are passed back to the skeleton to be sent back to the client.
8. The skeleton packages the data back to the stub.
9. The stub sends the return values and exception back to the client application.

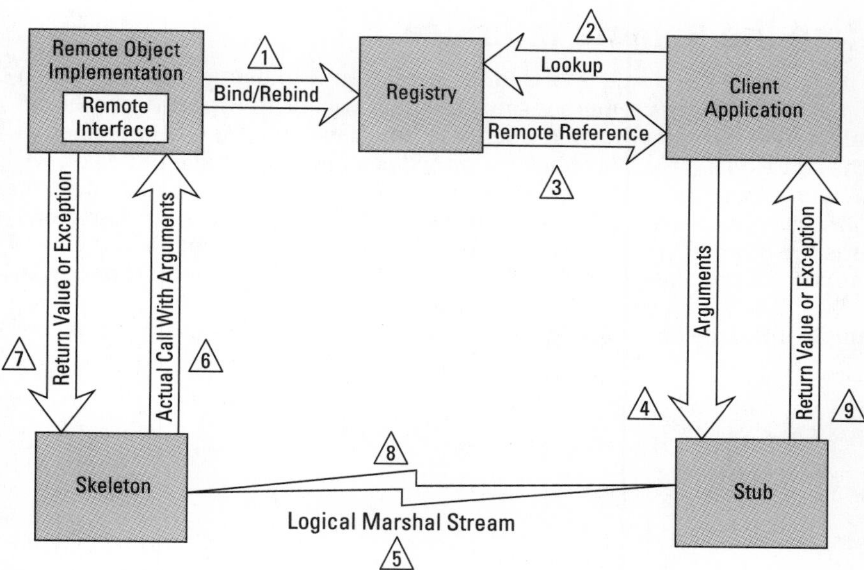

Figure 8-4: Steps involved in RMI

Up and running with RMI

So far, we have looked into the RMI architecture and the various concepts around RMI. It is time now to get into the real-world implementation of an RMI system. We shall now build an Echo Server using the RMI technology. An Echo Server is a server application that listens on a standard port for incoming messages. Any message the server receives is returned to the client from which the request originates. As we write the example, we assume that all the files written are placed under c:\.

Here are the basic steps involved in building the RMI system:

1. Define the `Remote` interface.
2. Implement the `Remote` interface.
3. Compile the server source.

4. Generate stubs and skeletons.
5. Start the RMI registry, and register the server.
6. Develop the client application.
7. Compile the client source and run the client.

Define the Remote interface

The first step in a remote method implementation is to define methods which can be accessed by clients remotely. Any class that wishes to export its methods should define those methods in a separate interface and provide implementation for the same. The `java.rmi` package provides an interface called `Remote`, which all interfaces should extend so that they can be accessed remotely. Any client that requires access to a remote method is returned a handle to the interface that houses the remote method. The interface returned to the client should extend the `java.rmi.Remote` interface directly or indirectly through other interfaces.

A sample interface definition for our Echo Server example is shown in Listing 8-4.

Listing 8-4

```
package servletbible.ch08.examples;

import java.rmi.Remote;
import java.rmi.RemoteException;

/**
 * Remote interface for the EchoServer
 * @author ServletBible
 **/
public interface EchoServer extends java.rmi.Remote {

    /**
     * Returns a string to the caller
     * @return A string
     * @throws RemoteException
     **/
    public String echo(String message) throws
java.rmi.RemoteException;
}
```

In this example, we have defined a public interface called `EchoServer`, which extends the `java.rmi.Remote`. The interface should be defined as public so that the clients can import it into their code. The interface defines one method called `echo()`, which takes a `String` parameter and returns a `String` parameter as output. The `echo()` method throws an exception of type `java.rmi.RemoteException`. All remote methods defined in the `Remote` interface should throw `RemoteException`. Any error that occurs during the remote method call results in a `RemoteException` being generated by the RMI system. Clients that call the remote method must enclose the method call in a try/catch block or should, in turn, throw the exception forward. Henceforth, all references to the `Remote` interface refer to an interface that has extended `java.rmi.Remote` either directly or indirectly.

The `java.rmi.Remote` interface does not contain method declarations within itself. It is a dummy interface similar to `java.io.Serialization`. It is a tag we attach to the interfaces to signify that they are exportable and can be made available to clients. The exporting of the objects is done by the methods in the `UnicastRemoteObject` class.

Implement the Remote interface

After the `Remote` interfaces are defined, the next step is to provide implementations to the methods defined in the `Remote` interface. In our example, the remote implementation implements the `EchoServer` interface we have defined and provides implementation for the `echo()` method defined as part of this interface. Let's build this class in steps, carefully analyzing each step that needs to be performed.

We begin the code with importing the necessary classes for the program. They are `RemoteException` and `UnicastRemoteObject`:

```
import java.rmi.RemoteException;
import java.rmi.server.UnicastRemoteObject;
```

The next step is to provide the definition of the class that implements the `Remote` interface we defined earlier. The new class should also extend a class called `UnicastRemoteObject`, which is part of the `java.rmi.server` package. What is the purpose of extending `UnicastRemoteObject`? `UnicastRemoteObject` is responsible for exporting all the `Remote` interfaces that the class implements so that the clients can access them. In some situations, you may need to extend your implementation class from another base class. In such situations, extending from `UnicastRemoteObject` is not possible because Java does not support inheriting more than one class at the same time (multiple inheritance). The `UnicastRemoteObject` class provides a method called `exportObject()`, which can be used in such situations. The `exportObject()` method takes a reference to the object to be exported as a parameter and makes it available to clients. For our example, we extend the `UnicastRemoteObject` to export the `Remote` interfaces.

The following code snippet shows you how to do this:

```
public class EchoServerImpl extends UnicastRemoteObject
        implements EchoServer {
```

After the class is defined, define a constructor to the class. All constructors of classes that extend `UnicastRemoteObject` should throw a `RemoteException`. This is because the base class (`UnicastRemoteObject`) constructors throw a `RemoteException` when there is a problem in instantiating the remote object.

The following code snippet explains this process:

```
public EchoServerImpl() throws RemoteException {
    super();
    System.out.println( "EchoServerImpl::constructor" );
}
```

The call to the `super()` method invokes the super class's constructor. It is not mandatory, but it is a good coding practice to do so.

The next step in implementing the remote object is to provide the implementation to all the interfaces this class implements. In our example, we implement one interface, and it contains only one method. Also in our example, the `echo()` method accepts a `String` parameter as input. It prints the `String` received from the client on the server's console and returns the same `String` object to the client.

```
    public String echo(String message) throws RemoteException {
        System.out.println("Received and Echoing back message :
" + message);
        return message;
    }
```

We have now completed all the necessary steps to provide implementation for the `Remote` interface we defined in the previous step. The complete implementation is in Listing 8-5.

Listing 8-5

```
package servletbible.ch08.examples;

import java.rmi.RemoteException;
import java.rmi.server.UnicastRemoteObject;

/**
 * This class is a simple example of a RMI Server
 * @author
```

```
 **/
public class EchoServerImpl extends UnicastRemoteObject
        implements EchoServer {

    /**
     * Do nothing constructor
     * @throws RemoteException
     **/
    public EchoServerImpl() throws RemoteException {
        super();
        System.out.println( "EchoServerImpl::constructor" );
    }

    /**
     * @return String
     * @throws RemoteException
     **/
    public String echo(String message) throws RemoteException {
        System.out.println("Received and Echoing back message : " +
message);
        return message;
    }
}
```

Compile the server source

After the Remote interface and the implementation are created, they can be compiled with the Java compiler. Issue the following command to compile the two files. This generates EchoServer.class and EchoServerImpl.class:

```
c:\> javac -d . EchoServer.java
c:\> javac -d . EchoServerImpl.java
```

Generate stubs and skeletons

After the Remote interface and remote implementation are compiled and class files are generated, the next step is to create stubs and skeleton for the remote object. We have seen that stubs are client-side proxies for the remote object. The stub represents the server and accepts all calls from the client on behalf of the server, routes the call to the server, waits for a response from the server, and passes the response to the client. Skeletons, on the other hand, reside on the server and accept all the invocation requests that originate from the stub, pass the request to the server, get the result from the server, and send it back to the stub. All marshaling and unmarshaling of data is done by the stub and skeleton. From the application programmer point of view, we have to generate the stubs and skeletons and let the RMI runtime do the rest of the work. The JDK provides us with a tool that helps in generating the stubs and skeletons.

RMI compiler

The RMI compiler (rmic) is responsible for generating stub and skeleton code from the remote object implementation. Figure 8-5 depicts the role of the RMIC in generating stubs and skeletons.

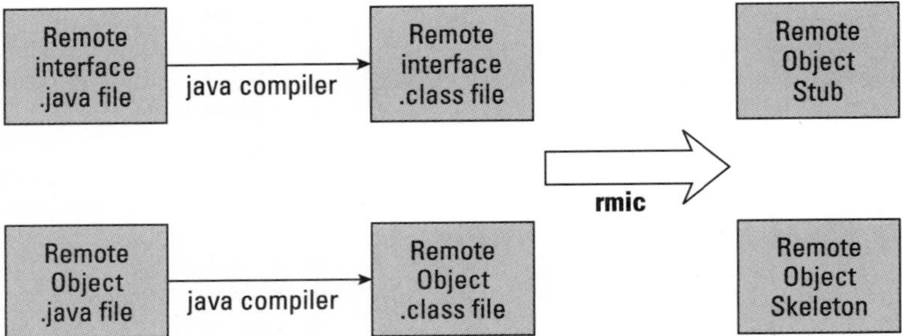

Figure 8-5: Role of RMIC in generating stubs and skeletons

Here is the general form of invoking RMIC:

```
c:\> rmic <options> <class names>
```

Some important options used with RMIC are listed in Table 8-1.

Table 8-1
Options for RMIC

Method	*Description*

`-classpath path`	Specifies the path RMIC uses to look up classes. This option overrides the default or the `CLASSPATH` environment variable if it is set. Directories are separated by semicolons. Thus, the general format for the *path* is:
	`.;<your_path>`
	For example:
	`.;C:\usr\local\java\classes`

Method	Description
`-d directory`	Specifies the destination root directory for the generated class hierarchy. You can use this option to specify a destination directory for the stub, tie, and skeleton files. For example, the command Windows: `C:\> rmic -d C:\java\classes foo.MyClass` places the stub and skeleton classes derived from `MyClass` into the directory `C:\java\classes\foo`. If the `-d` option is not specified, the default behavior is as if "`-d` ." were specified; the package hierarchy of the target class is created in the current directory, and stub/skeleton files are placed within it. Note that in previous versions of RMIC, if `-d` was not specified the package hierarchy was *not* created, and the output files were placed directly in the current directory.
`-g`	Enables generation of debugging tables. Debugging tables contain information about line numbers and local variables, information used by Java debugging tools. By default, only line numbers are generated.
`-always or -alwaysgenerate`	Forces regeneration even when existing stubs/ties/IDL are newer than the input class
`-keep or -keepgenerated`	Retains the generated `.java` source files for the stubs and skeletons and writes them to the same directory as the `.class` files
`-nowarn`	Turns off warnings. If used, the compiler does not print warnings.
`-sourcepath path`	Specifies where to find user source files
`-vcompat`	By default, creates stubs and skeletons compatible with both 1.1 and 1.2 JRMP stub protocol versions.
`-verbose`	Causes the compiler and linker to print messages about what classes are being compiled and what class files are being loaded
`-v1.1`	Creates stubs and skeletons for 1.1 JRMP stub protocol version
`-v1.2`	Creates stubs for 1.2 JRMP stub protocol version only

`<class name>` is the name of the class file that contains the remote object implementation. The class name without the extension must be provided. More than one class file can be passed to the `rmic`.

The RMI compiler can be used only on class files that implement one or more interface extended from `java.rmi.Remote`. For the `EchoServer` example, the stubs and skeletons can be generated by invoking `rmic` on `EchoServerImpl.class`. Upon completion, two files are generated through the `EchoServerImpl_Stub.class` and `EchoServerImpl_Skel.class`. Here's an example:

```
c:\> rmic -d . servletbible.ch08.examples.EchoServerImpl
```

Start the RMI registry and register the server

By now, we have completed all the steps involved in creating a remote object. The next step is to create an instance of the remote object and register it with the RMI registry so that the remote object can start listening for incoming requests from clients. In this section, we see how to write code to register the remote object with the registry, bind the remote object with the registry, and run the server application.

As always, we begin with the package definition and the necessary import statements. These are shown in the following code fragment:

```
package servletbible.ch08.examples;

import java.rmi.*;
import java.rmi.registry.*;
```

The next step is to define a class and a `main()` method for the class. We also define the necessary constants used in the program. In our case, we define the default port under which the RMI registry has to be started.

```
/**
 * This class registers EchoServerImpl with the RMI registry
 * @author
 **/
public class EchoServerSetup {

    public static final int REG_DEFAULT_PORT = 1099;
    /**
     * Main method
     * @param args Command-line arguments
     **/
    public static void main( String[] args ) {
```

After we have defined `main()` method, we check if there are any command-line arguments that are passed. In our example, the port number can be passed as a command-line argument. If there are no command-line arguments, we default to the standard registry port of 1099.

```
        int port = 0;

        try {

                System.out.println("Number of arguments : " +
```

```
args.length);

                if (args.length > 0) {
                    port = Integer.parseInt(args[0]);
                } else {
                    port = REG_DEFAULT_PORT;
                }
```

After checking for the port and setting the appropriate value, we attempt to create the registry. This is done by using the `LocateRegistry.createRegistry()` method. We have to supply the port number at which the registry has to be created and listen for incoming connections. If `createRegistry()` is unable to create the registry by using the port specified, a `RemoteException` is thrown. For the sake of simplicity, we assume that a `RemoteException` thrown while attempting to create the registry means that the registry is already running in the port specified.

```
                // Try to create the registry using the port
specified.
                Registry reg = LocateRegistry.createRegistry(port);


            } catch(RemoteException e) {
                // Do nothing. Registry already exists

            }

        System.out.println("Registry created successfully and running
on port number " + port);
```

Note

It is not mandatory that the RMI registry should be created with the `LocateRegistry.createRegistry()` method. RMI provides us with a command-line tool that creates a registry in a particular port we specify. This tool is called `rmiregistry`. If we start the RMI registry using the command-line tool, the preceding step can be omitted. Programs can bind to the well-known port at which the registry has been started. However, the `createRegistry()` method provides greater flexibility to detect whether the registry is running or not and to take appropriate actions.

After the registry is created and running on the port specified, the next step is to install a security manager, which defines the security environment that governs the operation of the remote object:

```
        try {

            // Set the security manager
            System.setSecurityManager( new RMISecurityManager() );
```

After the security manager is installed, create an instance of the remote object, and bind the object to the registry. For binding the object to the registry, use the `Naming.rebind()` method call:

```
            // Create a new object of EchoServerImpl
            EchoServerImpl server = new EchoServerImpl();

            String rmiURL = "rmi://localhost:" + port +
"/EchoServer";

            // Bind this object with the RMI registry
            Naming.rebind( rmiURL, server );

            System.out.println("Successfully bound the server to the
registry with the name EchoServer");
        } catch( Exception e ) {
            e.printStackTrace();
        }
    }
}
```

We have now completed the setup application responsible for creating the registry and registering the remote object. We have to compile this application and run the same so that the remote object can start listening for requests from clients. The following commands enable you to do this:

```
c:\> javac -d . EchoServerSetup.java
c:\> java servletbible.ch08.examples.EchoServerSetup
```

When the following commands are issued, the remote object is registered and waits for client requests. The diagram in Figure 8-6 shows a running instance of the RMI server application we have developed.

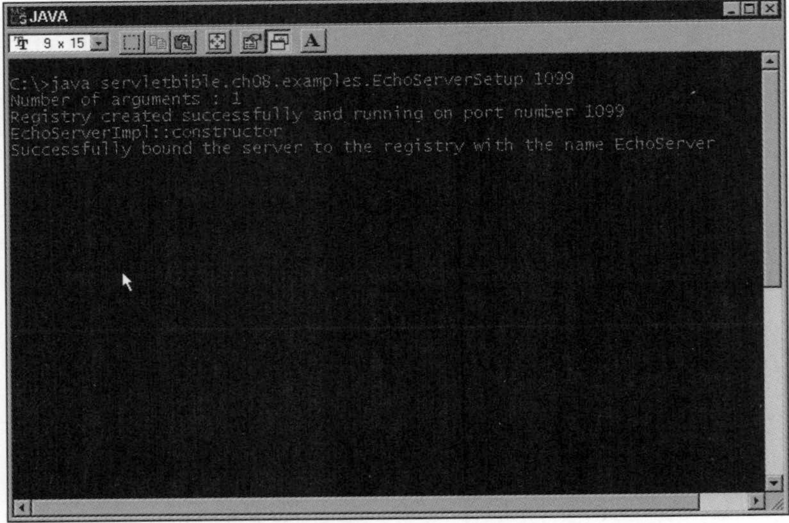

Figure 8-6: DOS Window showing the running instance of the RMI server application

Listing 8-6 shows the complete code listing of the setup application for reference.

Listing 8-6

```
package servletbible.ch08.examples;

import java.rmi.*;
import java.rmi.registry.*;

/**
 * This class registers EchoServerImpl with the RMI registry
 * @author
 **/
public class EchoServerSetup {

    public static final int REG_DEFAULT_PORT = 1099;
    /**
     * Main method
     * @param args Command-line arguments
     **/
    public static void main( String[] args ) {

        int port = 0;

        try {

                System.out.println("Number of arguments : " +
args.length);

                if (args.length > 0) {
                    port = Integer.parseInt(args[0]);
                } else {
                    port = REG_DEFAULT_PORT;
                }

                // Try to create the registry using the port
specified.
                Registry reg = LocateRegistry.createRegistry(port);


            } catch(RemoteException e) {
                // Do nothing. Registry already exists
                System.out.println("Exception while creating the
registry :-" + e.getMessage());
                return;
            }

        System.out.println("Registry created successfully and running
```

Continued

Listing 8-6 (continued)

```
on port number " + port);

        try {

            // Set the security manager
            System.setSecurityManager( new RMISecurityManager() );

            // Create a new object of EchoServerImpl
            EchoServerImpl server = new EchoServerImpl();

            String rmiURL = "rmi://localhost:" + port +
"/EchoServer";

            // Bind this object with the RMI registry
            Naming.rebind( rmiURL, server );

            System.out.println("Successfully bound the server to the
registry with the name EchoServer");

        } catch( Exception e ) {
            e.printStackTrace();
        }
    }
}
```

Develop the client application

It is time now for us to build the client that can utilize the services exposed by the remote object. The client should first contact the registry and get a reference to the remote object. When the remote object is available, the client can call the methods exposed by the remote object. The first few lines of code in the client are shown in the following snippet.

The client imports the necessary packages and defines a `main()` method. It also defines a `String` which holds the data to be sent to the remote object. In our case, the `String` variable holds the data the user types in the console.

```
package servletbible.ch08.examples;

import java.rmi.*;
import java.io.*;

/**
 * This class is the client for EchoServer
 * @author
 **/
```

```
public class EchoClient {

    public static final int REG_DEFAULT_PORT = 1099;

    /**
     * Main method
     * @param args Command-line arguments
     **/
    public static void main( String[] args ) {

        int port = 0;
        try {

            if (args.length > 0) {
                port = Integer.parseInt(args[0]);
            } else {
                port = REG_DEFAULT_PORT;
            }

            String messagetoserver=" ";
```

The next step is to install a security manager that governs the environment under which the remote object operates. Installing the security manager ensures that the client resources are well protected from the remote object.

```
            // Set the security manager
            System.setSecurityManager( new RMISecurityManager() );
```

The next step is the most important part in the client application. We now have to bootstrap the client with a registry and get a reference to the remote object. This is done by using the `java.rmi.Naming` class. The `Naming` class provides a lookup method that contacts the registry and obtains a reference to the remote object. The `lookup()` method accepts one argument through the URL containing the location of the RMI registry and the name of the resource in the registry the client wishes to access. The `lookup()` method returns a object of type `Object`. It has to be typecasted to the remote interface of the server the client wishes to access. In our example, there is only one remote interface defined (`EchoServer`). Hence, we typecast the return value to `EchoServer`:

```
            String rmiURL = "rmi://localhost:" + port +
"/EchoServer";

            // Look up EchoServer in the RMI registry
            EchoServer server = (EchoServer) Naming.lookup(rmiURL);
```

When the client obtains the reference to `EchoServer`, the client can invoke methods defined in the `EchoServer` interface. The client now reads for input from the console and sends it to the remote `echo()` method. The return value from the `echo()` method is printed on the client's console output.

```
            // Invoke the method
            System.out.println("Connection with the Echo Server
successful");
            System.out.println("Enter some text to see it echoed back
to you.");
            System.out.println("Type quit to end the session");

            BufferedReader brdr = new BufferedReader(new
InputStreamReader(System.in));

            while (!messagetoserver.equals("quit")) {
                messagetoserver = brdr.readLine();
                System.out.println( server.echo(messagetoserver) );
            }

        } catch( Exception e ) {
            e.printStackTrace();
        }
    }
}
```

The complete code listing is shown in Listing 8-7.

Listing 8-7

```
package servletbible.ch08.examples;

import java.rmi.*;
import java.io.*;

/**
 * This class is the client for EchoServer
 * @author
 **/
public class EchoClient {

    public static final int REG_DEFAULT_PORT = 1099;

    /**
     * Main method
     * @param args Command-line arguments
     **/
    public static void main( String[] args ) {

        int port = 0;
        try {

            if (args.length > 0) {
```

```
                port = Integer.parseInt(args[0]);
            } else {
                port = REG_DEFAULT_PORT;
            }

            String messagetoserver=" ";

            // Set the security manager
            System.setSecurityManager( new RMISecurityManager() );

            String rmiURL = "rmi://localhost:" + port +
"/EchoServer";

            // Look up EchoServer in the RMI registry
            EchoServer server = (EchoServer) Naming.lookup(rmiURL);

            // Invoke the method
            System.out.println("Connection with the Echo Server
successful");
            System.out.println("Enter some text to see it echoed back
to you.");
            System.out.println("Type quit to end the session");

            BufferedReader brdr = new BufferedReader(new
InputStreamReader(System.in));

            while (!messagetoserver.equals("quit")) {
                messagetoserver = brdr.readLine();
                System.out.println( server.echo(messagetoserver) );
            }

        } catch( Exception e ) {
            e.printStackTrace();
        }
    }
}
```

Compile the client source and run the client

The client code can be compiled and executed with the following commands. After the client is running, you can provide input and see it being echoed to you. The program can be ended by typing **quit**. The output of the client is shown in the following Figure 8-7.

```
C:\> javac -d . EchoClient.java
C:\> java servletbible.ch08.examples.EchoClient
```

Figure 8-7 shows the output after the client had called the remote object and displayed the results.

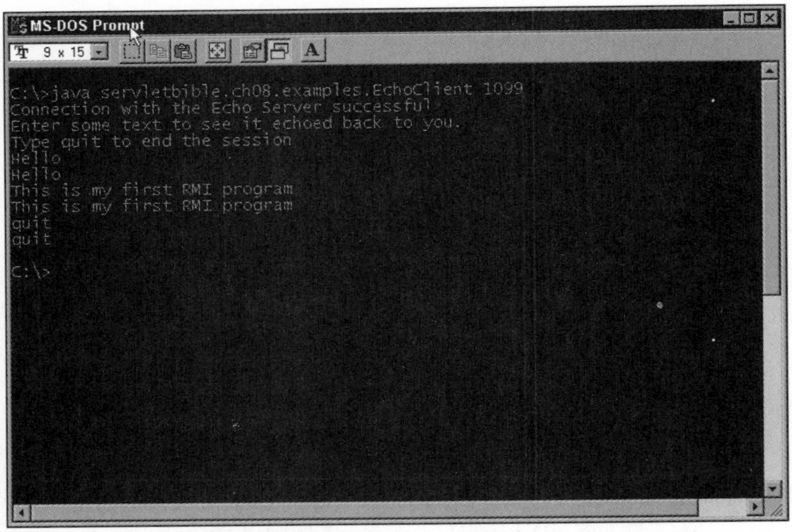

Figure 8-7: EchoClient calling the remote method and getting the results echoed

Security Issues When Dealing with RMI

In the example we've just completed, we have purposely ignored the description of the following line from the `EchoClient.java` program and `EchoServerSetup.java` program.

```
// Set the security manager
System.setSecurityManager( new RMISecurityManager() );
```

The network is never a secure place. Malicious code could be loaded onto the system, or someone may be waiting for an opportunity to access sensitive data. To attempt to resolve this problem, RMI requires that a security manager be explicitly set in the Java RMI program.

The `RMISecurityManager` is a subclass of `java.lang.SecurityManager` that has been set up to be used as the default security manager for RMI applications. It prevents the unauthorized loading of stubs and skeletons from different hosts, thereby ensuring that stub classes load necessary classes over the network.

Example RMI Stock Quote Server

With the solid grounding we have obtained on the RMI technology, let's now try to implement a more complex real-time example. The application we are going to write here is a stock quote server. A stock quote server is an application that keeps track of stock prices of publicly traded companies, the stock fluctuations for a particular period, and related details. Users accessing this application can get up-to-date information for the stocks that interest them. Stock quotes are constantly updated on a database maintained on the server. The RMI server program provides methods to inquire about the current stock price of a particular company's stock. It also provides a service that displays the stock information of all the companies in its database. The stock quote server accesses the database by using JDBC API to fetch information.

While designing this application, we follow the same basic steps we follow in the `EchoServer` example to define the various methods and functionality. The various server components that have to be created are provided in Table 8-2.

Table 8-2
Components of the Stock Quote Server

Filename	*Description*
`StockServer.java`	The `StockServer.java` file defines the Remote interface and exposes all the services made available from the stock quote server.
`StockServerImpl.java`	The `StockServerImpl.java` is the remote object implementation of the `StockServer` interface. It provides implementation for all the methods defined in the `StockServer` interface. It accesses the database by using JDBC calls to retrieve data.
`StockServerSetup.java`	The `StockServerSetup` creates the RMI registry and an instance of the stock quote server, binding the server to the registry so that the service is made available to clients.
`stocks.mdb`	The stocks.mdb file is an MS Access database used by our sample server application. It defines the tables that provide the necessary information regarding the stock details of all the companies.

The `StockServer.java` file defines the remote interface for the stock server program. It has to extend the `java.rmi.Remote` interface and provide method declarations for all the methods that will be exposed by this RMI server. The `StockServer.java` interface defines the methods listed in Table 8-3.

Table 8-3
Methods Defined in StockServer.java

Filename	***Description***
`getCurrentPrice`	Returns the last traded price for a particular stock.
`getDetailPrice`	Returns detailed price information for a particular stock. Detailed information will include the 52 week high, 52 week low, day high, day low etc.
`getAllPrices()`	Returns the last traded price information for all the stocks available in the server.
`first()`	Helper method to navigate an array of stock information. Used in conjunction with getAllPrices().
`last()`	Helper method to navigate an array of stock information. Used in conjunction with getAllPrices().
`next()`	Helper method to navigate an array of stock information. Used in conjunction with getAllPrices().
`prev()`	Helper method to navigate anarray of stock information. Used in conjunction with getAllPrices().
`getSymbol()`	Returns the symbol name for a particular stock.
`getName()`	Returns the Name of the company which is identified by a particular stock symbol.
`getLastTradedPrice()`	Returns the last traded price information for a particular stock.
`getYearHigh()`	Returns the 52 week high price for a particular stock
`getYearLow()`	Returns the 52 week low price for a particular stock.
`getDayHigh()`	Returns the highest price for the day for a particular stock.
`getDayLow()`	Returns the lowest price for the day for a particular stock.
`getPreviousDayClose()`	Returns the previous day closing price for a particular stock.

Listing 8-8 provides the complete implementation of the various components described in Table 8-3.

Listing 8-8

```
/**
* File : StockServer.java
*
* @contains interface definitions for the StockServer
* remote interface.
*/

package servletbible.ch08.examples.stockserver;

import java.rmi.*;

public interface StockServer extends Remote
{
    // Define all the interfaces that are
    // accessible to the clients.

    public String getCurrentPrice(String symbol) throws
RemoteException;

    public boolean getDetailPrice(String symbol) throws
RemoteException;

    public boolean getAllPrices() throws RemoteException;

    public boolean first() throws RemoteException;
    public boolean last() throws RemoteException;
    public boolean next() throws RemoteException;
    public boolean prev() throws RemoteException;

    public String getSymbol() throws RemoteException;
    public String getName() throws RemoteException;
    public String getLastTradedPrice() throws RemoteException;
    public String getYearHigh() throws RemoteException;
    public String getYearLow() throws RemoteException;
    public String getDayHigh() throws RemoteException;
    public String getDayLow() throws RemoteException;
    public String getPreviousDayClose() throws RemoteException;
}
```

The next step in writing the stock quote server application is to provide an implementation class for the `StockServer` remote interface that we just completed. `StockServerImpl.java` provides a complete implementation for the `StockServer` interface. It implements all the methods that are defined in the `StockServer` interface. In addition to providing implementation to the methods defined in `StockServer` interface, the `StockServerImpl` class defines vector variables that hold the data retrieved from the database. The `getXXX()` methods connect to the stock server database, retrieve information, and populate the variables that are defined for that purpose.

Listing 8-9 provides the complete implementation of `StockServerImpl.java` class.

Listing 8-9

```
/**
* File : StockServerImpl.java
*
* @contains implementation to all methods
* defined in StockServer remote interface.
*/

package servletbible.ch08.examples.stockserver;

import java.rmi.*;
import java.rmi.server.*;
import java.util.*;
import java.sql.*;

public class StockServerImpl extends UnicastRemoteObject implements
StockServer
{

    public StockServerImpl() throws RemoteException
    {
        currentIndex = -1;

            // Create vectors to hold the return values
            // from the database.
        Symbol = new Vector();
        Name = new Vector();
        LastTradedPrice = new Vector();
        YearHigh = new Vector();
        YearLow = new Vector();
        DayHigh = new Vector();
        DayLow = new Vector();
        PreviousDayClose = new Vector();

    }

// Implementation of all the remote methods.

    public String getCurrentPrice(String symbol) throws
RemoteException
    {
        try {
```

```
                    // Initialize the JDBC driver and obtain
                    // a connection from the database.
            Class.forName("sun.jdbc.odbc.JdbcOdbcDriver") ;
            Connection con =
DriverManager.getConnection("jdbc:odbc:stockdsn","","");

            Statement st = con.createStatement() ;

                    // Query the database for the symbol
                    // requested by the client

            ResultSet rs = st.executeQuery("Select Symbol,
LastTradedPrice from stocktable where symbol = '" + symbol + "'");

            if (rs.next()){
                            // Initialize the vector.
                Symbol.setSize(0);
                LastTradedPrice.setSize(0);

                            // Add the results from the database to
the Vector.
                Symbol.addElement(rs.getString("Symbol"));

LastTradedPrice.addElement(rs.getString("LastTradedPrice"));


                            // Position the value for currentIndex
to
                            // the first available record and set
the
                            // maxsize so as to control traversing.
                currentIndex = 0;
                maxsize = 1;

                            // Close the resultset, statement and
                            // connection objects
                rs.close();
                st.close();
                con.close();
                //System.out.println("Successful");
                return (String)LastTradedPrice.elementAt(0);
            }

        }
        catch(Exception e) {
            e.printStackTrace() ;
        }

            // If the query to database is not successful, set the
            //index to -1 so that it signifies a empty result set.

        currentIndex = -1;
```

Continued

Listing 8-9 (continued)

```
        maxsize = -1;

        return null;

    }

    public boolean getDetailPrice(String symbol) throws
RemoteException
    {
        try {
                    // Initialize the JDBC driver and obtain
                    // a connection from the database.

            Class.forName("sun.jdbc.odbc.JdbcOdbcDriver") ;
            Connection con =
DriverManager.getConnection("jdbc:odbc:stockdsn","","");

            Statement st = con.createStatement() ;

                    // Query the database for the symbol
                    // requested by the client

            ResultSet rs = st.executeQuery("Select * from stocktable
where symbol = '" + symbol + "'");

            if (rs.next()) {

                Symbol.setSize(0);
                Name.setSize(0);
                LastTradedPrice.setSize(0);
                YearHigh.setSize(0);
                YearLow.setSize(0);
                DayHigh.setSize(0);
                DayLow.setSize(0);
                PreviousDayClose.setSize(0);
                     // Add the results from the database
                     // to the Vector.

                Symbol.addElement(rs.getString("Symbol"));
                Name.addElement(rs.getString("Name"));

LastTradedPrice.addElement(rs.getString("LastTradedPrice"));
                YearHigh.addElement(rs.getString("YearHigh"));
                YearLow.addElement(rs.getString("YearLow"));
                DayHigh.addElement(rs.getString("DayHigh"));
                DayLow.addElement(rs.getString("DayLow"));

PreviousDayClose.addElement(rs.getString("PreviousDayClose"));
```

```
                                // Position the value for currentIndex
to
                                // the first available record and set
the
                                // maxsize so as to control traversing.
                    currentIndex = 0;
                    maxsize = 1;
                                // Close the resultset, statement and
                                // connection objects

                    rs.close();
                    st.close();
                    con.close();
                    //System.out.println("Successful");
                    return true;
                }

        }
        catch(Exception e) {
            e.printStackTrace() ;
        }

              // If the query to database is not successful, set the
              //index to -1 so that it signifies a empty result set.

        currentIndex = -1;
        maxsize = -1;

        return false;
    }

    public boolean getAllPrices() throws RemoteException
    {
        try {

            Class.forName("sun.jdbc.odbc.JdbcOdbcDriver") ;
            Connection con =
DriverManager.getConnection("jdbc:odbc:stockdsn","","");

            Statement st = con.createStatement() ;
            ResultSet rs = st.executeQuery("Select * from
stocktable");

            Symbol.setSize(0);
            Name.setSize(0);
            LastTradedPrice.setSize(0);
            YearHigh.setSize(0);
            YearLow.setSize(0);
            DayHigh.setSize(0);
            DayLow.setSize(0);
            PreviousDayClose.setSize(0);
```

Continued

Listing 8-9 *(continued)*

```
            maxsize = 0;
                     // Iterate through all the records in the
                     // resultset and add them to the vector.

            while (rs.next()) {

                Symbol.addElement(rs.getString("Symbol"));
                Name.addElement(rs.getString("Name"));

LastTradedPrice.addElement(rs.getString("LastTradedPrice"));
                YearHigh.addElement(rs.getString("YearHigh"));
                YearLow.addElement(rs.getString("YearLow"));
                DayHigh.addElement(rs.getString("DayHigh"));
                DayLow.addElement(rs.getString("DayLow"));

PreviousDayClose.addElement(rs.getString("PreviousDayClose"));
                            // Increment the maxsize by 1 for each
iteration.
                maxsize = maxsize + 1;
            }


            currentIndex = 0;


            rs.close();
            st.close();
            con.close();
            //System.out.println("Successful");
            return true;


        }
        catch(Exception e) {
            e.printStackTrace() ;
        }

        currentIndex = -1;
        maxsize = -1;

        return false;

    }

     // Positions the currentIndex to the first record
    public boolean first()  throws RemoteException
    {
        if (maxsize > 0)
        {
```

```
            currentIndex = 0;
            return true;
        }
        else // no records
            return false;
    }

    // Positions the currentIndex to the last record
    public boolean last()  throws RemoteException
    {
        if (maxsize > 0)
        {
            currentIndex = maxsize - 1;
            return true;
        }
        else // no records
            return false;
    }

    // Advances the currentIndex forward by 1 position
    public boolean next() throws RemoteException
    {
        if (maxsize == -1)
        {
            // No records exists
            return false;
        }

        currentIndex++;

        if(currentIndex >= 0 && currentIndex < maxsize)
        {
            return true;
        }
        else
            return false;
    }

    // Moves the currentIndex backward by 1 position
    public boolean prev() throws RemoteException
    {
        if (maxsize == -1)
        {
            // No records exists
            return false;
        }

        currentIndex--;

        if(currentIndex >= 0 && currentIndex < maxsize)
        {
```

Continued

Listing 8-9 *(continued)*

```
            return true;
        }
        else
            return false;
    }

    public String getSymbol() throws RemoteException
    {
        if(currentIndex < maxsize)
            return getSymbol(currentIndex);
        else
            return null;
    }

    public String getName() throws RemoteException
    {
        if(currentIndex < maxsize)
            return getName(currentIndex);
        else
            return null;
    }

    public String getLastTradedPrice() throws RemoteException
    {
        if(currentIndex < maxsize)
            return getLastTradedPrice(currentIndex);
        else
            return null;
    }
    public String getYearHigh() throws RemoteException
    {
        if(currentIndex < maxsize)
            return getYearHigh(currentIndex);
        else
            return null;
    }
    public String getYearLow() throws RemoteException
    {
        if(currentIndex < maxsize)
            return getYearLow(currentIndex);
        else
            return null;
    }
    public String getDayHigh() throws RemoteException
    {
        if(currentIndex < maxsize)
            return getDayHigh(currentIndex);
        else
            return null;
    }
```

```
public String getDayLow() throws RemoteException
{
    if(currentIndex < maxsize)
        return getDayLow(currentIndex);
    else
        return null;
}
public String getPreviousDayClose() throws RemoteException
{
    if(currentIndex < maxsize)
        return getPreviousDayClose(currentIndex);
    else
        return null;
}

public String getSymbol(int index)
{
    return (String)Symbol.elementAt(index);
}

public String getName(int index)
{
    return (String)Name.elementAt(index);
}

public String getLastTradedPrice(int index)
{
    return (String)LastTradedPrice.elementAt(index);
}

public String getYearHigh(int index)
{
    return (String)YearHigh.elementAt(index);
}

public String getYearLow(int index)
{
    return (String)YearLow.elementAt(index);
}

public String getDayHigh(int index)
{
    return (String)DayHigh.elementAt(index);
}

public String getDayLow(int index)
{
    return (String)DayLow.elementAt(index);
}

public String getPreviousDayClose(int index)
```

Continued

Listing 8-9 (continued)

```
    {
        return (String)PreviousDayClose.elementAt(index);
    }


    private Vector Symbol;
    private Vector Name;
    private Vector LastTradedPrice;
    private Vector YearHigh;
    private Vector YearLow;
    private Vector DayHigh;
    private Vector DayLow;
    private Vector PreviousDayClose;

    private int currentIndex;
    private int maxsize;
}
```

With the stock server interface and implementation classes complete, we now have to write a setup class that will register the stock server object with the RMI registry and create an instance of a stock server remote object so that it can serve client requests. The `StockServerSetup.java` does this job.

Listing 8-10 shows `StockServerSetup.java`, which does the registering and running of the stock server remote object.

Listing 8-10

```
/**
* File : StockServerSetup.java
*
* @creates the registry and binds the StockQuote
* @server with the registry.
*/


package servletbible.ch08.examples.stockserver;

import java.rmi.*;
import java.rmi.registry.*;

/**
 * This class registers StockServerImpl with the RMI registry
 * @author
 **/
```

```
public class StockServerSetup {

     public static final int REG_DEFAULT_PORT = 1099;
     /**
      * Main method
      * @param args Command-line arguments
      **/
     public static void main( String[] args ) {

         int port = 0;

         try {
                 // Check for any command line arguments
                 System.out.println("Number of arguments : " +
args.length);

                      // Retrieve the port number from the command
                      // line. If not supplied, set a default value.
                 if (args.length > 0) {
                     port = Integer.parseInt(args[0]);
                 } else {
                     port = REG_DEFAULT_PORT;
                 }

                 // Try to create the registry using the port
specified.
                 Registry reg = LocateRegistry.createRegistry(port);


             } catch(RemoteException e) {
                 // Do nothing. Registry already exists
                 System.out.println("Exception while creating the
registry :-" + e.getMessage());
                 return;
             }

        System.out.println("Registry created successfully and running
on port number " + port);

        try {

            // Set the security manager
            System.setSecurityManager( new RMISecurityManager() );

            // Create a new object of StockServerImpl
            StockServerImpl server = new StockServerImpl();

            String rmiURL = "rmi://localhost:" + port +
"/StockServer";

            // Bind this object with the RMI registry
```

Continued

Listing 8-10 *(continued)*

```
            Naming.rebind( rmiURL, server );

            System.out.println("Successfully bound the server to the
registry with the name StockServer");

            return;
        } catch( Exception e ) {
            e.printStackTrace();
        }
    }
}
```

Example Servlet Accessing the Stock Quote Server

With the stock quote server application now complete, let's try to create a client application that makes use of the services the stock quote server provides. In this example, we create a servlet that accesses the remote object to obtain stock information and displays the details to browser-based clients.

This application is a minor attempt to show how Web applications can be extended to make use of the services of components that already exist (in our case, the stock quote server). A normal Web application, which contains only servlets and HTML code, is composed of two tiers. By making the servlet access the RMI server component residing in a different location, we extend the application to the third tier. In a similar way, we can extend this application to n-tiers by making use of the components already on the market, thereby not reinventing the wheel. We are able to develop applications that are reliable and efficient within a shorter time than it takes to develop all the components from the scratch.

The servlet can be invoked in two ways. If the servlet is invoked without any `GET` or `POST` parameters, the servlet presents the user with a form where the user can enter the symbol of the stock he or she is interested in and can obtain the quote. The user can choose among three options: to get the current price of the stock, to get detailed information on the stock, or to list all stock prices.

Listing 8-11 shows the `StockServlet` code.

Listing 8-11

```
/**
* File : StockServlet.java
*
* @servlet client that accesses the StockServer
* @to retrieve stock information.
*/


package servletbible.ch08.examples.stockserver;

import javax.servlet.* ;
import javax.servlet.http.* ;
import java.rmi.*;
import java.io.* ;
import servletbible.ch08.examples.stockserver.*;


public class StockServlet extends HttpServlet {

    /**
     * Initializes this servlet
     *
     * @param cfg ServletConfig object
     * @throws ServletException When an exception occurs
     */
    public void init(ServletConfig cfg) throws ServletException {
        super.init(cfg) ;
    }

    /**
     * Checks for request parameters. If there are no
     * request parameters, a default HTML screen is
     * posted, else, the request parameters are passed
     * for further processing.
     *
     * @param req Request object
     * @param res Response object
     * @throws ServletException When an exception occurs
     * @throws IOException When an exception occurs
     */
    public void doGet(HttpServletRequest req,
        HttpServletResponse res)
        throws ServletException, IOException {

        PrintWriter out = res.getWriter() ;
        if (req.getParameter("opt")==null) {
```

Continued

Listing 8-11 *(continued)*

```
            out.println("<HTML><HEAD><TITLE>RMI Stock Price
example</TITLE><BODY><CENTER>");
            out.println("<FORM
action=\"/servlet/servletbible.ch08.examples.stockserver.StockServlet
\">");
            out.println("<NOBR><INPUT name=symbol size=25><INPUT
type=submit value=\"Get Quotes\">");
            out.println(" <SELECT name=opt><OPTION selected
value=cp>Current Price</OPTION>");
            out.println("<OPTION value=dp>Detailed
Price</OPTION><OPTION value=ap>All Stock Prices</OPTION>");

out.println("</SELECT></NOBR></FORM></CENTER></BODY></HTML>");

        }
        else {
            doPost(req,res) ;
        }
    }

    /**
     * Process the request parameter and invoke appropriate
     * remote methods.
     * @param req Request object
     * @param res Response object
     * @throws ServletException When an exception occurs
     * @throws IOException When an exception occurs
     */
    public void doPost(HttpServletRequest req,
        HttpServletResponse res)
        throws ServletException, IOException {

        PrintWriter out = res.getWriter() ;

        try {

            out.println("<HTML><HEAD><TITLE>RMI Stock Price
example</TITLE><BODY><CENTER>");
            out.println("<FORM
action=\"/servlet/servletbible.ch08.examples.stockserver.StockServlet
\">");
            out.println("<NOBR><INPUT name=symbol size=25><INPUT
type=submit value=\"Get Quotes\">");
            out.println(" <SELECT name=opt><OPTION selected
value=cp>Current Price</OPTION>");
            out.println("<OPTION value=dp>Detailed
Price</OPTION><OPTION value=ap>All Stock Prices</OPTION>");
            out.println("</SELECT></NOBR></FORM>");
```

```
            out.println("<TABLE border=0 cellPadding=4 cellSpacing=0
width=100%>");
            out.println("<TBODY><TR bgColor=#6699cc><TD><FONT
face=arial>");

out.println("<B><BIG>Quotes</BIG></B></FONT></TD></TR></TBODY></TABLE
>");

            // Set the security manager
            System.setSecurityManager( new RMISecurityManager() );

            String rmiURL = "rmi://localhost:" + "1099" +
"/StockServer";

            // Look up EchoServer in the RMI registry
            StockServer ssObj = (StockServer) Naming.lookup(rmiURL);

            // Invoke the method
            String symbol = req.getParameter("symbol");

            if (req.getParameter("opt").equals("cp"))
            {
                // Invoke the remote method getCurrentPrice()
                String price = ssObj.getCurrentPrice(symbol);

                // Display the results in a table to the user
                out.println("<TABLE><TBODY><TR><TD align=middle
colSpan=2>");
                out.println("<TABLE border=1 cellSpacing=0
width=100%>");
                out.println("<TBODY><TR bgColor=#dcdcdc>");
                out.println("<TH noWrap>Symbol</TH><TH colSpan=2
noWrap>Last Traded Price</TH></TR>");
                out.println("<TR align=right>");
                out.println("<TD align=left noWrap>");

                out.println(symbol);

                out.println("</TD>");
                out.println("<TD align=left noWrap>");

                out.println(price);

                out.println("</TD></TR></TBODY></TABLE>");
                out.println("</TD></TR></TBODY></TABLE>");

            }
            else if (req.getParameter("opt").equals("dp"))
            {
                // Invoke the remote method getDetailPrice()
                if (ssObj.getDetailPrice(symbol))
                {
```

Continued

Listing 8-11 *(continued)*

```
            // Display the results in a table to the user

                out.println("<TABLE><TBODY><TR><TD align=middle
colSpan=2>");
                out.println("<TABLE border=1 cellSpacing=0
width=100%>");
                out.println("<TBODY><TR bgColor=#dcdcdc>");
                out.println("<TH noWrap>Symbol</TH><TH colSpan=2
noWrap>Name</TH>");
                out.println("<TH noWrap>Last Traded Price</TH><TH
colSpan=2 noWrap>Year High</TH>");
                out.println("<TH noWrap>Year Low</TH><TH
colSpan=2 noWrap>Day High</TH>");
                out.println("<TH noWrap>Day Low</TH><TH colSpan=2
noWrap>Previous Day Close</TH></TR>");

                out.println("<TR align=right><TD align=left
noWrap>");
                out.println(ssObj.getSymbol());
                out.println("</TD><TD align=left noWrap>");
                out.println(ssObj.getName());
                out.println("</TD><TD align=left noWrap>");
                out.println(ssObj.getLastTradedPrice());
                out.println("</TD><TD align=left noWrap>");
                out.println(ssObj.getYearHigh());
                out.println("</TD><TD align=left noWrap>");
                out.println(ssObj.getYearLow());
                out.println("</TD><TD align=left noWrap>");
                out.println(ssObj.getDayHigh());
                out.println("</TD><TD align=left noWrap>");
                out.println(ssObj.getDayLow());
                out.println("</TD><TD align=left noWrap>");
                out.println(ssObj.getPreviousDayClose());

                out.println("</TD></TR></TBODY></TABLE>");
                out.println("</TD></TR></TBODY></TABLE>");

            }
        }
        else if (req.getParameter("opt").equals("ap"))
        {
            // Invoke the remote method getAllPrices()
            if (ssObj.getAllPrices())
            {
            // Display the results in a table to the user
                out.println("<TABLE><TBODY><TR><TD align=middle
colSpan=2>");
                out.println("<TABLE border=1 cellSpacing=0
```

```
width=100%>");
                        out.println("<TBODY><TR bgColor=#dcdcdc>");
                        out.println("<TH noWrap>Symbol</TH><TH colSpan=2
noWrap>Name</TH>");
                        out.println("<TH >Last Traded Price</TH><TH
colSpan=2 >Year High</TH>");
                        out.println("<TH >Year Low</TH><TH colSpan=2 >Day
High</TH>");
                        out.println("<TH >Day Low</TH><TH colSpan=2
>Previous Day Close</TH></TR>");

                        do
                        {
                            out.println("<TR align=right><TD align=left
noWrap>");

                            out.println(ssObj.getSymbol());
                            out.println("</TD><TD align=left noWrap>");
                            out.println(ssObj.getName());
                            out.println("</TD><TD align=left noWrap>");
                            out.println(ssObj.getLastTradedPrice());
                            out.println("</TD><TD align=left noWrap>");
                            out.println(ssObj.getYearHigh());
                            out.println("</TD><TD align=left noWrap>");
                            out.println(ssObj.getYearLow());
                            out.println("</TD><TD align=left noWrap>");
                            out.println(ssObj.getDayHigh());
                            out.println("</TD><TD align=left noWrap>");
                            out.println(ssObj.getDayLow());
                            out.println("</TD><TD align=left noWrap>");
                            out.println(ssObj.getPreviousDayClose());

                            out.println("</TD></TR>");
                        } while (ssObj.next());

                        out.println("</TBODY></TABLE>");
                        out.println("</TD></TR></TBODY></TABLE>");

                    }
                }

                out.println("</CENTER></BODY></HTML>");

            }
            catch(Exception e)
            {
                out.println("Exception occured" + e.getMessage());
            }

    }
}
```

Figures 8-8 through 8-11 show the stock quote server in action.

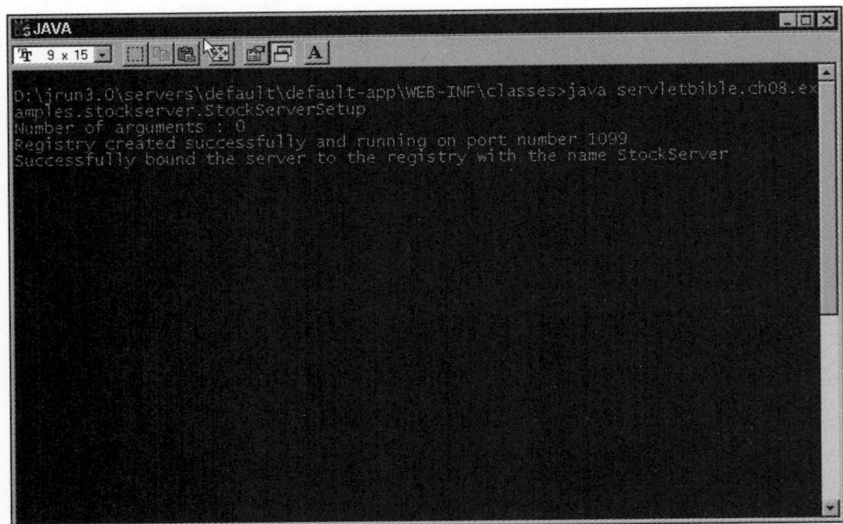

Figure 8-8: Stock quote server in action

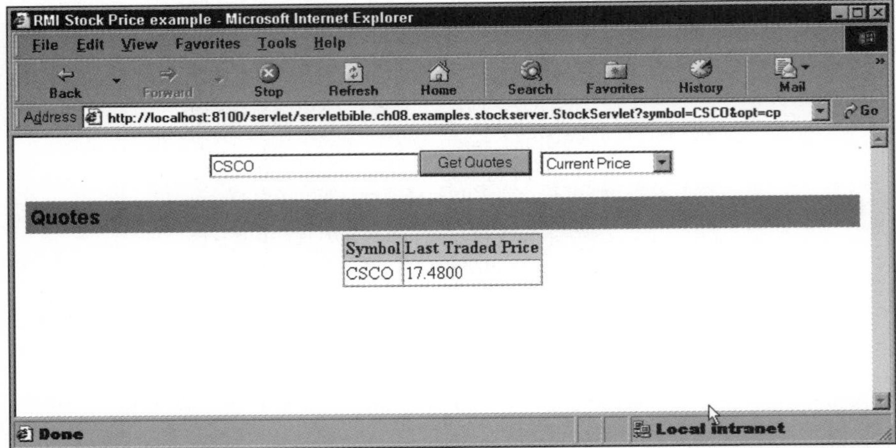

Figure 8-9: Example servlet accessing the stock quote server and retrieving results

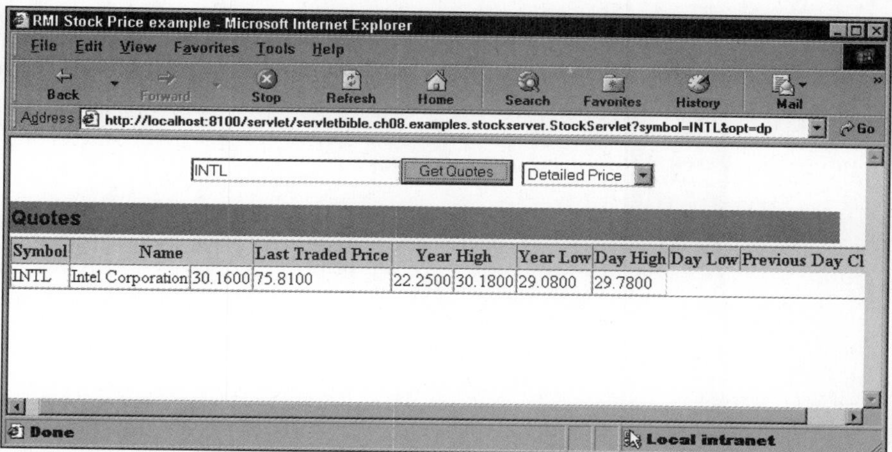

Figure 8-10: Example servlet accessing the stock quote server and retrieving the results

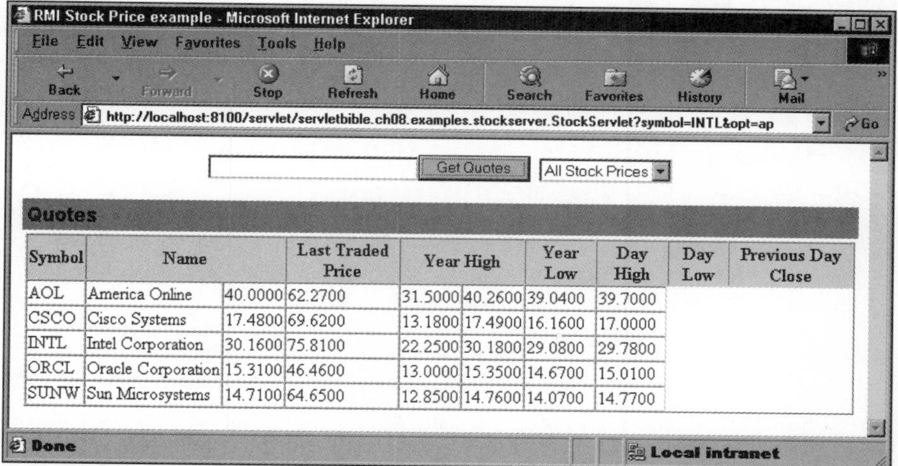

Figure 8-11: Example servlet accessing the stock quote server and retrieving the results

Summary

In this chapter, we discussed the need for distributed systems and the various technologies available to develop distributed applications. We then examined the RMI architecture in detail. We also saw how RMI makes writing distributed applications easier and how it provides an object-oriented solution to writing distributed applications. In addition, we discussed the concepts of marshaling and unmarshaling in detail. We then looked into a sample server application that examines the steps involved in writing RMI applications. Toward the end of the chapter, we developed a sample servlet-based client application that accesses an RMI server object, thus extending the three-tier architecture to n-tiers.

✦ ✦ ✦

Servlet Communications

✦ ✦ ✦ ✦

In This Chapter

Communication and data exchange between applets and servlets

Communication between servlets

Servlet chaining

Servlet nesting and servlet filters

✦ ✦ ✦ ✦

Applet-Servlet Communication

An applet is a Java program that executes on the Web browser. When embedded in a Web page, an applet is transported over the Internet from the server and is installed and executed in the browser automatically. Java applets have limited access to client resources so that they do not disturb data integrity and do not introduce the risk of viruses. Java applets can also use a JDBC connection or distributed objects. The Java applet allows more complex user-interface options than HTML combined with either CGI or Java servlets. However, the Java applet requires a Java-enabled Web browser. Table 9-1 lists the advantages of applets over HTML.

Table 9-1
Advantages of Applets vs. HTML

Applets	*HTML*
Applets allow complex GUI widgets such as grids, spin controls, and scrollbars.	These widgets are not available to HTML.
Applets allow local validation of data the user enters.	Local validation of data is possible by using HTML combined with JavaScript, but variances in JavaScript implementations make JavaScript difficult to use in most cases.
An applet can use the database to perform a list of values lookups and data validation.	HTML (even if combined with JavaScript) cannot do this without invoking a CGI or servlet program and drawing a new HTML page.
Once an applet is downloaded, the amount of data transferred between the Web browser and the server is reduced.	HTML requires that the server transfer the presentation of the data (the HTML tags) along with the data itself. The HTML tags can easily be one-fourth to one-half of the data transferred from the server to the client.

Applet-servlet communication is possible through the following communications:

- Tunneling (HTTP communication)
- Socket communication
- Remote Method Invocation (RMI)

Applet-servlet communication with HTTP tunneling

Accessing HTML form data on the server side is simple by calling the method `HttpRequest.getParameter("Parameter Name")`. While using an applet, a mechanism is needed for the applet to communicate with the servlet. The information entered in the applet GUI components has to be passed to the servlet. Because servlets support the HTTP/CGI interface, we can communicate with the servlet over HTTP socket connections.

HTTP tunneling is the process of creating a subprotocol over an HTTP protocol. The subprotocol contains information required to invoke an object on the Web server, invoke the required method, and get the returned results. A subprotocol concentrates on a specific task without any concern for the transport of data packets between the client and the server. HTTP communications can be one of the following:

✦ Text-based communication
✦ Object-based communication

Text-based HTTP communication

For versions prior to JDK 1.1, applet-to-servlet communication was possible through text-based HTTP communication only. With JDK 1.0.2, only basic scalar data types could be read and written for transmission, and other types had to be packed as a combination of basic types. While writing data, it had to have an indicator so that the type of data was known for reading. Formatting the responses is required in text-based communication.

For text-based HTTP communication, the applet must open a connection to the specified servlet URL. The `java.net.URLConnection` class is used to open the connection to the servlet:

```
URL url=new
URL("http:\\localhost:8100\\servlet\\emp?emp_id="+id_value);
URLConnection servletConnection = url.openConnection();
```

The URL object's `openConnection` method returns an `InputStream` object that contains the response. Once this connection is made, the applet can attain an output stream or input stream on the servlet:

```
InputStream input = servletConnection.getInputStream();
```

The applet can send data to the servlet by sending a `GET` or a `POST` method. If a `GET` method is used, the applet must URL-encode the name/value pair parameters into the URL string. For example, if we want to send the name/value pair of `emp_id=id_value`, our servlet URL resembles:

```
http:\\localhost:8100\\servlet\\emp?emp_id=id_value
```

Listing 9-1 shows HTTP communication using the `GET` method. The applet creates a user interface in which an employee ID can be entered to search for employee details (see Figure 9-1). The applet communicates to the servlet through the HTTP `GET` method. The servlet retrieves the details from the database and returns its response. The applet, in turn, displays employee details (see Figure 9-2).

Listing 9-1

```
import java.applet.*;
import java.awt.*;
import java.awt.event.*;
import java.net.*;
import java.io.*;
```

Continued

Listing 9-1 *(continued)*

```
/*
 * EmployeeSearch applet displays text box for
 * employee id.  After entering id, when the
 * Search button is clicked, it communicates with a
 * servlet and fetches the employee information
 * and displays it in text boxes inside the applet
 */

public class EmployeeSearchApplet extends Applet {

     // Text box to hold employee id, name and city
     TextField txtId,txtName,txtCity;

     // initialize the applet
     public void init() {
          // Labels
          Label lblEmpId, lblName, lblCity, lblEmpty;

          // Search button
          Button btnSearch;

          // Grid Bag Layout for the applet
          GridBagLayout gbLayout;
          GridBagConstraints gbConstraints;

          // Set font
          setFont(new Font("Times-Roman",Font.PLAIN,15));

          // Initialize Labels
          lblEmpId=new Label("Enter Employee ID");
          lblName=new Label("Name");
          lblEmpty=new Label("");
          lblCity=new Label("City");

          // Initialize Text Boxes
          txtId=new TextField(25);
          txtName=new TextField(25);
          txtCity=new TextField(25);

          // Initialize Search button
          btnSearch=new Button("Search Employee Details");

          // Initialize Grid Bag Layout
          gbLayout=new GridBagLayout();

          // Initialize Grid Bag constraints
          gbConstraints=new GridBagConstraints();
```

```
        // set layout
        setLayout(gbLayout);

        //add the labels and textfields to the applet
        gbConstraints.weightx=1;
        gbConstraints.weighty=0;
        gbConstraints.anchor=GridBagConstraints.WEST;
        gbConstraints.insets=new Insets(3,3,3,3);
        gbConstraints.gridwidth=1;
        add(lblEmpId,gbConstraints);

        gbConstraints.gridwidth=GridBagConstraints.REMAINDER;
        gbConstraints.insets=new Insets(0,5,3,0);
        add(txtId,gbConstraints);

        gbConstraints.insets=new Insets(3,3,3,3);
        gbConstraints.gridwidth=1;
        add(lblName,gbConstraints);

        gbConstraints.gridwidth=GridBagConstraints.REMAINDER;
        gbConstraints.insets=new Insets(0,5,3,0);
        add(txtName,gbConstraints);

        gbConstraints.insets=new Insets(3,3,3,3);
        gbConstraints.gridwidth=1;
        add(lblCity,gbConstraints);

        gbConstraints.gridwidth=GridBagConstraints.REMAINDER;
        gbConstraints.insets=new Insets(0,5,3,0);
        add(txtCity,gbConstraints);
        add(btnSearch,gbConstraints);

        gbConstraints.weightx=1;
        gbConstraints.weighty=1;
        add(lblEmpty,gbConstraints);

        // Add action listener to button and listen for events

        btnSearch.addActionListener(new ActionListener() {
            public void actionPerformed(ActionEvent ae) {
                // calls search method when button is clicked
                search();
            }
        });
    }

    // search method gets the employee id entered
    // and makes a call to the servlet to retrieve
    // the employee details.  It then populates the
    // respective text boxes.
```

Continued

Listing 9-1 *(continued)*

```
    private void search() {

        // get the employee id keyed in
        String empId=txtId.getText();

        try {

            // Initialize URL to call the servlet
            URL url=new
URL("http:\\\\localhost:8100\\\\servlet\\\\servletbible.ch09.examples.
EmployeeSearchServlet?empId="+empId);

            // Open the connection to servlet.
            URLConnection servletConnection =
url.openConnection();

            // get the InputStream from the servlet
            InputStream input =
servletConnection.getInputStream();
            BufferedReader br=new BufferedReader(new
InputStreamReader(input));

            int i=0;
            // variable to hold the output
            String searchOutput[] = new String[4];

            // read from InputStream
            while((searchOutput[i]=br.readLine())!=null) {
                i++;
            }
            br.close();
            // set the values read into the text boxes
            txtName.setText(searchOutput[0]);
            txtCity.setText(searchOutput[1]);
        } catch(Exception e) {
            // Exception occurred during search
            e.printStackTrace();
            // Display message in text boxes
            txtName.setText("Search Failed either because ");
            txtCity.setText("data was not found or some exception
occured");
        }
    }
}
```

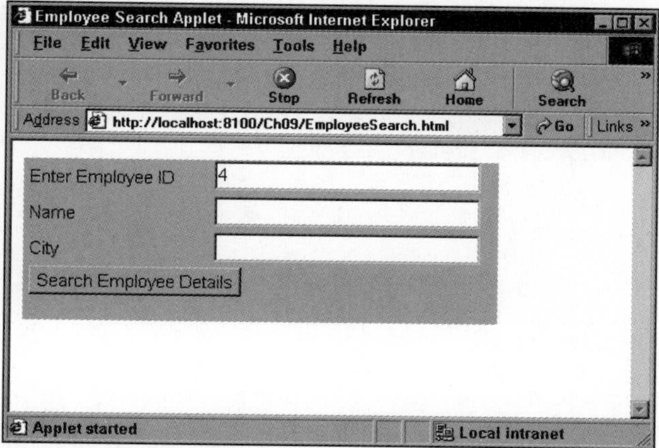

Figure 9-1: The user enters the employee ID to search employee details using HTTP communication.

Listing 9-2

```
package servletbible.ch09.examples;

import javax.servlet.*;
import javax.servlet.http.*;
import java.io.*;
import java.util.*;
import java.sql.*;

/*
 * EmployeeSearchServlet takes in the employee id
 * from the parameter passed from the applet.  It
 * searches for the database for that id and outputs
 * the name and city fields
 */
public class EmployeeSearchServlet extends HttpServlet {

     public void doGet(HttpServletRequest req,HttpServletResponse
res) throws ServletException,IOException {
          // Set the contenty type to text/plain
          res.setContentType("text/plain");

          // get the PrintWriter object
          PrintWriter out=res.getWriter();
          // getConnection method returns a
          // connection to the Employee database
          Connection con=getConnection();
```

Continued

Listing 9-2 (continued)

```
          if(con != null) {
               // Request the employee Id passed as parameter
               String empId=req.getParameter("empId");

               // Fetch the details
               String[] empDetails = fetchDetails(con,empId);

               // Send data
               out.println(empDetails[0]);
               out.println(empDetails[1]);
          } else {
               // Connection was not successful, return proper
messages
               out.println("Could not establish ");
               out.println("connection to database");
          }
          // Close the connection
          try {
               con.close();
          } catch(SQLException se) {
               se.printStackTrace();
          }
          // flush the output and close
          out.flush();
          out.close();
     }

     public void doPost(HttpServletRequest req,HttpServletResponse
res) throws ServletException,IOException {
          doGet(req,res);
     }

     private Connection getConnection() {
          Connection con = null;
          try {

               // Instantiate JDBC-ODBC driver
               Class.forName("sun.jdbc.odbc.JdbcOdbcDriver");
               // Get the connection
               con=DriverManager.getConnection("jdbc:odbc:Employee");

          } catch (SQLException e) {
               // Error getting connection
               System.out.println(e);
          } catch (ClassNotFoundException e) {
               // Error loading JDBC-ODBC
               System.out.println(e);
          }
          return con;
     }
```

```
    private String[] fetchDetails(Connection con, String empId) {
        // Variable to hold the result
        String[] empDetails = new String[2];
        try {
            Statement st=con.createStatement();
            // Execute the query and get the ResultSet object
            ResultSet rs=st.executeQuery("select name,city from
personal where empId = " + empId );
            // Move the cursor to the row fetched
            rs.next();
            // Fetch name and city
            empDetails[0] = rs.getString("name");
            empDetails[1] = rs.getString("city");
            // Close ResultSet
            rs.close();
            // Close Statement
            st.close();

        } catch (SQLException se) {
            // Error processing the query
            se.printStackTrace();
            // Send error message
            empDetails[0] = empDetails[1] = "Error accessing
database";
        }
        return empDetails;
    }
}
```

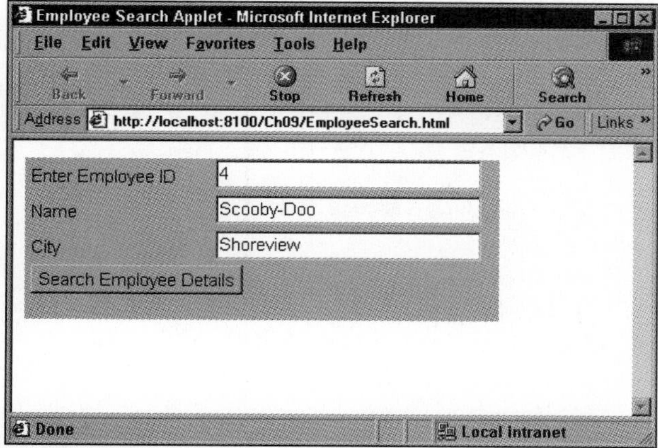

Figure 9-2: An applet displaying the employee details using HTTP communication

If a POST method is used, you can send any form of data (plain text, binary, and so on) to a servlet. The java.net.URLConnection class is used to open a connection to the specified servlet:

```
URL url=new URL("http:\\localhost:8100\\servlet\\emp");
URLConnection servletConnection = url.openConnection();
```

The URL object's openConnection returns an InputStream object that contains the response. Once this connection is made, the applet can get an output stream or input stream on the servlet:

```
InputStream input = servletConnection.getInputStream();
```

Now appending to the URL does not send data. The URL connection is informed that data is sent over the output stream and accepts input:

```
servletConnection.setDoInput(true);
servletConnection.setDoOutput(true);
```

The following method instructs that the connection not use cached versions of the URL:

```
servletConnection.setUseCaches(false);
```

The content type should be set in the HTTP request header. The following method sets the content type in the HTTP request header to the MIME-type application/octet stream. The application/octet stream MIME type allows us to send binary data:

```
servletConnection.setRequestProperty
                ("Content-Type", "application/octet-stream");
```

Now the applet can get input and output streams on the servlet. It can write data to the servlet and read the response:

```
DataOutputStream output = new
DataOutputStream(servletConnection.getOutputStream());
output.writeInt(id_value);
output.flush();
output.close();
InputStream input = servletConnection.getInputStream();
BufferedReader br=new BufferedReader(new InputStreamReader(input));
int i=0;
while((st[i]=br.readLine())!=null) {
i++;
}
```

The servlet must handle the type of data the applet sends. Thus, applets can communicate with servlets by using the GET and POST methods, but they must URL encode each name/value pair while using the GET method.

Object-based HTTP communication

With the introduction of object serialization in JDK 1.1, applet-servlet communication is now possible through object-based HTTP communication. Applets and servlets exchange Java objects, eliminating the issues of formatting the data types. Object serialization eliminates the low-level details of saving and restoring the object. To serialize a Java object, you must implement the `java.io.Serializable` interface. The values of the data members are saved. Later, the object can be deserialized with the values of its data members intact. A Java object can be serialized and deserialized over socket-output streams and socket-input streams.

Listing 9-3 shows object-based HTTP communication. The applet creates a user interface in which an employee ID can be entered to search for employee details. The `java.net.URLConnection` class is used to open a connection to the specified servlet.

The URL connection is informed that data is sent over the output stream and accepts input:

```
servletConnection.setDoInput(true);
servletConnection.setDoOutput(true);
```

The following method instructs that the connection not use cached versions of the URL:

```
servletConnection.setUseCaches(false);
```

The content type should be set in the HTTP request header. The following method sets the content type in the HTTP request header to the MIME-type application/octet stream:

```
servletConnection.setRequestProperty
                ("Content-Type", "application/octet-stream");
```

The application/octet stream MIME type allows us to send binary data.

Now the applet can get input and output streams on the servlet. It can write data to the servlet and read the response. Here, data is sent as a serialized object by using the `writeObject` method of `ObjectOutputStream` class:

```
ObjectOutputStream output = new
ObjectOutputStream(servletConnection.getOutputStream());
output.writeObject(new Integer(id_value));
   output.flush();
```

The servlet retrieves details from the database and returns a response as a serialized object. The `Employee` class implements the `Serializable` interface. The applet deserializes the object and then reads the object by using the `readObject` method of `ObjectInputStreamClass`. The object should be cast to its appropriate class (the `Employee` class, in this case):

```
InputStream input = servletConnection.getInputStream();
ObjectInputStream ob = new ObjectInputStream(input);
Employee em=(Employee)ob.readObject();
String s1=em.getName();
String s2=em.getCity();
```

Listing 9-3

```
import java.applet.*;
import java.awt.*;
import java.awt.event.*;
import java.net.*;
import java.util.*;
import java.io.*;

/*
 * EmployeeSearch applet displays text box for
 * employee id.  After entering id, when the
 * Search button is clicked, it communicates with a
 * servlet and fetches the employee information
 * and displays it in text boxes inside the applet
 */

public class ObjectBasedSearch extends Applet {

     // Text box to hold employee id, name and city
     TextField txtId,txtName,txtCity;

     // initialize the applet
     public void init() {
          // Labels
          Label lblEmpId, lblName, lblCity, lblEmpty;

          // Search button
          Button btnSearch;

          // Grid Bag Layout for the applet
          GridBagLayout gbLayout;
          GridBagConstraints gbConstraints;

          // Set font
          setFont(new Font("Times-Roman",Font.PLAIN,15));

          // Initialize Labels
          lblEmpId=new Label("Enter Employee ID");
          lblName=new Label("Name");
          lblEmpty=new Label("");
          lblCity=new Label("City");

          // Initialize Text Boxes
          txtId=new TextField(25);
          txtName=new TextField(25);
```

```
txtCity=new TextField(25);

// Initialize Search button
btnSearch=new Button("Search Employee Details");

// Initialize Grid Bag Layout
gbLayout=new GridBagLayout();

// Initialize Grid Bag constraints
gbConstraints=new GridBagConstraints();

// set layout
setLayout(gbLayout);

//add the labels and textfields to the applet
gbConstraints.weightx=1;
gbConstraints.weighty=0;
gbConstraints.anchor=GridBagConstraints.WEST;
gbConstraints.insets=new Insets(3,3,3,3);
gbConstraints.gridwidth=1;
add(lblEmpId,gbConstraints);

gbConstraints.gridwidth=GridBagConstraints.REMAINDER;
gbConstraints.insets=new Insets(0,5,3,0);
add(txtId,gbConstraints);

gbConstraints.insets=new Insets(3,3,3,3);
gbConstraints.gridwidth=1;
add(lblName,gbConstraints);

gbConstraints.gridwidth=GridBagConstraints.REMAINDER;
gbConstraints.insets=new Insets(0,5,3,0);
add(txtName,gbConstraints);

gbConstraints.insets=new Insets(3,3,3,3);
gbConstraints.gridwidth=1;
add(lblCity,gbConstraints);

gbConstraints.gridwidth=GridBagConstraints.REMAINDER;
gbConstraints.insets=new Insets(0,5,3,0);
add(txtCity,gbConstraints);
add(btnSearch,gbConstraints);

gbConstraints.weightx=1;
gbConstraints.weighty=1;
add(lblEmpty,gbConstraints);

// Add action listener to button and listen for events

btnSearch.addActionListener(new ActionListener() {
     public void actionPerformed(ActionEvent ae) {
          // calls search method when button is clicked
```

Continued

Listing 9-3 *(continued)*

```
                    search();
                }
            });
        }

        // search method gets the employee id entered
        // and makes a call to the servlet to retrieve
        // the employee details.  It then populates the
        // respective text boxes.
        private void search() {

            // get the employee id keyed in
            String empId=txtId.getText();

            try {

                // Initialize URL to call the servlet
                URL url=new
URL("http:\\localhost:8100\\servlet\\servletbible.ch09.examples.
ObjectBasedSearchServlet");

                 // Open the connection to servlet.
                 URLConnection servletConnection =
url.openConnection();
                System.out.println("Point 1");
                // Set client caching to false
                servletConnection.setUseCaches(false);

                // Enable I/O through the connection
                servletConnection.setDoInput(true);
                servletConnection.setDoOutput(true);

                // set request content type to object type
                servletConnection.setRequestProperty("Content-Type",
"application/octet-stream ");

                // gets the InputStream on the servlet  and send
employee
                //id to the servlet
                ObjectOutputStream output = new
ObjectOutputStream(servletConnection.getOutputStream());

                // Pass the employee ID
                output.writeObject(new Integer(empId));

                // flush and close the output
                output.flush();
                output.close();

                // get the InputStream from the servlet and read the
                //Employee  object
```

```
                InputStream input =
servletConnection.getInputStream();
                ObjectInputStream ois = new ObjectInputStream(input);

                // Get the employee object
                Vector emp=(Vector)ois.readObject();
                ois.close();

                // Get the details
                String name=(String) emp.elementAt(0);
                String city=(String) emp.elementAt(1);

                 // set the values read into the text boxes
                 txtName.setText(name);
                 txtCity.setText(city);
                 System.out.println("Finished Applet...");
           } catch(Exception e) {
                // Exception occurred during search
                e.printStackTrace();
                // Display message in text boxes
                txtName.setText("Search Failed either because ");
                txtCity.setText("data was not found or some exception
occured");
           }
      }
}
```

Listing 9-4 shows the servlet, which searches employee details from the database and returns the serialized `Employee` object by using the `writeObject` method of `ObjectOutputStream`.

Listing 9-4

```
package servletbible.ch09.examples;

import javax.servlet.*;
import javax.servlet.http.*;
import java.io.*;
import java.util.*;
import java.sql.*;

/*
 * EmployeeSearchServlet takes in the employee id
 * from the parameter passed from the applet.  It
 * searches for the database for that id and outputs
 * the name and city fields
 */
```

Continued

Listing 9-4 *(continued)*

```
public class ObjectBasedSearchServlet extends HttpServlet {

     public void doGet(HttpServletRequest req,HttpServletResponse
res) throws ServletException,IOException {
          //open InputStream
          ObjectInputStream input=new
ObjectInputStream(req.getInputStream());
          // open OutputStream
          ObjectOutputStream output=new
ObjectOutputStream(res.getOutputStream());
          try {
               // read the employee id sent by the applet
               Integer empId=(Integer)input.readObject();
               // Set the contenty type to application/octet-stream
               res.setContentType("application/octet-stream");
               // getConnection method returns a
               // connection to the Employee database
               Connection con=getConnection();
               Vector emp = new Vector();;
               if(con != null) {
                    // Fetch the details
                    String[] empDetails =
fetchDetails(con,empId.toString());
                    emp.add(0, new String(empDetails[0]));
                    emp.add(1, new String(empDetails[1]));
               } else {
                    // Connection was not successful, return proper
messages
                    emp.add(0, new String("Could not establish"));
                    emp.add(0, new String("connection to database"));
               }

               // Close the connection
               try {
                    con.close();
               } catch(SQLException se) {
                    se.printStackTrace();
               }

               // Send data
               output.writeObject(emp);
          } catch(Exception e) {
               System.out.println(e.getMessage());
               e.printStackTrace();
          }

          // flush the output and close
          output.flush();
          output.close();
     }
```

```
	public void doPost(HttpServletRequest req,HttpServletResponse
res) throws ServletException,IOException {
		doGet(req,res);
	}

	private Connection getConnection() {
		Connection con = null;
		try {

			// Instantiate JDBC-ODBC driver
			Class.forName("sun.jdbc.odbc.JdbcOdbcDriver");
			// Get the connection
			con=DriverManager.getConnection("jdbc:odbc:Employee");

		} catch (SQLException e) {
			// Error getting connection
			System.out.println(e);
		} catch (ClassNotFoundException e) {
			// Error loading JDBC-ODBC
			System.out.println(e);
		}
		return con;
	}

	private String[] fetchDetails(Connection con, String empId) {
		// Variable to hold the result
		String[] empDetails = new String[2];
		try {
			Statement st=con.createStatement();
			// Execute the query and get the ResultSet object
			ResultSet rs=st.executeQuery("select name,city from
personal where empId = " + empId );
			// Move the cursor to the row fetched
			rs.next();
			// Fetch name and city
			empDetails[0] = rs.getString("name");
			empDetails[1] = rs.getString("city");
			// Close ResultSet
			rs.close();
			// Close Statement
			st.close();

		} catch (SQLException se) {
			// Error processing the query
			se.printStackTrace();
			// Send error message
			empDetails[0] = empDetails[1] = "Error accessing
database";
		}
		return empDetails;
	}
}
```

The employee details are stored in a vector, and the vector is passed to the applet through the `writeObject` method of the `ObjectOutputStream` class. The `fetchDetails` method retrieves the employee name and city for the employee ID passed as a parameter.

An object-based HTTP communication example: FileSearch servlet

Listing 9-5 shows object-based HTTP communication. The applet communicates with the servlet to read the serialized object `CmdResult`. Deserializing the object, the applet displays the list of directories and files in a tree. The code listing consists of the following:

- ✦ `FileViewer.jsp`, which embeds the applet
- ✦ The applet `RemoteFile.java`, which uses HTTP communication to read and deserialize the `CmdResult` object. It displays the directories and files in a hierarchy in a tree.
- ✦ The servlet `FileSearch.java`, which sends the `CmdResult` object to the applet
- ✦ A class `CmdResult.java`, which is the serialized object the servlet returns

Listing 9-5

```
<html>
<body>
<jsp:plugin
 type="applet"
 code="RemoteFile.class"
 codebase="/"
    width="640"
    height="400"
</jsp:plugin>
</body>
   </html>
```

The JSP file in Listing 9-5 embeds the applet `RemoteFile.java`.

In Listing 9-6, the applet contains `JScrollPane` with `JTree` to show the hierarchical view of directories and files. The `getContentPane` method is used to get the container:

```
Container co=getContentPane();
```

Listing 9-6

```
import javax.swing.*;
import javax.swing.tree.*;
import java.applet.*;
import java.awt.*;
import java.awt.event.*;
import java.net.*;
import java.io.*;
import java.util.*;

public class RemoteFile extends JApplet {
  JTree tree;
  DefaultMutableTreeNode node;

  public void init() {

    Button   b=new Button("List Directories & Files");
    Container co=getContentPane();
    co.setLayout(new BorderLayout());

    // creates the  top node
     node= new DefaultMutableTreeNode("Server");

    // creates the tree
     tree=new JTree(node);
     int v=ScrollPaneConstants.VERTICAL_SCROLLBAR_AS_NEEDED;
     int h=ScrollPaneConstants.HORIZONTAL_SCROLLBAR_AS_NEEDED;

    // creates the scrollpane
     JScrollPane scrollpane=new JScrollPane(tree,v,h);
     co.add(scrollpane,BorderLayout.CENTER);
     co.add(b,"South");

       // register for action event and handle it
       b.addActionListener(new ActionListener() {
      public void actionPerformed(ActionEvent ae) {
        search();
      }
    });
    }

     void search() {

    try {
URL url=new URL("http://localhost:8100/servlet/FileSearch");
// open connection using openConnection()
  URLConnection servletConnection = url.openConnection();
  servletConnection.setUseCaches(false);
  servletConnection.setDoInput(true);
  servletConnection.setDoOutput(true);
```

Continued

Listing 9-6 (continued)

```
 servletConnection.setRequestProperty
            ("Content-Type", "application/octet-stream ");

 // get the InputStream
 InputStream input = servletConnection.getInputStream();
 ObjectInputStream ob = new ObjectInputStream(input);
// Deserialize and read the CmdResult object
CmdResult em=(CmdResult)ob.readObject();
// call getResult() method of CmdResult class
Hashtable v=em.getResult();
Enumeration e=v.keys();
     DefaultMutableTreeNode dd[]=new
     DefaultMutableTreeNode[8];

int ii=0;
while(e.hasMoreElements()) {
String d=(String)e.nextElement();
// create subtree containing directories
dd[ii]=new DefaultMutableTreeNode(d);
// add the subtree to the top node
node.add(dd[ii]);

Vector vec=(Vector)v.get(d);
Enumeration enum=vec.elements();
// get the list of files in each directory and add them
//to the directory subtree
while(enum.hasMoreElements()) {
 dd[ii].add(new
 DefaultMutableTreeNode(""+enum.nextElement()));
}
ii++;
}
ob.close();
   }
   catch(Exception e) {
    try{
      e.printStackTrace();
    }catch(Exception ee){
    }
   }
    }
  }
```

The following code creates the root node for the tree:

```
node= new DefaultMutableTreeNode("Server");
```

The following code creates the tree:

```
tree=new JTree(node);
```

The following code creates a scroll pane and adds the tree to it:

```
int v=ScrollPaneConstants.VERTICAL_SCROLLBAR_AS_NEEDED;
int h=ScrollPaneConstants.HORIZONTAL_SCROLLBAR_AS_NEEDED;
JScrollPane scrollpane=new JScrollPane(tree,v,h);
co.add(scrollpane,BorderLayout.CENTER);
```

The `java.net.URLConnection` class is used to open a connection to the specified servlet:

```
URL url=new URL("http://localhost:8100/servlet/FileSearch");
URLConnection servletConnection = url.openConnection();
```

The URL connection is informed that data be sent over the output stream and accepted through the input stream:

```
servletConnection.setDoInput(true);
servletConnection.setDoOutput(true);
```

The following method instructs that the connection not use cached versions of the URL:

```
servletConnection.setUseCaches(false);
```

The content type should be set in the HTTP request header. The following method sets the content type in the HTTP request header to the MIME type application/octet stream:

```
servletConnection.setRequestProperty
            ("Content-Type", "application/octet-stream");
```

The application/octet stream MIME type allows us to send binary data.

The applet deserializes the object then and reads the object by using the `readObject` method of `ObjectInputStreamClass`. The object should be cast to its appropriate class (`CmdResult`, in this case):

```
InputStream input = servletConnection.getInputStream();
ObjectInputStream ob = new ObjectInputStream(input);
CmdResult em=(CmdResult)ob.readObject();
```

Using the `getResult` method of the `CmdResult` object, a hashtable containing a key/value pair of directories and files is obtained.

```
Hashtable v=em.getResult();
```

The following code obtains an enumeration of directories by using the `keys` method of the `Hashtable` class:

```
Enumeration e=v.keys();
DefaultMutableTreeNode dd[]=new DefaultMutableTreeNode[8];
int ii=0;
while(e.hasMoreElements())
String d=(String)e.nextElement();
```

The `DefaultMutableTreeNode` constructor creates a subtree for each directory, and the `add` method adds each directory to the root node `Server`:

```
dd[ii]=new DefaultMutableTreeNode(d);
node.add(dd[ii]);
```

Using the `get` method of `Hashtable`, a vector containing the list of files in this directory is obtained:

```
Vector vec=(Vector)v.get(d);
```

Listing 9-7 adds this list of files to the directory subtree:

```
Enumeration enum=vec.elements();
while(enum.hasMoreElements()) {
dd[ii].add(new DefaultMutableTreeNode(""+enum.nextElement()));
}
```

Listing 9-7

```
import java.io.*;
import java.util.*;

/**
 * Stores the result of client request
 */
public class CmdResult implements Serializable {

    // Stores the result of client request
    private boolean error = false;
    // If successful, store the filenames and directory names
    private Hashtable result = null;
    // If unsuccessful, stores the error message associated with it
    private String errorMessage = null;

    /**
     * Creates new CmdResult
     *
     * @param error Status of the client request
     * @param result Hashtable of file or directory names
     * @param errorMessage Error message
```

```
     */
    public CmdResult( boolean error, Hashtable result, String
errorMessage ) {
        this.error = error;
        this.result = result;
        this.errorMessage = errorMessage;
    }

    /**
     * Creates new CmdResult
     *
     * @param error Status of the client request
     * @param errorMessage Error message
     */
    public CmdResult( boolean error, String errorMessage ) {
        this( error, null, errorMessage );
    }

    /**
     * Creates new CmdResult
     *
     * @param result Hashtable of file or directory names
     */
    public CmdResult(Hashtable result ) {
        this( false, result, null );
    }

    /**
*
     * @return String error message
     */
    public String getErrorMessage() {
        return errorMessage;
    }

    /**
     * Returns status of the client request
     *
     * @return boolean status of the client request
     */
    public boolean isError() {
        return error;
    }

    /**
     * Returns the Hashtable of file or directory names

*/
    public Hashtable getResult() {
        return result;
    }
}
```

In the servlet in Listing 9-8, the following code gets the list of directories:

```
File ff=new File("\\");
File[] roots=ff.listRoots();
```

Listing 9-8

```
import java.io.*;
import javax.servlet.http.*;
import javax.servlet.*;
import java.util.*;

public class FileSearch extends HttpServlet{

     public  void doGet(HttpServletRequest req,HttpServletResponse
     res) throws ServletException, IOException {
    doPost(req,res);
     }

  public void doPost(HttpServletRequest req,HttpServletResponse
  res) throws ServletException, IOException {
    ObjectOutputStream oos=null;
    try {
     Hashtable files=new Hashtable();
     File ff=new File("\\");

     // gets the list of directories
     File[] roots=ff.listRoots();

     for(int j=0;j<roots.length;j++)   {
       System.out.println(roots[j]);
       File f=new File((roots[j]).toString());
       File d[]=null;

       // get the list of files in each directory
       d=f.listFiles( new FileFilter() {
        public boolean accept( File file ) {
         return file.isFile();
        }
       });
       if(d!=null) {
        Vector fv=new Vector();

        for(int i=0;i<d.length;i++)  {
         // add the files to the vector
         fv.add(d[i].getName());
        }

        // put directory/files pair into the Hashtable
        files.put(roots[j].toString(),fv);
```

```
      }
    }

    // Instantiate a new CmdResult object
  CmdResult result = new CmdResult( files );
  res.setContentType("application/octet-stream");

   // open output stream
   oos = new ObjectOutputStream( res.getOutputStream() );
   // write the serialized object
   oos.writeObject(result);
   oos.flush();
  }
     catch( Exception e ) {
       e.printStackTrace();
       try {
        // We encountered an error
        // Notify the client of the error
        CmdResult result = new CmdResult(true,e.getMessage());
        oos.writeObject( result );
        oos.flush();
        oos.close();
       } catch( Exception e1 ) {
           e1.printStackTrace();
       }
     }
     }
    }
```

The following code iterates through all the directories and creates a file object for the current directory:

```
for(int j=0;j<roots.length;j++)
File f=new File((roots[j]).toString());
```

Using the `listFiles` method of the `File` object, the following code snippet retrieves the list of files in this directory:

```
File d[]=null;
d=f.listFiles( new FileFilter() {
                    public boolean accept( File file ) {
                        return file.isFile();
                    }
                }
            );
```

The `add` method of the `Vector` object adds the list of files in the current directory to vector `fv`:

```
if(d!=null) {
Vector fv=new Vector();
for(int i=0;i<d.length;i++)  {
System.out.println(d[i].getName());
fv.add(d[i].getName());
}
```

The `put` method of the `Hashtable` puts the key/value pair of the directory and file-list vector into the `Hashtable` `files`:

```
files.put(roots[j].toString(),fv);
```

Next, the program instantiates a new `CmdResult` object with the `files` `Hashtable`:

```
CmdResult result = new CmdResult(files);
```

The `setContentType` of the `Response` object is used to set the content type to `application/octet-stream`:

```
res.setContentType("application/octet-stream");
```

The following code opens the output stream to write the serialized object:

```
oos = new ObjectOutputStream( res.getOutputStream() );
```

Using `writeObject` of `ObjectOutputStream` sends the serialized `CmdResult` object back to the applet:

```
oos.writeObject(result);
oos.flush();
```

Interservlet Communication

In the first half of this chapter, we examined how communication servlets communicate with applets. Now, let's examine how servlets with other servlets.

Servlet chaining

Servlet chaining involves sending the output from one servlet to the input of another servlet. The output of the last servlet in the chain is sent as a response to the client. Servlets in the chain can handle the body content of the previous servlet's output. They can also process header values by adding, changing, or suppressing the response headers of the previous servlet. Chaining provides a new functionality by helping to split the job among a list of servlets.

Servlet chaining can be implemented in the following ways:

- ✦ Explicit chaining by servlet aliasing
- ✦ MIME-type chaining
- ✦ HTML requests

Explicit chaining by servlet aliasing

Servlet aliasing helps in implementing chaining by explicitly specifying the servlets and their order for certain requests. In servlet aliasing, a chain consists of servlets that are comma-separated and listed in the sequence of the chain. A single alias name or servlet name is given for the chain. When a client sends a request for the alias name or servlet name of the chain, it invokes the first servlet in the chain. Its output is passed to the next servlet. This continues until the output of the last servlet is sent to the client. The output of the previous servlet in the chain can be read by using `InputStream`, returned by `getInputStream`, or `Reader`, returned by `getReader` of `HttpServletRequest`. Employ the following steps to enable chaining by using servlet aliasing in JRun:

1. Write and compile the servlets to be chained.
2. Start the JRun Management console.
3. Click the required JRun server, and expand the Web-applications item.
4. Click the Web application containing the servlets for which you want to enable servlet chaining (see Figure 9-3).
5. In the Servlet URL Mappings panel, click Edit (see Figure 9-4).
6. Type the alias name that clients type in a URL to invoke the first servlet in the chain.
7. In the Servlet Invoked field, type the servlets in the chain by using a comma-separated list (see Figure 9-5). Use the servlet names specified in the Servlet Definitions panel, and click Update.

MIME type chaining

MIME type chaining triggers the next servlet automatically when a predecessor servlet returns the response of an associated MIME type. In MIME type chaining, a servlet is registered for a particular MIME type. When another servlet sends output of the same MIME type, the registered servlet handles the output.

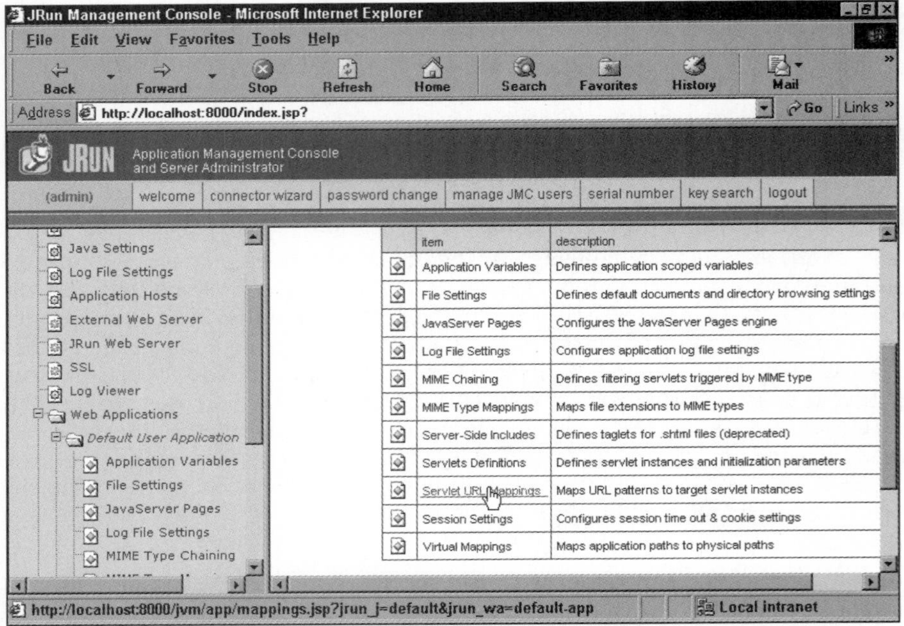

Figure 9-3: The user clicks the Servlet URL Mapping link for chaining by servlet aliasing.

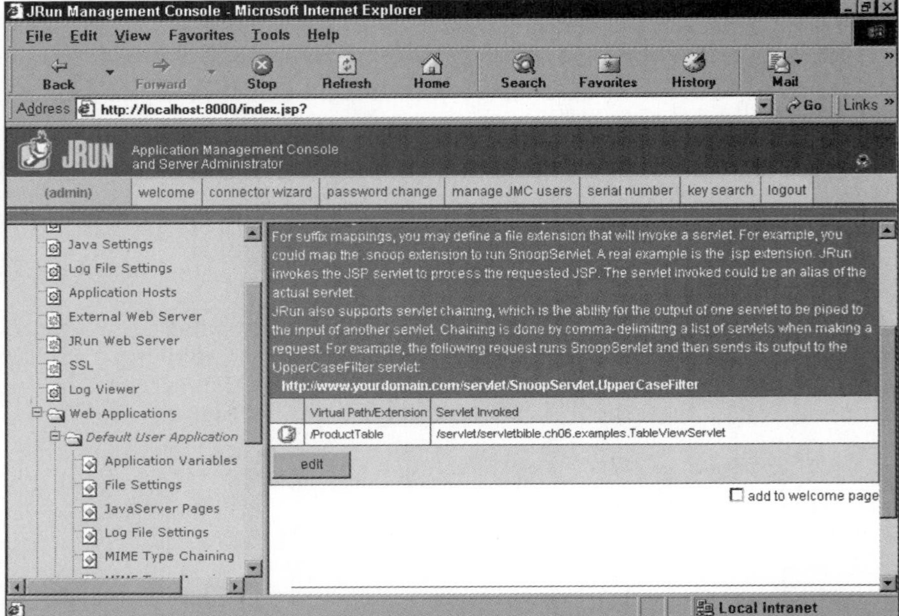

Figure 9-4: Click edit in the Servlet URL Mapping panel to define the servlets to be chained.

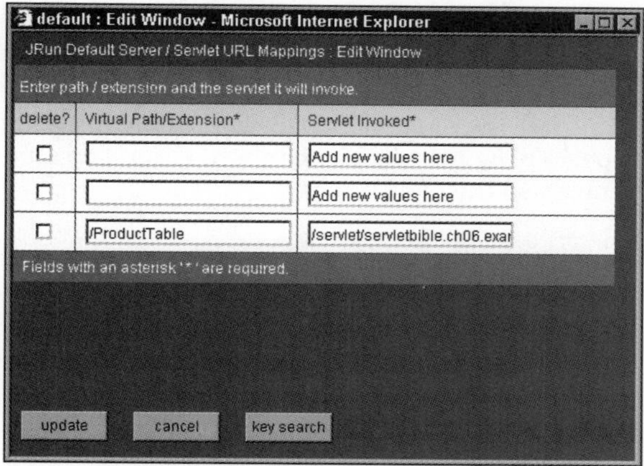

Figure 9-5: Enter the list of servlets in the Servlet Invoked field and chain path/extension in the virtual-path field.

Follow these steps to enable chaining by using servlet aliasing in JRun:

1. Write and compile the servlets to be chained. Start the JRun Management console. Click the required JRun server, and expand the Web-applications item. Click MIME Chaining. The MIME Type Mappings panel displays (see Figure 9-6).

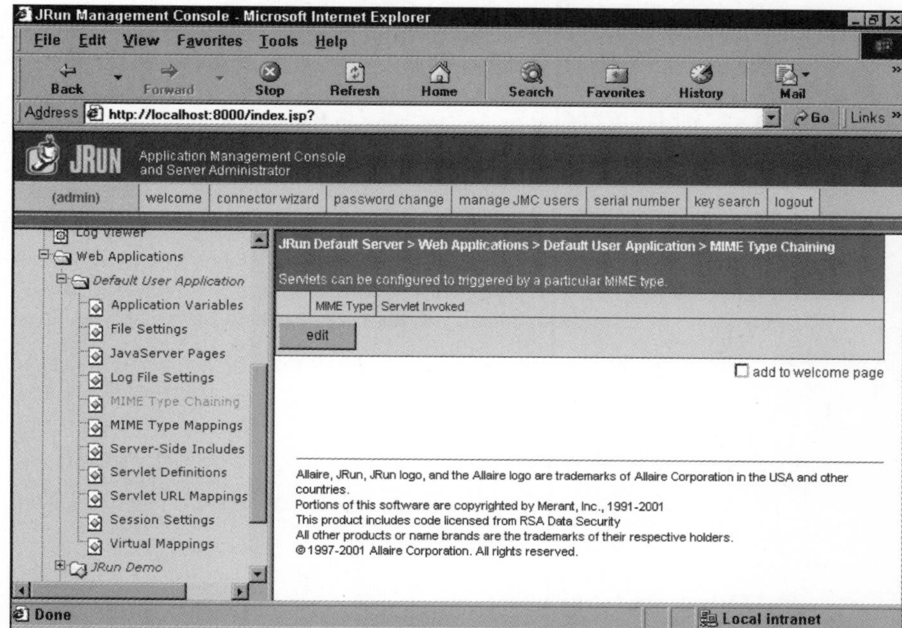

Figure 9-6: Click Edit to open the MIME Type Mappings window to register servlets for MIME type chaining.

2. Click Edit. The MIME Type Settings window opens. In the MIME Type field, enter the MIME type in the form of xxx/yyy (for example, **text/vnd.wap.wml**, **text/plain**, **text/html**, **image/gif**, **image/jpg**).
3. In the Servlet Invoked field, enter the name of the servlet (or an alias) to be triggered by that MIME type (see Figure 9-7). You can also enter a chain of servlets, separated by commas, in this field.
4. To delete a MIME filter, select its Delete? checkbox.
5. To apply your changes, click Update.
6. Restart your JRun server.

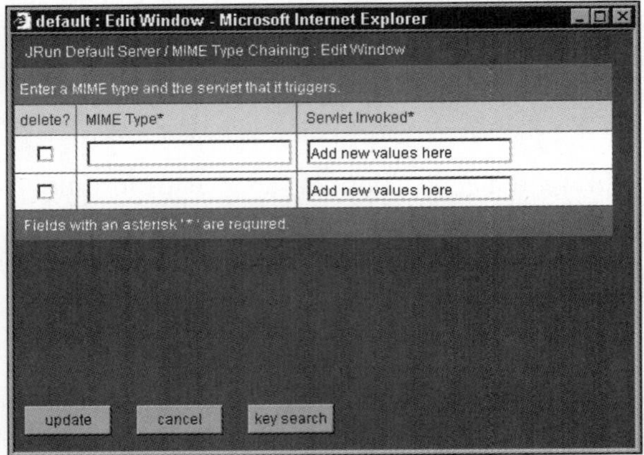

Figure 9-7: Enter the list of servlets to be invoked in the Servlet Invoked field and MIME type in the MIME Type Extension field.

Listing 9-9 illustrates MIME type chaining. Here, the second servlet, `XMLFilter`, is invoked when the response type of the first servlet is `text/xml`. The second servlet uses SAX API for parsing the XML file and sends HTML output to the client. The second servlet reads the XML file location from the first servlet and parses it by using SAX API.

The code listing consists of four files:

- ✦ An XML file to be parsed: `Book.xml`
- ✦ The first servlet, `MimeFilter`, with its response type `text/xml`, which writes the XML file path
- ✦ The second servlet, `XMLFilter`, which parses the XML document and writes HTML output to the client

✦ A Java class SAX1 that handles the events the parsing triggers. This class has an accessor method, which returns a `Hashtable`. The `Hashtable` contains an element/value pair of XML elements and its corresponding values.

Using the steps stated previously, set the MIME type chaining for text/xml for the `XMLFilter` servlet, as shown in Figure 9-8. Type **text/xml** in the MIME type and **XMLFilter** in the Servlet Invoked field. Click the Update button and restart the server.

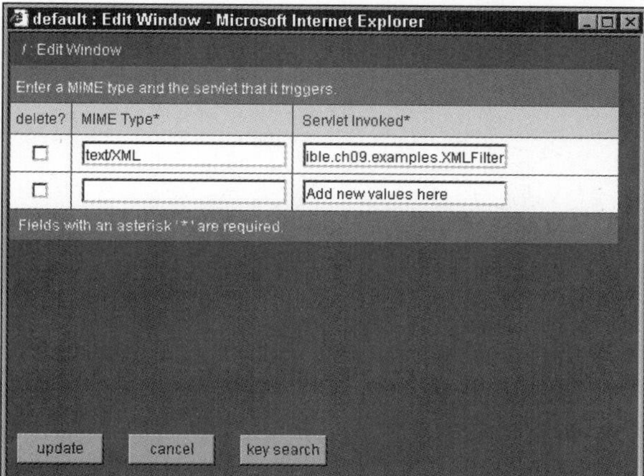

Figure 9-8: Enter the servlet (XMLFilter) to be invoked in the Servlet Invoked field and MIME type (text/xml) in the MIME Type Extension field.

Listing 9-9

```
  <?xml version="1.0"?>
  <BOOK>
  <TITLE>Servlets Bible</TITLE>
  <AUTHOR>Ritchie</AUTHOR>
  <PUBLISHER>Willy</PUBLISHER>
  <PRICE >800</PRICE>
</BOOK>
```

Listing 9-10

```
package servletbible.ch09.examples;
import javax.servlet.*;
import javax.servlet.http.*;
import java.io.*;
```

Continued

Listing 9-10 *(continued)*

```
import java.util.*;
import java.sql.*;

public class MimeFilter extends HttpServlet {

public void doGet(HttpServletRequest req,HttpServletResponse
res)
throws ServletException,IOException {

// Mime Type of response is set to 'text/xml'
res.setContentType("text/xml");
PrintWriter out=res.getWriter();
String file="c:\\book.xml";

// writes the path of XML document
out.println(file);
out.flush();
}
}
```

In Listing 9-11, the XML document path is read from the first servlet. Then the instance of `SAXParser` (which is used in parsing the XML document) is obtained by using the `newSAXParser` method of the `SAXParserFactory` class. Using the `parse` method of `SAXParser`, the parsing of the XML document starts. The events triggered are handled by `SAX1`, which implements the `HandlerBase` interface. Then, using the `getTable` method of `SAX1`, it gets the `Hashtable` containing the elements and data of the XML document. Then it writes the results as HTML data to the client.

Listing 9-11

```
import javax.servlet.*;
import javax.servlet.http.*;
import java.util.Hashtable;
import java.util.Enumeration;
import java.io.*;
import javax.xml.parsers.SAXParserFactory;
import javax.xml.parsers.SAXParser;
import org.xml.sax.*;


public class XMLFilter extends HttpServlet {

public void doGet(HttpServletRequest req,HttpServletResponse
res)
throws ServletException,IOException {
```

```
res.setContentType("text/html");
PrintWriter out=res.getWriter();

// reads the path of XML document from the first servlet
BufferedReader br=req.getReader();
String file=null;
try {
 file=br.readLine();
}
catch(IOException e) {
 System.out.println(e);
}
File f=new File(file);
FileReader fr=new FileReader(f);

     try {

//Instance of SAXParserFactory created
SAXParserFactory spf=SAXParserFactory.newInstance();

// SAXParser instantiated using SAXParserFactory's //newSAXParser()
method
SAXParser sp=spf.newSAXParser();

// Get instance of event handler class which implements //HandlerBase
and handles the events triggered
SAX1  handler=new SAX1();

// parser started using parse( ) method of SAXParser
sp.parse(new InputSource(fr),handler);

// Get the Hashtable using accessor method getTable() of //SAX1
Hashtable cfg=handler.getTable();

// returns enumeration of keys in Hashtable
Enumeration en= cfg.keys();
out.println("<html><table align=center width=50% border=5 ");

//enumerates all elements in Hashtable and writes the //object,key
values in a table format to the client
while(en.hasMoreElements())
{
      String s=(String) en.nextElement();

out.println("<tr><td>"+s+"</td><td>"+cfg.get(s)+"</td></tr>");
}
out.println("</table></html>");
out.flush();
 }catch(Exception e) {
     }
   }
 }
```

In Listing 9-12, HandlerBase is implemented to handle the events triggered during parsing. Methods such as startDocument, endDocument, startElement, and endElement are invoked when an XML tag is recognized. This interface also defines the characters and processingInstruction methods, which are invoked when the parser encounters the text in an XML element or in an inline processing instruction, respectively.

Listing 9-12

```
import java.io.*;
import java.util.*;
import org.xml.sax.*;

 public  class SAX1 extends HandlerBase{

   Hashtable tb=new Hashtable();
   String cu,cv,sr;

   public void setTable(Hashtable ta) {
     tb=ta;
   }


// Accessor method returning the Hashtable with the parsed
// results
public Hashtable getTable() {
  return tb;
}

   // called at start of Document
public void startDocument ()throws SAXException {
}

// called at end of Document
public void endDocument()throws SAXException {
}

// invoked at start of a new element
public void startElement (String name, AttributeList attrs)
throws SAXException {
 cu=name;
}

   // invoked at end of the  element
public void endElement (String name)throws SAXException {
 //adds element/value pair to Hashtable after checking for
 // closing element tag
     if(cu.equals(name))
   tb.put(cu,cv);
   }
```

```
   // invoked when data is encountered for an element
   public void characters (char buf [], int offset, int len)
   throws SAXException {
     // Data characters are converted into String
sr = new String(buf, offset, len);
     cv=sr;
   }
 }
```

The `startElement` method is invoked when an element (`<TITLE>`, for instance) is encountered. The element's value is stored in a variable `cu`.

The method `characters` is called when element data (`Servlets Bible`, for example, is encountered and is stored in `cv`.

The method `endElement` is called when the end of the element (say, `</TITLE>`) is encountered. Now the element/value pair is stored in `Hashtable` by using the `put` method of `Hashtable`.

The final HTML output to the client is shown in Figure 9-9.

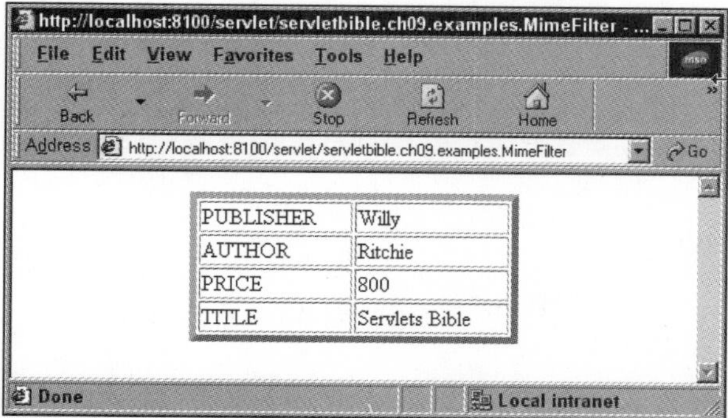

Figure 9-9: The user requests the MIMEFilter servlet and receives final HTML output from the XMLParser servlet invoked by MIME type chaining.

Chaining using HTML requests

When a list of servlets in the chain is specified as an HTTP request, servlet chaining is allowed. JRun allows chaining using HTML requests.

Listing 9-13 shows a chain in which the second servlet reads the plain text of the first servlet and converts the text into uppercase letters, returning the output (shown in Listing 9-14).

Listing 9-13

```
import javax.servlet.*;
import javax.servlet.http.*;
import java.io.*;

public class smallCase extends HttpServlet {

  public void doGet(HttpServletRequest req,HttpServletResponse
  res) throws ServletException,IOException {
res.setContentType("text/plain");
PrintWriter out=res.getWriter();
out.println(" this is an example of servlet chaining which converts
lowercase to uppercase letters");
out.flush();
  }
 }
```

Listing 9-14

```
import javax.servlet.*;
import javax.servlet.http.*;
import java.io.*;

public class UpperCase extends HttpServlet {

  public void doGet(HttpServletRequest req,HttpServletResponse
  res) throws ServletException,IOException {
     res.setContentType("text/html");
 PrintWriter out=res.getWriter();
 BufferedReader br=req.getReader();
 out.println("<html><body bgcolor=cyan><h1>Servlet
 Chaining</h1><hr><br>");
 String st;

 // reads the output of first servlet and sends output to
 client in uppercase
 while((st=br.readLine())!=null){
  out.println(st.toUpperCase()+"\n");
  out.flush();
 }

     }
}
```

Type the HTTP request as a list of servlets in the chain, as follows:

```
http://localhost:8100/servlet/smallCase,UpperCase
```

You can see the final output in Figure 9-10.

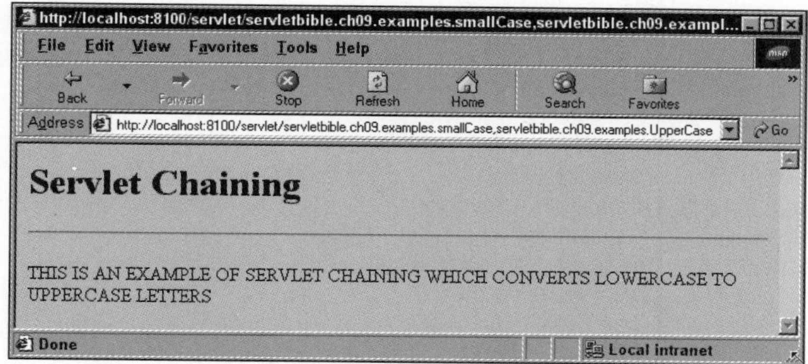

Figure 9-10: Servlet chaining using the HTTP requests method

Servlet nesting

When a servlet is executing, it can use the `RequestDispatcher` interface to invoke another resource (servlet, HTML files, and so on) on the server, so that its response can include the content the invoked resource generates. The servlet can forward its request to the invoked resource.

An object implementing the `RequestDispatcher` interface is obtained by using the `getNamedDispatcher` method of the `ServletContext` object, which returns the `RequestDispatcher` object for the named servlet.

The `getRequestDispatcher` method of the `ServletContext` object returns the `RequestDispatcher` object for the resource at the specified path.

You can get a `RequestDispatcher` from either a request or the Web context; however, the two approaches produce slightly different results. The method takes the path to the requested resource as an argument. A request can take a relative path (one that does not begin with a '/'), but the Web context requires an absolute path. If the resource is not available, or if the server has not implemented a `RequestDispatcher` object for that type of resource, the `getRequestDispatcher` method will return null. Your servlet should be prepared to deal with this condition through servlet exception handling.

The include method

The include method of the RequestDispatcher object helps in including contents of another text file, HTML file, servlet, JSP file, and so on. Before calling the include method, or after calling it, the calling servlet can write its response to ServletOutputStream or PrintWriter. To pass any data to the target servlet or JSP page, the ServletRequest object's setAttribute method can be used.

If the RequestDispatcher object wraps a static resource, the include method enables programmatic server-side includes. For example, if the RequestDispatcher object wraps a text file, its text is copied into the output stream. This text can include HTML tags. If the RequestDispatcher object wraps a Web component such as a servlet/JSP page, the include method invokes the servlet/JSP page, sends the request, executes the Web component, and includes the result in the response of the calling servlet. An included Web component can access the request object and write to a response, but it cannot set headers or call methods modifying the response headers.

Listing 9-15 shows how the first servlet (IncSer) uses the include method of the RequestDispatcher object to invoke the second servlet (Inc) and includes the second servlet's output in its final response.

Listing 9-15

```
import javax.servlet.*;
import javax.servlet.http.*;
import java.io.*;

public class IncSer1 extends HttpServlet {

     public void doGet (HttpServletRequest request,
  HttpServletResponse response)
  throws ServletException, IOException {

    PrintWriter out = response.getWriter();
//sets the attribute object and its value
request.setAttribute("Name","James");
request.setAttribute("Subject","Java Servlets");

// RequestDispatcher object for the servlet 'Inc' is
//obtained

RequestDispatcher
rd=getServletContext().getRequestDispatcher("/servlet/Inc1");

// output of first servlet
out.println("<body bgcolor=\"#ffffff\">" +
    "<center>" + "<hr> <br>  " + "<h1>" +
```

```
"<font size=\"+3\" color=\"#CC0066\">Welcome to Servlet
Bible </font>" );

    // include() method includes the output of second servlet
    rd.include(request,response);
  }
}
```

The second servlet in Listing 9-16 uses the `getAttribute` method of the request object to get the values the first servlet sets, and its output is sent back to the first servlet. The first servlet, in turn, sends the final response to the client.

Listing 9-16

```
import javax.servlet.*;
import javax.servlet.http.*;
import java.io.*;

public class Incl extends HttpServlet {
   public void doGet (HttpServletRequest request,
   HttpServletResponse response)
   throws ServletException, IOException {
      // gets the attribute values set by first servlet
      Object name=request.getAttribute("Name");
      Object title= request.getAttribute("Subject");
           PrintWriter out = response.getWriter();

      // output written here is sent to first servlet and
      //included in its final response to client.
      out.println("<br>");
      out.println(" User Name  : "+name+"\n");
      out.println("<br> Subject opted : "+title);
   }
}
```

The final output to the client is shown in Figure 9-11.

The forward method

The `forward` method of the `RequestDispatcher` object helps in forwarding a client request to another servlet, HTML file, and so on. Here, the calling servlet can perform initial work before passing the request to the called resource. The called resource sends the final response to the client.

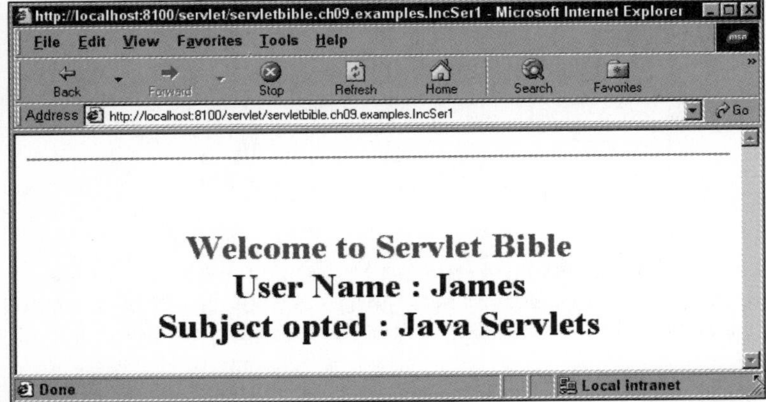

Figure 9-11: The final response of the IncSer servlet includes the output of the Inc servlet by using the include( ) method of RequestDispatcher.

If the servlet has accessed a `ServletOutputStream` or `PrintWriter` object, the `forward` method throws an `IllegalStateException`. The `include` method can be used if an output stream has already been created.

The following listing shows how the `forward` method is used to forward the request to the second servlet, which sends the final output:

```
public void doGet (HttpServletRequest request,
HttpServletResponse response)
throws ServletException, IOException {
  request.setAttribute("Name","James");
request.setAttribute("Subject","Java Servlets");
RequestDispatcher
rd=getServletContext().getRequestDispatcher("/servlet/Inc1");
rd.forward(request,response);
 }
```

Here, the first servlet cannot use the output stream. The final output to the client is from the second servlet.

Servlet filters

The servlet filter is an object that can transform the header and/or content of a request or modify a response. A filter can intercept a servlet before or after it is invoked, examine a request, modify the request headers and request data, and modify the response headers and response data.

Filters are used for logging, authentication, image filtering, data compression, stream tokenizing, encryption, XML transformation, and so on.

A filter should implement the `javax.servlet.Filter` interface and define its three methods: `init`, `doFilter`, and `destroy`. The following list explains the life cycle of the filter:

- `void init(FilterConfig config) throws ServletException`: The server calls `init(FilterConfig)` only once in its life cycle. This method prepares the filter for service. This method also sets the filter's configuration object.
- `void doFilter(ServletRequest req, ServletResponse res, FilterChain chain) throws IOException, ServletException`: Filtering work is done in this method. This method is called any number of times for requests specially set up to use the filter. In its `doFilter` method, each filter receives the current request and response, as well as a filter chain containing the filters that must be processed. In the `doFilter` method, a filter may do what it wants with the request and response. The filter then calls `chain.doFilter()` and transfers control to the next filter. When that call returns, a filter can, at the end of its own `doFilter` method, perform additional work on the response. If the filter needs to stop the processing request and get control of the response, it cannot call the next filter.
- `void destroy()`: This is called after the filter comes out of service . The server calls the `destroy` method to indicate that the filter's service has concluded.

Before Servlet API 2.3, the life cycle involved a `setFilterConfig(FilterConfig)` method also.

The `FilterConfig` interface has methods to retrieve the filter's name, its `init` parameters, and the active servlet context.

Summary

In this chapter, we have seen what applet-servlet communication is and how effectively it can be used. We also have seen the various types of applet-servlet communication. Also, we delved into how a servlet can communicate with another servlet.

In the next chapter, you will learn about a useful technique for presenting the same content in multiple pages: server side includes.

✦ ✦ ✦

CHAPTER 10

Building Server-Side Includes

✦ ✦ ✦ ✦

In This chapter

Understanding server side includes (SSI)

Using SSI

Using servlets to code SSI

Building a navigation bar by using SSI

Useful examples of SSI

✦ ✦ ✦ ✦

You know that servlets can be invoked through GET and POST requests. You can also invoke them through server side includes (or SSI), which allow for the inclusion of servlets into HTML pages to construct dynamic pages. As the servlet is embedded in the HTML page, it is invoked just before the server delivers the HTML page to the client. After the servlet has executed, the content it generates is included at the point where it has been called in the HTML page. The invocation process is illustrated in Figure 10-1.

Note

SSIs can be used only with Web servers that have complete support for servlets and allow servlet invocation through SSI.

The servlet is embedded into the HTML page similarly to the way applets are embedded. Applets are embedded into HTML pages by using the <APPLET> ... </APPLET> tags. Similarly, we embed servlets into HTML pages with the starting <SERVLET> and closing </SERVLET> tags. HTML pages that include servlets with the use of the <SERVLET> tags have the extension .shtml. This extension tells the Web server to expect an embedded servlet that will need to be parsed and invoked. In order to include a servlet in an SHTML page, the servlet must be developed and compiled before you include it in the SHTML page by using the <SERVLET> tags.

SSIs are most useful in situations in which you have common elements in several Web pages. SSIs allow you to consolidate common code and to include it in the appropriate pages. In addition, they provide a consequential benefit that allows you to update the common servlet, automatically reflecting changes in all the pages that have the servlet embedded in them. In cases in which large numbers of pages need dynamic content, centralizing common elements saves time.

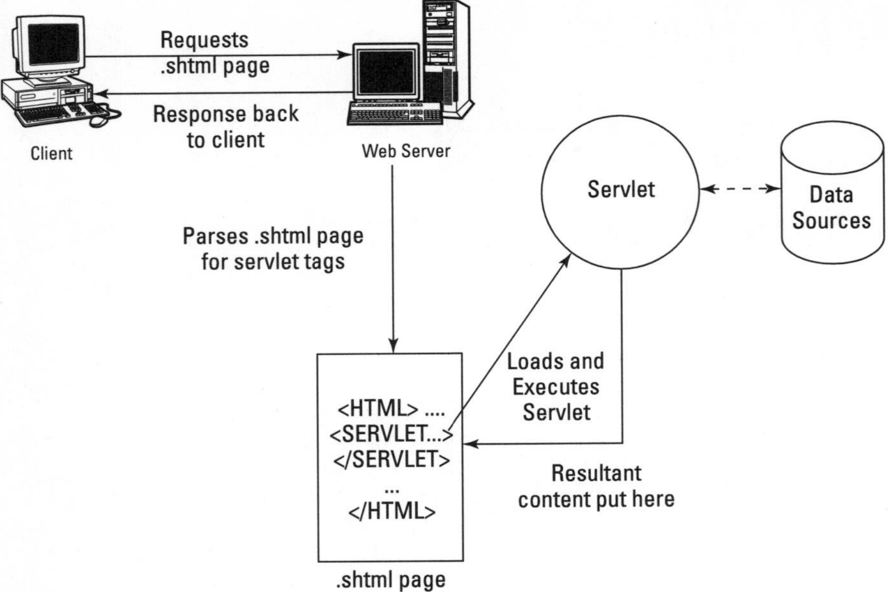

Figure 10-1: SSI servlet invocation

The main problem with using SSIs is that they are costly in the way of performance and server resources. As indicated in Figure 10-1, SHTML pages need to be parsed for the `<SERVLET>` tags and, therefore, load more slowly in the browser. This process eats server resources and is most noticeable in pages that have multiple or large numbers of servlet includes.

SSI Syntax

The syntax for embedding servlets into an SHTML page resembles the syntax for embedding applets in HTML pages. It appears generally in the following format:

```
<SERVLET NAME=SERVLETALIAS CODE=CLASSFILE CODEBASE=PATH>
<PARAM NAME=PARAM1 VALUE=VALUE1>
<PARAM NAME=PARAM2 VALUE=VALUE2>
...
</SERVLET>
```

The exact syntax of the servlet tags may vary among Web-server implementations; however, the servlet tags all follow a format similar to the preceding format used in Allaire's JRun.

The <PARAM> tags are optional, allow extra parameters to be passed to the servlet, and are used in the same way as in the embedding of applets.

Now we look at a simple example of an SSI by using the preceding syntax. Listing 10-1 provides this example.

Listing 10-1

```
<HTML><HEAD><TITLE> Hello World SSI </TITLE></HEAD>
<BODY>
<SERVLET NAME="HelloWorld" CLASS=
servletbible.ch10.examples.HelloServlet.class">
</SERVLET>

</BODY>
</HTML>
```

Figure 10-2 depicts the Hello World SSI after it has been processed and as it would appear in your browser.

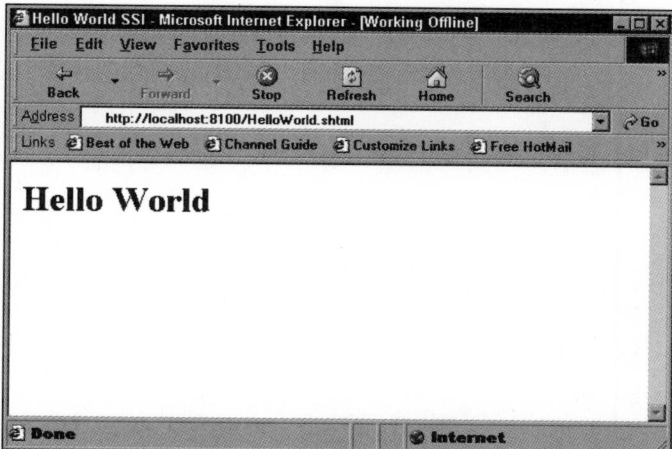

Figure 10-2: Hello World SHTML page

As you can see, this SHTML page resembles an HTML page embedding a java applet. Listing 10-1 calls the servlet in Listing 10-2. After the servlet is processed, its content ("<H1> Hello World </H1>") is placed where the servlet tags are. The servlet tags themselves are not visible in the client's browser.

Listing 10-2

```
package servletbible.ch10.examples;

import javax.servlet.*;
import javax.servlet.http.*;
import java.io.*;


public class HelloServlet extends HttpServlet {

/**
 * As you can see in this servlet we override the service
 * method rather than doGet or doPost.
 *
 */

public void service(HttpServletRequest req, HttpServletResponse res)
throws ServletException, IOException  {

res.setContentType("text/html");
PrintWriter out = res.getWriter();
out.println("<H1> Hello World </H1>");

    }

  }
```

The following example in Listings 10-3 and 10-4 illustrates how we can use the `param` tag with SSIs.

Listing 10-3

```
<HTML><HEAD><TITLE> Greetings </TITLE></HEAD>
<BODY>
<SERVLET NAME="GreetingServlet" CLASS="
 servletbible.ch10.examples.GreetingServlet.class">
<PARAM NAME="PERSON" VALUE="Ramesh">
</SERVLET>
</BODY>

  </HTML>
```

"Ramesh" is passed to the servlet, which then uses it to create the greeting message. The servlet that goes with this SSI appears in Listing 10-4.

Listing 10-4

```
package servletbible.ch10.examples;

import javax.servlet.*;
import javax.servlet.http.*;
import java.io.*;


public class GreetingServlet extends HttpServlet {

public void service(HttpServletRequest req, HttpServletResponse res)
throws ServletException, IOException  {

res.setContentType("text/html");
PrintWriter out = res.getWriter();

String name = req.getParameter("person");
out.println("<H1>Greetings "+ name +"</H1>");

    }

  }
```

Figure 10-3 shows the output of this SSI that appears in the browser.

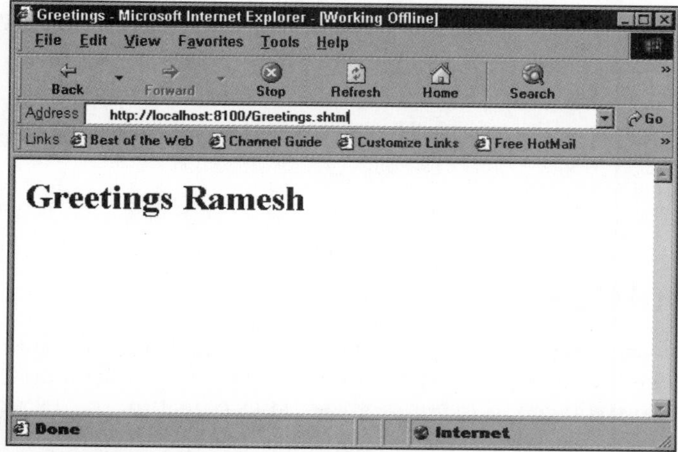

Figure 10-3: Greeting SSI

SSIs with JRUN

Developing SSIs to execute on JRUN is slightly different from developing them to execute on most Web servers. JRUN defines and executes SSIs in the form of taglets. In this chapter, examples are written in the standard SSI syntax by using the `<servlet>` tag.

To configure SSIs with JRUN, map the servlet to the tag you specify (taglet).

To configure taglets, follow these steps:

1. In the JRUN Management Console, sequentially select machine name ⇨ JRUN server name ⇨ Web applications ⇨ application name ⇨ Server-Side Includes.
2. In this window, select edit.
3. Enter the taglet name and the corresponding servlet that will be executed. For example, enter `<hello>` as the taglet name and `servletbible.ch10.examples.HelloServlet` for the corresponding servlet. Embedding the `<hello>` tag in the SHTML page calls and executes the `HelloServlet` class.
4. To apply the changes, click the Update button and restart the JRUN server.

The corresponding SHTML page should be placed under the Web server's document root (the location where you place your HTML pages).

To refer to the servlet, use the taglet name you have specified; in this example, call/execute the servlet by inserting the `<hello>` tag.

If you have overridden the `init()` method in your servlet and it requires initialization parameters, add the initialization parameters in the Servlet Definitions panel. To do this, follow these steps:

1. In the JRUN Management Console, sequentially select machine name ⇨ JRUN server name ⇨ Web applications ⇨ application name ⇨ Servlet Definitions.
2. In the Servlet Definitions panel, select edit.
3. In the `InitArguments` property, enter the parameter name and value.
4. Select Update to apply the changes.

More SSI Examples

The most common use of SSIs is the inclusion of the servlet for common page elements such as HTML headers, footers, and toolbars on Web sites. In the following example, you look at how you can incorporate these types of features into your Web site.

Page headers and footers

First, we construct the header of the document. The SHTML page supplies the title parameter to generate the title of the Web page (shown in Listing 10-5).

Listing 10-5

```
<servlet name="PageHeader" class="servletbible.ch10.examples.PageHeader.class">
<param name="title" value="Page Elements">
</servlet>
<!-- end of page header include -->
<br><br>
<FONT FACE="Arial">
 The above header was generated with the Page Header servlet.
 </FONT>
</body>

  </html>
```

Figure 10-4 depicts the output of the Header SSI that produces a page header only.

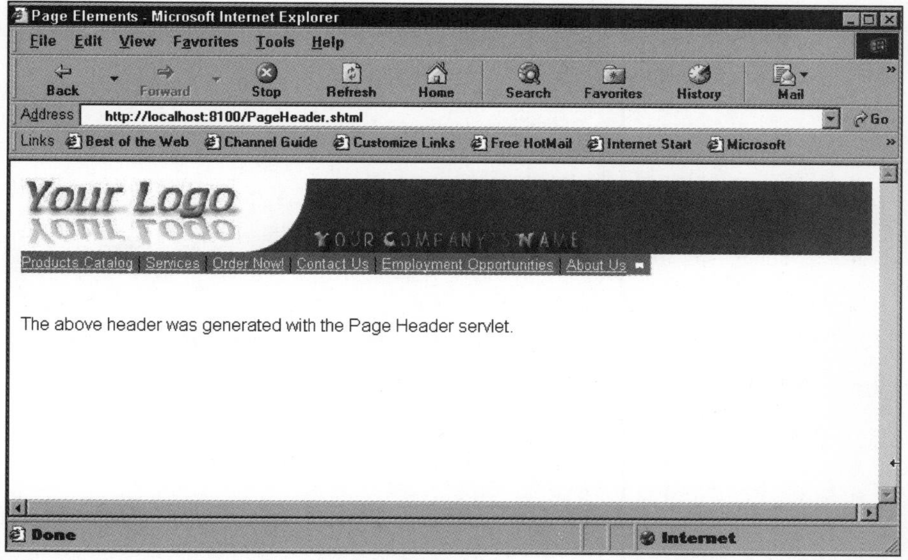

Figure 10-4: SHTML page with header only

The corresponding servlet that generates the preceding header is in Listing 10-6 The links in the header (and footer to follow) have been disabled and replaced with an anchor. Later in this chapter, we convert the page header servlet into a navigation bar.

Listing 10-6

```
package servletbible.ch10.examples;

import javax.servlet.*;
import javax.servlet.http.*;
import java.io.*;


public class PageHeader extends HttpServlet {

public void service(HttpServletRequest req, HttpServletResponse res)
throws ServletException, IOException
        {

        res.setContentType("text/html");
        PrintWriter out = res.getWriter();

     servletbible.utils.HtmlUtils hu = new servletbible.utils.HtmlUtils();


        String title = req.getParameter("title");
                out.println(hu.createHtmlHeader(title));

                out.println("<TABLE WIDTH=\"760\" CELLPADDING=\"0\"
CELLSPACING=\"0\" BORDER=\"0\">");
                out.println(hu.getTR());
                out.println(hu.getTD(261));
                out.println("<IMG SRC=\"images/yourlogo.jpg\" WIDTH=200
HEIGHT=68 BORDER=0><IMG SRC=\"images/whiteroundquarter.gif\" WIDTH=61
HEIGHT=68 BORDER=0></TD>");
                out.println("<TD WIDTH=499 BGCOLOR=\"#1842B5\" HEIGHT=68
valign=\"bottom\">");
                out.println("<img src=\"images/yourcompanysname.gif\"
border=0 width=241 height=21></TD></TR></TABLE>");
                out.println("<TABLE CELLPADDING=0 CELLSPACING=0
BGCOLOR=\"#FF0000\" BORDER=0>");
                out.println(hu.getTR());
                out.println("<TD HEIGHT=20>");
                out.println("<A HREF=\"#\"><FONT FACE=\"Arial\" SIZE =2
COLOR=\"BEIGE\"> Products Catalog </FONT></A>");
                out.println(hu.getClosedTD());
                out.println("<TD HEIGHT=20> | </TD>");
                out.println("<TD HEIGHT=20>");
                out.println("<A HREF=\"#\"><FONT FACE=\"Arial\" SIZE =2
```

```
COLOR=\"BEIGE\"> Services </FONT></A>");
                out.println(hu.getClosedTD());
                out.println("<TD HEIGHT=20> | </TD>");
                out.println("<TD HEIGHT=20>");
                out.println("<A HREF=\"#\"><FONT FACE=\"Arial\" SIZE =2
COLOR=\"BEIGE\"> Order Now! </FONT></A>");
                out.println(hu.getClosedTD());
                out.println("<TD HEIGHT=20> | </TD>");
                out.println("<TD HEIGHT=20>");
                out.println("<A HREF=\"#\"><FONT FACE=\"Arial\" SIZE =2
COLOR=\"BEIGE\"> Contact Us </FONT></A>");
                out.println(hu.getClosedTD());
                out.println("<TD HEIGHT=20> | </TD>");
                out.println("<TD HEIGHT=20>");
                out.println("<A HREF=\"#\"><FONT FACE=\"Arial\" SIZE =2
COLOR=\"BEIGE\"> Employment Opportunities </FONT></A>");
                out.println(hu.getClosedTD());
                out.println("<TD HEIGHT=20> | </TD>");
                out.println("<TD HEIGHT=20>");
                out.println("<A HREF=\"#\"><FONT FACE=\"Arial\" SIZE =2
COLOR=\"BEIGE\"> About Us </FONT></A>");
                out.println(hu.getClosedTD());
                out.println("<TD><IMG SRC=\"images/corner.gif\" BORDER=0
WIDTH=22 HEIGHT=20></TD>");
                out.println(hu.getClosedTD());
                out.println(hu.getClosedTR());
                out.println("</TABLE>");
        out.flush();
        out.close();

        }
}
```

Now we add the page footer to the document as we did for the header and implement an SHTML page that includes both a header and footer (shown in Listing 10-7).

Listing 10-7

```
<servlet name="PageHeader"
class="servletbible.ch10.examples.PageHeader.class">
<param name="title" value="Page Header">
</servlet>
<!-- end of page header include ‡

<br><br>
<FONT FACE="Arial">
 The above header was generated using server side includes.
```

Continued

Listing 10-7 *(continued)*

```
</FONT>
<br><br>
<!-- Beginning of page footer include -->
<servlet name="PageFooter"
class="servletbible.ch10.examples.PageFooter.class">
</servlet>
</body>
</html>
```

This SHTML page calls the page-header servlet in Listing 10-6 along with the footer servlet in Listing 10-8 to generate the page.

Listing 10-8

```
package servletbible.ch10.examples;

import javax.servlet.*;
import javax.servlet.http.*;
import java.io.*;


public class PageFooter extends HttpServlet {

public void service(HttpServletRequest req, HttpServletResponse res)
throws ServletException, IOException
    {

    res.setContentType("text/html");
    PrintWriter out = res.getWriter();

    servletbible.utils.HtmlUtils hu = new servletbible.utils.HtmlUtils();

        out.println("<HR WIDTH=\"75%\" ALIGN =\"LEFT\">");
        out.println("<table border=0 cellspacing=0 cellpadding=0
align=\"left\">");
        out.println(hu.getTR("left"));
        out.println("<td align=\"left\">");
        out.println("<a href=\"#\"><FONT FACE=\"Arial\" SIZE =1>Products
Catalog</a> | </FONT>");
        out.println("<a href=\"#\"><FONT FACE=\"Arial\" SIZE =1>
Services</a> | </FONT>");
        out.println("<a href=\"#\"><FONT FACE=\"Arial\" SIZE =1>Order
Now!</a> | </FONT>");
        out.println("<a href=\"#\"><FONT FACE=\"Arial\" SIZE =1>Contact
Us</a> | </FONT>");
```

```
        out.println("<a href=\"#\"><FONT FACE=\"Arial\" SIZE =1>Employment
Opportunities</a> | </FONT>");
        out.println("<a href=\"#\"><FONT FACE=\"Arial\" SIZE =1>About
Us</a></FONT>");
        out.println(hu.getClosedTD());
        out.println(hu.getClosedTR());
        out.println("</TABLE>");
        out.println(hu.getBR(1));
        out.println("<FONT FACE=\"Arial\" SIZE =1><I>");
        out.println("Best Viewed using Netscape 4.0 and above or Internet
Explorer 4.0 and above.");
        out.println("This site requires a JavaScript enabled browser.
</I></FONT>");

    out.flush();
    out.close();

    }

  }
```

The resulting page appears as in Figure 10-5.

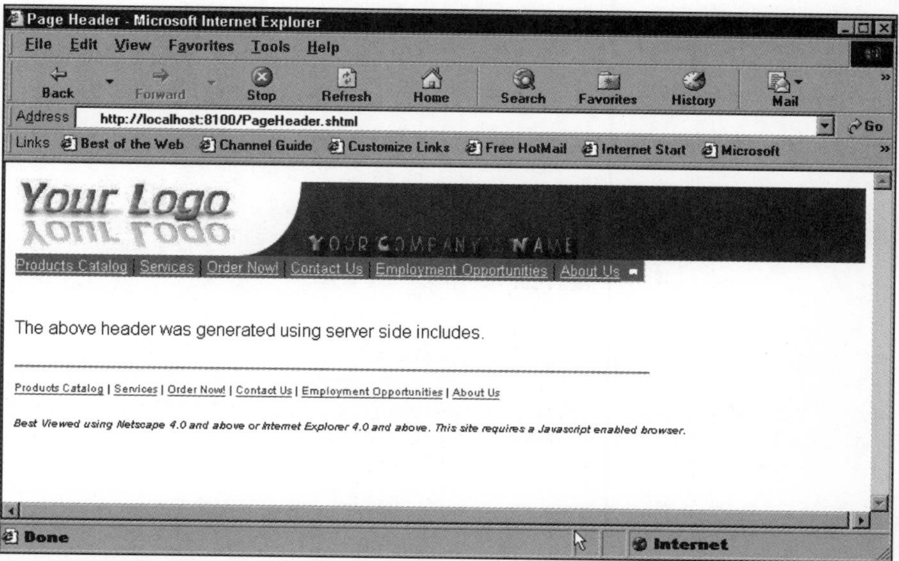

Figure 10-5: SHTML page with header and footer

If you have a site incorporating a header and/or footer on every page using SSIs, you need only a modification and recompilation of the appropriate servlets to update the entire site. The code for the header and footer is contained in a centralized location, making maintenance easy.

Date

Another common element used in sites is the display of dates. We modify the `Date` servlet from Chapter 2 to incorporate it by using SSIs (shown in Listing 10-9) The parameter the SHTML page supplies is the format the date should be displayed in (in this case, `'MMMMMMMMM dd yyyy'`).

Listing 10-9

```
package servletbible.ch10.examples;

import java.io.*;
import java.text.*;
import java.util.*;
import javax.servlet.*;
import javax.servlet.http.*;

/**
 * This is a simple servlet that displays the date in a
 * given string format.
 */
public class DateServlet2 extends HttpServlet {

    String todaysDate;


public void service(HttpServletRequest request, HttpServletResponse
response)
 throws ServletException,IOException {

        PrintWriter out = response.getWriter();
        response.setContentType("text/html");

        SimpleDateFormat d2cformatter = new
SimpleDateFormat(request.getParameter("DateFormat"));
        todaysDate = d2cformatter.format(new Date());

        out.println(todaysDate);
        out.flush();
      out.close();

    }
}
```

Listing 10-10ontains the code for the corresponding SHTML page for the `Date` Servlet.

Listing 10-10

```
<servlet name="PageHeader"
class="servletbible.ch10.examples.PageHeader.class">
<param name="title" value="Page Header">
</servlet>
<br><br>
<FONT FACE="Arial">
The above header was generated using server side includes on

<servlet name="Date" class="
servletbible.ch10.examples.DateServlet2.class">
<param name="DateFormat" value="MMMMMMMMM dd yyyy">
</servlet>
. </FONT>
<br><br>
<servlet name="PageFooter"
class="servletbible.ch10.examples.PageFooter.class">
</servlet>
</body>
</html>
```

Random image rotator

Many sites use random rotation to cycle through different images or banner ads for each site visit. The example in Listing 10-11 randomly selects an image from a list of ten to be displayed. You can apply this random rotation mechanism to randomly display banner advertisements, site headlines, photos/images, and other such content.

Listing 10-11

```
<html><head><title> Image Rotator </title></head>
<body>
<div align="center">
<IMG SRC="images/<servlet name="ImageRotator"
class="servletbible.ch10.examples.ch10.ImageRotator.class">
</servlet>" border="0">
</div>
</body>
</html>
```

Listing 10-12 uses an arbitrary vector, containing the ten images to be randomly selected. You may choose to implement this rotator by obtaining the list of images in a different way (for example, from a database or perhaps through loading a properties file).

Listing 10-12

```
package servletbible.ch10.examples;

import java.io.*;
import java.text.*;
import java.util.*;
import javax.servlet.*;
import javax.servlet.http.*;

public class ImageRotator extends HttpServlet {

public void service(HttpServletRequest request, HttpServletResponse
response)
 throws ServletException,IOException {

        PrintWriter out = response.getWriter();
        response.setContentType("text/html");

        // instantiate the java.util.Random class
        Random r = new Random();

        // get a random integer
        int num = r.nextInt();

// modulus by 10 will get integers to a maximum of up to ten
        int random_num = num % 10;

// we dont want negative numbers so add 10 to keep within 1 to 10 range.
        if (random_num < 1) random_num = random_num + 10;


        Vector imageList = new Vector(10);
        imageList.addElement("image1.jpg");
        imageList.addElement("image2.jpg");
        imageList.addElement("image3.jpg");
        imageList.addElement("image4.jpg");
        imageList.addElement("image5.jpg");
        imageList.addElement("image6.jpg");
        imageList.addElement("image7.jpg");
        imageList.addElement("image8.jpg");
        imageList.addElement("image9.jpg");
        imageList.addElement("image10.jpg");


        out.println(imageList.get(random_num).toString());
```

```
        out.flush();
      out.close();

    }
}
```

Initialization

Under certain circumstances, to optimize performance, it is advantageous to preload code. For example, if your servlet requires the use of a file or some other resource, it is a good idea to load and/or read necessary data before the servlet is invoked. To do this, override the `init()` method as follows:

```
public void init(ServletConfig config) throws ServletException
{
super.init(config);

Properties prop = new Properties();
try {
prop.load(new FileInputStream("infile.properties");
.
.
}
catch (IOException ioe) {
..
}
}
```

In this case, we load a properties file beforehand. We may use the data loaded in the `Properties` object later in the servlet.

SSI Navigation Bar

The page header servlet can be modified into a navigation bar that can be used to navigate a Web site. Make modifications by following a few simple steps.

Add the page links into the servlet:

```
out.println("<A HREF=\"products.shtml\"><FONT FACE=\"Arial\" SIZE =2
COLOR=\"BEIGE\"> Products Catalog </FONT></A>");
```

To know what page you are on, add a `Page` parameter to the SHTML page of each page in the site:

```
<PARAM NAME="Page" VALUE="products">
```

The navigation bar servlet must read in this parameter so that you can check and determine whether or not to enable or disable the link.

```
String page = req.getParameter("Page");
```

Add the checking condition to check the page the client is currently on and the code to print without the link in that case.

```
if (page.equals("products"))
{
out.println("<FONT FACE=\"Arial\" SIZE =2 COLOR=\"BEIGE\">
 Products
Catalog </FONT>");
}
else {
out.println("<A HREF=\"products.shtml\"><FONT FACE=\"Arial\" SIZE =2
COLOR=\"BEIGE\"> Products Catalog </FONT></A>");
}
```

If you have visited the products catalog page, it appears as in Figure 10-6.

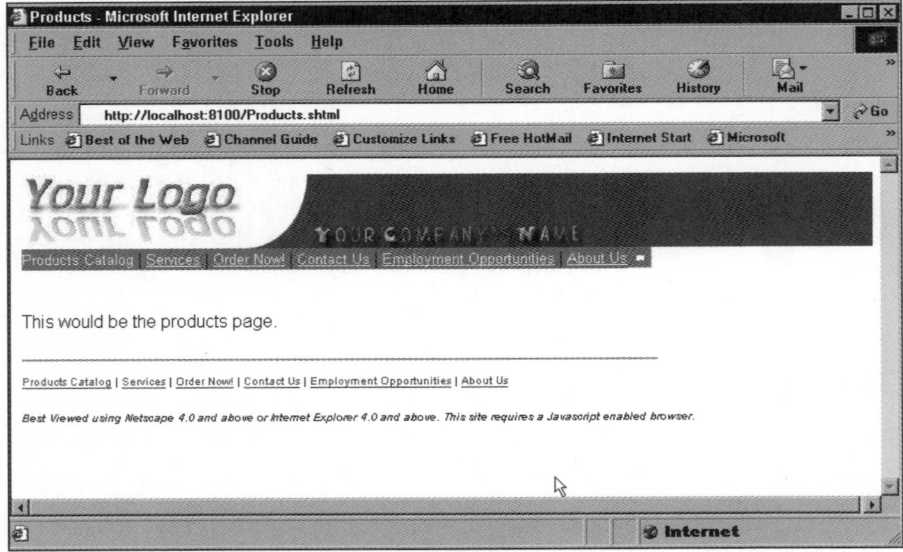

Figure 10-6: Products catalog page

The other pages render in the same manner, as in Figure 10-7.

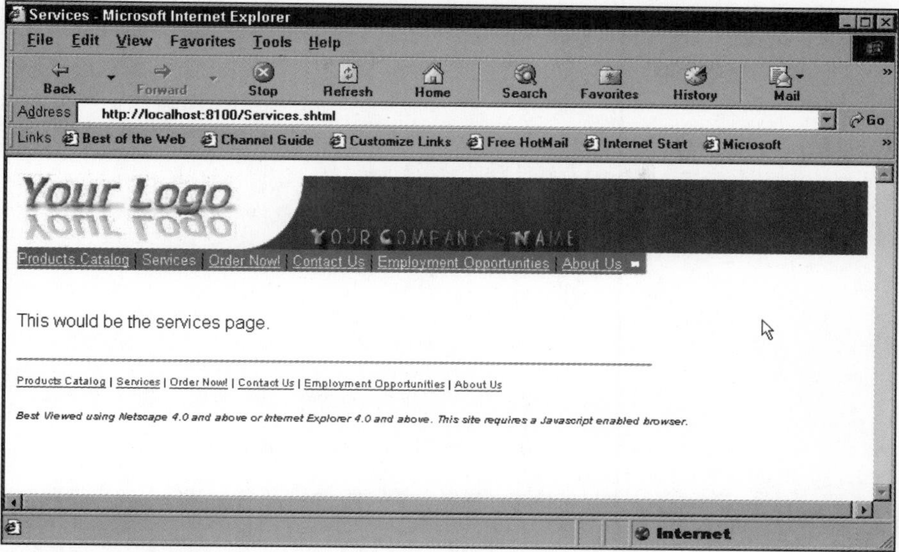

Figure 10-7: Services page

The code for the entire navigation servlet should be like that of Listing 10-13.

Listing 10-13

```
package servletbible.ch10.examples;

import javax.servlet.*;
import javax.servlet.http.*;
import java.io.*;


public class NavBar extends HttpServlet {

public void service(HttpServletRequest req, HttpServletResponse res)
throws ServletException, IOException
    {

        res.setContentType("text/html");
        PrintWriter out = res.getWriter();

    servletbible.utils.HtmlUtils hu = new servletbible.utils.HtmlUtils();

        String page = req.getParameter("Page");
```

Continued

Listing 10-13 *(continued)*

```
        String title = req.getParameter("title");
                out.println(hu.createHtmlHeader(title));
                out.println("<TABLE WIDTH=\"760\" CELLPADDING=\"0\"
CELLSPACING=\"0\" BORDER=\"0\">");
                out.println(hu.getTR());
                out.println(hu.getTD(261));
                out.println("<IMG SRC=\"images/yourlogo.jpg\" WIDTH=200
HEIGHT=68 BORDER=0><IMG SRC=\"images/whiteroundquarter.gif\" WIDTH=61
HEIGHT=68 BORDER=0></TD>");
                out.println("<TD WIDTH=499 BGCOLOR=\"#1842B5\" HEIGHT=68
valign=\"bottom\">");
                out.println("<img src=\"images/yourcompanysname.gif\"
border=0 width=241 height=21></TD></TR></TABLE>");
                out.println("<TABLE CELLPADDING=0 CELLSPACING=0
BGCOLOR=\"#FF0000\" BORDER=0>");
                out.println(hu.getTR());
                out.println("<TD HEIGHT=20>");

        if (page.equals("products"))
        {
                out.println("<FONT FACE=\"Arial\" SIZE =2 COLOR=\"BEIGE\">
Products Catalog </FONT>");
        }
        else {
                out.println("<A HREF=\"products.shtml\"><FONT
FACE=\"Arial\" SIZE =2 COLOR=\"BEIGE\"> Products Catalog </FONT></A>");
        }

                out.println(hu.getClosedTD());
                out.println("<TD HEIGHT=20> | </TD>");
                out.println("<TD HEIGHT=20>");

        if (page.equals("services"))
        {
                out.println("<FONT FACE=\"Arial\" SIZE =2 COLOR=\"BEIGE\">
Services </FONT>");
        }
        else {
                out.println("<A HREF=\"services.shtml\"><FONT
FACE=\"Arial\" SIZE =2 COLOR=\"BEIGE\"> Services </FONT></A>");
        }


                out.println(hu.getClosedTD());
                out.println("<TD HEIGHT=20> | </TD>");
```

```
                out.println("<TD HEIGHT=20>");

        if (page.equals("order"))
        {
                out.println("<FONT FACE=\"Arial\" SIZE =2 COLOR=\"BEIGE\">
Order Now! </FONT>");
        }
        else {
                out.println("<A HREF=\"order.shtml\"><FONT FACE=\"Arial\"
SIZE =2 COLOR=\"BEIGE\"> Order Now! </FONT></A>");
        }



                out.println(hu.getClosedTD());
                out.println("<TD HEIGHT=20> | </TD>");
                out.println("<TD HEIGHT=20>");

        if (page.equals("contact"))
        {
                out.println("<FONT FACE=\"Arial\" SIZE =2 COLOR=\"BEIGE\">
Contact Us </FONT>");
        }
        else {
                out.println("<A HREF=\"contact.shtml\"><FONT
FACE=\"Arial\" SIZE =2 COLOR=\"BEIGE\"> Contact Us </FONT></A>");
        }

                out.println(hu.getClosedTD());
                out.println("<TD HEIGHT=20> | </TD>");
                out.println("<TD HEIGHT=20>");

        if (page.equals("employment"))
        {
                out.println("<FONT FACE=\"Arial\" SIZE =2 COLOR=\"BEIGE\">
Employment Opportunities </FONT>");
        }
        else {
                out.println("<A HREF=\"employment.shtml\"><FONT
FACE=\"Arial\" SIZE =2 COLOR=\"BEIGE\"> Employment Opportunities
</FONT></A>");
        }

                out.println(hu.getClosedTD());
                out.println("<TD HEIGHT=20> | </TD>");
                out.println("<TD HEIGHT=20>");

        if (page.equals("about"))
        {
                out.println("<FONT FACE=\"Arial\" SIZE =2 COLOR=\"BEIGE\">
About Us </FONT>");
        }
```

Continued

Listing 10-13 *(continued)*

```
        else {
                out.println("<A HREF=\"about.shtml\"><FONT FACE=\"Arial\"
SIZE =2 COLOR=\"BEIGE\"> About Us </FONT></A>");
        }



                out.println(hu.getClosedTD());
                out.println("<TD><IMG SRC=\"images/corner.gif\" BORDER=0
WIDTH=22 HEIGHT=20></TD>");
                out.println(hu.getClosedTD());
                out.println(hu.getClosedTR());
                out.println("</TABLE>");
        out.flush();
        out.close();
    }
}
```

Each of the SHTML pages that include this navigation bar should have code resembling this format, with the inclusion of the title and page parameters:

```
<SERVLET NAME="NavigationBar"
class="servletbible.ch10.examples.NavBar.class">
<PARAM NAME="title" VALUE="Products">
<PARAM NAME="Page" VALUE="products">
</SERVLET>
```

Summary

In this chapter, you have learned what SSIs are and how to create your own SSIs by developing SHTML pages that invoke your servlets. You are also aware of the benefits code centralization offers. In addition, you have been provided with some examples of where you can use SSIs in your Web application.

The next chapter teaches you to manage sessions in a Web application by using the three major techniques of UR: rewriting, hidden form fields, and cookies. You will learn how to use the `Session` class, and you will be shown how to build your own shopping cart with session management techniques in place.

✦ ✦ ✦

Cookies and Session Management

✦ ✦ ✦ ✦

In This Chapter

An overview of session management

URL rewriting

Hidden fields

Cookies

Session management using the Servlet API (HTTPSession)

A shopping cart example

✦ ✦ ✦ ✦

You may be aware that HTTP is a *stateless* protocol. Although stateless protocols have many advantages over stateful protocols, they present significant technical challenges. For example, a lack of state information may prevent the server from identifying each client. This may prevent you from having user-defined preferences, as the server can't distinguish one user from another. Fortunately, this is not always a problem, as we have methods that allow us to add state to HTTP. In this chapter, we explore the session-management methods and session-management mechanisms built into Servlet API.

After reading this chapter, you should have a clear understanding of stateless protocol and how state can be added to HTTP by using objects provided in the Servlet API. Specifically, this chapter covers the following topics:

- ✦ Stateless protocol
- ✦ Sessions
- ✦ Session-management methods
- ✦ Session management with the Servlet API

Stateless Protocol

A protocol is said to be *stateless* if it can't remember previous connections and can't distinguish one client's request from that of another. In stateless protocol, each request is processed with no prior knowledge of previous requests. HTTP falls under this category. On the other hand, FTP (File Transfer Protocol) is stateful because it does not require you to create a new connection for every request. After the user logs in, FTP server maintains the user's credentials throughout the session. Because HTTP is stateless, there is no predefined way to track requests from the same user.

Understanding Sessions

In the conventional sense, a *session* is a persistent network connection between two host machines. Here, the session is over as soon as the connection between these hosts is closed. However, we are not interested in this type of session. Rather, let's focus on another type of session called the HTTP session or a virtual session. This type of session involves a virtual connection with the client rather than the physical connection. Let's first examine what is meant by a virtual connection as we understand an HTTP session.

In HTTP, each connection between the client and server is very brief. (HTTP 1.1 has provisions for *persistent* connections, however.) This is an inherent trait of stateless protocol. To illustrate this, let's explore a stateless protocol transaction. It goes like this: The client establishes a connection with the server, requests a specific resource, gets the response, and closes the connection. Because the connection is not persistent, the tie between the server and the client is closed after the connection is closed. Even if the same client issues another request, the server cannot associate this request with the previous one. This presents significant challenges to the HTTP protocol. This may result in the following problems:

- ✦ If the server requires authentication (for example, a client must log in), the client must identify itself to the server for every request. The server doesn't realize that this client has been authenticated already because the connection between the two has been lost.
- ✦ Storing client-specific information (for example, a chosen product list in a shopping cart application) is not possible because the server can't distinguish one client from another.

The solution to these problems is to establish a persistent virtual connection between the client and server. A *virtual connection* associates each request the server receives with the client that has issued the request. This is possible by requiring the client to return a piece of information with every request the client issues to the server. The server uses this piece of information (usually called a session ID) to identify the client that issued the request and to associate this request with the previous requests received from the same client. This solves the problems mentioned previously. These virtual connections are called sessions. *Sessions* are used to maintain state and the identity of the client across requests.

In the conventional session, all client requests are associated by the fact that they share the same network connection. In an HTTP session, however, requests are identified by their session IDs. A conventional session refers to the duration of time the network connection is active. Similarly, a virtual connection refers to the duration of time the virtual connection is active. In a nutshell, an HTTP session is a series of associated requests in which the client can be uniquely identified. This association exists for a specific period of time and is configurable in the Web server.

The conventional session expires when the network connection is closed, but the HTTP session remains active between requests. You might be asking, "When does an HTTP session expire?" The duration of the HTTP session can be configured for a servlet. The session remains active, as long as each request is received within a specified time. When a request is received from the client after the specified amount of time, the server ends the session and the client has to log in again. Expiring sessions in this way ensures that old sessions are not using server resources. Expiring the session means removing the session ID and the associated data from server storage.

Session-Management Methods

State information can be passed between the server and the client through multiple methods. We explore the various techniques for session management in this chapter. These methods include implementing rewritten URLs, using hidden fields, using cookies to pass state information, and using SSL sessions.

Storing session information in the URL (rewritten URLs)

Methods that add state to a stateless protocol such as HTTP have one thing in common: They must allow the server to send session information to the client with the assurance that the client will return that information with every request. In this method, every URL the servlet uses is rewritten to include the session ID. (This may not be true if the browser supports cookies.) An example follows:

```
http://www.myserver.com/someapp/somepage.jsp;jsessionid=12345678
```

A *cookie* is a small piece of information the server sends to the client. The client returns this information with every request based on the parameters the server sets. We explore cookies in detail later in this chapter.

In this URL, `jsessionid=12345678` is a key-value pair that holds the session ID. (Refer to `ftp://ftp.isi.edu/in-notes/rfc2396.txt` for more information about URLs.) The browser (the client) returns this information with every request to the server. Let's see an example of how this information is stored:

```
<HTML>
<BODY>
<FORM NAME="SomeServlet;jsessionid=12345678" METHOD=POST>
.
.
.
<INPUT TYPE=TEXT ...>
.
.
.
</FORM>
<A HREF="YetAnotherServlet;jsessionid=12345678>Click here to
continue</A> <BR>
</BODY>
</HTML>
```

In this example, all the links in the form are encoded with the session ID. This ensures that session information is passed to the server regardless of the HTTP method used.

Session Management Using Hidden Fields

Hidden fields in the HTML form are the most commonly used mechanism for storing session information. A *hidden field* is similar to an ordinary input field in HTML. The only difference is that the hidden field doesn't have an associated user-interface element. This imposes the restriction that the client can't modify the values of these variables. When the form that contains these hidden fields is submitted, the values of these fields are sent with the request. On the server side, these values are received as request parameters. One important thing to remember is that the hidden-variable mechanism works only when the form is submitted, not when you follow the links.

Let's write an example that uses hidden variables to store state information:

```
<HTML>
<HEAD>
<TITLE>Hidden Variables Example</TITLE>
<BODY>
<FORM ACTION=SampleServlet METHOD=post>
Please enter your name:
<INPUT TYPE=TEXT NAME=UserName VALUE="">
<BR>
<INPUT TYPE=SUBMIT>
</FORM>
</BODY>
</HTML>
```

This form allows the user to enter his or her name and to submit this information to the server. This information is transmitted to the server as a name/value pair part of the HTTP POST request. The POST request looks like the following:

```
POST /SampleServlet HTTP/1.0
User-Agent: Mozilla/4.75 [en] (WinNT; I)
Accept: image/gif, image/jpeg, */*
Content-Length: 15

UserName=kr
```

On receiving the POST request from the client, the server extracts the username by using the method getParameter() of the HTTPServletRequest object. The server uses this information for generating the next page. We have a problem now: Other pages in the application do not have access to this username. To solve this problem, the server stores this username in a hidden variable in all the forms it generates after the first page. This ensures that the username is available to all the pages.

The following example shows how the server stores the username in the hidden variable:

```
<HTML>
<BODY>
<FORM ACTION=SampleServlet METHOD="POST">
<INPUT TYPE=TEXT ...>
.
.
.
<INPUT TYPE=HIDDEN NAME=UserName VALUE="Kr">
.
.
.
</FORM>
</BODY>
</HTML>
```

Notice how the username is stored in the form in a hidden variable. Generally, a hidden-variable mechanism is used in conjunction with the rewritten URLs mentioned here.

Session Management with Cookies

A cookie is a simple piece of information stored on the client, on behalf of the server. This information is returned to the server with every request to the server, until it expires. When an HTTP server receives a request, in addition to the requested document, it may choose to return some state information a cookie-enabled browser stores on its behalf. This information includes a URL range within which the information should be returned to the server. The URL range comprises the domain name and some path within the domain. Whenever the browser requests a resource, it checks the URL against the URL range of all available cookies. If a match is found, that cookie is also returned with the request. This helps the server overcome the stateless nature of HTTP protocol.

Cookie Support in the Servlet API

Servlet API defines a class called `Cookie` in the `javax.servlet.http` package. This class encapsulates an HTTP cookie. It simplifies the process of setting information on cookies.

The constructor of the `Cookie` looks like the following:

```
public Cookie( String name, String value )
```

The following line initializes a `Cookie` object:

```
Cookie cookie = new Cookie( "userid", "Kr" );
```

The preceding is quite simple. Setting other attributes of the cookie is as easy as setting the one shown. The following code explains how you can create a typical `Cookie` object:

```
Cookie cookie = new Cookie( "userid", "Kr" );
cookie.setDomain( "www.somesite.com" );
cookie.setPath( "/" );
cookie.setSecure( true );
```

After creating a cookie, send it to the client with the response. Servlet API provides an easy method for this process. The `HTTPServletResponse` class has a method named `addCookie()` that transmits the cookie to the client with the response. This method has the following syntax:

```
public void addCookie( Cookie cookie )
```

The `addCookie()` method can be called multiple times to set many cookies. Keep in mind that original specification allows only 20 cookies per server. If your browser follows this specification, some cookies may not be set on the client.

Table 11-1 lists all the methods in the `Cookie` class.

Table 11-1
Methods Available in the Cookie Class

Method	*Description*
`getComment()`	Returns the comment describing the purpose of this cookie or `null` if the cookie has no comment
`GetDomain()`	Returns the domain name set for this cookie
`GetMaxAge()`	Returns the maximum age of the cookie, specified in seconds, by default, `-1` indicating the cookie persists until browser shutdown
`getName()`	Returns the name of the cookie. The name cannot be changed after creation.
`getPath()`	Returns the path on the server to which the browser returns this cookie. The cookie is visible to all subpaths on the server.
`GetSecure()`	Returns `true` if the browser is sending cookies only over a secure protocol or `false` if the browser can send cookies by using any protocol
`getValue()`	Returns the value of the cookie
`getVersion()`	Returns the version of the protocol this cookie complies with. Version 1 complies with RFC 2109, and version 0 complies with the original cookie specification drafted by Netscape.
`setComment()`	Specifies a comment that describes a cookie's purpose. The comment is useful if the browser presents the cookie to the user. Netscape Version 0 cookies do not support comments.
`setDomain()`	Specifies the domain within which this cookie should be presented.
`setMaxAge()`	Sets the maximum age of the cookie in seconds. A positive value indicates that the cookie expires after that many seconds have passed. Note that the value is the *maximum* age at which the cookie expires, not the cookie's current age. A negative value means the cookie is not stored persistently and is deleted when the Web browser exits. A zero value causes the cookie to be deleted.
`setPath()`	Specifies a URL path to which the client should return the cookie. The cookie is visible to all the pages in the directory and subdirectories referenced by the URL. A cookie's path must include the servlet that set the cookie (for example, /catalog, which makes the cookie visible to all directories on the server under /catalog).

Continued

Table 11-1 (continued)

Method	Description
`setSecure()`	Indicates to the browser whether or not the cookie should only be sent using a secure protocol, such as HTTPS or SSL. The default value is false.
`setValue()`	Assigns a new value to a cookie after the cookie is created
`setVersion()`	Sets the version of the cookie protocol this cookie complies with. Version 0 complies with the original Netscape cookie specification.

The following code snippet sets two cookies on the client. This code calls the `addCookie()` method multiple times to set more than one cookie:

```
public void service( HttpServletRequest request,
     HttpServletResponse response )
     throws ServletException, IOException {

     response.setContentType( "text/html" );
     PrintWriter out = response.getWriter();

Cookie userid = new Cookie( "userid", "Kr" );
Cookie username = new Cookie( "username", "Ramesh" );

Response.addCookie( userid );
Response.addCookie( username );

out.println( "<HTML><BODY>This page sets two cookies" );
out.println( "</BODY></HTML>" );
out.flush();
out.close();
}
```

To delete a cookie, create a new `Cookie` object and invoke its `setMaxAge` method with a value of 0, as in the following example:

```
Cookie cookie = new Cookie( "userid", "" );
cookie.setMaxAge( 0 );
response.addCookie( cookie );
```

A cookie named `userid` must already be available on the client for this code to work.

Session Management with SSL Sessions

Secure Sockets Layer (SSL), the encryption technology used in the HTTPS protocol, has a mechanism built into it allowing multiple requests from a client to be unambiguously identified as part of an accepted session. A servlet container can easily use this data to serve as the mechanism for defining a session.

Refer to `http://home.netscape.com/eng/ssl3/draft302.txt` for more information on SSL sessions.

Session Management with the Servlet API

We can use the methods we have discussed to implement session management ourselves. Fortunately, session-management support is provided by the Servlet API and can be implemented easily. In this section, let's explore the session-management methods Servlet API provides.

The session-management implementation revolves around an interface called `HttpSession`. This object encapsulates the essential information of an HTTP session (such as session ID and other client-specific information). We can retrieve the object that implements the `HTTPSession` interface by using the `getSession()` method of the `HTTPServletRequest` interface. Table 11-2 briefly describes the methods `HTTPSession` supports.

Table 11-2
Methods the HTTPSession Interface Supports

Method	*Description*
`getAttribute()`	Returns the object bound with the specified name in this session or null if no object is bound under the name.
`getAttributeNames()`	Returns an enumeration of string objects containing the names of all the objects bound to this session.
`getCreationTime()`	Returns the time when this session was created, measured in milliseconds, since midnight January 1, 1970 GMT.
`getId()`	Returns a string containing the unique identifier assigned to this session. The identifier is assigned by the servlet container and is implementation dependent.

Continued

Table 11-2 (continued)

Method	*Description*
`getLastAccessedTime()`	Returns the last time the client sent a request associated with this session, as the number of milliseconds since midnight January 1, 1970 GMT. Actions your application takes, such as getting or setting a value associated with the session, do not affect access time.
`getMaxInactiveInterval()`	Returns the maximum time interval, in seconds, that the servlet container will keep this session open between client accesses. After this interval, the servlet container invalidates the session. The maximum time interval can be set with the `setMaxInactiveInterval` method. A negative time indicates the session should never timeout.
`invalidate()`	Invalidates this session and unbinds any objects bound to it.
`isNew()`	Returns true if the client does not yet know about the session or if the client chooses not to join the session. For example, if the server has used only cookie-based sessions and the client has disabled the use of cookies, a session is new on each request.
`removeAttribute()`	Removes the object bound with the specified name from this session. If the session does not have an object bound with the specified name, this method does nothing.
`setAttribute()`	Binds an object to this session by using the name specified. If an object of the same name is already bound to the session, the object is replaced.
`SetMaxInactiveInterval()`	Specifies the time, in seconds, between client requests before the servlet container will invalidate this session. A negative time indicates the session should never timeout.

The `HTTPSession` object contains most of the methods you use to manage session, but the `HTTPServletRequest` object also contains some useful methods. Table 11-3 describes several methods the `HTTPServletRequest` object supports that help in session management.

Table 11-3
Session-Management Methods Defined by HTTPServletRequest

Method	Description
`getRequestedSessionId()`	Returns the session ID the client specifies. This may not be the same as the ID of the actual session in use. For example, if the request has specified an old (expired) session ID and the server has started a new session, this method gets a new session with a new ID. If the request has not specified a session ID, this method returns `null`.
`getSession()`	Returns the current session associated with this request or, if the request does not have a session, creates one. This method is overloaded to take a boolean parameter indicating whether or not to create a new session if one does not exist.
`isRequestedSessionIdFromCookie()`	Checks whether the requested session ID has come in as a cookie.
`isRequestedSessionIdFromURL()`	Checks whether the requested session ID has come in as part of the request URL.
`isRequestedSessionIdValid()`	Checks whether the requested session ID is still valid.

The session-management mechanisms in the Servlet API use cookies by default. Cookies are used because of the extra effort required to implement rewritten URLs. However, the Servlet API provides methods to check whether the client supports cookies. If a client is not supporting cookies, rewritten URLs can be used as an alternative. The servlet in Listing 11-1establishes a session with the client and returns session information with each request.

Listing 11-1

```
package servletbible.ch11.examples;

import javax.servlet.*;
import javax.servlet.http.*;
import java.io.*;
import java.util.*;

/**
```

Continued

Listing 11-1 *(continued)*

```
 * Demonstrates session management mechanisms built
 * into the Servlet API.
 *
 */

public class SessionInfo extends HttpServlet {
     /**
      * Initializes this servlet. This method is called when the
      * servlet is first loaded.
      *
      * @param config ServletConfig object
      * @throws ServletException When an exception occurs
      */
     public void init( ServletConfig config )
throws ServletException {
          super.init( config );
     }

     /**
      * Handles HTTP GET request
      *
      * @param request HttpServletRequest object
      * @param response HttpServletResponse object
      *
      * @throws ServletException When an exception occurs
      * @throws IOException When an exception occurs
      */
     public void doGet( HttpServletRequest request,
HttpServletResponse response )
          throws ServletException, IOException {

          // Set the content type to HTML
          response.setContentType( "text/html" );

          // Get the output stream from the response object
          PrintWriter out = response.getWriter();

          // Get the session (Create a new one if required)
          HttpSession session = request.getSession( true );

          // Return the session information to the client
          out.println( "<HTML>" );
          out.println( "<HEAD>" );
          out.println( "<TITLE>Session info servlet</TITLE>" );
          out.println( "</HEAD>" );
          out.println( "<BODY>" );
          out.println( "<H3>Session Information</H3>" );
          out.println( "New Session: " + session.isNew() );
          out.println( "<BR>Session ID: " + session.getId() );
          out.println( "<BR>Creation Time: " +
```

```
session.getCreationTime() );
          out.println( "<BR>Last Accessed Time: " +
session.getLastAccessedTime() );
          out.println( "<BR>Max. Inactive Interval: " +
session.getMaxInactiveInterval() );

          out.println( "<H3>Request Information</H3>" );
          out.println( "Session ID from Request: " +
                    request.getRequestedSessionId() );
          out.println( "<BR>Session using cookie: " +
                    request.isRequestedSessionIdFromCookie() );
          out.println( "<BR>Session using rewritten URL: " +
                    request.isRequestedSessionIdFromURL() );
          out.println( "<BR>Sessin is VALID: " +
                    request.isRequestedSessionIdValid() );

          out.println( "</BODY>" );
          out.println( "</HTML>" );

          // Flush the output stream
          out.flush();

          // Close the output stream
          out.close();
     }

     /**
      * Handles HTTP POST request
      *
      * @param request HttpServletRequest object
      * @param response HttpServletResponse object
      *
      * @throws ServletException When an exception occurs
      * @throws IOException When an exception occurs
      */
     public void doPost( HttpServletRequest request,
HttpServletResponse response )
          throws ServletException, IOException {
          // Invoke doGet to process this request
          doGet( request, response );
     }

     /**
      * Returns a brief description about this servlet
      *
      * @return String description about this servlet
      */
     public String getServletInfo() {
          return "Servlet that returns Session information";
     }
}
```

Figure 11-1 displays the response to the client's initial request to `SessionInfo` servlet, and Figure 11-2 displays the response to the client's second request to `SessionInfo` servlet. Notice that the first request passed doesn't have an associated session ID (see Figure 11-1).

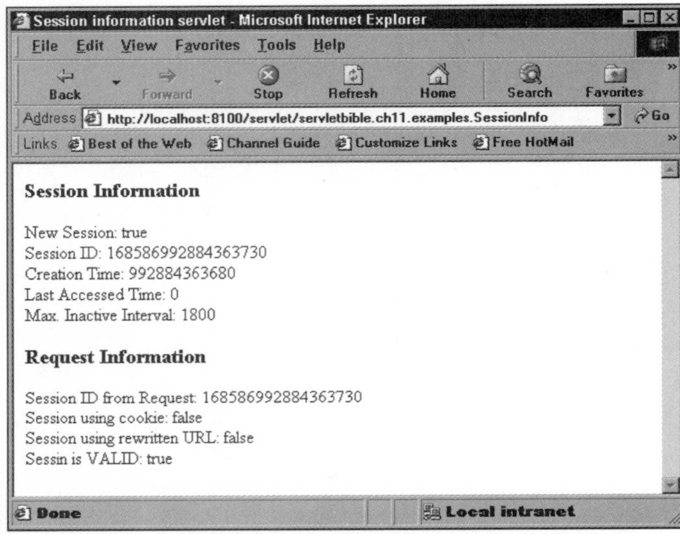

Figure 11-1: Response to the first request to SessionInfo servlet

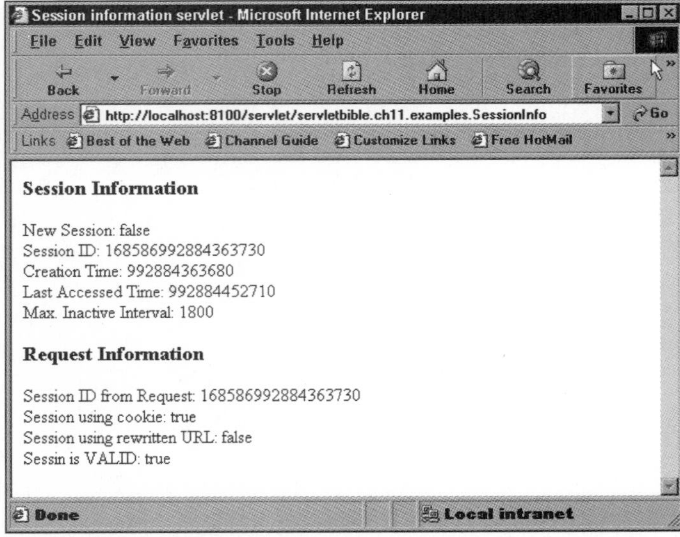

Figure 11-2: Response to the second request to SessionInfo servlet

Let's write another servlet that remembers the user's name and the number of times he or she has visited the site. This servlet prompts the user to enter his or her name. The servlet then demonstrates how session-management methods of the Servlet API can be used to remember the user's name and the number of times he or she has visited this site. The example in Listing 11-2 uses cookies for storing session information.

Listing 11-2

```
package servletbible.ch11.examples;

import javax.servlet.*;
import javax.servlet.http.*;
import java.io.*;
import java.util.*;

/**
 * Demonstrates session management mechanisms
 * built into the Servlet API. A session is established
 * with the client and user is prompted to enter his/her name.
 * User's name along with the number of times he/she visited
 * the site is stored in the session.
 *
 */

public class UserSession extends HttpServlet {
     /**
      * Initializes this servlet. This method is
      * called when the servlet is first loaded.
      *
      * @param config ServletConfig object
      * @throws ServletException When an exception occurs
      */
     public void init( ServletConfig config )
throws ServletException {
          super.init( config );
     }

     /**
      * Handles HTTP GET request
      *
      * @param request HttpServletRequest object
      * @param response HttpServletResponse object
      *
      * @throws ServletException When an exception occurs
      * @throws IOException When an exception occurs
      */
     public void doGet( HttpServletRequest request,
          HttpServletResponse response )
```

Continued

Listing 11-2 *(continued)*

```
          throws ServletException, IOException {

          String name = null;
          Integer hitCount = null;

          // Set the content type to HTML
          response.setContentType( "text/html" );

          // Get the output stream from the response object
          PrintWriter out = response.getWriter();

          // Get the session (Create a new one if required)
          HttpSession session = request.getSession( true );

          name = request.getParameter( "name" );

          // If session is new, this is the first request
          if( session.isNew() ) {
               // Request information from user
               out.println( "<HTML>" );
               out.println( "<HEAD>" );
               out.println( "<TITLE>User information</TITLE>" );
               out.println( "</HEAD>" );
               out.println( "<BODY>" );
               out.println( "<FORM NAME=userform" +
 "METHOD=post ACTION=servletbible.ch11.examples.UserSession>" );
               out.print  ( "<BR>Please enter your name: " );
               out.println( "<INPUT TYPE=text NAME=name>" );
               out.println( "<BR><BR><INPUT TYPE=submit>" );
               out.println( "</BODY>" );
               out.println( "</HTML>" );
          } else {
               // User has submitted the form
               // Name will be available in the request,
               // store it in the session

               if( name != null ) {
                    session.putValue( "name", name );
                    // This is the first request
                    hitCount = new Integer( 1 );
               } else {
                    name = (String) session.getValue( "name" );
                    hitCount = (Integer)
session.getValue( "hitCount" );
               }
               session.putValue( "hitCount",
new Integer( hitCount.intValue() + 1 ) );

               // Return the session information to the client
               out.println( "<HTML>" );
```

```
            out.println( "<HEAD>" );
            out.println( "<TITLE>Hello " + name + "!</TITLE>" );
            out.println( "</HEAD>" );
            out.println( "<BODY>" );
            out.println( "<H2>Hello " + name + "!</H2>" );
            out.println( "You have requested this page " +
hitCount.intValue() + " time(s)!" );
            out.println( "<BR><A HREF='UserSession'>" +
"Click here to continue</A>" );
            out.println( "</BODY>" );
            out.println( "</HTML>" );
        }
        // Flush the output stream
        out.flush();

        // Close the output stream
        out.close();
    }

    /**
     * Handles HTTP POST request
     *
     * @param request HttpServletRequest object
     * @param response HttpServletResponse object
     *
     * @throws ServletException When an exception occurs
     * @throws IOException When an exception occurs
     */
    public void doPost( HttpServletRequest request,
        HttpServletResponse response )
        throws ServletException, IOException {
        // Invoke doGet to process this request
        doGet( request, response );
    }

    /**
     * Returns a brief description about this servlet
     *
     * @return String description about this servlet
     */
    public String getServletInfo() {
        return "Servlet that stores user's name in the Session";
    }
}
```

Figure 11-3 shows the HTML generated by the code in Listing 11-3. When the form in Figure 11-3 is submitted, the form shown in Figure 11-4 is displayed. Whenever the *Click here to continue* hyperlink is clicked, the hit counter increases by one.

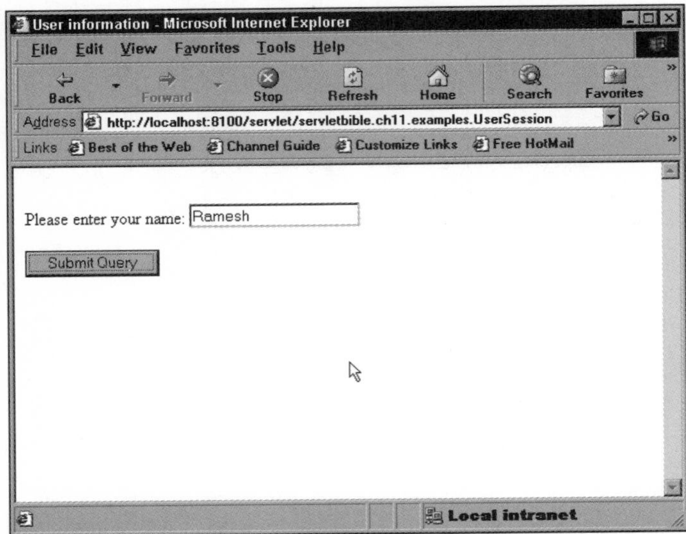

Figure 11-3: Response to the first request to UserSession servlet

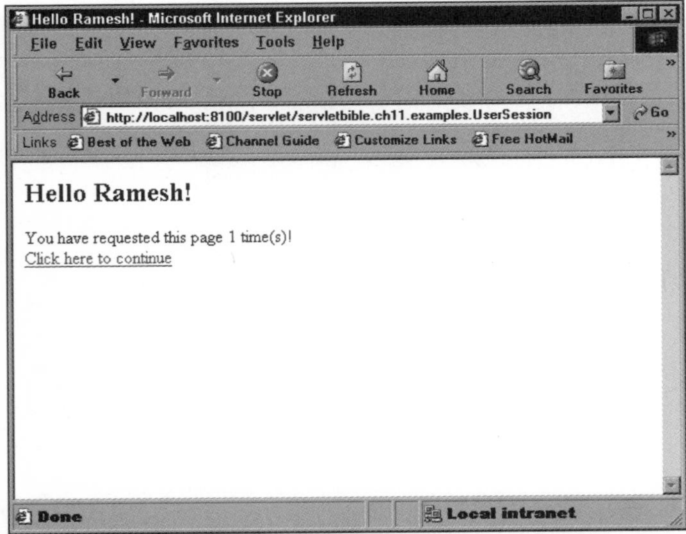

Figure 11-4: Response to the second request to UserSession servlet

URL rewriting

The previous example uses cookies for storing session information. Now it's time to look at an example that uses *rewritten URLs* for storing session information. This example uses the `HttpResponse`'s `encodeURL` method to encode the URL with the session ID. The code in Listing 11-3 does exactly this. Remember that cookie support must be turned off in your browser for this example to work as intended.

Listing 11-3

```
package servletbible.ch11.examples;

import javax.servlet.*;
import javax.servlet.http.*;
import java.io.*;
import java.util.*;

/**
 * Demonstrates session management mechanisms
 * built into the Servlet API. A session is established
 * with the client and user is prompted to enter his/her name.
 * User's name along with the number of times he/she visited
 * the site is stored in the session. This sample uses
 * rewritten URLs for storing session information.
 *
 * NOTE: Cookie support must be turned off in the browser.
 * Refer to your browser documentation on how to turn off
 * cookies
 *
 */

public class URLSession extends HttpServlet {
     /**
      * Initializes this servlet. This method is
      * called when the servlet is first loaded.
      *
      * @param config ServletConfig object
      * @throws ServletException When an exception occurs
      */
     public void init( ServletConfig config )
throws ServletException {
          super.init( config );
     }

     /**
      * Handles HTTP GET request
      *
      * @param request HttpServletRequest object
      * @param response HttpServletResponse object
      *
      * @throws ServletException When an exception occurs
      * @throws IOException When an exception occurs
      */
     public void doGet( HttpServletRequest request,
          HttpServletResponse response )
```

Continued

Listing 11-3 (continued)

```
        throws ServletException, IOException {

        String name = null;
        Integer hitCount = null;

        // Set the content type to HTML
        response.setContentType( "text/html" );

        // Get the output stream from the response object
        PrintWriter out = response.getWriter();

        // Get the session (Create a new one if required)
        HttpSession session = request.getSession( true );

        name = request.getParameter( "name" );

        // If session is new, this is the first request
        if( session.isNew() ) {
            // Request information from user
            out.println( "<HTML>" );
            out.println( "<HEAD>" );
            out.println( "<TITLE>User information</TITLE>" );
            out.println( "</HEAD>" );
            out.println( "<BODY>" );
            out.println( "<FORM NAME=userform METHOD=post" +
                " ACTION=" +
response.encodeURL( "URLSession" ) + ">" );
            out.print  ( "<BR>Please enter your name: " );
            out.println( "<INPUT TYPE=text NAME=name>" );
            out.println( "<BR><BR><INPUT TYPE=submit>" );
            out.println( "</BODY>" );
            out.println( "</HTML>" );
        } else {
            // User has submitted the form
            // Name will be available in the request,
            // store it in the session
            if( name != null ) {
                session.setAttribute( "name", name );
                // This is the first request
                hitCount = new Integer( 1 );
            } else {
                name = (String) session.getAttribute( "name" );
                hitCount = (Integer)
                    session.getAttribute( "hitCount" );
            }
            session.setAttribute( "hitCount",
                new Integer( hitCount.intValue() + 1 ) );

            // Return the session information to the client
            out.println( "<HTML>" );
            out.println( "<HEAD>" );
            out.println( "<TITLE>Hello " + name + "!</TITLE>" );
```

```
            out.println( "</HEAD>" );
            out.println( "<BODY>" );
            out.println( "<H2>Hello " + name + "!</H2>" );
            out.println( "You have requested this page " +
                 hitCount.intValue() + " time(s)!" );
            out.println( "<BR><A HREF='" +
                 response.encodeURL( "URLSession" ) +
                 "'>Click here to continue</A>" );
            out.println( "</BODY>" );
            out.println( "</HTML>" );
        }
        // Flush the output stream
        out.flush();

        // Close the output stream
        out.close();
    }

    /**
     * Handles HTTP POST request
     *
     * @param request HttpServletRequest object
     * @param response HttpServletResponse object
     *
     * @throws ServletException When an exception occurs
     * @throws IOException When an exception occurs
     */
    public void doPost( HttpServletRequest request,
         HttpServletResponse response )
         throws ServletException, IOException {
         // Invoke doGet to process this request
         doGet( request, response );
    }

    /**
     * Returns a brief description about this servlet
     *
     * @return String description about this servlet
     */
    public String getServletInfo() {
         return "Servlet that stores user's name in the Session";
    }
}
```

That's it. To encode the session ID into an URL, simply pass the URL to the `encodeURL()` method of the `HTTPServletRequest` object. One interesting fact about the previous example is that it works with both cookies and rewritten URLs The implementation of `encodeURL()` checks whether the browser supports cookies. If the browser does, it returns the URL unchanged. If the browser doesn't support cookies, the browser encodes the URL with the session ID. If cookie support is turned off in the browser, the output of the Listing 11-3 looks something like Figure 11-5.

Notice that session ID is encoded in the URL in the name `jsessionid`. It's good to use the `encodedURL()` method for all the URLs referred to in the servlet. This ensures the session integrity even if cookie support is disabled in the browser or if the browser doesn't support cookies at all.

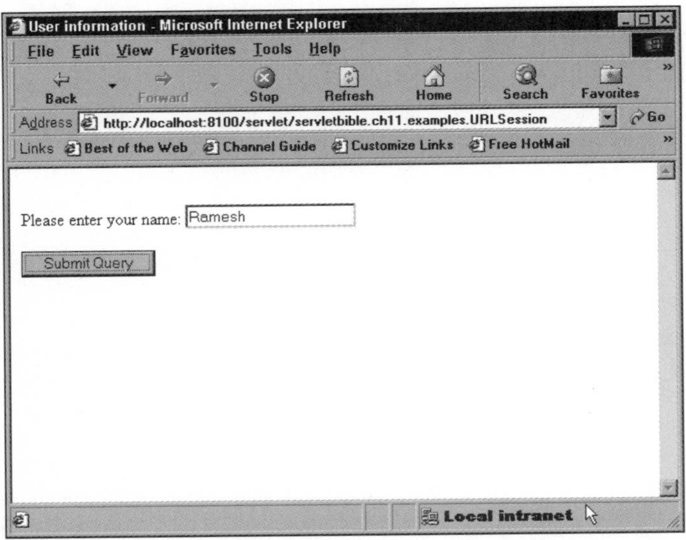

Figure 11-5: Response to the first request to URLSession servlet

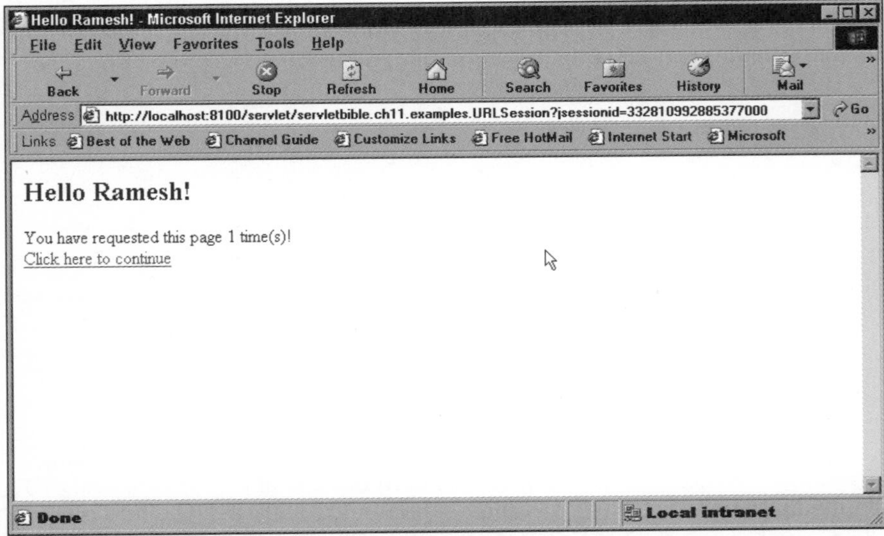

Figure 11-6: Response to the second request to URLSession servlet

A Shopping Cart Example

We have looked at various methods of session management and an example for each method. Now it's time to look at a solid example that uses session extensively. Let's write a very trivial shopping cart application using Servlet API.

This sample application uses a Microsoft Access database for storing data. This database has the following two tables:

- ✦ An Itemtable that stores details for the products
- ✦ An Usertable that stores details for users (such as the userid, password, and so on).

Tables 11-4 and 11-5 provide the database schema of these tables.

Table 11-4
Database Schema for the Item Table

Column Name	*Type*	*Description*
ItemCode	Text	This field stores the item code.
ItemDesc	Text	This field stores the item description.
Summary	Text	This field stores the detailed description of the item.
ItemPrice	Number	This field stores the unit price of the item.

Table 11-5
Database Schema for the User Table

Column Name	*Type*	*Description*
UserId	Text	This field stores the user ID.
Password	Text	This field stores the password for the user.
UserName	Text	This field stores the name of the user.
Address	Text	This field stores the address of the user.

The shopping cart application uses JDBC-ODBC bridge driver for connecting to the access database. This application uses JavaBeans for implementing some of the business logic.

Listing 11-4 models an item (a product) in the shopping cart application. It has various getter methods and setter methods for the attributes.

Listing 11-4

```
package servletbible.ch11.examples;

/**
 * Bean to hold the item information
 */
public class Item {

    public String itemCode ;
    public String itemDesc ;
    public String itemSummary ;
    public double itemPrice ;

    /**
     * GETTER methods
     */

    public String getItemCode() {
        return itemCode ;
    }

    public String getItemDesc() {
        return itemDesc ;
    }

    public String getItemSummary() {
        return itemSummary ;
    }

    public double getItemPrice() {
        return itemPrice ;
    }

    /**
     * SETTER methods
     */

    public void setItemCode(String itemCode ) {
        this.itemCode = itemCode ;
    }

    public void setItemDesc(String itemDesc) {
        this.itemDesc = itemDesc ;
    }

    public void setItemSummary(String itemSummary) {
```

```
        this.itemSummary = itemSummary ;
    }

    public void setItemPrice(double itemPrice) {
        this.itemPrice = itemPrice ;
    }

    public String toString() {
        return "ItemCode = " + itemCode + "ItemDesc = " +
            itemDesc + "ItemSummary = " + itemSummary +
            " ItemPrice = " + itemPrice ;
    }
}
```

Listing 11-5 manages all the items in this application. This class has the following responsibilities:

- ✦ Retrieving all the items from the Item table
- ✦ Retrieving information for an item (such as its description, price, and so on)
- ✦ Retrieving information for a set of items

Listing 11-5

```
package servletbible.ch11.examples;

import java.sql.* ;
import java.util.* ;

/**
 * Manager bean to handle item related transactions
 */
public class ItemManager {

    /**
     * Returns all the items from the <i>item</i> table
     *
     * @return Enumeration List of all items
     */
    public Enumeration getItemList() {
        try {
            Connection con = DBManager.getConnection() ;
            Statement st = con.createStatement() ;
            ResultSet rs = st.executeQuery("Select * from item") ;
            Vector itemList = new Vector() ;
            while (rs.next()) {
                Item myItem = new Item() ;
```

Continued

Listing 11-5 (continued)

```
                myItem.setItemCode(rs.getString("itemcode")) ;
                myItem.setItemDesc(rs.getString("itemdesc")) ;
                myItem.setItemSummary(rs.getString("summary")) ;
                myItem.setItemPrice(rs.getDouble("itemprice")) ;
                itemList.add(myItem) ;
            }
            rs.close();
            st.close();
            con.close();
            return itemList.elements() ;
        }
        catch(Exception e) {
            e.printStackTrace() ;
        }
        return null ;
    }

    /**
     * Returns the details for a particular item
     *
     * @param itemCode Item to get the details for
     * @return Item
     */
    public Item getItemDetails(String itemCode) {
        try {
            Connection con = DBManager.getConnection() ;
            Statement st = con.createStatement() ;
            ResultSet rs = st.executeQuery(
"Select * from item where itemcode = '" + itemCode + "'");
            if (rs.next()){
                Item myItem = new Item() ;
                myItem.setItemCode(rs.getString("itemcode")) ;
                myItem.setItemDesc(rs.getString("itemdesc")) ;
                myItem.setItemSummary(rs.getString("summary")) ;
                myItem.setItemPrice(rs.getDouble("itemprice")) ;
                return myItem ;
            }

        }
        catch(Exception e) {
            e.printStackTrace() ;
        }
        return null ;
    }

    /**
     * Returns the details for the given comma separated item codes
     *
     * @param itemCodes comma separated list of item codes
     */
    public Enumeration getSelectedItems(String itemCodes) {
```

```
        try {
            Connection con = DBManager.getConnection() ;
            Statement st = con.createStatement() ;
            ResultSet rs = st.executeQuery(
                "select * from item where itemcode in (" +
                itemCodes + ")" ) ;
            Vector itemList = new Vector() ;
            String last = null;
            while (rs.next()){
                Item myItem = new Item() ;
                myItem.setItemCode(rs.getString("itemcode")) ;
                myItem.setItemDesc(rs.getString("itemdesc")) ;
                myItem.setItemSummary(rs.getString("summary")) ;
                myItem.setItemPrice(rs.getDouble("itemprice")) ;
                itemList.add(myItem) ;
            }
            return itemList.elements() ;
        }
        catch(Exception e) {
            e.printStackTrace() ;
        }
        return null ;
    }
}
```

Listing 11-6 shows a class (a simple database manager). It has one method `getConnection()`, which returns a new JDBC connection every time it is called. This class can be extended to support database pooling.

Listing 11-6

```
package servletbible.ch11.examples;
import java.sql.* ;

/**
 * Bean for handling database connections.
 * Enhance the getConnection method to provide connection
 * pooling support or other support
 *
 */
public class DBManager {
    /**
     * Returns a new JDBC connection
     *
     * @return Connection New JDBC Connection
     */
    public static Connection getConnection() {
```

Continued

Listing 11-6 *(continued)*

```
        try {
            Class.forName("sun.jdbc.odbc.JdbcOdbcDriver") ;
            return (DriverManager.getConnection("jdbc:odbc:carteg","","") );
        }
        catch(Exception e) {
            e.printStackTrace() ;
        }
        return null ;
    }
}
```

Listing 11-7 shows a class (a simple user manager). It has one method `validate()`, which validates the given userid and password against the values in the database. It returns true if the given values are valid.

Listing 11-7

```
package servletbible.ch11.examples;

import java.sql.* ;

/**
 * Manager Bean for handling user table related operations
 *
 */
public class UserManager {

    /**
     * Validates the userid and password
     *
     * @param userId User id
     * @param passwd Password
     * @return boolean true - if the user is valid
     */
    public boolean validate(String userId, String passwd) {
        try {
            Connection con = DBManager.getConnection() ;
            Statement st = con.createStatement() ;
            ResultSet rs = st.executeQuery(
                "Select * from user where userid = '" +
                 userId + "' and password = '" + passwd + "'") ;
            if (rs.next()){
                rs.close();
                st.close();
                con.close();
```

```
                return true;
            }
        }
        catch(Exception e) {
            e.printStackTrace() ;
        }
        return false ;
    }
}
```

This servlet in Listing 11-8 provides the user with a login form and prompts for userid and password (shown in Figure 11-7). After the user submits the form, the servlet validates the entered userid and password against the values in the database by using the `validate()` method of the `UserManager` class. If the entered information is valid, the servlet puts an entry in the session and forwards the request to the page that displays the list of products.

Notice the use of `encodeURL()` method for all the URLs referred to in the servlet. This enables the servlet to work with rewritten URLs when cookie support is not available in the browser.

Listing 11-8

```
package servletbible.ch11.examples;

import javax.servlet.* ;
import javax.servlet.http.* ;
import java.io.* ;
import servletbible.ch11.examples.*;

/**
 * A shopping cart login servlet
 */

public class LoginServlet extends HttpServlet {

    /**
     * Initializes this servlet
     *
     * @param cfg ServletConfig object
     * @throws ServletException When an exception occurs
     */
    public void init(ServletConfig cfg)
throws ServletException {
        super.init(cfg) ;
    }
```

Continued

Listing 11-8 *(continued)*

```
    /**
     * Prompts the use to enter userid and password
     *
     * @param req Request object
     * @param res Response object
     * @throws ServletException When an exception occurs
     * @throws IOException When an exception occurs
     */
    public void doGet(HttpServletRequest req,
        HttpServletResponse res)
        throws ServletException, IOException {

        PrintWriter out = res.getWriter() ;
        if (req.getParameter("login")==null) {
            out.println("<html><body><center>") ;
            out.println("<form name = 'loginform' method = 'post'><table>") ;
            out.println("<tr><td>Enter username:</td>") ;
            out.println("<td><input type='text' name='userid'></td></tr>") ;

            out.println("<tr><td>Enter password:</td>") ;
            out.println("<td><input type='password' name='passwd'></td></tr>");
            out.print("<tr><td><input type = 'submit' " );
            out.println("name = 'login' value='Login'></td></tr>") ;
            out.println("</table></form></center></body></html>") ;
        }
        else {
            doPost(req,res) ;
        }
    }

    /**
     * Validates the userid and password
     *
     * @param req Request object
     * @param res Response object
     * @throws ServletException When an exception occurs
     * @throws IOException When an exception occurs
     */
    public void doPost(HttpServletRequest req,
        HttpServletResponse res)
        throws ServletException, IOException {

        PrintWriter out = res.getWriter() ;
        String userId, passwd ;
        UserManager login = new UserManager() ;
        if ((req.getParameter("userid")!=null) &&
(req.getParameter("passwd")!=null)) {
            userId = (String) req.getParameter("userid") ;
            passwd = (String) req.getParameter("passwd") ;
```

```
                // If successful login
                if (login.validate(userId,passwd)){
                    HttpSession session = req.getSession() ;
                    session.setAttribute("userId",userId) ;
                    RequestDispatcher rd = getServletContext().
                        getRequestDispatcher(res.encodeURL("/showlist"));
                    rd.forward(req,res) ;
                }
                out.println("<html><body><center>Invalid userid or password<br>");
                out.println("<a href='" +
                    res.encodeURL("login") + "'>Click here to relogin</a>") ;
                out.println("</body></html>") ;
            }
            else {
                out.print("Login Failed! Please enter valid" );
                out.println( "login details and click login" ) ;
                out.println("<a href = '" + res.encodeURL( "login" ) +
                    "'>click here</a>") ;
            }
        }
    }
```

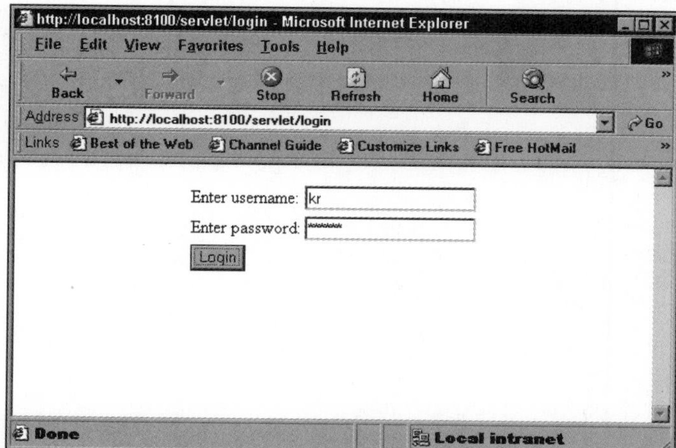

Figure 11-7: The Login Servlet for the shopping cart example

The servlet in Listing 11-9 provides the user with the list of products from the Item table. When an item is clicked, the selected item's itemcode is passed to the `ShowDesc`. It also has hyperlinks for the following:

✦ Viewing the items in the virtual shopping cart

✦ Checking out the items in the cart

✦ Logging out of the system

Listing 11-9

```
package servletbible.ch11.examples;
import javax.servlet.* ;
import javax.servlet.http.* ;
import java.io.* ;
import java.util.* ;
import servletbible.ch11.examples.*;

/**
 * Servlet to show the items available in the site
 */
public class ShowList extends HttpServlet {

    /**
     * Initializes this servlet
     *
     * @param cfg ServletConfig object
     * @throws ServletException When an exception occurs
     */
    public void init(ServletConfig cfg) throws ServletException {
        super.init(cfg) ;
    }

    /**
     * Handles HTTP GET request
     *
     * @param req Request object
     * @param res Response object
     * @throws ServletException When an exception occurs
     * @throws IOException When an exception occurs
     */
    public void doGet(HttpServletRequest req,
        HttpServletResponse res)
        throws ServletException, IOException {
        doPost(req,res) ;
    }

    /**
     * Displays the list of items
     *
     * @param req Request object
     * @param res Response object
     * @throws ServletException When an exception occurs
```

```
     * @throws IOException When an exception occurs
     */
    public void doPost(HttpServletRequest req,
        HttpServletResponse res)
        throws ServletException, IOException {
        PrintWriter out = res.getWriter() ;
        ItemManager itemMgr = new ItemManager() ;
        out.println("<html><body><center>") ;
        HttpSession session = req.getSession() ;
        if (session.getAttribute("userId")!=null) {
            out.println("Welcome " + session.getAttribute("userId") + "!" ) ;
            Enumeration list = itemMgr.getItemList() ;
            out.print("<table border = 1><tr><th>");
            out.println("Commodity</th><th>Price</th></tr>") ;
            while (list.hasMoreElements()) {
                Item item = (Item) list.nextElement() ;
                out.println("<tr valign = top><td><a href='");
                out.println(res.encodeURL("showdesc") + "?itemcode="+
                    item.getItemCode() + "'>" + item.getItemDesc() +
                    "</td><td align = right>" + item.getItemPrice()
                    + "</a></td></tr>") ;
            }
            out.println("</table>") ;
        }
        else{
            out.println("Session not bound") ;
        }
        out.println("<br><br><br>") ;
        out.println("<a href='" + res.encodeURL("checkout") +
            "'>Proceed to check out </a><br>") ;
        out.println("<a href='" + res.encodeURL("viewcart") +
            "'>View shopping cart</a><br>") ;
        out.println("<a href='" + res.encodeURL("logout") +
            "'>Click here to logout</a><br>") ;
        out.println("</center></body></html>") ;
    }
}
```

The class in Listing 11-10 displays the selected items detailed descriptions and prices (shown in Figure 11-8). Users have the following options in this page:

✦ They can add this item to the virtual shopping cart.

✦ They can proceed to checkout.

✦ They can view the items in the virtual shopping cart.

✦ They can navigate to the product list page.

✦ They can log out of the system.

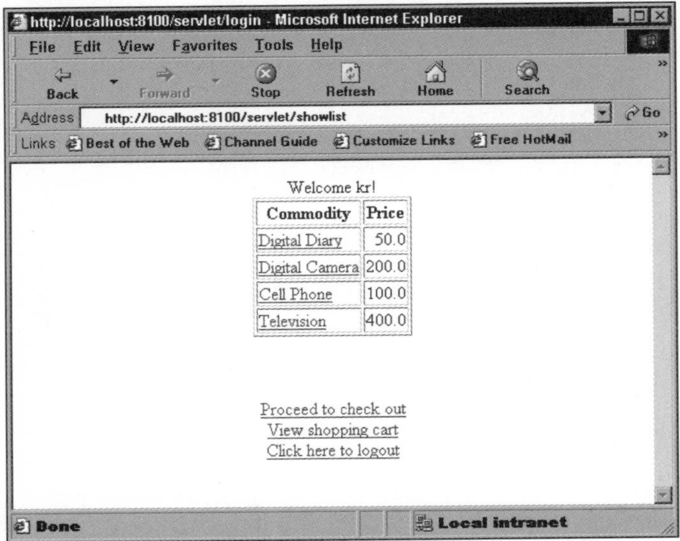

Figure 11-8: The Show List servlet displays the list of items in the shopping cart.

Listing 11-10

```
package servletbible.ch11.examples;
import javax.servlet.* ;
import javax.servlet.http.* ;
import java.io.* ;
import java.util.* ;
import servletbible.ch11.examples.*;

/**
 * Servlet to show item descriptions and summary
 */
public class ShowDesc extends HttpServlet {

    /**
     * Initializes this servlet
     *
     * @param cfg ServletConfig object
     * @throws ServletException When an exception occurs
     */
    public void init(ServletConfig cfg)
throws ServletException {
        super.init(cfg) ;
    }

    /**
```

```
     * Displays the details of the selected item
     *
     * @param req Request object
     * @param res Response object
     * @throws ServletException When an exception occurs
     * @throws IOException When an exception occurs
     */
    public void doGet(HttpServletRequest req,
        HttpServletResponse res)
        throws ServletException, IOException {

        PrintWriter out = res.getWriter() ;
        ItemManager itemMgr = new ItemManager() ;
        HttpSession session = req.getSession() ;
        out.println("<html><body>") ;
        if (session.getAttribute("userId")!=null) {
            out.println("Welcome " +
                session.getAttribute("userId") + "!" ) ;
            String code ;
            if (req.getParameter("itemcode")!=null) {
                code = (String) req.getParameter("itemcode") ;
                Item item = itemMgr.getItemDetails(code);
                out.print("<table border = 1><tr><th>" );
                out.print( "Commodity</th><th>Summary</th>" );
                out.println( "<th>Price</th></tr>" );
                out.println("<tr><td valign = top>" +
                    item.getItemDesc() + "</td><td valign = top width = 300 >"+
                    item.getItemSummary() + "</td><td valign = bottom >" +
                    item.getItemPrice() + "</td></tr>") ;
                out.println("</table>") ;
                out.println("<br><br><br><a href='" +
                    res.encodeURL( "addtocart" ) +
                    "?itemcode=" +
                    code + "'> Add this Item to cart </a><br>") ;
                out.println("<a href='" + res.encodeURL("checkout" ) +
                    "'>Proceed to check out </a><br>") ;
                out.println("<a href='" + res.encodeURL("showlist") +
                    "'>Continue shopping </a><br>") ;
                out.println("<a href='" + res.encodeURL("viewcart") +
                    "'>View shopping cart</a><br>") ;
                out.println("<a href='" + res.encodeURL("logout") +
                    "'>Click here to logout</a>") ;
            }
            else {
                out.println("The specified Item is no longer available") ;
            }
        }
        else{
            out.println("Session time out error") ;
        }
        out.println("</body></html>") ;
    }
}
```

The class in Listing 11-11 adds the selected item to the virtual shopping cart (shown in Figure 11-9). It gets the vector from the session, adds the selected item to it, and returns this vector to the session. After adding the item to the cart, the user is provided with the following options:

- ✦ Displaying the product-list page
- ✦ Logging out of the system

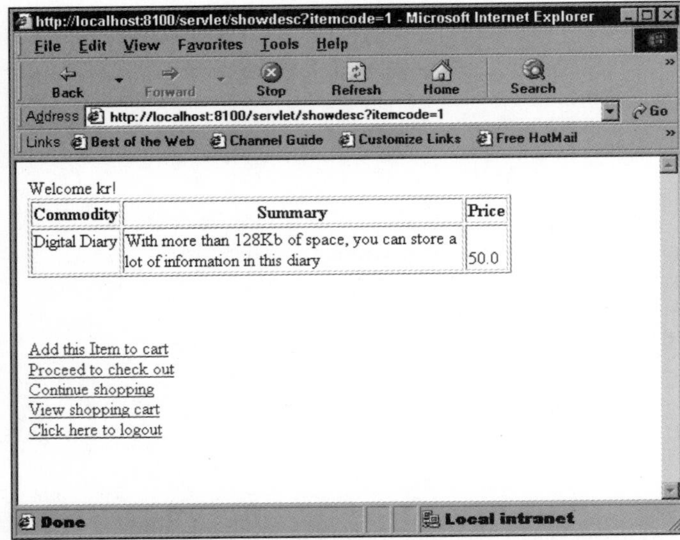

Figure 11-9: Shows the description of a particular item in the shopping cart

Listing 11-11

```
package servletbible.ch11.examples;
import javax.servlet.* ;
import javax.servlet.http.* ;
import java.io.* ;
import java.util.* ;
import servletbible.ch11.examples.*;

/**
 * Servlet to add items to cart
 *
 */
public class AddToCart extends HttpServlet {

    /**
     * Initializes this servlet
```

```
     *
     * @param cfg ServletConfig object
     * @throws ServletException When an exception occurs
     */
    public void init(ServletConfig cfg) throws ServletException {
        super.init(cfg) ;
    }

    /**
     * Addes the selected item to the cart
     *
     * @param req Request object
     * @param res Response object
     * @throws ServletException When an exception occurs
     * @throws IOException When an exception occurs
     */
    public void doGet( HttpServletRequest req, HttpServletResponse res )
        throws ServletException, IOException {
        PrintWriter out = res.getWriter() ;

        HttpSession session = req.getSession() ;
        if (session.getAttribute("userId")!=null) {
            String userId = (String) session.getAttribute( "userId" ) ;
            out.println( "<html><body><center>" ) ;
            out.println( "Welcome " + userId + "!" ) ;

            // Get the selected item from the request and add it to the cart
            if (req.getParameter("itemcode")!=null) {
                String code = (String) req.getParameter("itemcode") ;
                ItemManager itemMgr = new ItemManager() ;
                Item item = itemMgr.getItemDetails(code) ;
                Vector selectedItems ;
                if (session.getAttribute(userId)!=null) {
                    selectedItems = (Vector) session.getAttribute(userId) ;
                }
                else{
                    selectedItems = new Vector() ;
                }
                selectedItems.add( item ) ;
                session.setAttribute(userId,selectedItems) ;
                session.setAttribute(code,item) ;
                out.print("<br><br>The item was added to " );
                out.println( "your shopping cart<BR><br>" ) ;
                out.println("<a href='" + res.encodeURL("showlist") +
                    "'>Click here to continue shopping</a>") ;
                out.println("<br><a href='" + res.encodeURL("logout") +
                    "'>Click here to Logout</a>") ;
            }
        }
        else{
            out.println("Session timeout error") ;
        }
    }
}
```

The class in Listing 11-12 displays the items in the virtual shopping cart. It gets the list of selected products from the session and displays them. Users have the following options:

- ✦ They can delete items by marking the checkbox to the left of each item (shown in Figure 11-11).
- ✦ They can navigate to the product list page.
- ✦ They can log out of the system.

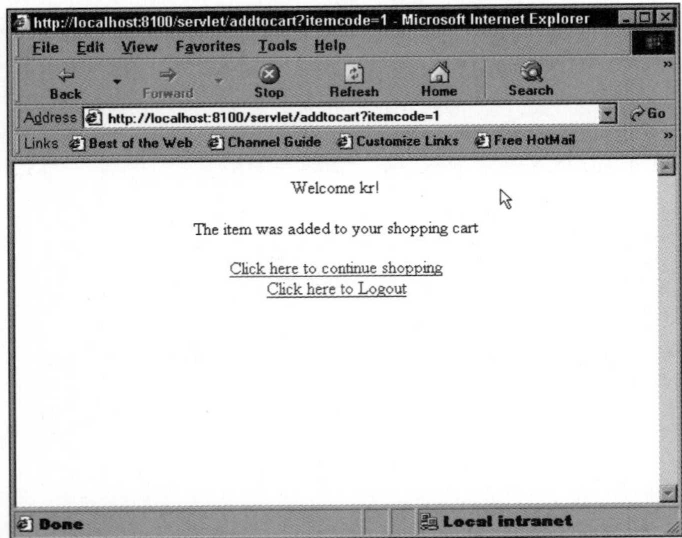

Figure 11-10: Shopping cart displaying the items after an item is added to cart

Listing 11-12

```
package servletbible.ch11.examples;
import javax.servlet.* ;
import javax.servlet.http.* ;
import java.io.* ;
import java.util.* ;
import servletbible.ch11.examples.*;

/**
 * Servlet to display the status of the shopping cart at any given time
 */
public class ViewCart extends HttpServlet {

    /**
```

```
 * Initializes this servlet
 *
 * @param cfg ServletConfig object
 * @throws ServletException When an exception occurs
 */
public void init(ServletConfig cfg) throws ServletException {
    super.init(cfg) ;
}

/**
 * Handles HTTP GET request
 *
 * @param req Request object
 * @param res Response object
 * @throws ServletException When an exception occurs
 * @throws IOException When an exception occurs
 */
public void doGet(HttpServletRequest req,
    HttpServletResponse res)
    throws ServletException, IOException {
    doPost(req,res) ;
}

/**
 * Displays the virtual shopping cart
 *
 * @param req Request object
 * @param res Response object
 * @throws ServletException When an exception occurs
 * @throws IOException When an exception occurs
 */
public void doPost(HttpServletRequest req,
    HttpServletResponse res)
    throws ServletException, IOException {
    PrintWriter out = res.getWriter() ;
    ItemManager itemMgr = new ItemManager() ;
    out.println("<html><body><center>" );
    out.println( "<form name='deleteform' method = 'post' " );
    out.println( "action = '" + res.encodeURL("deleteitems") + "'>") ;
    HttpSession session = req.getSession() ;
    if (session.getAttribute("userId")!=null) {
        String userId = (String) session.getAttribute("userId") ;

        out.println("Welcome " + userId + "!" ) ;
        Vector selectedItems ;
        if (session.getAttribute(userId)!=null) {
            selectedItems = (Vector) session.getAttribute(userId) ;
            Enumeration list = selectedItems.elements() ;
            out.println("<table border = 1><tr><th>" );
            out.println("Commodity</th><th>Price</th></tr>") ;

            while (list.hasMoreElements()) {
```

Continued

Listing 11-12 *(continued)*

```
                    Item item = (Item) list.nextElement() ;
                    out.println("<tr><td valign = top>");
                    out.println("<input type='checkbox' name='" +
                        item.getItemCode() +
                        "'><a href='" + res.encodeURL("showdesc") +
                        "?itemcode="+item.getItemCode()+"'>" +
                        item.getItemDesc() + "</td><td align = right>" +
                        item.getItemPrice() + "</a></td></tr>") ;
                }
                out.println("</table>") ;
                out.println("<br><br><br><a href='javascript:remove()'>" );
                out.println("Delete selected items</a>") ;
            }
            else {
                out.println("<br>The cart is empty") ;
            }
        }
        else{
            out.println("Session timeout error") ;
        }
        out.println("<br><br><br><a href='" +
            res.encodeURL("showlist") +
            "'>Click here to continue shopping</a>") ;
        out.println("<br><a href='" +
            res.encodeURL("logout") +
            "'>Click here to logout</a>") ;
        out.println("</form></body>") ;
        out.println("<script language = 'javascript'>") ;
        out.println("function remove() { ") ;
        out.println("document.deleteform.submit(); ") ;
        out.println("}</script></html>") ;
    }
}
```

The class in Listing 11-13 displays the items in the shopping cart and the price of each item. It also displays the total price of all the items (shown in Figure 11-12). Users have the following options in this page:

✦ They can go to the product-listing page.

✦ They can log out of the system.

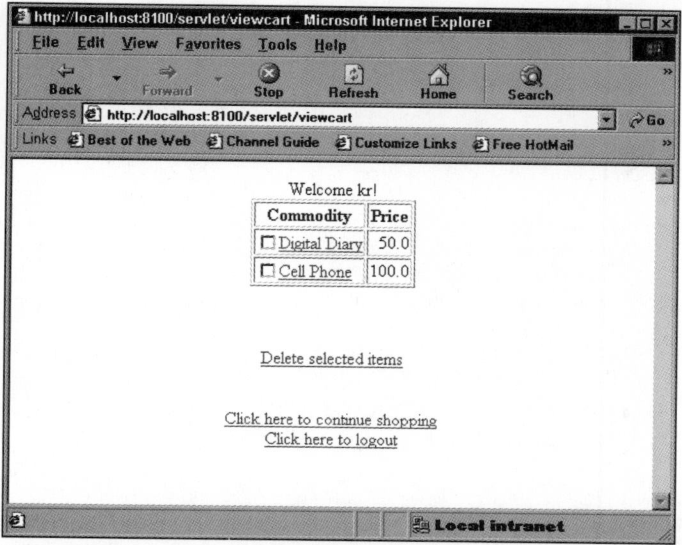

Figure 11-11: View Cart displays all the items in the shopping cart

Listing 11-13

```
package servletbible.ch11.examples;
import javax.servlet.* ;
import javax.servlet.http.* ;
import java.io.* ;
import java.util.* ;
import servletbible.ch11.examples.*;

/**
 * Servlet to show the items selected in the check out counter
 *
 */
public class CheckOut extends HttpServlet {

    /**
     * Initializes this servlet
     *
     * @param cfg ServletConfig object
     * @throws ServletException When an exception occurs
     */
    public void init(ServletConfig cfg)
throws ServletException {
        super.init(cfg) ;
```

Continued

Listing 11-13 *(continued)*

```
    }

    /**
     * Handles HTTP GET request
     *
     * @param req Request object
     * @param res Response object
     * @throws ServletException When an exception occurs
     * @throws IOException When an exception occurs
     */
    public void doGet(HttpServletRequest req,
HttpServletResponse res)
        throws ServletException, IOException {
        doPost(req,res) ;
    }

    /**
     * Checks out the selected items
     *
     * @param req Request object
     * @param res Response object
     * @throws ServletException When an exception occurs
     * @throws IOException When an exception occurs
     */
    public void doPost(HttpServletRequest req,
HttpServletResponse res)
        throws ServletException, IOException {
        PrintWriter out = res.getWriter() ;
        ItemManager itemMgr = new ItemManager() ;
        out.print("<html><body><center>" );
        out.print("<form name='deleteform' " );
        out.println( "method = 'post' action = '" +
            res.encodeURL("deleteitems") + "'>" ) ;
        HttpSession session = req.getSession() ;
        if (session.getAttribute("userId")!=null) {
            String userId = (String) session.getAttribute("userId") ;

            out.println("Welcome " + userId + "!") ;
            Vector selectedItems ;
            if (session.getAttribute(userId)!=null) {
                selectedItems = (Vector) session.getAttribute(userId) ;
                Enumeration list = selectedItems.elements() ;
                out.print("<table border=1><tr><th>Commodity");
                out.println("</th><th>Price</th></tr>") ;
                double total = 0;
                while (list.hasMoreElements()) {
                    Item item = (Item) list.nextElement() ;
                    out.println("<tr><td valign = top>" + item.getItemDesc() +
                        "</td><td align = 'right'>" + item.getItemPrice() +
                        "</td></tr>") ;
                    total = total + item.getItemPrice() ;
```

```
                }
                out.println("<tr><td> </td><td> </td></tr>") ;
                out.println("<tr><td> </td><td> </td></tr>") ;
                out.println("<tr><td align = right>Total</td>" );
                out.println("<td align = right>" + total + "</td></tr>") ;
                out.println("</table>") ;
            }
            else {
                out.println("<br>The cart is empty") ;
            }
        }
        else{
            out.println("Session timeout error") ;
        }
        out.println("<br><br><br><a href='" + res.encodeURL( "showlist" ) +
            "'>Click here to continue shopping</a>") ;
        out.println("<br><a href='" + res.encodeURL( "logout" ) +
            "'>Click here to logout</a>");
        out.println("</form></body>") ;
        out.println("<script language = 'javascript'>") ;
        out.println("function remove() { ") ;
        out.println("document.deleteform.submit(); ") ;
        out.println("}</script></html>") ;
    }
}
```

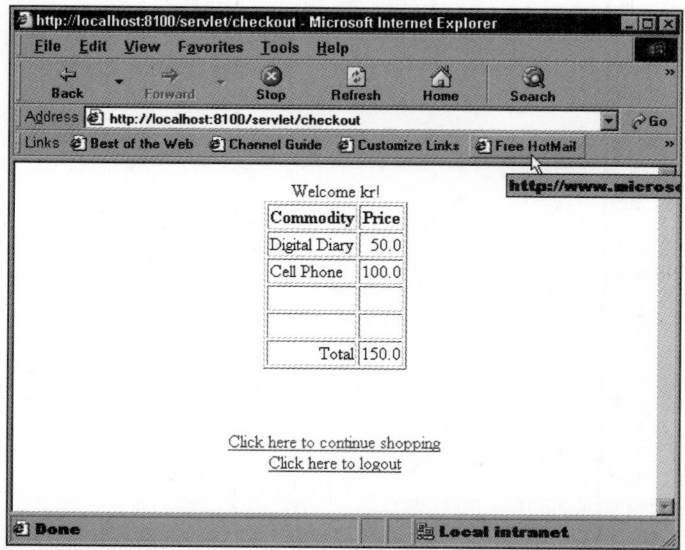

Figure 11-12: Shopping cart displaying a list of items checked out

The user is returned to the login page after the logout option has been selected (as shown in Figure 11-13).

Listing 11-14

```
package servletbible.ch11.examples;

import javax.servlet.* ;
import javax.servlet.http.* ;
import java.io.* ;
import servletbible.ch11.examples.*;

/**
 * Logs out the current user
 *
 */

public class LogoutServlet extends HttpServlet {

    /**
     * Initializes this servlet
     *
     * @param cfg ServletConfig object
     * @throws ServletException When an exception occurs
     */
    public void init(ServletConfig cfg) throws ServletException {
        super.init(cfg) ;
    }

    /**
     * Prompts the use to enter userid and password
     *
     * @param req Request object
     * @param res Response object
     * @throws ServletException When an exception occurs
     * @throws IOException When an exception occurs
     */
    public void doGet(HttpServletRequest req,
        HttpServletResponse res)
        throws ServletException, IOException {

        HttpSession session = req.getSession();
        String userId = (String) session.getValue( "userId" );
        session.removeValue( "userId" );
        session.removeValue( userId );
        RequestDispatcher dispatcher = getServletContext().
            getRequestDispatcher( "/login" );
        dispatcher.forward( req, res );
    }
```

```
    /**
     * Validates the userid and password
     *
     * @param req Request object
     * @param res Response object
     * @throws ServletException When an exception occurs
     * @throws IOException When an exception occurs
     */
    public void doPost(HttpServletRequest req,
        HttpServletResponse res)
        throws ServletException, IOException {
        doGet( req, res );
    }
}
```

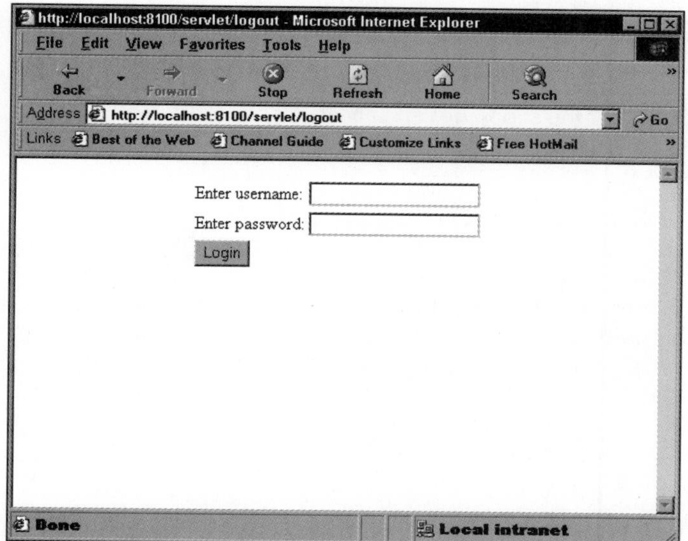

Figure 11-13: Logout servlet

The screen in Figure 11-14 shows the settings in JRun3.0 that need to be completed prior to running the shopping cart sample.

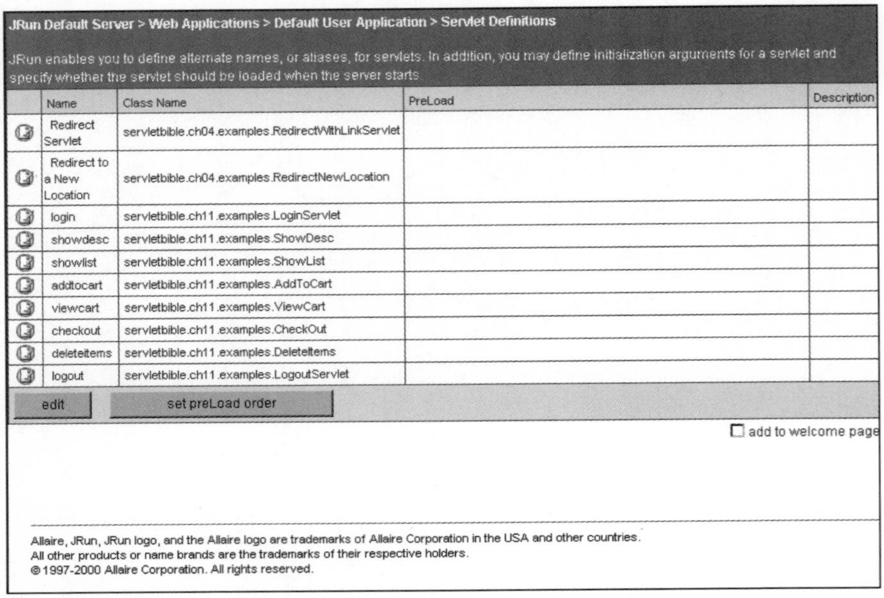

JRun Default Server > Web Applications > Default User Application > Servlet Definitions

JRun enables you to define alternate names, or aliases, for servlets. In addition, you may define initialization arguments for a servlet and specify whether the servlet should be loaded when the server starts.

	Name	Class Name	PreLoad	Description
	Redirect Servlet	servletbible.ch04.examples.RedirectWithLinkServlet		
	Redirect to a New Location	servletbible.ch04.examples.RedirectNewLocation		
	login	servletbible.ch11.examples.LoginServlet		
	showdesc	servletbible.ch11.examples.ShowDesc		
	showlist	servletbible.ch11.examples.ShowList		
	addtocart	servletbible.ch11.examples.AddToCart		
	viewcart	servletbible.ch11.examples.ViewCart		
	checkout	servletbible.ch11.examples.CheckOut		
	deleteitems	servletbible.ch11.examples.DeleteItems		
	logout	servletbible.ch11.examples.LogoutServlet		

edit | set preLoad order

☐ add to welcome page

Allaire, JRun, JRun logo, and the Allaire logo are trademarks of Allaire Corporation in the USA and other countries.
All other products or name brands are the trademarks of their respective holders.
© 1997-2000 Allaire Corporation. All rights reserved.

Figure 11-14: Jrun settings for the shopping cart servlet

Summary

In this chapter, you learned about sessions and the various ways to manage sessions and session information. We discussed session management support in the Servlet API. We also wrote a simple Shopping Cart application using session-management techniques.

✦ ✦ ✦

Security and Servlets

In This Chapter

Basic authentication

Digest authentication

Form-based authentication

Authorization

LDAP security

Servlets are useful in developing Web applications, and any Web application worth its salt should provide adequate security when deployed on the Internet. Because servlets are Java code, you have a whole range of Java Security APIs and extensions at your disposal. The security concepts and mechanisms explained in this chapter provide a basic understanding of servlet security and are intended to serve as guidelines.

Authentication

Authentication is the process by which users' access privileges are verified prior to their entering a Web site's protected area. HTTP authentication refers to the authentication scheme defined in HTTP protocol. The philosophy behind an HTTP authentication scheme is simple. The Web browser should provide adequate credentials to access protected realms.

When a Web browser requests a secure page, the Web server sends back a 401 unauthorized status code in its response with a WWW-Authenticate header. The Web browser sends the request again providing the client credentials, reciprocating the authentication challenge contained in the WWW-Authenticate header. If the Web server finds the credentials adequate, it returns the requested page. Otherwise it returns the 401 unauthorized response again. There are two major HTTP authentication approaches: basic authentication and digest authentication.

Basic authentication

The onus of authentication is on the Web server in the case of basic authentication. When the Web browser requests a protected page, the Web server returns the 401 unauthorized response with the authentication challenge in the WWW-Authenticate header, consisting of the token `Basic` and the name of the protected realm. The Web browser displays a dialog box requiring the user to enter a username and password.

Base64 is a method of encoding arbitrary data as plain ASCII text.

The Web browser base64-encodes the username and password and transmits the same to the Web server as plain text. The Web server base64-decodes the data and compares the username-password combination against its own internal value. The Web server lets the user access the page if the credentials are adequate.

```
import javax.servlet.*;
import javax.servlet.http.*;
import java.io.*;
import java.util.*;


public class BasicAuthentication extends HttpServlet{

 public void init(ServletConfig config) throws ServletException
{
  super.init(config);
  }

 public void doGet(HttpServletRequest req, HttpServletResponse
res)
     throws ServletException, IOException{

  res.setContentType("text/plain");
  PrintWriter out = res.getWriter();
  String authentication = req.getHeader("Authorization");

  boolean authenticated = false ;
  if(authentication == null)
  {
    // Do Nothing !
  }
  else if(authentication.toUpperCase().startsWith("BASIC "))
  {
    // Strip the prefix
    String cipher = authentication.substring(6);
    sun.misc.BASE64Decoder base64decoder = new
sun.misc.BASE64Decoder();
    // Decode the base64 encoded Username password combination
    String decipher = new
String(base64decoder.decodeBuffer(cipher));
```

```
      if(decipher.equals("Open:Sesame"))
      {
        out.println("Authenticated");
        authenticated = true;
      }
    }

    if(!authenticated)
    {
      res.setHeader("WWW-Authenticate", "BASIC
  realm=\"ServletBible\"");
      res.sendError(res.SC_UNAUTHORIZED);
    }

   }

  }
```

Digest authentication

In the case of basic authentication, the username and password are transmitted as plain text, and hence they are readily vulnerable to eavesdropping. An obvious way out is to encrypt the data before it is transmitted, using a secure algorithm such as MD5 encryption algorithm. This is the basis behind a variation of basic authentication known as *digest authentication.*

This again is exposed to replay attack—that is, an eavesdropper can intercept the encrypted message and pass the same back to the Web server to impersonate an authentic user. To alleviate this, digest authentication employs the technique of passing the nonce. The Web server generates the nonce uniquely and randomly each time a URI (Universal Resource Identifier) is requested by the Web browser. The Web browser produces a digest using username, password, URI, and the nonce value. Since the nonce value is uniquely generated each time, the replay attack will be futile, as the digest will consist of an old nonce value.

Form-based authentication

Form-based authentication entails letting the user log in via a particular logon page, storing the login information in Session, and checking whether the logged-in user has adequate credentials by using this Session information if the user attempts to access protected resources.

Lazy form-based authentication approaches intend to authorize the users just in time—that is, just when they try to access protected pages. The benefit of this approach over using a form that requires the user to log in at the very start of the session, irrespective of whether the user may then proceed to browse only nonprotected pages, is that users need not wait for authentication unless they really access protected resources. The majority of sites use form-based authentication rather than HTTP authentication, because reliance on HTTP authentication might lead to proprietary solutions that work only with specific Web server and browser combinations. However, form-based authentication involves checking against the session information for each and every page access, which slows down the access slightly.

After the Login, you can indicate that the user has logged in, as here:

```
// Get the session object
HttpSession session = request.getSession(true);
// Put the indicator flag in the Session variable
Session.putValue("logged", true);
```

Thus the information that the user has successfully logged in is stored in a session variable.

While accessing a protected resource, this can be checked as follows:

```
// Get the session object
HttpSession session = request.getSession(true);
// Get the indicator flag from the Session variable
Boolean logged = false ;
logged = Session.getValue("logged");
if(!logged)
{
 // Redirect to login page
 response.sendRedirect(loginURL) ;
      }
// Do something with the protected resource
```

Authorization

Authorization entails protection through security policies that prevent unauthorized code connecting to systems not intended. Two types of authorization are *code authorization* and *caller authorization*. Authorization happens after authentication.

Code authorization

Code authorization entails limiting the classes available to JVM that the servlet engine uses. `CLASSPATH` should be devoid of unnecessary entries.

Caller authorization

Caller authorization involves establishing the identity and credentials of the caller before allowing access to protected resources. J2EE provides support for *role-based authorization*. A security role provides an abstraction of a group of users requiring similar privileges. Examples of roles include manager, customer, and so on.

Role-based authorization can be either *declarative* or *programmatic*. Servlet specification provides for declarative role-based authorization through deployment descriptors. The servlet can use the following for programmatic authorization of roles:

```
HttpServletRequest.isUserInRole("customer")
```

Java security

The concept of the Java Security model is fairly straightforward. It is based on granting or restricting the functionality available to the user through an access control list. In the Java Security API, there is a `java.security.acl` package that contains security system classes in Java.

A Java Security Principal is an entity of distinct identity, such as an individual user or program in execution. For instance, consider a `java.security.Principal` called `customer`, as shown here:

```
Principal customer = new PrincipalImpl ("customer");
```

You can create a `Permission` object to represent the capability to create an order. Permission is symbolic and conceptual, and the logic to restrict or allow the user to perform a particular task must be implemented in code, as follows:

```
Permission canOrder = new PermissionImpl ("canOrder");
```

Now you can create an Access Control List entry:

```
Acl accessControlList = new AclImpl (owner, "OrderEntryAcl");
AclEntry aclControlEntry = new AclEntryImpl (customer);
aclControlEntry.addPermission(canOrder);
accessControlList.addEntry(owner, aclControlEntry);
boolean canCustomerOrder = accessControlList.checkPermission(customer,
canOrder);
```

LDAP Security

LDAP stands for *Lightweight Directory Access Protocol*. LDAP provides directory service. It can store any kind of information in a tree-like structure. An LDAP server restricts the users that can add, read, or update the information in the directory-tree structure.

Various versions of the LDAP support various types of authentication. The LDAP v2 defines three types of authentication: *anonymous*, *simple* (clear-text password), and *Kerberos v4*. The LDAP v3 supports three types of authentication: *anonymous*, *simple*, and *SASL*. SASL stands for *Simple Authentication and Security Layer* (RFC 2222).

It specifies a challenge-response protocol. By using SASL, the LDAP supports any kind of authentication the client and server can negotiate.

By using the `Context.SECURITY_AUTHENTICATION` environment property, you can specify the authentication mechanism:

- `sasl_mechanism`: Use SASL mechanism names separated by spaces. (For example, CRAM-MD5 to use CRAM-MD5.)
- `none`: Use no authentication (anonymous).
- `simple`: Use weak authentication (plain-text password).

By default, authentication mechanism is `none`. If authentication information is specified by the client without express specification of the `Context.SECURITY_AUTHENTICATION` property, the authentication mechanism becomes `simple`.

Every entry has a primary key called the *Distinguished Name* (*DN*). For simple authentication, the client passes the fully qualified DN of the user and password in clear text to the LDAP server. Since this is vulnerable to security risks, SSL is used in conjunction with simple authentication by several LDAP server so as to send the authentication information encrypted.

For simple authentication, set `Context.SECURITY_AUTHENTICATION` to `simple`. Also set the `Context.SECURITY_PRINCIPAL` to the fully qualified DN of the entity to be authenticated. Set `Context.SECURITY_CREDENTIALS` with password.

See the following example using simple authentication. Perform the following steps to install an LDAP server in your machine:

1. Download JavaLDAP server from `http://javaldap.sourcefourge.net` and extract the zip file to a directory.
2. Download SNACC for Java from the IBM Alphaworks site at `http://alphaworks.ibm.com`. The zip file may not have a `.jar` file prebuilt. You may need to create a `.jar` file out of the files in the classes directory.

   ```
   <snacc-installation-dir>\classes> jar cvf  ibmasn1.jar com
   ```
3. Download Xerces XML parser from `http://xml.apache.org`.
4. Download JNDI module from `java.sun.com`.
5. Copy the following files from JNDI and download to the `<jdk-installation>\jre\lib\ext` directory:

   ```
   jaas.jar,ldap.jar,ldapbp.jar,providerutil.jar
   ```
6. Copy the `.jar` files from Xerces and SNACC to the `<ldap-installation-dir>` directory.

7. Modify `javaldap.bat` in `<ldap-installation-dir>` to include `ibmasn1.jar` and `xerces.jar` in the `CLASSPATH`.
8. Modify `build.bat` to point to the correct JDK bin directory.
9. Run `javaldap.bat`.
10. Run `build.bat`.
11. Modify `backends.prop` in `<ldap-installation-dir>` to have only the following lines:

```
backend.num=1
backend.0.root=o=Ramesh Krisnaswamy
backend.0.type=org.javaldap.server.backend.BackendMemory
```

12. Add the following line to the end of the `acls.prop` file:

```
o=Ramesh Krisnaswamy|subtree#grant:r,b,t#[all]#public:
```

13. In the `javaldap.prop` file, replace `10389` with `389` in the following line. This changes the ldap port to 389.

```
javaldap.server.port=10389
```

14. Now we are all set to run the server. Run the server by using the following command:

```
java org.javaldap.server.LDAPServer
```

Make sure that the `<ldap-installation-dir>` directory is added to the `CLASSPATH`.

15. Run the following file to add an entry to the LDAP server:
    - `AddEntry.java`: Use this file to populate the LDAP server.

```
package servletbible.ch14.examples;

import javax.naming.*;
import javax.naming.directory.*;
import java.util.*;

public class AddEntry {
     public static void main( String[] args ) {
          try {
               Hashtable props = new Hashtable();

               props.put( Context.PROVIDER_URL, "ldap://localhost:389" );
               props.put( Context.INITIAL_CONTEXT_FACTORY,
"com.sun.jndi.ldap.LdapCtxFactory" );
               props.put( Context.SECURITY_PRINCIPAL, "cn=Admin" );
               props.put( Context.SECURITY_CREDENTIALS, "manager" );
```

```
                DirContext ctx = new InitialDirContext( props );
                try {
                    System.out.println( ctx );
                    Attribute objClasses = new BasicAttribute("objectclass");
                    objClasses.add("top");
                    objClasses.add("person");
                    objClasses.add("organizationalPerson");
                    objClasses.add("organizationalUnit");
                    objClasses.add("inetOrgPerson");
                    objClasses.add("userPassword");
                    Attribute cn = new BasicAttribute("cn", "Ramesh
Krishnaswamy");
                    Attribute sn = new BasicAttribute("sn", "Krishnaswamy");
                    Attribute l = new BasicAttribute("l", "Chennai");
                    Attribute ou = new BasicAttribute("ou", "Development");
                    Attribute up = new BasicAttribute("userPassword",
"allowme");
                    String dn = "cn=Ramesh Krishnaswamy, c=IN, o=ServletBible
Inc";

                    Attributes orig = new BasicAttributes();
                    orig.put(objClasses);
                    orig.put(ou);
                    orig.put(cn);
                    orig.put(l);
                    orig.put(sn);
                    orig.put(up);
                    ctx.createSubcontext(dn, orig);
                } catch( Exception e ) {
                    e.printStackTrace();
                }


            } catch( Exception e ) {
                e.printStackTrace();
            }
        }
}
```

If you run the following program, an entry for the user is added to the LDAP server.

Now that an entry is added to the LDAP server, the following servlet pseudo-code illustrates the use of LDAP for authentication and access control. The following servlet employs simple authentication, but you can choose any authentication mechanism. Here, if the entry is present in the LDAP server, the search returns the results, and — voila! — the user is allowed to access protected resources. Otherwise access is restricted for the user.

```
import javax.servlet.*;
import javax.servlet.http.*;
import javax.naming.*;
```

```
import javax.naming.directory.*;
import java.util.*;

public class LDAPServlet extends HttpServlet
{
    DirContext ctx ;
    public void init()
    {
        Hashtable env;
        try
        {
            //connect to LDAP Server
            env = new Hashtable();
            env.put(Context.INITIAL_CONTEXT_FACTORY,
            "com.sun.jndi.ldap.LdapCtxFactory");
            env.put(Context.SECURITY_AUTHENTICATION, "simple");
            env.put(Context.PROVIDER_URL,
"ldap://localhost:389");
            env.put(Context.SECURITY_PRINCIPAL, "cn=manager");
            env.put(Context.SECURITY_CREDENTIALS, "password");
            ctx = new InitialDirContext(env);
        }
        catch(Exception e)
        {
            e.printStackTrace();
        }
}

public void doPost(HttpServletRequest req, HttpServletResponse
res)
{
try
{
SearchControls search = new SearchControls();
search.setSearchScope(SearchControls.SUBTREE_SCOPE);
NamingEnumeration results = ctx.search("", "(sn=Krishnaswamy)",
search);
if (results != null )
{
    // Give access to protected resources
}
else
{
   // Restrict access to protected resources
}


}
catch(Exception e)
{
e.printStackTrace();
}
}
}
```

SASL authentication

SASL, which is supported by LDAP v3 but not LDAP v2, provides pluggable authentication. Thus LDAP server and client can negotiate even custom mechanisms for authentication. Some of the SASL mechanisms are as follows:

- Anonymous (RFC 2245)
- CRAM-MD5 (RFC 2195)
- Digest-MD5 (RFC 2831)
- External (RFC 2222)
- Kerberos V4 (RFC 2222)
- Kerberos V5 (RFC 2222)
- SecurID (RFC 2808)
- Secure Remote Password (`draft-burdis-cat-srp-sasl-04.txt`)
- S/Key (RFC 2222)
- X.509 (`draft-ietf-ldapext-x509-sasl-03.txt`)

Summary

In this chapter, you have learned the various security mechanisms for servlets You have learned the basics of authentication and authorization by using servlets.

✦ ✦ ✦

Beyond Servlets: JavaServer Pages

P A R T

✦ ✦ ✦ ✦

In This Part

✦ ✦ ✦ ✦

Introducing JSP

✦ ✦ ✦ ✦

In This Chapter

Introducing JSP basics

Understanding the syntax and semantics of JSP

Understanding JavaBean characteristics

Using JSP standard-action tags

✦ ✦ ✦ ✦

Using JavaBeans in JSP

In this chapter, we look into another exciting Web application development environment: Java Server Programming (JSP). Normally, JSP coexists with servlets acting as presentation components in a Web application. In this chapter, we give an introduction to what JSP is and the process behind JSP. Next we focus on the syntax and semantics of JSP. This chapter also introduces JavaBeans and how they can be used with JSP. The chapter explains in detail the elements of JSP with examples wherever appropriate.

Introducing JavaServer Pages

How does an HTML file interspersed with Java code look? That's how a typical JSP file looks. JSP is no different from other Web-development languages. It produces dynamic HTML. But the advantage here is that its Web applications can be developed rapidly. A JSP is unstructured when compared with a servlet and contains bits and pieces of Java code scattered throughout an HTML file. The programmer need not worry about how his or her code in JSP is interpreted; the Web server takes care of this process. Ultimately a JSP file is converted to a servlet by the Web server and is processed like a normal servlet. We see more of how this happens throughout this chapter.

Why do I need JSP? Why can't I use servlets instead? Servlets offer more structured Java code than JSP offers. JSPs are particularly useful on the presentation layer of the application. In fact, JSPs and servlets work together efficiently in a well-designed Web application. We see more of how we can effectively use JSPs and servlets in the next chapter when we deal with the Model View Controller (MVC) architecture.

An application can be divided into three layers: namely, the presentation layer, business layer and data layer. The presentation layer is responsible for the user interface. The business layer deals with logic and manipulating data to the application requirement. The data layer stores and retrieves data from database systems.

Refer to Chapter 13 for more on design patterns and MVC architecture.

The programmer has the choice to use servlets, JSPs, or both; but, as mentioned previously, a JSP takes much less time to code than a servlet. For example, a "Hello World" JSP file looks something like this:

```
<%@page language="java"%>
<html>
<body>
<h1>
<%="Hello World"%>
</h1>
</body>
</html>
```

Compare this with the servlet we discuss in Chapter 1. The inference is that JSPs are simple and easy to write. An added advantage to writing a JSP is that you don't need to compile the `.jsp` file; it is ready for use right away. The next section describes how the JSP works and how the Web server converts the JSP into a servlet automatically. In the preceding program, a couple of statements that start and end with `<%` and `%>` symbols identify that whatever they contain is processed by the server and does not appear as part of the HTML sent to the client. More explanations on JSP syntax come later.

Behind the scenes

A Web server's job is to send the requested HTML file to the client. In addition, a Web server can have a *Container* to which control is given in case the requested file is not an HTML file. Earlier Web servers acted as file servers and responded to clients by sending static HTML pages. Because dynamic Web-page generation has become popular, most Web servers have built-in containers as well as providing support to add-on containers. JRun is an application server that can serve static HTML files as well as process JSP files and servlets. It has a built-in servlet engine to process servlets and a built-in JSP compiler called `jsp.jikes`, which is part of the JSP engine, to compile JSP files into servlets.

We have stated that a JSP is internally converted into a servlet when executed. Let's look at the process behind the "Hello World" example. Imagine the file

`HelloWorld.jsp` is present under the root directory of the default server in JRun. Assume that we try to access this file from the browser on the machine on which the JRun server is running. In this case, the host name is `localhost` or 127.0.0.1. The URL is

```
http://localhost:8100/HelloWorld.jsp
```

The browser contacts JRun and places the request, passing the filename as `HelloWorld.jsp`. After checking for the file in the appropriate path, JRun identifies that the file is not an HTML but is a `.jsp`. The handle is passed to the JSP engine, which checks whether a compiled servlet exists in the `Web-inf\jsp` directory. If it does not exist or if there is any change in the existing file, the JSP engine calls the `jsp.jikes` compiler to compile the JSP file into a servlet. If there are any syntax and/or semantic errors during compilation, the servlet code is not generated, and the errors are thrown back to the browser.

A semantic error in a program is an error where the meaning of some aspect of a program is nonsense. An analogy to this is "Strength is sweet." Even though the sentence is well formed it is nonsense. Similarly, in programming semantic errors occur. For example, a function defined to return an integer value and declared to return another data type is a semantic error.

If the compilation is successful, the result is a `.java` file, which is the servlet code. Typically, the `.java` file generated by JRun is of the format

```
jrun_<directory name>_<directory name>..._<jsp file
name>xxxxxx.java
```

xxxxxx represents a code generated and suffixed by JRun. When we invoke the `HelloWorld.jsp` file from our browser for the first time, the following Java file is generated under the `Web-inf\jsp` directory:

```
jrun_HelloWorld2ejspf.java
```

After the Java file is generated, it is compiled, and a `.class` file is generated. Control is then passed to the servlet engine, and the rest is history. The generated servlet class is loaded into memory and is available for subsequent requests of the JSP file. (Notice a delay the first time a JSP file is requested.) Figure 13-1 illustrates the entire process.

The servlet generated by the JSP request contains a `_jspService()` method, which contains code to return the HTML file. Listing 13-1 presents the code JRun generates for `HelloWorld jsp`.

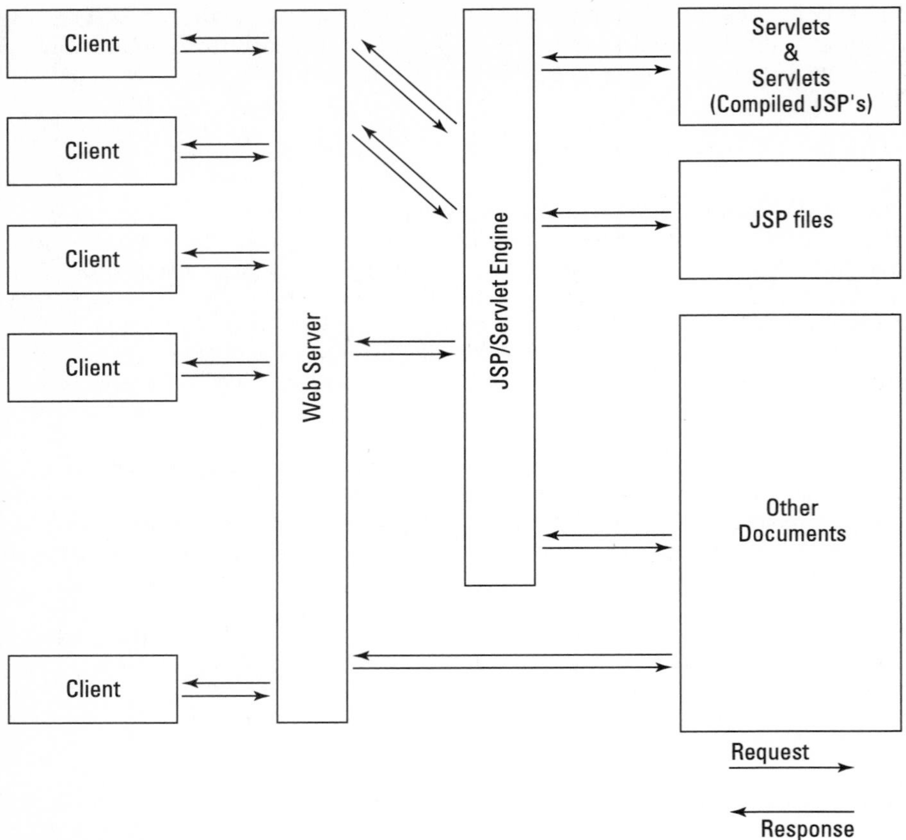

Figure 13-1: JSP request processing

Listing 13-1

```
// Generated by JRun, do not edit


import javax.servlet.*;
import javax.servlet.http.*;
import javax.servlet.jsp.*;
import javax.servlet.jsp.tagext.*;
import allaire.jrun.jsp.JRunJSPStaticHelpers;


public class jrun__HelloWorld2ejspf extends
allaire.jrun.jsp.HttpJSPServlet implements
allaire.jrun.jsp.JRunJspPage
{
    private ServletConfig config;
```

```
    private ServletContext application;
    private Object page = this;
    private JspFactory __jspFactory =
JspFactory.getDefaultFactory();

    public void _jspService(HttpServletRequest request,
HttpServletResponse response)
          throws ServletException, java.io.IOException
    {
        if(config == null) {
            config = getServletConfig();
            application = config.getServletContext();
        }
        response.setContentType("text/html; charset=ISO-8859-
1");
        PageContext pageContext =
__jspFactory.getPageContext(this, request, response,  null,
true, 8192, true);
        JspWriter out = pageContext.getOut();
        HttpSession session = pageContext.getSession();




        try {


    out.print("\r\n<html>\r\n<body>\r\n<h1>\r\n");

out.print("Hello Simplest World");
out.print("\r\n</h1>\r\n</body>\r\n</html>\r\n");


        } catch(Throwable t) {
            if(t instanceof ServletException)
                throw (ServletException) t;
            if(t instanceof java.io.IOException)
                throw (java.io.IOException) t;
            if(t instanceof RuntimeException)
                throw (RuntimeException) t;
            throw JRunJSPStaticHelpers.handleException(t,
pageContext);

        } finally {
            __jspFactory.releasePageContext(pageContext);
        }
    }



      private static final String[] __dependencies__ =
{"/HelloWorld.jsp",null};
```

Continued

Listing 13-1 *(continued)*

```
    private static final long[] __times__ = {989453837908L,0L};

    public String[] __getDependencies()
    {
        return __dependencies__;
    }

    public long[] __getLastModifiedTimes()
    {
        return __times__;
    }

    public int __getTranslationVersion()
    {
        return 14;
    }

}
```

Even though the code seems less understandable, look at the set of `out.print` statements in the `_jspService()` method, which outputs the HTML. These are the statements that we wrote in the `HelloWorld.jsp` that are converted. All the other statements are generated by JRun and vary across Web servers.

When a client requests a JSP file and a compiled servlet is not available or needs to be recompiled, the Web server goes through a process of compiling the JSP into a servlet.

Every Web server that can process JSP comes with a necessary Java API that can be used to compile a JSP file into a servlet. Normally the APIs are packed into a JAR file called `servlet.jar` and are placed in the library directory of the Web server. You can look at the servlet API in `http://java.sun.com/products/servlet/2.3/javadoc/index.html`.

The generated servlet file extends a class called `HttpJSPServlet`, which is in the `jsp.jar` file under the `lib` directory of JRun. This class contains the following methods:

- ✦ `jpsInit()` — This method is called when the JSP is initialized. This is equivalent to the `init()` method in the servlet. Programmers can do some initialization work to override this method.
- ✦ `jspDestroy()` — This method, similar to the servlet's `destroy()` method, is called when the JSP engine is going to destroy the JSP. Programmers can close connections to the database (if any) and free memory by destroying objects.

✦ `_jspService()`—This is the method where all HTML code goes. It is the equivalent of `service()` method in servlets. The method runs in threaded mode. For each client's request, a thread runs this method to satisfy the request. The method is abstract in class and is generated by the JSP engine; also, it should not be overridden by programmers. The method takes the `HttpServletRequest` and `HttpServletResponse` objects as parameters. This makes it clear that the request and response objects can be used within JSP without the need of importing the `javax.servlet.http.*` package.

When the JSP engine receives a request for a JSP page for the first time, the `jspInit()` method, if one exists, is invoked, and the `_jspService()` method is invoked. The `_jspService()` method is called thereafter to process subsequent requests from clients. The `jspDestroy()` method is called when the JSP engine finds that a JSP has to be destroyed – for example, in the event of the Web server being shutdown.

JSP Syntax and Semantics

JSP coding is not so different from coding programs in Java. Hence, you do not need to go through the process of learning a new language. All Java coding syntax and semantics apply for JSP, too. But there is a minor difference in the way a variable or an expression has to be embedded between HTML codes. A JSP code starts either with "<%" or a JSP tag. JSP follows the strict rule, as in XML, that all opening tags should have a corresponding closing tag. Thus, "<%" has a closing "%>" and a JSP tag has a corresponding closing JSP tag. All code that needs to be processed by the JSP engine is called *JSP elements*. All others are *templates,* and the JSP engine ignores them.

A JSP tag has a name and optional or required attributes similar to an HTML tag. Within the opening tag and the closing tag is the body section. The following is an example:

```
<jsptag attribute1="value" attribute2="value >
     ...body...
</jsptag>
```

There are certain rules to be followed when handling JSP tags:

✦ A JSP tag should have a corresponding closing JSP tag. If the JSP tag does not have a body, it can be closed on the same line by ending with a "/>" as in the following example:

```
<jsptag attribute1="value" attribute2="value"/>
```

✦ An attribute value should always be included within double quotes. Even though this rule is not a must in the HTML convention, it is strict in JSP.

✦ The escape sequence character (\) can be used to include special and reserved characters into the attribute value.

```
<jsptag myQuote="\"This comes within double quote\""
attribute2="value"/>
```

JSP elements can be classified in five categories: directives, declarations, scriptlets, expressions, and standard actions. The next several sections explain these elements in detail.

Directives

A JSP directive acts as a source of vital information to the JSP engine. There are three types of directives:

✦ page directive — Gives information on that page

✦ include directive — Gives information on any file that needs to be included

✦ iaglib directive — Gives a list of custom tags mentioned in the Uniform Resource Identifier (URI) used in this page.

page directive

A `page` directive provides information about the page to the JSP engine. A page directive can appear anywhere in the JSP and any number of times. Except for the import attribute, the other attributes can appear only once throughout the page. All page directives are gathered by the JSP engine and are affected to that page. Table 13-1 lists the attributes, what they are for, and their default values (if not given).

Table 13-1
page Directive Attributes

Attribute	*Description*
`language`	The `language` attribute defines the scripting language this page uses. At present, JSP engines in all Web servers understand only Java, but this attribute has its presence with the future languages in mind. The default value for this attribute is `"java"`.
`extends`	This attribute should be used when the compiled JSP must extend the mentioned class as a super class. We have seen, by default, that the generated servlet code extends from the JRun implemented class `"HttpJSPServlet"`. If any other class is mentioned as super class, the mentioned super class must implement all the necessary functions for running the servlet. It is advised not to use this attribute. If unspecified, this attribute is not taken into consideration.

Attribute	*Description*
`import`	This is similar to the import in a normal Java file. It includes all the classes in the package specified. The packages are delimited by commas (,). This attribute, if unmentioned, is not considered.
`session`	This is a Boolean value that specifies whether session handling is acceptable in this page. By default, the value is true.
`buffer`	This value identifies the buffer size. After filling the buffer, the output is dumped to the output stream. If the value is "`none`," no buffering happens and the output is transmitted to the output stream directly. The default value is Web-server specific.
`autoFlush`	When the buffer is full, if `autoFlush` is `"true"` the buffer is flushed to the output stream. If the attribute value is `"false"`, after the buffer is full a runtime exception occurs. By default, the value is `"true"`.
`isThreadSafe`	This is a Boolean value indicating whether the page is thread safe. If the value is `"false"`, all client requests are queued up and processed one by one. The default value is `"true"`.
`info`	This is a string normally used to describe the function the page performs. This attribute is not considered if unspecified.
`isErrorPage`	This is used to determine whether this page acts as an error page. If so, this page's URL can be used as a value for the `errorPage` attribute to transfer control to this page in case of errors. An instance-variable exception of type `java.lang.Throwable` is available for the page to identify the exception and to take appropriate action. By default, the value of this attribute is `"false"`.
`errorPage`	This is a string describing the URL of the page to which control has to be transferred if any exception is thrown during the runtime of this page. The page catches an object of type `Throwable` and passes it to the page mentioned in the `errorPage` attribute, which processes the error. The error page to which control is transferred should have a page directive with the attribute `isErrorPage` set to `"true"`.
`contentType`	This defines the character encoding and MIME type of the response. The default value is `"text/html"`.

include directive

The `include` directive includes the specified file's content into this page during translation time. The file included should be available in the path mentioned. Also, the contents of the included file should be a static page, such as an HTML file, but cannot be another JSP page.

The only attribute in this directive is `file`; it takes in a string value holding the filename with the path.

```
<%@ include file="/Hello/HelloWorld.html" %>
```

Let's see an example of the `page` directive and the `include` directive used in a JSP page. Listing 13-2 shows the JSP code that uses these two directives.

Listing 13-2

```
<%@ page language="java" import="java.util.*" info="A page
using page and include directive"%>
<html>
<body>
<title>
An example JSP page using page and include directive
</title>
<h2>
<%="This statement comes from the JSP Page" %>
</h2>
<p>
<h3>
<BR>
<%
     Date dt = new Date();
%>
Today's date is <%=dt%>
</h3>
<p>
<%@ include file="include.html" %>
</body>
</html>
```

The following is the source for the `include.HTML` file:

```
<h3>
This statement comes from the file included using the include
directive
</h3>
```

The program is very simple; it displays a line from the JSP and a line from the HTML. The HTML file is included by using the `include` directive. The statement

```
<%="This statement comes from the JSP Page" %>
```

is a JSP *expression*, and the block

```
<%
      Date dt = new Date();
%>
```

is a *scriptlet*. Both the expression and scriptlet are discussed in detail in the sections "Expressions" and "Scriptlets." Note that we use the `import` statement to import the package `java.util`, which enables us to use the `Date` object within the scriptlet. As shown in Figure 13-2, the JSP page displays today's date and time and a statement from the static HTML page.

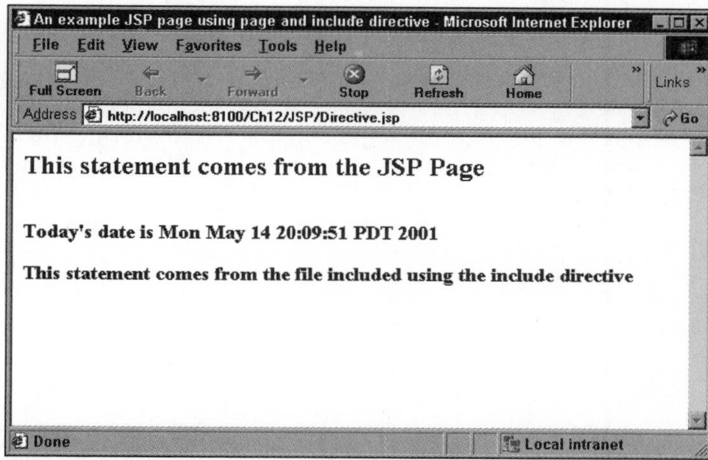

Figure 13-2: A JSP page displayed in a browser by using the page and include directives

taglib directive

The `taglib` directive is used to embed custom user-defined tags in the current page. The tags are defined in a Tag Library Descriptor (TLD) document. The TLD document is passed as a value to the `uri` attribute. The JSP engine refers to the file represented in the `uri` attribute to take necessary action when a custom-user tag is encountered. There can be more than one `taglib` directive used in a single page. To identify a TLD document corresponding to a tag, it is prefixed with a name, which is passed as a value to the `prefix` attribute. This also ensures that even if there are tags with the same name, but defined in two or more TLD documents, they can be uniquely identified with the prefix name.

```
<%@ taglib uri="/Hello/Hello.tld" prefix="world" %>
```

The `uri` and `prefix` attributes are compulsory; and, if they are not present, a translation error is thrown. After the `taglib` directive is defined, all tags in the TLD document can be used anywhere in the page. Using the tag is similar to using other JSP tags and follows the same rules.

```
<world:hello>
     body
</world:hello>
```

A prefix cannot have the following reserved words: `java`, `javax`, `jsp`, `jspx`, `servlet`, `sun`, and `sunw`.

The taglib directive was not clear till JSP 1.0 but is now widely used and recognized by all the major Web servers.

A TLD document is written in XML notation. Tags that offer related functionality should be grouped together. Typically, a Java class file is associated with a tag, which implements the relevant function the tag is supposed to perform. The following code segment is pseudo-code representing the format of a TLD document and is not a working code segment:

```
<taglib>
    <tlibversion>
        Version number of tag library (required)
    </tlibversion>
    <jspversion>
        Version number of JSP this document is designed to work
(optional).
    </jspversion>
    <shortname>
        A short name to this document (required).
    </shortname>
    <uri>
        Unique string (optional).
    </uri>
    <info>
        Text giving description about the tag library
(optional).
    </info>
</taglib>
<tag>
    <name>
        Define the tag name (required)
    </name>
    <tagclass>
        String representing the java class file along with package name.
The class file should be placed under the Web-
inf/classes directory of JRun (required).
    </tagclass>
    <teiclass>
        Specifies the class which will be the subclass of
javax.servlet.jsp.tagext.TagExtraInfo class. It is used when
```

```
the tag defines scripting variables or if validation of the tag
has to be performed during the translation time (optional).
    </teiclass>
    <bodycontent>
        can  be anyone of the values.
        tagdependent - the body contains statements that are not JSP.
        JSP - the body contains JSP code
        empty - there is no body for this tag (optional default
value is JSP).
    </bodycontent>
    <attribute>
        defines the attributes for this tag. Each attribute is
enclosed within <attribute> and </attribute>
        <name>
            name of the attribute (required).
        </name>
        <required>
            a boolean value to identify whether this
attribute is required or not (optional and by default false).
        </required>
        <rtexprvalue>
            a boolean value which tells whether scriptlet
expression values can be assigned as value to this attribute
(optional and by default false).
        </rtexprvalue>
    </attribute>
    <attribute>
    .
        .
    .
    </attribute>
</tag>
<tag>
.
.
.
</tag>
```

Let's examine a small TLD document as follows:

```
<?xml version="1.0" encoding="ISO-8859-1" ?>
<!DOCTYPE taglib SYSTEM "http://java.sun.com/j2ee/dtds/web-
jsptaglibrary_1_1.dtd">
<taglib>
<tlibversion>1.0</tlibversion>
<jspversion>1.1</jspversion>
<shortname>dt</shortname>
<info>Gets the current System date</info>
<tag>
<name>today</name>
<tagclass>servletbible.ch12.examples.tagclass.MyDateClass
</tagclass>
</tag>
</taglib>
```

The first two statements describe that this document is in XML notation, that it is of `taglib` type, and that the standards for TLD are available at `http://java.sun.com/j2ee/dtds/web-jsptaglibrary_1_1.dtd`. Now look into the `MyDateClass` code in Listing 13-3.

Listing 13-3

```
package servletbible.ch12.examples.tagclass;

import javax.servlet.jsp.*;
import javax.servlet.jsp.tagext.*;
import java.util.*;

/**
* MyDateClass gets the current date and writes it
* to the output stream
*/
public class MyDateClass extends TagSupport {
    /**
    * doEndTag method is called at end of Tag
    * returns EVAL_PAGE - continue evaluation of the body
    */
    public int doEndTag() throws JspException {
        try {
            Date dt = new Date();
            pageContext.getOut().write(dt.toString());
        } catch(java.io.IOException ioe) {
            throw new JspException("Exception occured during doEndTag : " +
ioe.getMessage());
        }
        return EVAL_PAGE;
    }
}
```

The `javax.servlet.jsp.tagext` package in the servlet API defines all the classes necessary to translate the tag libraries. The `TagSupport` class has the necessary methods, which are executed upon encountering a tag. Here we extend this class and override the `doEndTag()` method, which gets triggered when the closing tag is encountered. The `PageContext` object is automatically available through this class. Through the `PageContext` object, we have access to the output stream, and we can write the output. Inside this method, we create a `Date` object and write it to the output stream.

Finally, look at `taglib.jsp` file in Listing 13-4, which holds the include directive.

Listing 13-4

```
<%@ page language="java"%>
<%@ taglib uri="/Ch12/TagLibs/CurrentDate.tld" prefix="date"%>
<html>
<title>
An example to illustrate taglib directive
</title>
<body>
<h3>
Today's date is
<date:today/>
</h3>
</body>
</html>
```

We provide the TLD file in the URI and set the prefix attribute to `"date"`. Note the use of `<date:today/>`. This refers to the TLD file and to the tag `today` and loads the `MyDateClass` class. If the class overides the `doStartTag()` method, it is executed. Because the tag ends without body, the `doEndTag()` method of `MyDateClass` is executed; thus, the server's current date and time are displayed, as shown in Figure 13-3.

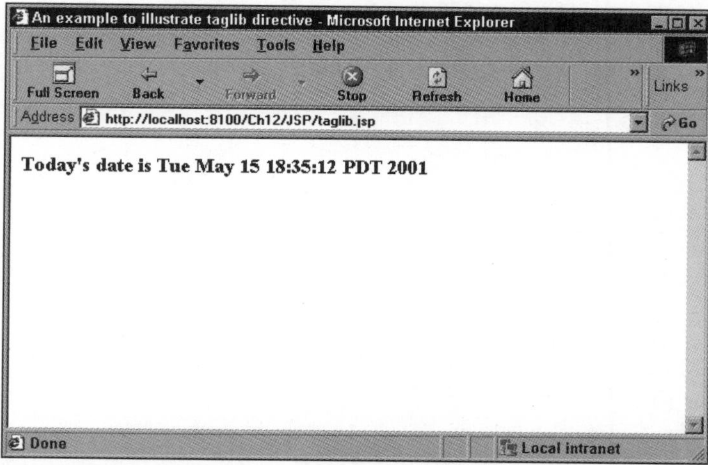

Figure 13-3: A JSP page displayed in a browser by using the taglib directive

Script elements

Script elements are JSP elements, which can be Java statements, declarations, methods, and expressions. Basically, script elements can be categorized into three types:

- Declarations
- Scriptlets
- Expressions

Let's look at these in detail.

Declarations

JSP pages can have variables and methods defined, as in a Java program. Variable declarations and method definitions are embedded within a special set of tags, "<%!" and "%>". The declared variables and methods have class scope and are available throughout the JSP page. The variables are initialized when the compiled servlet class is loaded. The declaration of a variable and definition of a method can be performed at any point in a JSP page. Listing 13-5 shows an example (factorial.html) that displays the factorial of a given number.

Listing 13-5

```
<html>
<body>
<form name="frmFactorial" method=post action="getfact.jsp">
<table border=0>
    <tr>
        <td>
            Enter a positive number
        </td>
        <td>
            <input type=text name="number" value=""></input>
        </td>
    </tr>
    <tr>
        <td align=center colspan=2>
            <input type=submit value="Get Factorial">
            </input>
        </td>
    </tr>
</table>
</form>
</body>
</html>
```

It's a simple HTML that displays a text box and submits the page to getfact.jsp. Listing 13-6 shows the getfact.jsp file.

Listing 13-6

```
<%@ page language="java" import="java.io.*" %>
<html>
<body>
<%!
// number will store the number that was keyed in from the html
String number;

public int getFactorial() {
    int i;
    try {
//    Try to parse the value and get an integer value
    i = Integer.parseInt(number);
    } catch (NumberFormatException nfe) {
//        Not a number, so return -1
        return -1;
    }
//    Negative number entered, so return -1
    if(i < 0) return -1;
//    Factorial for 0 and 1 is 1, so return 1
    if(i < 2) return 1;

//    Calculate the factorial
    int fact=1;
    for(int j=2;j<=i;j++) fact *= j;
    return fact;
}
%>
<h3>
<%
//Get the number from the HTML using request
number=request.getParameter("number");
%>
<!-- Display the factorial -->
Factorial of <%=number%> is <%=getFactorial()%>
</h3>
</body>
</html>
```

In the `page` directive, we use the `import` attribute and import the package `java.io`, because we use `NumberFormatException` later in the code. After the `<body>` tag comes our declaration, starting with "`<%!`" The number variable stores the number entered in the HTML page in the form of a string because we get it from the request object. In the `getFactorial()` method, the string value is parsed and stored into a variable `i`. If it is not a number, the `parseInt()` method throws a `NumberFormatException`; we catch it and return a -1 to indicate that the method has returned an error.

If the string contains a number, we check whether it is a negative number by checking if it is less than zero. In this case, we return a -1 value. If everything is okay, we compute the factorial and return the value.

After the declaration block comes a scriptlet (code embedded within "`<%`" and "`%>`"),which we learn more about in the next session. For now, this block has a statement that uses the request object to get the value of the number keyed in the HTML page.

The variable declaration and method definition come within the servlet code generated by the JSP engine. Listing 13-7 shows the Java code generated by the JSP compiler for the factorial example JSP page.

Listing 13-7

```
// Generated by JRun, do not edit


import javax.servlet.*;
import javax.servlet.http.*;
import javax.servlet.jsp.*;
import javax.servlet.jsp.tagext.*;
import allaire.jrun.jsp.JRunJSPStaticHelpers;



import java.io.*;public class jrun__Ch12__JSP__getfact2ejsp15
extends allaire.jrun.jsp.HttpJSPServlet implements
allaire.jrun.jsp.JRunJspPage
{
    private ServletConfig config;
    private ServletContext application;
    private Object page = this;
    private JspFactory __jspFactory =
JspFactory.getDefaultFactory();

    public void _jspService(HttpServletRequest request,
HttpServletResponse response)
         throws ServletException, java.io.IOException
    {
        if(config == null) {
            config = getServletConfig();
            application = config.getServletContext();
        }
```

```
        response.setContentType("text/html; charset=ISO-8859-
1");
        PageContext pageContext =
__jspFactory.getPageContext(this, request, response,  null,
true, 8192, true);
        JspWriter out = pageContext.getOut();
        HttpSession session = pageContext.getSession();



        try {


    out.print("\r\n<html>\r\n<body>\r\n");
out.print("\r\n<h3>\r\n");

//Get the number from the HTML using request
number=request.getParameter("number");

    out.print("\r\n<!-- Display the factorial -->\r\nFactorial
of ");

out.print(number);
out.print(" is ");

out.print(getFactorial());
out.print("\r\n</h3>\r\n</body>\r\n</html>\r\n");


        } catch(Throwable t) {
            if(t instanceof ServletException)
                throw (ServletException) t;
            if(t instanceof java.io.IOException)
                throw (java.io.IOException) t;
            if(t instanceof RuntimeException)
                throw (RuntimeException) t;
            throw JRunJSPStaticHelpers.handleException(t,
pageContext);

        } finally {
            __jspFactory.releasePageContext(pageContext);
        }
    }



// number will store the number that was keyed in from the html
String number;
```

Continued

Listing 13-7 *(continued)*

```
public int getFactorial() {
    int i;
    try {
//    Try to parse the value and get an integer value
    i = Integer.parseInt(number);
    } catch (NumberFormatException nfe) {
//        Not a number, so return -1
        return -1;
    }
//    Negative number entered, so return -1
    if(i < 0) return -1;
//    Factorial for 0 and 1 is 1, so return 1
    if(i < 2) return 1;

//    Calculate the factorial
    int fact=1;
    for(int j=2;j<=i;j++) fact *= j;
    return fact;
}
    private static final String[] __dependencies__ =
{"/Ch12/JSP/getfact.jsp",null};

    private static final long[] __times__ = {990059361726L,0L};

    public String[] __getDependencies()
    {
        return __dependencies__;
    }

    public long[] __getLastModifiedTimes()
    {
        return __times__;
    }

    public int __getTranslationVersion()
    {
        return 14;
    }

}
```

Look at the code at the end of the `_jspService()` method. We have the variable `number` declared, followed by the `getFactorial()` method as it appears in the JSP page with all the comments. Figures 13-4 and 13-5 show the HTML page and the factorial output the JSP page generates.

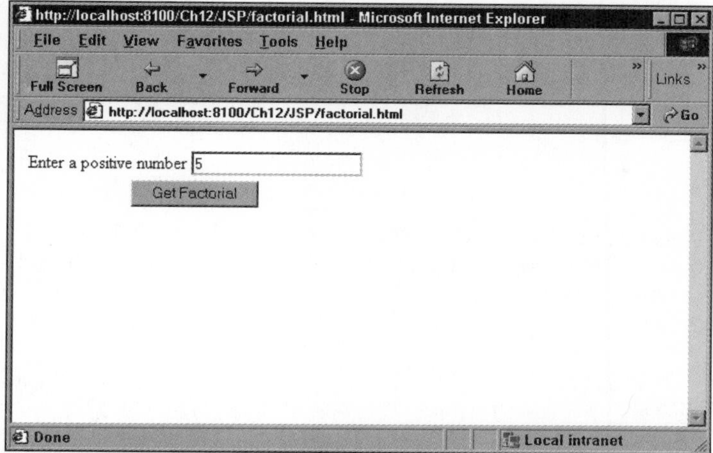

Figure 13-4: Enter a number and calculate the factorial.

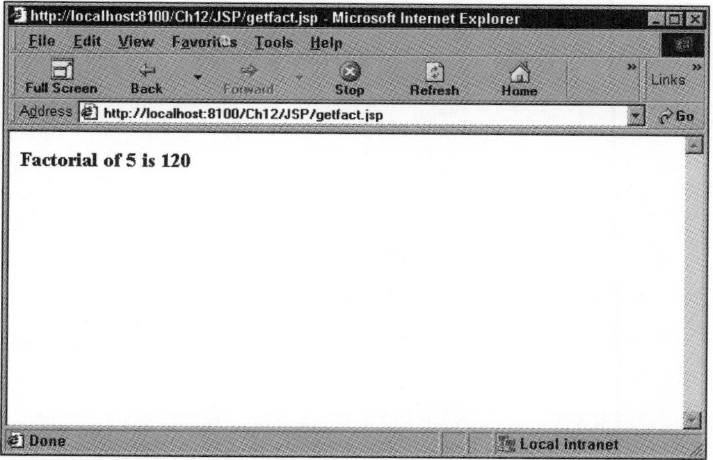

Figure 13-5: Display the factorial of the given number.

Scriptlets

A scriptlet is a block of Java code embedded in the `service()` method of the servlet. Thus, the code is executed on every client's request. Any number of scriptlets can appear within a JSP page. All Java code that appears in scriptlets is embedded in the servlet in the same order in which it is imbedded in the JSP page. A scriptlet starts with "<%" and ends with "%>". The body contains Java code, which performs some functionality to modify the objects and variables available to it.

The factorial program in Listing 13-7 does not display an error message in case the number entered is invalid; instead, it displays the value -1. We can incorporate this validation with the help of scriptlets. The HTML form-action tag has to be changed to point to the modified JSP page — `getfactValidate.jsp`.

```
<form name="frmFactorial" method=post
action="getfactValidate.jsp">
```

We modify the `getfact.jsp` file with the following code and save it as `getfactValidate.jsp`. This code (Listing 13-8) also switches back to the HTML page, if the number entered is invalid, through the use of the `<meta>` HTML tag.

Listing 13-8

```
<%@ page language="java" import="java.io.*" %>
<html>
<%!
// number will store the number that was keyed in from the html
String number;

public int getFactorial() {
    int i;
    try {
//    Try to parse the value and get an integer value
    i = Integer.parseInt(number);
    } catch (NumberFormatException nfe) {
//        Not a number, so return -1
        return -1;
    }
//    Negative number entered, so return -1
    if(i < 0) return -1;
//    Factorial for 0 and 1 is 1, so return 1
    if(i < 2) return 1;

//    Calculate the factorial
    int fact=1;
    for(int j=2;j<=i;j++) fact *= j;
    return fact;
}
%>

<%
//Get the number from the HTML using request
number=request.getParameter("number");

// Get the factorial
int fact = getFactorial();
String msg;

// If fact is less than zero then an invalid number was
```

```
// entered
if(fact<0) {
//    Display an error message and show the HTML page again after
// 3 seconds
%>
<meta http-equiv="refresh" content="3;url=factorialValid.html">
<%
    msg = "Please enter a valid number";
}
else {
//    Display the factorial
    msg = "Factorial of " + number + " is " + fact;
}
%>
<body>
<h3>
<!-- Display the message -->
<%=msg%>
</h3>
</body>
</html>
```

The scriptlet that comes after the declaration block contains the validation section. We get the number by using the request object and then call the `getFactorial()` method, storing the result in a variable called `fact`. Now we check whether the value of `fact` is negative. If it is negative, we frame the `<meta>` tag with a refresh rate of three seconds and transfer control back to `factorialValid.html` as follows:

```
.
.
if(fact<0) {
//    Display an error message and show the html page again
after
// 3 seconds
%>
<meta http-equiv="refresh" content="3;url=factorialValid.html">
<%
    msg = "Please enter a valid number";
}
else {
//    Display the factorial
    msg = "Factorial of " + number + " is " + fact;
}
%>
.
```

If the user enters an invalid number, the scriptlet displays an error message, as shown in Figure 13-6.

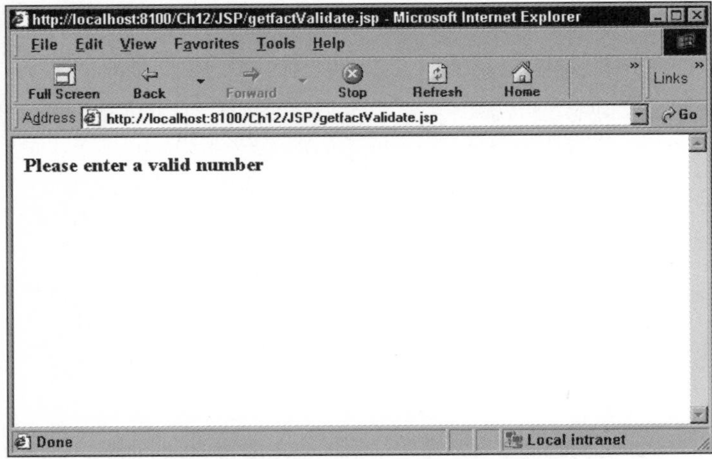

Figure 13-6: If an invalid number is entered, getFactorial displays an error message.

When we want to output some HTML between the body of the scriptlet, we end the scriptlet there, write the HTML, and again open a new scriptlet tag, whose body becomes a continuation of the code from the previous scriptlet. This becomes clear when you look at the servlet code generated for the preceding set of statements under the `_jspService()` method. The following code segment is taken from the servlet generated by JRun:

```
.
.
.
if(fact<0) {
//    Display an error message and show the html page again
after
// 3 seconds

    out.print("\r\n<meta http-equiv=\"refresh\"
content=\"3;url=factorialValid.html\">\r\n");

msg = "Please enter a valid number";
}
else {
//    Display the factorial
    msg = "Factorial of " + number + " is " + fact;
}
.
.
```

The HTML portion alone is translated into `out.print` statements and the Java code in the scriptlet is retained as it is in the servlet code.

HTTP-EQUIV Attribute

A `meta` element provides information about the current HTML page. The tag contains attribute/value pairs. `<http-equiv>` is used to supply information an HTTP-server can use to generate extra HTTP headers. `<http-equiv>` can take the following values:

- `content-type`—This allows MIME character-set information to be embedded in the HTML document.
- `expires`—This sets the expiration date and time for this page. If the date set is before today's date, a request for the page is obtained from the server but is not taken from the cache. Using this approach, loading the page from the client machine's cache can be avoided.
- `refresh`—This tells the browser that the page should be refreshed after a specified number of seconds.
- `set-cookie`—This sets the cookie on the client machine with the name/value pair specified in the `content` attribute.

The `content` attribute gets values based on the values of the `<http-equiv>` attribute.

Expressions

An expression outputs a value or result of an expression or a variable's value to the client through the response object. This is a shortcut notation for outputting values, and we have seen the usage of expressions in all the JSP examples we have examined. An expression starts with "<%" immediately followed by an "=" and then followed by a value, an expression, or a variable. The following is a valid expression:

```
<%=number1 + " multiplied by " + number2 + " gives " +
number1*number2%>
```

number1 and *number2* are numeric values. If any special character such as the quote (") has to be included, the escape sequence (\") can be used. The following is an example:

```
<%="\"This statement appears within quotes\""%>
```

Comments

In the JSP page, we encounter JSP tags, Java code in the scriptlet, and HTML. These three have their own commenting styles. Of course, Java code commenting with `//` and `/*...*/` applies here too. Comments in Java code also appear in the generated servlet code. Comments in HTML begin with `<!--` and are ended by `-->`. This comment appears on the HTML page sent to the client. JSP comments start with `<%--` and end with `--%>`. Whatever JSP, HTML, or Java code is contained within these tags is ignored by the JSP engine during compilation. The following is an example of a JSP comment:

```
<%--
JSP comment starts here
<%@ page import="java.util.*"%>
<h1> Hello World </h1>
<%
String s = new String("Hello");
%>
JSP comment ends here
--%>
<html>
<body>
<h1>
<%="Hello World"%>
</h1>
</body>
</html>
```

Before we go into JSP action commands, take a look at creating JavaBeans, as some JSP tags are related to them. Readers who are familiar with JavaBeans can skip the next section.

JavaBean Characteristics

A JavaBean can be defined as a software component delivering functionality to various applications that need such functionality. In what way is a JavaBean different from a Java class? A mere walkthroughof JavaBean code and an ordinary Java class can offer no insight. But a JavaBean follows a certain specification called *software-component specification*. A Java class may be called a JavaBean when it adheres to this specification.

A JavaBean can reside anywhere on the network and can be utilized by any application. If such is the case, a Bean instance can also be persistent for later use. So a JavaBean should implement the `java.io.Serializable` interface. The `Serializable` interface helps in transmitting the Bean data in the form of byte streams on the network or by saving it to disk for later use. The `Serializable` interface does not have any function prototype declared in it, but it's an indication that the object implementing it can be persistent.

The classes and interfaces in the `java.beans` package help a programmer or an Integrated Development Environment (IDE) to parse through a Bean and identify its properties, methods, and events. The component specification contains the necessary instructions to use these classes. The current specification version is 1.01 and is available at `http://java.sun.com/products/javabeans/docs/spec.html`. JavaBeans encapsulate data and provide methods to access or modify data. The data is hidden from other classes, so they cannot directly access it.

JavaBeans as software components have one or more of the following characteristics:

✦ Properties and customization

✦ Event handling

✦ Introspection

✦ Persistence and packaging

✦ Interoperation

Let's look into these characteristics individually.

Properties and customization

Properties are attributes pertaining to that component. For example, a visual component consists of foreground color and font properties. In nonvisual components, the properties hold information that helps in performing some operation; for example, in a Math Bean, a property called operator might hold the operator symbol, such as +, -, * or /, based on which an operation is performed between two numbers.

A property might be initialized when the Bean is instantiated or can be set during runtime. Setting a property during design or runtime is called the *customization* of that property. A property can be accessed or set using the appropriate get and set methods. If the Bean has a property named *value,* it should have the `int getValue()` and `setValue(int value)` methods. Properties can be categorized into three types:

✦ *Indexed properties* — These properties are arrays and can hold multiple values. There is a pair of get and set methods. One get method retrieves the entire array and the other retrieves a particular item in the array. Similarly, one set method sets a new array of values to the property and another sets a value in the particular index of the array. The following is the list of method prototypes in case the property is indexed:

```
public <property type>[] get<Property name>();
public <property type> get<property name>(int index);
public void set<property name>(<property type>[] value);
public void set<property name>(int index,<property type>
value);
```

✦ *Bound properties* — Bound properties notify other objects that the property value has changed. This can be an indication to the event-receiving object to take some action.

✦ *Constrained properties* — When a Bean receives an event or a value from another object, causing an illegal value to be assigned to the property, the Bean can reject the event. Such a property is called a *constrained property.*

Event handling

When there are two or more Beans involved in an application, the Beans can communicate with each other through event handling. The introduction of new event-handling mechanisms in JDK 1.1 helps in achieving a way to notify objects through event firing. An object wishing to receive an event registers itself to that event's listener. An object wishing to send an event fires that event. A typical example of such a mechanism is a pie chart updating itself when values change in a spreadsheet. The pie chart component registers itself for value-change events of the spreadsheet. The spreadsheet component, on the other hand, fires a value-change event when data is modified in one of its cells. The pie chart component updates the chart every time it receives a value-change event.

A component's set property method can also reject an event if the property is a constrained property. A property should be able to identify the event, and other information such as the changed value, to determine its action. A class that extends the `java.util.EventObject` class can act as an event object and can be passed along with the event.

The Bean that wants to receive an event has to implement the `java.beans.PropertyChangeListener` interface and define the `propertyChange()` method as shown here:

```
import java.beans.*;

public class EventReceivingBean implements
Serializable,PropertyChangeListener {
.
.
.
public void propertyChange (PropertyChangeEvent pce) {
.
// event received, do the necessary action
.
}
.
.
.
}
```

A Bean that wants to notify the objects registered for an event has to have a method to add the listener object to the `addPropertyChangeListener()` method of the `java.beans.PropertyChangeSupport` class, as follows:

```
import java.beans.*;

public class EventFiringBean {

    private PropertyChangeSupport pcs;
    private int value; // a property
    .
    .
    EventFiringBean() {
        super();
```

```
        pcs = new PropertyChangeSupport();
        .
        .
    }
    public void addEventListener(PropertyChangeListener pcl) {
        // register the listener
        pcs.addPropertyChangeListener(pcl);
    }
    public void removeEventListener(PropertyChangeListener pcl)
{
        // Un-register the listener
        pcs.removePropertyChangeListener(pcl);
    }

    // property value's get method
    public int getValue() {
        return value;
    }
    // property value's set method
    public void setValue(int value) {
        int oldValue = this.value;
        this.value = value;
        // Property has changed, so notify all the objects
registered to listen to this event
        firePropertyChange("value",new Integer(oldValue), new
Integer(value));
    }
    .
    // some more methods
}
```

Note that the `firePropertyChange()` method takes three parameters. The first parameter is the property name, the second parameter is the old value of the property, and the third parameter is the new value of the property. Because the second and third parameters accept only an object, in the preceding code fragment the `int` data type is wrapped into an `integer` object.

Introspection

Introspection means to examine a class's public methods and members. Java's built-in *reflection* mechanism helps in parsing a class and identifying the properties of the Bean. The IDEs, which support Beans, identify the public methods and properties of the Bean through reflection. A program or an IDE that wants to extract information about a Bean requests a `BeanInfo` object. To return a `BeanInfo` object, the Bean class should have implemented the `BeanInfo` interface. The `BeanInfo` object has methods to retrieve information about the Bean, such as the properties, methods, and events. If the Bean has not implemented the BeanInfo interface, the program or IDE can parse for the get and set methods, and if a corresponding member exists, the member is taken as a property.

Persistence and packaging

What if a Bean's state has to be availed by many applications on the Internet? The best way to achieve this is to store the Bean in the form of binary large object (blob) data. This can be retrieved and changed to its original format whenever needed. Object serialization achieves persistence of an object. When there are many Beans that need to be persistent, all can be written to a physical storage and can be packaged into a JAR file to be extracted whenever needed.

Interoperation

JavaBeans have been designed to work with other software-component technologies such as ActiveX, OLE, and OpenDoc. Existing applications might have some components developed in any of the other component technologies. It might not be a feasible solution to discard them and create new components using Java. Because JavaBeans provide support to other component technologies, integrating all the components solves the problem.

This concludes a brief introduction to JavaBeans. Every topic in Java is a world in itself to explore. In the next section, we continue with JSP standard action tags.

JSP Standard Action Tags

Action tags perform actions such as instantiating an object or making changes to an object's state. Certain actions are dependent upon the previous page's data. JSP defines certain standard action tags that need to be supported by all Web servers that support JSP. The following are the standard JSP action tags:

```
<jsp:useBean>
<jsp:getProperty>
<jsp:setProperty>
<jsp:param>
<jsp:include>
<jsp:forward>
<jsp:plugin>
```

Any other user-defined tags or tags defined by the Web server are implemented through `taglib` directive, which we have seen already in the section "taglib directives." Let's look into the standard action tags.

<jsp:useBean>

The `<jsp:useBean>` tag includes a Bean in the page, thereby enabling the page to access the Bean's properties through the Bean's get and set methods. The Bean's public methods can also be accessed after the Bean is instantiated through this tag. The prototype of this tag is as follows:

```
<jsp:useBean id="name used to refer"
scope="page|request|session|application" beanName="bean class
name" class="class name" type="type name"/>
```

Any of the combinations of `beanName`, `className`, and `type` attributes can be used.

✦ The `id` attribute holds the name for the Bean used to refer to this Bean in the page. This is how we define a variable name and use that name in Java code.

✦ The `scope` determines the life period of the Bean. The `scope` can be one of four values:

- `page` — The Bean object is alive till this page exists and is available to the `service()` method of the servlet generated. Thus, the object is available for every client request to this page.
- `request` — When the scope attribute holds a "request" value, the object has its life as long as the `HttpRequest` object is available, even though the request might be passed or forwarded through chaining to different pages. An object with the request scope is distinct to each and every client.
- `session` — An object with the session scope is available for use throughout the client session. Once instantiated, the object can be accessed by any JSP page by using the `HttpSession` object's `getAttribute()` method. The generated servlet contains the `HttpSession` object's `setAttribute()` method to hold the object as a session variable. When the client terminates his or her session, the object gets destroyed. The object is unique to each client.
- `application` — The most persistent of all is the object whose scope is of type application. The object, once instantiated, is available to all the clients and remains alive till the server is shutdown. Hence, the object is not unique to clients, and all clients access the same object instance.

✦ The `beanName` attribute specifies the class name of the Bean, including the package name if any. If the beanName is specified, the `typeName` attribute should also be mentioned.

✦ The `type` mentions the type of the object. The Java type-casting convention is followed here also, and the class name mentioned in this attribute should be the object's super class, an interface, or the class itself. This defaults to the object's class name.

✦ The `class` attribute is the simplest form and is equivalent to giving both the beanName attribute and the type attribute the same value.

Even the type attribute alone can be given and acts similarly to giving the class attribute.

<jsp:getProperty>

The `<jsp:getProperty>` standard action gets the property value from the Bean and writes it to the output stream. The prototype of this property is as follows:

```
<jsp:getProperty name="bean name" property="property name"/>
```

- ✦ The `name` is the Bean name specified in the `id` attribute of the `jsp:useBean` tag.
- ✦ The `property` tag holds one of the properties defined in the JavaBean.

<jsp:setProperty>

The `<jsp:setProperty>` tag sets the value specified in the Bean's property by calling its set method internally. The format of this tag is

```
<jsp:setProperty name="bean name" property="property name|*"
param="parameter name" value="value"/>
```

- ✦ The `name` is the Bean name specified in the `id` attribute of the `jsp:useBean` tag.
- ✦ The `property` attribute can hold either a property name or a "*". When "*" is used, all parameters are parsed, and the values are updated to all the properties matching the parameters. This is done through the *introspection* of the Bean. Refer to more on introspection in the previous section titled "Java Bean characteristics." If this value is used, the `param` and `value` attributes cannot be used.
- ✦ The `param` attribute provides the parameter name. It is not mandatory that the parameter name of the control given in the HTML match the property name. If the property name and the name given to the control in the HTML are different, the `param` attribute can be used to provide the actual parameter name.
- ✦ The `value` attribute holds the value to be set to the property. The value can be a literal value or an expression evaluated during execution of the JSP. The `value` attribute is used when the value does not come from user input and has to be set explicitly from the code.

The `param` and `value` attributes cannot be used together.

The `<jsp:useBean>`, `<jsp:getProperty>`, and `<jsp:setProperty>` are the standard action tags used in connection with JavaBeans. The next example illustrates JavaBeans and these tags in action. The example attains employee information from the user and displays the same in the next screen. When the entry screen is shown, the default property values from the Bean are displayed. When the page is submitted, all the values keyed in are stored in the Bean and displayed. For simplicity's sake, let's take an Employee Bean, which holds the employee code, employee name, age, and e-mail address. These four variables form the properties for the Bean and are initialized to some default values in the constructor. Listing 13-9 shows the `EmployeeBean.java` code.

Listing 13-9

```
package servletbible.ch12.examples.beans;

/*
 * Employee Bean is a simple java bean
 * which has Employee Code, name, age
 * and Email as properties.
 */

public class EmployeeBean {
    // Employee Code
    private int eCode;

    // Employee Name
    private String name;

    // Age of the employee
    private int age;

    // Email address of the employee
    private String email;

    // getter method for Employee Code
    public int getECode() {
        return eCode;
    }
    // setter method for Employee Code
    public void setECode(int eCode) {
        this.eCode=eCode;
    }

    // getter method for employee name
    public String getName() {
        return name;
    }
    // setter method for employee name
    public void setName(String name) {
        this.name=name;
    }

    // getter method for employee age
    public int getAge() {
        return age;
    }
    // setter method for employee age
    public void setAge(int age) {
        this.age=age;
    }

    // getter method for employee Email address
```

Continued

Listing 13-9 *(continued)*

```
    public String getEmail() {
        return email;
    }
    // setter method for employee Email address
    public void setEmail(String email) {
        this.email = email;
    }

    // Bean constructor
    public EmployeeBean() {
        // Initialize employee code to some 3 digit random
number
        eCode = (int) (Math.random()*1000);

        // Initialize employee name
        name = "Your Name";

        // Initialize employee age
        age = 25;

        // Initialize employee Email address
        email = "yourname@host.com";
    }
}
```

For each of the variables defined, we have the corresponding get and set methods. A property can be accessed or modified through these methods because the variables are declared private. The `eCode` is initialized to a three-digit random number.

Listing 13-10 shows the JSP code, `BeanExample.jsp`, which displays the entry screen.

Listing 13-10

```
<%@ page language="java"%>
<%-- Use Employee Bean for this page --%>
<jsp:useBean id="empBean"
beanName="servletbible.ch12.examples.beans.EmployeeBean"
type="servletbible.ch12.examples.beans.EmployeeBean"
scope="page"/>
<%-- This will initialize the bean with default values provided
in the constructor --%>
<html>
<title>
```

```
Get Employee Information
</title>
<body>
<form id="frmEmployee" name="frmEmployee" method=post
action="BeanExampleOutput.jsp">
<table border=0>
    <tr>
        <td>
            Employee Code
        </td>
        <td>
            <%-- Use jsp:getProperty to get employee code -
%>
            <input type=text id="eCode" name="eCode"
value='<jsp:getProperty name="empBean" property="eCode"/>'>
            </input>
        </td>
    </tr>
    <tr>
        <td>
            Employee Name
        </td>
        <td>
            <%-- Use jsp:getProperty to get employee name -
%>
            <input type=text id="name" name="name"
value='<jsp:getProperty name="empBean" property="name"/>'>
            </input>
        </td>
    </tr>
    <tr>
        <td>
            Age
        </td>
        <td>
            <%-- Use jsp:getProperty to get employee age --%>
            <input type=text id="age" name="age"
value='<jsp:getProperty name="empBean" property="age"/>'>
            </input>
        </td>
    </tr>
    <tr>
        <td>
            E-Mail
        </td>
        <td>
            <%-- Use jsp:getProperty to get employee Email
address --%>
            <input type=text id="email" name="email"
```

Continued

Listing 13-10 *(continued)*

```
value='<jsp:getProperty name="empBean" property="email"/>'>
            </input>
        </td>
    </tr>
    <tr>
        <td colspan=2>
            <!-- Submit data -->
            <input type=submit id="btnSubmit"
name="btnSubmit" value="Submit">
            </input>
        </td>
    </tr>
</table>
</form>
</body>
</html>
```

The employee Bean is instantiated using the `<jsp:useBean>`, and the scope is set to `page`, which means the object expires after execution of this page. The Bean `"empBean"` is used to retrieve the initial values of the Bean using the `<jsp:getProperty>` and is assigned to the text boxes. Note the name of the text boxes in the HTML. They have the same name as the property name in the Bean. This is helpful when we look into the code for displaying the information entered in this screen. Pressing the Submit button takes you to the `BeanExampleOutput` page, as shown in Figure 13-7.

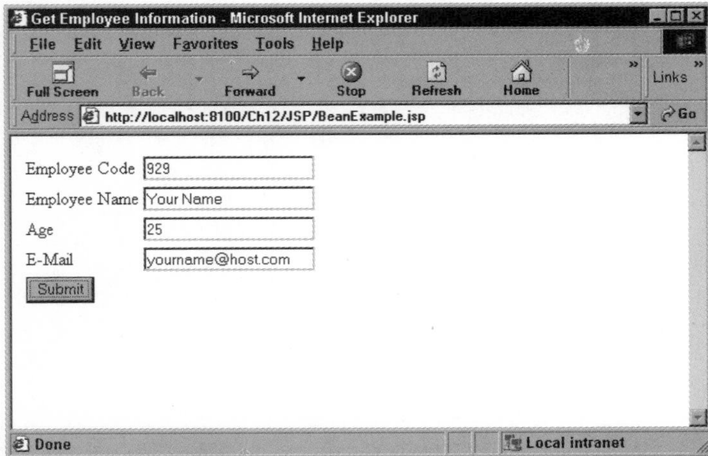

Figure 13-7: HTML form showing initial values of employee information

Listing 13-11 shows the JSP code (`BeanExampleOutput.jsp`) that displays the information keyed in by using the `BeanExample` page.

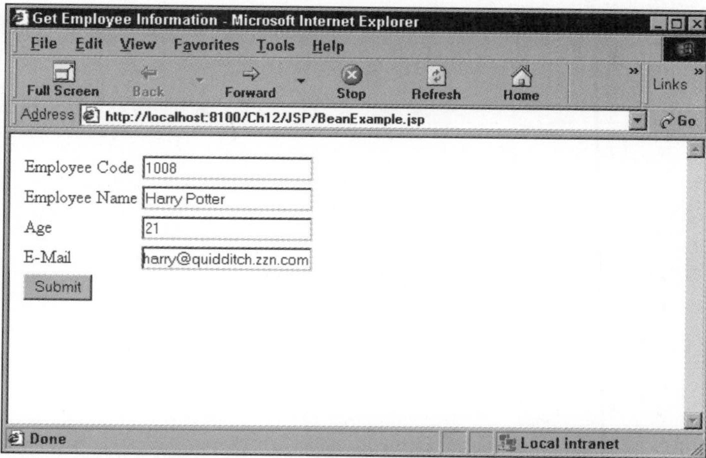

Figure 13-8: HTML form displayed after entry of employee information

Listing 13-11

```
<%@ page language="java"%>
<%-- Use Employee Bean for this page --%>
<jsp:useBean id="empBean"
class="servletbible.ch12.examples.beans.EmployeeBean"
scope="request"/>
<%-- jsp:setProperty will request all the values from
    the previous page and calls the appropriate setter
    methods to set all the properties
--%>
<jsp:setProperty name="empBean" property="*"/>
<html>
<title>
Get Employee Information from previous page
</title>
<body>
<form id="frmEmployee" name="frmEmployee" method=post>
<h3>
Employee Information you keyed in
</h3>
<table border=0>
    <tr>
        <td>
            Employee Code
```

Continued

Listing 13-11 *(continued)*

```
        </td>
        <td>
            <%-- Another way to get the property value is
                to use the bean name and call the get method
                directly.
            --%>
            <%=empBean.getECode()%>
        </td>
    </tr>
    <tr>
        <td>
            Employee Name
        </td>
        <td>
            <%=empBean.getName()%>
        </td>
    </tr>
    <tr>
        <td>
            Age
        </td>
        <td>
            <%=empBean.getAge()%>
        </td>
    </tr>
    <tr>
        <td>
            E-Mail
        </td>
        <td>
            <%=empBean.getEmail()%>
        </td>
    </tr>
</table>
</form>
</body>
</html>
```

In this example, we instantiate the employee Bean with `request` scope, which allows us to retrieve the values from the previous page. Note the property value as `"*"` in the `<jsp:setProperty>`. This sets all the properties to the values entered in the previous page. The JSP processor parses the Bean, identifies all the properties and the names of the text boxes that match the property names, and calls the appropriate set methods to store the text boxes' values. If introspection were not there, we would have to write four `<jsp:setProperty>` tags as follows:

```
<jsp:setProperty name="empBean" property="eCode"
param="eCode"/>
```

```
<jsp:setProperty name="empBean" property="name" param="name"/>
<jsp:setProperty name="empBean" property="age" param="age"/>
<jsp:setProperty name="empBean" property="email"
param="email"/>
```

Even though coding the preceding statements does not pose any error, think of writing *n* x 10 `<jsp:setProperty>` tags instead of one, when there are *n* properties defined in the Bean. There is one more way to get values from the Bean. We can directly use the Bean name and call the get method to retrieve values. Figure 13-9 shows the employee information entered in the form from the previous page displayed in the browser.

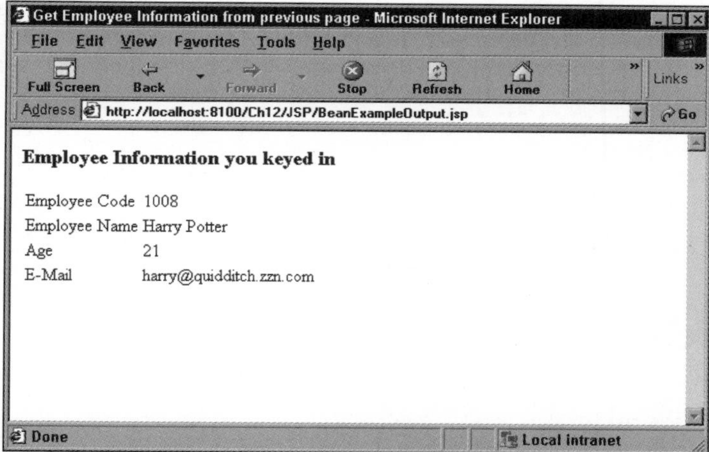

Figure 13-9: Employee information displayed from the previous page

<jsp:param>

The `<jsp:param>` tag is used to define user-defined parameters, which can be used with the `<jsp:include>` and `<jsp:forward>` tags. The prototype is as follows.

```
<jsp:param name="parameter name" value="value"/>
```

`name` is the parameter name; the `value` attribute holds the value.

<jsp:include>

`<jsp:include>` allows including another page embed within this page. The difference between this tag and the `include` directive is that this page allows inclusion of another dynamic page, whereas an `include` directive does not. The `include` directive is taken care of during compilation, whereas the `include` tag is handled during request processing. The included page has access only to the JspWriter object, and it cannot set headers or cookies. The format of the tag is:

```
<jsp:include page="resource" flush="true|false"/>
```

✦ The page attribute holds the resource URL. The resource can either be specified with the physical path or the relative path. A runtime exception is thrown if the resource specified cannot be located.

✦ If the flush attribute is true, the buffer is flushed before the inclusion of this file.

The <jsp:include> tag can have a body containing the <jsp:param> tags. If the included resource is another JSP page, all the parameters created within this tag using <jsp:param> along with the existing parameters can be accessed in the included file by using the request object. The parameter value can be retrieved by using the request.getParameter() method, as shown here:

```
<jsp:include page="myPage.jsp" flush="true">
    <jsp:param name="hello" value="hello world"/>
    .
    .
</jsp:include>
```

<jsp:forward>

<jsp:forward> transfers control to another JSP page, a servlet, or a static HTML page. Here is the format:

```
<jsp:forward page="url"/>
```

After the JSP engine encounters this tag, the execution stops and control is transferred to the page specified in the page attribute. If the output stream is not buffered and this page generates output, the page throws a java.lang.IllegalStateException.

We write some JSP code that utilizes the <jsp:param>, <jsp:include>, and <jsp:forward> tags. We have already seen the BeanExample.jsp code, which displays the employee code, name, age, and e-mail address and displays default values from the Employee Bean. Using the <jsp:include> tag, we add two more fields: city and state. These are included by using the <jsp:include> tag from another page: SomeMoreValues.jsp. Listing 13-12 shows the modified BeanExample.jsp, stored into a new file: IncludeParam.jsp.

Listing 13-12

```
<%@ page language="java"%>
<%-- Use Employee Bean for this page --%>
```

```
<jsp:useBean id="empBean"
beanName="servletbible.ch12.examples.beans.EmployeeBean"
type="servletbible.ch12.examples.beans.EmployeeBean"
scope="page"/>
<%-- This will initialize the bean with default values provided
in the constructor --%>
<html>
<title>
Get Employee Information
</title>
<body>
<form id="frmEmployee" name="frmEmployee" method=post
action="ForwardPage.jsp">
<table border=0>
    <tr>
        <td>
            Employee Code
        </td>
        <td>
            <%-- Use jsp:getProperty to get employee code --
%>
            <input type=text id="eCode" name="eCode"
value='<jsp:getProperty name="empBean" property="eCode"/>'>
            </input>
        </td>
    </tr>
    <tr>
        <td>
            Employee Name
        </td>
        <td>
            <%-- Use jsp:getProperty to get employee name --
%>
            <input type=text id="name" name="name"
value='<jsp:getProperty name="empBean" property="name"/>'>
            </input>
        </td>
    </tr>
    <tr>
        <td>
            Age
        </td>
        <td>
            <%-- Use jsp:getProperty to get employee age --%>
            <input type=text id="age" name="age"
value='<jsp:getProperty name="empBean" property="age"/>'>
            </input>
        </td>
    </tr>
    <tr>
        <td>
            E-Mail
```

Continued

Listing 13-12 *(continued)*

```
        </td>
        <td>
            <%-- Use jsp:getProperty to get employee Email
address --%>
            <input type=text id="email" name="email"
value='<jsp:getProperty name="empBean" property="email"/>'>
            </input>
        </td>
    </tr>
    <%-- Here we include another JSP page passing in a parameter
--%>
    <jsp:include page="SomeMoreValues.jsp" flush="true">
        <%-- pass a parameter, city with default value --%>
        <jsp:param name="city" value="Shoreview"/>
    </jsp:include>
    <tr>
        <td colspan=2>
            <!-- Submit data -->
            <input type=submit id="btnSubmit"
name="btnSubmit" value="Submit">
            </input>
        </td>
    </tr>
</table>
</form>
</body>
</html>
```

Note that within the table, before we place the Submit button, we use the `<jsp:include>` tag and include the file `"SomeMoreValues.jsp"`. We also pass one more parameter, `"city"`, with the default value `"Shoreview"`, which can be accessed by the included page. Let's look into the `"SomeMoreValues.jsp"` code in Listing 13-13.

Listing 13-13

```
<%@ page language="java"%>
<tr>
    <td>
        City
    </td>
    <td>
        <%-- Get the param value passed --%>
        <input type=text id="city" name="city"
```

```
value='<%=request.getParameter("city")%>'>
        </input>
    </td>
</tr>
<!-- add one more value -->
<tr>
    <td>
        State
    </td>
    <td>
        <input type=text id="state" name="state"
value="Minnesota">
        </input>
    </td>
</tr>
```

This example shows just a part of the HTML (it doesn't have a header or body). We use the `request.getParameter()` method to get the value passed as a parameter in the body of `<jsp:include>`. We also define a new text field, `state`. The screen is as shown in Figure 13-10 when `IncludeParam.jsp` is executed.

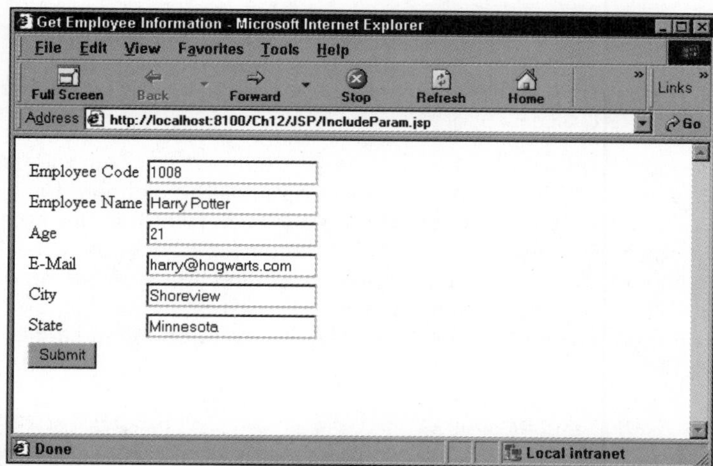

Figure 13-10: Employee information form with two new fields added

Pressing the Submit button takes you to `ForwardPage.jsp`, shown in Listing 13-14.

Listing 13-14

```
<%@ page language="java"%>
<%
//    Get all the values from the previous page

    String ecode = request.getParameter("eCode");
    String name = request.getParameter("name");
    String age = request.getParameter("age");
    String email = request.getParameter("email");
    String city = request.getParameter("city");
    String state = request.getParameter("state");

// Frame it into a single string

    String empInfo = "Mr./Ms. " + name + "\n";
    empInfo += city + ", " + state + "\n\n";
    empInfo +=     "ecode: " + ecode + "\n";
    empInfo += "age  : " + age + "\n";
    empInfo += "email: " + email;
%>
<jsp:forward page="InfoPage.jsp">
<%-- Declare a parameter passing in the framed string as value,
    so that the forwarded page can request it --%>
    <jsp:param name="info" value="<%=empInfo%>"/>
</jsp:forward>
```

When the JSP engine executes a `<jsp:include>` tag, it embeds it within the page specified in the `page` attribute. If necessary, it also compiles the included page, if the page included is another dynamic page. The result is a servlet that is a combination of the page and the included page. Thus, all the parameters in the actual page, as well as in the included page, are available for request on submission of the page. In `ForwardPage.jsp`, we retrieve all the values by using the `request.getParameter()` method, and we frame the address information into a single string variable, `empInfo`.

We call the `<jsp:forward>` tag, passing in `"InfoPage.jsp"` as the page attribute. We also declare a `<jsp:param>`, `"info"`, passing the value of `empInfo` as its value. Thus, `empInfo` is available to `InfoPage.jsp` through the parameter information. Listing 13-15 shows the code for `InfoPage.jsp`.

Listing 13-15

```
<%@ page language="java"%>
<html>
<title>
Employee Information
```

```
</title>
<body>
<b>
Employee Information
</b>
<%-- request the info from the ForwardPage --%>
<textarea cols=60 rows=6 readonly>
<%=request.getParameter("info")%>
</textarea>
</body>
</html>
```

InfoPage.jsp displays the employee information in a text area. The final screen is shown in Figure 13-11.

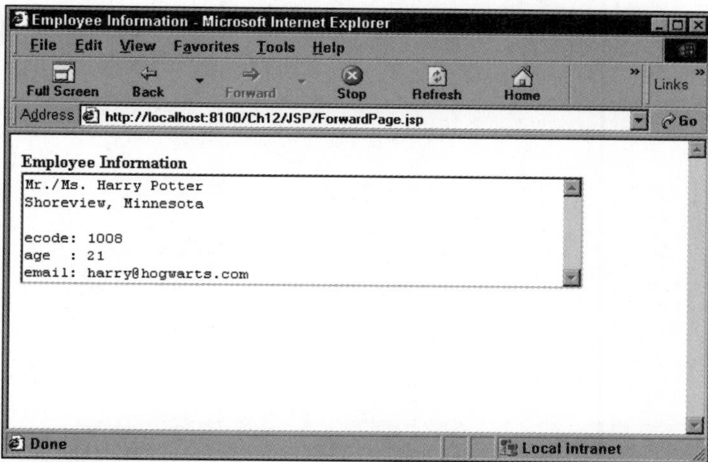

Figure 13-11: Updated employee information displayed in the browser

Note that none of the entry screens incorporate validations. You can add your own client-side scripting to validate the fields.

Validation using JavaScript is covered in Chapter 5.

<jsp:plugin>

The `<jsp:plugin>` tag can be used to embed objects such as an applet or a visual Bean component from the client end (that is, the browser). It is similar to the `<applet>` or the `<object>` tag. The following is the prototype:

```
<jsp:plugin type="bean|applet" code="object code"
codebase="object codebase" align="alignment"
archive="archiveList" height="height" hspace="hspace"
width="width" nspluginurl="url" iepluginurl="url"/>
```

Although most of the attributes are similar to the HTML tag's attributes, `nspluginurl` and `iepluginurl` need some explanation. Nothing is special about them. These two attributes specify the URL where the Java Runtime Environment (JRE) plug in can be downloaded for Netscape and Internet Explorer, respectively. This is needed only if the client machine requires a Java plug-in. Listing 13-16 shows the code for `InfoPage.jsp`, modified to include an applet by using `<jsp:plugin>`.

Listing 13-16

```
<%@ page language="java"%>
<html>
<title>
Employee Information
</title>
<body>
<jsp:plugin type="applet" code="MyApplet" height="100"
width="100"/>
<b>
Employee Information
</b>
<%-- request the info from the ForwardPage --%>
<textarea cols=60 rows=6 readonly>
<%=request.getParameter("info")%>
</textarea>
</body>
</html>
```

Objects accessible within a JSP page

A JSP page, by default, has access to various objects, some of which are listed here:

- `request` **object** — The `request` object, an instance of `javax.servlet.ServletRequest`, is passed as a parameter to the `_jspService()` method and is available within the method. So all scriptlet code, expressions, and standard action tags have access to this object. But the declaration blocks in a JSP page do not have access to it because they are declared and defined out of the `_jspService()` method.
- `response` **object** — The `response` object is similar to the `request` object and is available throughout the page.

- `session` object — The `session` object is an instance of `javax.servlet.http.HttpSession`. This object is useful mainly for keeping track of session objects, adding objects, and removing objects that are available throughout the session. This object has the session scope. When the session attribute in the page directive holds a "false" value, session management is turned off. A reference to the `session` object in any other pages results in a translation error. By default, the `session` object is available even though session handling is not used in the application.
- `application` object — The `application` object is available throughout the life of the Web server and is available to all the applications. This is an instance of `javax.servlet.ServletContext`.
- `pageContext` object — The server-specific features are included in a special class called `PageContext` in the `javax.servlet.jsp` package. This object encapsulates the page context of a particular JSP page.
- `out` object — The `out` object is available throughout the page and is an instance of the `PrintWriter` object. This object is used to write data to the client. The output stream can be buffered, and the buffer size can be adjusted. The buffer can also be turned off so that data is flushed immediately after writing.
- `config` object — The `config` object holds the configuration information of the servlet and is available with page scope.
- `page` object — The JSP itself is referenced through this object and can be accessed throughout the page.
- `exception` object — This object can be used to trace runtime exceptions. But this object is available only for an error page on which a page directive with the `isErrorPage` attribute is set to "true." The object is of type `java.lang.Throwable`.

Summary

In this chapter, we provided an overview of JSP, a discussion of the JSP's process, syntax, and semantics. You learned about three directives (`page`, `include`, and `taglib`) and JavaBeans and their characteristics such as properties, customization, event handling, introspection, persistence, and packaging.

We discussed firing events from one Bean that can be captured by another Bean and declaring variables and defining methods that can be used within the JSP by using the declaration block. We covered scriptlets containing Java code to perform certain actions on objects and expressions that are shortcuts to output to a client, the result of an expression, or a variable. You learned about the three ways to comment in a JSP file and the objects available to a JSP page.

With the standard action tags in JSP, we saw how JSP can utilize JavaBeans with the help of the `<jsp:useBean>`, `<jsp:getProperty>`, and `<jsp:setProperty>` tags, and we examined the other standard action tags: `<jsp:param>`, `<jsp:forward>`, and `<jsp:plugin>`. Finally, we looked at JSP examples using JSP directives and tags, some of them using the JavaBeans.

In the next chapter, we look into a design pattern that utilizes the power of JSP, servlets, and JavaBeans.

✦ ✦ ✦

CHAPTER 14

The Model View Controller (MVC) Architecture

✦ ✦ ✦ ✦

In This Chapter

Design patterns and their use in software development

The MVC architecture

Advantages of using MVC architecture

Servlets, JSP, JavaBeans, and MVC architecture

Build a simple Shopping cart using MVC architecture

✦ ✦ ✦ ✦

Patterns are a set of documented procedures that help programmers in developing software in an architectural way. Patterns aren't languages themselves, and you can't build applications with just the patterns. Patterns are guides to programmers in developing applications in an efficient way. They also serve as guides in avoiding pitfalls. These pitfalls are problems that you face in applications that are already developed. They pose a "never-do-it-like-this-again" warning. Upon developing applications, you will find do's and don'ts for subsequent development of applications that fall under the same domain.

A pattern becomes mature as you use it in developing applications. A pattern's value adds up as users recognize its effectiveness in the applications that you develop by using the architecture that the pattern describes. Design patterns take years to evolve, and they are under constant research by IT organizations. Pattern specifications express a tradeoff between the positives and negatives of a particular architecture. These design patterns are well documented and function like a handbook to software developers. Patterns also describe the "costs" that you incur in obtaining the solution to a problem. The pattern developers don't concentrate on how and what tools and programming constructs you should use in designing a pattern; rather, they concentrate on the document containing patterns that developers who've built successful applications have used. Patterns aren't quantitative but are qualitative in defining concrete solutions to problems. Good patterns come from experience and how long people have used them.

The study of patterns occurs not only in software, but also in many other fields, such as construction, music, and anthropology. Software patterns initially evolved after the object-oriented programming approach came into existence. Although a lot of work's gone on in developing patterns for object-oriented application development, consistent work's also been underway on the development of patterns for efficient, reliable, and scalable software in the area of concurrent and distributed programming. More work is going on right now in integrating software patterns with existing solutions and software processes. If you can read, understand, and implement a software design patterns correctly, there is a good chance you will be able to produce high quality software.

Introduction to MVC Architecture Design Pattern

The Model View Controller (MVC) architecture divides an application into three parts, referred to in its name. MVC was introduced in the context of Smalltalk development, where developers needed to present the graphical interface for a work that another module did. Subsequently, MVC gained its popularity — and was widely used in developing efficient applications such as CAD/CAM. Each part of the MVC architecture — the Model, the View, and the Controller — plays a role in completing an application. We describe each one in detail in the following sections. One of the key benefits in separating code into these parts and layers is that you can drastically reduce maintenance work if modifications are requested. For example, if the user interface requires a change, only code in the view layer need be changed (that is, only code for the user interface needs be changed without affecting the other parts of the system). You will then be able to have different views listen to the same data.

Model

A *model* takes care of holding data and contains code to manipulate data. A model encodes the business logic of an application. The model is also responsible for holding the state of an object. You can access the state, the data, and the functionality of the model through its public methods. A model registers all the views and notifies them of the data change so that the registered views are updated with the latest data. The `java.util.Observable` class helps in achieving this task.

View

A *view* presents the data to the user through a user interface. A user also keys in the data through this user interface. You can understand a view as a graphical interface for a model. You can associate more than one view with a model. A CAD/CAM application is a good example in which you view data graphically in different renderings.

After the user keys in data, the view notifies the controller that the input data has been entered, which then takes the appropriate action for updating the model. A view implements the `java.util.Observer` interface to get the notification of the change in data from the model.

Controller

A *controller* couples the model and view and integrates the application. After a view notifies the controller of user input, the controller notifies the model of the data change. The model then notifies all the views registered so that they change accordingly. A controller is basically a listener.

The diagram in Figure 14-1 shows the MVC architecture.

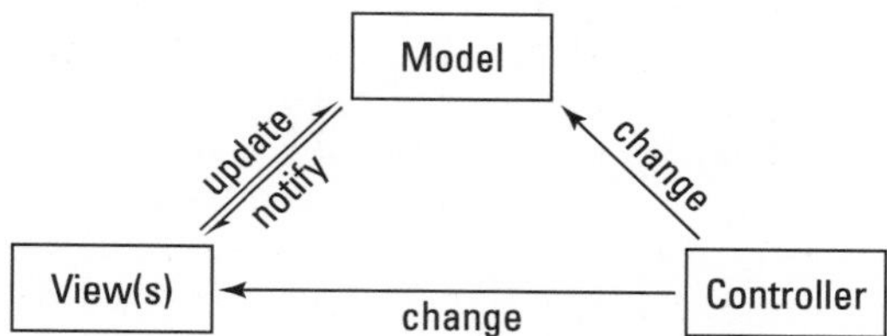

Figure 14-1: MVC architecture

To take an analogy from daily life, we can say that our bodies function much like the MVC pattern.

What happens as you read the statement "The rose is beautiful"? Your eye is the *view* here. The eye doesn't know what a rose is or what "beautiful" means. Our nerves, which transmit information from the eye to the brain, are *controllers*. Our brain is a complex model, which incorporates data and data-processing logic. It follows these steps:

1. What you see goes in through your eye as an image, and your brain matches these patterns that it received to identify letters, group the letters together to form the word, and group the words again to create the sentence.
2. Next it parses the statement for meaning, and again a breakup occurs as the brain splits up the words.
3. The brain maps the word *rose* against a picture of a rose that is in your mind.
4. The brain associates the concept *beautiful* to a feeling.

These steps summarize what your brain does — and a lot more processes occur in between these steps.

Here the model is only one thing, the brain, but everyone has different views and different controllers. Eye, ear, nose, mouth, skin, and so on are all views, and the different nerves that transmit information to or from these views are controllers. We're not actually aware of the model, the different views, and the controllers' individual functionality, but they're well synchronized, and the output seems to emanate from a single function. We can quote many day-to-day examples similar to this one, all of which follow the MVC pattern.

A type of software application that we can best quote as an example of an MVC is a spreadsheet. A spreadsheet application uses data values, which it maps to different graphical charts. If the data changes, all the charts update their views automatically. Another example is CAD/CAM software, which projects graphic models in different perspectives and views based on its data.

The model and the views bond only during the application's runtime. During its compile time, the model is neither aware of the object that it's to notify nor when a state change occurs in its data. It also doesn't know from which object it may receive the notification to update its data's state. A view doesn't know from where the data may come and which object it must notify if the user keys in new values. A controller contains the code to bind the model and the view. The controller registers the view and the model to listen to certain notifications so that they can update themselves.

MVC in Java

Java's Swing, which is a part of the JFC (Java Foundation Classes), is based on the MVC architecture. The Swing architecture is little modified from the original MVC in that it creates the view and the controller for a User Interface (UI) component. Most of the components have an associated model, which takes care of data storage as well as the state of the component. With the use of the JDK 1.1 event model, the model layer notifies the views. The notification can consist of a simple alert or contain information about the event. Simple notification merely informs the views that a change occurred in the data and doesn't tell the views what data changed. Notification can also include information on what data changed and the new value of that data.

You can also apply MVC to Java applications by using the `Observer/Observable` objects. An *observer* is any object that wants to receive notification if the state of another object changes. An observable object has methods to change the data and its state. An object can register with the observable object to be notified of the observable object's state. If you use these two objects in the context of MVC, the model is an object that extends the `Observable`, and all the view objects that are interested in the state change of the model must implement the `Observer` interface. The notification happens automatically between the model and the views after these objects use the `Observable` and `Observer` objects, respectively, and the controller binds them together. The view and the controller contain the instances of the model, so they can access the data inside the model.

The `Observer` interface contains the following method:

```
public void update(Observable o, Object arg)
```

This method is called after the `Observable` object calls a `notifyObservers` method to indicate a state change. `o` is the `Observable` object, and `arg` is the arguments passing to the `notifyObservers` method.

The `Observable` class contains the methods described in Table 14-1.

Table 14-1
Methods of the Observable class

Method	***Description***
`void addObserver(Observer o)`	Adds the observer to the list of objects interested in the state change of this object. An object can be registered only once.
`int countObservers()`	Returns the number of observers registered with this object.
`protected void clearChanged()`	Identifies that the object has no more changed state. Subsequently the `hasChanged` method returns false.
`void deleteObserver(Observer o)`	Deletes the `Observer o` from the list of observers.
`void deleteObservers()`	Removes all the observers registered with this object.
`boolean hasChanged()`	Tests whether this object's state has changed.
`void notifyObservers()`	If the `hasChanged` method returns `true`, indicating that the object's state has changed, this method notifies all the observers registered with this object. It then calls the `clearChanged` method.
`void notifyObservers(Object arg)`	Same as the preceding method, except that an object that may be of use to the observers is passed as an argument.
`protected void setChanged()`	Identifies that this object has changed its state. After this method, the `hasChanged` method returns `true`.

A model extends the `Observable` class. If the model wants to inform the observers that its state has changed, it calls the `setUpdate` method, followed by the `notifyObservers` method. A typical code segment is as follows:

```
import java.util.*;
.
.
class ModelClass extends Observable {
      .
      private String newState;
      .
      void setNewObjectState(String newState) {
            // set the new value
            this.newState = newState;
            .
            .
            // call the setChanged method to
            // indicate the state change
            setChanged();
            // notify observers
            notifyObservers();
      }
      .
      .
      .
}
```

A view that wants to be notified of an object's change implements the `Observer` interface. The `update` method is called automatically if a notification is received. The programmer can code this method to take advantage of the notification and update itself with the model's data change. A view would look like the following code segment:

```
import java.util.*;
.
.
class ViewClass implements Observable {
      .
      .
      // Variable to hold the model
      private ModelClass mc;
      .
      ViewClass(ModelClass mc) {
            // store the instance of model
            this.mc = mc;
            .
            .
      }
      public void update(Observable obs, Object o) {
            // Model's state has changed.
```

```
                // Update the view using the model's instance
                .
                .
                .
        }
        .
        .
        .
}
```

Finally, the controller takes its place in tying up the model and the view. A controller's code contains code statements similar to the code that follows:

```
import java.util.*;
.
.
class ControllerClass {
        .
        // Create some object
        String newState;
        .
        public void tieModelAndView() {
                // Initalize our local object
                newState = new String("new state");
                //create instance of model
                ModelClass mc = new ModelClass();

                // create instance of view
                ViewClass vc = new ViewClass();

                // register view with model.
                mc.addObserver(vc);

                // the following should
                // notify the view automatically
                mc.setNewObjectState(newState);
                .
                .
        }
        .
        .
}
```

After the `ControllerClass` calls the `setNewObjectState` method of the model class, the method sets its local variable to the passed value. Then it calls the `setChanged` method to mark that the object's state has changed. Afterward, the `ModelClass` calls the `notifyObservers` method to notify the observers — the `ViewClass` in this case.

An example using Observer and Observable

Now let's look into a small MVC application that uses the `Observer` and `Observable` objects. This application automatically converts the distance that you enter in any one of the units (for example, miles, kilometers, and meters) to the other units. Here you find three views, one for each unit of measurement. The model uses a single private variable to store the miles. The methods do the conversion to the respective units. Initially let's look at the code for the model. `DistanceModel.java` is the file, and the code in it appears in Listing 14-1.

Listing 14-1

```
package servletbible.ch13.examples;

import java.util.*;

class DistanceModel extends Observable {
     // variable to store the mile value
     private double mile ;

     /**
       * setMile method sets the mile value
       * and notifies the observers
       */
     public void setMile(double mile) {
          this.mile=mile;
          setChanged();
          notifyObservers();
     }

     /**
       * setKM method converts the kilometer
       * to mile and stores it in the mile variable.
       * Finally it notifies the observers
       */
     public void setKM(double km) {
          this.mile = km/1.6094;
          setChanged();
          notifyObservers();
     }

     /**
       * setMeter method converts the meter
       * to mile and stores it in the mile variable.
       * Finally it notifies the observers
       */
     public void setMeter(double meter) {
          this.mile = meter/1609.4;
          setChanged();
          notifyObservers();
     }
```

```
    /**
     * getMile returns mile
     */
    public double getMile() {
        return mile;
    }

    /**
     * getKM returns value of mile in Kilometer
     */
    public double getKM() {
        return mile*1.6094;
    }

    /**
     * getMeter returns value of mile in Meter
     */
    public double getMeter() {
        return mile*1609.4;
    }

}
```

The code is pretty simple and self-explanatory. The `DistanceModel` contains the `get` and `set` methods for getting and setting the unit values. Notice that only the mile value is stored, as you can manipulate the other values with this value.

Next let's look at the views. The code is similar for all the views, except for the label name, frame title, and the window position. So let's look into one view.

The code for the other two views viz., `KMView.java` and `MeterView.java`, are available in the book's CD-ROM.

Listing 14-2 shows the view and is in the file `MileView.java`.

Listing 14-2

```
package servletbible.ch13.examples;

import java.util.*;
import java.awt.*;
import java.awt.event.*;
import java.text.*;

class MileView implements Observer {
```

Continued

Listing 14-2 *(continued)*

```
// frame
Frame mileFrame;

// text box for entering mile
TextField txtMile;

// model
DistanceModel model;

/**
 * The constructor accepts the model
 * as parameter and does the initialization
 * of the frame, text field and events.
 */
MileView(DistanceModel model) {
     // assign model to the local variable
     this.model = model;

     // register this view with the observable model
     model.addObserver(this);

     // create frame
     mileFrame = new Frame("Miles - Enter value and press enter");

     //create textbox for entering Mile
     txtMile = new TextField("",15);

     // set the layout
     mileFrame.setLayout(new FlowLayout());

     //set resizable false
     mileFrame.setResizable(false);

     // add the label
     mileFrame.add(new Label("Miles"));

     // add text box
     mileFrame.add(txtMile);

     // add action listener to listen for text box changes
     txtMile.addActionListener(new MileListener());

     // add window listener
     mileFrame.addWindowListener((WindowListener)(new WindowAdapter() {
          public void windowClosing(WindowEvent we) {
               // hide frame and exit
               mileFrame.setVisible(false);
               System.exit(0);
```

```
            }
        }));

        // set the bounds and make it visible
        mileFrame.setBounds(10,10,325,60);
        mileFrame.setVisible(true);
    }

    /**
     * The inner class MileListener implements ActionListener
     * and is used for handling events with the Mile Text box
      */
    class MileListener implements ActionListener {
        public void actionPerformed(ActionEvent ae) {
            double mile = 0.0;
            try {
                // Get the text box value and
                // convert it to a double value
                mile = Double.valueOf(txtMile.getText()).doubleValue();

                // check if its not less than 0
                if (mile < 0) {
                    txtMile.setText("");
                    txtMile.requestFocus();
                    return;
                }
            }
            catch (NumberFormatException e){
                    // Not a number
                    txtMile.setText("");
                    txtMile.requestFocus();
                    return;
            }

            // set the mile in model
            model.setMile(mile);
        }
    }

    // Event from Observable,
    // value has changed, update the text box
    public void update(Observable obs,Object obj) {
        // Use decimal format to format the number
        // to five decimal places
        DecimalFormat dm = new DecimalFormat("#0.00000");
        String mile = dm.format(model.getMile());
        txtMile.setText(mile);
    }
}
```

The view's constructor takes in a parameter of type `DistanceModel`. The view is registered with the `Observable` object by using the `addObserver` method. A frame is created and a label and a text box are added to the frame. Next, an action listener is added to the text box to listen to the change in the text box. Here you need to trap just the "Enter" key. Adding an action listener suffices the need. To accomplish this task, an inner class is defined, which implements the `ActionListener` interface. The `ActionListener` interface could be implemented in the main class itself, but here, a class for handling the event is dedicated for the text box alone, because you don't need to process any other events. An anonymous class is added to listen to the window-closing event, in which case the frame is made invisible and the application exits.

The `update` method gets the new data from the model, formats the number, and sets it to the text box. Notice that the text box is validated; it accepts only positive numbers. The kilometer view and the meter view are similar code, except for the label change. To tie up the model and the view, you need a controller, which is what we're going to see next. Listing 14-3 shows the code inside `MVC.java`, which does the job of a controller.

Listing 14-3

```
package servletbible.ch13.examples;

/**
 * MVC is the controller class which
 * ties up the views and the model
 * and is the starting point for this example.
 */
public class MVC {
     public static void main(String[] args) {
          //create model
          DistanceModel model = new DistanceModel();

          // create views
          new MeterView(model);
          new KMView(model);
          new MileView(model);
     }

  }
```

That's a simple example. It creates the model and the views by passing the model as a parameter. That binds everything together, and the application is ready to run. Figure 14-2 shows the application in action.

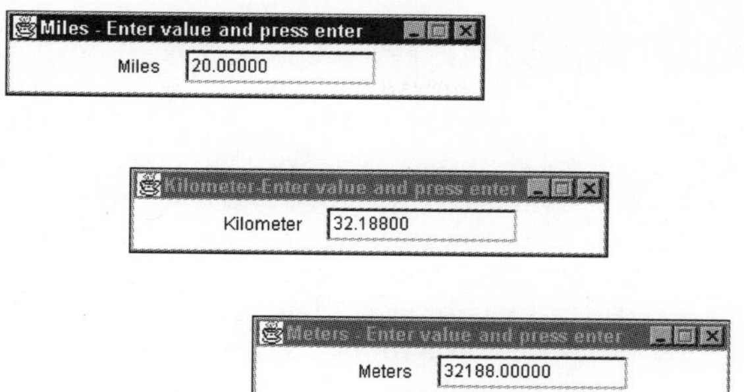

Figure 14-2: Example of MVC architecture using Observer/Observable

Advantages of Using MVC Architecture

Following are the advantages of using the MVC architecture:

- It divides the entire application into business model, view, and controller, which maps to logic, presentation, and event handling, respectively. You can concentrate on each of these parts individually.
- A code change in either the model, view, or controller layers has minimal or no effect in the operation of the other layers. It may require minor or no changes of code to the other layers.
- Dividing the application into logical components gives you maximum reusability of the user interface and of the business logic through many applications that belong to the same domain area.
- You can change the component's or the view's design and behavior dynamically based on the model's data.
- Different views can use a single model to project the data in different ways.
- If technological change is necessary, you need to change only the view and the controller; the model remains the same. If the application shifts to a Web-based application, for example, you can still use the model.

MVC applications have components that are loosely coupled and highly cohesive. Using MVC architecture for very small applications creates components that have minimal or no function, thereby creating unnecessary code complexity and runtime overhead.

Servlets, JSP, JavaBeans, and MVC

You can categorize a Web application into a three-tiered architecture: the presentation tier, the business logic tier, and the service/data tier. You can map these three tiers to the MVC architecture, with the business logic serving as the model, the presentation tier functioning as the view, and the service/data tier acting as the controller. The service tier and the data tier may again be physically separated. The service tier receives a change notification from the view and can access the model to update the data. The view can access the model to get the information and update itself.

So what's the advantage of using this architecture? As in the advantages for MVC, you can have multiple views for the same model. Here, each view can exist in a different environment. One may cater to Web browsers on a PC, and another may cater to smart browsers present on a wireless device, but both views use the same model to get the information. Figure 14-3 gives a pictorial representation of a three-tiered architecture mapping to the components of MVC.

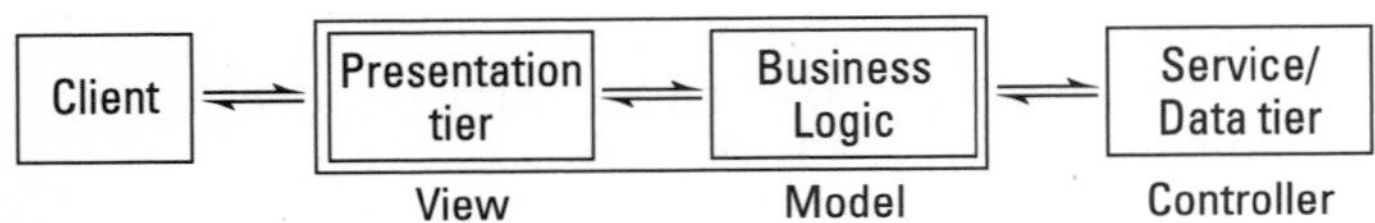

Figure 14-3: A three-tiered architecture mapping to components of MVC

You can effectively use servlets, JSP, and JavaBeans to implement MVC architecture in a Web application. You can best use JSPs for generating HTML dynamically. Hence, they can act as a view. JavaBean components, which are visual components, can also act as a view. A nonvisual JavaBean component is useful for encapsulating data that are easily accessible to other objects. Hence they can act as a model. The servlets can act as controllers, which receive data from the client and pass that data on to the model for updating to the database. They can also act as an intermediary in getting data from the bean and passing that data on to the view. A JSP can also act as a controller, but because the code that you write doesn't have any presentation aspect and you're using pure Java code, servlets are preferable. Similarly, you can also use a servlet for a view. Ultimately, the choice of JSP or a servlet for a controller or a view lies in the hands of the designer/developer of the application. Figure 14-4 shows these technologies used in conjunction with MVC.

Every Web application needs an entry point. A static HTML-based application isn't necessarily accessible from a specific page, but generally a Web application needs a starting point and a way of going through in a logical flow. Users shouldn't have access directly to an in-between page on the first go. A controller program helps in providing an entry point to an application and prevents users from directly accessing an intermediate page without going through the logical flow. Moreover, if you don't maintain a correct flow for the application, you have no guarantee that all the attributes related to the application initialized correctly.

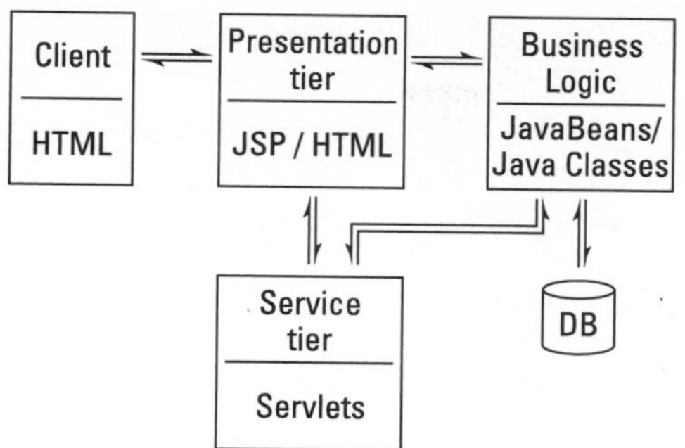

Figure 14-4: Servlets, JSP, and JavaBeans used in MVC architecture

Case Study: A Simple Shopping Cart Example Using MVC Architecture

This section deals with a shopping-cart example that uses the MVC architecture. Shopping carts are a feature of many dot.com Web sites. Here, we just concentrate on developing the shopping cart part, which you can extend or modify to any domain. We take the stationery items that people can order online.

Our example performs the following jobs:

- Because a user must log in before he can use the shopping cart, the example starts with a login screen, and the user must enter his username and the password. If the authentication is successful and the user is a valid user, the application takes the user in.
- A product catalog screen appears. The product code, description, price, and the unit of measurement appear in a table format.
- The user can click the product description to add the item to his shopping cart.
- After a user selects the product, a product-ordering screen appears, which prompts the user for the quantity of the product that he needs.
- After the user enters a valid quantity value and submits it, the application adds the product to his shopping cart.
- After placing the item in the shopping cart, the application returns the user to the product catalog page.
- The `Shopping Cart` link takes the user to his cart, where he can view the items he's ordered so far.
- The details on the shopping-cart page includes product code, product description, date ordered, price of the product, quantity ordered, and the total amount of the order.

- The user can delete the items from the shopping cart by clicking the `Delete` link.
- The user can return to the product-catalog screen by clicking the `Product Catalog` link.
- Clicking the `Logout` link logs out the user. This action opens the login screen.

Our example doesn't perform the following tasks:

- This example doesn't provide screens for adding new users or modifying their profiles.
- The application is restricted to adding items to the shopping cart and removing items from the shopping cart. It can't check out the items.
- If a user adds items to the shopping cart, the application doesn't update the quantity on hand in the database, because this value updates only if an actual check out occurs, and we don't implement the check-out screen here.

You can take up these points as an exercise to complete the application. The main idea of this example is to demonstrate the MVC architecture.

We use an MS Access database that we call `Inventory.mdb`, which is present on the CD-ROM. Tables 14-2 through 14-6 are present in the Inventory database. The database is designed in MS Access.

Table 14-2
Table: User

Field Name	*Data Type*	*Length (bytes)*	*Remarks*
Userid	Text	50	Primary key
Password	Text	15	Required
Firstname	Text	50	Required
Lastname	Text	50	Required
Email	Text	25	Required
Address	Text	100	Required
City	Text	50	Required
State	Text	25	Required
Zip	Text	8	Required

Table 14-3
Table: Product

Field Name	*Data Type*	*Length (bytes)*	*Remarks*
Productid	Number (Integer)	8	Primary Key
ProductDescription	Text	70	Required
Price	Number (Double)	8	Required
QOH	Number (Double)	8	Required (QOH – Quantity on Hand)
ROL	Number (Double)	8	Required (ROL – Reorder Level)
Units	Text	4	Required

Table 14-4
Table: Cart

Field Name	*Data Type*	*Length (bytes)*	*Remarks*
Orderid	Number (Integer)	8	Primary key
Userid	Text	50	Foreign key, refers to user table, Required
productid	Number (Integer)	8	Foreign key, refers to product table, Required
Date	Date/Time	8	Required
quantity	Number (Double)	8	Required

Table 14-5
Table: Purchase

Field Name	*Data Type*	*Length (bytes)*	*Remarks*
productid	Number (Integer)	8	Foreign key, refers to product table, Required
date_of_purchase	Date/Time	8	Required
quantity	Number (Double)	8	Required

Table 14-6
Table: Sales

Field Name	*Data Type*	*Length (bytes)*	*Remarks*
Userid	Text	50	Foreign key, refers to user table, Required
productid	Number (Integer)	8	Foreign key, refers to product table, Required
date_of_sales	Date/Time	8	Required
quantity	Number (Double)	8	Required

Although we don't use the Sales and Purchase tables, you can use them during the expansion of the application.

We use JavaBeans, servlets, JSP pages, and a few Java interfaces. The Java interfaces define constants that we use to describe the database information, table information, and the field information. Let's look into these Java interfaces first. The following are the three interfaces that we use:

- ✦ `DBConnectionInfo.java`: Contains the driver and the database URL information.
- ✦ `TableName.java`: Contains the table names in the database.
- ✦ `FieldName.java`: Contains the field names of all the tables.

The `DBConnectionInfo` interface defines constants that we use to connect to the database. The `TableName` and `FieldName` interfaces define constant string variables, which we use while framing SQL query in the Bean classes. Listings 14-4, 14-5, and 14-6 give the code listings for these interfaces.

Listing 14-4

```
package servletbible.ch13.examples;

/**
* DBConnectionInfo defines connection information
* for Inventory database.
*/

public interface DBConnectionInfo {
     // JDBC-ODBC driver
     public final String DRIVER = "sun.jdbc.odbc.JdbcOdbcDriver";
     // DSN for Inventory database
```

```
    public final String DBURL = "jdbc:odbc:Inventory";
}
```

Because we're using an MS Access database, we use the JDBC-ODBC Bridge to connect to the database. The DRIVER variable holds the driver provided by Sun for JDBC-ODBC Bridge. The DBURL holds the Data Source Name (DSN) Inventory to connect to the inventory database.

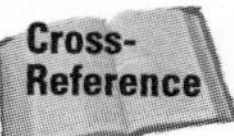

Chapter 2 provides a detailed explanation on how to create a DSN.

Listing 14-5 and 14-6 are TableName.java and FieldName.java, respectively.

Listing 14-5

```
package servletbible.ch13.examples;

/**
* TableName interface defines String constants
* that hold the table names in the Inventory database.
*These constants are used when framing a query.
*/

public interface TableName {
     // User Table
     public final String USER = "user";
     // Product Table
     public final String PRODUCT = "product";
     // Purchase Table
     public final String PURCHASE = "purchase";
     // Sales Table
     public final String SALES = "sales";
     // Shopping Cart table
     public final String CART = "cart";
}
```

Listing 14-6

```
package servletbible.ch13.examples;

/**
* FieldName interface defines String constants
```

Continued

Listing 14-6 *(continued)*

```
* that hold the field names from all the tables
* in the Inventory database. These constants are
* used when framing a query.
*/

public interface FieldName {
     /**
     * Table: User
     */
     // User ID
     public final String USER_ID = "Userid";
     // Password
     public final String PASSWORD = "password";
     // First Name
     public final String FIRST_NAME = "firstName";
     // Last Name
     public final String LAST_NAME = "lastName";
     // E-Mail id
     public final String EMAIL = "email";
     // Address
     public final String ADDRESS = "address";
     // City
     public final String CITY = "city";
     // State
     public final String STATE = "state";
     // Zip
     public final String ZIP = "zip";

     /**
     * Table: Product
     */
     // Product ID
     public final String PRODUCT_ID = "productid";
     // Product Description
     public final String PRODUCT_DESCRIPTION = "productDescription";
     // Price of product
     public final String PRICE = "price";
     // Quantity on Hand
     public final String QUANTITY_ON_HAND = "qoh";
     // Reorder Level
     public final String REORDER_LEVEL = "rol";
     // Unit measurement
     public final String UNITS = "units";

     /**
     * Table: Purchase
```

```
    * Includes product id
    */
    // Date of Purchase
    public final String DATE_OF_PURCHASE = "date_of_purchase";
    // Quantity purchased
    public final String QUANTITY = "quantity";

    /**
    * Table: Sales
    * Includes userid, productid and quantity
    */
    // Date of Sales
    public final String DATE_OF_SALES = "date_of_sales";

    /**
    * Table: cart
    * Includes userid, productid and quantity
    */
    // Order Id, together with user id forms unique key
    public final String ORDER_ID = "orderid";
    // Shopping date
    public final String DATE_OF_SHOPPING = "date";
}
```

Some of the fields in tables are foreign keys referring to other tables and have the same field names. Therefore, tables holding common field names we define in a constant string variable once. The comments indicate the fields that are already defined but not defined again. The `Userid` field, for example, is present in the user, product, and cart tables, but we define it only once, in defining the fields in the user table.

In the future, if the field names change in the database, only the constant values in these interfaces must be changed. This reduces the pain of replacing the values in all the queries in the application.

The models

Next, we create JavaBeans relevant to our application scope. The Beans act as models storing data and business logic. We need a connection Bean, which creates a new connection to the database. Creating a new instance of this Bean creates a new connection to the database. Whenever a connection is necessary, we can use the `getConnection` method that we define in this Bean. Listing 14-7 is the code for `ConnectionBean`.

Listing 14-7

```
package servletbible.beans;

import java.sql.*;
import java.io.*;

/*
 * ConnectionBean initializes connection to database
 */
public class ConnectionBean {
     protected Connection connection = null;
     private String driver;
     private String url;
     // Constructor takes the driver and url as parameters
     public ConnectionBean(String driver, String url) {
          // store driver and url
          this.driver = driver;
          this.url = url;
          // create a connection
          connection = createConnection(driver,url);
     }

     // createConnection creates a new connection
     private Connection createConnection(String driver, String url) {
          Connection connection = null;
          try {
               // Load the driver
               Class.forName(driver);
               // Establish Connection
               connection = DriverManager.getConnection(url);
               // Successful connection
               System.out.println("Established Connection");
          } catch(ClassNotFoundException cnfe) {
               // Error loading driver
               System.out.println("Could not load driver: " + driver);
               cnfe.printStackTrace();
          } catch(SQLException se) {
               // Error establishing connection
               System.out.println("Could not open connection to URL: " + url);
               se.printStackTrace();
          }
          return connection;
     }

//     get and set methods for connection
     public Connection getConnection() {
          // if connection is null, create new connection
          if(connection == null) {
               connection = createConnection(driver,url);
          }
          return connection;
     }
```

```
	public void setConnection(Connection connection) {
		this.connection = connection;
	}

//	closeConnection closes the connection
	public boolean closeConnection() {
		if(connection != null) {
			try {
				// close connection
				connection.close();
				// return true to indicate successful closing
				return true;
			} catch(SQLException se) {
				// error occurred during connection close
				se.printStackTrace();
				// return false to indicate error
				return false;
			}
		}
		// Connection already null, return true
		return true;
	}
}
```

The constructor of the `ConnectionBean` class takes in the driver and database URL as parameters. The driver and database URL are stored for future references. The constructor then calls the `createConnection` method to create a connection. The `createConnection` method loads the driver and the connection is established using the `DriverManager`'s `getConnection` method. The `getConnection` and `setConnection` methods are used to get and set the connection. The `closeConnection` method closes the connection and returns a Boolean value to indicate whether the operation was successful.

Next, we present the `UserBean`, which has the attributes and corresponding `get` and `set` methods to fill in the details for a user. `UserBean.java` is presented in Listing 14-8.

Listing 14-8

```
package servletbible.beans;

import java.sql.*;
import servletbible.ch13.examples.*;

/*
```

Continued

Listing 14-8 *(continued)*

```
 * UserBean encapsulates all data from the user table
 * and contains method to authorize a user
 */
public class UserBean {
     protected String userID;
     protected String password;
     protected String firstName;
     protected String lastName;
     protected String email;
     protected String address;
     protected String city;
     protected String state;
     protected String zip;

//     get and set methods for User Id
     public String getUserID() {
          return userID;
     }
     public void setUserID(String userID) {
          this.userID = userID;
     }

//     get and set methods for Password
     public String getPassword() {
          return password;
     }
     public void setPassword(String password) {
          this.password = password;
     }

//     get and set methods for First Name
     public String getFirstName() {
          return firstName;
     }
     public void setFirstName(String firstName) {
          this.firstName = firstName;
     }

//     get and set methods for Last Name
     public String getLastName() {
          return lastName;
     }
     public void setLastName(String lastName) {
          this.lastName = lastName;
     }

//     get and set methods for E-mail
     public String getEmail() {
          return email;
     }
     public void setEmail(String email) {
```

```
        this.email = email;
    }

//    get and set methods for Address
    public String getAddress() {
        return address;
    }
    public void setAddress(String address) {
        this.address = address;
    }

//    get and set methods for City
    public String getCity() {
        return city;
    }
    public void setCity(String city) {
        this.city = city;
    }

//    get and set methods for State
    public String getState() {
        return state;
    }
    public void setState(String state) {
        this.state = state;
    }

//    get and set methods for ZIP
    public String getZip() {
        return zip;
    }
    public void setZip(String zip) {
        this.zip = zip;
    }

//    validateUser method authenticates a user
    public boolean validateUser(Connection con) {
        // if connection is null return false to indicate error
        if(con == null) return false;
        // flag to indicate user is valid or not
        boolean flag=false;
        try {
            // create Statement
            Statement st = con.createStatement();
            // Frame SQL
            /*
                select * from user where
                ucase(user_id) = '<uppercase of getUserID()>'
                and password = '<getPassword()>'
             */
            String sql = "Select * from " + TableName.USER;
            sql += " where ucase(" + FieldName.USER_ID + ") = '";
```

Continued

Listing 14-8 *(continued)*

```
                sql += getUserID().toUpperCase() + "' and ";
                sql += FieldName.PASSWORD + " = '" + getPassword() + "'";
                // execute query
                ResultSet rs = st.executeQuery(sql);
                if(rs.next()) {
                     // Yes user and password ok,
                     // fill other details in the bean
                     // User ID
                     setUserID(rs.getString(FieldName.USER_ID));
                     // First Name
                     setFirstName(rs.getString(FieldName.FIRST_NAME));
                     // Last Name
                     setLastName(rs.getString(FieldName.LAST_NAME));
                     // E-mail
                     setEmail(rs.getString(FieldName.EMAIL));
                     // Address
                     setAddress(rs.getString(FieldName.ADDRESS));
                     // City
                     setCity(rs.getString(FieldName.CITY));
                     // State
                     setState(rs.getString(FieldName.STATE));
                     // Zip
                     setZip(rs.getString(FieldName.ZIP));
                     flag = true;
                }
                // close resultset
                rs.close();
                // close statement
                st.close();
                // return flag
                return flag;
           } catch(SQLException se) {
                // some error occurred during database operation
                se.printStackTrace();
                // return false to indicate error
                return false;
           }
      }
}
```

`UserBean` contains properties for all the fields in the user table. It also has a method called `validateUser`. The method accepts a `Connection` object as a parameter. The method verifies whether the `Userid` and `password` values in the Bean are valid. If they're valid, the method sets all the other user information into the attributes of the Bean. Take a look at the query while comparing the

UseridUserid. The program converts both the UseridUseridfield in the user table and the value in the Bean to uppercase. The ramification is that Userid can be case insensitive. For example dd, DD, dD, and Dd are identified as same user.

Next comes the ProductBean, which is used to fill up the product details. Listing 14-9 is the code in ProductBean.java.

Listing 14-9

```
package servletbible.beans;

import java.sql.*;
import java.util.*;
import servletbible.ch13.examples.*;

/*
 * ProductBean is a JavaBean which encapsulates
 * data in the product table. Contains methods
 * to get all products and add a product to shopping cart
 */
public class ProductBean {
     protected int productID;
     protected String productDescription;
     protected double price;
     protected double qoh;
     protected double rol;
     protected String units;
     protected double qtyRequired;

     public ProductBean() {
          super();
          // initialize to default values
          productID = 0;
          productDescription = "";
          price = 0.0;
          qoh = 0.0;
          rol = 0.0;
          units = "";
          qtyRequired = 0.0;
     }

//     get and set methods for Product ID
     public int getProductID() {
          return productID;
     }
     public void setProductID(int productID) {
          this.productID = productID;
```

Continued

Listing 14-9 *(continued)*

```
    }

//     get and set methods for Product Description
    public String getProductDescription() {
        return productDescription;
    }
    public void setProductDescription(String productDescription) {
        this.productDescription = productDescription;
    }

//     get and set methods for Price
    public double getPrice() {
        return price;
    }
    public void setPrice(double price) {
        this.price = price;
    }

//     get and set methods for Quantity on Hand
    public double getQoh() {
        return qoh;
    }
    public void setQoh(double qoh) {
        this.qoh = qoh;
    }

//     get and set methods for Reorder Level
    public double getRol() {
        return rol;
    }
    public void setRol(double rol) {
        this.rol = rol;
    }

//     get and set methods for unit of measurement
    public String getUnits() {
        return units;
    }
    public void setUnits(String units) {
        this.units = units;
    }

//     get and set methods for quantity required
    public double getQtyRequired() {
        return qtyRequired;
    }
    public void setQtyRequired(double qtyRequired) {
        this.qtyRequired = qtyRequired;
```

```
    }

//    getProductByKey returns a Product Bean
//    with data for a product represented by
//    Product ID
    public ProductBean getProductByKey(int productID,Connection con) {
        ProductBean pb = new ProductBean();
        try {
            // if connection is null return null
            if (con == null) return null;

            // create a Statement object
            Statement st = con.createStatement();

            // Frame SQL
            /*
                select * from product
                where product_id = <productID>
            */
            String sql = "Select * from ";
            sql += TableName.PRODUCT + " where ";
            sql += FieldName.PRODUCT_ID + " = ";
            sql += productID;

            // execute query
            ResultSet rs = st.executeQuery(sql);
            if(rs.next()) {
                // set all values
                // Product ID
                pb.setProductID(productID);
                // Product Description
                pb.setProductDescription(
                    rs.getString(FieldName.PRODUCT_DESCRIPTION)
                );
                // Price of the product
                pb.setPrice(rs.getDouble(FieldName.PRICE));
                // Quantity on Hand
                pb.setQoh(rs.getDouble(FieldName.QUANTITY_ON_HAND));
                // Reorder Level
                pb.setRol(rs.getDouble(FieldName.REORDER_LEVEL));
                // Unit of measurement
                pb.setUnits(rs.getString(FieldName.UNITS));
            }
            // close resultset
            rs.close();
            // close statement
            st.close();
            // return bean
            return pb;
        } catch(SQLException se) {
```

Continued

Listing 14-9 *(continued)*

```
                // error occurred during database operation
                se.printStackTrace();
                // return null to indicate error
                return null;
           }
      }

      // getAllProducts method returns a collection
      // of ProductBeans
      public Vector getAllProducts(Connection con) {
           // Vector to hold all the product beans
           Vector vt = null;
           // if connection is null return null
           if(con == null) return null;
           try {
                // create vector
                vt = new Vector();
                // create Statement object
                Statement st = con.createStatement();
                // Frame SQL
                /*
                     select product_id, product_description,
                     price,units from product
                 */
                String sql = "Select ";
                sql += FieldName.PRODUCT_ID + ",";
                sql += FieldName.PRODUCT_DESCRIPTION + ",";
                sql += FieldName.PRICE + ",";
                sql += FieldName.UNITS;
                sql += " from " + TableName.PRODUCT;

                // execute query
                ResultSet rs = st.executeQuery(sql);
                int index = 0;
                while(rs.next()) {
                     // Create ProductBean
                     ProductBean pb = new ProductBean();
                     // Add values
                     // Product ID
                     pb.setProductID(rs.getInt(FieldName.PRODUCT_ID));
                     // Product Description
                     pb.setProductDescription
(rs.getString(FieldName.PRODUCT_DESCRIPTION));
                     // Product Price
                     pb.setPrice(rs.getDouble(FieldName.PRICE));
                     // Unit of Measurement
                     pb.setUnits(rs.getString(FieldName.UNITS));
                     // add bean to vector
                     vt.add(index,pb);
                     index++;
```

```
                }
                // close resultset
                rs.close();
                // close statement
                st.close();
                // return vector of product beans
                return vt;
            } catch (SQLException se) {
                // error occured during database operation
                se.printStackTrace();
                // return null to indicate error
                return null;
            }
        }
}
```

The ProductBean contains one attribute more than does the product table. It uses the qtyRequired attribute if the user places an order for an item. The value that the user enters is held in this variable. The Bean has two methods, getProductByKey and getAllProducts, to get a single product referenced by a productid and to get all the products respectively. The getAllProducts method is useful in displaying the product catalog.

The getProductByKey method takes the productid and the Connection object as parameters. It retrieves all the information from the database based on the productid and puts all the other information relating to that product into the Bean.

The getAllProducts method retrieves all the records from the product table. For each record, a new ProductBean is created, and all the information pertaining to the product in that record is stored. Then the Bean is added to a Vector object. The index variable is used to increment the element position of the vector. After all the records process, the vector holding all the ProductBeans is returned.

CartBean has attributes and methods to set and get values for the cart table. It also has a method to add, delete, and view items in the shopping cart for the Userid passed as parameter. Listing 14-10 shows CartBean.java.

Listing 14-10

```
package servletbible.beans;

import java.sql.*;
import java.util.*;
import java.text.*;
```

Continued

Listing 14-10 *(continued)*

```
    import servletbible.ch13.examples.*;

/*
 * CartBean is JavaBean for Shopping cart.
 * Encapsulates data from the cart table plus
 * product description and price.
 */
public class CartBean {
     protected long orderID;
     protected String userID;
     protected int productID;
     protected java.util.Date date;
     protected String productDescription;
     protected double price;
     protected double quantity;

//     get and set methods for Order ID
     public long getOrderID() {
          return orderID;
     }
     public void setOrderID(long orderID) {
          this.orderID = orderID;
     }

// get and set methods for User ID
     public String getUserID() {
          return userID;
     }
     public void setUserID(String userID) {
          this.userID = userID;
     }

// get and set methods for Product ID
     public int getProductID() {
          return productID;
     }
     public void setProductID(int productID) {
          this.productID = productID;
     }

// get and set methods for Date
     public java.util.Date getDate() {
          return date;
     }
     public void setDate(java.util.Date date) {
          this.date = date;
     }

// get and set methods for product description
     public String getProductDescription() {
          return productDescription;
```

```
        }
        public void setProductDescription(String productDescription) {
            this.productDescription = productDescription;
        }

//      get and set methods for price
        public double getPrice() {
            return price;
        }
        public void setPrice(double price) {
            this.price = price;
        }

//      get and set methods for quantity
        public double getQuantity() {
            return quantity;
        }
        public void setQuantity(double quantity) {
            this.quantity = quantity;
        }

//      viewCart method retrieves all the products ordered
//      by user represented by userId.
        public Vector viewCart(Connection con, String userId) {
            //
            Vector vt = null;
            // if connection not available return null to indicate error
            if (con == null) return null;
            try {
                // create a new vector
                vt = new Vector();

                // create Statement object
                Statement st = con.createStatement();

                // Frame the sql
                /*
                    Select c.order_id,c.user_id,c.product_id,
                    c.date_of_shopping,p.product_description,
                    p.price,c.quantity from cart c,product p
                    where p.product_id = c.product_id and
                    ucase(c.user_id) = 'uppercase of <userId>'
                    order by c.date_of_shopping
                 */
                String sql = "Select c." + FieldName.ORDER_ID;
                sql += ",c." + FieldName.USER_ID;
                sql += ",c." + FieldName.PRODUCT_ID;
                sql += ",c." + FieldName.DATE_OF_SHOPPING;
                sql += ",p." + FieldName.PRODUCT_DESCRIPTION;
                sql += ",p." + FieldName.PRICE;
                sql += ",c." + FieldName.QUANTITY;
```

Continued

Listing 14-10 *(continued)*

```
            sql += " from " + TableName.CART + " c," + TableName.PRODUCT + " p
where ";
            sql += "p." + FieldName.PRODUCT_ID + "=c." +
FieldName.PRODUCT_ID;
            sql += " and ucase(c." + FieldName.USER_ID + ") = '" +
userId.toUpperCase() + "' ";
            sql += "order by c." + FieldName.DATE_OF_SHOPPING;

            // Execute the query
            ResultSet rs = st.executeQuery(sql);
            int index=0;

            // Loop through the result set
            while(rs.next()) {
                // create new Cart Bean instance
                CartBean cb = new CartBean();

                // set all the values
                // Order ID
                cb.setOrderID(rs.getInt(FieldName.ORDER_ID));
                // User ID
                cb.setUserID(rs.getString(FieldName.USER_ID));
                // Product ID
                cb.setProductID(rs.getInt(FieldName.PRODUCT_ID));
                // Date
                cb.setDate(rs.getDate(FieldName.DATE_OF_SHOPPING));
                // Product Description
                cb.setProductDescription
(rs.getString(FieldName.PRODUCT_DESCRIPTION));
                // Price
                cb.setPrice(rs.getDouble(FieldName.PRICE));
                // Quantity
                cb.setQuantity(rs.getDouble(FieldName.QUANTITY));

                // Add the bean to vector
                vt.add(index,cb);
                index++;
            }
            // Close resultset
            rs.close();
            // Close statement
            st.close();
            return vt;
        } catch(SQLException se) {
            // Error during stack operation
            se.printStackTrace();
            // return null to indicate error
            return null;
        }
    }
```

```
    // deleteItem method deletes an item represented by
    // order id from the cart for the user represented by userId
    public boolean deleteItem(Connection con, int orderId, String userId) {
        // if connection is null return false to indicate error
        if(con == null) return false;
        try {
            // create Statement object
            Statement st = con.createStatement();

            // Frame SQL
            /*
                delete from cart where order_id = <orderId>
                and ucase(user_id) = '<uppercase of userId>'
             */
            String sql = "delete from " + TableName.CART;
            sql += " where " + FieldName.ORDER_ID + " = ";
            sql += orderId + " and ucase(" + FieldName.USER_ID + ") = '" +
userId.toUpperCase() + "'";

            // execute update
            st.executeUpdate(sql);

            // deletion successful, return true to indicate success
            return true;
        } catch (SQLException se) {
            // error occured during database operation
            se.printStackTrace();
            // return false to indicate error
            return false;
        }
    }
    // addToCart method adds a product to cart for the
    // user represented by userId
    public boolean addToCart(Connection con,ProductBean pb,String userId) {
        // if connection is null return null
        if (con == null) return false;
        try {
            // get the next order Id
            int nextOrderId = getNextOrderID(con,userId);
            // if nextOrderId returned is zero, there
            // was some problem getting one, hence return false
            if (nextOrderId == 0) return false;
            // create Statement object
            Statement st = con.createStatement();

            // Get current date
            java.util.Date dt = new java.util.Date();
            // Format it to dd mmm yyyy using DateFormat object
            DateFormat df = DateFormat.getDateTimeInstance
(DateFormat.LONG,DateFormat.SHORT);
            String date = df.format(dt);
```

Continued

Listing 14-10 *(continued)*

```
            // Frame SQL
            /*
                 insert into cart values(<nextOrderId>,
                 <pb.getProductID(),<date>,<pb.getQtyRequired()>)
             */
            String sql = "insert into ";
            sql += TableName.CART + " values(";
            sql += nextOrderId + ",";
            sql += "'" + userId + "',";
            sql += pb.getProductID() + ",'";
            sql += date + "',";
            sql += pb.getQtyRequired() + ")";
                 // execute update
            st.executeUpdate(sql);
            //close statement
            st.close();
            // successful operation. return true
            return true;
       } catch(SQLException se) {
            // some error occured during database operation
            se.printStackTrace();
            // return false to indicate error
            return false;
       }
  }

  // getNextOrderID method returns
  // the next orderID number available in the cart table
  private int getNextOrderID(Connection con, String userId) {
       int nextOrderID = 0;
       try {
            // create Statement
            Statement st = con.createStatement();
            // Frame SQL
            /*
                 select max(order_id) as maxOrd
                 from cart where user_id = '<userId>';
             */
            String sql = "select max(" + FieldName.ORDER_ID + ") as maxOrd ";
            sql += "from " + TableName.CART + " where ";
            sql += FieldName.USER_ID + " ='" + userId + "'";
            // execute query
            ResultSet rs = st.executeQuery(sql);
            if(rs.next()) {
                 // next order id is maximum order id + 1
                 nextOrderID = rs.getInt("maxOrd") + 1;
            }
```

```
            else {
                 // cart table is empty, this is the first order
                 nextOrderID = 1;
            }
            // close resultset
            rs.close();
            // close statement
            st.close();
            // return next order id
            return nextOrderID;
       } catch(SQLException se) {
            // some error has occured during database operation
            se.printStackTrace();
            // return 0 to indicate error
            return 0;
       }
  }
}
```

The CartBean has four methods, apart from holding the properties of the cart table, and a couple extra attributes. The viewCart method returns a collection of CartBeans containing the items that the user orders, which the userid parameter represents.

An item in the shopping cart is uniquely identified by the combination of Orderid and Userid. The Orderid is generated by using the getNextOrderID method. The method gets the maximum Orderid for a particular Userid, present in the cart table. It then increments that value by one and returns the value. If the resulting query is empty, the method returns a value of one (indicating the first item in the cart for the user). If the method returns a zero value, it indicates a database error.

The addItem method adds a new item to the cart for the user, which the userid parameter represents. It first calls the getNextOrderID method to get the next Orderid for a Userid. The method also takes in a ProductBean as a parameter to update the product information. It gets the productid and the required quantity value from the bean. The current date it obtains from the Date object, which is formatted to the long date type (for example, 27 Jun 2001), and it concatenates it along with the insert query.

The deleteItem method deletes an item that orderid and userid represent. The values are obtained as parameters, and the record is deleted from the table.

Note Notice that all the Beans are under the package servletbible.beans. We haven't coded a JavaBean for the purchase and sales tables, as we don't use these tables in our application scope.

Now that we've looked into the beans, we're ready to create the views and controllers by using JSP pages and servlets.

The views and controllers

From here, we look at the JSP pages and servlets in the order of flow for the application. Figure 14-5 depicts the flow of the shopping cart application.

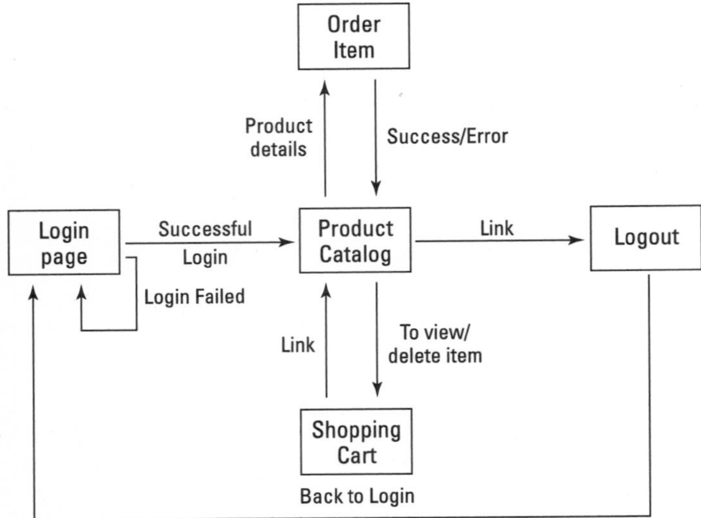

Figure 14-5: Shopping Cart application flow

Our application's starting point is at `http://<host name>:<port number>/ShoppingCart/Welcome.html`.

The `Welcome.html` file does a simple job of dividing the screen into two frames. The top frame isn't visible because its height is zero. The bottom page loads the login page. Why do we do things this way? If the starting page is a frame page, the subsequent pages are called from the frames and don't reflect the URL of the page in the browser's URL location box. Any subsequent pages loaded that are bookmarked will not be displayed when opening the bookmark. The bookmark will take you to the login screen. Our screen design, by default, doesn't contain frames, but just to accomplish this, we divide the screen into two frames and set the top frame's height to zero. Listing 14-11 gives the HTML code.

Listing 14-11

```
<html>
<title>Shopping Cart</title>
```

```
<frameset rows="0%,100%">
     <frame frameborder=0 NORESIZE>
     <frame id=CartFrame name=ContentFrame frameborder=0 NORESIZE
src="/ShoppingCart/Login.jsp">
</frameset>
</html>
```

The login page displays two text boxes, one to enter the `Userid` and the other to enter the password. Control returns to this page if the `Userid` and/or password isn't valid or someone clicks the `Logout` link in any of the screens. Listing 14-12 is the code for `Login.jsp`.

Listing 14-12

```
<%--
Login.jsp displays a login screen to log into the
application.
--%>

<%@page language="java"%>
<%
// msgStatus holds any status value that has to be
// checked before displaying this page
String msgStatus = request.getParameter("msgStatus");

if (msgStatus != null) {
//     If the value is "LoginFail" then this page is again
//     displayed because of a login failure
     if(msgStatus.equalsIgnoreCase("LoginFail")) {
//          Insert a global script that gets executed
//          before the page is loaded.  This script
//          displays an error message
%>
          <script language="JavaScript">
          alert("Invalid username and or password. Please try again.");
          </script>
<%
     }
}
%>
<html>
<head>
<!--
initialization function for the page
gets invoked on body onload event
-->
```

Continued

Listing 14-12 *(continued)*

```
<script language="JavaScript">
function init() {
//     Set the focus to the user id text box
     document.frmLogin.userID.focus();
}
</script>
</head>
<body onload=init()>
<%--
On submission of this page, the servlet ProcessLogin
is called which authorizes the user
--%>
<form id=frmLogin name=frmLogin method=Post action="/servlet/
servletbible.ch13.examples.ProcessLogin">
<table height="100%" width="100%" cellpadding=0 cellspacing=0 border=0>
<tr>
     <td>
     </td>
</tr>
<tr>
     <td align=center>
        <table border=0>
        <tr>
            <td>
               <font face="Courier New" size=+1>
               <b>
               Login Name
               </b>
               </font>
            </td>
            <td>
               <font face="Courier New" size=+1>
               <!-- User ID text box -->
               <input type=text id=userID name=userID value="">
               </input>
               </font>
            </td>
        </tr>
        <tr>
            <td>
               <font face="Courier New" size=+1>
               <b>
               Password
               </b>
               </font>
            </td>
```

```
            <td>
               <!-- Password text box -->
               <input type=password id=password name=password value=""
class=TBox>
               </input>
            </td>
        </tr>
        <tr>
            <td colspan=2 align=center>
               <font face="Courier New" size=+1>
               <b>
               <!-- Submit page -->
               <input type=submit id=btnSubmit name=btnSubmit value=Login>
               </input>
               </b>
               </font>
            </td>
         </tr>
        <table>
     </td>
</tr>
<tr>
     <td>
     </td>
</tr>
</table>
</form>
</body>
</html>
```

The login screen opens on two cases: if the user isn't valid and if someone clicks the Logout link. If it's an invalid user, the URL holds a parameter msgStatus with a value of LoginFail. Initially, the value of the msgStatus parameter is checked for this value. If it does contain this value, a JavaScript is framed to trigger the error message. Notice that this script is global and executes along the flow of the HTML. The remaining HTML centers the text boxes within the page with the help of the <table> tag. Figure 14-6 shows the login screen.

The ProcessLogin servlet performs the validation of the Userid and password. If you click the Login button on the login page, control transfers to this servlet. This servlet acts as a controller in getting the event from the JSP and communicates with the respective model to authenticate the user. Listing 14-13 shows the ProcessLogin servlet code.

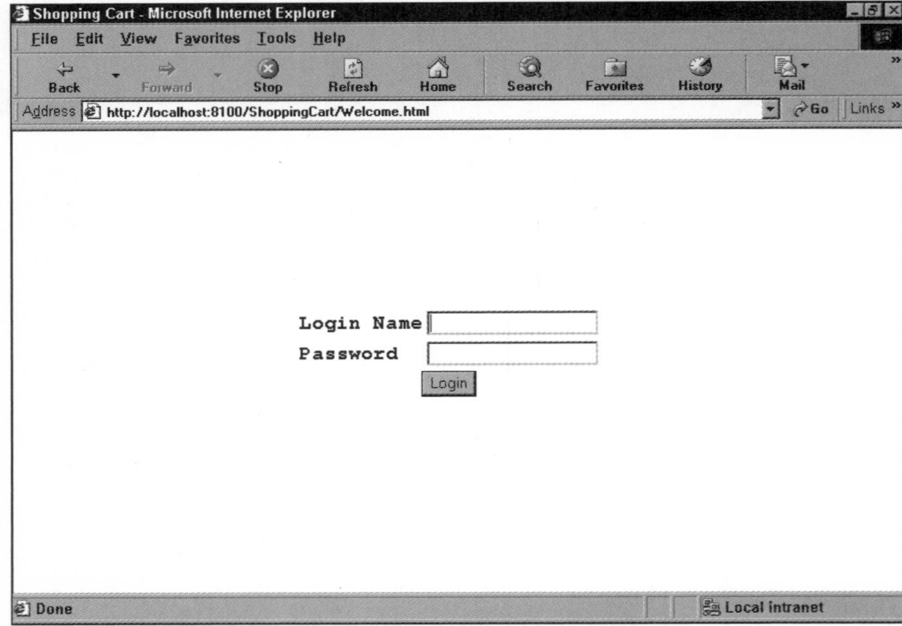

Figure 14-6: Login screen

Listing 14-13

```
package servletbible.ch13.examples;

import javax.servlet.*;
import javax.servlet.http.*;
import java.io.*;
import servletbible.beans.*;

/**
  * ProcessLogin servlet uses the UserBean's
  * validateUser method to authenticate the
  * user id.and the password, and calls the
  * appropriate page.
  */
public class ProcessLogin extends HttpServlet
{

     public void service(HttpServletRequest request, HttpServletResponse response)
throws ServletException, IOException
     {
          HttpSession session;

          // get session object
```

```
        session = request.getSession();

        // get the connection object stored in the session
        servletbible.beans.ConnectionBean cb = (servletbible.beans.ConnectionBean)
session.getAttribute("DBConnection");

        // If connection bean does not exist, create one
        if(cb == null) {
             // get the connection information from the DBConnectionInfo
interface
             cb = new servletbible.beans.ConnectionBean
(DBConnectionInfo.DRIVER,DBConnectionInfo.DBURL);
             // add it to session
             session.setAttribute("DBConnection",cb);
        }

        // get the user bean stored in the session
        servletbible.beans.UserBean ub = (servletbible.beans.UserBean)
session.getAttribute("User");

        // If User Bean does not exist in session, create one
        if(ub == null) {
             ub = new servletbible.beans.UserBean();
             // add it to session
             session.setAttribute("User",ub);
        }
        Boolean sin = (Boolean) session.getAttribute("SomebodyIn");
        if(sin == null) {
             session.setAttribute("SomebodyIn",new Boolean("false"));
        }
        // set the values keyed in, in the login page
        ub.setUserID(request.getParameter("userID"));
        ub.setPassword(request.getParameter("password"));

        // call the validateUser method to check if the user exists
        if(ub.validateUser(cb.getConnection())) {
             // Valid user. Set the SomebodyIn session variable
             // to a value of true.
             session.setAttribute("SomebodyIn",new Boolean("true"));

             // forward the page to ProductCatalog page
             getServletConfig().getServletContext().getRequestDispatcher
("/ShoppingCart/ProductCatalog.jsp?msgStatus=LoginOk" + "").forward
(request, response);
        } else {
             // either user does not exist, or the password is incorrect
             // call back Login page
             getServletConfig().getServletContext().getRequestDispatcher
("/ShoppingCart/Login.jsp?msgStatus=LoginFail" + "").forward(request, response);
        }
   }
}
```

The servlet first gets the HttpSession object. It then retrieves the ConnectionBean object. If this servlet is invoked for the first time in this session, the return value is null. In that case, a new ConnectionBean object is created and stored in the session as a DBConnection attribute. The ConnectionBean class has a constructor that establishes the connection. Notice that the string constants from the DBConnectionInfo interface pass as parameters to the constructor.

The Userid must be stored in a UserBean after the user is authorized. This bean must remain available throughout the session. Hence a new UserBean must be created and be stored in the session. Similar to what occurs with the ConnectionBean, a check is made to determine whether a UserBean already exists in the session. If it is not available, a new instance is created. A session variable, SomebodyIn, is a flag to identify whether a user's logged in. This flag value is used in subsequent pages to confirm a valid flow of the application. The UserBean's setUserID and setPassword methods are used to store the Userid and password the user enters. These values are obtained by using the HttpServletRequest object request that comes as a parameter to the service method. Then a call to the validateUser method of the UserBean is made. The method returns a true value if the user is a valid user. If true, the session variable SomebodyIn is set to a true value and the control transfers to the product catalog page with the msgStatus parameter set to a value of LoginOk. If the user is invalid, the validateUser method returns a false value, in which case the control transfers back to the login page, with the parameter msgStatus holding a value of LoginFail. Figure 14-7 depicts the screen on an invalid authorization.

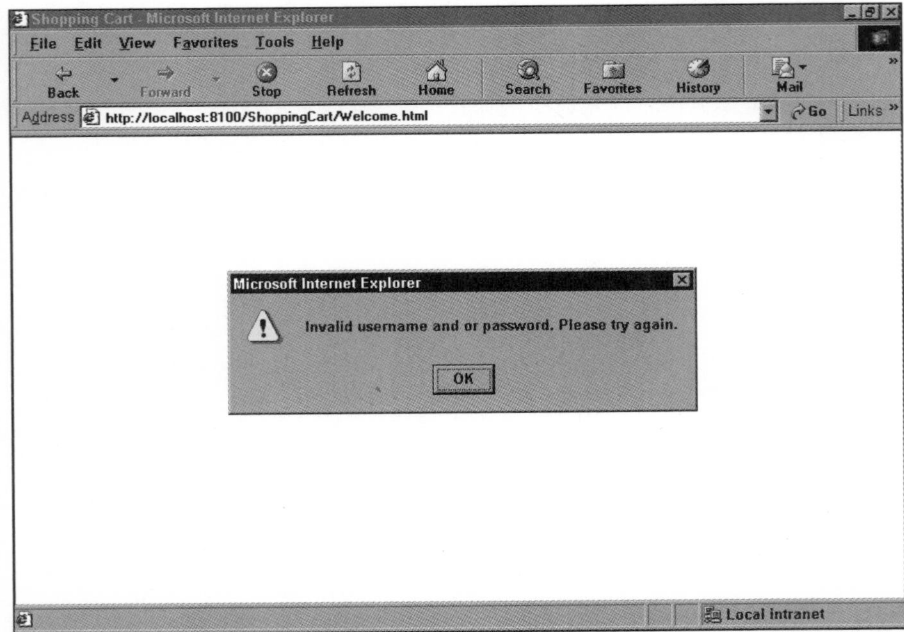

Figure 14-7: Invalid Userid/password

The product catalog page displays the list of products available. The user can click a product description to order that product. Listing 14-14 is the code present in `ProductCatalog.jsp`.

Listing 14-14

```
<%--
ProductCatalog page displays all the products available.
A link is provided for every product. Clicking the product
leads to the order form page.
--%>

<%@page language="java" import="java.sql.*,java.util.*"%>
<%!
// session variable
private HttpSession session;

// connection variable
private Connection con;

%>
<%
// get session
session=request.getSession();
// Check if user has logged in
Boolean b = (Boolean) session.getAttribute("SomebodyIn");
if(b==null || !b.booleanValue()) {
//     user not logged in, transfer the page to Welcome.html
%>
     <html>
     <head>
     <script language="JavaScript">
     window.open("Welcome.html","_self");
     </script>
     </head>
     </html>
<%
     //stop processing, user has not logged in
     return;
}
// Get Connection Bean stored in the session
servletbible.beans.ConnectionBean cb = (servletbible.beans.ConnectionBean)
session.getAttribute("DBConnection");

// get the connection
con = cb.getConnection();
%>
<html>
```

Continued

Listing 14-14 *(continued)*

```
<body>
<form id=frmCatalog name=frmCatalog>
<table border=0 cellpadding=0 cellspacing=0 width="50%">
<tr>
<td align=left>
<!-- Link to view Shopping Cart -->
<a href="/ShoppingCart/ShoppingCart.jsp">Shopping Cart</a>
</td>
<td align=right>
<!-- Link for logging out -->
<a href="/ShoppingCart/Logout.jsp">Logout</a>
</td>
</tr>
</table>
<br>
<%
// msgStatus holds status value to be processed
String msgStatus = request.getParameter("msgStatus");

if(msgStatus != null) {
     if(msgStatus.equalsIgnoreCase("LoginOk")) {
          // This page has come after the user has logged in
          servletbible.beans.UserBean ub = (servletbible.beans.UserBean)
session.getAttribute("User");

          // Get user name to display a welcome message
          String userName = ub.getFirstName() + " " + ub.getLastName();
%>
          <!-- Welcome message -->
          <h3>Welcome <%=userName%>, to Shopping Cart</h3>
<%
     } else if(msgStatus.equalsIgnoreCase("ProAdded")) {
          // This page has come after a product
          // has been successfully added to the cart.
          // Display product added message
%>
          <h3>Product added to Shopping Cart</h3>
<%
     } else if(msgStatus.equalsIgnoreCase("ProAddErr")) {
          // This page has come after an error during
          // addition of a product in the cart.
          // Display the error message
%>
          <h3>Could not add product to Shopping Cart due to Database error</h3>
<%
     }
}
%>
<p>
<h2>Product Catalog</h2>
```

```
<%-- Create instance of ProductBean --%>
<jsp:useBean id="proBean" class="servletbible.beans.ProductBean" scope="page"/>

<%
// Get all the products calling the getAllProducts method.
// The connection to the database is passed as a parameter
Vector vt = proBean.getAllProducts(con);

if(vt == null || vt.size()==0) {
     // either an error occured or the product table is empty
%>
     <br><h3>Could not complete Database operation. Try again ....</h3>
<%
}
else {
     // Display all the products
%>
     <h3>Click on any of the product description to add to Cart.</h3>
     <table border=1 cellpadding=0 cellspacing = 0 width="70%">
     <tr bgcolor=#DDDDDD>
     <th>
     Product ID
     </th>
     <th>
     Product Description
     </th>
     <th>
     Price (in Rs.)
     </th>
     <th>
     Units
     </th>
     </tr>
<%
     // go through the vector
     for (int i=0;i < vt.size(); i++) {
          servletbible.beans.ProductBean pb = (servletbible.beans.ProductBean)
vt.elementAt(i);
%>
          <tr>
               <td>
                    <!-- Product ID -->
                    <%=pb.getProductID()%>
               </td>
               <td>
                    <!-- Product Description with link -->
                    <%--
                         The product id and product description are
                         passed as parameter
                    --%>
                    <a href="/ShoppingCart/OrderForm.jsp?prdId=<%=pb.getProductID
```

Continued

Listing 14-14 *(continued)*

```
()%>&prdDesc=<%=pb.getProductDescription()%>">
                    <%=pb.getProductDescription()%>
                    </a>
               </td>
               <td align=right>
                    <!-- Price -->
                    <%=pb.getPrice()%>
               </td>
               <td align=center>
                    <!-- Unit of Measurement -->
                    <%=pb.getUnits()%>
               </td>
          </tr>
<%
     }
%>
     </table>
<%
}
%>
<br>
<table border=0 cellpadding=0 cellspacing=0 width="50%">
<tr>
<td align=left>
<!-- Link to view Shopping Cart -->
<a href="/ShoppingCart/ShoppingCart.jsp">Shopping Cart</a>
</td>
<td align=right>
<!-- Link for logging out -->
<a href="/ShoppingCart/Logout.jsp">Logout</a>
</td>
</tr>
</table>
</form>
</body>
</html>
```

Initially, a check is made to determine whether any user's logged in. The session variable `SomebodyIn` tells whether somebody's in. If the value is `null` or `false`, control goes back to the Welcome page, which displays the login page. If everything is OK, an instance of `ConnectionBean` is obtained and the `getConnection` method of the `ConnectionBean` returns a connection handle.

The message status of this page can come in three flavors: If the value of `msgStatus` parameter is `LoginOk`, this screen comes after a successful login. If the `msgStatus` is

ProAdded, the user's added an item into the shopping cart successfully and returned back to this page. If the msgStatus is ProAddErr, some error occurred during the addition of an item into the shopping cart, and the control returns to this page. Appropriate messages appear on-screen for all these status messages.

A user can also reach this page without any message status by clicking the link on the order form page or from the shopping cart page.

A new instance of ProductBean is created using the <jsp:useBean> JSP tag. Using this instance, a call to the getAllProducts method returns a Vector object holding a collection of ProductBeans. Then the program goes through a loop, processing each element in the vector. All the products appear in a table format. Each product appears as a row in the table. The product description appears as a link. On clicking the link, the user goes to the order page. Links across the pages enable the user to view the shopping cart and to log out of the application. The Logout link always takes the user to the login page. Figure 14-8 shows the product catalog page.

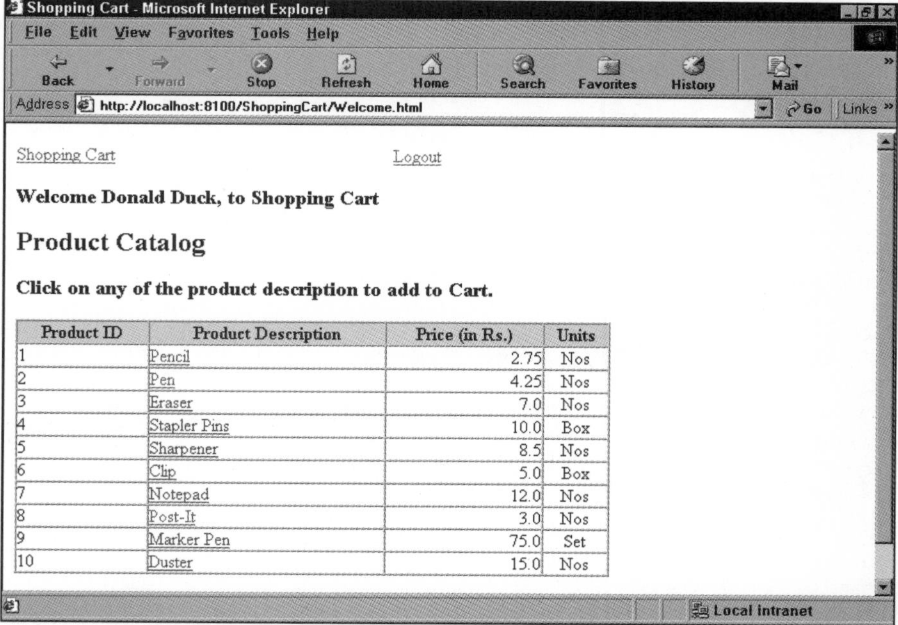

Figure 14-8: Product catalog page after a successful login

If the user clicks a product, the control transfers to the order page. The order page comes from the JSP page OrderForm.jsp, which is shown in Listing 14-15.

Listing 14-15

```
<%--
OrderForm displays a page to enter the quantity
of the product selected from the product catalog page
--%>

<%@page language="java"%>
<%!
// session variable
private HttpSession session;
%>
<%
//get the session variable
session=request.getSession();

// Check if user has logged in
Boolean b = (Boolean) session.getAttribute("SomebodyIn");
if(b==null || !b.booleanValue()) {
//     user not logged in, transfer the page to Welcome.html
%>
     <html>
     <head>
     <script language="JavaScript">
     window.open("Welcome.html","_self");
     </script>
     </head>
     </html>
<%
     //stop processing, user has not logged in
     return;
}
//get the product details passed as parameter
String prdId = request.getParameter("prdId");
String prdDesc = request.getParameter("prdDesc");

// If parameters are missing by any chance
// transfer the control to previous page
// which should be product catalog page

if(prdId == null || prdDesc == null) {
%>
     <html>
     <head>
     <script language="JavaScript">
     history.go(-1);
     </script>
     </head>
     </html>
<%
     // stop processing and return
     return;
}
```

```
%>
<html>
<head>
<script language="JavaScript">
// validateQuantity function validates
// the quantity of product needed, entered
// by the user.
function validateQuantity() {
     // get the value from text box.
     var qty = document.frmOrder.qtyRequired.value;

     // parse the text into float value.
     // If its not a number (NaN) parseFloat returns NaN
     var num = parseFloat(qty);

     // NaN value can be checked using the isNaN function
     // If its not a number or the quantity is less than
     // or equal to zero display error message
     if(isNaN(num) || num <= 0.0) {
          alert("Enter a valid numeric value");
          document.frmOrder.qtyRequired.value = "";
          document.frmOrder.qtyRequired.focus();
          return;
     }

     //quantity ok, submit the page
     document.frmOrder.submit();
}
</script>
</head>
<body>
<%-- On submitting the page, control is transferred
to SubmitOrder page --%>
<form id=frmOrder name=frmOrder action="/ShoppingCart/SubmitOrder.jsp">
<table border=0 cellpadding=0 cellspacing=0 width="50%">
<tr>
    <td align=left>
       <!-- Link to Product Catalog page -->
       <a href="ProductCatalog.jsp">Product Catalog</a>
    </td>
    <td align=center>
       <!-- Link to Shopping Cart page -->
       <a href="ShoppingCart.jsp">Shopping Cart</a>
    </td>
    <td align=right>
       <!-- Link for logging out -->
       <a href="Logout.jsp">Logout</a>
    </td>
</tr>
</table>
<br>
<table>
```

Continued

Listing 14-15 *(continued)*

```
<tr>
    <td>
       Product ID
    </td>
    <td>
       <!-- Display Product ID in a readonly text box -->
       <input type=text id=productID name=productID value=<%=prdId%> ReadOnly>
       </input>
    </td>
</tr>
<tr>
    <td>
       <!-- Display Product Description in a readonly text box -->
       Product Description
    </td>
    <td>
       <input type=text id=productDescription name=productDescription
        value=<%=prdDesc%> ReadOnly>
       </input>
    </td>
</tr>
<tr>
    <td>
       Quantity Required
    </td>
    <td>
       <!-- Textbox for entering quantity required -->
       <input type=text id=qtyRequired name=qtyRequired value="">
    </td>
</tr>
<tr>
    <td colspan=2 align=center>
       <!-- Button which transfers control to Submit Order page
after validating the quantity -->
       <input type=button id=btnSubmit name=btnSubmit value="Continue >>>"
       onclick=validateQuantity()>
       </input>
    </td>
</tr>
</table>
<br>
<table border=0 cellpadding=0 cellspacing=0 width="50%">
<tr>
    <td align=left>
       <!-- Link to Product Catalog page -->
       <a href="ProductCatalog.jsp">Product Catalog</a>
    </td>
    <td align=center>
<!-- Link to Shopping Cart page -->
```

```
<a href="/ShoppingCart/ShoppingCart.jsp">Shopping Cart</a>
    </td>
    <td align=right>
       <!-- Link for logging out -->
       <a href="/ShoppingCart/Logout.jsp">Logout</a>
    </td>
</tr>
</table>
</form>
</body>
</html>
```

After checking whether a user's logged in and the flow of the application is intact, the program checks whether the necessary parameters, `prdId` and `prdDesc`, have valid values. These parameters pass from the product catalog page. The productid and the description appear in a read-only text box. The generated HTML also displays a text box for entering the quantity that the user requires for the product that he's selected to order. This text box accepts a positive numeric value, which the JavaScript function `validateQuantity` validates. If the entered quantity is valid, control transfers to the `SubmitOrder` JSP page, which creates a `ProductBean` and stores the values for updating. Figure 14-9 shows the order form page.

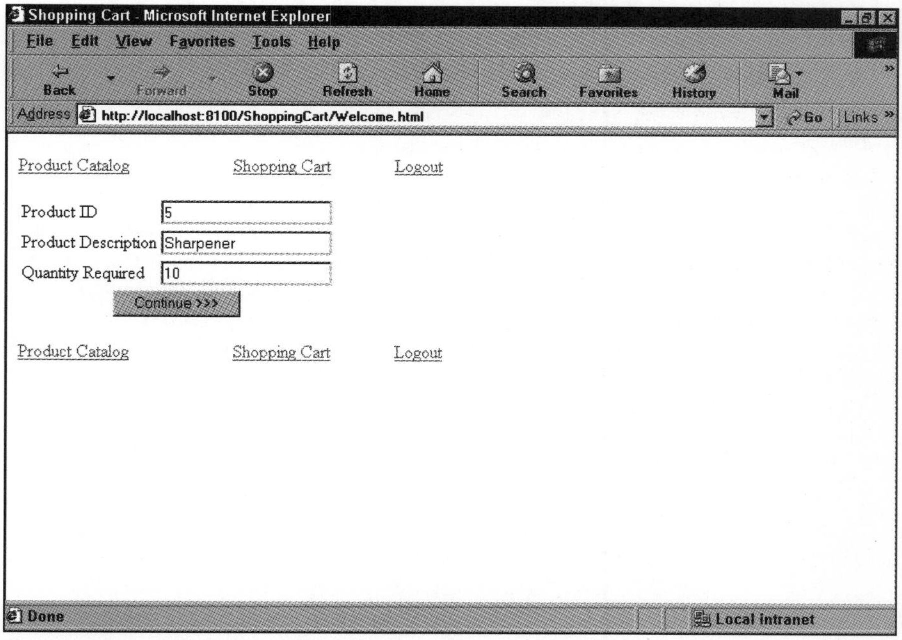

Figure 14-9: Order form page

The SubmitOrder JSP page is an intermediary that encapsulates the data pertaining to the product that the user ordered into a new ProductBean. After doing that, the page forwards the control to the OrderForm servlet, which takes care of calling the appropriate Bean's method to update the information in the database. The functionality that the SubmitOrder JSP page performs could very well occur in the OrderForm servlet. The main idea here is to demonstrate that JSP pages can also act as intermediary pages apart from their usual usage as views. We know that, finally, all JSP pages convert to servlets and are executed to generate the static HTML. Listing 14-16 is SubmitOrder.jsp.

Listing 14-16

```
<%--
SubmitOrder.jsp is an intermediate page.
The Page initializes a ProductBean, setting the id,
description and quantity required and forwards the
page to OrderForm servlet
--%>
<%@page language="java"%>
<jsp:useBean id="proBean" class="servletbible.beans.ProductBean"
scope="request"/>
<jsp:setProperty name="proBean" property="productID"/>
<jsp:setProperty name="proBean" property="productDescription"/>
<jsp:setProperty name="proBean" property="qtyRequired"/>
<jsp:forward page="/servlet/servletbible.ch13.examples.OrderForm"/>
```

The ProductBean is initialized with the request scope. The <jsp:setProperty> tag sets the values of the productid, description, and quantity. Then the control transfers to the OrderForm servlet.

The service method in the OrderForm servlet handles the request from the SubmitOrder JSP page. The ProductBean is requested from the SubmitOrder page. A new instance of CartBean is created. The UserBean and the ConnectionBean are obtained from the session. The addToCart method in the CartBean is invoked, passing the Connection object, ProductBean and the Userid as parameters. If the method is successful, control transfers to the product catalog page, with the msgStatus parameter set to ProAdded; otherwise, the status is set to ProAddErr. Listing 14-17 is the OrderForm.java servlet code.

Listing 14-17

```
package servletbible.ch13.examples;

import javax.servlet.*;
import javax.servlet.http.*;
```

```
import java.io.*;
import java.sql.*;
import servletbible.beans.*;

/*
 * OrderForm servlet gets the Product Bean created
 * by the SubmitOrder jsp page and calls the
 * addToCart method which adds the product to
 * Shopping cart, and transfers the control back
 * to the Product Catalog page with appropriate message
 */
public class OrderForm extends HttpServlet
{
    public void service(HttpServletRequest request, HttpServletResponse response)
throws ServletException, IOException
  {

        // Get the session variable
        HttpSession session = request.getSession();

        // Check if user logged in/session expired
        Boolean b = (Boolean) session.getAttribute("SomebodyIn");
        if(b==null || !b.booleanValue()) {
             // user not logged in or session expired
             getServletConfig().getServletContext().getRequestDispatcher
("/ShoppingCart/Welcome.html").forward(request, response);
             return;
        }

        //Get the Product Bean created in Submit Order intermediate page
        servletbible.beans.ProductBean pb = (servletbible.beans.ProductBean)
request.getAttribute("proBean");

        // Create a cart bean
        servletbible.beans.CartBean carb = new servletbible.beans.CartBean();

        // Get user information from User Bean
           servletbible.beans.UserBean ub = (servletbible.beans.UserBean)
session.getAttribute("User");
           String userId = ub.getUserID();

        // Get Connection Bean
        servletbible.beans.ConnectionBean cb = (servletbible.beans.ConnectionBean)
session.getAttribute("DBConnection");

        // Get connection handle
        Connection con = cb.getConnection();

        String page = "/ShoppingCart/ProductCatalog.jsp?";
```

Continued

Listing 14-17 *(continued)*

```
          /*
           * addToCart method in Product Bean adds the product
           * to the shopping cart against the user logged in.
           * If the operation is successful, it returns a true
           * value otherwise a false value.  Takes the connection
           * object and user id as parameter
           */
          if(carb.addToCart(con,pb,userId)) {
               // Product added successfully,
               // pass message status as ProAdded
               page += "msgStatus=ProAdded";
          }
          else {
               // Error occured during addition.
               // pass message status as ProAddErr
               page += "msgStatus=ProAddErr";
          }
          // forward the page to ProductCatalog
          getServletConfig().getServletContext().getRequestDispatcher
(page).forward(request, response);
     }
}
```

The `OrderForm` servlet is a controller and does the job of receiving the event and calling the appropriate model's methods. Figure 14-10 presents the product catalog page after adding an item into the shopping cart.

Figure 14-11 shows the product catalog page when a database error occurs after adding an item into the shopping cart.

The major code that's left out is the view/delete shopping cart code. Listing 14-18 is `ShoppingCart.jsp`.

Listing 14-18

```
<%--
ShoppingCart.jsp displays the Shopping cart for the user
who has logged in.  The user can also delete the product
he had added to the cart.  The delete link calls this same
page
--%>

<%@page language="java" import="java.sql.*,java.util.*,java.text.*"%>
%>
```

Continued

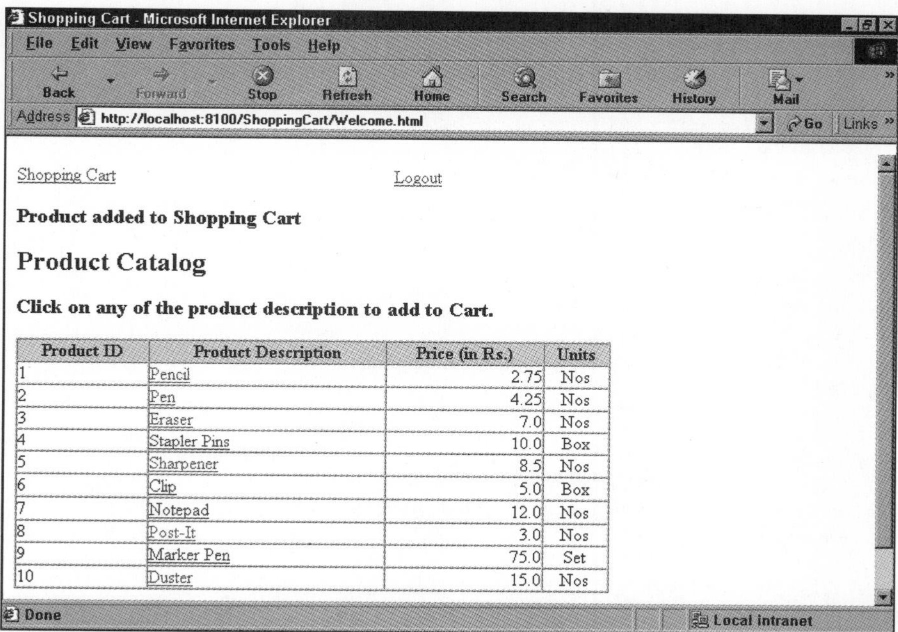

Figure 14-10: Product catalog page after successful addition of an item into the shopping cart

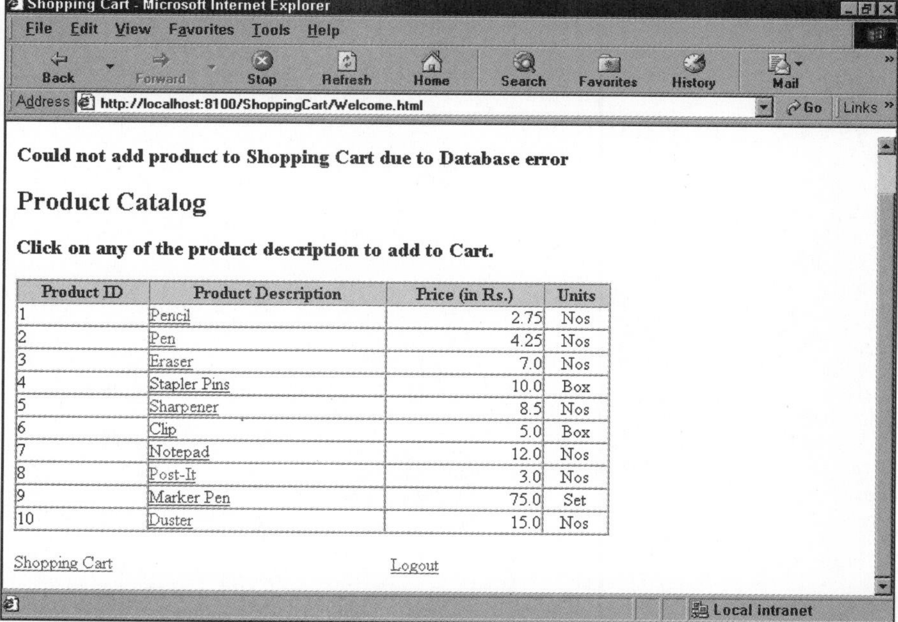

Figure 14-11: Product catalog page after a database error while adding an item into the shopping cart

Listing 14-18 *(continued)*

```
<%!
// session variable
private HttpSession session;
//connection handle
private Connection con;
%>
<%
// get session variable
session=request.getSession();
// Check if user has logged in
Boolean b = (Boolean) session.getAttribute("SomebodyIn");
if(b==null || !b.booleanValue()) {
//      user not logged in, transfer the page to Welcome.html
     <html>
     <head>
     <script language="JavaScript">
     window.open("/ShoppingCart/Welcome.html","_self");
     </script>
     </head>
     </html>
<%
     //stop processing, user has not logged in
     return;
}
// Get the connection bean
servletbible.beans.ConnectionBean cb = (servletbible.beans.ConnectionBean)
session.getAttribute("DBConnection");
// Get the connection handle
con = cb.getConnection();
%>
<%-- Instantiate the cart bean --%>
<jsp:useBean id="cartBean" class="servletbible.beans.CartBean" scope="page"/>
<html>
<body>
<form id=frmCart name=frmCart>
<table border=0 cellpadding=0 cellspacing=0 width="50%">
<tr>
<td align=left>
<!-- Link to Product Catalog page -->
<a href="/ShoppingCart/ProductCatalog.jsp">Product Catalog</a>
</td>
<td align=right>
<!-- Link for logging out -->
<a href="/ShoppingCart/Logout.jsp">Logout</a>
</td>
</tr>
</table>
<br>
<%
// Get User Bean from Session
servletbible.beans.UserBean ub = (servletbible.beans.UserBean)
```

```
session.getAttribute("User");
//Get user name
String userName = ub.getUserID();

// msgStatus holds any status value to be processed
String msgStatus = request.getParameter("msgStatus");
if(msgStatus != null) {
     if(msgStatus.equalsIgnoreCase("DeleteItem")) {
     // Delete clicked, get the Order Id
     String orderId = request.getParameter("orderId");
          // Call the deleteItem method in Cart Bean.
          // Returns true if deletion successful
          // otherwise returns false
          if(cartBean.deleteItem(con,Integer.parseInt(orderId),userName)) {
               // Display deleted
%>
               <h3>Deleted item from Shopping Cart</h3>
<%
          }
          else {
               // Could not delete. Display error message
%>
               <h3>Could not delete item from Shopping Cart due to Database
error</h3>
<%
          }
     }
}
%>
<p>
<h2>Shopping Cart</h2>
<%
// Get all the products in the cart for the user.
// viewCart method in Cart Bean takes connection object
// and user name
Vector vt = cartBean.viewCart(con,userName);
if(vt == null) {
     // Some database error occured. Display error message.
%>
     <h3>Could not complete Database operation. Try again ....</h3>
<%
}
else if(vt.size() == 0) {
     // Cart is empty
%>
     <h3><I>Shopping Cart is empty</I></h3>
<%
}
else {
     // Display all the items in a table
%>
     <table border=1 cellpadding=0 cellspacing = 0 width="90%">
```

Continued

Listing 14-18 *(continued)*

```
     <tr bgcolor=#DDDDDD>
          <th>
             
          </th>
          <th>
            Product ID
          </th>
          <th>
            Product Description
          </th>
          <th>
            Date
          </th>
          <th>
            Price
          </th>
          <th>
            Quantity
          </th>
          <th>
            Amount
          </th>
     </tr>
<%
     double price;
     double quantity;
     double amount;
     // DateFormat object to format date in dd mmm yyyy format
     DateFormat df = DateFormat.getDateInstance(DateFormat.LONG);

     //DecimalFormat object to format decimal value
     DecimalFormat dcmlf = new DecimalFormat("#,##0.00");
     String dt;
     String amt;
     for (int i=0;i < vt.size(); i++) {
          // Each element in the vector is a Cart Bean instance
          servletbible.beans.CartBean cab = (servletbible.beans.CartBean)
vt.elementAt(i);

          // Get price
          price = cab.getPrice();

          // Get Quantity
          quantity = cab.getQuantity();

          // Compute Amount
          amount = quantity*price;

          // Format amount
          amt = dcmlf.format(amount);
```

```
            // Get date and format in dd mmm yyyy
            dt = df.format(cab.getDate());
%>
            <tr>
                 <td>
                 <%--
                      Delete link, pass DeleteItem message status
                      and Order Id.
                 --%>
                 <a href="/ShoppingCart/ShoppingCart.jsp?msgStatus=
DeleteItem&orderId=<%=cab.getOrderID()%>">
                 Delete
                 </a>
                 </td>
                 <!-- Product ID -->
                 <td align=center>
                      <%=cab.getProductID()%>
                 </td>
                 <!-- Product Description -->
                 <td>
                      <%=cab.getProductDescription()%>
                 </td>
                 <!-- Date -->
                 <td align=center>
                      <%=dt%>
                 </td>
                 <!-- Product Price -->
                 <td align=right>
                      <%=price%>
                 </td>
                 <!-- Quantity Ordered -->
                 <td align=right>
                      <%=quantity%>
                 </td>
                 <!-- Amount -->
                 <td align=right>
                      <%=amt%>
                 </td>
            </tr>
<%
     }
%>
     </table>
<%
}
%>
<br>
<table border=0 cellpadding=0 cellspacing=0 width="50%">
<tr>
<td align=left>
<!-- Link to Product Catalog page -->
<a href="/ShoppingCart/ProductCatalog.jsp">Product Catalog</a>
```

Continued

Listing 14-18 *(continued)*

```
</td>
<td align=right>
<!-- Link for logging out -->
<a href="/ShoppingCart/Logout.jsp">Logout</a>
</td>
</tr>
</table>
</form>
</body>
</html>
```

The shopping cart JSP code does the job of showing the items in the cart, as well as deleting the item from the cart. After the routine of checking whether a user's logged in, the code checks for the `msgStatus` parameter. If it contains a value of `DeleteItem`, the user's opted to remove an item from the cart, in which case the Orderid also comes as a parameter. The Userid can be obtained from the `UserBean`, which is in the session. An instance of the `CartBean` is created, and the `deleteItem` method is called, passing the database connection handle, Orderid, and the Userid as parameters. The output of the delete operation appears on screen, and the items in the cart appear on screen again. If the `msgStatus` parameter is `null`, the `viewCart` method of the `CartBean` is called. The method returns a `Vector` object, which holds all the information. The `Vector` is processed element by element and appears in a table format. A link for deleting an item is provided as the first column in the table. Notice how the `href` attribute is coded in the anchor tag:

```
<a href="/ShoppingCart/ShoppingCart.jsp
?msgStatus=DeleteItem&orderId=<%=cab.getOrderID()%>">
```

The value that the `getOrderID` method returns is embedded within the URL as a value to the `orderid` parameter. Clicking this link is going to call the same page but with the necessary parameters for deleting the item. Figure 14-12 displays the shopping cart screen.

Figure 14-13 shows the empty shopping cart screen.

The left-out code is `Logout.jsp`, which is what Listing 14-19 provides.

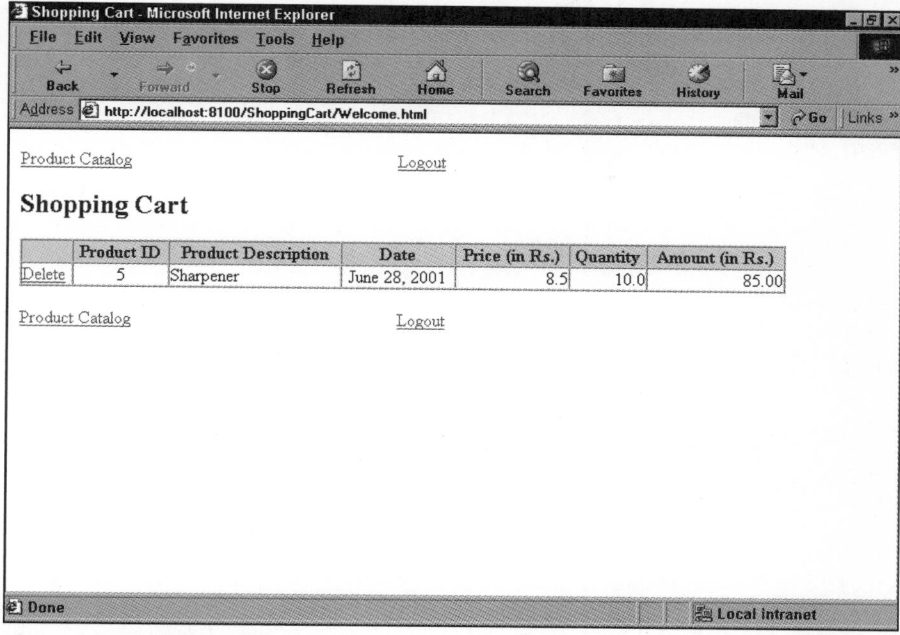

Figure 14-12: Shopping cart

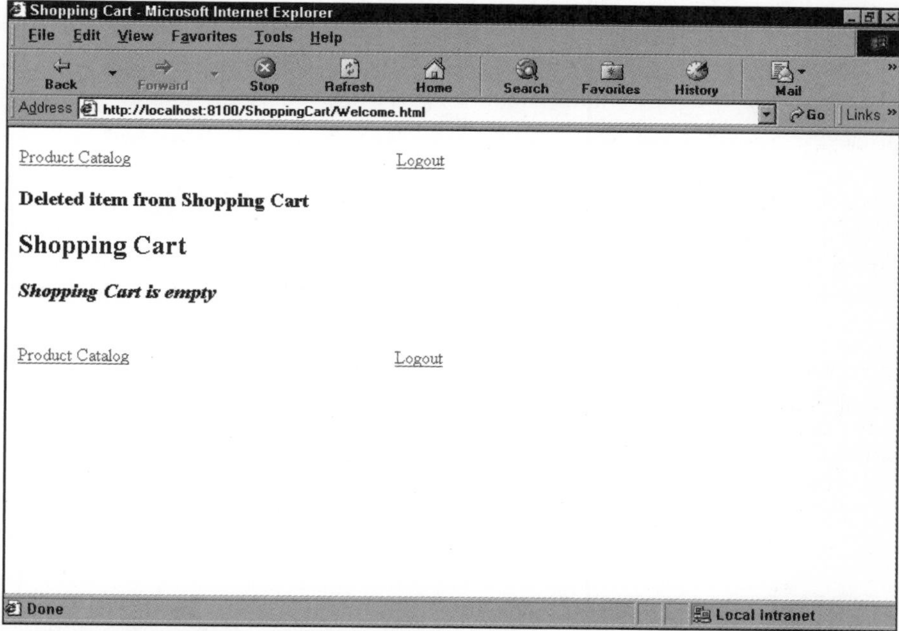

Figure 14-13: Shopping cart when empty

Listing 14-19

```
<%--
Logout JSP page removes the variables in the session, and
closes the database connection
--%>

<%@page language="java" import="java.sql.*"%>
<%!
// session variable
private HttpSession session;
// connection handle
private Connection con;
%>
<%
session=request.getSession();
Boolean b = (Boolean) session.getAttribute("SomebodyIn");
if(b!=null && b.booleanValue()) {
     // Get Connection Bean
     servletbible.beans.ConnectionBean cb = (servletbible.beans.ConnectionBean)
session.getAttribute("DBConnection");
     // Close connection
     cb.closeConnection();
     // Remove user variable from session
     session.removeAttribute("User");
     // Remove Connection Bean from session
     session.removeAttribute("DBConnection");
}
%>
<html>
<head>
<script language="JavaScript">
// transfer the control to Welcome.html
window.open("/ShoppingCart/Welcome.html","_self");
</script>
</head>
</html>
```

The code is a piece of cake and does a cleanup job. It closes the connection handle by calling the `closeConnection` method of the `ConnectionBean`. It then removes all the session variables and finally forwards the page to `Welcome.html`, which shows the login page. The `Logout.jsp` is called after the user clicks the `Logout` link, which is present in the product catalog page, order form page, and shopping cart page.

The main idea of this case study is to demonstrate the MVC architecture. If you go through the code thoroughly, you see that the entire application divides up into presentation code, business logic code, and the controller, which binds the first two. A controller can be either a servlet or a JSP page, but usually only a servlet takes up the controller's job, as a JSP page is mainly for use in embedding HTML dynamically and is more presentation oriented. Nevertheless, the option of using a servlet or a JSP is at the discretion of the programmer. The advantage in our application is that, if you need to change the look and feel of the application , you need to change only on the views or the JSP pages and need not touch the model's code. Similarly, if you need to make a change in the business logic, you need only to add new methods in the model's classes and make very minor changes needs in a controller or a view.

Summary

In this chapter, we briefly discuss design patterns, examine what an MVC architecture is, and the advantages of using an MVC architecture. We show you how you can use MVC in Java applications by using the `Observable/Observer` objects, how you can apply MVC in designing Web applications, and how you can implement it by using JavaBeans, JSP pages, and servlets. Finally, we provide a case study that develops shopping-cart examples by using the MVC architecture.

Coming up is the final part of this book, which deals with servlets and security and provides some tips on building a good Web application.

✦ ✦ ✦

CHAPTER 15

Servlets and JSP Tips and Tricks

In This Chapter

Troubleshooting

Logging

Using property files

Scheduling tasks

Documenting your application

Troubleshooting Servlets

A browser may fail to invoke a servlet for several reasons. One way to discover the problem is to check the log files the Web server provides. JRun records all events, errors, and system messages in log files. Three log files, `default-event.log`, `default-err.log`, and `default-out.log`, are created for the default application. Similarly, three log files, `admin-event.log`, `admin-err.log`, and `admin-out.log`, are created for the Admin application. The event log stores all the events such as loading classes, calling the `init` and `destroy` methods of servlets, and so on. The error log stores all exceptions thrown during the execution of a servlet. The out log stores all messages that need to be output to the console.

When a servlet is not working, the first way to know what the problem might be is to check the error log. If an exception has occurred during the execution of the servlet, a stack trace of the exception should have been recorded in the log file.

If the servlet uses package names, make sure the servlet is called with the proper package name prefixed. The most important thing is to check whether the servlet class is under the appropriate directory of the Web application. In the case of JRun, the servlet class files should be under the `WEB-INF\classes` directory.

One common problem that arises when the servlet class is not declared as public is that a 500 Internal Server Error occurs, and the error is not logged. Make sure the servlet is declared public.

Another common mistake occurs if an HTML page makes a post request to the servlet, but the servlet has only the doGet method or vice versa. This returns a 405 - Resource not allowed error. The best solution, if you are not sure which method to code, is to code one method and call it from the other method, as shown here:

```
.
.
public void doPost(HttpServletRequest request,
HttpServletResponse response) throws ServletException,
IOException {
     doGet(request,response);
}
```

Writing the service() method can also solve this problem and can handle both GET and POST requests. The service() method has priority over the doGet() and doPost() methods. Thus, if the service method is present along with a doGet() and/or doPost() method, only the service method is executed.

Debugging a servlet follows the same procedure as debugging a Java application. Either the System.out.println can be used, or messages can be output along with the HTML. But, in the latter case, it's also necessary to remove them after debugging is complete.

Troubleshooting JSP

Most Web servers that support compilation and execution of JSP pages to servlets display error messages if they encounter problems during compilation. These error messages are shown to the client's browser as a static HTML. Usually, these errors occur if the JSP syntax and semantics are not followed properly.

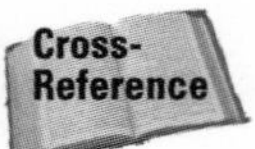

Chapter 12 and Appendix D provide the syntax and semantics for JSP.

Some Integrated Development Environment (IDE) applications support systematic debugging. This allows the programmer to go through the code step by step, simultaneously keeping track of the values and attributes of objects. For developers, whose master editor is a notepad or some sleek text editor, the best way to debug is through comments in the HTML or by directly displaying the values in the HTML. Displaying values in the HTML might alter the look and feel of the page, so it is necessary that the statements for debugging be removed after they are complete.

Errors may occur after the JSP has been converted to a servlet. These errors can be fixed in a manner similar to fixing a problem in a servlet. See the previous section, which discusses troubleshooting servlets.

Log Writer

As we have discussed already in the first section of this chapter, JRun maintains log files to store events, errors, and application-generated messages. But the problem here occurs if more than one application is running on the server. In this case, the events, errors, and console messages from all the applications are logged into the three files JRun provides by default.

One solution is that JRun can be set up to log events, errors, and console messages to a user-defined file for every application created in JRun. A separate environment can be created for every application. This creates a separated directory structure. To do this, log into the Admin module.

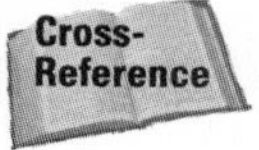

See Chapter 2 for more on the JRun Admin modules.

To create a new Web application, click the Web Applications link. This pops a new screen on the right pane (Figure 15-1). Click the Create an Application link.

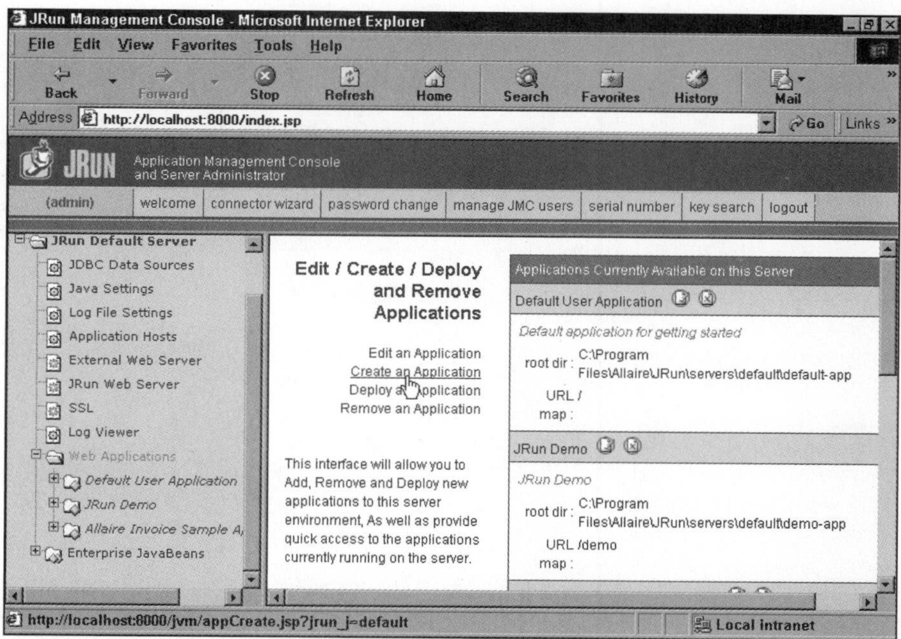

Figure 15-1: The Web Applications screen on JRun Admin

Select the Default Server (Figure 15-2). Provide the application name, the URL, and the application root directory.

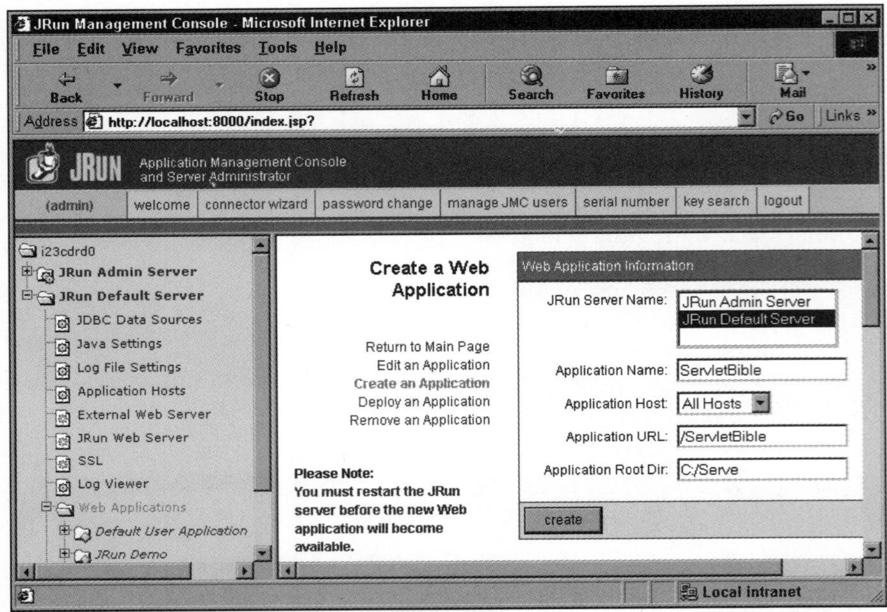

Figure 15-2: Create a new Web application.

JRun creates the following directory structure:

```
<application directory>
          |
          |
          +--WEB-INF
                |
                |
                +--classes
                |     |
                |     +-<empty>
                |
                +--lib
                |    |
                |    +-<empty>
                |
                +--web.xml
```

The HTML and JSP pages can be put under the root application directory or directories created under it. All servlet class files go under the classes directory under the WEB-INF directory.

The new application has a list of environmental variables that can be set up. This can be seen on the left menu when the Web Applications menu is expanded (Figure 15-3).

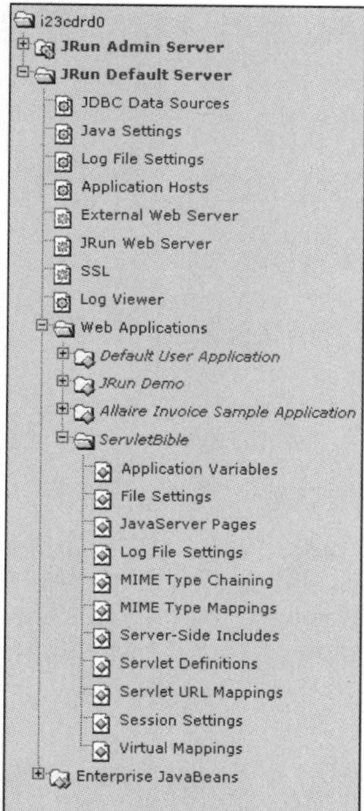

Figure 15-3: After creating a new Web application

Click Log File Settings, and press the Edit button that appears on the right pane of the screen. This pops up a new screen. Scroll down to the Event Log section. By default, the log path that appears in the text box is

```
{jrun.rootdir}/logs/{jrun.server.name}-event.log
```

`jrun.rootdir` is the JRun's root directory. `jrun.server.name` represents the server under which the application is running. In this case, it is the default server. To store the logs in the application's directory, change the value of the Event Log to the following value (shown in Figure 15-4):

```
{webapp.rootdir}/logs/{webapp.name}-event.log
```

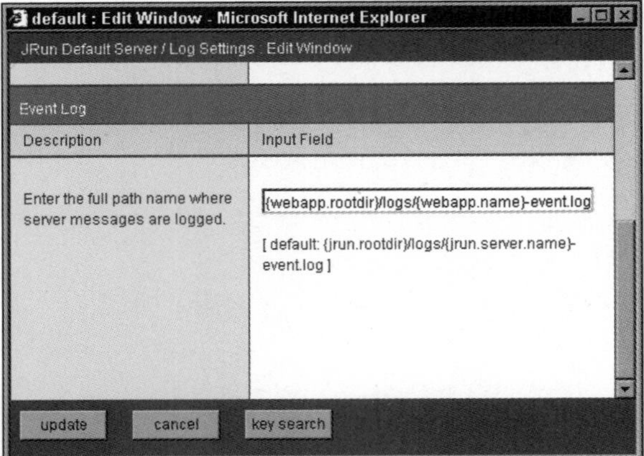

Figure 15-4: Edit the Event Log path.

This logs all events under the application's log directory.

The Web application can also write its own log file to record more information specific to the application. This provides more control and can also be useful for debugging the application. Listing 15-1 shows how to create a log file. This example is the same as the `TableViewServlet` example in Chapter 6, but it has additional statements to log in information and errors.

Listing 15-1

```
package servletbible.ch15.examples;

import javax.servlet.*;
import javax.servlet.http.*;
import java.io.*;
import java.sql.*;

/**
* Table View servlet. Displays the records in the Product
* table from the Inventory database.  The trace and error
* message if any are logged to TableView.log file under
* the logs directory.
*/

public class TableViewServlet2 extends HttpServlet
{

     //     Connection object to hold the database connection.

    Connection con;
```

```
    // PrintWriter object to write to the log file
    PrintWriter pw = null;

    // init method initializes the JDBC-ODBC connection
     public void init() {
              try {
                   // Initialize the PrintWriter object
                   // The directory default-app/Ch15/Logs should
exist
                   // under the default Web server
                   pw = new PrintWriter(new FileWriter("default-
app/Ch15/Logs/TableView.log",true));
              } catch (IOException ie) {
                   System.out.println("Error during log file
open");
                   ie.printStackTrace(System.out);
              }

              try {
                   // Get Date
                   java.util.Date d = new java.util.Date();
                   // Append date and time to log file
                   if (pw != null) {
                        pw.println(d);
                        pw.flush();
                   }
                   // Get the JDBC-ODBC connection
                   Class.forName("sun.jdbc.odbc.JdbcOdbcDriver");

                   if(pw != null) {
                        pw.println("Loaded JDBC-ODBC driver");
                        pw.flush();
                   }
                   // Inventory is the DSN name
                   con =
DriverManager.getConnection("jdbc:odbc:Inventory");

                   if(pw != null) {
                        pw.println("Connection Established to
Inventory database");
                        pw.flush();
                   }
              } catch (ClassNotFoundException cnfe) {
                   // Error during class load
                   if(pw != null) {
                        // flush stack trace to log
                        cnfe.printStackTrace(pw);
                        pw.flush();
                   } else {
```

Continued

Listing 15-1 *(continued)*

```
                    System.out.println("Could not load Jdbc-
Odbc driver");
                }
            } catch(SQLException se) {
                // Error during connection
                if(pw != null) {
                    // flush stack trace to log
                    se.printStackTrace(pw);
                    pw.flush();
                } else {
                    System.out.println("SQL Exception
caught!");
                }
            }

    }

    /**
    * Override the doGet method
    *
    * @param request the client's request
    * @param response the servlet's response
    */
    public void doGet(HttpServletRequest request,
HttpServletResponse response) throws ServletException, IOException
      {
                /**
            * Sets the content type
            */
                response.setContentType("text/html");

                // Log Date and Time
                if (pw != null) {
                    java.util.Date d = new java.util.Date();
                    pw.println(d);
                    pw.flush();
                }

            PrintWriter out = response.getWriter();

            /**
            * Prints the records in Product table.
            */
            out.println("<html><head><title>Table View
Servlet</title></head><body>");
                out.println("<H1>Table: Prodcut</H1>");

                /**
```

```
                * getRecords method gets the detail from the
                * table and forma a html table
                */
            out.println(getRecords());

            out.println("</body></html>");
                out.close();
    }

    private String getRecords()
    {
        String html = "";
        try {
            if (pw != null) {
                pw.println("Preparing to fetch records from
product table..");
                pw.flush();
            }
            // Create a statement
            Statement stmt = con.createStatement();

            if (pw != null) {
                pw.println("Executing query \"Select * from
product\"");
                pw.flush();
            }

            // Create a resultset passing the query to
executeQuery method
            ResultSet rs = stmt.executeQuery("Select * from
product");

            /**
            * ResultSetMetaData stores information about
            * the column names, their types etc.
            */
            ResultSetMetaData rsmd = rs.getMetaData();

            //get the column count
            int colCount = rsmd.getColumnCount();
            html = "<table cellspacing=0 cellpadding=0
border=1>";

            // take the field names to display them as table
header
            for(int i=1;i<=colCount;i++) {
                html += "<th>";
                html += rsmd.getColumnName(i);
                html += "</th>";
```

Continued

Listing 15-1 *(continued)*

```
            }

            if (pw != null) {
                pw.println("Processing the result set and
populating in HTML table");
                pw.flush();
            }

            // Go through the result set to fetch records
            while(rs.next()) {
                html += "<tr>";
                /**
                * Get the data type of each column and based on
that
                * use the getXXX method in the ResultSet object
                */
                for(int i=1;i<=colCount;i++) {
                    html += "<td>";

                    // Types object has the list of all data
types supported in standard SQL
                    // getColumnType gets a data type for a
particular column
                    switch(rsmd.getColumnType(i)) {
                        case Types.INTEGER:
                            html += rs.getInt(i);
                            break;
                        case Types.FLOAT:
                            html += rs.getFloat(i);
                            break;
                        case Types.DOUBLE:
                                html += rs.getDouble(i);
                            break;
                        case Types.VARCHAR:
                            html += rs.getString(i);
                            break;
                    }
                    html += "</td>";
                }
                html += "</tr>";
            }
            html += "</table>";

            if (pw != null) {
                pw.println("Closing ResultSet and Statement");
                pw.flush();
            }
```

```
                // Close the result set and statement
                rs.close();
                stmt.close();

                // return HTML
                return html;
            } catch(SQLException se) {
                // some error occured during database operation
                // Log the error
                if (pw != null) {
                    pw.println("Error occured during database
operation.");
                    se.printStackTrace(pw);
                    pw.flush();
                }
                else {
                    se.printStackTrace();
                }

                // return error message
                return se.getMessage();
            }
        }
        public void destroy() {
            try {
                // Close the connection
                if (pw != null) {
                    pw.println("Closing Connection to Inventory
database..");
                    pw.flush();
                }
                con.close();
            } catch(SQLException se) {
                if (pw != null) {
                    pw.println("Error closing Connection");
                    pw.flush();
                }
                else {
                    System.out.println("Error closing Connection");
                }
            }
            // Close log file
            if(pw != null)
                pw.close();
        }
}
//End of TableViewServlet2 Servlet
```

In the `init` method, the log file is opened and assigned to a `PrintWriter` object. The path of the file should exist; otherwise, a `FileNotFoundException` occurs. The `flush` method of the `PrintWriter` object makes sure the output is flushed immediately.

Note how we dump the stack trace when an exception occurs. All exceptions inherit the `Exception`, class and the `Exception` class extends the `java.lang.Throwable` class. The `Throwable` class has a method called `printStackTrace`. This method takes a `PrintWriter` object as parameter. Thus, passing the `pw` object in Listing 15-1 to this method dumps the stack trace to the file. Figure 15-5 displays a sample log file generated.

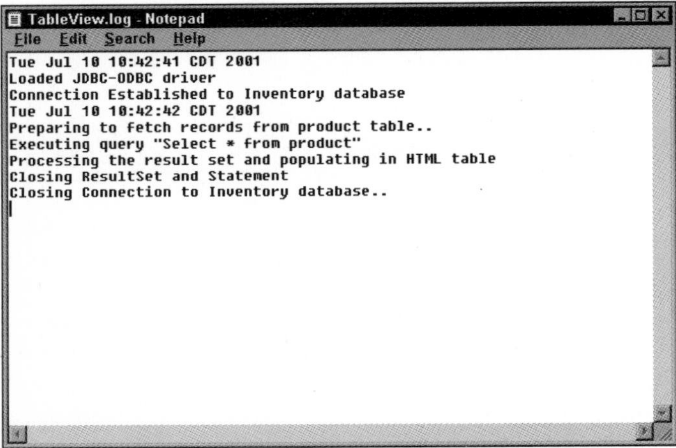

Figure 15-5: Log file generated after running TableViewServlet2 servlet

We've illustrated a sample and simple custom log generation. When dealing with applications such as the Shopping Cart example we see in Chapter 13, a separate set of classes can be dedicated to dealing with storing information, errors, and debugging messages. More functionality, such as file rolling and error severity, can be added.

Property Files

Property files are useful for attaining and storing key value pairs in files. When an application needs to use a lot of parameters or attributes, it is best to store them in a property file and to access it from the application. A property file is just like another text file with a key value pair. The key is identification, and the value is a definition to the key. When property files are used, new attributes can be added to the file but not to the code. Similarly, any value change needs to be reflected only in the property file, reducing the time taken to compile the code and restart everything. The `Properties` class in the `java.util` package has the necessary methods to manipulate property files. It extends `HashtableProperties` to incorporate some of its functionality. The following lists the functionality the `Properties` class provides:

- Loading key/value pairs into a `Properties` object from a file or stream
- Retrieving a value based on its key
- Listing all keys and their values
- Enumerating over the keys
- Saving properties to a file or stream

Table 15-1 shows the methods available in the `Properties` class.

Table 15-1
Properties class methods

Method	*Description*
`String getProperty(String key)`	Returns the value for the key specified in the parameter
`String getProperty(String key, String defaultValue)`	Same as the preceding but returns the default value instead of `null` if the key is not found
`void list(PrintStream out)`	Lists all the key value pairs to the specified output stream
`void list(PrintWriter out)`	Same as the preceding
`void load(InputStream in)`	Loads the key value pairs from the given input stream
`Enumeration propertyNames()`	Gives an enumeration of all the keys in this property object
`Object setProperty(String key, String value)`	Sets the key value property. This method internally calls the `put` method of the `HashtableProperties` class. Because property files can hold only strings, only string objects are accepted for the key value pair.
`void store(OutputStream out, String header)`	Sends all key value pairs to the stream. The method sends the data in a format that can be retrieved by using the `load` method. Header information is also sent to the output stream.

Here is an example of using the Properties class. The GetData HTML gets two values for attributes: name and age. Then it calls a servlet named PropertyDisplay, which stores the values into a property file, retrieves the values from the property file, and displays them. The GetData HTML displays two text boxes: one for name and one for age (Figure 15-6). After the user presses Submit, control is transferred to the PropertyDisplay servlet. Listing 15-2 is the GetData.html.

Listing 15-2

```
<html>
<title>
     Property File Example
</title>
<body>
<form id=frmProp name=frmProp method=post
action="/servlet/servletbible.ch15.examples.PropertyDisplay">
<table border=0>
<tr>
     <td>
          Name
     </td>
     <td>
          <input type=text id=txtName name=txtName>
          </input>
     </td>
</tr>
<tr>
     <td>
          Age
     </td>
     <td>
          <input type=text id=txtAge name=txtAge>
          </input>
     </td>
</tr>
<tr>
     <td colspan=2>
          <input type=Submit id=btnSubmit name=btnSubmit>
          </input>
     </td>
</tr>
</table>
</form>
</body>
</html>
```

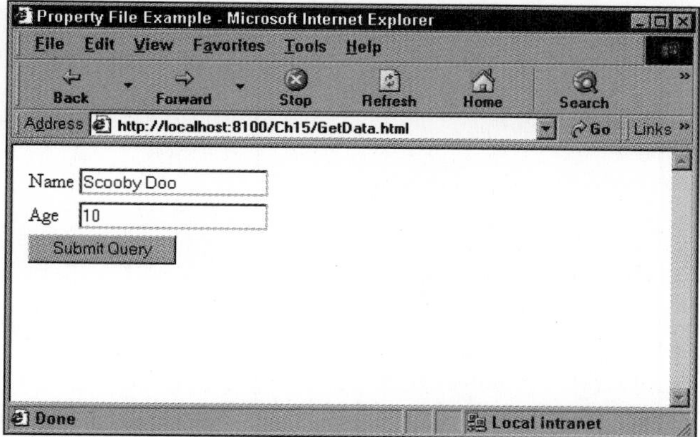

Figure 15-6: GetData HTML getting name and age from the user

Listing 15-3 is the code for the `PropertyDisplay.java` file. The program opens a `FileOutputStream` object, `fos`, with the property filename. Note that the path given along with the filename has to exist. A new `Properties` object, `p`, is created. Then the code gets the values for name and age that are entered in the previous page through the `request` object. If these values are not `null`, they are stored in the `Properties` object by calling the `setProperties` method. Then a call to the `store` method on the `Properties` object `p` is called, with `fos` as a parameter that stores the `Name` and `Age` attributes in the property file.

Listing 15-3

```
package servletbible.ch15.examples;

import javax.servlet.*;
import javax.servlet.http.*;
import java.io.*;
import java.util.*;

/*
 * PropertyDisplay servlet, gets the information from the
 * previous page, stores it in the property file and
 * retrieves it back and displays it
 */
```

Continued

Listing 15-3 *(continued)*

```
public class PropertyDisplay extends HttpServlet
{

     public void doPost(HttpServletRequest request,
HttpServletResponse response) throws ServletException, IOException {
          /**
          * Sets the content type
          */
          response.setContentType("text/html");
          PrintWriter out = response.getWriter();
          out.println("<html><title>Property File
Example</title><body>");
          try {
               // Open the property file for writing
               // Path has to exist
               FileOutputStream fos = new FileOutputStream("default-
app/Ch15/Property/personal.property");

               // Create Properties object
               Properties p = new Properties();

               // Get name and age from previous page
               String name = request.getParameter("txtName");
               String age = request.getParameter("txtAge");

               // If both of them are not null store it in the
               // property file
               if(name != null && age != null) {
                    p.setProperty("Name",new String(name));
                    p.setProperty("Age",new String(age));
                    p.store(fos,"Personal");
               }

               // close output stream
               fos.close();

               // Open the property file for reading
               // Path has to exist
               FileInputStream fis = new FileInputStream("default-
app/Ch15/Property/personal.property");

               // Load the properties
               p.load(fis);

               // Get the properties
               name = p.getProperty("Name");
               age = p.getProperty("Age");
```

```
                // Display the properties
                out.println("Values stored and retrieved from
property file");
                out.println("<br>");
                out.println("Name: " + name + "<br>");
                out.println("Age: " + age);
            } catch(IOException ioe) {
                // Display exception
                out.println("Exception occured :<br>");
                out.println(ioe.getMessage());
            }
            out.println("</body></html>");
            out.close();
        }

        public void doGet(HttpServletRequest request,
HttpServletResponse response) throws ServletException, IOException {
            doPost(request,response);
        }
}
```

After storing the values, a `FileInputStream` object, `fis`, is opened to retrieve the attributes from the property file. The Name and Age attributes are retrieved using the `getProperty` method of the `Properties` object, `p`. These values are then sent back to the client by embedding them in the HTML (Figure 15-7).

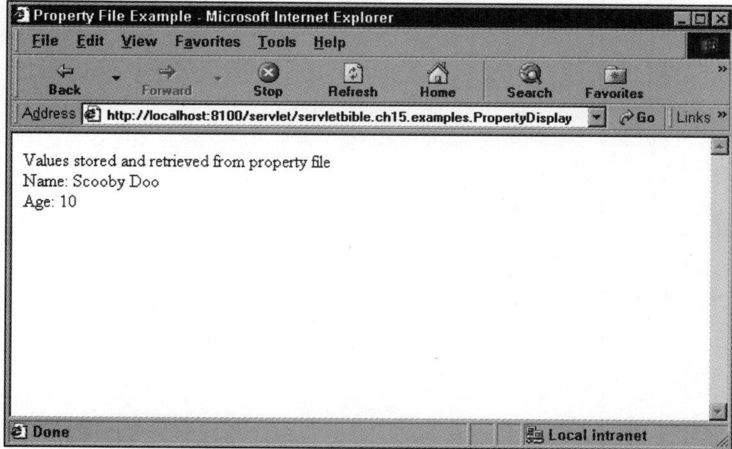

Figure 15-7: PropertyDisplay servlet displaying values from the property file

The following is the content of the property file `personal.property`:

```
#Personal
#Tue Jul 10 15:53:13 CDT 2001
Name=Scooby\ Doo
Age=10
```

Look at the header. The value `Personal` is passed as a parameter to the `store` method. The second line holds the date and time the property file is created. Also note that spaces are separated with the escape sequence "\ ".

Property files can be best used to store information related to database connections and file locations in the application. These values have the scope of change in the future. Thus, by storing them in a property file, altering the values of these attributes does not affect the code in any way.

Synchronization

One of the problems developers face is how to deal with concurrent requests on shared/common resources. For example, one thread may require write access to a particular file, while another thread may want to read it at the same time and still another thread may want write access. We need to avoid the situation in which competing threads deny each other access to the resource, thus preventing program flow from occurring (also known as *deadlock*). Java assists you in this area by providing the `synchronized` reserved word. In the previous example, modules of code involved in performing file access and read/write operations are known as the critical components of the program.

For example, look at the following snippet:

```
public static synchronized void AppendFile(File fname,String
fileEntry) {

        BufferedWriter bw = null;

        try
        {
            bw = new BufferedWriter(new FileWriter(fileName, true));
            bw.write(fileEntry);
            bw.newLine();
            bw.flush();
            bw.close();

        }
        catch (IOException ioe) {
        System.out.println(ioe);
        }

    }
```

In this snippet, we have the method AppendFile, and the critical code is the body of this method. In appending data to a file, we want to allow one-at-a-time access to the file. By placing the keyword static in front of the method, we ensure that only one instance of this method is running. By placing the synchronized keyword in front of the respective method, we ensure sequential access to file resources and data integrity in the file.

In reality, synchronization is a much more complex problem than depicted here. The synchronized Java reserved word is a transparent solution that assists in dealing with this problem by allowing concurrent requests (to shared/common resources) to be processed equitably.

Scheduling Tasks

The java.util package of the Java language contains a couple of classes that are very useful in scheduling tasks: Timer and TimerTask. The Timer class is used to create Timer objects and to set the respective time(s) at which the scheduled task is executed. The TimerTask class implements the Runnable interface, and it is in this class that the code is placed (that is, the run() method of the class).

Now we look at an example of how we can schedule a task to run at a specified time. First, we instantiate the Timer class and declare the time at which we want to run the task, as follows:

```
import java.util.*;

Timer timer = new Timer();
Date time = new Date(60000 + System.currentTimeMillis());
```

Here we set the time to run the scheduled task to be one hour after running this program. The final step is to use the schedule() method to schedule the task to be run, as follows:

```
// Here we are instantiating the created task class
task tk = new task;

timer.schedule(tk, time);
```

tk refers to an instance of the task class. task contains the work performed one hour after the current time.

The task class extends the abstract class TimerTask and overrides the run() method in which the code for the work to be done is contained:

```
class task extends TimerTask{
        public void run(){
           // The code for the task should go here.
```

```
    }
}
```

If we take a basic example and put this together, we may get something like this:

```
import java.util.*;

public class Schedule {
    public static void main(String args[]) {
        Timer timer = new Timer();
        Date time = new Date(System.currentTimeMillis() + 5000);

        task tk = new task();

        timer.schedule(tk, time);

    }
}

class task extends TimerTask{
        public void run(){
        System.out.print("Hello World");
         }
        }
```

In this example, we have a program scheduled to print `Hello World` in the console five seconds after we execute the `Schedule` class.

The `Timer` class can also be used to run tasks repeatedly at specified periods. We can simply use the `scheduleAtFixedRate` method to do this. If we modify the code from `timer.schedule(tk, time)` to `timer.scheduleAtFixedRate(tk, 10000, 2000)`, the first `Hello World` is printed on the screen after 10 seconds, and every other `Hello World` is printed on the screen two seconds after the previous one. Refer to the `Timer` and `TimerTask` classes in the API to see the available methods in these classes.

Flushing the Output Stream

When the output stream's `close` or `flush` method is called, the buffer is cleared, and all the output is transmitted to the client. Sometimes it may be necessary to flush the buffer more than once within the same program. This forces information to the client before the complete page is sent. This might be useful when some banner has to be displayed on the page and the page might take some processing time before it is displayed. The disadvantage of flushing the output stream is that after the stream is flushed it has to establish a new connection with the Web server to transmit data. When there are lot of images to be loaded in a page, frequent flushing forces all text to the client while the images are loading.

Here is sample code that flushes some output and waits for five seconds before it completes transmitting the complete page:

```
package servletbible.ch15.examples;

import javax.servlet.*;
import javax.servlet.http.*;
import java.io.*;

/*
 * This servlet displays a message and
 * waits for 5 seconds to complete the
 * final message
 */
public class Flush extends HttpServlet
{

     public void service(HttpServletRequest request,
HttpServletResponse response) throws ServletException, IOException {
          // Sets the content type
          response.setContentType("text/html");

          PrintWriter out = response.getWriter();

          out.println("<html><body>");
          out.println("Before Flushing.....<br>");

          // Flush the output
          out.flush();

          try {
               // sleep for 5 secs
               Thread.sleep(5000);
          } catch(InterruptedException ie) {
               ie.printStackTrace();
          }

          // Display the final message
          out.println("After sleeping for 5 secs, the page is
complete");
          out.println("</body></html>");
          out.close();
     }
}
```

Note **This example might not work on a browser that does not support loading of partial data.**

This code is self-explanatory. To make the client wait, the code purposefully makes the servlet execution thread sleep for five seconds. Before the thread sleeps, the output stream is flushed. This forces the statement `out.println("Before Flushing.....")` to be sent to client. The client displays this message; finally, after five seconds, the final message is displayed. Figures 15-8 and 15-9 show the output generated.

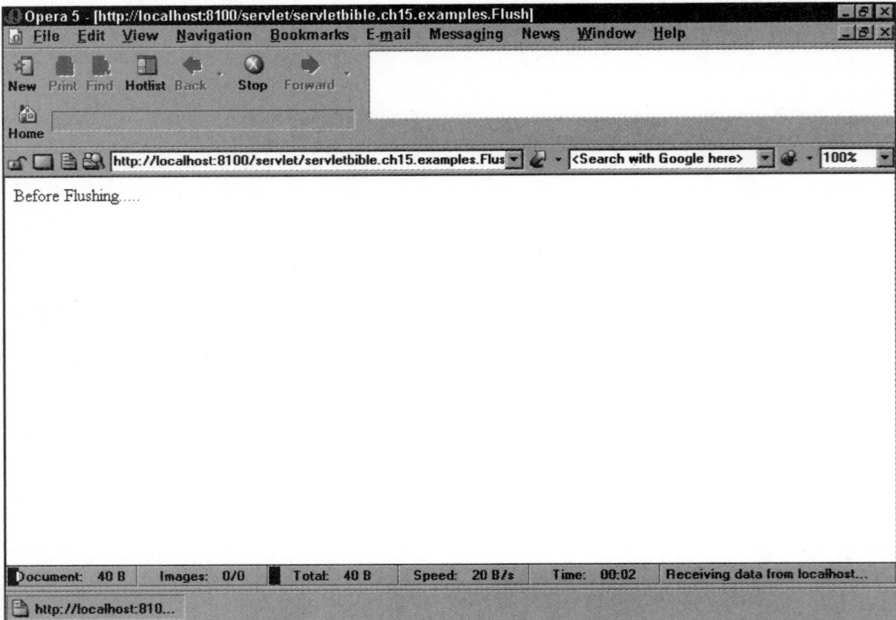

Figure 15-8: After displaying the first message, the client waits for the remaining page.

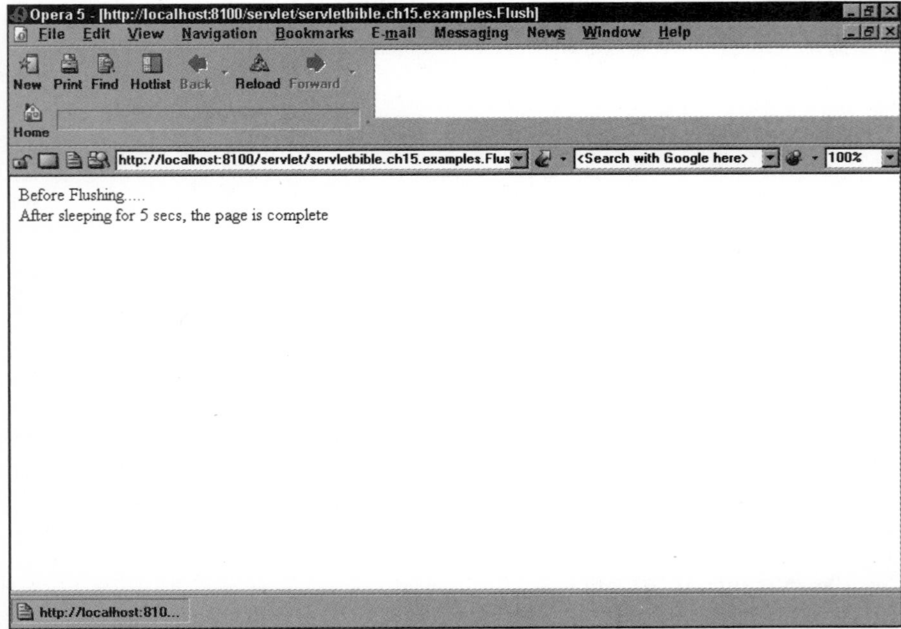

Figure 15-9: After five seconds, the page is displayed in entirety.

Documenting with Javadoc

Javadoc is a tool included in the Java Development Kit (JDK) to create API documentation for your application. The Javadoc executable is located in the `bin` directory of the JDK, so you can call Javadoc on the command line, assuming that you have the JDK `bin` directory in your `CLASSPATH`. You can run Javadoc on individual `.java` source files or on an entire package. Javadoc works by looking for a specific commenting style and tags in your code. These are then picked out, and the appropriate HTML files are generated.

To use Javadoc with your application, follow a specific commenting style for your classes and respective methods. This commenting style consists of embedding specific tags into the comment. The JavadocJavadoc tool uses the text appearing after these tags to generate the API documentation.

First, we look at the specific tags and then at how they can be used to construct Javadoc style comments.

Javadoc Tags

The following list defines the Javadoc tags and the order in which tags should appear:

- `@author`
- `@version`
- `@param`
- `@return`
- `@exception`
- `@see`
- `@since`
- `@serial`
- `@deprecated`
- `@link`

@author name

This tag is used to specify the author of the class. Multiple authors should be listed in chronological order, with the creator of the class at the top. If the author of the class is not known, use the word *unascribed* after the `@author` tag.

@version text

The text specified contains the version number of the JDK in which the current method or class belongs.

@param parameter_name description
This tag is used to specify the parameter names (excluding data type) and a description of the parameter of the current method being documented. For each parameter, a new `@param` tag should be used in the comments. Each parameter should be specified in the order in which it appears in the method's argument.

@return description
This tag specifies a description of what the current method returns. This tag does not need to be specified for methods that return nothing (that is, void methods) nor for constructors.

@exception Exception_Name description
The exceptions the method throws should be included using this tag. The description should indicate when the method might throw the exception. If using Javadoc versions 1.2 and higher, you can also use the `@throws` tag in place of the `@exception` tag, as they are synonymous. Multiple exceptions should be listed in alphabetical order.

@see reference_text/link
This tag is used to specify either text or a link to point to a reference of some sort. This tag creates a "See Also" followed by the reference text and/or link in documentation for the current class/method. The reference text/link can appear in a number of formats, either as a plain string or an HTML for a link (i.e. `<A HREF....>..</A>`).

@since version_number
This tag specifies the JDK version in which current class or member has existed.

@serial description
Classes that implement the `Serializable` interface should have their respective methods used to write data documented with the inclusion of this tag. The description should specify a description of the field (and acceptable values) being written with the current method.

@deprecated comment/link
This tag is used to specify from where the current method has been deprecated and perhaps a link to the replacement method, if any.

@link #anchor method_name
This special tag can be used with other tags to provide links to other methods. For example, this can be used in conjunction with the `@see` tag to provide a link.

The `#anchor` might look as follows:

```
@link #getHtmlFooter() getHtmlFooter
```

This creates a link pointing to the getHtmlFooter method (anchor) in the generated HTML files.

Javadoc Commenting

Now that we have an understanding of the basic Javadoc tags, we can construct Javadoc comments. All Javadoc comments are enclosed in box style as follows:

```
/**
* Comments would go here.
* @tags would go underneath.
*/
```

A one-line version looks like this:

```
/** Comments here */
```

One of the useful features of Javadoc is that it allows you to embed HTML into comments. If you wish to emphasize a keyword, you can enclose it in <b> tags in the comment itself. By convention, any code (consisting of Java reserved words, package names, classes, method names, and so on) is enclosed in the <code> tag. This is purely for stylistic purposes.

Now we look at an example Javadoc comment used for documenting a particular class:

```
/**
* HtmlUtils is a utility class used to simplify the process
* of constructing and returning HTML to be used in
* sending a response to the client.
*
* @author Suresh Rajagopalan
* @since JDK 1.3
*/
```

Default constructors can be documented in this manner:

```
/**
* Default empty constructor for HtmlUtils
*/
```

Documenting methods follows a pattern similar to the class comment; however, the @author is not needed in this case:

```
/**
* The <code>createHtmlHeader</code> method is used to construct *
the opening tags of a HTML document for the specified title.
*
* @param title This is the title located at the top of the
```

```
* browser for each HTML document
*
* @return The HTML string containing the opening portion of a   *
HTML document
*/
```

Running Javadoc

After you have completed documenting your application by using the Javadoc commenting style, you can use the Javadoc tool to generate HTML.

Javadoc comes with many options. These can be viewed by entering at the command line `Javadoc -help`.

This allows you to see a list of available switches and what they can be used to do.

To document a single program, enter at the command line

```
javadoc HelloWorld.java
```

This generates HTML API for the `HelloWorld` program. To generate this HTML in a specific directory, use -d switch and specify the directory as follows:

```
javadoc -d c:\servletbible\docs HelloWorld.java
```

To document multiple programs:

```
javadoc -d directory [directory of Program if any]\Program1.java [directory of
Program if any]\Program2.java
```

You can even use wildcards in the Javadoc tool. For example:

```
javadoc -d *.java
```

This generates the documentation for all Java files in the current directory.

To document a single package from the package directory:

1. Change to the base directory of the package to be documented.
2. Enter the following:

```
javadoc -d c:\servletbible\docs servletbible.ch11.examples
```

An example of documenting multiple packages from any directory:

```
javadoc -d c:\servletbible\docs -sourcepath c:\development\
servletbible.ch06.examples servletbible.ch11.examples
```

Here we have used the sourcepath switch to tell the Javadoc tool the path-search order in which to locate the packages:

For more information on Javadoc, visit the Javadoc homepage at http://java.sun.com/j2se/javadoc/index.html.

Summary

This chapter offers some tips on what can be used to enhance or improve your Web application in select areas. Some of the key tips you have picked up in this chapter include how to debug your servlets, how to troubleshoot problems with your JSP, documenting and using the Javadoc tool, scheduling tasks using the Timer class, using property files in your application, and how to flush a servlet's output stream.

As you gain more experience in servlet and JSP development, you may learn or develop your own set of ideas and tips to enhance performance or reduce maintenance work on Web applications.

Happy coding!

✦ ✦ ✦

What's on the CD-ROM

This appendix provides you with information on the contents of the CD-ROM that accompanies this book. For the latest and greatest information, please refer to the ReadMe file located at the root of the CD-ROM. Here is what you will find:

- ✦ System Requirements
- ✦ Using the CD-ROM with Windows, Linux, and the Macintosh
- ✦ What's on the CD-ROM
- ✦ Troubleshooting

System Requirements

Make sure that your computer meets the minimum system requirements listed in this section. If your computer doesn't match up to most of these requirements, you may have a problem using the contents of the CD-ROM.

For Windows 9*x*, Windows 2000, Windows NT4 (with SP 4 or later), Windows Me, or Windows XP:

- ✦ A PC with a Pentium processor running at 166 Mhz or faster
- ✦ At least 32MB of total RAM installed on your computer; for best performance, we recommend at least 64MB
- ✦ Ethernet network interface card (NIC) or modem with a speed of at least 28,800 bps
- ✦ A CD-ROM drive

For Linux:

- ✦ A PC with a Pentium processor running at 166 Mhz or faster
- ✦ At least 32MB of total RAM installed on your computer; for best performance, we recommend at least 64MB
- ✦ An Ethernet network interface card (NIC) or modem with a speed of at least 28,800 bps
- ✦ A CD-ROM drive

Using the CD-ROM with Windows

To install the items from the CD-ROM to your hard drive, follow these steps:

1. Insert the CD into your computer's CD-ROM drive.
2. A window will appear with the following options: Install, Explore, Links, and Exit.
   - **Install:** Gives you the option to install the supplied software and/or the author-created samples on the CD-ROM
   - **Explore:** Allows you to view the contents of the CD-ROM in its directory structure
   - **Links:** Opens a hyperlinked page of Web sites
   - **Exit:** Closes the autorun window

If you do not have autorun enabled, or if the autorun window does not appear, follow these steps to access the CD-ROM:

1. Click Start ⇨ Run.
2. In the dialog box that appears, type ***d*:\setup.exe**, where *d* is the letter of your CD-ROM drive. This will bring up the autorun window described earlier.
3. Choose the Install, Explore, Links, or Exit option from the menu. (See Step 2 in the preceding list for a description of these options.)

Using the CD-ROM with Linux

To install the items from the CD-ROM to your hard drive, follow these steps:

1. Log in as root.
2. Insert the CD into your computer's CD-ROM drive.
3. If your computer has Auto-Mount enabled, wait for the CD-ROM to mount. Otherwise, do one of the following:

- **Command-line instructions:** At the command prompt, type

  ```
  mount /dev/cdrom /mnt/cdrom
  ```

  (This will mount the "cdrom" device to the mnt/cdrom directory. If your device has a different name, then exchange "cdrom" with that device name — for instance, "cdrom1".)
- **Graphical instructions:** Right-click on the CD-ROM icon on the desktop and choose Mount CD-ROM from the selections. This will mount your CD-ROM.

4. Browse the CD-ROM and follow the individual installation instructions for the products listed in this appendix.
5. To remove the CD from your CD-ROM drive, do one of the following:
   - **Command-line instructions:** At the command prompt, type

     ```
     umount /mnt/cdrom
     ```

   - **Graphical instructions:** Right-click on the CD-ROM icon on the desktop and choose UMount CD-ROM from the selections. This will mount your CD-ROM.

What's on the CD-ROM

The following sections provide a summary of the software and other materials you'll find on the CD-ROM.

Author-created material

All author-created material from the book, including code listings and samples, are on the CD-ROM in the folder named "Author."

Applications

The following applications are on the CD-ROM:

✦ The Apache Web Server (Open Source), from The Apache Software Foundation

✦ Versions available for Windows and UNIX

✦ The Apache HTTP Server site is located at `http://httpd.apache.org/`.

✦ Instructions for how to compile the source are provided in the appendix.

Binary distributions can be found at http://httpd.apache.org/dist/httpd/binaries/linux/ (Linux) or `http://httpd.apache.org/dist/httpd/binaries/win32/` (Windows)

To install using the Windows Installer Version (*.msi), you will need the latest version of the Windows Installer which can be downloaded from Microsoft's Web site at `http://www.microsoft.com`.

Forte for Java Community Edition (freeware), from Sun Microsystems

Versions available for Windows, Linux, and Solaris

Visit Forte for Java's Web site at `http://www.sun.com/forte/ffj/` for more information and product updates.

Forte for Java is a powerful and extensible integrated development environment for developing J2EE applications.

Java 2 Software Development Kit Standard Edition (freeware), from Sun Microsystems

Version 1.3 for Windows

The Java home page is located at `http://java.sun.com/`.

This is Sun's Java Development Kit, which is required to develop Java applications.

JRUN Server (30-day trial), from Macromedia Inc.

Versions available for Windows

The JRUN home page is located at `http://www.macromedia.com/software/jrun/`.

A servlet and JSP engine, JRUN is powerful and can be plugged into most popular servers, such as Netscape Enterprise Server, IIS, and Microsoft Personal Web Server. A fully functional evaluation and a licensed version are available. JRUN includes powerful visual tools called JRUN Studio, which can be used for developing rapid Web applications.

LiteWebSever (freeware), from Gefion Software

Versions available for Windows and UNIX (multi-platform version)

LiteWebServer is located at `http://www.gefionsoftware.com`.

This is a simple Web server that supports servlets and is written in Java. It has support for the Servlet 2.1 API and CGI 1.1. It is easy to set up and has a Web-based GUI for administration.

Jakarta Tomcat Servlet Container (Open Source), from the Apache Software Foundation

Versions available for Windows and UNIX

The Tomcat home page is located at `http://jakarta.apache.org/tomcat/`.

Tomcat is an open source servlet container. It can act as a standalone server for developing servlets or be integrated with the Apache Web Server. Jakarta Tomcat always has support for the latest servlet API. Tomcat also has support for JSP. It is free, but an open source can be difficult to configure.

Visual Slickedit (30-day trial), from Microedge Inc.

Versions available for Windows and UNIX

The Visual Slickedit home page is located at `http://www.slickedit.com`.

One of my personal favorites for IDEs, Visual Slickedit has support for numerous languages and comes with myriad features.

WebServer Stress Tool (30-day trial), from Paessler Tools

Versions available for Windows

The Paessler Tools home page is located at `http://web-server-tools.com/tools/`.

This is a load-testing tool that can simulate large volumes of users accessing your application and allow you to determine the performance of your application as well as any bugs that may have resulted due to high loads.

Shareware programs are fully functional trial versions of copyrighted programs. If you like particular programs, register with their authors for a nominal fee and receive licenses, enhanced versions, and technical support. *Freeware programs* are copyrighted games, applications, and utilities that are free for personal use. Unlike shareware, these programs do not require a fee or provide technical support. *GNU software* is governed by its own license, which is included inside the folder of the GNU product. See the GNU license for more details.

Trial, demo, or evaluation versions are usually limited either by time or functionality (such as being unable to save projects). Some trial versions are very sensitive to system date changes. If you alter your computer's date, the programs will time out and will no longer be functional.

Troubleshooting

If you have difficulty installing or using any of the materials on the companion CD-ROM, try the following solutions:

- **Turn off any anti-virus software you may have running.** Installers sometimes mimic virus activity and can make your computer incorrectly believe that it is being infected by a virus. (Be sure to turn the anti-virus software back on later.)
- **Close all running programs.** The more programs you're running, the less memory is available to other programs. Installers also typically update files and programs; if you keep other programs running, installation may not work properly.
- **Reference the ReadMe file.** Please refer to the ReadMe file located at the root of the CD-ROM for the latest product information at the time of publication.

If you still have trouble with the CD-ROM, please call the Hungry Minds Customer Care phone number: (800) 762-2974. Outside the United States, call (317) 572-3994. You can also contact Hungry Minds Customer Service by e-mail at `techsupdum@hungryminds.com`. Hungry Minds will provide technical support only for installation and other general quality control items; for technical support on the applications themselves, consult the program's vendor or author.

✦ ✦ ✦

The Servlet API

The classes, interfaces, and exceptions of the Servlet 2.2 API are covered in this appendix. The following packages of the Servlet 2.2 API are covered in this order:

- javax.servlet
- javax.servlet.http

These packages make up the presentation tier of the J2EE Architecture. Each class in these packages and its members are summarized.

Public members, private members, and protected members are indicated.

Deprecated classes, interfaces, methods, and attributes have not been included in this appendix.

javax.servlet

Table B-1
Interfaces, Classes, and Exceptions of the javax.servlet Package

Interfaces	*Classes*	*Exceptions*
`RequestDispatcher`	`GenericServlet`	`ServletException`
`Servlet`	`ServletInputStream`	`UnavailableException`
`ServletConfig`	`ServletOutputStream`	
`ServletContext`		
`ServletRequest`		
`ServletResponse`		
`SingleThreadModel`		

Interfaces of the javax.servlet package

RequestDispatcher

Description:

An interface used to dispatch (by forwarding) requests from the client to the appropriate resource (that may be another servlet or JSP or HTML page) on the server. A RequestDispatcher object can be created and used through the `ServletContext().getRequestDispatcher(String url)` method.

Method summary:

- `void forward(ServletRequest request, ServletResponse response)` **throws** `ServletException, IOException`
- `void include(ServletRequest request, ServletResponse response)` **throws** `ServletException, IOException`

These are public members.

Method Name	*Description*
`forward`	Forwards requests to other resources
`include`	Includes the output of another resource in the calling servlet's response

Servlet

Description:

The interface that contains the method signatures that all servlets must implement. These are the methods of the servlet life cycle, including `init()`, `service()` and `destroy()`.

Method summary:

- `void destroy()`
- `ServletConfig getServletConfig()`
- `String getServletInfo()`
- `void init(ServletConfig config)`**throws** `ServletException`
- `void service(ServletRequest request, ServletResponse response)` **throws** `ServletException, IOException`

These are public members.

Method Name	*Description*
`destroy`	This method is called by the Web server's servlet container to unload the servlet from memory, garbage collecting the servlet and any resources it holds.
`getServletConfig`	This retrieves a `ServletConfig` object provided for the `init` method. This object contains the initialization parameters for the servlet.
`getServletInfo`	This retrieves general information about the servlet where implemented by the servlet's developer.
`init`	When the servlet is instantiated, this method is called. After executing successfully, the servlet can process requests.
`service`	This is the method the servlet container calls to process/handle client requests.

ServletConfig

Description:

A container for initialization parameters to be passed to the servlet during the servlet's initialization.

Method summary:

- String getInitParameter
- Enumeration getInitParameterNames
- ServletContext getServletContext
- String getServletName

These are public members.

Method Name	*Description*
getInitParameter	Returns the value of the specified parameter name. If the parameter does not exist, null is returned.
getInitParameterNames	Returns an enumeration of names of the servlet's initialization parameters. If no initialization parameters exist for the servlet, null is returned. These names are contained in the ServletConfig object used in the init call of the servlet.
getServletContext	This returns the ServletContext object (used in the init call of the servlet).
getServletName	The name of the servlet instance is returned.

ServletContext

Description:

Contains the methods necessary for servlets to obtain information about the servlet container and its environment.

This interface is a component of the ServletConfig object.

Method summary:

- java.lang.Object getAttribute(String name)
- Enumeration getAttributeNames()
- ServletContext getContext(String URIPath)
- String getInitparameter(String name)
- Enumeration getInitparameterNames()
- int getMajorVersion()
- String getMimeType(String filename)
- int getMinorVersion()

- `RequestDispatcher getNamedDispatcher(String name)`
- `String getRealPath(String path)`
- `RequestDispatcher getRequestDispatcher(String path)`
- `URL getResource(String path)` **throws** `MalformedURLException`
- `InputStream getResourceAsStream(String path)`
- `String getServerInfo()`
- `void log(String message)`
- `void log(String message, java.lang.Throwable te)`
- `void removeAttribute(String name)`
- `void setAttribute(String name, java.lang.Object obj)`

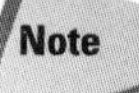

These are public members.

Method Name	***Description***
`getAttribute`	Retrieves the value of the specified name of the servlet containers' attribute. If the value does not exist, null is returned.
`getAttributeNames`	Retrieves the available servlet containers' attributes as an enumeration.
`getContext`	Retrieves a `ServletContext` object for the specified absolute URL. If the URL is not available or is in the incorrect format, null is returned.
`getInitParameter`	See `ServletConfig.getInitParameter`.
`getInitParameterNames`	See `ServletConfig.getInitParameterNames`.
`getMajorVersion`	Returns the number of the major version of the servlet API the servlet container supports
`getMimeType`	Returns the MIME type of the filename supplied
`getMinorVersion`	Returns the number of the minor version of the servlet API the servlet container supports
`getNamedDispatcher`	For the specified servlet name, a `RequestDispatcher` object is returned.
`getRealPath`	Returns the absolute path that is mapped with the specified virtual path
`getRequestDispatcher`	For the specified path to a server-side resource, a `RequestDispatcher` object is returned.

Continued

Method Name	*Description*
`getResource`	For the specified relative path, the URL of the mapped resource is returned. If no resource is mapped to the specified path, null is returned.
`getResourceAsStream`	For the specified relative path, the mapped resource is returned as an `InputStream` object. If no resource is mapped to the specified path, null is returned.
`getServerInfo`	Returns the name and version of the server/servlet container where the servlet is being executed
`log(String message)`	Appends the specified message to the servlet container log file
`log(String message, java.lang.Throwable te)`	Appends the specified message and the throwable exceptions' stack trace to the servlet container log file
`removeAtrribute`	Given the name of attribute, this method removes it from the servlet context.
`setAttribute`	For the given attribute name, the link to the specified object is stored in the servlet context.

ServletRequest

Description:
Contains the methods necessary for servlets to obtain information about the clients' request

Method summary:

- `java.lang.Object getAttribute(String name)`
- `Enumeration getAttributeNames()`
- `String getCharacterEncoding()`
- `int getContentLength()`
- `String getContentType()`
- `ServletInputStream getInputStream()` throws `IOException`
- `Locale getLocale`
- `Locale getLocales`
- `String getParameter(String name)`
- `Enumeration getParameterNames()`
- `String getParameterValues(String name)`

- `String getProtocol`
- `BufferedReader getReader()` **throws** `IOException`
- `String getRealpath(String path)`
- `String getRemoteAddr()`
- `String getRemoteHost()`
- `RequestDispatcher getRequestDispatcher()`
- `String getScheme()`
- `String getServerName()`
- `int getServerPort()`
- `boolean isSecure()`
- `void removeAttribute(String name)`
- `void setAttribute(String name, java.lang.Object obj)`

These are public members.

Method Name	***Description***
`getAttribute`	See `ServletContext.getAttribute(String name)`.
`getAttributeNames`	See `ServletContext.getAttributeNames()`.
`getCharacterEncoding`	Returns the type of character encoding used. If none is used, null is returned.
`getContentLength`	Returns in bytes the length of the request. If the length cannot be determined, -1 is returned.
`getInputStream`	Retrieves the request as binary data in the form of a `ServletInputStream`. An `IllegalStateException` is thrown if the `getReader()` method has already been called.
`getLocale`	The preferred Locale of the client is returned.
`getLocales`	Returns an enumeration of the preferred Locales of the client
`getParameter`	The value of the request-parameter name specified is returned. If the value does not exist, null is returned.
`getParameterNames`	Returns an Enumeration of all the available parameter names in the request
`getParameterValues`	Returns the values of the specified parameter name in an array of String objects

Continued

Method Name	Description
getProtocol	Returns the protocol name and version used in the request.
getReader	Similar to getInputStream but returns the request in the form of a BufferedReader. An UnsupportedEncoding Exception is thrown if the request cannot be decoded. If getInputStream() has already been called, an Illegal StateException is thrown. An IOException is thrown if an input/output error has occurred.
getRealPath	See ServletContext.getRealPath.
getRemoteAddr	Returns the IP address of the client making the request
getRemoteHost	Returns the host name of the client making the request
getRequestDispatcher	See ServletContext.getRequestDispatcher.
getScheme	Returns the scheme used to make the request (for example, HTTPS, FTP or HTTP).
getSeverName	Returns the host name of the server that has received the request
getServerPort	Returns the port number of the server where the request has been received
isSecure	Returns a Boolean value indicating whether the request has been made and received through a secure medium/channel
removeAttribute	See ServletContext.removeAttribute.
setAttribute	See ServletContext.setAttribute.

ServletResponse

Description:
Contains the methods necessary for servlets to generate and send a response to the client

Method summary:

- void flushBuffer() throws IOException
- int getBufferSize()
- String getCharacterEncoding()
- Locale getLocale()
- ServletOutputStream getOutputStream() throws IOException
- PrintWriter getWriter() throws IOException
- boolean isCommitted()

- `void reset()`
- `void setBufferSize(int buffer_size)`
- `void setContentLength(int length)`
- `void setContentType(String content_type)`
- `void setLocale(Locale locale)`

These are public members.

Method Name	*Description*
`flushBuffer`	Clears the buffer and sends its data to the client. A call to this method sets the status codes and response headers.
`getBufferSize`	Returns the size of the buffer used in the response. A 0 is returned if no buffering has been used.
`getCharacterEncoding`	See `ServletRequest.getCharacterEncoding`.
`getLocale`	Returns the Locale to be used in the response.
`getOutputStream`	Returns the `ServletOutputStream` to be used to construct the response. An `IllegalStateException` is thrown if the `getWriter` method has already been called.
`getWriter`	Returns a `PrintWriter` object that can be used to write character text to the client. The `setContentType` method must be used first to commit the character encoding of the text being sent. If the character encoding set is not available, an `UnsupportedEncodingException` is thrown. An `IllegalStateException` is thrown if the `getOutputStream` method has already been called.
`isCommitted`	Returns a Boolean indicating whether the response has been committed (that is, if the status codes and response headers have been set).
`reset`	Clears the buffer, status codes, and response headers. An `IllegalStateException` is thrown if this method is called when the response has been committed.
`setBufferSize`	Sets the value of the buffer size to be used in the response. An `IllegalStateException` is thrown if any part of the body of the response has been written.
`setContentLength`	Sets the Content-Length header with the specified value of the length of the content being sent to the client
`setContentType`	Sets the type of the content sent to the client
`setLocale`	Sets the locale of the response being sent to the client

SingleThreadModel

Description:
This is an empty interface that can be implemented to ensure that the implementing servlet is executed sequentially (that is, handles requests one at a time).

Classes of the javax.servlet package

GenericServlet

Description:
An abstract class that uses `ServletConfig` and `ServletContext` objects (that have been created during the servlets' initialization) to implement a basic protocol-independent servlet. To create your own GenericServlet you only need override the service method.

Interfaces implemented:
`Servlet`, `ServletConfig`, and `Serializable` (from the `java.io` package)

Constructor:
`GenericServlet()`: a default empty constructor

This is a public member.

Use the `init` method to perform any initialization work.

Method summary:

- `void destroy()`
- `String getInitParameter(String name)`
- `Enumeration getInitParameterNames()`
- `ServletConfig getServletConfig()`
- `ServletContext getServletContext()`
- `String getServletInfo()`
- `String getServletName()`
- `void init(ServletConfig config)`**throws** `ServletException`
- `void init()`**throws** `ServletException`

- `log(String message)`
- `log(String message, java.lang.Throwable te)`
- `abstract void service(ServletRequest request, ServletResponse response)` **throws** `ServletException, IOException`

These are public members.

Method Name	*Description*
`destroy`	Used by the servlet container to unload the servlet from memory. See `Servlet.destroy`.
`getInitParameter`	See `ServletConfig.getInitParameter`.
`getInitParameterNames`	See `ServletConfig.getInitParameterNames`.
`getServletConfig`	See `Servlet.getServletConfig`.
`getServletContext`	See `ServletConfig.getServletContext`.
`getServletInfo`	See `Servlet.getServletInfo`.
`getServletName`	See `ServletConfig.getServletName`.
`init(ServletConfig config)`	Be sure to call `super.init(config)` if you are overriding this method. See `Servlet.init`.
`init`	A duplicate convenience method used in place of `init(ServletConfig config)` to initialize without having to call `super.init(config)`.
`log(String message)`	See `ServletContext.log(String message)`.
`log(String message, Throwable te)`	See `ServletContext.log(String message, Throwable te)`.
`service`	This method is always called by the servlet container to process/handle client requests.

ServletInputStream

Description:

This is an abstract subclass of the input stream class, which provides the means to read data from clients' requests. The object is accessible through the `ServletRequest.getInputStream` method.

Constructor:

- `ServletInputStream();` a default empty constructor

This is a protected member.

Method summary:

- `int readLine(byte b[], int offset, int length)` throws `IOException`

These are public members.

Method Name	*Description*
`readLine`	Reads the specified number of bytes or until a newline character is reached from input stream. The data that is read (starting from the specified offset) is put into the byte array. On completion, the number of bytes that have been read is returned. If the end of the stream is reached, -1 is returned.

ServletOutputStream

Description:

An abstract subclass of the output stream class that is utilized to write a response to the client. The object is accessible through the `ServletResponse.getOutputStream` method.

Constructor:

- `ServletInputStream();` a default empty constructor

This is a protected member.

Method summary:

- `void print(boolean b)`throws `IOException`
- `void print(char c)`throws `IOException`
- `void print(double d)`throws `IOException`
- `void print(float f)`throws `IOException`
- `void print(int i)`throws `IOException`

- `void print(long l)`**throws** `IOException`
- `void print(String s)`**throws** `IOException`
- `void println()`**throws** `IOException`
- `void println(boolean b)`**throws** `IOException`
- `void println(char c)`**throws** `IOException`
- `void println(double d)`**throws** `IOException`
- `void println(float f)`**throws** `IOException`
- `void println(int i)`**throws** `IOException`
- `void println(long l)`**throws** `IOException`
- `void println(String s)`**throws** `IOException`

These are public members.

Method Name	***Description***
`print(..)`	Writes the specified value to the client in the primitive type specified (`boolean`, `char`, `double`, `float`, `int`, `long` or `String`) without a carriage-return, line-feed character at the end.
`println`	Writes a carriage-return, line-feed character to the client
`println(..)`	Writes the specified value to the client in the primitive type specified (`boolean`, `char`, `double`, `float`, `int`, `long` or `String`) with a carriage-return, line-feed character at the end

Exceptions of the javax.servlet package

ServletException

Description:

Base exception for servlets, thrown to signal a problem with the servlet

Constructor:

- `ServletException()`; used to construct a new `ServletException`

This is a public member.

Method summary:

- ✦ `ServletException(String message)`
- ✦ `ServletException(String message, Throwable rootCause)`
- ✦ `ServletException(Throwable rootCause)`
- ✦ `Throwable getRootCause()`

These are public members.

Method Name	*Description*
`ServletException(..)`	A new `ServletException` is constructed including the specified message and/or the message of the root cause of the exception
`getRootCause`	Returns the root-cause exception that has triggered the `ServletException`

UnavailableException

Description:

A subclass of the `ServletException` that is thrown to signal that a servlet is temporarily or permanently unavailable and that the servlet cannot handle the request.

Constructor:

- ✦ `UnavailableException(String message)`; used to construct a new `UnavailableException` with a description of the exception
- ✦ `UnavailableException(String message, int seconds)`; used to construct a new `UnavailableException` with a description of the exception and a time estimate of how long the services for that servlet will be unavailable.

These are public members.

Method summary:

- ✦ `int getUnavailableSeconds()`
- ✦ `boolean isPermanent()`

These are public members.

Method Name	*Description*
`getUnavailableSeconds`	Returns the time estimate, in seconds, of how long the services of the unavailable servlet will be unavailable
`isPermanent`	Returns a Boolean indication of whether the servlet's services will be permanently unavailable

javax.servlet.http

Table B-2
Interfaces and Classes of the javax.servlet.http Package

Interfaces	*Classes*
`HttpServletRequest`	`Cookie`
`HttpServletResponse`	`HttpServlet`
`HttpSession`	`HttpSessionBindingEvent`
`HttpSessionBindingListener`	`HttpUtils`

Interfaces of the javax.servlet.http package

HttpServletRequest

Description:

This interface is essentially a representation of an HTTP request and can be used to get information about the HTTP request being made. It is a subclass of `ServletRequest` from the `javax.servlet` package.

Method summary:

- ✦ `String getAuthType()`
- ✦ `String getContextPath()`
- ✦ `Cookie getCookies()`
- ✦ `long getDateHeader(String name)` throws `IllegalArgumentException`
- ✦ `String getHeader(String name)`

- `Enumeration getHeaderNames()`
- `int getIntHeader(String name)` **throws** `NumberFormatException`
- `String getMethod()`
- `String getPathInfo()`
- `String getPathTranslated()`
- `String getQueryString()`
- `String getRemoteUser()`
- `String getRequestedSessionId()`
- `String getRequestURI()`
- `String getServletPath()`
- `HttpSession getSession()`
- `HttpSession getSession(boolean create)`
- `boolean isRequestedSessionIdFromCookie()`
- `boolean isRequestedSessionIdFromUrl()`
- `boolean isRequestedSessionIdFromURL()`
- `boolean isRequestedSessionIdFromValid()`
- `boolean isUserInRole()`

These are public members.

Method Name	***Description***
`getAuthType`	Returns the type-authentication scheme used, such as BASIC or SSL. A null is returned if no authentication scheme was used.
`getContextPath`	Returns the part of the URL that represents the context of the request
`getCookies`	Returns an array of the cookies sent with the request. If no cookies have been sent, null is returned.
`getDateHeader`	Returns the specified header as a Date in long form (as the number of milliseconds from Jan 1st , 1970). This can be used with HTTP headers such as 'If-Modified-Since.' If the specified header does not exist, a -1 is returned. If the header cannot be converted to a date, an `IllegalArgumentException` is thrown.
`getHeader`	The value of the specified header is returned. A null is returned if the header does not exist in the request.

Method Name	Description
getHeaderNames	An enumeration of request-header names is returned. If no headers are found in the request, a null or empty enumeration is returned.
getIntHeader	Returns the specified header in the form of an int type. If the specified header cannot be found then a -1 is returned. If the specified header cannot be converted into an integer, a `NumberFormatException` is thrown.
getMethod	Returns the type of HTTP method (for example, `GET` or `POST`) used to make the request.
getPathInfo	Returns additional path information of the URL with which the client has made a request. This information is a subset of the full URL that starts after the servlet path and ends before the query string. A null is returned if this information does not exist.
getPathTranslated	Returns the preceding path in the form of a real path. A null is returned if the preceding path does not exist.
getQueryString	Returns the query string contained in the URL with which the request has been made. A null is returned if no query string exists.
getRemoteUser	If the client making the request has been authenticated, the login id is returned; otherwise, a null is returned.
getRequestedSessionId	Returns the session id the client provides. If no session id is specified in the client's request, a null is returned.
getRequestURI	Returns a subset of the first line of the HTTP request, starting from the URL and ending with the query string (if any).
getServletPath	Returns a subset of the URL (with which the client has made a request) that contains the servlet name and path but excludes additional path information (if any).
getSession	Returns the session object linked with the request. If no session is associated with the request, a new session is established.
getSession (boolean create)	This is like the preceding description. If the create Boolean value specified is true, it creates a new session (if one does not exist with the request) or returns an existing open session. If the create value specified is false and an existing session is open, that session is returned; otherwise, a null is returned.

Continued

Method Name	*Description*
isRequestedSession IdFromCookie	Returns true if the requested session id is contained in the cookie that comes with the request. Otherwise, false is returned.
isRequestedSessionId FromURL	Returns true if the requested session id is contained in URL with which the client has made the request. Otherwise, false is returned.
isRequestedSessionId FromValid	Returns true if the requested session id matches the associated open session. If the session has been invalidated or has expired, a false is returned.
isUserInRole	Returns true if the client has been authenticated with the specified role.

HttpServletResponse

Description:
This interface is essentially a representation of an HTTP response and can be used to construct or modify an HTTP response. It is a subclass of `ServletResponse` from the `javax.servlet` package.

Attribute summary:
The following attributes represent HTTP status code headers.

- `static final SC_ACCEPTED`
- `static final SC_BAD_GATEWAY`
- `static final SC_BAD_REQUEST`
- `static final SC_CONFLICT`
- `static final SC_CONTINUE`
- `static final SC_CREATED`
- `static final SC_EXPECTATION_FAILED`
- `static final SC_FORBIDDEN`
- `static final SC_GATEWAY_TIMEOUT`
- `static final SC_GONE`
- `static final SC_HTTP_VERSION_NOT_SUPPORTED`
- `static final SC_INTERNAL_SERVER_ERROR`

- static final SC_LENGTH_REQUIRED
- static final SC_METHOD_NOT_ALLOWED
- static final SC_MOVED_PERMANENTLY
- static final SC_MOVED_TEMPORARILY
- static final SC_MULTIPLE_CHOICES
- static final SC_NON_AUTHORITATIVE_INFORMATION
- static final SC_NOT_ACCEPTABLE
- static final SC_NOT_FOUND
- static final SC_NOT_IMPLEMENTED
- static final SC_NOT_MODIFIED
- static final SC_NO_CONTENT
- static final SC_OK
- static final SC_PARTIAL_CONTENT
- static final SC_PAYMENT_REQUIRED
- static final SC_PRECONDITION_FAILED
- static final SC_PROXY_AUTHENTICATION_REQUIRED
- static final SC_REQUESTED_RANGE_NOT_SATISFIABLE
- static final SC_REQUEST_ENTITY_TOO_LARGE
- static final SC_REQUEST_TIMEOUT
- static final SC_REQUEST_URI_TOO_LONG
- static final SC_RESET_CONTENT
- static final SC_SEE_OTHER
- static final SC_SERVICE_UNAVAILABLE
- static final SC_SWITCHING_PROTOCOLS
- static final SC_UNAUTHORIZED
- static final SC_UNSUPPORTED_MEDIA_TYPE
- static final SC_USE_PROXY

Note These are public members.

Method summary:

- void addCookie(Cookie cookie)
- void addDateHeader(String name, long date)
- void addHeader(String name, String value)
- void addIntHeader(String name, String value)
- boolean containsHeader(String name)
- String encodeRedirectURL(String url)
- String encodeURL(String url)
- void sendError(int sc) **throws** IOException
- void sendError(int sc, String message) **throws** IOException
- void sendRedirect(String location) **throws** IOException
- void setDateHeader(String name, long date)
- void setHeader(String name, String value)
- void setIntHeader(String name, int value)
- void setStatus(int sc)

Note These are public members.

Method Name	***Description***
addCookie	Sends the specified cookie to the client in the response.
addDateHeader	Adds the specified response header with the specified date to the response. The date is in long format and is the number of milliseconds from Jan 1st, 1970.
addHeader	Adds the specified response header with the specified String value to the response.
addIntHeader	Adds the specified response header with the specified integer value to the response.
containsHeader	Used to determine if the specified response header contains a value. It returns true if the response header contains the value.
encodeRedirectURL	Returns an encoded URL to be used for the sendRedirect method. Logic is in place in this method to determine whether the session id will also be included in the encoding of the URL.
encodeURL	Returns an encoded version of the specified URL, including the session id where appropriate (for example, browser does not support cookies).

Method Name	*Description*
`sendError(int sc)`	Sends the appropriate error response to the client based on the status code specified. Once this method has been called, the response is committed. If this method has been called after the response has been committed, an `IllegalStateException` is thrown.
`sendError(int sc, String message)`	This is the same as the preceding description; however, the error response may include the specified descriptive message.
`sendRedirect`	This method commits the response by setting the `sc_moved_temporarily` and redirecting the client to the specified location. If the response has been committed, an `IllegalStateException` is thrown.
`setDateHeader`	Sets the value of the specified response header with the specified date value. The date is in long format and is the number of milliseconds from Jan 1st, 1970.
`setHeader`	Sets the value of the specified response header with the specified string value.
`setIntHeader`	Sets the value of the specified response header with the specified integer value.
`setStatus`	Sets the specified status code that will be used in the response.

HttpSession

Description:

A `HttpSession` is a way to establish data persistence throughout the duration of users' visits to the Web site or for the specified amount of time using the `setMaxInactiveInterval` method. This persistence can be established through the user of cookies or URL rewriting. Users and their corresponding sessions are identified through a unique session id. The `HttpSession` interface is the means through which sessions can be created and through which information about the users' sessions can be acquired.

Method summary:

- `java.lang.Object getAttribute(String name)`
- `Enumeration getAttributeNames()`
- `long getCreationTime()`
- `String getId()`
- `long getLastAccessedTime()`

- `int getMaxInactiveInterval()`
- `void invalidate()`
- `boolean isNew()`
- `void removeAttribute(String name)`
- `void setAttribute(String name, java.lang.Object value)`
- `void setMaxInactiveInterval(int interval)`

These are public members.

For all the methods of the session interface, an `IllegalStateException` is thrown if the method is called when the session has expired or been invalidated.

Method Name	***Description***
`getAttribute`	Returns the object with the specified name from the session. A null is returned if no object of the specified name is found.
`getAttributeNames`	Returns an enumeration of all object names held in the current session.
`getCreationTime`	Returns the time for which the current session has been created in milliseconds (since Jan 1st 1970).
`getId`	Returns the session id of the current session.
`getLastAccessedTime`	Returns the time in milliseconds (since Jan 1st 1970) when the client last placed a request for the current session.
`getMaxInactiveInterval`	Returns the maximum amount of time in milliseconds (since Jan 1st 1970) for which the session will be kept open between client requests. If the time has lapsed, the servlet container renders the session expired.
`invalidate`	Terminates and removes any objects associated with the current session.
`isNew`	Returns true if the client has not yet used the session that has recently been created.
`removeAttribute`	Removes the specified object associated with the current session.
`setAttribute`	Associates the specified object with the current session by using the specified name to identify the object.
`setMaxInactiveInterval`	Allows you to set the maximum amount of time in milliseconds for which the session will be kept open between client requests. If a negative time value is specified, the session remains open until it is invalidated and does not timeout.

HttpSessionBindingListener

Description:

A subclass of `java.util.EventListener` used to notify the registered class or classes when an object is bound or unbound from a session. The class can register itself by implementing this interface.

Method summary:

- `void valueBound(HttpSessionBindingEvent event)`
- `void valueUnbound(HttpSessionBindingEvent event)`

These are public members.

Method Name	*Description*
`valueBound`	Uses the `HttpSessionBindingEvent` event to notify the registered class or classes that the object has been bound to the session.
`valueUnbound`	Uses the `HttpSessionBindingEvent` event to notify the registered class or classes that the object has been unbound from the session.

Classes of the javax.servlet.http package

Cookie

Description:

A cookie is a small chunk of information sent to the user agent. It is sent back to the server on subsequent requests. It stores information in the form of name and value pairs. Cookies are commonly used in session management to identify the client and the session they are associated with. The `Cookie` class can be used to create and send cookies as part of the response sent to the client. It also allows for the retrieval of information contained in the cookie and about the cookie.

Constructor:

- `Cookie(String name, String value);` use this constructor to instantiate a cookie object with the specified name and value.

This is a public member.

Attribute summary:

- ✦ `comment`
- ✦ `domain`
- ✦ `maxAge`
- ✦ `name`
- ✦ `path`
- ✦ `secure`
- ✦ `value`
- ✦ version

These are private members.

Attribute Name	*Description*
`comment`	A string containing the description/purpose of the cookie. The default value is null.
`domain`	A string containing the domain name for the cookie.
`maxAge`	An integer containing the maximum the cookie can last before it expires.
`name`	A string containing the name of the cookie.
`path`	A string containing the path on the server to which the cookie is accessible.
`secure`	A Boolean flag that indicates whether the cookie is accessible via a secure protocol such as HTTPS.
`value`	A string containing the value of the cookie.
`version`	An integer value containing the version protocol the cookie conforms to. A 0 value indicates compliance with the original Netscape specification. A 1 indicates compliance with the RFC 2109 specification.

Method summary:

- ✦ `java.lang.Object clone()`
- ✦ `String getComment()`
- ✦ `String getDomain()`
- ✦ `int getMaxAge()`
- ✦ `String getName()`
- ✦ `String getPath()`
- ✦ `boolean getSecure()`

- `String getValue()`
- `int getVersion()`
- `void setComment(String description)`
- `void setDomain(String pattern)`
- `void setMaxAge(int age)`
- `void setPath(String path)`
- `void setSecure(boolean flag)`
- `void setValue(String value)`
- `void setVersion(int version)`

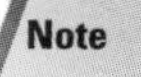

These are public members.

Method Name	*Description*
`clone`	Makes a copy of the cookie object and returns it.
`getComment`	Returns the value of the comment attribute or null if there is no assigned value.
`getDomain`	Returns the value of the domain attribute or null if no domain has been set.
`getMaxAge`	Returns the value of the `maxAge` attribute. A -1 value indicates that the cookie remains active until the browser is shutdown.
`getName`	Returns the value of the name attribute.
`getPath`	Returns the value of the path attribute.
`getSecure`	Returns the value of the Boolean flag secure.
`getValue`	Returns the value contained in the cookie.
`getVersion`	Returns the value of the version attribute.
`setComment`	Sets the comment attribute with the specified value.
`setDomain`	Sets the domain attribute with the specified value.
`setMaxAge`	Sets the `maxAge` attribute with the specified value. Setting A 0 value causes the cookie to be deleted.
`setPath`	Sets the path (and the subdirectories through which the cookie will be accessible).
`setSecure`	Sets the value of the secure attribute. This signals to the client's browser that the cookie should be accessed and sent via a secure protocol such as HTTPS.
`setValue`	Sets the actual value the cookie should store.
`setVersion`	Sets the value of the version attribute.

HttpServlet

Description:
An abstract subclass of the `GenericServlet` that provides the means to create servlets that can be executed using the HTTP.

Interfaces implemented:
`Serializable`

Constructor:

- `HttpServlet();` default empty constructor

This is a public member.

Method summary:

- `void doDelete(HttpServletRequest req, HttpServletResponse res)` **throws** `ServletException, IOException`
- `void doGet(HttpServletRequest req, HttpServletResponse res)` **throws** `ServletException, IOException`
- `void doOptions(HttpServletRequest req, HttpServletResponse res)` **throws** `ServletException, IOException`
- `void doPost(HttpServletRequest req, HttpServletResponse res)` **throws** `ServletException, IOException`
- `void doPut(HttpServletRequest req, HttpServletResponse res)` **throws** `ServletException, IOException`
- `void doTrace(HttpServletRequest req, HttpServletResponse res)` **throws** `ServletException, IOException`
- `long getLastModified(HttpServletRequest req)`
- `void service(HttpServletRequest req, HttpServletResponse res)` **throws** `ServletException, IOException`

The preceding are protected members.

- `void service(ServletRequest req, ServletResponse res)` **throws** `ServletException, IOException`

The preceding is a public member.

Method Name	*Description*
doDelete	Override this method to handle delete requests. These delete requests may remove files from the server.
doGet	Override this method to handle HTTP GET requests. The content in this method is executed if the servlet is called from the browser.
doOptions	Returns in the form of a header the HTTP methods the server supports.
doPost	Override this method to handle HTTP POST requests.
doPut	Override this method to handle put requests. HTTP PUT requests may be used to add files to the server.
doTrace	This method can be used to handle TRACE requests. This method need not be overridden, as it is used to return the request headers.
getLastModified	Returns the time the request has been modified in milliseconds (since Jan 1st 1970).
service(HttpServlet Request req, HttpServlet Response res)	This method is executed for all HTTP requests and appropriately dispatches the request/response to the appropriate method.
service(ServletRequest req, ServletResponse res)	Can be used to dispatch protocol-independent requests to the appropriate method.

HttpSessionBindingEvent

Description:

A subclass of the EventObject sent as a parameter to the object that implements the HttpSessionBindingListener interface at the point where an object is bound to, or unbound from, a session

Constructor:

HttpSessionBindingEvent(HttpSession session, String name); creates the event sent to the registered listener object to notify it that the object has been bound to, or unbound from, the session

Attribute summary:

- ✦ `name`

Attribute Name	*Description*
`name`	An attribute containing the identifier of the object that has been bound to, or unbound from, the session

Method summary:

- ✦ `String getName()`
- ✦ `HttpSession getSession()`

These are public members.

Method Name	*Description*
`getName`	Returns the value of the name attribute
`getSession`	Returns the session the object has been bound to or unbound from

HttpUtils

Description:

As its name suggests, this class contains some useful utility methods that can be used in servlet development.

Constructor:

- ✦ `HttpUtils();` instantiates a new `HttpUtils` object.

This is a public member.

Method summary:

- ✦ `static StringBuffer getRequestURL(HttpServletRequest req)`
- ✦ `static Hashtable parsePostData(int length, ServletInputStream in)`
- ✦ `static Hashtable parseQueryString(String s)`

These are public members.

Method Name	Description
getRequestURL	Returns a complete URL without the query string
parsePostData	Returns a Hashtable object with name-value pairs of the form information that has been posted. If form data is in an invalid format, an IllegalStateException is thrown.
parseQueryString	Returns a Hashtable object with name-value pairs of the query string. If the query string is in an invalid format, an IllegalStateException is thrown.

✦ ✦ ✦

Servlet Engines

✦ ✦ ✦ ✦

This appendix lists some of the common servlet engines used for servlet development and hosting and provides URLs for various servlet engines.

Servlet Engines

Servlet engines are required in order to host and execute servlets and JSP's. Numerous engines can be used for servlet development and production environments. The following sections provide information on common servlet engines and where you can find them.

Tomcat

Tomcat, from the Apache Software Foundation, is one of the most popular servlet engines. Tomcat can act as a stand-alone server for developing servlets or can be integrated with the Apache Web Server. Tomcat always supports the latest servlet API. In addition, Tomcat supports JSP. Tomcat is free and open source; however, it may be difficult to configure. You can find Tomcat at:

```
http://jakarta.apache.org/tomcat/index.html
```

NetForge

NetForge, by Novacode, is a simple Web server that supports servlets and is written in Java. NetForge supports the Servlet 2.1 API and CGI 1.1. It is easy to set up and has a Web-based GUI for administration. You can find NetForge at:

```
http://www.novocode.com/
```

JRun

A servlet and JSP engine, Allaire's JRun is powerful and can be plugged into most popular servers such as Netscape Enterprise Server, IIS, and Microsoft Personal Web Server. Fully functional evaluation and licensed versions are available. JRun offers a powerful visual tool called JRun Studio that can be used for developing rapid Web applications. You can find JRun at:

```
http://www.allaire.com/products/jrun/
```

The Orion Application Server

The Orion Application Server supports J2EE services: EJB 1.1; Servlet 2.2; JSP 1.1; JTA 1.0.1; JNDI 1.2; JDBC 2.0; and JMS 1.0. In addition, Orion can automatically compile servlets, JSP and related classes, and beans that reduce development and testing cycles. Like Resin (described later), Orion is quite fast; however, its documentation may be inadequate. The Orion Server is good value in the application-server market in terms of features and cost. You can find Orion at:

```
http://www.orionserver.com/
```

iPlanet

In terms of performance (in particular with SSL transactions) and scalability, iPlanet, by Sun and Netscape Alliance, does not match WebSphere or WebLogic; however, in terms of cost, iPlanet wins. iPlanet has an excellent GUI for administration, which makes it easy to manage and configure. Gradually, iPlanet is working its way up the ladder of the application-server market. You can find iPlanet at:

```
http://www.iplanet.com/
```

WebLogic

WebLogic, by BEA Systems, is a leader in the application-server market. WebLogic has unparalleled features. It is J2EE compliant and comes with native drivers for most major databases. BEA caters to various organizations, as WebLogic comes in three flavors: Server, Enterprise, and Express. You can find WebLogic at:

```
http://www.beasys.com/
```

WebSphere

WebSphere, by IBM, is one of the primary competitors in the application-server market. WebSphere is targeted for enterprise-level applications. This product's focus, among its many features, is performance and scalability. WebSphere integrates with other IBM products such as IBM's Visual Age for Java, used as a Java IDE. WebSphere has won many awards as the best Web-application server on the market; however, it is also quite expensive. You can locate WebSphere at:

```
http://www.ibm.com/software/webservers/appserv/enterprise.html
```

jo! Web server

jo! is a small servlet engine from tagtraum industries that supports the Servlet 2.2 API and JSP 1.1. jo! not only automatically reloads servlets and JSP's but reloads WAR files. jo! supports SSI through the `<servlet>` tag. You can find jo! at:

```
http://www.tagtraum.com/
```

Enhydra

Enhydra is one of the few open-source application servers on the market. It supports the Servlet 2.2 and JSP 1.1 API's. Enhydra comes with an XML engine. The enterprise version of Enhydra is currently under development, but you can find it at:

```
http://www.enhydra.org/
```

eWave and ServletExec

eWave and ServletExec, by Unify Corporation, are popular Web servers that can be used for Solaris, Windows, Mac OS, HP-UX, and Linux. Although a free evaluation version disables administration utilities and advanced features, a fully functional ServletExec is available for purchase. It provides HTML-based remote administration for maximum browser compatibility and is easy to use. Unify's eWave, with its Web server, provides a free servlet debugger. You can locate eWave and ServletExec at:

```
http://www.unifyewave.com/products/engine_access.htm
```

Resin

Caucho Technology's Resin claims to be the fastest for processing servlet and JSP requests. One of its best features is automatic class loading. This is most useful in development environments so you don't have to recycle your server every time you modify the servlet. Resin supports the Servlet 2.3 API and JSP 1.2. Resin gives Web developers the ability to choose the right language for their tasks. Resin has a built-in XSL (XML Stylesheet Language) parser that can be used to format XML. Resin is free for development, and you can find it at:

```
http://www.caucho.com/download/
```

LiteWebServer

LiteWebServer, by Gefion Software, is a pure, Java-based Web server that supports the Servlet 2.2 and JSP 1.1 API's. It is small, free, and easy to use and set up. LiteWebServer is recommended for servlet development, personal use, or a small Intranet. You can locate LiteWebServer at:

```
http://www.gefionsoftware.com
```

✦ ✦ ✦

APPENDIX D

JSP Syntax Sheet

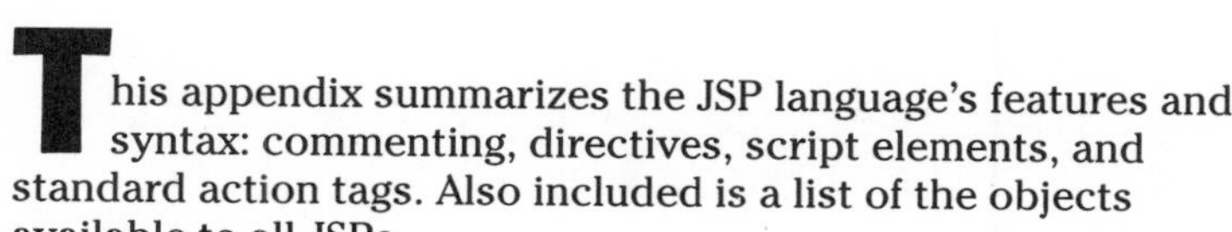

This appendix summarizes the JSP language's features and syntax: commenting, directives, script elements, and standard action tags. Also included is a list of the objects available to all JSPs.

Comments in JSP

There are three ways comments can be created in JSP; they appear in the following syntax:

```
<%-- comment text here --%>
```

This is equivalent to the HTML style of commenting (that is, `<!-- comment -->`). However, unlike the HTML comment, the JSP comment is not visible to the client browsers in the page source of the document.

```
<% // a single line comment %>
```

This is the Java style of commenting for single line comments. The text that appears after the `//` is not visible to the client in the page source of the document and is not used by the servlet engine for compilation or execution.

```
<% /* This is the Java
    * multi line style of commenting.
    */
 %>
```

Comments between the `/*` and the `*/` are treated in the same manner as the Java single line comment.

Directives

JSP has the three directives: `page`, `include`, and `tag-lib`. These directives are prefixed by the @ symbol.

Directive: `page`

Example Syntax: `<%@ page language="java" import="java.util.*" %>`

Attributes:

```
language = "java"

extends = "package.class "

import = "package.class | package .*"

session = "true|false"

buffer = "none|xkb", where x is a positive integer representing
the number of kilobytes of the buffer size.

autoFlush = "true|false"

isThreadSafe = "true|false"

info = "a text description or comment"

errorPage = "/error.jsp", this is the relative path of default
error page.

contentType = "MIME Type; charset =character set to be used if
any"

isErrorPage = "true|false"
```

Description: A page directive provides information about the page to the JSP engine. Page directives can appear anywhere and any number of times on the page. Each attribute, however, can appear only once. The page directive affects only the page in which it is specified.

Directive: `include`

Example Syntax: `<%@ include file="/header.html" %>`

Attributes:

`file = "page.html"` where `page.html` represents the relative URL of the file to be included in the JSP

Description: The `include` directive allows you to include a static file's content into this page.

Directive: `tag-lib`

Example Syntax: `<%@ uri = "/tags/Hello.tld" prefix = "servlet-bible" %>`

Syntax of the Custom tag as follows:

```
<prefix:tag attribute="value"/> [.. </prefix:tag>]
```

Attributes:

`uri = "/tags/Hello.tld"` , The `uri` is the relative path to the Tag Library Descriptor.

prefix = "servletbible"

Description: The `tag-lib` directive is used to embed custom user-defined tags in the current page. The tags are defined in a Tag Library Descriptor (TLD) document.

Script Elements

Declarations

Example Syntax: `<%! int counter = 0; %>`

Description: The declaration element is used to declare variables and methods that will be used in the JSP.

Expressions

Syntax: `<%=expression %>`

Description: Expressions are used to send output (that may be through the value of a variable or the value the expression returns) to the client through the response object. The `<%=` is essentially equivalent to `out.print` or `out.println` in Java.

Scriptlet

Syntax: `<% .. %>`

Description: Scriptlets are essentially the Java code embedded between the `<%` and `%>` tags.

Standard Action Tags

These are tags provided by the JSP language to perform specific actions. The prefix of these tags is the language JSP.

Tag: `forward`

Example Syntax: `<jsp:forward page="/page.jsp" />`

Attributes:

```
page="/page.jsp | <%=expression%>"
```

The page attribute is the relative URL of the page to which the user is forwarded. That page can be evaluated dynamically by using an expression.

Description: Forwards the user to the specified URL. The control of the response object is transferred to the specified resource.

Tag: `include`

Example Syntax: `<jsp:include page="/page.jsp" />`

Attributes:

```
page="/page.jsp | <%=expression%>"
```

The page attribute is the relative URL of the page that will be included. As with the forward tag, the page attribute can be evaluated dynamically using an expression.

```
flush = "true|false"
```

If the flush attribute is set to true, the output buffer is flushed before the specified page is included.

Description: Allows the specified document to be included as part of the response sent to the user.

Tag: `plugin`

Example Syntax:

```
<jsp:plugin type="applet" code="servletbible.HelloWorld" codebase="/applets/"
height="50" width="100">
<jsp:params>
<jsp:param name="font" value="Arial" />
</jsp:params>
<jsp:fallback> Your browser does not have support for Java applets
</jsp:fallback>
</jsp:plugin>
```

Attributes:

```
type = "bean|applet"

code = "package.class"

codebase = "/directory"
```

directory represents the relative path that leads to the applet or bean on the Web server.

```
name = "instance name"

align = " top|bottom|middle|left|right"

archive = "URI"

height = "pixel height"

width = "pixel width"

hspace = "pixels left/right"

vspace = "pixels top/bottom"

jreversion = "1.3"
```

Version number of the Java Runtime Environment

```
nspluginurl = "URL of plugin for netscape browsers"

iepluginurl = "URL of plugin for internet explorer browsers"
<jsp:fallback>
```

This content between this tag is displayed if the `plugin` is not supported.

Description: Similar to the HTML applet tag, this `plugin` tag is used to embed and execute Java applets or beans.

Tag: `useBean`

Example Syntax:

```
<jsp:useBean id="empBean"

beanName="servletbible.ch12.examples.beans.EmployeeBean"
type="servletbible.ch12.examples.beans.EmployeeBean" scope="page" />

[</jsp:useBean>]
```

Attributes:

```
id = "bean instance name"
scope = "page|request|session|application"
class = "package.class"
type = "package.class"
beanName = "package.class|<%=expression%>"
```

Description: This tag is used to instantiate a bean for the duration of the specified scope. The JSP has access to the bean and its properties for the duration of the scope.

Tag: `getProperty`

Example Syntax: `<jsp:getProperty name="empBean" property="eCode" />`

Attributes:

```
name = "bean instance name"
property = "property to retrieve"
```

Description: This tag is used to retrieve the value of the specified property from the instantiated bean.

Tag: `setProperty`

Example Syntax: `<jsp:setProperty name="empBean" property="age" param="age"/>`

Attributes:

```
name = "bean instance name"
property = " * | property to which the value is being set"
```

A * indicates that all the form parameters will be set to the corresponding bean properties of identical name.

```
param = " request parameter name "
```

The `request parameter name` must match a corresponding bean property.

```
value = "value of property to be set | <%=expression%>"
```

Description: This tag is used to set properties into the instantiated bean. The values are preserved for the duration of the scope specified in the `useBean` tag.

JSP Accessible Objects

All JSPs have access to the following objects and their respective methods.

request object

This object is an instance of `javax.servlet.ServletRequest`. This object is unique for every request the client makes. The object's scope (the duration at which values are held) is at the request level (that is, until the request is complete).

response object

This object is an instance of the `java.servlet.ServletResponse`. Its scope is at the page level.

session object

This object is an instance of `javax.servlet.HttpSession`. It is useful in JSPs to keep track of the active session. The values held in this object last for the duration of the client's session. (This may be a set time interval such as 20 minutes.)

application object

This object is an instance of `javax.servlet.ServletContext`. The scope of this object is for the duration of time the Web server is active.

pageContext object

This object is an instance of the `javax.servlet.jsp.PageContext` class and holds Web-server-specific features. The object also encapsulates the page context of the JSP.

config object

This object is an instance of `javax.servlet.ServletConfig` and holds configuration information at the scope of the page level.

page object

The JSP itself is an instance of this object (`java.lang.Object`).

out object

This object is an instance of the `PrintWriter` and is used to write data to the client through the output stream of the JSP.

exception object

This object is any exception thrown (that is, an instance of `java.lang.Throwable`) to the JSP at runtime. The `errorPage` directive accesses this object to perform its action.

✦ ✦ ✦

APPENDIX E

Elements of the Hypertext Transfer Protocol

HTTP Exchange

HTTP is a mechanism through which clients can request access to resources on a remote server. HTTP transactions consist of the request/response itself, the appropriate headers followed by a blank line and finally entity body/content.

The following steps take place in this exchange:

1. The client sends a request through the user-agent.

   A sample request header looks like this:

   ```
   GET /default/index.html HTTP/1.0
   Referer: http://www.hungryminds.com/
   Accept: text/html, image/gif, */*
   Accept Language: en-us
   Accept-Encoding: gzip, deflate
   User-Agent: Mozilla/4.0 (compatible; MSIE
   5.0; Windows NT, DigExt)
   Host: hungryminds.com
   Connection: Keep-Alive
   ```

2. The server processes the request.
3. The server then sends a response (first, a status code to indicate the status of the client's request, followed by the response headers, then a blank line and finally the requested document/resource itself).

A sample request header looks like this:

```
HTTP 1.0 200 OK
Last-modified: Wednesday, 13-May-99 11:22:32 GMT
Content-length: 415
Content-type: text/html; charset=ISO-8859-1
```

4. The user-agent reads the response header and/or document body and renders the view to the client.

CGI Environment Variables

The values of these variables are accessible through their respective methods (that can be found in either `HttpServletRequest` or `ServletContext`) as shown in Table E-1.

Table E-1
CGI Variables

Variable Name	*Description*	*Accessible Method*
`AUTH_TYPE`	The authentication scheme the server uses to protect the server-side program.	`GetAuthType`
`CONTENT_LENGTH`	The length (number of bytes) of the content sent as a `POST` request. This value represents the size of the data making up the input stream sent to the servlet.	`GetContentLength`
`CONTENT_TYPE`	The type of content sent to the server for requests that have attached data, such as `POST` or `PUT`.	`GetContentType`
`DOCUMENT_ROOT`	The root directory under which the documents and programs reside for the server-side application.	`getServletContext().getRealPath("/index.jsp")`
`PATH_INFO`	This is additional path information located in the URL but not including the query string. For example, in the URL `www.hungryminds.com/default/applications/index.jsp`, the `PATH_INFO` contains `/default/applications`.	`GetPathInfo`

Variable Name	*Description*	*Accessible Method*
PATH_TRANSLATED	This is the PATH_INFO value; however, it is converted from virtual paths into absolute paths on the server.	GetPathTranslated
QUERY_STRING	This is information sent as name/value pairs in the URL as a GET request.	GetQueryString
REMOTE_ADDR	The IP address of the client making the request.	GetRemoteAddr
REMOTE_HOST	The host name of the client making the request.	GetRemoteHost
REMOTE_USER	If the client has been authenticated, this value contains the username.	GetRemoteUser
REQUEST_METHOD	The type of HTTP request the client has made (for example, GET or POST).	GetMethod
SCRIPT_NAME	The name of the server-side program being executed.	GetServletPath
SERVER_NAME	The hostname of the server under which the current program is being executed.	GetServerName
SERVER_PORT	The port on the server where communications transactions can take place (for example, '80' for HTTP transactions.	GetServerPort
SERVER_PROTOCOL	The protocol name and version number the server supports to handle and process requests.	GetProtocol
SERVER_SOFTWARE	The name and version of the Web-server software being used to handle requests.	getServletContext().getServerInfo()

Table E-2 outlines additional HTTP header variables (prefixed by HTTP_) that the client may send. The server may exclude headers that have already been processed or exclude them due to its environment limitations.

These variables are accessible in the following format, request.getHeader ("Header-Name"). The HTTP_, and should not be included in the header name.

For example, accessing the value of the HTTP_ACCEPT header, is done in this format:

```
request.getHeader("Accept")
```

and in the HTTP_ACCEPT_LANGUAGE header as follows:

```
request.getHeader("Accept-Language")
```

Table E-2
HTTP_ Header Variables

Variable Name	*Description*
HTTP_ACCEPT	This header contains the MIME types that the client can accept/support.
HTTP_ACCEPT_LANGUAGE	The ISO code for the language the client supports. For example, 'en-us' is English as of the United States.
HTTP_ACCEPT_CHARSET	The character set the client has accepted (for example, iso-8859-1).
HTTP_CONNECTION	The type of HTTP connection requested (for example, 'Keep-Alive' or 'Close').
HTTP_COOKIE	The cookie value(s) sent as part of the request.
HTTP_ACCEPT_ENCODING	The encoding methods the client supports (for example, gzip).
HTTP_HOST	The hostname of the client making the request.
HTTP_PRAGMA	May contain directives such as 'no-cache'.
HTTP_REFERER	The URL of the page that refers the user to the current resource.
HTTP_USER_AGENT	Indicates the software the client uses to make requests. This header usually contains the browser name and version, for example, Mozilla/4.0 (compatible; MSIE 5.0; Windows NT, DigExt).

HTTP Headers

The following section summarizes some useful request/response headers in the HTTP 1.1 protocol.

You can find the detailed HTTP 1.1 RFC on the CDROM that accompanies this book.

Request headers

Accept

This indicates the media or MIME types that are acceptable as a response by the client. The * character is used to group MIME types into ranges. A header value of `*/*` indicates all MIME types. A `type/*` indicates support for all subtypes of the `type`.

Accept-Charset

This header field is used to indicate the supported character sets of the client (for example, iso-8859-5, unicode-1-1, and so on.

Accept-Encoding

This defines the content coding the client accepts.

Accept Language

This defines the set of client-preferred natural languages. These are represented by ISO codes (for example, en-us).

Authorization

A client can use this field to authenticate itself with the server.

From

This field often contains the e-mail address of the person controlling the user agent making the HTTP request.

Host

This field specifies the host and port number of the client that can be obtained from the original URI/URL or referring resource. This field must be included in all HTTP 1.1 requests.

If-Modified-Since

This field indicates to the server that the client wants the requested resource only if it has changed after the specified date. If the resource has not been modified, a status code 304 is returned.

If-Match

A client that has obtained one or more resources can verify those entities by including a list of their associated entity tags in this header field. This header is useful in PUT requests.

If-None-Match

Associated with If-Match; if none of the entity tags match, a status code 412 should be returned.

If-Range

If the client has a partial/partially current copy of the requested documents, this field can be used to retrieve only out-of-date documents.

If-Unmodified-Since

Similar to the If-Modified-Since field; if the requested resource/document has been modified since the specified date, the server must not perform the requested operation. A status code 412 is returned. This is most useful in PUT requests/operations.

Proxy-Authorization

This allows clients to identify themselves to proxies requiring authorization.

Range

An optional field the client can use to obtain missing parts of the requested document.

Referer

This field lets the client (optionally) specify the URL from which the request URL has been obtained.

User-Agent

This field contains information about the user agent and the type of user agent originating the request.

Response Headers

Age

Indicates an estimate of the amount of time that has passed, according to the server, since the response was last created.

Location

This contains the location to which the client may be directed (the current location of the requested resource).

Public

This header contains the request methods the server allows and supports.

Retry-After

This indicates the date and time at which the requested resource may be available. A time value is specified in seconds. The client can attempt to retry the request after the specified interval or at the specified time.

Server

This header contains the server name and version information processing the request.

This header may specify additional information about the response that the response-status code may not completely indicate. Refer to the RFC for more information about the currently defined warning codes.

General headers

These common headers can be used in requests and responses.

Cache-Control

This field contains cache-control directives that must be followed by caching mechanisms through the request-response chain.

Connection

This contains the preferred options for a particular connection. The `Keep-Alive` option signals that a persistent connection be used. HTTP 1.1 provides for the `close` option that signals for the closure of connection and indicates that a persistent connection is not required.

Date

Contains the date and time stamp at which the transaction has been generated.

HTTP Status Codes

Status codes are used in the HTTP to indicate (in the header part of the response) the status of request the user agent makes. Five classes of status codes indicate particular types of responses. Each of the status codes corresponds to an attribute (`SC_Name`) in the `HttpServletResponse` interface used to generate a response to the client. The following section summarizes the available status codes (in their respective classes) in the HTTP 1.1 standard.

Informational status codes 1XX

This class of codes is used for informational and provisional responses.

100 continue

This is used to indicate that the server has received the request and that the client should continue sending the complete request if it is not already doing so.

101 switching protocols

This indicates that the server accepts the client's request (through the Upgrade header field) to change the protocol.

Successful status codes 2XX

The 2XX range of status codes indicates to the client that the request has been successfully received and accepted.

200 OK

This indicates that the request has been successfully received and accepted; the response follows.

201 created

The server has successfully processed the request through the creation of a new resource. The URL of this resource is provided in the Location header field.

202 accepted

The request has been accepted by the server; however, further processing is required.

203 nonauthoritative information

The response being sent is not final/complete. The original document is not being returned to the client, however a copy of the original document is being returned.

204 no content

The request has been successfully processed by the server; however; there is no new content to provide to the client. Therefore, the current view in the client's browser is preserved. This status code is useful in cases in which you want to fulfill a request without updating the client's current browser view.

205 reset content

Similar to the 204 status; the request has been fulfilled; however, there is no new content to be displayed. The 205 status code causes the current view on the client to be reset/refreshed to clear any input that the client may have entered in form fields. This is particularly useful in situations in which a client may want to fill out the same form repeatedly with different information.

206 partial content

The server has fulfilled a part of the request (for the requested resource).

Redirection status codes 3XX

The 3XX range is used in the case of redirection or in cases in which the client requires further action to process the request. If the requested resource has changed locations, the server may respond with the current location of the resource in the response header. The client may make a subsequent request for the resource with the new location, or the server may simply redirect the client to the new location.

300 multiple choices

The requested resource is located in several locations (provided to the client). The server can indicate its preference in the location the client should go to by including the URL in the Location header field.

301 moved permanently

As the name suggests, the requested resource has a new permanent location contained in the Location header field.

302 moved temporarily

The resource has temporarily been relocated to the new URL provided in the Location header field.

303 see other

The resource can be found at the new location and should be accessed using the GET request method rather than POST.

304 not modified

This is used where the request has been accepted; however, the requested resource (using the GET method) has not been modified.

305 use proxy

This indicates to the client that the requested resource should be requested by using a proxy that is accessible at the location specified in the Location header field.

Client error-status codes 4XX

The 4XX range of status codes is used by the server to indicate to the client that there is an error with the client or with the request the client has made. These status codes are followed up with an explanation of the error.

400 bad request

The server has been unable to interpret the request, as the client has sent the request in an invalid format.

401 unauthorized

The current resource cannot be accessed, as a WWW-Authenticate header field has not been provided to authenticate the user. The user must authenticate himself or herself before attempting to access the requested resource.

402 payment method

This is a provisional code for future use.

403 forbidden

The client is denied access to the requested resource (authentication does not help).

404 not found

The requested resource cannot be found at the specified URL.

405 method not allowed

The requested resource cannot be requested using that particular type of HTTP request method.

406 not acceptable

The requested resource cannot be supplied using the media formats that the client can accept (that is, what has been specified in the Accept header field).

407 proxy authentication required

This is similar to the 401 status code in that the requested resource cannot be accessed without proxy authentication. The client must make the request with an applicable Proxy-Authorization header field.

408 request timeout

The server has timed out the request the client has made, as it has taken too long in making the request. The request being made may have taken an inadequate amount of time due to high network traffic. The client may repeat this request.

409 conflict

This can be returned when the request cannot be fulfilled, as there is some conflict with the current state of the resource and as the client can resolve this (perhaps through a resubmission of the request).

410 gone

This indicates that the requested resource is no longer available and that no location to the new address is specified. This code is returned in cases in which site owners want all links to the address to be removed.

411 length required

The client must send the request with the Content Length header value specified in order for the server to process the request.

412 precondition failed

One or more of the request header values has deemed to be false when evaluated on the server.

413 request entity too large

The requested resource is deemed to be too large to fulfill the request at this time. If the server can fulfill the request at a later time, the server may specify the Retry-After header value.

414 request-URI too long

The server cannot fulfill this GET request, as the URI/URL with which the request is being made is too long for the server to interpret.

415 unsupported media type

The server cannot process the request, as the entity body is in a format that is not supported on the server (using that HTTP request method).

Server error-status codes 5XX

The 5XX range indicates an error with the server in the attempt to process the request. These codes are accompanied by a reason why the request has been fulfilled.

500 internal server error

When the server or server-side application encounters a situation that is not taken care of, this results in the response not being sent or in a malformed response.

501 not implemented

This is returned when the server does not cater to the requested functionality in order to process the request.

502 bad gateway

This is returned when the server, in an attempt to process the request, has received a bad response from another server that was needed to complete the request.

503 service unavailable

The server cannot supply the requested resource, as it maybe overloaded or is in need of maintenance. If the outage time is known, a value may be supplied in the Retry-After header field.

504 gateway timeout

This is similar to the 502 status code; however, the server has timed out the response it has been receiving from the other server it has been attempting to access.

505 HTTP version not supported

As the name suggests, the request cannot be fulfilled, as the server does not support the version of the HTTP being used to make the request.

✦ ✦ ✦

Apache and Tomcat Configuration

The Apache Web server is widely used today. It is a free, open-source Web server that can be downloaded from the Internet (at `www.apache.org`). It is developed by a group interested in promoting open-source software on the Web.

Tomcat is a Servlet/JSP engine capable of handling requests to servlets and JSP applications on the Web. It provides a reference implementation to the latest servlet and JSP specifications of Sun Microsystems. Tomcat is developed by the Jakarta group (a division of Apache) as one of its various subprojects.

At the time of this writing, the latest releases of Apache and Tomcat are Apache 1.3.20 and Tomcat 3.2.3, respectively. Work is underway for the release of Apache 2.0 and Tomcat 4.0, but both are in beta stages. For this appendix, we use Apache 1.3.20 and Tomcat 3.2.3.

You can find the latest versions of Apache and Tomcat on the accompanying CD-ROM.

This appendix is divided into two sections. In the first section, we look at installing and configuring the Apache Web server. The second section deals with installing and configuring the Tomcat engine and integrating Tomcat with the Apache Web server.

Apache Installation

The Apache Web server is primarily designed to run on the UNIX platform. By popular demand, the Apache server has been ported to other platforms also. In this section, we cover installing the Apache server on two platforms: Windows and UNIX.

Compiling Apache for Microsoft Windows

The Apache Web server can be installed on all Windows systems running Windows 2000/NT/98/95. However, among the Windows family, it is often advised to install Apache on Windows 2000 or NT Server to get the maximum benefits. The Apache Web server is available in two forms for installation:

✦ **Binary distribution** — This distribution contains the Apache source files compiled for the win32 platform. The binary distribution is available as `.msi` packages on the Apache Web site. Microsoft Installer (`.msi`) is Microsoft's new format for packaging installation files. The Microsoft Installer comes built in with Windows 2000. For other versions of Windows (NT/98/95), the Microsoft installer can be downloaded from the Microsoft Web site.

✦ **Source distribution** — This distribution contains the entire source for Apache in a `.zip` file. Source files need to be compiled and linked with the appropriate modules to get Apache up and running. To make life simpler, the source distribution comes with installation scripts that help in compiling the source in the proper sequence and linking the appropriate modules.

For this discussion, we use the source distribution to install the Apache Web server.

The Apache source distribution can be found on the accompanying CD-ROM. Alternatively, you can download the same from `http://www.apache.org`.

Any software installation comes with a checklist of to-do's that need to be completed before beginning any successful installation. The following points need to be taken care of before you compile and install Apache:

✦ The Apache server for Windows requires a Visual C++ compiler to compile all source files. Ensure that Microsoft VC++ 5.0 or 6.0 is installed and is working properly before beginning the installation.

✦ If you choose to compile source files from the command-line environment instead of from the Visual Studio GUI, you need `vcvars32.bat`, which helps set the environment for compilation. The batch file can be found in the `vc98/bin` folder in the Visual Studio directory in the case of VC++ 6.0

✦ You also need the awk utility in the `<visual studio installation directory>/bin` folder. For this discussion, I will assume that Visual Studio is installed in C:\Program files \VisualStudio. The awk utility is internally used by installation scripts to construct and install the binaries for the win32 platform. The awk does not come with the Visual Studio installation. You can download it from http://cm.bel-labs.com/cm/cs/who/bwk/awk95.exe. After downloading, rename the file as awk.exe and copy it to the aforementioned folder.

We are now ready to compile the source and begin the installation process. Unpack the Apache distribution into an appropriate directory. Open a command-line prompt, and change to the src subdirectory of the Apache distribution.

Set up the environment for compilation and installation by running the vcvars32.bat present in the C:\Program Files\VisualStudio\VC98\bin folder or the location appropriate to your system from the command prompt.

The master Apache makefile instructions are in the Makefile.win file. To compile Apache on Windows, use one of the following commands:

`nmake /f Makefile.win _apacher` **(release build)**

`nmake /f Makefile.win _apached` **(debug build)**

Both compile Apache. The latter includes debugging information in the resulting files, making it easier to find bugs and track down problems.

The following projects under the Apache source are compiled to generate Apache.exe in the following order:

- ap.dsp
- ApacheOS.dsp
- gen_test_char.dsp
- gen_uri_delims.dsp
- regex.dsp
- Win9xConHook.dsp
- ApacheCore.dsp
- Apache.dsp
- mod_auth_anon.dsp
- sdbm.dsp
- mod_auth_dbm.dsp
- mod_auth_digest.dsp
- mod_cern_meta.dsp

- mod_digest.dsp
- mod_expires.dsp
- mod_headers.dsp
- mod_info.dsp
- mod_proxy.dsp
- mod_rewrite.dsp
- mod_speling.dsp
- mod_status.dsp
- mod_usertrack.dsp
- htdigest.dsp
- htpasswd.dsp
- logresolve.dsp
- rotatelogs.dsp
- xmltok.dsp
- xmlparse.dsp

Once all the modules are compiled without errors, install the files by issuing the following command from the command prompt:

`nmake /f Makefile.win installr INSTDIR=`*`c:\ServerRoot`* **(for release build)**

`nmake /f Makefile.win installd INSTDIR=`*`c:\ServerRoot`* **(for debug build)**

`INSTDIR` specifies the location where all the Apache files have to be installed. If this argument is omitted, installation occurs in `\Apache` on the current drive.

The directory structures for the installed files follow:

- *c:\ServerRoot*\Apache.exe — Apache program
- *c:\ServerRoot*\ApacheCore.dll — Apache runtime [shared library]
- *c:\ServerRoot*\Win9xConHook.dll — Win9x console fixups [shared library]
- *c:\ServerRoot*\xmlparse.dll — XML parser [shared library]
- *c:\ServerRoot*\xmltok.dll — XML token engine [shared library]
- *c:\ServerRoot*\bin*.exe —- Administration programs
- *c:\ServerRoot*\cgi-bin — Example CGI scripts

- `c:\ServerRoot\conf` — Configuration files directory
- `c:\ServerRoot\icons` — Icons for FancyIndexing
- `c:\ServerRoot\include\*.h` — Apache header files
- `c:\ServerRoot\htdocs` — Welcome `index.html` pages
- `c:\ServerRoot\htdocs\manual` — Apache documentation
- `c:\ServerRoot\lib` — Static library files
- `c:\ServerRoot\libexec` — Dynamic link libraries
- `c:\ServerRoot\logs` — Empty logging directory
- `c:\ServerRoot\modules\mod_*.so` — Loadable Apache modules

Apache can also be compiled by using VC++'s Visual Studio development environment. To simplify this process, a Visual Studio workspace, `Apache.dsw`, is provided in the `src` folder. This workspace exposes the entire list of working `.dsp` projects required for the complete Apache binary release. It includes dependencies between projects to assure that they are built in the appropriate order. InstallBin is the top-level project that builds all others and installs compiled files in their proper locations.

While compiling through the Visual Studio development environment, care must be taken to build all dependent projects first. To simplify the process, dependencies between all projects are defined in the Microsoft Visual Studio workspace file `Apache.dsw`. `Apache.dsw` is also set as the default project. Hence, building `Apache.dsw` ensures that all subprojects are built in order.

Compiling Apache for Linux

In this section, let's see how to install Apache under a Linux platform. The installation procedure specified here applies to all UNIX flavors. As in the case of Windows, the UNIX version of Apache comes in binary distribution and source distribution.

For Linux systems, Apache binaries are available in RPM format. Users comfortable with installing rpm format files may download these from the Apache Web site.

Before compiling Apache from the source distribution, you must take care of the following:

- An A C compiler such as gcc or its equivalent must be available.
- A make utility such as make or equivalent must be available.
- Tools such as gunzip and tar must be available.

After ensuring that the prerequisites are taken care of, download the Linux version of the Apache source distribution from the Apache Web site. The Apache source distribution is normally available in compressed archive format with a .gz extension. Let's assume that the downloaded file is available in the root user's home directory /root.

Unzip and expand the compressed archive by issuing the following commands:

```
# gunzip apache_1.3.20.tar.gz
# tar -xvf apache_1.3.20.tar
```

These commands create a folder with the name apache_1.3.20, and all the files in the compressed archive are expanded into this location with the appropriate directory structure.

Under the apache_1.3.20 folder, you find a file named configure, which is a shell script responsible for compiling source files and making the Apache source ready for installation. From this step onward, the entire installation should be carried out under the root user. Issue the following command from the command prompt:

```
# ./configure
```

Here is the output of the command:

```
Configuring for Apache, Version 1.3.20
 + using installation path layout: Apache (config.layout)
Creating Makefile
Creating Configuration.apaci in src
Creating Makefile in src
 + configured for Linux platform
 + setting C compiler to gcc
 + setting C pre-processor to gcc -E
 + checking for system header files
 + adding selected modules
 + checking sizeof various data types
 + doing sanity check on compiler and options
Creating Makefile in src/support
Creating Makefile in src/regex
Creating Makefile in src/os/unix
Creating Makefile in src/ap
Creating Makefile in src/main
Creating Makefile in src/lib/expat-lite
Creating Makefile in src/modules/standard
```

The configure script creates the make files necessary for compiling the Apache source. The configure script also sets the default path under which Apache is installed: /usr/local/apache. However, you can alter this by passing the install location as a parameter to configure the script. Use ./configurehelp to see the list of available options.

Once the necessary scripts are available, you can compile the source by issuing the following command from the prompt:

```
# make
```

The make command compiles all source files and dependent files in the specified order and makes the system ready for installation. Once make completes its job, the Apache Web server can be installed by issuing the following command:

```
# make install
```

After a successful installation, the following message appears in the command prompt:

```
+--------------------------------------------------------+
| You now have successfully built and installed the      |
| Apache 1.3 HTTP server. To verify that Apache actually |
| works correctly you now should first check the         |
| (initially created or preserved) configuration files   |
|                                                        |
|   /usr/local/apache/conf/httpd.conf                    |
|                                                        |
| and then you should be able to immediately fire up     |
| Apache the first time by running:                      |
|                                                        |
|   /usr/local/apache/bin/apachectl start                |
|                                                        |
| Thanks for using Apache.       The Apache Group        |
|                                http://www.apache.org/  |
+--------------------------------------------------------+
```

Starting and Stopping Apache

On Windows

There are two ways of starting and stopping the Apache Web server in Windows. This depends on the way in which Apache has been installed. If Apache is installed from a binary distribution (.exe or .msi), the installation process installs Apache as a service on Windows NT/2000. In such cases, the Apache service can be started or stopped by using the Services control panel.

Apache Web server can be started by issuing the following command from the command prompt:

```
D:\ApacheServer1.3.20>apache -k start
```

On Windows NT/2000, we can instruct the installer to run Apache as a service. In such cases, the Apache Web server can be started or stopped using the Services option in the control panel.

What follows are the various options that can be supplied to Apache.exe:

```
D:\ApacheServer1.3.20>apache -h
Usage: APACHE.EXE [-D name] [-d directory] [-f file] [-n service]
                  [-C "directive"] [-c "directive"] [-k signal]
                  [-v] [-V] [-h] [-l] [-L] [-S] [-t] [-T]
  -D name           : define a name for use in <IfDefine name> directives
  -d directory      : specify an alternate initial ServerRoot
  -f file           : specify an alternate ServerConfigFile
  -C "directive"    : process directive before reading config files
  -c "directive"    : process directive after  reading config files
  -v                : show version number
  -V                : show compile settings
  -h                : list available command line options (this page)
  -l                : list compiled-in modules
  -L                : list available configuration directives
  -S                : show parsed settings (currently only vhost settings)
  -t                : run syntax check for config files (with docroot check)
  -T                : run syntax check for config files (without docroot check)
  -n name           : name the Apache service for -k options below;
  -k stop|shutdown : tell running Apache to shutdown
  -k restart        : tell running Apache to do a graceful restart
  -k start          : tell Apache to start
  -k install   | -i: install an Apache service
  -k config         : reconfigure an installed Apache service
  -k uninstall | -u: uninstall an Apache service
```

On Linux

Apache on Linux can be started by using a shell script provided for that purpose. The shell script is apachectl and can be found under the bin directory in the Apache installation.

Assuming Apache is installed in /usr/local/apache, you can start Apache by issuing the following command from the command prompt:

```
$ /usr/local/apache/bin/apachectl start
```

The various options provided by apachectl can be obtained by using the following command:

```
$ /usr/local/apache/bin/apachectl help

usage: /usr/local/apache/bin/apachectl
(start|stop|restart|fullstatus|status|graceful|configtest|help)

start      - start httpd
stop       - stop httpd
restart    - restart httpd if running by sending a SIGHUP or start if
             not running
```

```
fullstatus - dump a full status screen; requires lynx and mod_status enabled
status     - dump a short status screen; requires lynx and mod_status enabled
graceful   - do a graceful restart by sending a SIGUSR1 or start if not running
configtest - do a configuration syntax test
help       - this screen
```

Configuring Apache

The heart of Apache is a configuration file that contains all the settings Apache uses. Apache uses a default-configuration file called `httpd.conf` that resides in the `conf` directory under the Apache installation. Whenever the Apache Web server starts, it reads this configuration file to initialize itself. It is not mandatory that all configuration settings be mentioned in `httpd.conf`. If you want to use a different configuration file, you can specify it with the `-f` option while starting Apache.

Apache also contains two more configuration files in addition to `httpd.conf`, which it uses to initialize itself during startup. The files are `srm.conf` and `access.conf` and are present in the `conf` directory under Apache installation. The `srm.conf` contains all resource-configuration directives, and `access.conf` contains all access-control directives. Apache processes `httpd.conf`, `srm.conf`, and `access.conf` in the order specified to read the configuration information. The latest versions of Apache have deprecated usage of these files. All entries specified as part of these files are now moved to `httpd.conf`, thereby providing a single place to configure and control the Apache Web server.

In addition to the configuration files just mentioned, Apache provides `.htaccess` files in which configuration information can be specified. These files reside in each virtual directory defined in the Web server and control the configuration information for files and directories under the specified directory. An important thing to be noted about `.htaccess` files is that they are read for each request to that directory, unlike other configuration files, such as `httpd.conf`, which is read only once during the start or restart of the Web server.

Configuration directive

Any configuration file Apache reads has to specify configuration information in the form of *directives*. Directives follow a specialized syntax and carry a specific meaning that instructs Apache to perform a particular action. A configuration file can contain one or more directives. Each directive carries one or more arguments necessary to carry out the specified action. Directives may contain one or more directives under them. The nesting of directives is governed by the context in which a particular directive is being used. Apache reads each directive line by line and performs the necessary associated action.

Configuration context

Any directive specified in a server configuration file is governed by a *context*. A context defines the section in the configuration file where a particular directive can be used. Apache defines four different contexts:

- **server config:** — This means the directive may be used in the server-configuration files (for example, `httpd.conf`, `srm.conf`, and `access.conf`), but *not* within any `<VirtualHost>` or `<Directory>` containers. The directive is not allowed in `.htaccess` files. Directives specified in this context are applicable to the entire server.
- **virtual host:** — This context means that the directive may appear inside `<VirtualHost>` containers in server-configuration files. Directives specified in this context are effective only to the virtual host under which they are specified. They do not affect any resource outside the defined virtual host.
- **directory:** — A directive marked *valid* in this context may be used inside `<Directory>`, `<Location>`, and `<Files>` containers in server-configuration files. Directives specified in this context are applicable only to the directory under the control of this context.
- **`.htaccess`:** — If a directive is valid in this context, it can appear inside per-directory `.htaccess` files. Directives specified in this context are applicable to all files and subdirectories that exist in the same directory as the `.htaccess` file.

Each directive specifies the context in which it can be used. A directive may be specified in more than one context. In such cases, an override attribute is associated with the context that specifies which context has to be chosen. For example, take a `DirectoryIndex` directive. The `DirectoryIndex` directive sets the list of resources to look for when the client requests an index of the directory by specifying a slash (/) at the end of the directory name. The context for this directive can be server config, virtual host, directory, or `.htaccess`. Assume that this directive is specified at the server config context and `.htaccess` context of a particular directory. Assuming the override behavior is set to true, the `DirectoryIndex` argument specified in the `.htaccess` file takes precedence over the one specified in the server config context whenever a client requests an index of the particular directory.

Common configuration directives

In this section, let's look into the most commonly used configuration directives that help us configure the Apache Web server. As we discuss each directive, we also will see the context in which the directive is applicable.

ServerRoot directive

Syntax: `ServerRoot` *`directory name`*

Example: `ServerRoot /usr/local/apache` (on Linux)

`ServerRoot "d:/ApacheServer1.3.20"` (on Windows)

Context: server config

The ServerRoot directive sets the directory in which the server is installed. Typically, it contains subdirectories such as conf and logs. Relative path references to other configuration files specified in the httpd.conf are taken as relative to this directory.

Listen directive

Syntax: Listen [*IP-address*:]*port*

Context: server config

Example: Listen 3000

Listen 192.21.7.109:4000

The Listen directive instructs Apache to listen to more than one IP address or port. By default, it responds to requests on all IP interfaces, but only on the port the Port directive provides. It tells the server to accept incoming requests on the specified port or address-and-port combination. If only the port number is specified, the server listens to the given port on all network interfaces instead of to the port the Port directive provides. If an IP address is given as well as a port, the server listens on the given port and network interface.

Note that you may still require a Port directive so that URLs that Apache generates that point to your server will still work. Multiple Listen directives may be used to specify a number of addresses and ports to listen to. The server responds to requests from any of the listed addresses and ports.

Port directive

Syntax: Port *number*

Example: Port 80

Context: server config

The Port directive specifies the port number Apache uses to listen to incoming requests. By default, the port on which the Web server listens is 80. The number argument can range from 0 to 65535; some port numbers (especially those below 1024) are reserved for particular protocols. Therefore, you must be careful while selecting a port.

If any Listen or BindAddress directives are specifying a number, Port has no impact on the address where the server listens.

ServerName directive

Syntax: `ServerName` *`fully-qualified-domain-name`*

Example: `ServerName www.servletbible.com`

Context: server config, virtual host

The `ServerName` directive sets the hostname of the server and is used when creating redirection URLs. `ServerName` allows you to set a host name that is sent back to clients for your server if it is different from the host name the program produces (that is, using "www" instead of the host's real name). The name defined here must be a valid DNS name for the host. If the host doesn't have a registered DNS name, enter the IP address.

DocumentRoot directive

Syntax: `DocumentRoot` *`directory-filename`*

Example: `DocumentRoot /usr/local/apache/htdocs` (Linux)

`DocumentRoot "d:/ApacheServer1.3.20/htdocs"` (Windows)

Context: server config, virtual host

The `DocumentRoot` directive specifies the default directory for the Web server that contains all the files that can be served upon a client request. All sections of the URL after the `http://ipaddress:port/` section are searched under the `DocumentRoot`. However, this default-search behavior can be overridden if the `Alias` directive is specified.

<Directory> directive

Example:

```
<Directory />
Options FollowSymLinks
AllowOverride None
</Directory>
```

Context: server config, virtual host

This directive opens a section enclosing a group of directives that apply to the named directory and its subdirectories. Any directive allowed in a directory context may be used. The directory argument is either a directory path or a wildcard pattern for a directory path. If multiple sections match a directory (or its parent directories) containing a document, the sections are applied in order, beginning with the shortest match first, interspersed with directives from the `.htaccess` files along the path to the directory.

Options directive

Syntax: `Options [+|-]option [[+|-]option] ...`

Example: `Options FollowSymLinks MultiViews`

Context: server config, virtual host, directory, `.htaccess`

The `Options` directive controls which server features are available in a particular directory. The option can be set to `None`, in which case none of the extra features are enabled. The `All` option enables all options except for `MultiViews`. This is the default setting. The `ExecCGI` allows execution of CGI scripts. `FollowSymLinks` allows the server to follow symbolic links in a specified directory. `Includes` indicates that server-side includes are permitted. `IncludesNOEXEC` allows server-side includes, but the `#exec` command and `#include` of CGI scripts are disabled. `Indexes` generates a default index page if no index page is specified for the requested URL. If a URL that maps to a directory is requested and there is no `DirectoryIndex` (for example, `index.html`) in that directory, the server returns a formatted listing of the directory.

AllowOverride directive

Syntax: `AllowOverride All|None|directive-type [directive-type]`

Example: `AllowOverride All`

Context: directory

When the server finds an `.htaccess` file (as specified by `AccessFileName`), it needs to know which directives declared in that file can override access information provided at a higher context than the current one. The `AllowOverride` directive allows you to specify what directives can be overridden in the current context.

When this directive is set to `None`, `.htaccess` files are completely ignored. In this case, the server does not attempt to read `.htaccess` files in the file system.

When this directive is set to `All`, any directive that has the `.htaccess` context is allowed in `.htaccess` files.

The *`directive-type`* can be one of the following groupings of directives:

✦ **`AuthConfig`:** Allows use of the authorization directives (`AuthDBMGroupFile`, `AuthDBMUserFile`, `AuthGroupFile`, `AuthName`, `AuthType`, `AuthUserFile`, `Require`, and so on)

✦ **`FileInfo`:** Allows use of the directives controlling document types (`AddEncoding`, `AddLanguage`, `AddType`, `DefaultType`, `ErrorDocument`, `LanguagePriority`, and so on)

- **`Indexes`:** Allows use of the directives controlling directory indexing (`AddDescription`, `AddIcon`, `AddIconByEncoding`, `AddIconByType`, `DefaultIcon`, `DirectoryIndex`, `FancyIndexing`, `HeaderName`, `IndexIgnore`, `IndexOptions`, `ReadmeName`, and so on)
- **`Limit`:** Allows use of the directives controlling host access (`Allow`, `Deny`, and `Order`)
- **`Options`:** Allows use of the directives controlling specific directory features (`Options` and `XBitHack`)

Order directive

Syntax: `Order` *`ordering`*

Default: `Order Deny,Allow`

Context: directory, `.htaccess`

The `Order` directive controls the default access state and the order in which `Allow` and `Deny` directives are evaluated. Ordering is one of the following:

- **`Deny,Allow`:** `Deny` directives are evaluated before `Allow` directives. Access is allowed by default. Any client that does not match a `Deny` directive or does match an `Allow` directive is allowed access to the server.
- **`Allow,Deny`:** `Allow` directives are evaluated before `Deny` directives. Access is denied by default. Any client that does not match an `Allow` directive or does match a `Deny` directive is denied access to the server.
- **`Mutual-failure`:** Only hosts that appear on the `Allow` list and do not appear on the `Deny` list are granted access. This ordering has the same effect as `Order Allow,Deny` and is deprecated in favor of that configuration.

Keywords may only be separated by a comma; no white space is allowed between them. Note that, in all cases, every `Allow` and `Deny` statement is evaluated.

In the following example, all hosts in the `apache.org` domain are allowed access; all other hosts are denied access:

```
Order Deny,Allow
Deny from all
Allow from apache.org
```

In the next example, all hosts in the `apache.org` domain are allowed access, except for hosts in the `foo.apache.org` subdomain. All hosts not in the `apache.org` domain are denied access because the default state is to deny access to the server.

```
Order Allow,Deny
Allow from apache.org
Deny from foo.apache.org
```

On the other hand, if the `Order` in the last example is changed to `Deny,Allow`, all hosts are allowed access. This happens because, regardless of the actual ordering of the directives in the configuration file, the `Allow from apache.org` is evaluated last and overrides the `Deny from foo.apache.org`. All hosts not in the `apache.org` domain are allowed access because the default state changes to *allow*.

The presence of an `Order` directive can affect access to a part of the server, even in the absence of accompanying `Allow` and `Deny` directives, because of its effect on the default-access state. For example:

```
<Directory /www>
  Order Allow,Deny
</Directory>
```

This denies all access to the `/www` directory because the default access state is set to *deny*.

The `Order` directive controls the order of access-directive processing only within each phase of the server's configuration processing. This implies, for example, that an `Allow` or `Deny` directive occurring in a `<Location>` section is always evaluated after an `Allow` or `Deny` directive occurring in a `<Directory>` section or an `.htaccess` file, regardless of the setting of the `Order` directive. For details on the merging of configuration sections, see the documentation on how `Directory, Location` and `Files` sections work.

DirectoryIndex directive

Syntax: `DirectoryIndex` *`local-url`* `[`*`local-url`*`] ...`

Default: `DirectoryIndex index.html`

Context: server config, virtual host, directory, `.htaccess`

The `DirectoryIndex` directive sets the list of resources to look for when the client requests an index of the directory by specifying a slash (/) at the end of the directory name. *`Local-url`* is the URL of a document on the server relative to the requested directory; it is usually the name of a file in the directory. Several URLs may be given, in which case the server returns the first it finds. If none of the resources exist and the `Indexes` option is set, the server generates its own listing of the directory.

AccessFileName directive

Syntax: `AccessFileName` *`filename`* `[`*`filename`*`] ...`

Example: `AccessFileName .htaccess my.htaccess`

Context: server config, virtual host

When returning a document to the client, the server looks for the first existing access-control file from this list of names in every directory of the path to the document (if access-control files are enabled for that directory). The default file name is `.htaccess`.

`AccessFileNames` usually start with a period (.) so that they are treated as hidden files on UNIX systems. On a Windows system, files starting with a period are not allowed, so a different name has to be specified.

Alias directive

Syntax: `Alias` *`url-path directory-filename`*

Example: `Alias /myalias/ "d:/mynewdirectory/"`

Context: server config, virtual host

The `Alias` directive allows documents to be stored in the local file system other than under the `DocumentRoot`. URLs with a path beginning with *`url-path`* are mapped to local files beginning with *`directory-filename`*.

Example: `Alias /image /ftp/pub/image`

A request for `http://myserver/image/foo.gif` causes the server to return the file `/ftp/pub/image/foo.gif`.

Note that if you include a trailing / on the `url-path`, the server requires a trailing / to expand the alias. That is, if you use `Alias /icons/ /usr/local/apache/icons/`, the `url /icons` is not aliased.

Note that you may need to specify additional `<Directory>` sections that cover the destination of aliases. Aliasing occurs before `<Directory>` sections are checked, so only the destination of aliases is affected. (Note, however, that `<Location>` sections are run through once before aliases are performed, so they do apply.)

Logging in Apache

Apache Web server maintains a record of all the operations it has performed in log files. Apache uses two main log files: `access.log` and `error.log`. They can be found in the `logs` subdirectory of the Apache installation directory.

Access logs

The access log file records all access to the Web server from any host. The access log provides important information, such as which resources are accessed from the server and the IP address of the client that has accessed the particular resource. The access log also specifies the HTTP request method and version number, in addition to other things. The default location of the access log is in the `logs` subdirectory of the Apache installation root. However, it can be modified by using the following entry in `httpd.conf`:

```
CustomLog logs/access.log common
```

Error logs

The error log file is located in the same location as the access log. Apache records messages regarding any error in the error log. The error log also contains diagnostic and informative messages such as server startup, server shutdown, and so on. The location of the error log can be controlled by the `error log` directive in the `httpd.conf` file.

```
ErrorLog logs/error.log
```

The log level for error messages stored in the error log can be controlled by the `LogLevel` directive.

```
LogLevel level
```

Possible values for the level are shown in Table F-1.

Table F-1
Log Levels and Their Meanings

Level	***Description***
`Emerg`	Emergencies – system is unusable
`Alert`	Action must be taken immediately.
`Crit`	Critical conditions
`Error`	Error conditions
`Warn`	Warning conditions
`Notice`	Normal but significant condition
`Info`	Informational
`Debug`	Debug-level messages

Tomcat Installation

Tomcat is a servlet and JSP reference implementation from Sun. It is available as a free download from `http://jakarta.apache.org`. Tomcat is designed to function as a standalone server or in tandem with other servers. For purposes of simplicity, we will first look into installing and configuring Tomcat as a standalone server. Later, we will look into how we can configure Tomcat with Apache so that they work together.

Installing and configuring Tomcat

Tomcat server can be installed and configured in more than one way. It can be set up to function as an in-process server, out-of-process server, or standalone server. For the purposes of our discussion, we will look at how to install and configure Tomcat as a standalone server. A later section covers installing and configuring Tomcat as an out-of-process server for Apache Web server.

The Tomcat installation as a standalone server involves a few steps, and they are common for both Windows and Linux:

1. Download the binary distribution of Tomcat from `http://jakarta.apache.org/tomcat`.
2. Unzip the distribution to a local directory on the server.
3. Ensure that JDK is installed and available.
4. Set the path to environment variables that Tomcat uses.
5. Start the Tomcat server.

On Windows

The binary distribution of Tomcat for Windows comes as a zip file and can be unzipped using any uncompress utility available for Windows. Uncompress the Tomcat distribution to `c:\Jakarta-tomcat-3.2.3`.

Now set the path to the `JAVA_HOME` variable. This is required for Tomcat to find the location of the JDK installed on the local system.

On a Windows NT/2000 system, you can set the variable in the following location:

Control Panel ➪ System ➪ Advanced ➪ Environment Variables

The next step is to set the value of the `TOMCAT_HOME` variable. Set this value to where the binary distribution of Tomcat has been extracted. In our case, it is `c:\Jakarta-tomcat-3.2.3`.

With this, the installation of Tomcat is complete. We are not ready to start the Tomcat server. The preceding commands can be set in the `autoexec.bat` so that these variables are available when we launch Tomcat from a command window.

On Linux

The binary distribution for Linux comes as a `gzipped` file. It can be uncompressed using the following command:

```
$ gunzip jakarta-tomcat-3.2.3.tar.gz | tar -xvf
```

Set the path of `JAVA_HOME` using the following command:

```
$ JAVA_HOME=/usr/local/jdk1.2.2; export JAVA_HOME
```

Set the path to the Tomcat home directory as follows:

```
$ TOMCAT_HOME=/usr/local/jakarta-tomcat-3.2.3; export TOMCAT_HOME
```

The preceding command can be included in `.bash_profile` so that the variables are set every time the user logs in.

Starting and stopping Tomcat

Once Tomcat is installed, Tomcat can be started on a Windows system using the following command from the command prompt:

```
C:\> cd jakarta-tomcat-3.2.3
C:\jakarta-tomcat-3.2.3> cd bin
C:\jakarta-tomcat-3.2.3\bin> startup.bat
```

To shut down Tomcat, run the `shutdown.bat` file present in the `bin` directory of the Tomcat installation.

On a Linux/UNIX system, Tomcat can be started as follows:

```
$ cd /usr/local/jakarta-tomcat-3.2.3/bin
$ ./startup.sh
```

To shut down Tomcat on a Linux system, run the `shutdown.sh` shell script from the `bin` directory of the Tomcat installation.

The Tomcat installation can be tested by issuing the following URL from a browser: `http://localhost:8080`.

The output in the browser after issuing this command should appear as in Figure F-1.

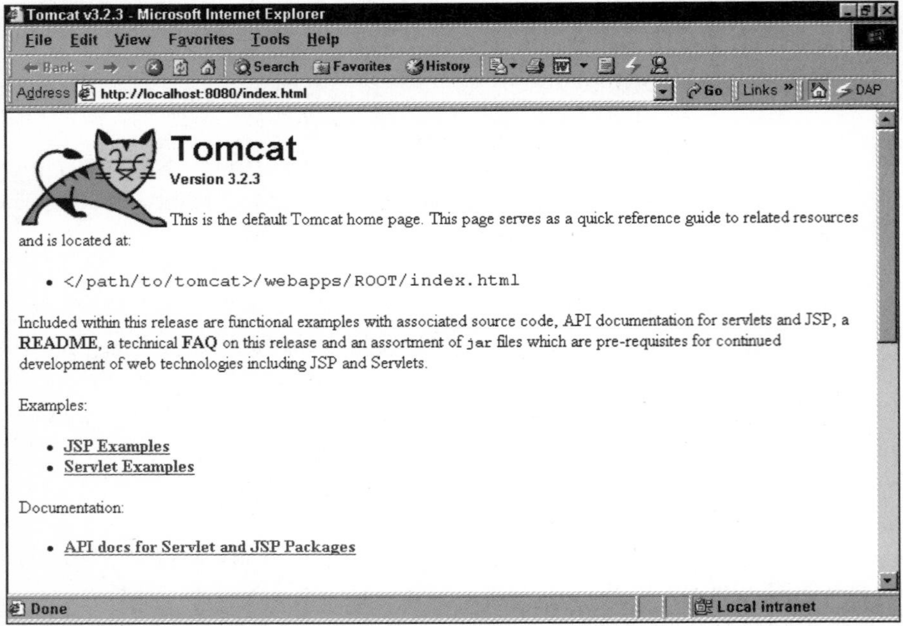

Figure F-1: Tomcat installation

Tomcat directory structure

After a successful installation of Tomcat, the directory resembles the entries in Table F-2.

Table F-2
Tomcat Directory Structure

Directory Name	*Description*
`bin`	Contains startup/shutdown scripts
`conf`	Contains various configuration files, including `server.xml` (Tomcat's main configuration file) and `web.xml`, which sets default values for the various Web applications deployed in Tomcat
`doc`	Contains miscellaneous documents regarding Tomcat

Directory Name	*Description*
`lib`	Contains various `jar` files Tomcat uses. On UNIX, any file in this directory is appended to Tomcat's `CLASSPATH`.
`logs`	This is where Tomcat places its log files.
`src`	The servlet API's source files. Don't get excited, though: These are only the empty interfaces and abstract classes that should be implemented by any servlet container.
`Webapps`	Contains sample Web applications
`work`	Automatically generated by Tomcat, this is where Tomcat places intermediate files (such as compiled JSP files) during its work. If you delete this directory while Tomcat is running, you will not be able to execute JSP pages.
`classes`	You can create this directory to add classes to the `CLASSPATH`. Any class you add to this directory finds its place in Tomcat's `CLASSPATH`.

Configuring Tomcat

The heart of Tomcat configuration lies in two files:

- `server.xml` — Contains all global configuration settings.
- `web.xml` — Contains context-related configuration information.

Let's look into the configuration of these files in detail.

server.xml

`server.xml` is Tomcat's main configuration file. It can be found in the `conf` directory in the Tomcat installation. It serves two goals:

- It provides initial configuration for Tomcat components.
- It specifies the structure for Tomcat, letting Tomcat boot and build itself by instantiating components as specified in `server.xml`.

The important elements in `server.xml` are described in Table F-3.

Table F-3
Elements in the server.xml File

Element	*Description*
Server	This is the topmost element in the file server.xml. The server defines a single Tomcat server. Generally, you should not bother with this too much. A Server element can contain elements of type Logger and ContextManager.
Logger	This element defines a logger object. Each logger has a name to identify it, as well as a path to the log file to contain the logger output and a verbosityLevel (that specifies the log level). Currently, there are loggers for the servlets (where the ServletContext.log() goes), JSP files, and the Tomcat runtime.
ContextManager	A ContextManager specifies the configuration and structure for a set of ContextInterceptors, RequestInterceptors, and contexts and their connectors. The ContextManager has a few attributes that provide it with the following: •The debug level used for logging debug messages •The base location for webapps/, conf/, logs/, and all defined contexts. It is used to start Tomcat from a directory other than TOMCAT_HOME. •The name of the working directory •A flag to control whether stack traces and other debug information are included in the default responses
ContextInterceptor RequestInterceptor	These interceptors listen for certain events that happenin & the ContextManager. For example, the ContextInterceptor listens for startup and shutdown events of Tomcat, and the RequestInterceptor watches the various phases that user requests need to pass if is serviced. Tomcat's administrator doesn't need to know much about the interceptors. A developer, on the other hand, should know that this is how global types of operations can be implemented in Tomcat (for example, security and per-request logging).

Element	*Description*
`Context`	Each `Context` represents a path in the Tomcat hierarchy where you place a Web application. A Tomcat context has the following configuration: •The path where the context is located. This can be a full path or relative to the `ContextManager`'s home. •A debug level used for logging debug messages •A reloadable flag When developing a servlet, it is very convenient to have Tomcat reload it upon change; this lets you fix bugs and have Tomcat test the new code without the need to shut down and restart. To turn on servlet reloading, set the reloadable flag to true. Detecting changes, however, is time consuming; moreover, because new servlets are getting loaded in a new class-loader object, there are cases in which this class-reloading trigger casts errors. To avoid these problems, set the reloadable flag to false; this disables the autoreload feature.

web.xml

`web.xml` contains information related to Web-application configuration. The servlet 2.2 specification introduced the notion of a Web configuration that all servlet containers should adhere to while creating and deploying Web applications. Tomcat lets the user define default `web.xml` values for all contexts by putting a default `web.xml` file in the `conf` directory. When constructing a new context, Tomcat uses the default `web.xml` file as the base configuration and the application-specific `web.xml` (the one located in the application's `WEB-INF/web.xml`) to overwrite these defaults.

Web applications

According to the servlet 2.2 specification, a "Web Application is a collection of servlets, HTML pages, classes, and other resources that can be bundled and run on multiple containers from multiple vendors." Simply stated, a Web application is anything that resides in the Web layer of an application. Every Web application has one `ServletContext`. The `ServletContext` of one Web application does not clash with another.

A Web application consists of the following items:

- ✦ Servlets
- ✦ JSP
- ✦ Utility classes
- ✦ Static documents (HTML, images, sounds, and so on)
- ✦ Client-side applets, JavaBeans, and classes
- ✦ A deployment descriptor and metainformation about the application

Directory structure for Web applications

A Web application contains a structure hierarchy of directories within itself. Each directory is used to store a specific component of the application. Any Web application that has to be deployed in Tomcat has to conform to the directory structure. Table F-4 shows the directory structure of a sample Web application named `test` and what each of its directories should contain. Each of these directories should be created from the `<SERVER_ROOT>` of the servlet container. An example of a `<SERVER_ROOT>`, using Tomcat, is `/jakarta-tomcat-3.2.3/webapps`.

Table F-4
Directory Structure for a Web Application

Directory	*Description*
`/test`	This is the root directory of the Web application. All JSP, HTML, and image files are stored here.
`/test/WEB-INF`	This directory contains all resources related to the application that are not in the document root of the application. This is where your Web-application deployment descriptor is located. Note that the `WEB-INF` directory is not part of the public document. No files contained in this directory can be served directly to a client.
`/test/WEB-INF/classes`	This directory is where servlets and utility classes are located.
`/test/WEB-INF/lib`	This directory contains Java archive files that the Web application depends upon. For example, this is where you place a `JAR` file that contains a JDBC driver.

The Web-application deployment descriptor

The deployment descriptor is the heart of all Web applications. The deployment descriptor is an XML file named `web.xml` located in the `/<SERVER_ROOT>/applicationname/WEB-INF/` directory. It describes configuration information for the entire Web application. For our application, the location of the web.xml file is the /<SERVER_ROOT>/test/WEB-INF/ directory. Information contained in the deployment descriptor includes the following elements:

- ServletContext Init parameters
- Localized content
- Session configuration
- Servlet/JSP definitions
- Servlet/JSP mappings
- Mime type mappings
- Welcome file list
- Error pages
- Security

The following code snippet contains a limited example of a Web-application deployment descriptor. As we progress through this series, we will look at the web.xml file and its elements in much more detail.

```
<web-app>
  <display-name>TEST WEB Application</display-name>
  <session-timeout>30</session-timeout>
  <servlet>
    <servlet-name>EchoServlet</servlet-name>
    <servlet-class>request.EchoServlet</servlet-class>
    <load-on-startup>1</load-on-startup>
  </servlet>
</web-app>
```

In this example, we are setting three application-level elements. The first application-level elements is <display-name>. This element simply describes the name of the Web application.

The second application-level element is <session-timeout>. This element controls the lifetime of the application's HttpSession object. The <session-timeout> value we have used tells the JSP/servlet container that the HttpSession object becomes invalid after 30 minutes of inactivity.

The last application-level element is <servlet>. This element defines a servlet and its properties.

Deploying Web applications in Tomcat

Now that we have seen the structure of a Web application and the various components, let's create a sample Web application. We create a Web application called mywebapp, insert some sample JSP and servlets, and access them from a browser.

First, we create the directory structure for the mywebapp Web application. Create a directory called mywebapp under <SERVER_ROOT>/webapps, and create all subdirectories as specified in the previous section.

Create a web.xml text file in the WEB-INF directory under mywebapp, and add the following entries to it:

```
<?xml version="1.0" encoding="ISO-8859-1"?>
<!DOCTYPE web-app
PUBLIC "-//Sun Microsystems, Inc.//DTD Web Application 2.3//EN"
"http://java.sun.com/j2ee/dtds/web-app_2_3.dtd">
<web-app>
</web-app>
```

The next step in creating a Web application is to create a ServletContext. The ServletContext acts as a container for the Web application and provides an interface between the servlet container and the Web application. The ServletContext has to be added in the server.xml file in Tomcat. Add the following entry to the server.xml file to create a context for mywebapp.

```
<Context path="/mywebapp" docBase="mywebapp" debug="0" reloadable="true" />
```

In this entry, path refers to the virtual path reference the user uses to refer to this Web application. The docbase tells the servlet container the physical location of the Web application.

Add a JSP and test the Web application. To add a JSP to a Web application, create a JSP in a text editor, and save it to the Web application root directory. In our example, the JSP has to be saved to <SERVER ROOT>/webapps/mywebapp. Add a small snoop JSP to our Web application. Name the file snoop.jsp. Listing F-1 shows the code for the JSP.

Listing F-1

```
<html>
<!--
  Copyright (c) 1999 The Apache Software Foundation.  All rights
  reserved.
-->

<body bgcolor="white">
<h1> Request Information </h1>
<font size="4">
```

```
JSP Request Method: <%= request.getMethod() %>
<br>
Request URI: <%= request.getRequestURI() %>
<br>
Request Protocol: <%= request.getProtocol() %>
<br>
Servlet path: <%= request.getServletPath() %>
<br>
Path info: <%= request.getPathInfo() %>
<br>
Path translated: <%= request.getPathTranslated() %>
<br>
Query string: <%= request.getQueryString() %>
<br>
Content length: <%= request.getContentLength() %>
<br>
Content type: <%= request.getContentType() %>
<br>
Server name: <%= request.getServerName() %>
<br>
Server port: <%= request.getServerPort() %>
<br>
Remote user: <%= request.getRemoteUser() %>
<br>
Remote address: <%= request.getRemoteAddr() %>
<br>
Remote host: <%= request.getRemoteHost() %>
<br>
Authorization scheme: <%= request.getAuthType() %>
<br>
Locale: <%= request.getLocale() %>
<hr>
The browser you are using is <%= request.getHeader("User-Agent") %>
<hr>
</font>
</body>
</html>
```

To run the example, restart Tomcat. After Tomcat restarts, the Web application can be accessed by using the following URL: `http://locahost:8080/mywebapp/snoop.jsp`.

The output is shown in Figure F-2.

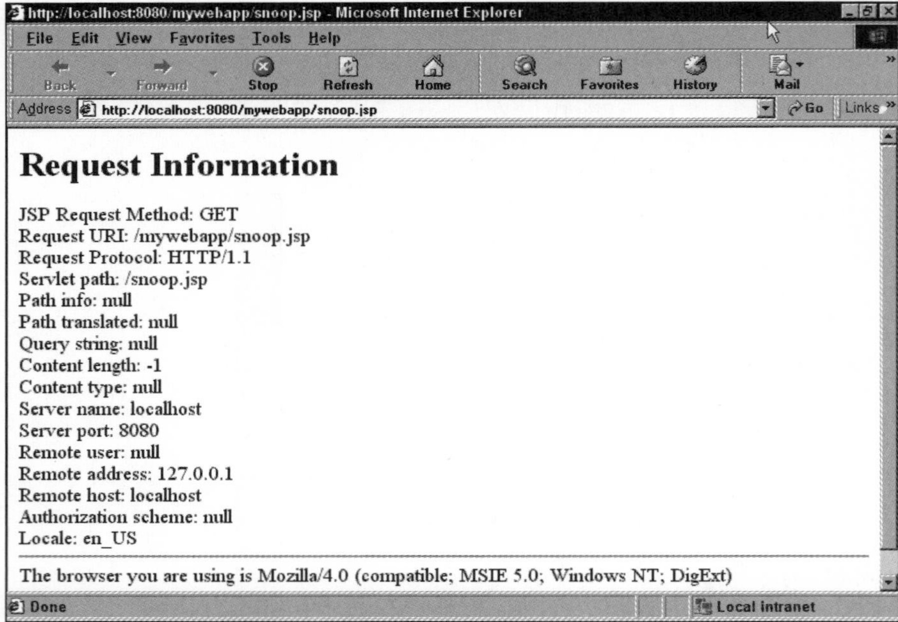

Figure F-2: Snoop JSP

Now that we have added a JSP, let's add a servlet and configure the servlet. Write a small `HelloWorld` servlet to illustrate this.

Compile this servlet by using JDK. Create a directory called `classes` under `WEB-INF` and copy `HelloWorld.class` to this directory.

Next, edit the `web.xml` file, and add the following entries:

```
<servlet>
  <servlet-name>
      HelloWorld
  </servlet-name>
  <servlet-class>
      HelloWorld
  </servlet-class>
</servlet>
<servlet-mapping>
    <servlet-name>
        HelloWorld
    </servlet-name>
    <url-pattern>
        /Hello
    </url-pattern>
</servlet-mapping>
```

Restart the Tomcat server after adding these entries to `web.xml`. The `HelloWorld` servlet can then be accessed by using the following URL: `http://localhost:8080/mywebapp/Hello`.

The output is shown in Figure F-3:

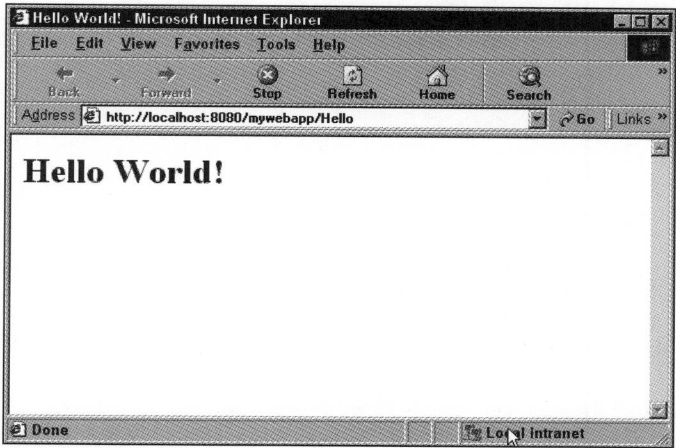

Figure F-3: HelloWorld servlet

The Glue!

Now you know how to install and configure Apache as a standalone Web server. You also saw how to configure Tomcat as a standalone server and how to deploy Web applications. Apache is optimal for serving static HTML files and images. Tomcat works well for serving dynamic Web pages such as servlets and JSP. How do we make the best use of both?

There has to be some mechanism by which static pages are served by Apache Web server and dynamic pages are served by Tomcat. The Web server must also have a mechanism to identify the requests it should forward to Tomcat and the requests it should handle by itself. The Apache group has made available a plug-in called `mod_jk`, which provides the glue between Apache and Tomcat. `mod_jk` intercepts all requests meant for Tomcat and forwards the requests to Tomcat server.

mod_jk

`mod_jk` is an Apache plug-in module that handles communication between Apache and Tomcat. It is available as a free download from the Apache Web site and is in two formats: binary and source. The binaries can be downloaded from http://jakarta.apache.org/builds/jakarta-tomcat/release/v3.3-m1/bin/.

The Linux version of mod_jk can be found in the Linux subdirectory, and the Windows version can be downloaded from the win32 subdirectory.

Configuring Apache to use mod_jk

The simplest way to configure Apache to use mod_jk is to turn on the Apache auto-configure setting in Tomcat and put the following Include directive at the end of your Apache httpd.conf file (make sure you replace *TOMCAT_HOME* with the correct path for your Tomcat installation):

```
Include TOMCAT_HOME/conf/mod_jk.conf-auto
```

Example:

```
Include /usr/local/jakarta-tomcat/conf/mod_jk.conf-auto
```

This tells Apache to use directives in the mod_jk.conf-auto file in the Apache configuration.

Custom configurations can be created by enabling autoconfiguration and copying the *TOMCAT_HOME*/conf/mod_jk.conf-auto file to your own configuration file, such as *TOMCAT_HOME*/conf/mod_jk.conf-local.

The basic configuration follows:

1. Instruct Apache to load Tomcat. This can be done with Apache's LoadModule and AddModule configuration directives.
2. Inform mod_jk of the location of your workers.properties file. Use the mod_jk JkWorkersFile configuration directive.
3. Specify a location where mod_jk is going to place its log file and a log level to be used. Use the JkLogFile and JkLogLevel configuration directives. Possible log levels are *debug*, *info*, *error*, and *emerg*, but *info* should be your default selection.
4. The directive JkLogStampFormat configures the date/time format found on the mod_jk log file. Using the strftime() format string, the date/time format is set by default to [%a %b %d %H:%M:%S %Y].

A simple example is to include the following lines in your httpd.conf file:

```
LoadModule     jk_module  libexec/mod_jk.so
AddModule      mod_jk.c
JkWorkersFile /usr/local/jakarta-tomcat/conf/workers.properties
```

```
JkLogFile       /usr/local/apache/logs/mod_jk.log
JkLogLevel      info
JkLogStampFormat "[%a %b %d %H:%M:%S %Y] "
```

Assigning URLs to Tomcat

If you have created a custom or local version of mod_jk.conf-local as noted previously, you can change settings such as the workers or the URL prefix.

Use the mod_jk JkMount directive to assign specific URLs to Tomcat. In general, the structure of a JkMount directive is

```
JkMount <URL prefix> <Worker name>
```

For example, the following directives send all requests ending in .jsp or beginning with /servlet to the ajp13 worker, but JSP requests to files located in /otherworker go to "remoteworker".

```
JkMount /*.jsp ajp13
JkMount /servlet/* ajp13
JkMount /otherworker/*.jsp remoteworker
```

You can use the JkMount directive at the top level or inside <VirtualHost> sections of your httpd.conf file.

✦ ✦ ✦

Index

Symbols & Numbers

A

B

Continued

D

E

Continued

K

L

M

N

O

P

Continued

T

Continued

X

Hungry Minds, Inc. End-User License Agreement

READ THIS. You should carefully read these terms and conditions before opening the software packet(s) included with this book ("Book"). This is a license agreement ("Agreement") between you and Hungry Minds, Inc. ("HMI"). By opening the accompanying software packet(s), you acknowledge that you have read and accept the following terms and conditions. If you do not agree and do not want to be bound by such terms and conditions, promptly return the Book and the unopened software packet(s) to the place you obtained them for a full refund.

1. **License Grant.** HMI grants to you (either an individual or entity) a nonexclusive license to use one copy of the enclosed software program(s) (collectively, the "Software") solely for your own personal or business purposes on a single computer (whether a standard computer or a workstation component of a multi-user network). The Software is in use on a computer when it is loaded into temporary memory (RAM) or installed into permanent memory (hard disk, CD-ROM, or other storage device). HMI reserves all rights not expressly granted herein.
2. **Ownership.** HMI is the owner of all right, title, and interest, including copyright, in and to the compilation of the Software recorded on the disk(s) or CD-ROM ("Software Media"). Copyright to the individual programs recorded on the Software Media is owned by the author or other authorized copyright owner of each program. Ownership of the Software and all proprietary rights relating thereto remain with HMI and its licensers.
3. **Restrictions on Use and Transfer.**
   - **(a)** You may only (i) make one copy of the Software for backup or archival purposes, or (ii) transfer the Software to a single hard disk, provided that you keep the original for backup or archival purposes. You may not (i) rent or lease the Software, (ii) copy or reproduce the Software through a LAN or other network system or through any computer subscriber system or bulletin-board system, or (iii) modify, adapt, or create derivative works based on the Software.
   - **(b)** You may not reverse engineer, decompile, or disassemble the Software. You may transfer the Software and user documentation on a permanent basis, provided that the transferee agrees to accept the terms and conditions of this Agreement and you retain no copies. If the Software is an update or has been updated, any transfer must include the most recent update and all prior versions.
4. **Restrictions on Use of Individual Programs.** You must follow the individual requirements and restrictions detailed for each individual program in Appendix A of this Book. These limitations are also contained in the individual license agreements recorded on the Software Media. These limitations may include a requirement that after using the program for a specified period of time, the user must pay a registration fee or discontinue use. By opening the Software packet(s), you will be agreeing to abide by the licenses and restrictions for these individual programs that are detailed in Appendix A and on the Software Media. None of the material on this Software Media or listed in this Book may ever be redistributed, in original or modified form, for commercial purposes.

5. **Limited Warranty.**

   (a) HMI warrants that the Software and Software Media are free from defects in materials and workmanship under normal use for a period of sixty (60) days from the date of purchase of this Book. If HMI receives notification within the warranty period of defects in materials or workmanship, HMI will replace the defective Software Media.

   (b) **HMI AND THE AUTHOR OF THE BOOK DISCLAIM ALL OTHER WARRANTIES, EXPRESS OR IMPLIED, INCLUDING WITHOUT LIMITATION IMPLIED WARRANTIES OF MERCHANTABILITY AND FITNESS FOR A PARTICULAR PURPOSE, WITH RESPECT TO THE SOFTWARE, THE PROGRAMS, THE SOURCE CODE CONTAINED THEREIN, AND/OR THE TECHNIQUES DESCRIBED IN THIS BOOK. HMI DOES NOT WARRANT THAT THE FUNCTIONS CONTAINED IN THE SOFTWARE WILL MEET YOUR REQUIREMENTS OR THAT THE OPERATION OF THE SOFTWARE WILL BE ERROR FREE.**

   (c) This limited warranty gives you specific legal rights, and you may have other rights that vary from jurisdiction to jurisdiction.

6. **Remedies.**

   (a) HMI's entire liability and your exclusive remedy for defects in materials and workmanship shall be limited to replacement of the Software Media, which may be returned to HMI with a copy of your receipt at the following address: Software Media Fulfillment Department, Attn.: *Java™ Servlet Programming Bible*, Hungry Minds, Inc., 10475 Crosspoint Blvd., Indianapolis, IN 46256, or call 1-800-762-2974. Please allow four to six weeks for delivery. This Limited Warranty is void if failure of the Software Media has resulted from accident, abuse, or misapplication. Any replacement Software Media will be warranted for the remainder of the original warranty period or thirty (30) days, whichever is longer.

   (b) In no event shall HMI or the author be liable for any damages whatsoever (including without limitation damages for loss of business profits, business interruption, loss of business information, or any other pecuniary loss) arising from the use of or inability to use the Book or the Software, even if HMI has been advised of the possibility of such damages.

   (c) Because some jurisdictions do not allow the exclusion or limitation of liability for consequential or incidental damages, the above limitation or exclusion may not apply to you.

7. **U.S. Government Restricted Rights.** Use, duplication, or disclosure of the Software for or on behalf of the United States of America, its agencies and/or instrumentalities (the "U.S. Government") is subject to restrictions as stated in paragraph (c)(1)(ii) of the Rights in Technical Data and Computer Software clause of DFARS 252.227-7013, or subparagraphs (c) (1) and (2) of the Commercial Computer Software - Restricted Rights clause at FAR 52.227-19, and in similar clauses in the NASA FAR supplement, as applicable.

8. **General.** This Agreement constitutes the entire understanding of the parties and revokes and supersedes all prior agreements, oral or written, between them and may not be modified or amended except in a writing signed by both parties hereto that specifically refers to this Agreement. This Agreement shall take precedence over any other documents that may be in conflict herewith. If any one or more provisions contained in this Agreement are held by any court or tribunal to be invalid, illegal, or otherwise unenforceable, each and every other provision shall remain in full force and effect.

Sun Microsystems, Inc. Binary Code License Agreement

READ THE TERMS OF THIS AGREEMENT AND ANY PROVIDED SUPPLEMENTAL LICENSE TERMS (COLLECTIVELY "AGREEMENT") CAREFULLY BEFORE OPENING THE SOFTWARE MEDIA PACKAGE. BY OPENING THE SOFTWARE MEDIA PACKAGE, YOU AGREE TO THE TERMS OF THIS AGREEMENT. IF YOU ARE ACCESSING THE SOFTWARE ELECTRONICALLY, INDICATE YOUR ACCEPTANCE OF THESE TERMS BY SELECTING THE "ACCEPT" BUTTON AT THE END OF THIS AGREEMENT. IF YOU DO NOT AGREE TO ALL THESE TERMS, PROMPTLY RETURN THE UNUSED SOFTWARE TO YOUR PLACE OF PURCHASE FOR A REFUND OR, IF THE SOFTWARE IS ACCESSED ELECTRONICALLY, SELECT THE "DECLINE" BUTTON AT THE END OF THIS AGREEMENT.

1. **License to Use.** Sun grants you a non-exclusive and non-transferable license for the internal use only of the accompanying software and documentation and any error corrections provided by Sun (collectively "Software"), by the number of users and the class of computer hardware for which the corresponding fee has been paid.
2. **Restrictions.** Software is confidential and copyrighted. Title to Software and all associated intellectual property rights is retained by Sun and/or its licensors. Except as specifically authorized in any Supplemental License Terms, you may not make copies of Software, other than a single copy of Software for archival purposes. Unless enforcement is prohibited by applicable law, you may not modify, decompile, or reverse engineer Software. You acknowledge that Software is not designed, licensed or intended for use in the design, construction, operation or maintenance of any nuclear facility. Sun disclaims any express or implied warranty of fitness for such uses. No right, title or interest in or to any trademark, service mark, logo or trade name of Sun or its licensors is granted under this Agreement.
3. **Limited Warranty.** Sun warrants to you that for a period of ninety (90) days from the date of purchase, as evidenced by a copy of the receipt, the media on which Software is furnished (if any) will be free of defects in materials and workmanship under normal use. Except for the foregoing, Software is provided "AS IS". Your exclusive remedy and Sun's entire liability under this limited warranty will be at Sun's option to replace Software media or refund the fee paid for Software.
4. **Disclaimer of Warranty.** UNLESS SPECIFIED IN THIS AGREEMENT, ALL EXPRESS OR IMPLIED CONDITIONS, REPRESENTATIONS AND WARRANTIES, INCLUDING ANY IMPLIED WARRANTY OF MERCHANTABILITY, FITNESS FOR A PARTICULAR PURPOSE OR NON-INFRINGEMENT ARE DISCLAIMED, EXCEPT TO THE EXTENT THAT THESE DISCLAIMERS ARE HELD TO BE LEGALLY INVALID.
5. **Limitation of Liability.** TO THE EXTENT NOT PROHIBITED BY LAW, IN NO EVENT WILL SUN OR ITS LICENSORS BE LIABLE FOR ANY LOST REVENUE, PROFIT OR DATA, OR FOR SPECIAL, INDIRECT, CONSEQUENTIAL, INCIDENTAL OR PUNITIVE DAMAGES, HOWEVER CAUSED REGARDLESS OF THE THEORY OF LIABILITY, ARISING OUT OF OR RELATED TO THE USE OF OR INABILITY TO USE SOFTWARE, EVEN IF SUN HAS BEEN ADVISED OF THE POSSIBILITY OF SUCH DAMAGES. In no event will Sun's liability to you, whether in contract, tort (including negligence), or otherwise, exceed the amount paid by you for Software under this Agreement. The foregoing limitations will apply even if the above stated warranty fails of its essential purpose.

6. **Termination.** This Agreement is effective until terminated. You may terminate this Agreement at any time by destroying all copies of Software. This Agreement will terminate immediately without notice from Sun if you fail to comply with any provision of this Agreement. Upon Termination, you must destroy all copies of Software.
7. **Export Regulations.** All Software and technical data delivered under this Agreement are subject to US export control laws and may be subject to export or import regulations in other countries. You agree to comply strictly with all such laws and regulations and acknowledge that you have the responsibility to obtain such licenses to export, re-export, or import as may be required after delivery to you.
8. **U.S. Government Restricted Rights.** If Software is being acquired by or on behalf of the U.S. Government or by a U.S. Government prime contractor or subcontractor (at any tier), then the Government's rights in Software and accompanying documentation will be only as set forth in this Agreement; this is in accordance with 48 CFR 227.7201 through 227.7202-4 (for Department of Defense (DOD) acquisitions) and with 48 CFR 2.101 and 12.212 (for non-DOD acquisitions).
9. **Governing Law.** Any action related to this Agreement will be governed by California law and controlling U.S. federal law. No choice of law rules of any jurisdiction will apply.
10. **Severability.** If any provision of this Agreement is held to be unenforceable, this Agreement will remain in effect with the provision omitted, unless omission would frustrate the intent of the parties, in which case this Agreement will immediately terminate.
11. **Integration.** This Agreement is the entire agreement between you and Sun relating to its subject matter. It supersedes all prior or contemporaneous oral or written communications, proposals, representations and warranties and prevails over any conflicting or additional terms of any quote, order, acknowledgment, or other communication between the parties relating to its subject matter during the term of this Agreement. No modification of this Agreement will be binding, unless in writing and signed by an authorized representative of each party.

Forte™ for Java™, Release 3.0 Community Edition Supplemental License Terms

These supplemental license terms ("Supplemental Terms") add to or modify the terms of the Binary Code License Agreement (collectively, the "Agreement"). Capitalized terms not defined in these Supplemental Terms shall have the same meanings ascribed to them in the Agreement. These Supplemental Terms shall supersede any inconsistent or conflicting terms in the Agreement, or in any license contained within the Software.

1. **Software Internal Use and Development License Grant.** Subject to the terms and conditions of this Agreement, including, but not limited to Section 4 (Java™ Technology Restrictions) of these Supplemental Terms, Sun grants you a non-exclusive, non-transferable, limited license to reproduce internally and use internally the binary form of the Software complete and unmodified for the sole purpose of designing, developing and testing your Java applets and applications intended to run on the Java platform ("Programs").
2. **License to Distribute Software.** Subject to the terms and conditions of this Agreement, including, but not limited to Section 4 (Java™ Technology Restrictions) of these Supplemental Terms, Sun grants you a non-exclusive, non-transferable, limited license to reproduce and distribute the Software in binary code form only, provided that (i) you distribute the Software complete and unmodified and only bundled as part of, and for the sole purpose of running, your Programs, (ii) the Programs add significant and primary functionality to the Software, (iii) you do not distribute additional software intended to replace any component(s) of the Software, (iv) for a particular version of the Java platform, any executable output generated by a compiler that is contained in the Software must (a) only be compiled from source code that conforms to the corresponding version of the OEM Java Language Specification; (b) be in the class file format defined by the corresponding version of the OEM Java Virtual Machine Specification; and (c) execute properly on a reference runtime, as specified by Sun, associated with such version of the Java platform, (v) you do not remove or alter any proprietary legends or notices contained in the Software, (v) you only distribute the Software subject to a license agreement that protects Sun's interests consistent with the terms contained in this Agreement, and (vi) you agree to defend and indemnify Sun and its licensors from and against any damages, costs, liabilities, settlement amounts and/or expenses (including attorneys' fees) incurred in connection with any claim, lawsuit or action by any third party that arises or results from the use or distribution of any and all Programs and/or Software.
3. **License to Distribute Redistributables.** Subject to the terms and conditions of this Agreement, including but not limited to Section 4 (Java Technology Restrictions) of these Supplemental Terms, Sun grants you a non-exclusive, non-transferable, limited license to reproduce and distribute the binary form of those files specifically identified as redistributable in the Software "RELEASE NOTES" file ("Redistributables") provided that: (i) you distribute the Redistributables complete and unmodified (unless otherwise specified in the applicable RELEASE NOTES file), and only bundled as part of Programs, (ii) you do not distribute additional software intended to supersede any component(s) of the Redistributables, (iii) you do not remove or alter any proprietary legends or notices contained in or on the Redistributables, (iv) for a particular version of the Java platform, any executable output generated by a compiler that is contained in the Software must (a) only be compiled from source code that conforms to the corresponding version of the OEM Java Language Specification; (b) be in the class file format defined by the corresponding version of the OEM Java Virtual Machine Specification;

and (c) execute properly on a reference runtime, as specified by Sun, associated with such version of the Java platform, (v) you only distribute the Redistributables pursuant to a license agreement that protects Sun's interests consistent with the terms contained in the Agreement, and (v) you agree to defend and indemnify Sun and its licensors from and against any damages, costs, liabilities, settlement amounts and/or expenses (including attorneys' fees) incurred in connection with any claim, lawsuit or action by any third party that arises or results from the use or distribution of any and all Programs and/or Software.

4. **Java Technology Restrictions.** You may not modify the Java Platform Interface ("JPI", identified as classes contained within the "java" package or any subpackages of the "java" package), by creating additional classes within the JPI or otherwise causing the addition to or modification of the classes in the JPI. In the event that you create an additional class and associated API(s) which (i) extends the functionality of the Java platform, and (ii) is exposed to third party software developers for the purpose of developing additional software which invokes such additional API, you must promptly publish broadly an accurate specification for such API for free use by all developers. You may not create, or authorize your licensees to create, additional classes, interfaces, or subpackages that are in any way identified as "java", "javax", "sun" or similar convention as specified by Sun in any naming convention designation.
5. **Java Runtime Availability.** Refer to the appropriate version of the Java Runtime Environment binary code license (currently located at `http://www.java.sun.com/jdk/index.html`) for the availability of runtime code which may be distributed with Java applets and applications.
6. **Trademarks and Logos.** You acknowledge and agree as between you and Sun that Sun owns the SUN, SOLARIS, JAVA, JINI, FORTE, and iPLANET trademarks and all SUN, SOLARIS, JAVA, JINI, FORTE, and iPLANET-related trademarks, service marks, logos and other brand designations ("Sun Marks"), and you agree to comply with the Sun Trademark and Logo Usage Requirements currently located at `http://www.sun.com/policies/trademarks`. Any use you make of the Sun Marks inures to Sun's benefit.
7. **Source Code.** Software may contain source code that is provided solely for reference purposes pursuant to the terms of this Agreement. Source code may not be redistributed unless expressly provided for in this Agreement.
8. **Termination for Infringement.** Either party may terminate this Agreement immediately should any Software become, or in either party's opinion be likely to become, the subject of a claim of infringement of any intellectual property right.

For inquiries please contact: Sun Microsystems, Inc. 901 San Antonio Road, Palo Alto, California 94303 (LFI#91205/Form ID#011801)

Terms and conditions of the license & export for Java™ 2 SDK, Standard Edition 1.3.1_01

Sun Microsystems, Inc. Binary Code License Agreement

READ THE TERMS OF THIS AGREEMENT AND ANY PROVIDED SUPPLEMENTAL LICENSE TERMS (COLLECTIVELY "AGREEMENT") CAREFULLY BEFORE OPENING THE SOFTWARE MEDIA PACKAGE. BY OPENING THE SOFTWARE MEDIA PACKAGE, YOU AGREE TO THE TERMS OF THIS AGREEMENT. IF YOU ARE ACCESSING THE SOFTWARE ELECTRONICALLY, INDICATE YOUR ACCEPTANCE OF THESE TERMS BY SELECTING THE "ACCEPT" BUTTON AT THE END OF THIS AGREEMENT. IF YOU DO NOT AGREE TO ALL THESE TERMS, PROMPTLY RETURN THE UNUSED SOFTWARE TO YOUR PLACE OF PURCHASE FOR A REFUND OR, IF THE SOFTWARE IS ACCESSED ELECTRONICALLY, SELECT THE "DECLINE" BUTTON AT THE END OF THIS AGREEMENT.

1. **License to Use.** Sun grants you a non-exclusive and non-transferable license for the internal use only of the accompanying software and documentation and any error corrections provided by Sun (collectively "Software"), by the number of users and the class of computer hardware for which the corresponding fee has been paid.
2. **Restrictions.** Software is confidential and copyrighted. Title to Software and all associated intellectual property rights is retained by Sun and/or its licensors. Except as specifically authorized in any Supplemental License Terms, you may not make copies of Software, other than a single copy of Software for archival purposes. Unless enforcement is prohibited by applicable law, you may not modify, decompile, or reverse engineer Software. You acknowledge that Software is not designed, licensed or intended for use in the design, construction, operation or maintenance of any nuclear facility. Sun disclaims any express or implied warranty of fitness for such uses. No right, title or interest in or to any trademark, service mark, logo or trade name of Sun or its licensors is granted under this Agreement.
3. **Limited Warranty.** Sun warrants to you that for a period of ninety (90) days from the date of purchase, as evidenced by a copy of the receipt, the media on which Software is furnished (if any) will be free of defects in materials and workmanship under normal use. Except for the foregoing, Software is provided "AS IS". Your exclusive remedy and Sun's entire liability under this limited warranty will be at Sun's option to replace Software media or refund the fee paid for Software.
4. **Disclaimer of Warranty.** UNLESS SPECIFIED IN THIS AGREEMENT, ALL EXPRESS OR IMPLIED CONDITIONS, REPRESENTATIONS AND WARRANTIES, INCLUDING ANY IMPLIED WARRANTY OF MERCHANTABILITY, FITNESS FOR A PARTICULAR PURPOSE OR NON-INFRINGEMENT ARE DISCLAIMED, EXCEPT TO THE EXTENT THAT THESE DISCLAIMERS ARE HELD TO BE LEGALLY INVALID.
5. **Limitation of Liability.** TO THE EXTENT NOT PROHIBITED BY LAW, IN NO EVENT WILL SUN OR ITS LICENSORS BE LIABLE FOR ANY LOST REVENUE, PROFIT OR DATA, OR FOR SPECIAL, INDIRECT, CONSEQUENTIAL, INCIDENTAL OR PUNITIVE DAMAGES, HOWEVER CAUSED REGARDLESS OF THE THEORY OF LIABILITY, ARISING OUT OF OR RELATED TO THE USE OF OR INABILITY TO USE SOFTWARE, EVEN IF SUN HAS BEEN ADVISED OF THE POSSIBILITY OF SUCH DAMAGES. In no event will Sun's liability to you, whether in contract, tort (including negligence), or otherwise, exceed the amount paid by you for Software under this Agreement. The foregoing limitations will apply even if the above stated warranty fails of its essential purpose.

6. **Termination.** This Agreement is effective until terminated. You may terminate this Agreement at any time by destroying all copies of Software. This Agreement will terminate immediately without notice from Sun if you fail to comply with any provision of this Agreement. Upon Termination, you must destroy all copies of Software.
7. **Export Regulations.** All Software and technical data delivered under this Agreement are subject to US export control laws and may be subject to export or import regulations in other countries. You agree to comply strictly with all such laws and regulations and acknowledge that you have the responsibility to obtain such licenses to export, re-export, or import as may be required after delivery to you.
8. **U.S. Government Restricted Rights.** If Software is being acquired by or on behalf of the U.S. Government or by a U.S. Government prime contractor or subcontractor (at any tier), then the Government's rights in Software and accompanying documentation will be only as set forth in this Agreement; this is in accordance with 48 CFR 227.7201 through 227.7202-4 (for Department of Defense (DOD) acquisitions) and with 48 CFR 2.101 and 12.212 (for non-DOD acquisitions).
9. **Governing Law.** Any action related to this Agreement will be governed by California law and controlling U.S. federal law. No choice of law rules of any jurisdiction will apply.
10. **Severability.** If any provision of this Agreement is held to be unenforceable, this Agreement will remain in effect with the provision omitted, unless omission would frustrate the intent of the parties, in which case this Agreement will immediately terminate.
11. **Integration.** This Agreement is the entire agreement between you and Sun relating to its subject matter. It supersedes all prior or contemporaneous oral or written communications, proposals, representations and warranties and prevails over any conflicting or additional terms of any quote, order, acknowledgment, or other communication between the parties relating to its subject matter during the term of this Agreement. No modification of this Agreement will be binding, unless in writing and signed by an authorized representative of each party.

Java™ 2 Software Development Kit (J2SDK), Standard Edition, Version 1.3.x Supplemental License Terms

These supplemental license terms ("Supplemental Terms") add to or modify the terms of the Binary Code License Agreement (collectively, the "Agreement"). Capitalized terms not defined in these Supplemental Terms shall have the same meanings ascribed to them in the Agreement. These Supplemental Terms shall supersede any inconsistent or conflicting terms in the Agreement, or in any license contained within the Software.

1. **Software Internal Use and Development License Grant.** Subject to the terms and conditions of this Agreement, including, but not limited to Section 4 (Java™ Technology Restrictions) of these Supplemental Terms, Sun grants you a non-exclusive, non-transferable, limited license to reproduce internally and use internally the binary form of the Software complete and unmodified for the sole purpose of designing, developing and testing your Java applets and applications intended to run on the Java platform ("Programs").
2. **License to Distribute Software.** Subject to the terms and conditions of this Agreement, including, but not limited to Section 4 (Java™ Technology Restrictions) of these Supplemental Terms, Sun grants you a non-exclusive, non-transferable, limited license to reproduce and distribute the Software in binary code form only, provided that (i) you distribute the Software complete and unmodified and only bundled as part of, and for the sole purpose of running, your Programs, (ii) the Programs add significant and primary functionality to the Software, (iii) you do not distribute additional software intended to replace any component(s) of the Software, (iv) you do not remove or alter any proprietary legends or notices contained in the Software, (v) you only distribute the Software subject to a license agreement that protects Sun's interests consistent with the terms contained in this Agreement, and (vi) you agree to defend and indemnify Sun and its licensors from and against any damages, costs, liabilities, settlement amounts and/or expenses (including attorneys' fees) incurred in connection with any claim, lawsuit or action by any third party that arises or results from the use or distribution of any and all Programs and/or Software.
3. **License to Distribute Redistributables.** Subject to the terms and conditions of this Agreement, including but not limited to Section 4 (Java Technology Restrictions) of these Supplemental Terms, Sun grants you a non-exclusive, non-transferable, limited license to reproduce and distribute the binary form of those files specifically identified as redistributable in the Software "README" file ("Redistributables") provided that: (i) you distribute the Redistributables complete and unmodified (unless otherwise specified in the applicable README file), and only bundled as part of Programs, (ii) you do not distribute additional software intended to supersede any component(s) of the Redistributables, (iii) you do not remove or alter any proprietary legends or notices contained in or on the Redistributables, (iv) you only distribute the Redistributables pursuant to a license agreement that protects Sun's interests consistent with the terms contained in the Agreement, and (v) you agree to defend and indemnify Sun and its licensors from and against any damages, costs, liabilities, settlement amounts and/or expenses (including attorneys' fees) incurred in connection with any claim, lawsuit or action by any third party that arises or results from the use or distribution of any and all Programs and/or Software.

4. **Java Technology Restrictions.** You may not modify the Java Platform Interface ("JPI", identified as classes contained within the "java" package or any subpackages of the "java" package), by creating additional classes within the JPI or otherwise causing the addition to or modification of the classes in the JPI. In the event that you create an additional class and associated API(s) which (i) extends the functionality of the Java platform, and (ii) is exposed to third party software developers for the purpose of developing additional software which invokes such additional API, you must promptly publish broadly an accurate specification for such API for free use by all developers. You may not create, or authorize your licensees to create, additional classes, interfaces, or subpackages that are in any way identified as "java", "javax", "sun" or similar convention as specified by Sun in any naming convention designation.
5. **Trademarks and Logos.** You acknowledge and agree as between you and Sun that Sun owns the SUN, SOLARIS, JAVA, JINI, FORTE, and iPLANET trademarks and all SUN, SOLARIS, JAVA, JINI, FORTE, and iPLANET-related trademarks, service marks, logos and other brand designations ("Sun Marks"), and you agree to comply with the Sun Trademark and Logo Usage Requirements currently located at http://www.sun.com/policies/trademarks. Any use you make of the Sun Marks inures to Sun's benefit.
6. **Source Code.** Software may contain source code that is provided solely for reference purposes pursuant to the terms of this Agreement. Source code may not be redistributed unless expressly provided for in this Agreement.
7. **Termination for Infringement.** Either party may terminate this Agreement immediately should any Software become, or in either party's opinion be likely to become, the subject of a claim of infringement of any intellectual property right.